Country	GNP per Capita	Real GDP per Capita	HDI	Population (millions)
France	20460	18430	0.927	57.1
Gabon	3980	3498	0.525	1.2
Gambia	360	763	0.215	0.9
Georgia	1780	3670	0.747	5.5
Germany	20510	19770	0.918	80.2
Ghana	420	930	0.382	16.0
Greece	6420	7680	0.874	10.2
Grenada	2300	3374	0.707	0.1
Guatemala	940	3180	0.564	9.8
Guinea	500	500	0.191	6.1
Guinea-Bissau	180	747	0.224	1.0
Guyana	300	1862	0.580	0.8
Haiti	380	925	0.354	6.8
Honduras	590	1820	0.524	5.5
Hong Kong	13580	18520	0.875	5.8
Hungary	2750	6080	0.863	10.5
Iceland	23230	17480	0.914	0.3
India	330	1150	0.382	880.1
Indonesia	610	2730	0.586	191.2
Iran	2410	4670	0.672	61.6
Iraq	1940 (1989)*	na	0.614	19.3
Ireland	11150	11430	0.892	3.5
Israel	12110	13460	0.900	5.1
Italy	18580	17040	0.891	57.8
Jamaica	1490	3670	0.749	2.5
Japan	26840	19390	0.929	124.5
Jordan	1060	2895	0.628	4.3
Kampuchea (Cambodia)	200	1250	0.307	8.8
Kazakhstan	2030	4490	0.774	17.0
Kenya	340	1350	0.434	25.3
Kuwait	11000 (1992)*†	13126	0.809	1.9
Kyrgyzstan	1160	3280	0.689	4.5
Laos	220	1760	0.385	4.5
Latvia	3920	7540	0.865	2.7
Lebanon	1400 *†	na	0.600	2.9
Lesotho	570	na	0.476	1.8
Liberia	440 (1989)*	na	0.317	2.8
Libya	5800 (1992)*†	na	0.703	4.9
Lithuania	2420	5410	0.868	3.8
Luxembourg	31860	20800	0.908	0.4
Madagascar	210	710	0.396	12.9

(Continued on inside back cover)

Contents

Preface

Everyone is aware of poverty, malnutrition, and other forms of human misery present in much of the world. The images caught on photos and films, especially of children, are compelling. Why does such misery occur? Is it inevitable? Can something be done to alleviate it or end it? Economic development is the field that deals with these momentous questions.

Our subject exhibits many contradictions. In recent years, some less developed countries (or LDCs) have been undergoing development at rates as rapid as the world has ever seen. At their current rates of growth, they will not be LDCs for much longer. In other countries, however, conditions have worsened seriously, with output having fallen by 20 percent or more over two or three decades, and with governments that have largely broken down. Some LDCs have recently chosen to let markets work and to avoid damaging government interventions in their economies, while others continue to employ counterproductive policies. A large increase in investment by the rich countries in the LDCs has taken place, but investors are fickle and a small minority of countries is receiving most of the money. High- and low-income countries have shown new willingness to reduce their trade barriers against one another, as seen in the Uruguay Round of trade negotiations. But concerns over competition for developed-country workers from low-wage labor in the LDCs promise to keep the issue of trade barriers alive. In many countries, health and education have improved, but high population growth threatens to undermine the gains. Especially where growth is most rapid, environmental concerns have surfaced, and some of these have global implications. Political instability in the LDCs seems more dangerous for world peace and prosperity than anything likely to arise in the developed countries. These questions are central to economic development.

The third edition of *Economic Development* addresses these issues while providing analysis of the basic theories of development. As in the past editions, a main distinguishing feature is the book's coverage of the international economic aspects of development. The discussion in Chapters 13 to 15 reflects my conviction that trade is now probably the single fastest path to development, but a path that could easily be closed off by the developed world. Developed-country trade barriers, often touched on only briefly in competing texts, receive a thorough treatment.

I have continued to try to produce a highly readable book, making the writing a literary effort as well as a pedagogical one. The material is intended to be understood by students who have taken only the first-year principles of an economics course. Although some boxed material is included for those economics majors who have taken intermediate theory, the body of the text does not require knowledge beyond an initial course. As in the past editions, the bibliographical referencing remains extensive, which should prove valuable to students and instructors alike. The endnotes at the conclusion of each chapter contain this referencing. By contrast the footnotes at the bottoms of the pages are intended to be read, and usually add human interest to the subject.

ORGANIZATION AND NEW FEATURES

The first chapter is an introduction to the field, emphasizing the disparate performance of the low-income countries and the need for the development of human capabilities as well as output growth. In this edition, the contrast between a human development approach and an approach emphasizing economic growth, and the importance of women in the development effort, have been expanded. Chapter 2 reflects my belief that the *measurement* of development (including national product and income, income distribution, and indicators of the "quality of life") should come early in the analysis. New in this chapter is an extended treatment of GDP corrected for purchasing power and the recent improvements to the UN's Human Development Index.

Chapter 3 is a survey of how countries develop. The initial lessons are drawn from the experiences of today's developed countries. The chapter then considers the very successful experience of the high-performing Asian economies—the earlier achievers, South Korea, Taiwan, Hong Kong, and Singapore, and three latecomers, Indonesia, Malaysia, and Thailand. The startling accomplishments of these countries are then contrasted to the equally startling deterioration in several countries elsewhere in an effort to identify general lessons. The chapter reflects the growing concern that development prospects can be devastated by "state failure" in the LDCs that do not allow market incentives to operate. In this edition, new emphasis is directed toward the problems of endemic corruption in many LDCs and the debate on the advantages of democracy over authoritarianism.

Chapters 4, 5, 6, and 7 are reorganized to cover the financing of economic development. Chapter 4 focuses on the role of capital investment in the LDCs and how domestic saving by households, businesses, and government promotes it. The account of the role of capital in development now reflects recent modifications in the modeling of economic growth, and the treatment of financial repression and the effect of low or negative real rates of interest on growth has been revised. Chapter 5 is new, containing material on government macroeconomic policy that formerly was included in other chapters. It presents analysis, including diagramming, of the effect of budget deficits and money creation, together with much new information on the successes and failures of macro stabilization and reform. Chapter 6 covers inflows of private foreign capital. The recent substantial rise in portfolio investment receives thorough coverage, as does direct investment by multinationals and the present state of the debt crisis in bank lending that was so damaging to the LDCs in the 1980s. Chapter 7 concludes the treatment of development finance by examining the role of foreign aid and the international agencies including the World Bank and the International Monetary Fund. It judges the debate on the efficacy of all of these, and adds recent analysis of the conditionality attaching to the financial flows from these sources.

Chapter 8 is a conventional approach to factor proportions, technology, and dualism in industry. It includes many real-world examples of the LDCs' problems in these areas, and a rewritten section on developed-countries' technological property and the LDCs.

Chapter 9 on population has undergone a major revision. It utilizes recent data indicating that a fast population increase does indeed harm economic growth in the LDCs. The emphasis is on the reasons why population growth has been rapid in the LDCs, why it can be damaging, and the actions countries might take to reduce population pressures.

Chapter 10, on "human capital," considers the importance of education, health, and nutrition as factors in raising productivity and as "basic needs." A new beginning section links inadequate human capital to low wages in the LDCs. It is followed by an updated approach to education, health, and nutrition that addresses the accumulation of more and better human capital.

In Chapter 11, on rural development, the sections on the spread of the high-yield varieties of foodstuffs and the consequences of their adoption, on rural credit problems, and on agricultural extension services are updated. They remain more comprehensive than in texts of comparable scope. The length and depth of coverage in this chapter fully reflect my belief that stimulating the rural sector of developing countries should have high priority.

Chapter 12, on industrialization in the LDCs, is new. Previous editions focused on planning at this point, while this edition considers and compares government failure and market failure. Today, comprehensive planning is distinctly out of fashion for very good reasons. Thus the selling-off of state enterprises receives thorough treatment here. But project appraisal and the linkage of investments are still valuable ideas, so I try to provide a more comprehensible treatment of cost-benefit analysis and shadow pricing than other development texts can offer. Much of the labor for an expansion of the urban sector of the LDCs is coming from a huge rural-to-urban migration, a discussion of which now finds a home in this chapter. An appendix covers technical aspects of the capital–output ratio.

Chapters 13, 14, and 15 consider the international economic aspects of development. Topics examined in detail include autarky and import substitution versus export promotion, prospects for the terms of trade, depreciation of the exchange rate as a strategy, and customs unions. The important subject of developed-country trade barriers receives a thorough treatment. The Uruguay Round promises a helpful reduction in these barriers in coming years, but if unskilled and semiskilled jobs in the developed countries are lost to imports from the LDCs—or if the public perceives that to be the case—a new era of protectionist trade barriers could easily emerge.

Chapter 16 considers the consequences for the environment of economic development. The rather sudden realization that serious environmental problems may be caused by the long-run growth of heavily populated LDCs is a disturbing element in our subject, one that received little attention until recently. The chapter assesses the dangers to the world environment, discusses how trade barriers based on environmental concerns may become common, and calls for an international organization to assess and police these issues. The book concludes with Chapter 17, a resumé of the lessons learned in the preceding chapters.

I recommend that students using this text be encouraged to purchase the latest issue of the World Bank's *World Development Report*, available from Oxford University Press. This will provide convenient access to the latest available data. If additional readings are desired, Gerald M. Meier's *Leading Issues in Economic Development*, also from Oxford University Press and available in a 1995 edition, serves as an excellent supplement. I cite *Leading Issues* more often than any other single nonstatistical source, only fitting since Professor Meier taught economic development at Wesleyan University when I was an undergraduate there.

ACKNOWLEDGMENTS

Numerous reviewers helped with suggestions and comments. I did not always accept their advice, and they are thus not responsible for any remaining flaws. But I accepted it very often with many resulting improvements. At some point in the life of this book, the manuscript has been read or comments have been received from Eliezer B. Ayal of the University of Illinois, Chicago Circle; William J. Barber of Wesleyan University; Wilson Brown of the University of Winnipeg; Robert Christiansen at the World Bank; Kong Chu of the Georgia Institute of Technology; Eugene R. Dykema of Calvin College; Evangelos M. Falaris of the University of Delaware; Patrick J. Gormely of Kansas State University; Ann Helwege of Tufts University; Whitney Hicks of the University of Missouri; Olu Onafowora of Susquehanna University; Abdul Turay of Radford University; C. R. Winegarden of the University of Toledo; and Harish C. Gupta, William E. Kuhn, and Hendrik van den Berg at the University of Nebraska. Their collective advice led to many alterations and improvements in the finished product. Over the years, Peter Kilby at Wesleyan University has provided encouragement and helpful comments.

The student assistants at Colby College who worked on the third edition were Azeen Chamarbagwala and Susan Hale.

I have heard it said that being an author means wearing a bathrobe late into the morning, asking for many cups of tea, and calling out frequently for synonyms and hyphenation rules. My wife knows how all-too-true this is. Thanks for bearing with me.

Jan S. Hogendorn
East Vassalboro, Maine

ABOUT THE AUTHOR

Jan S. Hogendorn is the Grossman Professor of Economics at Colby College. A graduate of Wesleyan University, he received his doctorate from the London School of Economics. He has been a visiting scholar at Oxford University and the University of Birmingham in England, Ahmadu Bello University in Nigeria, and Robert College (Bosporus University) in Turkey. His work has been supported by fellowships from the Danforth Foundation, the Guggenheim Foundation, the Mellon Foundation, and the Institute for European Studies, and he has been a Fulbright Scholar in England and Nigeria. Books by Professor Hogendorn have been published by Cambridge University Press, Oxford University Press, Academic Press, Addison-Wesley, and Prentice-Hall, as well as HarperCollins.

Chapter 1

Studying Economic Development

Economic development is the study of how human economic circumstances change over time and how they can be made to change. Development has a special immediacy because it grapples with human misery, poverty and disease, as well as the attempts to correct them. The closeness to these problems and the awareness that much will be gained by their elimination brings enormous human interest to the subject. Likewise, a first visit to a low-income country brings quick understanding why such a country may view its struggle to develop as a war, or even a great crusade. The topic holds center stage as the world comes to recognize that poverty is becoming an increasing threat to well-being everywhere.

Economic development is a grand subject that spans continents and disciplines; the sheer scale and scope of its coverage make it the broadest subset of economics.[1] In a sense it is also the oldest branch of the discipline, for obviously all of the early economists were dealing with development topics, many of them similar to what development economists deal with today.[2]

The study of economic development can be distilled into an elementary insight. It is the study of choice made necessary because resources—land, labor, physical and human capital, technology, and entrepreneurial ability—are scarce. Consider the production possibilities curve (PPC) of first-year economics courses. In Figure 1.1, curve 1 shows the combinations of food on the vertical axis and machinery on the horizontal that can be produced with a given resource endowment. The curve shows the trade-off between food and machinery production: greater quantities of food require a sacrifice of machinery; and more machinery means less food.

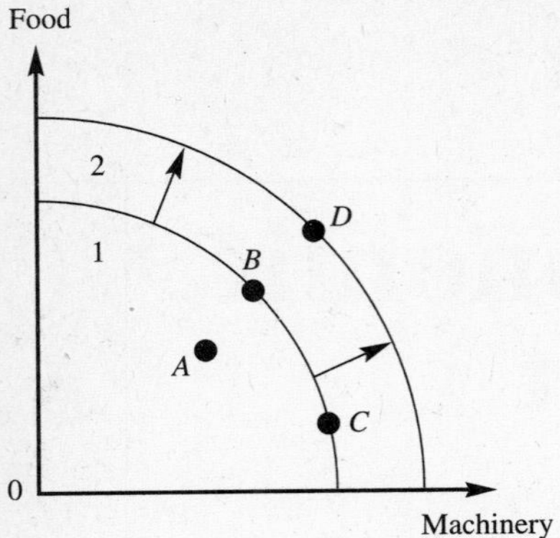

Figure 1.1 Development and the PPC. Economic development can be seen as a search for productive efficiency (attainment of a position on the PPC rather than inside it); allocative efficiency (a position on the PPC that provides an adequate balance in what is produced); and growth in the factors of production that leads to an outward movement of the PPC.

The basic concerns of economic development can be illustrated by means of a PPC diagram. These concerns are (1) The achievement of production efficiency, that is, utilizing available resources fully and at maximum efficiency so that the point of production is on the PPC, as at *B*, rather than below it, as at *A*. (2) Achievement of allocative efficiency, that is, ensuring that economic choices do not result in unwarranted over-emphasis on some forms of production and under-emphasis on others (for example, too much machinery and not enough food, as at *C*, where people go hungry not because production capacity is inadequate but because an inefficient production decision has been made. (3) Growth in the quantity and quality of productive resources, so that the PPC moves outward from curve 1 to curve 2, allowing actual production to rise, say to point *D*.

The first two considerations—productive and allocative efficiency—involve the study of economic pathologies that are potentially correctable, and we shall see that insights from the study of diseased economies can be penetrating.[3] Correction of these inefficiencies can often be accomplished rather rapidly if and when government policies are changed; they are mainly short-run problems. The third consideration, growth in the quantity and quality of resources, is a continuing process that takes a long time. It involves major questions such as what government policies can help to move the PPC outward and whether policies that succeed in some countries are transferable to others.

WHAT IS DIFFERENT ABOUT DEVELOPMENT ECONOMICS?

Much of the subject matter covered is familiar to every economist. Completely new tools for analysis have not usually been necessary, and the standard ones are drawn from every branch of the discipline. Though there used to be a school of thought that totally new models were needed to explain development adequately, today most of the standard conclusions of micro and macroeconomics are quite generally accepted even by many former skeptics.*

Yet some of the major approaches of development economics will seem unusual to a student brought up in the neoclassical tradition of supply and demand and equilibrium. These different approaches attempt to deal with a number of situations quite unlike those of conventional economics. The emphasis on sectoral and systemic transformation is probably the most important of these. Among the important examples of ongoing transformation are the shift in production from agricultural commodities and minerals ("primary products") to industrial output; the movement from small-scale to large-scale production and marketing; the effects of rapid population growth and the migration of enormous numbers of people from rural areas to cities; and the emergence of modern ways from old traditional socioeconomic patterns. Increasing modernity is seen when male dominion and low status of women are replaced by more equality between the genders, when extended families with relatives living together are succeeded by smaller nuclear families, or where closed and self-sufficient peasant villages are replaced by communities engaged in regional and international trade.

Usually these shifts are slow and, at any given moment, incomplete. Hence low-income economies often exhibit pervasive and persistent dualisms that, contrary to the neoclassical theories of markets and movements toward equilibrium, may not be rapidly self-correcting. Urban dualism is the existence of an informal, small-scale, labor-intensive, low-wage sector of highly competitive family and individual enterprises alongside a modern, capital-intensive, high-wage industrial sector. The modern sector may employ world-class technology, radically different from that in the informal sector, and often includes huge multinational firms as well as the large government firms (known as state operated enterprises, or SOEs) that frequently do not follow the conventional rules of profit maximization.

Rural dualism takes the form of small family farms, sometimes heavily engaged in the subsistence production of food and other products for the family's own use, alongside large plantations, state farms, and mining enterprises that use very different ratios of labor to capital and pay much higher wages. Markets can be highly fragmented with limited information and very high transactions costs. Sharecropping—where tenants share their income with landowners—may be prevalent, and frequently the major portion of credit to farmers is provided by these landowners. This low-wage agricultural sector, where production for subsistence is important, holds huge numbers of people, with inadequate opportunities for employing them elsewhere. Many migrate to the cities despite the strong possibility that they will end up employed only in the low-wage, informal sector.[4]

*A note for the already-knowledgeable: The flow of models has not been just one way. Some of the discoveries of development economics that have informed the work of other areas of the discipline include efficiency wages and pecuniary externalities, cost-benefit analysis, hysteresis, principal-agent models, and the crowding-in effect of public investment. See Bardhan, "Economics of Development and the Development of Economics," 129–142; and Alain de Janvry, Elisabeth Sadoulet, and Erik Thorbecke, "Introduction," *World Development* 21, no. 4 (April 1993): 565–575.

Often the dualism is compounded by a public policy of urban bias, with favoritism demonstrated toward the cities.

Another major difference in the economics of development concerns the role of government. Whereas the economies of the developed countries generally benefit from excellent if not perfect information about markets and low transactions costs in marketing, economic development must deal with situations where the information in markets is inadequate and transactions costs are high. Arguably, these economies are also less flexible, with economic change more difficult to bring about. Reasons for such inflexibility include institutions that do not work well, blockages, bottlenecks, rigidities, and lags that contribute to inelasticities in the supply of essential inputs, and imperfect markets. Enterprise may be deficient; responses slow or perverse. Lack of knowledge, inferior transport, poor communication, and an absence of a complete set of markets to ensure against risks of all kinds may hinder the path to equilibrium charted by supply and demand curves. One symptom of slow response by suppliers (that is, low elasticities of supply) might be that inflation is quick to occur and hard to control. Under such conditions, market pricing may work less efficiently.

To overcome these difficulties, it has long been understood that government has an important role. Indeed, at the dawn of development economics, governments were typically too small to carry out effective remedial policies. Later, many governments grew large, often too large, and many of their policies became counterproductive. Numerous prices were kept unchanged by government decisions. Included were foreign exchange rates, interest rates, prices charged by state enterprises, and prices paid for agricultural products. Some governments even tried to emulate the economic planning of the Soviet Union. These activities distorted the information carried by the price system and especially distorted the flow of investment. In many countries, they continue to do so.

Substantial evidence supports the view that a major reason countries are poor is because their policies are poor.[5] Their management inefficiencies in the public sector, often combined with political instability, are severe handicaps. The absence of sufficient administrative competence and organizational ability in government may actually be the greatest existing block to development. As a result, modern development economists face a major task concerning the role of governments. They must work to reinforce that role when it is helpful in mobilizing resources, allocating them efficiently, and raising productivity. But they must also work to downsize government activity when is not furthering these aims.[6] Knowing when to support government activity and when to criticize it is a talent that development economists must carefully cultivate.

DEVELOPMENT: AN INTERDISCIPLINARY SCIENCE

Development is an area of economics that must draw frequently on knowledge from other disciplines. This knowledge is not only useful but also critical for the work of the economist.[7] Law and order or the lack thereof, the degree of democracy and personal trust, behavior based on a desire for power as opposed to economic gain, the struggle of ethnic groups within a country, and the constraints of family and religion are all broadly important. But these institutional areas often are not defined or discussed very clearly by economists. Often insufficient work is done on how these factors influence the "economic" factors. Researchers may ignore these institutional areas or may acknowledge their existence and then, in effect, discount them by holding them constant, *ceteris paribus*. But these areas ought not to be overlooked by a development specialist: sociology, anthropology, political science, and history are all important to this field. This is no doubt one reason why an economist narrowly trained in the standard tools of the profession may feel uncomfortable with this subject and may in an understandable reaction accuse it of being "soft." Experienced development economists—not all of them, but many—cheerfully admit to this accusation and believe that wide application of the knowledge from other disciplines adds to the intellectual vitality of economic studies.

The development economist can profit also from some knowledge of personal psychology—how to deal with and understand people. If old policies are to be scrapped, new policies effectively implemented, or present policies appreciated and defended, then a convincing message must be conveyed to government administrators and politicians. These officials, with training and backgrounds different from economists, are often distrustful of academic models and, perhaps, of academics themselves. Also, these officials must consider political as well as economic realities. They know that a policy change, however much it contributes to efficiency, will have its losers, and the losers may possess political influence and economic power. Policies concerning taxes, subsidies, land, trade, foreign exchange, credit, and pricing of public goods have implications of penalty and reward for political enemies and supporters. Thus, the advice of the development economist, however sensible, may be rejected. A desire to promote national unity, heal ethnic divisions, or project an image of progress can also spur politicians toward economic programs that might appear less than fully rational to economists. Politicians might, therefore, give unexpected high priority to heavy industries such as steel, to a policy of import substitution to reduce national "dependence," to a "strong" foreign exchange rate, to modern tanks and planes for the military, to wide-bodied jets for the national airline and a superhighway to the airport, or to magnificent avenues and buildings in the capital city.[8]

In the face of all this, the economist who can present a model, expound it effectively, and explain the difficult points in an understandable and convincing way is an especially valuable person. There is abundant evidence that proper policy can promote development and that mistaken policy impedes it, which puts a grave responsibility on economists to communicate effectively. The field also calls for the perception that "first-best" solutions, representing the most sensible economic responses to problems, may for political reasons be less desirable than "second-best" solutions. The advisor who can work effectively within these constraints, recommending policies that can be adopted and that will work almost as well as the first best-policies, is a valuable person.[9] Yet it is also fair to say that it can be a great waste of time for an economist to try to convince politicians to change priorities if voters (or political supporters in countries that do not have elections) are not convinced first. A general lack of knowledge about economic policy can be a serious hindrance to the adoption of proper policy, and acquiring the education that could break this bottleneck would likely take a long time.

On Guard!

The student of this subject must be always on guard. The sheer vastness of development economics brings a pronounced tendency to generalize prematurely about what causes development.[10] Catchwords and nostrums of all kinds abound in the literature about less-developed countries. Beware the "hedgehog theories," to use the words of Isaiah Berlin—theories of single causation that reflect little complexity in a subject that is assuredly complicated. There is a danger in being tied to one approach. It is better to use the approaches that promise to yield the best results. The proponents of single-minded points of view are now perhaps somewhat less zealous and less partisan than they were only a short time ago. But a very useful trait for a development economist still is, as we shall see throughout this book, a healthy skepticism in the presence of "true believers" who profess to know exactly how development occurs and precisely what obstructs it. Perhaps even some humility is required—an appreciation of how little is sometimes known of the human and social constraints on progress.

To be sure, a development economist does not need to be a sociologist, anthropologist, political scientist, historian, practicing psychologist, skeptic, and humble student all at the same time. But openness to other disciplines helps to avoid the complaint of Friedrich von Hayek, who said that "nobody can be a great economist who is only an economist. . . . An economist who is only an economist is likely to be a nuisance if not a positive danger."

A TYPICAL LOW-INCOME COUNTRY?

The more than 150 countries that make up this research area have low incomes. Using gross national product (GNP) per capita as a measure, the 1994 *World Development Report* listed 42 "least-developed" low-income countries with per capita GNP of under \$675, and 66 middle-income countries with per capita GNP between \$675 and \$8356.* By contrast, 19 high-income industrial countries have GNP per capita above \$8356. Four economies, Israel, Hong Kong, Singapore, and the United Arab Emirates, have incomes large enough to qualify as high-income,

*GNP and income figures here and throughout are mostly the latest available at the time of writing, taken from tables 1, 1a, and 2 of the World Bank's *World Development Report 1994*. Current population figures are also in table 1. Most statistical data in the remainder of this book, when not otherwise footnoted, is either taken directly from the annex to the 1994 report, "World Development Indicators," or is calculated from it by the author. References to the *World Development Report* are hereafter cited as *WDR*.

but they are regarded as still having many of the characteristics of developing economies. (GNP data for most of these countries are shown on the endpapers.)

Table 1.1 contrasts the large population and low income of the less-developed countries with the small population and high income of the rich economies. Note the considerable disparity among regions. Some geographical areas (particularly sub-Saharan Africa) have performed far worse than others, for reasons we shall have to address.

Further broad similarities can be found among the less-developed economies. Almost always, the lower a country's level of income, the smaller the percent of its population employed in modern industry. There usually will be a large pool of underemployed labor and often much open unemployment in the cities, which has proven very difficult to absorb. The vast farming and service sectors will be low in productivity. Exports usually consist of only primary products and labor-intensive manufactures, the proceeds from which pay for the imports of essential capital goods that cannot be produced at home. The production of whatever goods are produced is often not as labor-intensive as might be presumed from the relative abundance of labor and scarcity of capital because of government economic policies. Whether low-income countries' exports are primary products or manufactured goods, their trade is for the most part with developed countries and not with each other.

Among the less-developed countries (LDCs) there is, however, tremendous diversity, and the economist must avoid the bad habit of lumping them together. Some countries are densely populated; others are not. Some are geographically big; some are little. Some are rich in natural resources; some are resource poor. Some are highly trade dependent (a high ratio of exports and imports to GNP); whereas some are not. Most were once colonies; only a few were not. The public servants of a number are generally honest in their dealings; but in many more they are corrupt. Some are democracies; some are authoritarian dictatorships; many lie somewhere in between. Adding to the diversity, there are examples of both very rapid and very slow growth in each of these groups.

TABLE 1.1 WORLD POPULATION AND INCOME

Area	Percent of World Population	Percent of World Income
Latin America and Caribbean	8.3	5.0
Sub-Saharan Africa	9.1	0.8
East Asia and Pacific	31.2	5.0
South Asia	21.5	1.7
High-income economies	15.4	78.8
(of which USA)	(4.7)	(26.2)

Source: Calculated from World Bank, *World Development Report 1993* (Washington, D.C., 1993), Tables A.2 and 1. The data are for 1991. World income is defined as gross national product. Geographical groupings do not add to 100% because of the exclusion from the table of the Middle East, North Africa, the former Communist countries of Eastern Europe, and the states that made up the old USSR.

There are other contrasts as well. The LDCs, with their very different types of governmental structures, have disparate attitudes toward government regulation of the economy. Some employ heavy protection against imports, while others have low barriers or even none at all (Hong Kong). Many direct their development efforts toward increasing the conventional measures of per capita income and output; others emphasize the creation of an economy that will foster national self-reliance and self-respect; until recently a number focused on the Marxian "modes of production" and movement toward a "socialist economy." But the recent collapse of Communist central planning has put into grave doubt the idea that there is an acceptable nonmarket, government-directed path to development.[11] The dwindling band of countries pursuing a traditional Marxian alternative now includes only Cuba and North Korea. (This book does not treat the reforming economies of Eastern Europe and the former Soviet Union, whose economic problems frequently have little in common with those of the "traditional" LDCs. For these reforming economies, specialized texts should be consulted.)

Possibly, the differences among countries and geographical areas will one day grow so pronounced that development economics as we know it will disappear, to be replaced by regional studies.[12] In any case, the differences point to the difficulty in finding universal solutions. Policies that work well to assist development in Southeast Asia may not necessarily succeed in sub-Saharan Africa. An awareness of diversity and what it means is a valuable trait for an economist to have.

The Recent Diverse Performance of the Low-Income Economies

With all the differences among the less-developed countries, there remains the common characteristic, the unifying theme so to speak, of poverty. The rapidity of economic growth thus becomes a central issue. In one sense the record is encouraging. Real per capita output growth for the low-income economies as a whole (second row of Table 1.2) has been about the same or superior to growth in the developed countries (first row) for many years.*

Taken as a broad average, the increase in developing-country output compares quite favorably to that of today's developed countries at the time they began their economic growth. For example, Britain at the start of the Industrial Revolution achieved less than 1% per capita growth annually from 1700 to 1780, while in its heyday from 1780 to 1880 its growth was still only about 1% per year. The United States registered less than 2% annual real per capita growth from 1840 to 1960.†

*China and India pull up the figures for the low-income countries substantially because their performance, particularly China's, was above average and because the figures are weighted by population. For a discussion of the figures and additional data, see International Monetary Fund (IMF), *World Economic Outlook 1994.*

†The historical growth rates in Britain and the United States have been studied by Simon S. Kuznets; the figures are from his *Modern Economic Growth: Rate, Structure, and Spread* (New Haven, 1966). No country could have averaged even 1% annual real growth for the last 500 years; extrapolating backward in time with that rate would have given them impossibly low incomes, below starvation levels, at the start of the period.

TABLE 1.2 ANNUAL PERCENTAGE CHANGES IN REAL PER CAPITA OUTPUT

	Average 1976–1985	1986	1987	1988	1989	1990	1991	1992	1993	1994
Industrial countries	2.2	2.3	2.6	3.7	2.5	1.6	−0.2	0.9	0.5	1.7
All LDCs	2.0	2.7	3.4	4.7	0.6	1.9	2.5	3.3	4.4	3.5
Asia	4.4	4.9	6.1	10.5	0.9	4.0	4.3	6.4	7.2	5.7
Latin America and Caribbean	0.9	1.9	1.2	−0.8	−0.8	−1.6	1.3	0.4	1.5	0.8
Africa	−0.4	−0.4	−1.3	1.2	0.9	−1.1	−1.0	−2.2	−1.5	0.6

Source: International Monetary Fund, *World Economic Outlook, 1994*, 109. Output is defined as real GDP. The 1994 figures are estimates.

Yet the broad averages conceal some very diverse performances, as shown in the last three rows of Table 1.2. Several important contributors to growth such as investment, the share of manufacturing in gross domestic product (GDP), and exports show the same wide disparities among continents that is shown by per capita output.

The figures make it obvious that Asia has fared exceedingly well. A number of countries in this area, including Hong Kong, Singapore, South Korea, and Taiwan in a "first wave" and, later, Indonesia, Malaysia, and Thailand in a second, are on the way to becoming members of the rich industrial world. Some examples of Asia's success are startling. In 1970, real per capita income in South Korea was 83% of the level in Brazil, while by 1990 it was 221%. In the same years, Thailand's income grew from 40% to 125% of Peru's income. China and India still have far to go, but China's recent growth has been explosive and India's has greatly improved. Among the few exceptions to strong Asian growth are Burma (Myanmar) and Cambodia.

Performance in Latin America and the Caribbean has generally been positive but far below Asian standards, and much better in the 1970s than in the 1980s. It has also been highly uneven; for example, in 1992 real growth in Argentina was 9% and in Chile 10%, while the economies of Brazil and Peru actually contracted. Many countries in the area are characterized by large inequality, high inflation, debt crises, and even for a few economic collapse. Major reasons for the poorer performance compared to Asia appear to include skewed landholding, inward-looking views of international trade, ethnic differences, and political and economic conflict between landed elites, urban commercial elites, and organized labor.[13]

Africa's economic showing has been doleful, actually negative, during many years of the last two decades, and its poorest countries now produce less per person than they did in 1960. Two-thirds of all the least-developed countries are located in sub-Saharan Africa. There are only a few exceptions (Botswana being the outstanding one) to the rule of low or negative per capita output growth in that part of the world. Africa's record is cause for great concern among economists and indeed for humanity in general, and the reasons underlying it are examined in Chapter 3.

Explaining the unequal record of growth among the continents is one of the great challenges of development economics, one that is taken up in many parts of this book. The variability—now greater than ever before, with record growth in some countries but *falling* output in 32 others between 1965 and 1990—makes political cohesion among the LDCs far more difficult to achieve. It also puts into doubt the theories that a colonial past can be a major cause of present underdevelopment. Asia had considerable colonization but registered annual growth in real per capita GDP of about 5% from 1987 to 1992; while Africa, which was heavily colonized, had a negative growth rate of –0.8% annually during the same period. Meanwhile, Latin America and the Caribbean (large portions of which have been independent for nearly two centuries) registered a negative growth of –0.2%.[14] The great disparity points to a conclusion that no single set of development principles may apply equally well to all countries.[15]

The Social Setting: Great Improvements but Great Obstacles

Social change in the low-income economies is also marked by huge diversities. Table 1.3 presents an optimistic view of the social setting in the middle column and a pessimistic view in the right-hand column. The glaring mixture of good news and bad news is apparent.

The rise in life expectancy mentioned in the table is extraordinary. In the developing countries it has risen as much in the past 30 years as it did in developed countries during the whole nineteenth century.

CLOSING THE GAP?

Whatever success has been registered by the low-income economies, closing the gap with the rich industrial countries in any reasonable time frame will be difficult if not impossible. In 1960, the richest 20% of the world's population had income levels that were about 30 times greater than the income of the poorest 20%. By 1990, the gap had grown to about 60 times.[16]

The sheer magnitude of the task is huge. Consider some facts.[17] Indian GDP per person in 1992 was $310. That was 1.33% of U.S. GDP per person, $23,240 in that year; Switzerland's per capita GDP was over $36,000. The LDCs' energy consumption per person is only 11% of the per capita energy used in the developed countries; for the lowest-income countries the figure is just 2.4%. In the rich industrial countries, for every 100,000 people there are 6 times more radios, 11 times more television sets, 15 times more telephones, 15 times more book titles published, and 17 times the number of cars. If the whole world were to be brought up to the income level of the developed countries, world output would have to be about 5 times larger, a very difficult proposition even if the effects on the world's resources and its environment are ignored.[18] Adding to the difficulty, real GDP growth in the LDCs fell substantially in the 1980s compared to what it had been from 1950 to 1975. The figure for the later period was nearly 60% lower.[19] The 1980s have therefore been called the "lost decade" for development.

TABLE 1.3 MIXED RESULTS IN SOCIAL PROGRESS FOR THE LOW-INCOME ECONOMIES

Subject	Good News	Bad News
Life expectancy	Increased by over a third in 30 years, to 63 years. Now over 70 years in 26 LDCs.	High death rates in the LDCs are due mainly to infant mortality, death of children from immunizable or treatable disease, and preventable deaths of women during childbirth.
Health	Two-thirds of the LDCs' population now has access to health services. Public spending on health as a proportion of GNP has doubled in the past 30 years.	Nearly 1.5 billion people do not have access to health services; 1.3 billion do not have access to safe water; in sub-Saharan Africa, one adult in 40 is HIV-positive.
Food, nutrition	From 1965 to 1990, the number of countries where the average person gets enough calories doubled from 25 to 50. Average calorie intake in 1965 was only 90% of requirements, but it was 107% by 1985.	Over 800 million people, about 15% of the world's population, do not get enough food to eat. One child in three is malnourished.
Education and literacy	In the last 20 years, primary school enrollment rose from less than 70% of school age children to well over 80%. Secondary school enrollment has nearly doubled from under 25% to 40%. Literacy has risen by more than one-third since 1970, to 65%.	Nearly one billion people, or 35% of the adult population, are illiterate. In numerous areas, 30% or more of primary school students drop out.
Income, poverty	In Asia, home of two-thirds of the population of the LDCs, per capita GNP growth in 1987–1992 was high, 4.7% per year.	About a third of the population of the LDCs (1.3 billion people) are in absolute poverty, defined as income too low to maintain adequate subsistence. In Africa, about half.
Children	In the last 30 years, infant mortality has been cut by more than half.	Malnutrition and disease kills 34,000 young children every day.
Women	From 1970 to 1990, the secondary school enrollment of girls rose from 17% to 36%.	Two-thirds of all illiterates in the LDCs are women; women get about half the higher education that men do.
Security	The end of the Cold War has meant that LDCs are no longer embroiled in superpower rivalries.	Wars, insurrections, and armed terrorism affect about 60 countries. About 35 million people are refugees.
Environment	In the last 20 years, the proportion of rural families with access to safe water has gone from under 10% to almost 60%	Tropical forests are being destroyed at a rate of about a football field every second. Fast economic growth in the LDCs could make the problem of world pollution much worse.

Source: United Nations Development Program, *Human Development Report 1991* (New York, 1991): 2–3, *1992* (New York, 1992): 14, and *1993* (New York, 1993): 12, as amended by the author.

The least-developed countries suffer an infant mortality rate 8.6 times higher and mortality in childbirth 30.4 times more often than developed countries. The number of doctors is only 6% of the number in rich countries per thousand of population (and only 1% in sub-Saharan Africa); the number of scientists and technicians, essential for technical progress, is 10%. The difference between birth and death rates is reflected in the rate of population growth; in the developed countries population increases at an annual rate of 0.6%, whereas in the least-developed countries the average is 2.8%.

THE ARITHMETIC OF GAP-CLOSING AND THE "RULE OF 72"

Economic growth, if rapid enough, could, of course, close any gap between low-income and rich countries. But arithmetic works against gap-closing. Mathematically, the absolute gap in output will increase whenever the ratio of per capita output, rich to low income, is greater than the inverse ratio of their growth rates. If Y is per capita output, $\%\Delta Y$ is the growth rate of output, A is the developed country, and B is the low-income country, then the gap between the world's rich and the world's poor will widen whenever

$$\frac{Y_A}{Y_B} > \frac{\%\Delta Y_B}{\%\Delta Y_A}$$

For example, if the growth rate of output per person for South Korea (B) is 6% and that for the United States (A) is 3%, and U.S. output per person is almost $24,000, then South Korea will be falling behind at its current per capita income of about $7,000. It would be closing the absolute gap only if its income exceeded $12,000; above that level the condition is satisfied that Y_A/Y_B be less than $\%\Delta Y_B/\%\Delta Y_A$.

Here is another way to look at this. The United States grew at 1.7% per year between 1980 and 1992. China's growth was much greater during this period, 7.6% per year. In 1992 U.S. per capita income was $23,240; the increment from 1.7% growth in that year would have been $395.08 per person. China's income was $470; 7.6% of that is $35.72 per person. So, despite China's much faster rate of growth, the absolute gap between the two countries became far wider, by about $359. (Obviously, whenever growth rates are faster in the rich countries than in the low-income countries, the gap between them will widen.) At present continental growth rates, only Asia has a reasonable hope of catching up, with an estimated gap-closing time of 250 years. Only ten countries could close the gap with the rich countries in a hundred years at today's rate of growth; fewer than 20 could in a thousand years. In any case, many of the economies of Africa and some in Latin America have been contracting.[20]

THE "RULE OF 72"

An interesting artifact of mathematics, the "Rule of 72," is helpful in calculating the rapidity of growth. Take any growth rate and divide it into 72. The result is the number of years needed to double income at that growth rate. Example: growth is 10% a year. 72/10 = 7.2. It will take 7.2 years for income to double. (If you were tempted to say it would take 10 years at 10% a year, you forgot about compounding.) The result is close to what would be obtained with a more sophisticated formula. The actual correct answer is 7.27 years.

Obstacles Posed by Policies in the Developed Economies

There is a close connection between macroeconomic policy in the world's developed economies and the prospects for development of low-income countries. Policies on the part of the rich can certainly hurt the prospects for the less-developed, raising the obstacles to development. The two most important policy decisions involve growth in the rich countries and their attitudes toward foreign trade.

Ever since about 1980, monetary policy has been used by the developed countries as their first line of defense against inflation. Simultaneously, an easy fiscal policy of low taxes, high spending, and considerable government borrowing on credit markets to finance the resulting budget deficits has found favor, at least tacitly. Tight money and extensive borrowing by governments resulted in the high real interest rates that have been characteristic of the 1980s and are continuing into the 1990s. These real rates, often at least twice as high as in the 1950s, 1960s, and 1970s, were quickly passed on to the LDCs. That posed a major burden for the countries that had borrowed heavily in the 1970s and was the major cause of the ongoing debt crisis. More generally, the high real interest rates reduced investment everywhere, in the rich and poor countries alike, slowing growth and limiting demand for exports from the LDCs.

Trade policy is the other potential obstacle. During the 1980s, trade barriers were raised in many developed countries, including the United States and Europe. The rise in trade protectionism was not a coincidence. The high real interest rates and slow economic growth in these regions meant that domestic producers often found themselves vulnerable to imports, and understandably, they lobbied for tariffs, quotas, and other forms of trade restriction. Especially in Europe, high unemployment was fertile ground for protectionist sentiment.

Slow growth, high interest rates, and trade barriers in the developed countries can all have a severe effect on the future prospects of the LDCs. A combination of stagnant developed-country GDP and trade protectionism would make it far more difficult for these countries to develop by means of an export strategy. It amounts to saying that, for the world's low-income countries, several major factors in their development are rather completely out of their control.

WHAT'S IN A NAME?

Probably no branch of economics has had more difficulty in finding acceptable names for its subject matter. The very concept of a developed country is itself unclear, being wholly relative to time and place. How can we say that there is today any developed country when in a century or two it may be (as, indeed, we all hope fervently) that the human condition is bettered beyond present expectation or belief. Egypt under the Pharaoh Ramses, China of the Ming and T'ang dynasties, India under the Mughals, Turkey under the Byzantines (Constantinople of the "gilded streets" wrote the scholar-monks of Europe during the Dark Ages), Tunisia in Roman times (called "the breadbasket of Rome" by the ancient Latin authors)—all were once regarded as among the richest in their world. At the start of the twentieth century Argentina had a per capita national income about as high as Germany, Australia, and Canada, and it was then considered to be a developed economy. But because of its poor economic policies, Argentina's growth slowed so seriously that today it is an LDC.

All of these countries have continued to grow, probably even in per capita terms, but their income levels have fallen far behind those of the rich countries, so people call them poor. In this sense all countries are developing. Poor and rich, we must always remember, are relative terms applicable only to a particular time and place. Keep this context in mind when we use the term *developed country*. Misunderstanding might be avoided by the qualified term *more-developed country* (MDC), which is now sometimes used, but it has the disadvantage of introducing yet another set of initials into a subject in which there are too many already, so we shall avoid it in this book. *Industrial country* could be employed instead, but some developed countries have a significantly larger industrial sector than others. Further, many people would undoubtedly, but incorrectly, associate industry with manufacturing, thus giving too little emphasis to the service sector that is growing everywhere in the developed countries.

Another aspect of appropriate naming is what to call a "poor" country.[21] The word *backward* was used in the nineteenth century, just as the expressions *rude* and *barbarous* had been employed in the eighteenth. These terms' negative reflection on race, religion, culture, and social institutions now cause acute embarrassment. The word *poor* is appropriate when used as a synonym for low income, but it is a stark term that may sometimes carry demeaning overtones toward cultural and social institutions, so it is often avoided. In fact, the unpleasantness of the condition means any label begins to wear badly with repetition, and the subject matter of this field has therefore been renamed not once but several times.

The names *undeveloped* and *underdeveloped* both had currency, and the latter term is still used. The new term became *developing country*, but for some nations this was patently not true.* It was followed soon after in the 1960s by *less-developed country* (LDC). The poorest in this group are sometimes classed as *least-developed countries* (LLDCs), or as *low-income countries* (LICs). At the other end of spectrum, LDCs that have made a success of growing through the

---

*A.K. Sen has trenchantly commented that calling a country that is regressing a "developing" country is like calling a hungry person an "eating person." Amartya Sen, "Economic Regress: Concepts and Features," *Proceedings of the World Bank Annual Conference on Development Economics 1993* (Washington, D.C., 1994), 316.

export of manufactures have received the name *newly industrializing countries* (NICs).*

The term *Third World* is in common use. It was apparently coined by the French demographer Alfred Sauvy in 1952, taken from the time of the French Revolution. The third estate was the commoners, distinct from the nobles and the clergy. The term is catchy and indeed has caught on.† In the same vein, the *First World* is the developed countries, the *Second World* is (or was) the Communist countries, and some use *Fourth World* to designate the least-developed countries. None of these other terms have any currency at all compared to the famous Third World. The third-place ranking of the LDCs in this list causes some resentment, and many scholars in these countries and elsewhere avoid using the term.

A much higher number, the Group of 77 (G-77), is in use. The G-77 is the LDC club in the United Nations that now actually contains far more members than that. The number signifies the 77 LDCs that attended the original meeting of the United Nations Conference on Trade and Development in 1964. A Group of 24 (G-24) influential LDCs often serves as the representative for the larger assembly. It consists of eight countries each from Africa, Asia, and Latin America. The G-24 may be found bargaining in international negotiations and frequently drafts policy recommendations directed to the developed countries' Group of 7 (G-7). The G-7's members are Canada, Britain, France, Germany, Italy, Japan, and the United States.

A geographical designation is also employed, the North for the developed countries and the South for the LDCs, reflecting the fact—we must examine whether it is coincidence—that most poor countries are located in the tropics. The author prefers the name *LDC* because it accurately reflects the knowledge that today many countries are relatively less developed than others. (Conveniently, it is also the shortest of the names.)

GROWTH VERSUS DEVELOPMENT

An important additional aspect of the choice of names lies in the use of the two terms *growth* and *development*. In the past, the two were used synonymously, and many writers still use them interchangeably.‡ But an important and useful distinction can be made. It is helpful to use the word *growth* broadly to refer to an increase in output or income and to reserve the term *development* for the underlying

*Those who worry that Hong Kong is not a country but a British territory modify NIC to NIE for newly industrializing economies. Their worry will not last much longer, of course, because Hong Kong is slated to be absorbed into China in 1997.

†I have also heard it said that Third World was a mistranslation of the French *tiers monde,* used by a journalist to describe the poorest one-third of the world's countries.

‡Similar near-synonyms exist in other major languages. In French, many authors use *croissance* and *développement* to mean the same thing; in German *Wachstum* and *Entwicklung* serve the same purpose; as do *crecimiento* and *desarrollo* in Spanish. See Fernand Braudel, *The Perspective of the World,* vol. 3 of *Civilization and Capitalism* (New York, 1984), 303.

structural, institutional, and qualitative changes that expand a country's capabilities. Essentially, the distinction implies that increases in output (GDP or GNP) may not always be very effective in attacking poverty among the poorest part of the population. The idea of economic development suggests that economic growth in output should be shared by a large portion of the population, and that the population is achieving not just a greater quantity of goods but a higher qualitative level of living.[22] The outcome is that development will most often mean growth as well, but growth unfortunately need not necessarily mean development.

Exactly what the word *development* conveys has been vehemently debated, a debate that is difficult to conclude because the term encompasses a large number of value judgments. There is no universally accepted standard for economic development, so perhaps a rough consensus is the best that can be expected. In this book we shall join the great majority of economists who have largely rejected the idea that some measure such as national product or national income is an adequate gauge of development. Product and income statistics are useful and important, to be sure, but development is a process of structural change in the way goods and services are produced and the way people live; understanding the process is central to the subject.

Let us then, noting the lack of consensus, begin with the following definition of development: the process through which over a long time period the real per capita income (output) of a country rises, with the understanding that not just an elite few but the general mass of population is the beneficiary of the increase. To this we add the further understanding, that the rise in income (output), if it is to be called development, must be accompanied by changes in basic conditions, including improved diet, better health, lower infant mortality rates, better clothing and housing, increased literacy, and an improved physical and cultural environment. Many development specialists would now include freedom to vote and freedom from discrimination as further considerations, for without the safety valve of democratic expression and protection from prejudice, it is more difficult for individuals to develop their capabilities fully. More accountability to the public by government officials would seem to be a necessary element in improving the institutions of the LDCs.

In short, not just output but the composition of output is important. The composition is a significant part of the quality of life. This quality goal is now considered to be of crucial significance by almost all development economists in determining whether progress has taken place. (The word *progress* could actually do more service in our subject, but it is now rarely used by economists.) Some attempts have recently been made to measure this broad concept, as in the human development index discussed in Chapter 2.

The Human Development Approach

The dichotomy between growth and development gave rise to the idea that human capacities and capabilities should be improved directly, before growing output would bring this about. This is called the human development approach. (An older idea, the basic needs approach, focused more narrowly on certain requirements such as enough food, improved sanitation, and the like. The term is now out of fashion; human development is a broader concept.) Advocates of the human development approach argue that the most fundamental requirements of the improvement of all people should be met before the less-essential needs of the few are met. This approach involves raising income-earning opportunities for the poor and public assistance in providing food, water, health services, sanitation, and education. All of these are intended to reach the lowest income groups and are expected to encourage their participation in the economy. The aim is to bring welfare improvements at lower levels of income in a shorter time than could be achieved by concentrating on output growth alone. Many supporters of the idea see traditional growth patterns as flawed "trickle-down" processes.

There is an element of controversy here, in that there may or may not be a significant trade-off between growth and early attention to human development in areas such as education, nutrition, and health. Some believe that only after productivity is raised—which economists consider the key to output and income growth—can a country be concerned with the other elements of human development. Doing it the other way around means higher government taxes to finance the programs at the expense of saving and investment, so in the long run lowering the welfare of all. Certainly there is the suspicion that early overemphasis on human development objectives can impede growth. Sri Lanka in the 1960s and 1970s, Jamaica in the 1970s, and Tanzania for many years are cited as classic examples. Others believe that improvements in the area of human development can raise productivity because productivity depends in part on health, nutrition, and education. Raising the quality of labor will thus raise output; arguably it will also reduce desired family size and lead to a more stable society with less civil disturbance.[23]

Although the controversy continues, there is strong evidence and considerable logic to show that growth and development, income increases, and the provision of basic social services do not represent a trade-off but are complementary goals. The likelihood of complementarity is suggested above. Greater resources lead to a greater command over food and health care, especially among the poorest, and are required to implement the direct provision of social services, which include better water, sanitation, health care facilities, immunization, and education. Therefore, growth promotes human development.[24] At the same time, the delivery of essential social services and development of human capabilities can stimulate output, and thus growth, through higher labor productivity.

The World Bank's *World Development Report 1990* focused on this topic. The thrust of that report indicates that, in the long run, a carefully designed strategy of providing social services to improve human resources and decrease poverty does not entail a negative trade-off with economic growth. In this view, the direct provision of social services is central to both growth and development.[25] The concept of growth with equity, rather than the concept of a struggle between growth and equity, appears to be gaining ground. Nowadays, many development economists can be found to argue that when an economy grows, it must be transformed. Growth and transformation are so closely linked, so these economists reason, that distinguishing between them is not very useful.[26]

ARE GROWTH AND DEVELOPMENT DESIRABLE?

An opinion is sometimes voiced that on balance economic growth and development are not desirable because their costs outweigh their benefits. The "no-growth" advocates base their position on the triple concerns of pollution, depletion of natural resources, and the psychic costs of a consumer society. These advocates argue that "progress" means pollution of the environment and the inevitable exhaustion of an already dwindling stock of natural resources (topics returned to in Chapter 16). Such "progress" means trading a poor life, but one that is calm and uncomplicated in a secure social structure and lived in a relatively clean environment, for impersonality, tension, unhappiness, rootlessness, and pollution; for the unworthy ends of acquisitiveness and materialism; for the monotonous and repetitive work that characterizes the assembly lines of the developed countries.[27]

The arguments are eminently debatable, but we shall spend little time here on this debate because in any practical sense the decision is not in our hands. There will be a relentless drive toward higher material standards of living because, like it or not, there is overwhelming evidence that the people of the LDCs and their political leaders, democratic or dictatorial, have wanted it, now want it, and will continue to strive for it. Quite obviously they consider the benefits to be far greater than the costs. It must be admitted at once that higher material standards of living do not necessarily make people happier. Richard Easterlin noted, in what is now known as the "Easterlin paradox," that opinion surveys in high-income countries do not reveal greater happiness than do similar surveys in low-income LDCs.[28] That paradox indicates that, broadly, the relationship of happiness and income level must to a large degree be one of position rather than an absolute. Such logic appears in conformity with historical experience. For example, Americans of average income in 1900, 1850, or 1800 would presumably have been desperately unhappy compared to Americans in the 1990s, whereas there is little credible evidence indicating anything of the kind.

Higher living standards do, however, serve in another role that can be considered even more important. They give people more control over their own lives by increasing the range of human choice. W. Arthur Lewis, in one of his most memorable passages, put it this way: "What distinguishes men from pigs is that men have greater control over their environment, not that they are more happy."[29] Karl Marx made the same point; he spoke of "replacing the domination of circumstances and chance over individuals by the domination of individuals over chance and circumstance."[30]

This is indeed what development offers to the people of the LDCs—it offers choice, the possibility that life will be more humane and at a higher standard. That standard is not necessarily just goods, though they are highly desired. People can afford to choose more leisure if they want, instead of facing the necessity of working constantly to survive. Activities can broaden to include art, music, reading, movies, and sports; it is surely no coincidence that in America football, baseball, and basketball and in Europe soccer all became popular in the 50 years before the First World War—fruits of economic growth, so to speak.

Another and somewhat different case can be made that a wider range of choices advances well-being. In a stagnant, no-growth economy, according to Kenneth Boulding of the University of Colorado,

> a gain by one person almost always has to be achieved at the cost of a loss by another. Under these circumstances, even personal betterment is viewed as a political struggle, for the person who moves to a better opportunity in effect pushes somebody else to a worse one.[31]

Boulding suggests that as a response to the intense political tensions, authoritarian governments will arise to solve them. Economic development can ease the tension because with development, when one person gets more, another person need not necessarily get less; the other person may get more, too. In short, without development an economy operates as a zero-sum game in which the gains to some are obtained by taking from others, whereas with development, the game can be positive sum, with some people gaining more than others do.

Women and the Desirability of Development

When Arthur Lewis wrote that men have greater control over their environment, not that they are more happy, he used the word men to mean all human beings. But his old-fashioned phrasing calls attention to an outstanding problem of development economics. As a group, women of the Third World are often a disadvantaged class compared to men. Because of this, women stand to be special beneficiaries of development. The literature on the role of women in development and the consequences for them is rapidly growing, and women's issues have become a major area of study.[32]

Women are often underpaid, overworked, and educated at perhaps half the percentages of men and boys. In rural Pakistan, for example, their literacy is just 2%, very far below that of males. In some countries women are legally unable to own property and vote, and often they have little say in whether to have more children.

Women obviously have an especially important part to play in population control and in human capital improvement through their nurturing, as discussed in Chapters 8 and 9, but their importance extends far beyond that. Their role is especially important when households are headed by women, which is true of approximately a quarter of the world's families. (In some areas, such as the Caribbean and South Africa, the figure reaches 40%.)

In the poorest LDCs, women tend the children, sew the clothes, do the washing by hand, haul the firewood, pound the grain, and carry the water. This last task may be especially onerous: in many areas, perhaps nine out of ten women have the task of fetching water from a village well or city standpipe, street faucet, or delivery truck; this task may consume more than an hour at a time and may be necessary several times a day.[33] The only opportunity women may have to leave their houses or fields may be to carry to market the goods the family wants to sell. Women working on farms grow half the world's food. In Africa their role is especially large; food crops are planted, weeded, and harvested by women, who also do most of the storing and food preparation. In some African countries women do over three-fourths of the agricultural work, largely with primitive tools and all in addition to other duties. (The men often work for wages on large farms or in cities.) But women own little land, receive few loans, and receive infrequent assistance from mostly male agricultural and development advisors. It is clear enough that for rural development to occur, the productivity of women must be increased and their influence utilized, a topic returned to in Chapter 10.

A striking statistic is that the much longer life expectancy of women in the developed world is not duplicated in many of the LDCs. While the margin of life expectancy for females over males in the developed countries in 1992 was six years (seven years in the United States), women do not maintain that advantage in many LDCs. The life expectancy of women is the about the same as men in Bangladesh, India, and Pakistan and is only two additional years on average in all low-income LDCs. The scope for improvement in this area as income grows is demonstrated by the much higher differential in the better-off LDCs—for example, an additional six years in the middle-income countries, the same as in the rich industrial countries.[34] According to the United Nations, because of this fact about 100 million women who would otherwise be alive are missing from the world's population. The reason is mainly maternal mortality in childbirth, which is 12 times higher per 1000 of population (and 30 times more in the least-developed) than in the developed countries. But some of it is due to poor treatment of female children, including the infanticide that still occurs in the male-favoring societies of some countries, the receipt of less food and medical care, and some neglect of elderly women. Arthur Lewis writes that

> it is open to men to debate whether economic progress is good for men or not, but for women to debate the desirability of economic growth is to debate whether women should have the chance to cease to be beasts of burden and to join the human race.[35]

Because the present situation for females is all too frequently marriage at 13 or 14, several children born before 20, rapid aging by 25, and perhaps toothlessness by 35, it is difficult to contest Lewis's conclusion.

Conclusion

The case for development would thus appear to be compelling, certainly to the people who would otherwise have to exist in a state of permanent poverty. Henceforth, we will assume that development is desirable for the world's poor countries because that is their choice. The remainder of the book will, therefore, not consider whether to develop but "how to develop." The organizational structure will be, first, to examine how growth and development are measured; second, to preview the causes of growth and development; third, to examine the causes of progress—capital, technology, labor and human capital, and international trade; and finally, to assess the degree to which environmental problems will be an obstacle.

NOTES

1. Compare Gerald M. Meier, *Emerging from Poverty: The Economics That Really Matters* (New York, 1984), 135. For recent extensive surveys of economic development, critical evaluations of the subject, and extended bibliographies, see (in alphabetical order): V. N. Balasubramanyam and Sanjaya Lall, eds., *Current Issues in Development Economics* (New York, 1991); P. T. Bauer, *The Development Frontier: Essays in Applied Economics* (Cambridge, Mass., 1991); Henry J. Bruton, "The Search for a Development Economics," *World Development* 13, nos. 10/11 (1985), 1099–1194; Hollis Chenery and T. N. Srinivasan, eds., *Handbook of Development Economics,* vols. 1 and 2 (Amsterdam, 1988 and 1989); Partha Dasgupta, *An Inquiry into Well-Being and Destitution* (Oxford, 1993); Norman Gemmell, ed., *Surveys in Development Economics* (Oxford, 1987); Deepak Lal, *The Poverty of Development Economics* (Cambridge, 1985); David Lehmann, ed., *Development Theory: Four Critical Studies* (London, 1979); W. A. Lewis, "The State of Development Theory," *American Economic Review* 74, no. 1 (1984): 1–10; Ian M. D. Little, *Economic Development: Theory, Policy, and International Relations* (New York, 1982); Gerald M. Meier, *Emerging from Poverty: The Economics that Really Matters* (New York, 1984); Gustav Ranis and T. Paul Schultz, eds., *The State of Development Economics* (Oxford, 1988); W. W. Rostow, *Theorists of Economic Growth from David Hume to the Present: With a Perspective on the Next Century* (Oxford, 1990); H. W. Singer, *Economic Progress and Prospects in the Third World: Lessons of Development Experience Since 1945* (Aldershot, 1993); A. H. Somjee, *Development Theory: Critiques and Explorations* (New York, 1991); Amartya K. Sen, "Development: Which Way Now," *Economic Journal* 93 (December 1983): 742–762; Nicholas Stern, "The Economics of Development: A Survey," *Economic Journal* 99, no. 397 (September 1989): 597–685; Lawrence H. Summers and Vinod Thomas, "Recent Lessons of Development," *World Bank Research Observer* 8, no. 2 (July 1993): 241–265; Francis X. Sutton, *A World to Make: Development in Perspective* (New Brunswick, N.J., 1990); and John Toye, *Dilemmas of Development: Reflections on the Counter-Revolution in Development Economics,* 2d ed. (Oxford, 1993). The history of the subject is nicely traced in biographical format by Gerald M. Meier and Dudley Seers, *Pioneers in Development* (New York, 1984), and in general by Singer, *Economic Progress and Prospects in the Third World: Lessons of Development Experience Since 1945.*
2. Pranab Bardhan, "Economics of Development and the Development of Economics," *Journal of Economic Perspectives* 7, no. 2 (Spring 1993): 129–142.
3. Bardhan, "Economics of Development and the Development of Economics," 129–142.
4. For some of these points see Joseph Stiglitz, "Economic Organization, Information, and Development," in Chenery and Srinivasan, *Handbook of Development Economics,* vol. 1, 96, and de Janvry, Sadoulet, and Thorbecke, "Introduction," 565–575.
5. See Gerald M. Meier, *Leading Issues in Economic Development,* 5th ed. (New York, 1989), 66.
6. J. B. Knight, "The Evolution of Development Economics," in Balasubramanyam and Lall, *Current Issues in Development Economics,* 12. The fixation of earlier development economics on the role of the state is noted by de Janvry, Sadoulet, and Thorbecke in their "Introduction" to a special issue of *World Development* 21, no. 4 (April 1993): 565–575. The issue focuses on the changing balance between the state and markets in the LDCs.
7. A work that emphasizes the merits of an interdisciplinary approach is A. H. Somjee, *Development Theory: Critiques and Explorations* (New York, 1991).

8. Some of the examples in the text are adapted from Little, *Economic Development: Theory, Policy, and International Relations.* Analyses of nationalist aims and their impact on economic performance are important new departures in development economics. Useful works are Dudley Seers, *The Political Economy of Nationalism* (New York, 1983); and Peter J. Burnell, *Economic Nationalism in the Third World* (Boulder, Colo., 1986).
9. See Meier, *Emerging from Poverty,* 228–230.
10. See Assar Lindbeck's comment in Sven Grassman and Erik Lundberg, eds., *The World Economic Order: Past and Prospects* (New York, 1981), 556–557.
11. Michael T. Rock, " 'Twenty-five Years of Economic Development' Revisited," *World Development* 21, no. 11 (November 1993): 1796.
12. Compare Little, *Economic Development,* 16.
13. Rock, " 'Twenty-five Years of Economic Development' Revisited," 1793, 1795.
14. The figures are from IMF, *World Economic Outlook 1993* (Washington, D.C., 1993), 44.
15. Toye, *Dilemmas of Development,* 39.
16. United Nations Development Program, *Human Development Report 1992,* p. 1. The *Human Development Report* is cited hereafter as *HDR.*
17. Most of the data in this paragraph are from *WDR 1994* and *HDR 1994,* and they apply to various years, mainly 1985 to 1992.
18. Toye, *Dilemmas of Development,* 7.
19. Rock, " 'Twenty-five Years of Economic Development' Revisited," 1796.
20. The idea for this paragraph was suggested by David Morawetz, *Twenty-Five Years of Economic Development, 1950 to 1975* (Baltimore, 1977), 26–30.
21. See Albert O. Hirschman, "The Rise and Decline of Development Economics," in Mark Gersovitz et al., eds., *The Theory and Experience of Economic Development* (London, 1982), 387–388.
22. Lyn Squire, "Fighting Poverty," *American Economic Review* 83, no. 2 (May 1993): 377–382.
23. Following Paul Streeten, "Human Development: Means and Ends," *American Economic Review Papers and Proceedings* 84, no. 2 (May 1994): 232–237.
24. Evidence to this effect is cited by Sudhir Anand and Martin Ravallion, "Human Development in Poor Countries: On the Role of Private Incomes and Public Services," *Journal of Economic Perspectives* 7, no. 1 (Winter 1993): 133–150.
25. Chapter 3 of *WDR 1990* examines the issue, as do all recent annual issues of *HDR.* For discussions of the subject, see Harsha Aturupane, Paul Glewwe, and Paul Isenman, "Poverty, Human Development, and Growth: An Emerging Consensus?" *American Economic Review Papers and Proceedings* 84, no. 2 (May 1994): 244–249; Streeten, "Human Development: Means and Ends," 232–237; Frances Stewart, *Basic Needs in Developing Countries* (Baltimore, 1985); Paul Streeten with Shahid Javed Burki, Mahbub Ul Haq, Norman Hicks, and Frances Stewart, *First Things First: Meeting Basic Human Needs in Developing Countries* (New York, 1981); and Stern, "The Economics of Development," 644–645. For a calculation that countries with life expectancy ten years higher than would have been predicted by their per capita income had a change in income of 0.7% to 0.9% better than expected see Norman Hicks, "Growth vs. Basic Needs: Is There a Trade-Off?" *World Development* 7, nos. 11/12 (1979): 985–994.
26. Robert Dorfman, "Review Article: Economic Development from the Beginning to Rostow," *Journal of Economic Literature* 29, no. 2 (June 1991): 573.
27. The consequences for development on traditional cultures is reviewed by Deepak Lal, *Cultural Stability and Economic Stagnation* (New York, 1988).

28. See R. A. Easterlin, "Does Economic Growth Improve the Human Lot? Some Empirical Evidence," in Paul A. David and Melvin W. Reder, eds., *Nations and Households in Economic Growth: Essays in Honor of Moses Abramovitz* (New York, 1974).
29. W. Arthur Lewis, *The Theory of Economic Growth* (London, 1955), 421.
30. Karl Marx and Friedrich Engels, *The German Ideology* (1846), quoted by Sen, "Development: Which Way Now," 754. A similar discussion by Sen can be found in his essay "The Concept of Development," in Chenery and Srinivasan, eds., *Handbook of Development Economics,* vols. 1, 13. For perceptive comments on how increasing the range of choice can be very painful in a traditional social setting, see Bruton, "The Search for a Development Economics," 1099–1124.
31. Kenneth E. Boulding, *Economics as a Science* (New York, 1970), 86.
32. To continue reading in this fascinating area, one might consult some of the following (in alphabetical order): Iftikhar Ahmed, *Technology and Rural Women* (London, 1985); Ester Boserup, *Woman's Role in Economic Development* (New York, 1970); Judith Bruce and Daisy Dwyer, eds., *A Home Divided: Women and Income in the Third World* (Stanford, Calif, 1988); Sue Ellen M. Charlton, *Women in Third World Development* (Boulder, Colo., 1984); Susan Joekes, *Women in the World Economy* (New York, 1987); M. Leahy, *Development Strategies and the Status of Women* (Boulder, Colo., 1986); Uma Lele, "Women and Structural Transformation," *Economic Development and Cultural Change* 34, no. 2 (January 1986): 195–221; M. Loutfi, *Rural Women: Unequal Partners in Development* (Geneva, 1983); Marilyn Waring, *If Women Counted* (New York, 1989); a special issue of *World Development* 17, no. 7 (July 1989), "Beyond Survival: Expanding Income-Earning Opportunities for Women in Developing Countries"; and a discussion in *WDR 1989,* 246–247.
33. See Barbara Herz, "Women in Development: Kenya's Experience," *Finance and Development* 26, no. 2 (1989): 44.
34. The differences between female and male life expectancies are from *WDR 1994,* Table 29.
35. Lewis, *Theory of Economic Growth,* 422.

Chapter 2

Measuring Development and Poverty

The debate on the meaning of economic progress—growth in output and income versus underlying change in a country's social and economic structure—is reflected in the methods used to measure movement in an economy. The standard measures of output and income are gross domestic product, gross national product, and national income.[1] These tools are universally used. There are substantial problems involved in the measurement of output and income, however. Even greater difficulties beset the employment of these tools to measure well-being, satisfaction, or levels of living, or to judge the progress of different countries or the same country over time. Uncritical use of output and income statistics can lead to poor policy, poor planning, and incorrect conclusions, so we shall examine carefully each of the potential problems.

The greatest of all the difficulties in attempting to judge levels of living involves the distribution of income and poverty. In some LDCs, the figures for output and income can be misleading because income is distributed in a highly unequal way, and a large proportion of the population is enmeshed in much greater poverty than the rest. Questions of income distribution and poverty are treated in the last half of the chapter.

PROBLEMS WITH MEASURING TOTAL OUTPUT AND INCOME

Various difficulties, some more serious than suggested in the neat quantitative tables of the international organizations, interfere with accurate measurement of total output and total income in the LDCs. We discuss a number of these issues.

Poverty and the Collection of Statistics

It generally follows that the poorer a country, the poorer its ability to collect statistics. No doubt some marketed product and the money income generated from that product get overlooked simply because a less-developed country is likely to have a less-developed statistical bureau. In some instances, the absence of data is so formidable that total output is not calculated at all. Other reasons for data unreliability or unavailability are war or internal unrest, and a political desire to conceal or alter the statistics. In doubtful cases, the World Bank does not publish the information in its annual *World Development Report*. Disconcertingly, the number of countries on this list has been rising. Included in 1994 were Afghanistan, Albania, Angola, Bahrain, Burma (Myanmar), Cambodia, Cuba, Djibouti, Eritrea, Haiti, Iraq, Lebanon, Liberia, Libya, Mongolia, North Korea, Somalia, Sudan, Syria, Vanuatu, Yemen, Zaire, and Zambia. Even when the information is published regularly, sometimes a revision will occur that is surprisingly large. For example, revision of the Nigerian national accounts in 1979 raised its national product since 1973 by over a third in some years.[2]

The Treatment of Subsistence Output Fundamental problems exist, however, even when statistical services are reasonably well organized and data are regularly available. Nonmarket transactions with no money flows, important in the LDCs, are exceedingly difficult to deal with. The subsistence sector of an LDC's economy—goods and services produced for one's own use, such as food, housing, do-it-yourself carpentry and construction, transportation, the water supply—is likely to be very large. The types of work typically done by women, including porterage, marketing in village markets, food preparation, and water provision, may be unpaid.[3] The phenomenon extends to exchanges within kinship groups in which relatives are helped not for pay but in return for some help tomorrow or to satisfy traditional obligations.

How is subsistence output treated? In a few cases the procedure of the developed countries is followed, and little or no attempt is made to value this type of production. The omission is a serious one, startling even, and the accuracy, and hence usefulness, of the national accounts are reduced accordingly. (United Nations statistical conventions for the national accounts have reduced the incidence of this practice, however, and have in this and many other ways improved the comparability of statistics.)

Most LDCs do attempt to value subsistence production. Where the attempt is made, however, problems immediately arise as to how much output has been produced and what prices should be used to value it. Take food as an example. Agricultural production figures are often not based on reliable data for acreage and yield.[4] After estimating production, however roughly, it is then necessary to decide on a price. For example, what price should be applied to a pound of homegrown yams consumed in Ghana? The market price? Which market? The town markets are divided from one another by a lack of transportation. What should be done about the wide seasonal price fluctuations? More disturbing, what if the goods, being mostly subsistence production, are traded on the market only in small quantities?

The demand curve for, say, bananas may be highly inelastic because of the limited market, which will thus be thin and volatile. A rise in banana output of 10% will have a substantial impact on price, perhaps a fall of 20%. Measuring all banana output, including subsistence output, in terms of market price would then paradoxically show the area to be worse off than before. As it is commonly true that the lower a country's income, the larger the subsistence sector as a proportion of the whole, then the resulting inaccuracy in the measurement of total output is relatively greater for the LDCs with the lowest income.

Statistical departments generally react to these problems in one of two ways. They use either a "high" or a "low" estimate for income from the subsistence sector. The motive to minimize subsistence income statistics stems from the connection between low income and some World Bank financing, credit terms from rich countries, or tariff preferences, all more liberal for the poorer LDCs. Arguing from a position of poverty also has a certain moral value in North–South negotiations. A motive to overstate is a government's desire to showcase its excellent performance for domestic or international political reasons. On occasion one finds even the statistical departments themselves owning up to the seriousness of the data weakness. There was once a sentence in the preface to the national accounts of Zambia, for instance, admitting that "the figures for subsistence output in the national accounts are purely token figures and it is important to remember that a revised scheme of evaluation would alter the results radically."[5] The same type of problem affects the measurement of output when barter occurs, rather than monetary transaction in markets. Seldom is the attempt made to estimate for the national accounts the value of goods exchanged by means of barter.*

*The problems of measurement were much greater for the LDCs that used the techniques of Marxian measurement. When output was measured according to Marxian principles, many services were excluded from the nation's total output. Measurement concentrated on the production of goods. On the side of national income, the Marxian theory that all value stems from labor content colored its view of capital, land, and natural resources and led to the exclusion of interest and rent. Marxist accounting included only that portion of services directly connected with goods production. "Nonproductive" services such as banking, health, education, and personal services were not included; neither was depreciation. The result was called net material product (NMP). The differences in measurement meant that national income and product figures for countries such as Afghanistan, Albania, Angola, Bénin, Cambodia, Congo, Cuba, Ethiopia, Guinea, Guinea-Bissau, Laos, Mongolia, Mozambique, Nicaragua, North Korea, Somalia, South Yemen, and Vietnam were at one time or another either excluded from the statistical tables of books on development economics, or were suspect—they were not comparable or were at least more difficult to compare with the GDP measures of the market economies. Other countries, such as Burma (Myanmar), Cape Verde, Guyana, Madagascar, São Tomé, and Seychelles were borderline cases. (It might be noted that at one time Communist countries were believed to inflate their figures for production for reasons of policy, principally propaganda and intimidation of potential enemies.) Now, however, almost all of these countries have shifted to standard accounting practices. See Paul Marer et al., *Historically Planned Economies: A Guide to the Data* (Washington, D.C., 1992), for comprehensive comparisons of 17 centrally planned economies with countries at similar levels of development. Methods are also assessed by Elio Lancieri, "Dollar GNP Estimates for Central and Eastern Europe 1970–90: A Survey and a Comparison with Western Countries," *World Development* 21, no. 1 (January 1993): 161–175.

The Underground Economy The output and income from unreported cash transactions and from illegal activities also present a problem. The inclusion of the underground economy of barter transactions, unreported cash transactions, and illegal activities would raise U.S. GDP anywhere from 3% to 20%, according to various estimates.[6] If, as appears to be the case, these types of transactions constitute a larger portion of an LDC's total output than of a developed country's, then including these transactions would raise income even more. India's underground economy is estimated to be about 30% of "legitimate" GDP; Taiwan's, 20% to 33%. The hidden economy of Burma (Myanmar) is very large, at perhaps 50%. (Burma/Myanmar recently canceled all its high-denomination bank notes in an attempt to make underground transactions more challenging.) It has been argued that over the development process, the size of a country's underground economy may follow a predictable pattern: rising in significance as the country's income rises, falling back as policies such as overly high taxes and penal import duties are put right, but rising again as the service sector grows and taxes can be more easily avoided.[7]

In a few countries (Burma/Myanmar, Bolivia, Colombia, Jamaica, Peru) illegal drug exports yield very large but uncounted revenues that are sometimes thought to be greater than from any other single export item.*

PROBLEMS WITH TOTAL OUTPUT AS A MEASURE OF WELFARE

If measurement is a problem, how much more difficult is the attempt to make any correlation between a country's total output or income (even if measured accurately) and that country's welfare or level of living. Any adequate principles of economics textbook covers in detail the traps—population, what goods, leisure, durables, psychic considerations, and income distribution issues—set for the unwary one who tries this in a developed country. The problems are even greater for an LDC.

Income and Population

Obviously, if the same total amount of total output or income is earned by two different size populations (say Japan with 125 million and Britain with 58 million), other things being equal, the individuals in the country with the smaller population will be better off. Aggregate measures are thus inappropriate, and it is customary to employ figures for per capita output and income.

The use of per capita figures introduces yet another risk of error because census data must be used. The United Nations has worked diligently to improve population estimates (see the endpapers of this book), but census data in LDCs can

*Cocaine is thought to be the most important export of Bolivia and Peru and probably the second-largest export of Columbia. *The Economist*, October 8, 1988.

still contain serious inaccuracies. In some rare cases, there has been no full census at all, as in the Republic of Guinea where population figures are based on a survey taken in 1954–1955. Sometimes the data are compiled when taxes are collected, so the tax evaders are not counted. Sometimes political power depends on census results, as when legislative seats are apportioned by population, so the counting is corrupted. The national censuses of 1962 and 1973 in Nigeria, black Africa's most populous and wealthy country, were voided for political reasons, and no other attempt has ever been made.[8] In Uruguay, following a census in 1907, politics prevented another until 1964. Lebanon has not had a national census since 1932. Seasonal migration interferes with accuracy. Nomads, who can move across borders as they choose, will do so when the census-cum-tax authorities pay a visit to collect the tax charged on cattle in some African countries.

Thus the use of questionable census data to compute total output per capita can cause even greater error in that figure than in output alone. (Understating total output and also understating population could, ironically and accidentally, decrease the degree of inaccuracy in output per capita. This presumably does sometimes occur.) Note in addition that some parts of total output are calculated using population figures. Census errors thus feed back into output itself.

Other Obstacles to Equating National Income and Product with Welfare

What Goods? An additional barrier to measurement is that the national accounts do not differentiate among goods being produced. Military goods? (Real national product in Hitler's Nazi Germany more than doubled before Germany's collapse in 1945; just before the Gulf War, Iraq's relatively high output was heavily weighted toward production for the military.) Capital goods, as in a country attempting to grow rapidly through heavy investment but with dire shortages of consumer goods? (China's investment is said to have reached 44% of output during the Great Leap Forward after 1958; the load was insupportably heavy, and the economy suffered severe damage.)[9] Manufactured goods fostered by government tariff protection, so that their recorded values are thereby inflated? Consumer goods, but with investment neglected so that a future penalty of reduced output must eventually be paid? Do some of the products in total output reduce the quality of life, as when more cars cause massive traffic jams in the cities or more telephones overload the system so less than half of the calls go through? Are the goods perhaps produced by unsafe methods, causing heavy pollution and even loss of life? In Bhopal, India, during 1984, a cloud of methyl isocyanate, accidentally released from an insecticide plant owned by a Union Carbide subsidiary, killed over 2000 people and injured tens of thousands more. More intentionally destructive, the West African nation of Guinea-Bissau in the 1980s was taking dangerously toxic U.S. and European waste materials for disposal, which for a time generated revenue totaling more than half the government's budget. The potential damage to local residents was given a very low weight. (Eventually, public outcry halted the practice.)

Many apparently innocent expenditures may lead to long-term environmental damage. The high dam at Aswan on the Nile caused downstream salinization in the Nile Delta. Salinization has also been extensive in Pakistan's irrigation dam and ditch program on the Indus River. Cutting trees for fuel and construction leads to deforestation. Because forested land holds rainfall runoff much better than denuded land, floods and landslides may result (as in Nepal) and hydroelectric dams may silt up (as in the Philippines).* In the national accounts all of these goods are lumped together with those that do no damage or have no adverse long-run economic consequences. Nothing is reflected in total output beyond the market value of the good or service produced.

Knowledge that a country could exhaust its minerals, cut its forests, pollute its air and water, fish out its fisheries, erode its land, and wear out its soils without these adverse consequences registering in the national accounts has disturbed many observers. A pioneering study undertaken by the World Resources Institute of Washington, D.C., showed what a difference is made if this is taken into account. It focused on Indonesia, where measured economic growth was 7.1% per annum from 1971 to 1984. The study indicated that if environmental depreciation had been taken into account using the same concept universally employed in the national accounts to depreciate capital (plant and equipment), then Indonesia's growth would have been only 4% rather than 7.1%. Indeed, because the LDCs depend more on natural resource production and suffer more damage from pollution than do the developed countries, accounting for environmental harm would presumably change the output totals of the former countries more than the latter.

Major work on a new system of environmentally adjusted accounts that takes into account depletion or degradation of natural resources has been pioneered by Norway and the Netherlands. In the LDCs, with U.N. help, environmental adjustment has been widely applied in Costa Rica, China, Mexico, and Papua New Guinea. Elsewhere, it is still uncommon. The United Nations now recommends regular calculation and publication of "satellite accounts" adjusted for environmental depreciation, but this adjustment is not a simple one to make and will presumably take a long time to accomplish.[10]

Notice also the problem in measuring total output when some goods are simply not available. What will the statistics have to say about the gasoline supply drying up because of congestion at the ports or some shortage of foreign exchange? Perhaps there is no bread because a license for wheat imports was mistakenly not issued one week. Perhaps the electricity goes off every evening between five and eight because the generators would otherwise be overloaded by the peak demand, so some sections of the power grid are simply shut off. Perhaps the antiquated water system is closed down during certain daylight hours because population has outgrown its capacity. All these things can and often do happen, but their crucial importance for welfare is not reflected in the national accounts. The gasoline,

---

**WDR 1984*, 95. In addition, there is the obvious increase in the price of the wood itself—for example, by ten times in Ethiopia during the 1970s. In that country wood now claims as much as 20% of household income.

bread, electricity, and water that are not sold are, of course, not included in total output, but periodic nonavailability of goods surely lessens welfare more than is indicated by the reduced figure. Permanent nonavailability has an even greater impact. The health of citizens is unlikely to be much better even after a 20% improvement in their income if there is neither a hospital nor a doctor within 100 miles.[11] Countries *A* and *B* might, therefore, have equal per capita income, but *A*'s citizens chase about frantically searching for needed goods whose supply has been interrupted, while *B*'s inhabitants find full shelves in the marketplaces and public services working well. The implications for welfare can be large.

The question of what goods make up total output is also influenced by geography, with distinct implications for the standard of living. In temperate zones heated homes and warm clothing are necessary. A country in those latitudes will have to devote a fair portion of its output just to ward off the cold, and it will have to have a higher output than a warm country in order to achieve welfare equality. Peru and Turkey suffer from earthquakes, and Bangladesh is hit by vicious cyclones (as hurricanes are called in the Bay of Bengal) almost every year, whereas other countries are not as subject to recurring natural disasters and not at all subject to cold. A given income does not provide equal welfare in different areas when there is a different bill for heated homes, warm clothing, and disaster relief.

Product Quality, Leisure, Durable Goods, Psychic Concerns We next examine the problem of product quality. One thousand dollars' worth of Volkswagen made in Germany may appear at first glance to be exactly the same as $1000 worth of the supposedly identical equivalent made in Brazil, but the quality of the product can differ substantially. Gasoline may be the regular price but the octane disconcertingly low, so that in many LDCs a high-performance car will not only knock but will run two or three minutes after the ignition is turned off because of carbon buildup. Weevils may be baked into bread and little pebbles may be found in rice, the first hard on the appetite, the second on the teeth. A dollar's worth of Indian cloth may wear out sooner, or later, than a dollar's worth of Philippine cloth. The competition that would force prices to reflect quality differences may meanwhile not be operating effectively because of high barriers to international trade.

Leisure is not included in the national accounts, and total output as a measure of welfare suffers accordingly. A rise in welfare because economic development allows an increase in leisure is not reflected in the accounts, nor is a fall in leisure if economic dislocation forces workers to take a second job or grow some of their own food.

Another anomaly is the treatment of durable goods. These goods—cars, stoves, refrigerators, and so forth—are conventionally put into GDP or GNP in the year they are produced and sold. Yet a durable good continues to perform an economic service long after its initial purchase. In theory one would want to measure not the purchase price of the durable good but the services that flow from it over the years. Obviously, the car that lasts 15 years and 150,000 miles yields more services than the car junked after four years and 40,000 miles.

From the standpoint of welfare, there are, therefore, two sides to this issue. Developed countries have more durable goods, and so their welfare is understated by their total output. Also important, however, is the fact that LDCs keep durables in service much longer. Welding car bodies, soldering loose connections, wiring up carburetors, cannibalizing radios, cars, and bicycles, all contribute to keeping durables in service much longer than they would be in a rich country. The welfare of an LDC is therefore also understated by its measured total output, possibly in greater proportion than that of a developed country. The other side of this particular coin is that the tension of daily life rises appreciably, which is perhaps most apparent to the casual visitor when a wheel on his or her taxi drops off. The poor condition of vehicles is certainly one reason why auto accidents kill far more people per mile traveled in the LDCs than in the developed countries—for example, 16 times more per vehicle-mile in Nigeria than in the United States.[12]

Finally, there is the familiar problem of the absence of psychic cost from the national accounts. There is no place in the accounting for working conditions and job satisfaction. Even if they had equal incomes, the farmer working in the enervating torrid heat and humidity of West Africa or Southeast Asia certainly would be in a different welfare position from the farmer in North America. One never gets completely acclimated—not even after a lifetime of adapting to the environment—to 100-degree heat, 95% humidity, and heavy labor with hand tools, all at the same time. For this reason alone, each dollar earned will come with more difficulty and psychic cost. Before World War II, much attention was given to this problem but unfortunately often with a connotation of racial inferiority. Gunnar Myrdal surveyed this question aptly in his *Asian Drama*.

> It needs to be explained . . . why the climatic factor is almost entirely neglected in the literature on development problems . . . , why there is so little specialized research on the economic effects of climate and the possibilities for their amelioration, and why the development plans of these countries are almost entirely silent on this subject. This present-day lack of interest in climatic conditions is in sharp contrast to the thinking about underdevelopment in pre-independence times. Among the stereotyped opinions then elaborated to explain the poverty of the underdeveloped countries—more specifically, the lack of drive, enterprise, and efficiency of other peoples—were theories that all this was attributable to the unbearable climate and its effects on soils, crops, animals, and people, and on the pattern of civilization in general. . . . It was a doctrine consonant with the vague beliefs in the racial inferiority of the colonial peoples. In any case, this pessimism supported the common view badly needed as a rationalization of Western colonial policy, that little could be done to improve the productivity of the colonies and the life of the colonial peoples. That this interest in the climatic conditions, and especially the glib popular theories concerning their effects, served opportunistic ends should not, of course, be taken to mean that these conditions are unimportant or even that all the observations made in the pre-independence era were incorrect. Yet the reaction to this type of thinking has been so complete that, as we have pointed out, climate is no longer discussed as an important factor in economic development.[13]

The point should not be ignored.[14] A hot, humid climate does interfere with work. An East African topsoil baked by the sun into an impenetrable hardpan surface can be abrasive enough to cause the rapid wearing out of iron and even steel plows; a tropical downpour can wash out a farm road or ruin an irrigation ditch in a few moments. Such frustrations have a psychic impact that does not appear directly in the national accounts; the ability to measure well-being is thus lessened.*

Problems with Using Total Output to Make Comparisons Over Time

Perhaps the most confusing use of the national accounts is the attempt to make comparisons with them. "India's output is now 40% larger than it was in 1980" is an example of comparison over time. Such statements are subject to serious questions regarding accuracy.

Any student of economics can explain that over time inflation will affect the figures for nominal income and product, which will make accurate comparison impossible without some adjustment for the price increases. This is accomplished by means of a weighted price index. But the less developed a country's statistical services, the less frequently one might expect adjustment in its price indexes. The commodities included and the weights used go out of date; it is not unknown for some indexes to have reflected the same commodities and weights for 20 and even 30 years. Although such cases are exceptional, it is common to find that the price indexes of LDCs are adjusted far less frequently than those of the developed world.

Problems with Using Output and Income Statistics to Make Comparisons Between Countries

"India's total output per capita is double that of Bangladesh" is an example of a comparison between countries. An immediate problem is encountered. To make any statement of this kind, one has to put the respective outputs into the same currency. Conventionally, the U.S. dollar is used as the measuring rod. So India's total output in rupees is converted into dollars at the prevailing exchange rate, and Bangladeshi total output in taka is also converted into dollars at its exchange rate. The two can then be compared with each other, to any other country whose output is converted into dollars, or directly to the total output of the United States. For

---

*Our discussion of GNP's imperfect ability to reflect welfare could go further afield into many aspects of social organization not closely associated with standard economics. Two such aspects are the possible presence of prejudice or an authoritarian government. Though practically no country is free from some aspect of one or the other, some countries clearly suffer more than others. Examples of prejudice in LDCs would include anti-Jewish in the Arab states; anti-Palestinian in Israel; anti-black among South Africa's whites and anti-Xhosa among its Zulus; anti-Indian in East Africa; anti-"untouchable," anti-Sikh and, anti-Muslim in India; anti-Kurd in Iraq; and anti-Chinese in parts of Southeast Asia. The litany appears, depressingly, very long. Where tension due to prejudice is at a high level, welfare is correspondingly reduced, but this does not appear in the GNP. The same is true for an authoritarian government. Life in Hitler's Nazi Germany seems to have had its parallels in the very recent history of some LDCs—for example, Cambodia, Equatorial Guinea, Iraq, Rwanda, Somalia, Uganda, and Zaire—in which a dollar's worth of national income presumably brought far less satisfaction to the recipient than it did in some more fortunate country. See W. Arthur Lewis, *Racial Conflict and Economic Development* (Cambridge, Mass., 1985).

many years the publications of the United Nations, the International Monetary Fund, and the World Bank did exactly that, converting local currencies into dollars so that comparisons of GNP, GDP, and national income could be made. It is still the most common form for showing differences in output and income.

There is, however, a serious flaw in the method. A country's exchange rate, whether it be rupees or any of a hundred other currencies, to the dollar, may not reflect closely the actual purchasing power of the money. Numerous currencies in the LDCs are fixed at some artificial level by the government, a level that may have little relation to supply and demand for that currency in international trade and on foreign exchange markets.* Buying and selling such a currency may even be prohibited except through the central bank. Little useful information may thus be conveyed by the official exchange rate, of which there may even be more than one if a multiple-rate system with preferences for exports and penalties for imports is in use. The official rate may be so far from what could be obtained on a free market that the statisticians employ a conversion factor in making their calculations. One proxy might be the rate for illegal foreign exchange transactions on a black market. Even the black-market rate, while an improvement, may not approximate a free-market equilibrium price because of the risks involved in buying or selling on that market.

Yet more discouraging for accurate comparison is that the problem persists even if the exchange rate is demonstrably a free-market equilibrium price that does yield useful information. Take a reasonably free-market rate such as 800 South Korean won equal to one U.S. dollar. This rate reflects the purchasing power of the dollar in Korea, or the won in the United States, over goods and services traded internationally. The rate, however, reflects only that, and the relative purchasing power over goods and services not in international trade is not shown by the foreign exchange rate. This shortcoming is sure to be important when comparing an LDC to any developed country because a large volume of goods and services never enters international trade at all. Included may be goods whose transport cost is high (fresh foods) or nearly impossible (house construction), and services (haircuts, domestic services, taxi rides) that are impossible to transport.

If the prices of the nontraded goods and services were proportional to the prices for goods in international trade, this would make no difference, and the foreign exchange rate would give an adequate comparison of the purchasing power of the two currencies. But the prices of nontraded goods are likely to differ substantially. In most LDCs, capital is ordinarily scarce, and labor is cheap. Goods embodying plentiful labor will thus be cheaper than in a developed country. Services usually embody more labor than capital, and so do many labor-intensive, unstandardized products that do not enter international trade. So we can assume that these nontraded goods and services are relatively cheaper in LDCs than are the traded goods.

It comes down to the probability that a dollar converted into a foreign currency will buy more in the foreign country than it will in the United States. In India,

*For a conspicuous example of what might happen, one day in 1986 the government of Uganda decreed that the Uganda shilling had tripled in value. See *The Economist*, June 20, 1987.

for example, the price for goods not entering international trade has been estimated at about 13% of the price in the United States. Similarly, a study by Lloyd Reynolds involving retail price information collected at Shanghai noted a large discrepancy in purchasing power. The same cereal diet, two-room apartment, and use of public transportation that cost $900 in Shanghai at the official dollar–yuan exchange rate would have cost $4800 in Ann Arbor, Michigan. Chinese per capita GNP of $470 per year (1992) looks much better in this light.[15]

This phenomenon was once often called the Gilbert and Kravis effect because Milton Gilbert and Irving Kravis first estimated how much the real income of a country might be understated through the use of foreign exchange rates. The original Gilbert and Kravis study showed per capita GNP in eight Western European countries and the United States during the 1950s, when labor was clearly much cheaper all over Europe than it was across the Atlantic. Gilbert and Kravis found that converting the GNPs into dollars at prevailing exchange rates undervalued 1955 output by 18% to 70% for the European countries studied. Subsequent studies of LDCs have estimated that use of the exchange rate for comparative purposes understates per capita GNP some 200% for countries with per capita output of $600, and understates it by an even greater 300% when per capita output is about $200. The same effect is true historically. Economic historians estimate that U.S. real per capita income in 1860 was probably nearly double the calculated figure when purchasing power adjustments are taken into account.[16]

Recently, the problem of using foreign exchange rates to make the conversion has grown much worse because fluctuations in the dollar of 10%, 20%, or even 30% a year have occurred against some foreign currencies. Indeed, currency markets can be quite volatile and market rates can "overshoot" due to speculative pressures. When exchange rates vary, GNP will shift, and the change can be large. For a dramatic case, consider that Japan's per capita GNP was 47% above Great Britain's in 1978, but 5% lower in 1980. The reason was not that Japan's growth suddenly slowed and Britain's spurted; quite the opposite, Japan's growth rate was much faster during the whole period. The entire explanation is that during those years the pound sterling appreciated against the dollar and the yen depreciated.[17] Rather frequently, a similar situation arises where growth in the quantity of output has been rapid, but a country's currency has depreciated against the dollar so that the appearance is that no growth has occurred in that country.

Correcting Total Output for Purchasing Power These problems with exchange rate conversion lay behind the World Bank's extended effort to recompute the national accounts to take account of purchasing power. The work began with an International Comparison Project (ICP), which was associated with the work of Irving Kravis, Alan Heston, and Robert Summers at the University of Pennsylvania.[18] The technique was to determine a weighted average world price for each of about 150 commodities. Professor Kravis has stated that this weighted price structure bears a very rough resemblance to the price structure of Italy.[19] In effect, a common measuring rod is established in the form of a set of average international prices. The idea is to get an "international dollar" with the same purchasing power over total foreign country GDP, so that the output of every country is valued by a single set of prices. The quantities of goods and services produced are valued at these international prices. A purchasing power parity foreign exchange rate is calculated on this basis.

Currently, annual estimates of GNP corrected for purchasing power are made for almost all the LDCs for which uncorrected data are available.* (The most recent data are shown on the endpapers.) Such estimates yield an outcome that is dramatically different from the orthodox method, as Table 2.1 shows. The difference in some sample per capita GDPs calculated by the purchasing power method as a percentage of the same GDPs calculated with official foreign exchange rates is shown in Table 2.2.

A major conclusion from the use of purchasing power adjustments is that when the adjustments are made, LDCs produce about 34% of world output rather than only about 18% when the figures are not adjusted. Ranked by unadjusted GDP, no developing country is in the world's ten largest economies. When adjusted by purchasing power, however, China is second, India is fifth, and Brazil and Mexico are ninth and tenth respectively. Two conclusions are that the world's income is not quite so badly distributed as the unadjusted data suggest, and the LDCs may be a healthier place for new investment than is sometimes assumed.[20] Irving Kravis once complained that

> as things are the enormous authority of our leading international institutions is placed behind numbers that are poorer measures of real comparative GDP than others that are available. The result is a constant stream of citations of erroneous international comparisons of national real products in newspapers, journals, and even in scholarly papers.[21]

Nowadays, however, the major international organizations such as the United Nations, the World Bank, and the International Monetary Fund (IMF) are giving more and more weight to output and income as adjusted for purchasing power.

Perhaps not surprisingly, given the political implications of this research (LDCs are not quite so poor as the usual statistics show), some LDCs have opposed the publication of these adjusted figures, and UN funding has sometimes been difficult to obtain. The purchasing power adjustments should not, however, lessen in any way our concern with poverty. They simply make our knowledge of it more accurate. A debate is taking place on some of the methods employed in making the adjustments. Some argue that the importance of developed countries in the weighted world-average price level skews the results (only slightly, argues Kravis) and whether the prices of services are treated correctly.[22] Other scholars argue that quality differences introduce a bias. Quality affects many areas, for example, clothing, where the "fashion content" of the clothing receives no weight. A wider range of choice may be available in one country than in another. In the LDCs, education usually has a low price, say for tuition. But how are we able to judge the effects of larger class size and the general abilities of the teachers on the quality of the education? Health and government services involve the same problem. Perhaps airfares are cheap in some given LDCs, but the old Ilyushin airliner is just holding

*One drawback of this type of accounting is that purchasing power surveys are not done every year. New surveys every five years is true of most countries. Annual changes are therefore mostly extrapolations from older information.

TABLE 2.1 GDP CALCULATED BY FOREIGN EXCHANGE CONVERSION AND BY PURCHASING POWER CONVERSION, 1991

	Per Capita GDP (in Dollars)	
	Foreign Exchange Conversion	Purchasing Power Conversion
Low-income LDCs	240	880
All LDCs	880	2,730
Developed countries	14,920	14,860

Source: HDR 1994, 165.

TABLE 2.2 GDP CALCULATED BY PURCHASING POWER METHOD AS PERCENT OF GDP CALCULATED BY FOREIGN EXCHANGE RATE METHOD, 1991 (IN DOLLARS)

Sri Lanka	530	Philippines	330
Pakistan	493	Mexico	233
Colombia	437	Japan	72
Kenya	397	Sweden	69
India	348	Switzerland	65

Source: HDR 1994, 164–165, 196.

together and "it comes when it comes. Maybe mañana." The purchasing power adjustments may not reflect any of this very accurately.[23] It should also be noted that the adjusted data do not take into consideration the missing products that are not available, the size of the underground economy, environmental depreciation, or a number of other problems already discussed in this chapter.

Other Indicators of Economic Progress

Cautions concerning product and income calculations in recent years have led to a search for various alternatives and supplements that would better reflect progress in human development and the level of living than the GDP does alone. Early attempts focused on indicators such as the percentage of the labor force in agriculture, literacy rates, school enrollments as a percentage of the relevant age group, life expectancy, infant mortality, and all the following measured per capita: calorie supply, energy consumption, number of vehicles, consumption of iron, steel, and cement, purchases of consumer durables, number of radios and telephones, consumption of meat, and quantity of letters mailed. Weights for leisure and income distribution were sometimes included.[24] But it has been generally accepted that problems beset such methods. The obvious difficulty is that combining them must involve weighting based on some system of values, and it is very difficult ever to reach a consensus.[25] Young people, for example, may prefer a good score in education to a good score in health, whereas old people might favor the reverse. Meat consumption in the list above would seem to be of far less interest in

India than in Argentina. The problem of the inability of parties to agree on a generally accepted list would seem serious.*

The Human Development Index Until quite recently the best known of these attempts was the physical quality of life index (PQLI) pioneered by the Overseas Development Council in Washington, D.C. It was simpler and less subject to debate over values than the more complicated attempts. The PQLI is an index number based on the percentages of literacy, infant mortality, and life expectancy rates, and for some time it was widely quoted. In 1990 the United Nations Development Program adopted that basic approach, throwing its support behind what it called the human development index (HDI). The HDI combines quality of life components with national product adjusted for purchasing power. HDI focuses on four basic variables: life expectancy, adult literacy, mean years of schooling, and real per capita GDP adjusted for purchasing power. On a scale where the best possible score is 1.0 and the worst is zero, the highest score in 1994 is Canada's 0.932. The United States, at 0.925, is eighth on the list, brought down by a slightly lower life expectancy (76 years) than some other countries have. Barbados is the highest-ranking LDC, with a score of 0.894. The lowest score recorded is for the Republic of Guinea, at 0.191, and eight of the next nine countries on the low end of the list are also in Africa.[26]

CALCULATING THE HDI

In each of the four categories, life expectancy, adult literacy, mean years of schooling, and real per capita GDP adjusted for purchasing power, a country's position is calculated by taking a maximum based on an estimate of the highest figure reasonably to be expected for about 30 years into the future, and a minimum based on the lowest reported values over about 30 years past. For example, maximum attainable average life expectancy reachable in the coming three decades is estimated to be about 85 years, whereas minimum life expectancy reported for any country over the past three decades is about 25 years. A country's reported life expectancy will thus fall somewhere between this maximum and minimum. Take Gabon in Africa as an example.[27] Its reported life expectancy is 52.9 years. Its ranking on life expectancy is calculated by finding where it lies in the range:

$$\frac{52.9 - 25.0}{85.0 - 25.0} = \frac{27.9}{60.0} = 0.465$$

In other words, Gabon's life expectancy score of 0.465 means that it lies somewhat below the halfway point in the best performance that can be

*Another and altogether different approach might be to measure well-being with reference to what use is made of available time: paid work, including breaks and travel; unpaid work on preparing food, obtaining water, child care, shopping and marketing, and so forth; sleep; and free time, including education, leisure, and recreation. This approach is examined by F. Thomas Juster, Paul N. Courant, and Greg K. Dow, "A Theoretical Framework for the Measurement of Well-Being," *Review of Income and Wealth* 27, no. 1 (1981); and see Nissel, "Indicators of Human Betterment," 18–21.

expected and the worst that has been registered. Using the same techniques, a similar ranking is determined for adult literacy (benchmarks 100% to 0%) and mean years of schooling (benchmarks 15 years and 0 years). In these two categories, Gabon 62.5% literacy and 2.6 mean years of schooling gives it scores of 0.625 (not terribly bad) and 0.173 (quite poor) respectively. These two scores are combined and weighted, with literacy given twice the weight as mean years of schooling. Thus,

$$2\,(0.625) + 0.173 = 1.423 \div 3 = 0.473$$

The final measure is real GNP adjusted for purchasing power, with benchmarks from $40,000 to $200. A declining weight is given to income above the poverty level, with the justification for the weighting being that decent living standards can be provided with much less income than is earned by the world's richest countries. Gabon's weighted score of 0.636 is relatively good among the LDCs. Gabon's "average deprivation" is the sum of these three index numbers divided by three, or

$$0.465 + 0.473 + 0.636 = 1.574 \div 3 = 0.525$$

Thus the human development index for Gabon is 0.525, 114th out of the 173 countries ranked.

The HDI results are sometimes quite different from the conventional ones. Take, for example, the case in Table 2.3. Côte d'Ivoire, in West Africa, surpasses Sri Lanka, in the Indian Ocean, by a comfortable margin, $680 to $500, when unadjusted per capita GNP is used as the measure. But in Côte d'Ivoire, life expectancy is just 52 years and only 56% of its adults are literate. In Sri Lanka, despite the recent ethnic troubles in that country, life expectancy is a substantial 71 years and adult literacy is a creditable 89%. Furthermore, adjusting for purchasing power reveals that prices are much lower in Sri Lanka than in Côte d'Ivoire: Sri Lankan GNP rises with adjustment for prices by a factor of 4.9, whereas Côte d'Ivoire's GNP rises by only 2.3. In the HDI, Côte d'Ivoire's score of .370 places it well down the list at number 136 whereas Sri Lanka's .665 is one of the best scores among the low-income LDCs, positioning it at number 90.

Note that the comparison is not as favorable to Sri Lanka as might be assumed. Overall that country's development effort can be viewed as inadequate given the excellent quality of its human resources. Its advantages have not led to strong growth in output and income.*

Only slightly less dramatic and involving two very important LDCs is the gap that appears between India and China when the human development index is used. Their 1991 GNPs' per capita were about the same, $370 in China and $330 in India. China is, however, far ahead in the HDI. Its life expectancy is 71 years, its literacy

*One reason for this is the racial division between Sinhalese and Tamils that in recent years has led to virtual civil war, tens of thousands of deaths, and very heavy economic damage. See *WDR 1991*, 39.

TABLE 2.3 COMPARISON OF CÔTE D'IVOIRE AND SRI LANKA BY MEANS OF GNP PER CAPITA AND WITH THE HUMAN DEVELOPMENT INDEX

	Per Capita GNP ($), 1991	Life Expectancy (Years), 1992	Adult Literacy (%), 1992	Schooling (Mean Years) 1992	Adjusted GNP ($) 1991	HDI
Côte d'Ivoire	680	52	56	1.9	1510	.370
Sri Lanka	500	71	89	7.2	2650	.665

Source: HDR 1994, tables 1 and 2.

rate is 80%, and price adjustment raises its GNP 8.0 times. India's life expectancy is 60 years, its literacy rate is 50%, and price adjustment raises its GNP only 3.5 times. Thus, China's score of 0.644 is well above the LDC average, whereas India's 0.382 is below average. Countries that rank high on the HDI compared to their output and income include Chile, China, Colombia, Costa Rica, Cuba, Guyana, Madagascar, Sri Lanka, Tanzania, and Uganda. Countries where the opposite is true include Algeria, Angola, Gabon, Guinea, Namibia, Saudi Arabia, Senegal, South Africa, and the United Arab Emirates. The greatest gap upward between the HDI and GNP is China (+49 places), while the greatest gap downward is Gabon (–72 places).[28] (The complete set of scores in the human development index is shown on the endpapers.)

As with all measurements of economic performance, the HDI has been subject to controversy, which in this case is a little more lively than most. One figure, the literacy rate, is thought to be somewhat weak. A country's own definition is used, and some of the data are old. Nineteen countries have no literacy data more recent than 1970, and for many more (41) the data come from the 1970s.[29] The HDI has been criticized for not distinguishing female from male human development, although the United Nations has recently responded by providing such calculations, which uniformly show male HDIs higher than those for females. No country in the world has an HDI score as good for females as for males.* The HDI has also been attacked for containing no reflection of unequal income distribution. Now, however, a distribution-adjusted index has been introduced and is regularly published alongside the standard HDI. (Income distribution is considered later in the chapter.) Income distribution adjustments reveal some striking disparities. For example, if South Africa's HDI (0.650) is calculated by race, among whites only it is 0.878 (just behind Spain in 24th place among the world's countries), but among blacks only the score plummets, putting the country in 123rd place, just ahead of Congo.[30]

Some critics are more stern. They ask why anyone believes it is necessary even to try to capture human development in just one number. Isn't comparing literacy and life expectancy a case of trying to add apples and oranges?[31] The respected Yale University economist T. N. Srinivasan is particularly outspoken.

> The HDI is conceptually weak and empirically unsound, involving serious problems of noncomparability over time and space, measurement errors, and biases. Meaningful

*The gender-sensitive index has difficulties of its own, particularly the measurement of female versus male incomes. It uses wages as a surrogate, but this cannot reflect non-monetized household work.

inferences about the process of development and performance as well as policy implications could hardly be drawn from variations in HDI.[32]

Clearly, as the critics charge, the HDI is arbitrary and that arbitrariness cannot be eliminated. But the HDI has also provided an eye-catching way to call attention to problems with the use of unadjusted GDP per capita.[33] It also now provides a convenient way to illustrate how certain social indicators behave over time on a country-by-country basis.* For all the weaknesses, it is well worth calculating the HDI.

POVERTY AND INCOME DISTRIBUTION

Perhaps the greatest of all the problems with measuring economic development is that GNP and income per capita say nothing at all about the distribution of the output and income. Including the income inequalities within countries, the richest 20% of the world's people get at least 150 times more income than the poorest 20%.[34] Of course, in market economies full equality of incomes is not a reasonable goal, for that would undercut the incentives of the market system. Yet the implications for welfare of overly great inequalities in income can be great, and income distribution issues have become central in the growth-versus-development debate. These issues are treated in detail in the remainder of this chapter.

Unequal distribution within a country can affect welfare negatively in several fairly obvious ways. When a small number of rich become more affluent at the expense of a mass of poor who are plunged more deeply into poverty, then health and nutrition problems are likely to arise, birth rates might rise to make up for the higher infant mortality, and social and political tension would almost inevitably increase. A study by Alberto Alesina and Roberto Perotti involving 70 countries during the period 1960 to 1985 suggests that income inequality leads to social discontent, which causes political and economic instability. In turn, they argue, this reduces investment and therefore economic growth. Alesina and Perotti developed an index of political instability based on the number of assassinations, the occurrence of domestic mass violence, coups and attempted coups, and the level of democracy. According to this index the more unequal a country's income distribution, the more politically unstable it is.[35] This is not to mention the ethical unacceptability of further impoverishing the poor to benefit those already much better off.

If democratic elections result in populist governments that attempt to carry out the will of the people, then large inequalities in income distribution can have other negative results. There is some evidence to indicate that in this situation, economic policies may be adopted that tax growth-promoting activities, such as investment, in order to make the income distribution more equal.[36]

Even if all incomes increase, but grow faster for the rich, then social and political tension may still result; but it may not if absolute incomes have more meaning

*Before changes in the procedure in 1994, it was not possible to make clear comparisons as to what was happening over time to a country's indicators.

for people than relative incomes, or if there seems to be a significant chance for the poor eventually to move into upper-income groups.[37]

The large potential impact of inequality on welfare is disturbing because data appear to support the belief that income distribution will be persistently less equal in LDCs than in developed countries. (Admittedly, the data are inadequate—only a few countries have good time-series data on distributional issues.) The first generation of development economists was little aware of how troublesome and long-lasting this condition could be.

Absolute Poverty

Economists use the term *absolute poverty* to describe that part of the population which falls below some minimally acceptable standard of living. This group falls below the level of income that, in the country concerned, will purchase output just adequate for subsistence. The measurement usually involves an estimate of the income needed to achieve some minimum level of sustenance (2250 calories per day in India's pioneering approach) plus some further estimate of the smallest amount of income needed for nonfood items, shelter, and clothing.*

Defining absolute poverty as income below $370 in 1985 dollars adjusted for purchasing power, the United Nations estimates that somewhat over 1 billion people are in this condition. That is about one-third of the population of the LDCs. In the least-developed LDCs, 31% of the urban population and 71% of the rural population live in absolute poverty.[38] (For middle-income countries, the figures are, understandably, much better, under 20% for both urban and rural populations.) Table 2.4 indicates that absolute poverty is sometimes elevated even in countries with relatively high incomes. None of the countries shown in Table 2.4 is classified

TABLE 2.4 PERCENTAGE OF POPULATION IN ABSOLUTE POVERTY, 1980–1990

	Urban	Rural
Ecuador	40	65
Guatemala	66	74
Jamaica	—	80
Morocco	28	45
Philippines	40	64

Source: HDR 1994, table 18.

*The usual technique is to measure the financial cost of obtaining a minimum necessary level of caloric needs and then multiply that by a factor to obtain the necessary spending for the nonfood items necessary for subsistence. See *HDR 1990*, 106. The tying of the absolute level to fulfillment of some minimum level of caloric needs appears reasonable but has also sparked controversy. Different climates and work environments lead to different caloric needs even for the same person; other requirements such as vitamins, protein, and so forth are not considered, and there has been debate on the appropriateness of the 2250-calorie benchmark. See Peter Cutler, "The Measurement of Poverty: A Review of Attempts to Quantify the Poor with Special Reference to India," *World Development* 12, nos. 11/12 (1984); 1119–1130. For a further discussion of alternative measurements, see *WDR 1990*, chapter 2.

among the poorest LDCs. Great differences exist in countries with relatively similar overall levels of per capita income. For example, India's figure for rural residents below the line of absolute poverty is 42%, whereas China's figure is just 13%. The absolute poverty figures leave some major questions unanswered. For example, it is important to know whether most of the absolutely poor are earning 98% of the poverty line figure or 50% of it, and the single figure does not express that. Even so, the wider availability of information on absolute poverty has been a welcome addition to the usefulness of the national accounts.

Table 2.5 shows another side to the poverty issue: the situation is much worse in sub-Saharan Africa and South Asia than it is anywhere else. Moreover, the table demonstrates that poverty has not been declining; it being about the same in 1985 and 1990. This lack of progress is disappointing.

It is striking that a transfer of income amounting to just 4% of the total GNP of the LDCs would raise everyone above the poverty line. Even with growth of just 1% per year, absolute poverty could be completely eliminated in just four to ten years, assuming all increases in income went to those in poverty.[39]

Poverty May Be Concentrated Geographically Within a Country The part of the population living in poverty may be concentrated geographically, with wide differences in income distribution existing among regions within individual LDCs. The income disparities among regions of the *developed* countries are for the most part rather slight. For example, income in the U.S. South is over 80% of the income level of the prosperous middle-Atlantic states. But LDCs face much more internal disparity. In Brazil, the state that contains Rio de Janeiro has an average income ten times that of the poor states in the northeast; these states have over half the country's poor but only about a quarter of its total population. The Shanghai region of China is more than 11 times richer than Guizhou Province, and the per capita income of China's eastern region is estimated to be 50% higher than that of the southern region. Western India's income is only 60% of eastern India's. Peru's coastal area has an income 12 times that of the Amazonian states. Similar comparisons can be drawn between Indonesia's rich Java to poor Sumatra, or Turkey's relatively wealthy Aegean Coast and Istanbul to the backward east. These

TABLE 2.5 PERCENTAGE OF POPULATION BELOW POVERTY LINE, 1985 AND 1990

	1985	1990
All LDCs	30.5	29.7
South Asia	51.8	49.0
East Asia	13.2	11.3
Sub-Saharan Africa	47.6	47.8
Latin America, Caribbean	22.4	25.5

Note: The poverty line used here is $370 annual income per capita in 1985 dollars adjusted for purchasing power.

Source: WDR 1992, 30.

and many similar examples make it clear that distribution is more unequal in the LDCs, and poverty can be heavily concentrated.*

Similarly, geographical disparities appear when the UN's human development index is calculated by region of a country. Among the few HDI calculations that have been made by region are those for Brazil and Nigeria. South Brazil is in forty-second place, equal to Portugal, while North Brazil is one-hundred-and-eleventh, equal to Bolivia. In Nigeria, one state (Bendel) has an HDI equal to Sri Lanka's high score, while Borno State's HDI is lower than that of any country (0.156 compared to Guinea's 0.191).

The Causes of Income Inequality

There are seven main causes for greater income inequality in the LDCs than in the developed countries. (1) Most important in some areas, land ownership and access to land are highly unequal for historical and social reasons. (2) Significant scarcities of professional and technical skills mean that the renumeration of teachers, engineers, scientists, computer specialists, economists, physicians, and the like may be driven up relative to the rest of the population, thereby ensuring unusual disparities in income. (3) Widespread existence of imperfect factor mobility, imperfect information, and monopoly power based on economic or political strength may make existing disparities difficult to close. (4) Inequalities can be perpetuated by a social structure that excludes people on the basis of caste, race, sex, or religion from jobs, land-holding, and other means to produce income. (5) Even where governments wish to move toward more equity, taxes and transfer payments are less effective in changing the distribution of income than they are in the developed world because the mechanisms themselves are less developed. (6) Government pricing policies, subsidies, taxes, credit, foreign exchange allocations, land policies, and the like may be used to reward supporters and penalize opponents and the powerless. (7) Population growth means an increase in the percent of young people in the population. Inequality rises even though the distribution of income stays the same within any given age group. Although this symptom is ultimately self-correcting, it is still real and appears in the statistics.

Unequal distribution is especially pronounced in parts of Central and South America, where land ownership is highly skewed. There the poorest fifth of the population receives only about half the income that this fifth receives in Africa and East Asia.[40] Income is also very unevenly distributed in some of the oil-producing states. But income inequality problems seem to affect all types of LDCs.

Measuring Income Inequality

Until the 1970s, there was little available information on income distribution, and change was difficult to assess.[41] Since that time, however, much more attention has been focused on the issue. Methods of measurement have been refined, and the

---

*The figures are, however, biased by different price levels in the regions. When data are available, they tend to show lesser differences when prices are taken into account. For example, in Brazil about one-third of the income difference between the rich southwest and the poor northeast is accounted for by price differences between the regions. See *WDR 1991*, 40–41.

data available have become much more comprehensive. Whether the data are uniformly better is open to question. Sometimes the figures for income distribution are calculated from very imperfect information, and less confidence should be placed in them than even in the figures for income and product.

The Lorenz Curve and Distribution by Quintiles Economists measure the degree of income inequality with the Lorenz curve, a graphical representation of data named after the American statistician Max Otto Lorenz, who developed it in 1905.[42] Figure 2.1 shows the percentage of income earned on the vertical axis and the percentage of the population earning that income on the horizontal axis. If income is distributed equally throughout the whole population, then the poorest 30% of the population earns 30% of the income (point *Y*), and 100% of the population earns 100% of the income (point *X*). If income is not distributed equally, then the poorest 30% of the population might earn only 10% of the income, as at point Z. If distribution is equal, then the Lorenz curve is a 45-degree line sloping

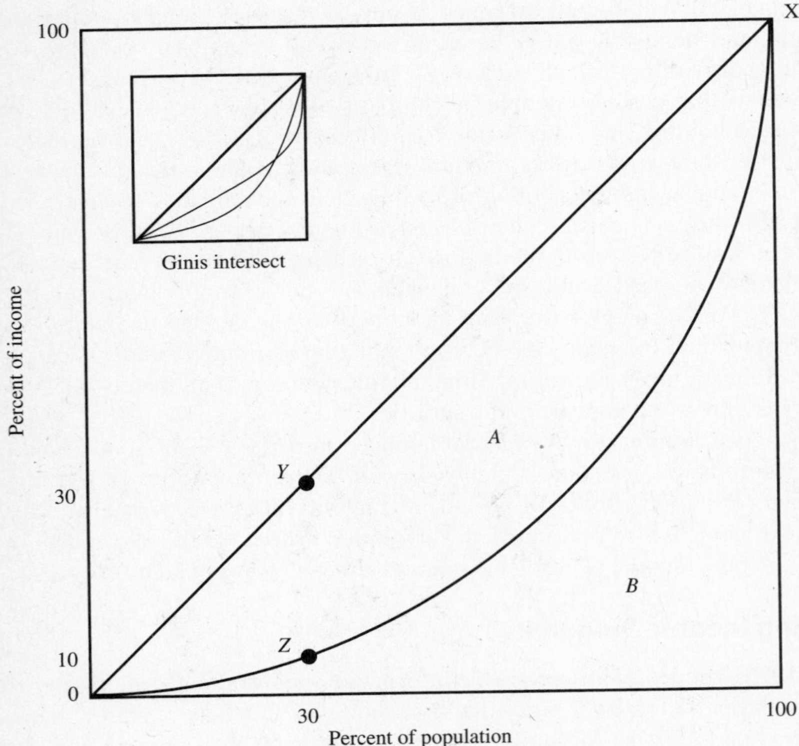

Figure 2.1 A Lorenz curve of income distribution shows the percentage of income earned by a given percentage of the population. At point Z, the poorest 30% of the population earns 10% of the income. The greater the bow, the greater the inequality of income. The calculation (*A*/*A* + *B*) is called the Gini coefficient. The higher the Gini coefficient, the greater the degree of income inequality.

up from the origin of the figure. If distribution is unequal, the curve is bowed away from the 45-degree line. The greater the bow, the larger the degree of inequality. A potential problem arises in the comparison of countries or time periods if two curves intersect (as in the inset of Figure 2.1). It is then hard to state which curve represents the greater inequality; a normative judgment must be made because some parts of society are more equal and some are less equal.

A Lorenz curve is rather cumbersome, and it is possible to present the same underlying information on distribution in a numerical format. The method favored by the World Bank is to array the distribution by quintiles (20% of the population). The data can be by household or by individuals.[43] For example, India's income distribution is given by quintiles in Table 2.6. The poorest 20% of the population earns 8.8% of the income; the richest quintile earns 41.3%. The figures can be added across columns. For example, the lowest 40% of the population by income earned 21.3% of all the income.

Some examples of especially great inequality and relatively less inequality are presented in Table 2.7, along with some developed country comparisons.

When comparing two countries, if one country has a greater percentage share of income accruing in at least one quintile below the highest, and its other three below the highest are at least equal, then that country is said to have "Lorenz dominance over" or to "Lorenz dominate" the other country. Sri Lanka, with percentage shares of 4.8, 9.5, 14.4, and 21.9 for the quintiles below the highest clearly "Lorenz dominates" Kenya's 3.4, 6.7, 10.7, and 17.3. Often, though, one country might have a higher share in one of the quintiles and a lower share in another, in which case the comparison is more ambiguous.

The Gini Coefficient Another method of comparison yields a number for each country derived from areas on the Lorenz curve diagram. Recall that the more unequal the distribution, the more bowed the Lorenz curve will be. The greater bow increases the area labeled A in Figure 2.1 and decreases the area labeled B. The calculation ($A/A + B$) is called the Gini coefficient, after Corrado Gini, the Italian statistician who first formulated it in 1912. The more unequal the distribution, the larger the area A and thus the higher the Gini coefficient.

Recent Gini calculations are given in Table 2.8(p. 47).* The high coefficients for many LDCs contrast with the much lower Ginis for most of the developed countries, usually in the low 0.30s (United States 0.38), and a few LDCs which exhibit Ginis at about the same level as in the developed countries.

The main problem with Ginis is that countries with quite different income distributions can have similar coefficients. This would be true when two Lorenz

*Other calculated Gini coefficients differing somewhat from those shown in the text are given in Lecaillon et al., *Income Distribution*, chap. 2. A world average Gini is a high 0.67. See Margaret E. Grosh and E. Wayne Nafziger, "The Computation of World Income Distribution," *Economic Development and Cultural Change* 34, no. 2 (1986): 347–359. In addition to the Gini coefficient, there is another method for measuring income distribution called a Theil index, named for Henri Theil. More advanced treatises in income distribution can be consulted for details.

TABLE 2.6 PERCENTAGE SHARE OF TOTAL DISPOSABLE HOUSEHOLD INCOME IN INDIA BY PERCENTILE POPULATION GROUPS

Lowest 20%	Second 20%	Third 20%	Fourth 20%	Highest 20%
8.8	12.5	16.2	21.3	41.3

Note: Though these data are recent, dating from 1989–1990, in many other LDCs studies on income distribution are carried out infrequently if at all, so there are large gaps in the published information.

Source: WDR 1994, 220.

TABLE 2.7 PERCENTAGES OF TOTAL DISPOSABLE HOUSEHOLD INCOME BY PERCENTILE POPULATION GROUPS

	Lowest 20%	Second 20%	Third 20%	Fourth 20%	Highest 20%
Panama	2.0	6.3	11.6	20.3	59.8
Brazil	2.1	4.9	8.9	16.8	67.5
Guatemala	2.1	5.8	10.5	18.6	63.0
Tanzania	2.4	5.7	10.4	18.7	62.7
Honduras	2.7	6.0	10.2	17.6	63.5
Kenya	3.4	6.7	10.7	17.3	61.8
Colombia	3.6	7.6	12.6	20.4	55.8
Zimbabwe	4.0	6.3	10.0	17.4	62.3
Venezuela	4.8	9.5	14.4	21.9	49.5
Peru	4.9	9.2	13.7	21.0	51.4
Morocco	6.6	10.5	15.0	21.7	46.3
China	6.4	11.0	16.4	24.4	41.8
South Korea	7.4	12.3	16.3	21.8	42.2
United Kingdom	4.6	10.0	16.8	24.3	44.3
United States	4.7	11.0	17.4	25.0	41.9
France	5.6	11.8	17.2	23.5	41.9
Germany	7.0	11.8	17.1	23.9	40.3
Japan	8.7	13.2	17.5	23.1	37.5

Note: The figures in the table are for widely different years.

Source: WDR 1994, table 30.

curves intersect, as in the inset to Figure 2.1. So the distribution by quintiles favored by the World Bank, even though it requires dealing with more than one number for each country, has gained favor.

Whatever technical measure is employed, any movement toward income equality in the LDCs has been limited. Typically in an LDC the richest 10% of the population still receives 30% to 40% of the pretax income, whereas in a developed country the richest 10% receives only 20% to 30%. (This relative difference, however, does not overcome the absolute difference. The rich in the developed countries are richer on average than the rich in the LDCs.)

TABLE 2.8 GINI COEFFICIENT, LATEST YEAR

Country	Gini	Country	Gini
Ecuador	0.66	Hong Kong	0.45
Jamaica	0.66	Sri Lanka	0.45
Honduras	0.62	Philippines	0.45
Sierra Leone	0.59	Costa Rica	0.42
Brazil	0.57	Singapore	0.42
Panama	0.57	India	0.42
Côte d'Ivoire	0.55	El Salvador	0.40
Nepal	0.53	Tunisia	0.40
Turkey	0.51	Bangladesh	0.39
Mexico	0.50	Egypt	0.38
Malaysia	0.48	United States	0.38
Thailand	0.47	South Korea	0.36
Chile	0.46	Pakistan	0.36
Iran	0.46	Peru	0.31
Colombia	0.45	Indonesia	0.31

Source: Taken where available from *HDR 1993,* table 18, and otherwise from earlier issues of the *HDR.* Gini coefficients are calculated infrequently. The data here are for various years, 1975 to 1988. The U.S. figure is from the *Statistical Abstract of the United States,* 1993, table 750.

The Debate on Whether Growth Makes Income Distribution Less Equal

For many years, a debate has been conducted on the relationship between growth and the distribution of income. One school of thought dating from work by Harvard University's Simon Kuznets in 1954 argues that trends in income distribution follow a pattern during the development process. According to this view, over time a curve plotting the Gini coefficient assumes an inverted U-shape as in Figure 2.2. Believers in the U-shape generally conceded, however, that the *U* has gradually sloping, rather than steep, sides, indicating that the tendency is relatively weak.[44]

There are indeed logical reasons to believe that an inverted *U* of Ginis could occur. A compelling one is that in a poor, stagnant economy, the onset of growth will raise some people's income (entrepreneurs, the skilled, those located where growth first occurs) before it touches others. Another reason involves the shift in a country's structure of production. A small structural change involving movement from a poor (rural) sector to a higher income (urban) sector could lead to increased inequality. A common-sense way of seeing this is to picture a society wherein the whole population, with equal incomes, is in agriculture. Then shift one person into a new, higher-paid industrial sector. Immediately, inequality increases and the Gini rises. This effect will be diluted as growth proceeds, but it will occur nonetheless.

A further cause of the inverted *U* might be that a very poor country has little population growth; death rates are too high to allow it. With income growth, population also grows, and this has an effect on the Gini. The percentage of younger people in the population increases; the weight of their low or nil incomes therefore rises; and the Gini indicates increased inequality. Morton Paglin showed in the 1970s that a third of all U.S. inequality is due to changes in the age–income profile, and, of course, U.S. population growth is relatively low.[45] The existence of an inverted U-shaped curve might indicate that to increase the equality of income

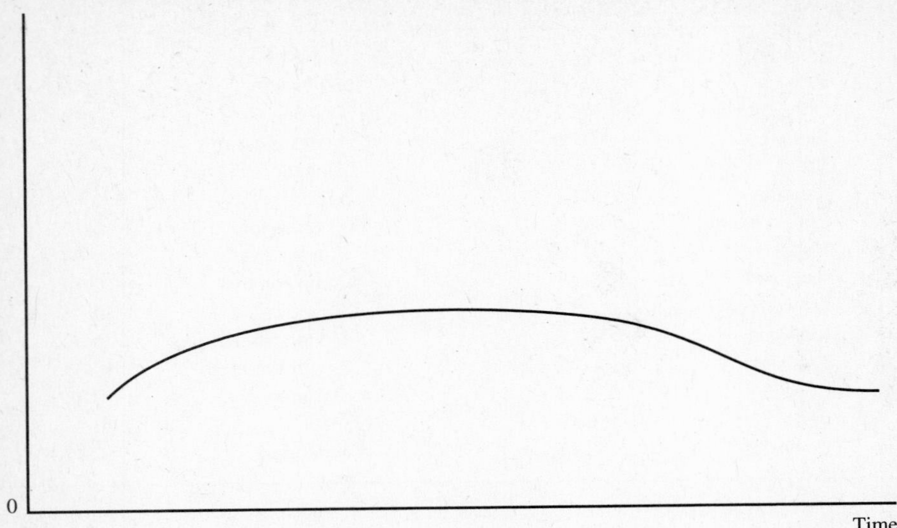

Figure 2.2 The suggested inverted U-shape of the Gini coefficient, with its implication that income distribution becomes less equal as development begins and becomes more equal as it progresses.

distribution in the medium term, special programs targeted toward distribution might be needed because growth in the same time period predictably will lessen equality.

The increasing equality shown by the right side of the *U* might logically be due to higher levels of education and skills, with a major effect on the poorer part of the population, a slowing of population growth, and a catching up by the retarded sectors of the economy.

The Kuznets Curve of Income Distribution The debate on whether growth brings a more or less equal distribution can conveniently be illustrated with a so-called Kuznets curve in Figure 2.3, named for the same Simon Kuznets, whose research on the matter was mentioned earlier. The per capita income of the top 40% of the population is plotted on the vertical axis and the per capita income of the bottom 60% on the horizontal axis. A Kuznets curve shows how income distribution changes as income grows. For example, a straight line through the origin shows unchanging income distribution with increasing income. So at point *A*, the top 40% of the population might be receiving $800 in income per person, and the bottom 60%, $200. Further up the curve at point *B*, economic growth has raised the figure for the top 40% to $1600 and the bottom 60% to $400. Note that points *A* and *B* show no change in distribution. If income growth is accompanied by a change in distribution, the Kuznets curve will not intersect the origin. If distribution is less equal—that is, richer people's incomes are expanding faster than poorer people's—the curve (dotted in the figure) intersects the horizontal axis. A Kuznets curve (dashed in the figure) intersecting the vertical axis represents more

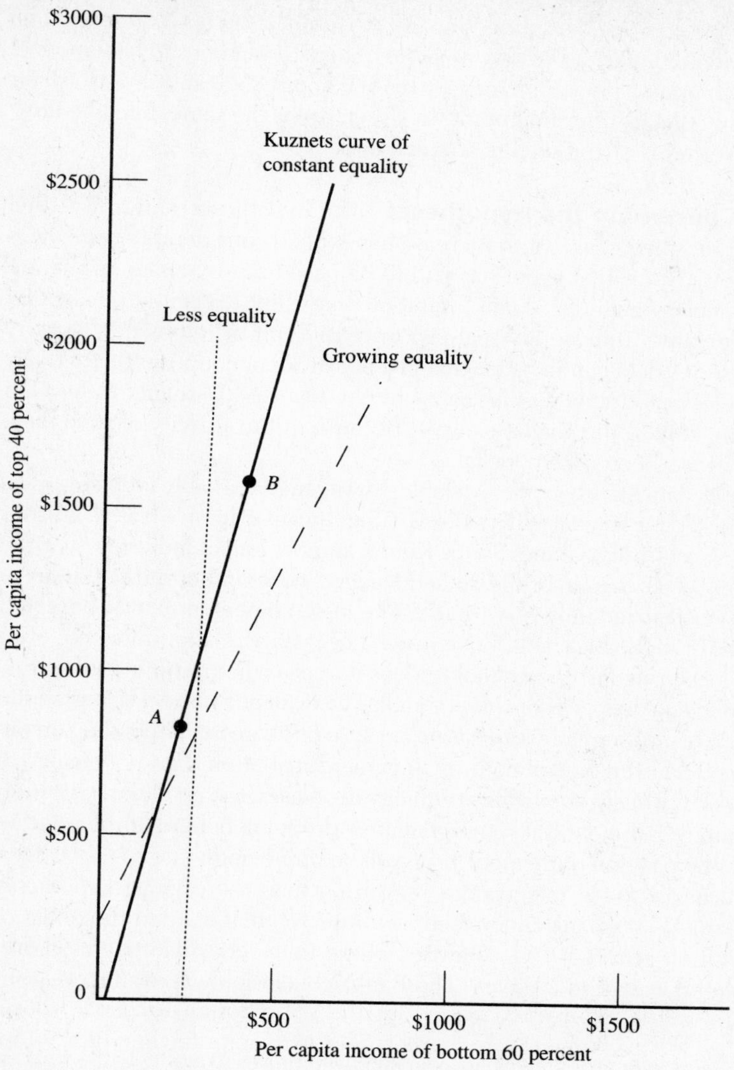

Figure 2.3 Kuznets curves indicate what happens to income distribution as economies grow. A straight-line Kuznets curve that hits the figure's origin signals unchanging income distribution; a curve that hits the horizontal (x) axis indicates decreasing equality; while a curve that hits the vertical (y) axis indicates increasing equality.

equality with income growth; that is, the incomes of the poor are expanding faster than the incomes of the rich.

Though Kuznets's own writing offered little evidence to support the claim, subsequent empirical research from cross-section analysis (that is, based on country comparisons), yielded the Kuznets curve in Figure 2.4. This curve, drawn as a heavy line, plots the combined cross-section information for over 50 countries. The curve exhibits a kink; that is, it shows a weak tendency for incomes to become less equal with growth up to a per capita income level of about $800 and shows a slight tendency to more equality after that point. In effect, this is the same outcome illustrated by the inverted U-shape of Gini coefficients.

Controversy Concerning the Hypothesis The hypothesis that growth first lessens equality and then causes it to increase has evoked considerable controversy. One major criticism is that proof has had to be based mostly on country comparisons (cross-section analysis). Data limitations have until recently meant that comparisons over time (time-series analysis) were difficult or impossible to carry out. Only time-series data can indicate that given individual countries are actually undergoing the lessened equality illustrated by the inverted U-shape of the Gini coefficient or the kink in the Kuznets curve. Because of the scarcity of such data, the theory has always been controversial.

As time-series data have become available, however, remarkably little empirical support has emerged for Kuznets's hypothesis.[46] Significant evidence from countries such as Taiwan, Costa Rica, China, South Korea, and Sri Lanka indicated that the process traced in the U-shaped or the kinked Kuznets curve either did not occur in these countries or occurred only very weakly. The lesson emerged that the inverted U-shape of Ginis or kinked Kuznets curve is not a necessary relationship. Nor, even where growth does bring lessened equality, does it appear that faster growth is systematically related to a deeper U or sharper kink. The evidence rather supported the conclusion that income inequality can either increase or decrease, depending on the policies employed and the type of country. Income distribution does not change in any inevitable way.[47] Finally, even where equality decreases, the result may not indicate absolute impoverishment but rather a relative dropping behind of the poor. In absolute terms, the position of the poor may well be improving.

These conclusions were much more reassuring than the original hypothesis. Then, in 1990, the World Bank announced new research that charted the effect of economic growth on poverty in 11 countries where time-series data are available. The period covered was 15 to 20 years. The Bank's conclusion was even more optimistic.

> In the low-income countries inequality consistently improves (contrary to the Kuznets hypothesis), and there is no case in which the effect of growth is offset by changes in inequality. . . . In short, growth reduces poverty.[48]

The World Bank ascribes the outcome to two major factors that are the result of public policy: labor markets being allowed to work so that the poorest, with only their labor power to offer, have been gaining from growth; and direct action by governments to bring productivity-increasing social services to the poor. These are major topics treated in detail later in this book.

To be sure, the sample size of countries with adequate time-series data on income distribution is small. But if subsequent research continues to cast doubt on the original Kuznets hypothesis, that would be good news. One of the great fears of development economists would have been laid to rest.

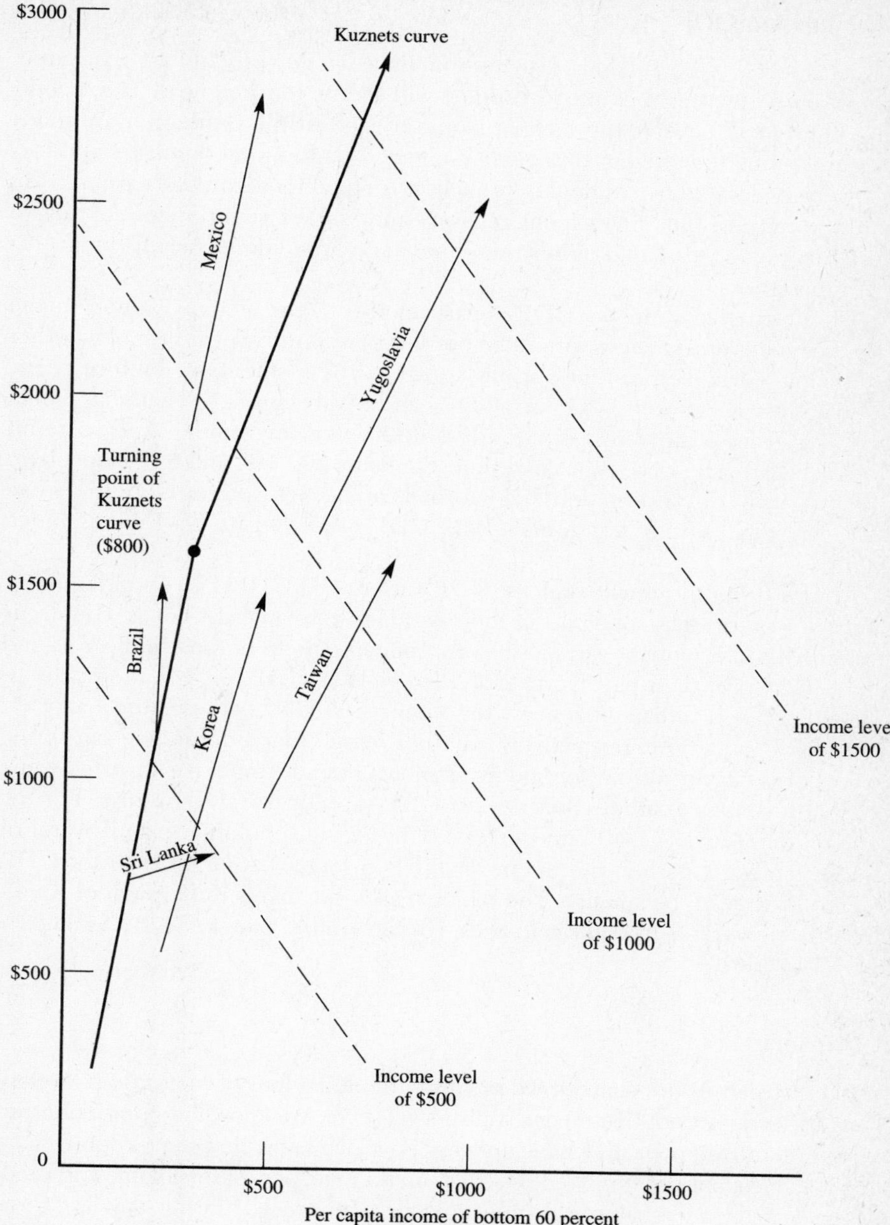

Figure 2.4 The kink in the Kuznets curve indicates a weak tendency for incomes to become less equal with growth up to a per capital income level of about $800 and a slight tendency to more equality after that point.

GNP Versus GDP

A last aspect of the income distribution issue is the probability that some income earned within a country's borders will accrue to foreigners. The technical definition of GNP is the factor income earned in the production of goods and services by the citizens of a given country. It is the total domestic and foreign output claimed by residents. As such, it is equal to all income earned from domestic output, plus investment receipts and worker remittances coming to residents from abroad, and minus these incomes earned domestically but accruing to foreigners.

An alternative concept, GDP, measures the factor income earned in the output of goods and services within the borders of a country regardless of whether the income earned from that output is claimed by residents or by foreigners. The difference between GNP and GDP can be substantial.[49] Thailand, Chile, and Mexico have all attracted considerable foreign investment, and so remit profits abroad. Their GDPs exceed their GNPs by 6%, 7%, and 6%, respectively. Payments of interest on debt held abroad can be a reason for GDP to exceed GNP. For this reason, Argentina's 1991 GDP exceeded its GNP by as much as 24%.

Under different circumstances, GNP can exceed GDP. For example, many emigrant workers may send part of their earnings to relatives at home. Hundreds of thousands of Egyptians work in the oil-producing states of the Middle East and send back part of their pay. Egypt's GNP exceeds its GDP by 15%. Many Philippine citizens and Indian citizens do the same; their GNPs are greater than their GDPs by 31% and 6%, respectively. Another reason that a difference can spring up concerns earnings from foreign investments. Saudi Arabia has invested some of its oil revenues in other countries; its GNP exceeds its GDP by 16%. For the same reason, Kuwait's GNP exceeded GDP by 52% just before the Gulf War. For all LDCs taken together, the figure for GNP is somewhat larger than for GDP, whereas it used to be smaller. The major reason for this is the growth of remittances from workers in other countries. (In the United States, GDP was 98.82% of GNP in 1991.)

Summary

In the first part of the chapter, we saw that the difficulties of measuring development are so significant that no one statistic will serve. We know that some countries are rich, some are poor, and some are very poor. We know that some countries are growing, and some are not. We know that, on average, per capita income and product have risen and that social indicators have improved during the last three decades; we also know that the percentage in absolute poverty as measured by income is still large. We should be exceedingly wary, however, of any statement of precision in these areas. For those seeking exactitude, a combination of real per capita output alongside a table of adjustments based on purchasing power and nonmonetary real indicators plus the United Nations' human development index will greatly lessen the margin of error.

So the measurement question really involves a value judgment. Perhaps a reasonable one is as follows: However inadequate total output is as a measuring rod, it is hard to imagine significant long-term development without reasonable growth in output. This statement as much as anything else explains the concentration on that much-maligned measure. But it is also important to study what has happened to unemployment, inequality, and the qualitative dimensions of poverty. If these are worsening, then even fast growth in per capita output is not the same as adequate development.

Finally, the emphasis in the last few pages on methods for measuring inequality and poverty reflects the extent to which "growth with equity" has become a core position among economists. The inclusion of equity goals was a long time in coming because development specialists were typically more concerned with efficiency goals involving a higher national product. As we saw in Chapter 1, although a conflict between economic growth and equity is possible and must be guarded against, there is evidence that the two goals are complementary rather than exclusive. That is excellent news, making the path toward economic development easier than it would be otherwise.

NOTES

1. For a recent survey, see Anwar M. Shaikh, *Measuring the Wealth of National Accounts* (Cambridge, 1994).
2. See Douglas Rimmer, *The Economies of West Africa* (New York, 1984), 268.
3. See Marilyn Waring, *If Women Counted* (New York, 1989).
4. From *WDR 1991*, 44.
5. From a lecture by A. D. Knox at the London School of Economics.
6. See Carol S. Carson, "The Underground Economy: An Introduction," *Survey of Current Business* (May 1984): 21–37.
7. *The Economist*, September 19, 1987.
8. See R. K. Udo, "Population and Politics in Nigeria," in J. C. Caldwell and C. Okonjo, *The Population of Tropical Africa* (London, 1968), for details of the withdrawal of the 1962 census.
9. Ding Chen, "The Economic Development of China," *Scientific American* 243, no. 3 (1980): I59.
10. See Ernst Lutz and Mohan Munasinghe, "Accounting for the Environment," *Finance and Development* 28, no. 1 (March 1991): 19–21; Malcolm Slesser and Jane King, "Resource Accounting: An Application to Development Planning," *World Development* 16, no. 2 (February 1988): 293–303; and Robert Repetto, "Nature's Resources as Productive Assets," *Challenge* 32, no. 5 (September/October 1989): 16–27.
11. From Amartya K. Sen, "Development: Which Way Now?" *Economic Journal* 93 (December 1983): 756.
12. *WDR 1980*, 54.
13. Gunnar Myrdal, *Asian Drama: An Inquiry into the Poverty of Nations* (New York, 1968), 678–679.
14. The subject has been treated by Andrew M. Kamarck, *The Tropics and Economic Development: A Provocative Inquiry into the Poverty of Nations* (Baltimore, 1976); and by B. F. Hodder, *Economic Development in the Tropics* (London, 1980).

15. Lloyd Reynolds, "China as a Less Developed Economy," *American Economic Review* 65, no. 3 (1975): 418–428; and the comments by Benjamin Higgins and Jean Downing Higgins, *Economic Development of a Small Planet* (New York, 1979), 283.
16. See Simon Kuznets, *Economic Growth of Nations: Total Output and Production Structure* (Cambridge, Mass., 1971).
17. Irving W. Kravis, "Comparative Studies of National Incomes and Prices," *Journal of Economic Literature* 22 (March 1984): 2.
18. Among the most important works on the International Comparison Project are, in chronological order, Irving B. Kravis, Alan W. Heston, and Robert Summers, *International Comparisons of Real Product and Purchasing Power* (Baltimore, 1978); Irving B. Kravis, Alan W. Heston, and Robert Summers, *World Product and Income: International Comparisons of Real Gross Product* (Baltimore, 1982); Robert Summers, Irving B. Kravis, and Alan W. Heston, "International Comparisons of Real Product and Its Composition: 1950–77," *Review of Income and Wealth* 26, no. 1 (March 1980): 19–66; Irving B. Kravis, "Comparative Studies of National Incomes and Prices," *Journal of Economic Literature* 22 (March 1984): 1–39; Robin Marris, "Comparing the Incomes of Nations: A Critique of the International Comparison Project," *Journal of Economic Literature* 22 (March 1984): 40–57; Irving B. Kravis, "The Three Faces of the International Comparison Project," *The World Bank Research Observer* 1, no. 1 (1986): 3–26; Robert Summers and Alan W. Heston, "A New Set of International Comparisons of Real Product and Price Levels Estimates for 130 Countries, 1950–1985," *Review of Income and Wealth* 31, no. 1 (1988): 1–25; Yoshimasha Kurabayashi and Itsuo Sakuma, *Studies in International Comparisons of Real Product and Prices* (New York, 1990); and Robert Summers and Alan Heston, "The Penn World Table (Mark 5): An Expanded Set of International Comparisons, 1950–1988," *Quarterly Journal of Economics* (May 1991).
19. Kravis, "Comparative Studies of National Incomes and Prices," 33.
20. See IMF, *World Economic Outlook 1993*, 116–119.
21. Kravis, "Comparative Studies of National Incomes and Prices," 37.
22. See Kravis, "Three Faces of the International Comparison Project," 21–22.
23. Points surveyed by Elio Lancieri, "Purchasing Power Parities and Phase IV of the International Comparison Project: Do They Lead to 'Real' Estimates of GDP and Its Components?" *World Development* 18, no. 1 (January 1990): 29–48.
24. Familiar attempts include Wilfred Beckerman, *International Comparisons of Real Incomes* (Paris, 1966); and Wilfred Beckerman and Robert Bacon, "The International Distribution of Incomes," in Paul Streeten, ed., *Unfashionable Economics* (London, 1970).
25. See Muriel Nissel, "Indicators of Human Betterment," in Kenneth E. Boulding, ed., *The Economics of Human Betterment* (Albany, NY, 1984), 15–35 (especially 28–29).
26. *HDR 1994*, 91–93.
27. See *HDR 1994*, 108 for the example.
28. *HDR 1993*, 11, 14; *HDR 1994*, 95.
29. T. N. Srinivasan, "Human Development: A New Paradigm or Reinvention of the Wheel," *American Economic Review Papers and Proceedings* 84, no. 2 (May 1994): 241.
30. *HDR 1994*, 98–99.
31. Michael Hopkins, "Human Development Revisited: A New UNDP Report," *World Development* 19, no. 10 (October 1991): 1469–1473. For further criticism, see Partha Dasgupta, *An Inquiry into Well-Being and Destitution* (Oxford, 1993), 78; and Mark McGillivray, "The Human Development Index: Yet Another Redundant Composite Development Indicator," *World Development* 19, no. 10 (October 1991): 1461–1468.

32. Srinivasan, "Human Development: A New Paradigm or Reinvention of the Wheel," 241.
33. Paul Streeten, "Human Development: Means and Ends," *American Economic Review Papers and Proceedings* 84, no. 2 (May 1994): 232–237.
34. *HDR 1992*, 1.
35. Alberto Alesina and Roberto Perotti, "Income Distribution, Political Instability, and Investment," *NBER Working Paper No. 4486*, 1994.
36. Torsten Persson and Guido Tabellini, "Is Inequality Harmful for Growth?" *American Economic Review* 84, no. 3 (June 1994): 600–621.
37. See Albert O. Hirschman, "The Changing Tolerance for Income Inequality in the Course of Economic Development," *Quarterly Journal of Economics* 87, no. 4 (1973): 544–566.
38. *HDR 1994*, 165.
39. Lyn Squire, "Fighting Poverty," *American Economic Review* 83, no. 2 (May 1993): 377–382; and Dasgupta, *An Inquiry into Well-Being and Destitution*, 80.
40. Michael T. Rock, " 'Twenty-five Years of Economic Development' Revisited," *World Development* 21, no. 11 (November 1993): 1794.
41. Gerald K. Helleiner, "The Refnes Seminar: Economic Theory and North–South Negotiations," *World Development* 9, no. 6 (1981): 542.
42. The methods for measuring income distribution receive a detailed study in Jacques Lecaillon et al., *Income Distribution and Economic Development: An Analytical Survey* (Geneva, 1984). There is an overview of the subject, with many citations, by William R. Cline, "Distribution and Development: A Survey of Literature," *Journal of Development Economics* 1 (1975): 359–400; and a thorough study by Gary S. Fields, *Poverty, Inequality, and Development* (Cambridge, 1980).
43. For a critical analysis see Lecaillon et al., *Income Distribution*.
44. Many tests of the proposition are discussed in Lecaillon et al., *Income Distribution*, 10–14.
45. See Morton Paglin, "The Measurement and Trend of Inequality: A Basic Revision," *American Economic Review* 65, no. 4 (1975): 598–609.
46. See in particular R.M. Sundrum, *Income Distribution in Less Developed Countries* (London, 1990); Gary S. Fields, "Income Distribution and Economic Growth," in Gustav Ranis and T. Paul Schultz, eds., *The State of Development Economics* (Oxford, 1988), 462, 469; Stern, "The Economics of Development: A Survey," citing S. Anand and S. M. R. Kanbar; and Rati Ram, "Economic Development and Income Inequality: Further Evidence on the U-Curve Hypothesis," *World Development* 16, no. 11 (November 1988): 1371–1376.
47. Gary S. Fields, "Income Distribution and Economic Growth," in Gustav Ranis and T. Paul Schultz, eds., *The State of Development Economics* (Oxford, 1988), 462, 469. Also see Albert Fishlow's comments on this essay in the same volume, 483, 485.
48. *WDR 1990*, 47. The percentage of the population in poverty fell in all 11 countries; the actual number of people in poverty fell in eight of these.
49. The figures in this paragraph are from *HDR 1994*, tables 26 and 27, and relate to 1991.

Chapter
3

What Causes Development?

An Overview

This chapter gives an overview of what are thought to be the main causes of economic development.[1] This view is based on the experience of today's low-income countries during the last quarter century and today's rich countries during their period of early development. The discussion serves an important purpose for the book as a whole in that it provides a broad framework for subsequent chapters that examine these causes in detail. We will find neither a single "engine" of causation nor any absolute barrier to development, but instead a group of six important factors that propel the process, their significance varying from country to country: (1) increased saving and investment and acquisition of appropriate technology, (2) structural transformation of the economy's production, (3) a growing foreign trade with close attention to comparative advantage, (4) an economic system that allows for efficient allocation, including increases in the efficiency of government, (5) human capital formation and human resource development, and (6) avoidance of unsustainable practices that would reverse the development process.

It should be understood that the process is not mechanical, automatic, or fully predictable. Progress in each of these areas appears valuable, but experience shows it may not always be a necessary condition for growth. Neither will it always be a sufficient condition. Following the recommended policies does not carry a guarantee of success, but proper policy certainly appears to improve the odds.

CRITICAL FACTORS FOR DEVELOPMENT

If indeed the six critical factors do improve the odds, that knowledge must stand as the greatest of all the contributions of development economics to practical affairs.[2] This entire book examines these eminently debatable issues in detail, while this part of the chapter represents an introduction to them. Recent econometric evidence is cited when available to lend a quantitative aspect to the relationships. Bear in mind that statistical correlations do not amount to proof, but they *are* indications that conclusions are reasonable and supportable.

Saving, Investment, and Technical Change

The first factor propelling the process of economic development is increased productivity through saving and investing a larger proportion of national income and product. Investment is the process by which capital is formed—the tools, machines, structures, inventories, and other man-made improvements to the economy. Capital, whether directly productive or for social improvement, is lacking in the underdeveloped world. There is less equipment per worker, often a shortage of housing and transport, low stocks of inventory, and frequently an inappropriate level of technology embodied in the capital. The lack of capital is caused by a low level of domestic saving and investment and limited investment from abroad. Saving is more difficult when incomes are low; borrowing abroad is expensive, and foreign aid is harder to obtain in sufficient quantity. From whatever the source, it is imperative that enough be saved and invested to increase the capital stock at a satisfactory rate. Economic theory suggests that capital accumulation should be productive in the low-income LDCs because of their great scarcity of capital. Econometric work suggests that in the average LDC, an increase in the proportion of investment to total output of one percentage point will raise annual output growth by 0.1 to 0.2 of a percentage point.[3] (The contribution to growth from investment in *equipment* is higher than for other forms of physical investment. Raising the ratio of investment in equipment to total output by one percentage point increases economic growth by 0.33 of a percentage point.)[4]

Yet the efficiency with which capital is used varies greatly. In the LDCs that are growing fastest, a dollar's worth of capital produces more than twice as much output as in the low-growth LDCs.[5]

It is also clear that innovation and technical change in the long run make investment more productive, and that has been central in the growth of today's rich countries. These are broad terms: technical change can include not only a better machine or computer but also the straightening of a production line, obtaining more miles per gallon, closing an inefficient factory, or using an improved fertilizer. Fortunately, there is great potential for technology in the LDCs to catch up with the more advanced countries. Unfortunately, that potential has yet to be realized in many countries.

With saving, investment, and technical change, the productivity of the labor force can be raised. Productivity growth, as opposed to growth in the physical quantities of inputs, appears to be the key to higher incomes per person.[6]

Now, however, there is far less confidence than formerly among development economists that this capital formation should be accomplished by active state intervention through planning and protection of the domestic market against foreign trade. (Deliberate government efforts to form capital in areas with widespread externalities, such as transport, communications, and education, have not suffered from this loss of faith.) This belief was a prominent feature of development economics 25 years ago. There are also serious concerns about the appropriate level of technology for the LDCs. Large parts of Chapters 4 to 8 address the subjects of capital formation and technology.

Structural Transformation

Structural transformation is a broad term that encompasses industrialization, urbanization, the shift from traditional to modern ways in the scale of production and marketing, the status of women, self-sufficiency versus commerce with others, and the view toward population size. We take up all of these in due course, but here we emphasize the structural change in the type of production.

There is a typical pattern of changes that affects the various sectors of an economy in a predictable way. These sectoral changes were first analyzed in detail by the British economist Colin Clark and are thought to apply widely among very diverse LDCs. The changes are certainly not linear and uniform, but to a greater or lesser degree they do occur in all countries. Every economy can be divided into three sectors: a primary sector producing the so-called primary products—agricultural commodities, minerals, and the like; a secondary sector producing manufactures; and a tertiary sector producing services. There is impressive evidence that with economic development, a movement occurs in the relative importance of these sectors.

In a typical low-income LDC, agriculture will make up the largest share of GNP, over 60% sometimes and often about 40%. Services (the tertiary sector) will also be large, perhaps 40% on the average, with many people engaged in petty trade, marketing, carrying goods from place to place, hauling water, and the like. When some development occurs, one expects growth in the secondary (manufacturing) sector and a drop in the primary and perhaps the tertiary sectors. Thus, between 1960 and 1992, the share of agriculture in the national product of low-income LDCs sank from about 50% to 30%, while the share of manufacturing rose from about 9% to 16%.

With further growth as a country rises in the ranks of the LDCs, there is usually a considerable fall in the size of the agricultural sector (the average output share for middle-income LDCs was 24% in 1960 and 12% in 1990). Manufacturing rises (25% in the upper-middle-income economies in 1990) to about the same share of production as in many developed countries. Numerous LDCs, including Argentina, Brazil, Korea, Mexico, Peru, the Philippines, Singapore, Taiwan, and Turkey, now exceed the U.S. share.[7] Services remain largely unchanged.

As a country enters the ranks of the developed, one expects a further decline in primary production (agriculture's share of national product averages only 4% in the developed countries and 2% in the United States) and a great rise in the tertiary, or service, sector (54% of national product in 1960 and usually 65% or more in most developed countries in 1992). Although the evidence of a growing service sector in many of the LDCs is limited, there is no doubt that at some point in the development process this sector rises in importance.*

The labor to be employed in the growing service sector becomes available when rising productivity, especially in agriculture, means less labor is required in other sectors. The fastest growth rates, incidentally, are usually found in the countries that are increasing the size of the secondary (manufacturing) sector, for it is here that productivity can grow most swiftly, hence leading to the fastest increase in output.

The sectoral changes that accompany development are not uniform because different countries move at different rates. Yet the changes occur in virtually all settings. It is a pity that they are much more certainly an effect of economic advance rather than its cause. If the sectoral movements were mainly causal, government planners could conceivably "jump the gun" in a deliberate attempt to speed up the process. Unfortunately, as we shall see in Chapters 4 and 12, premature alteration of a country's economic structure in the absence of a solid foundation of successful growth is likely to be a high-cost method for accomplishing little. That does not mean that structural questions can simply be left to sort themselves out without attention from governments. Growing numbers of development specialists now believe that a minimally acceptable level of services is a condition for successful development rather than just a result of it.

From the fact that agriculture sinks in importance with development, can that sector then be ignored? No. Improved performance of the agricultural sector can help greatly in the short run. In the typical low-income LDC, most people are small farmers, working manually with traditional techniques and low output per farmer. (At the beginning of the 1970s, an American agricultural worker produced an average output per day 34 times larger than an African or Asian worker.)[8] This is surely understandable. Poverty itself means low capital per farmer. A tropical climate, rainfall cycles that are damagingly erratic, or land that is too swampy or too dry all may be enemies requiring far more capital to rectify than is available. But there is plenty of experience to show that these small farmers are responsive to economic incentives and that proper policies can motivate them to raise production.

---

*One main reason for the movement to services as countries become wealthy is consumer demand, which shifts toward travel, entertainment, restaurant meals, health care, banking, stockbroking, and insurance as income rises. The increasing need for transport, distribution, and communications also contributes, as does the tendency for housewives to enter the labor force. Greater urbanization increases the need for police, sanitation workers, and city administrators. Finally, the service sector grows because, being lower in productivity, it offers greater opportunities for employment. For details, see the annual issues of *WDR* and *HDR*. For a survey see David L. McKee, *Growth, Development, and the Service Economy in the Third World* (New York, 1988). It should be noted that when structural transformation is expressed as a percentage of the labor force rather than as a share of GDP, these sectoral changes appear even more dramatic. Incomplete specialization of many individuals means, however, that the statistics are far less trustworthy and must be treated with care. See P. T. Bauer, *Reality and Rhetoric* (Cambridge, Mass., 1984), 10–11.

Unless both agricultural productivity and total farm production are increased, development will be difficult. The country that neglects agriculture will thus neglect the sector where, self-evidently for some of the least developed, it has the largest comparative advantage. If incomes do not advance in agriculture, the growth of domestic markets for a country's new output of manufactured goods will be limited.

Concentration on industry to the exclusion of agriculture will also lead to a problem of balance. A growing national income from new industries leads to a growing demand for agricultural commodities. Population growth leads in the same direction. If farm output does not increase to meet the new demand, how will an industrial labor force be fed? Through imports, perhaps, but LDCs already spend some 25% to 33% of the revenue generated from their exports on imported food. Balance of payments problems are likely to arise unless agriculture receives attention, and this will be more serious when foreign trade promotion is not a central feature in government economic policy. The results can include inflation, foreign exchange shortages, and hungry people.

Statistics indicate that on average the lower the overall growth of an LDC, the poorer its performance in the farm sector. High-growth LDCs have increased their agricultural output at a rate more than four times the level of the low-growth LDCs. The lesson seems clear enough that a stagnant agricultural sector is an inhibiting factor for development. The subject is treated in Chapter 11.

Foreign Trade

The third consideration is a country's foreign trade. Exports typically must move ahead rapidly, for only with the "push" of comparative advantage, doing what one does best, can a country reach income growth rates higher than are achieved from purely local activities. Without exports, the imports needed for development cannot be acquired. The only other possible means to pay for imports—an inflow of private foreign capital plus official loans and grants from the developed countries—seem very unlikely to alleviate this problem in the foreseeable future.

The role of imports in the process is often more crucial than is commonly realized. Worldwide, the chance to acquire highly desirable new goods that are not available locally has been a fundamental stimulant to productive human effort. Complex capital goods may be very expensive if purchased locally, or may not be available at all. The technology embodied in the capital may be procurable only through imports.

For a long time, the exports of LDCs did not rise as fast as those of the developed countries. The LDCs' share of the world's total exports, about one-quarter in 1955, had dropped to one-fifth ten years later. Modest growth has set in, however, and in 1992 the figure reached 21%. How are the LDCs to achieve acceptable export (and hence import) growth? They often find demand for the traditional plantation crops increasing relatively slowly. Minerals may be better, but they are depletable; in any case, many LDCs are poorly endowed with natural resources. Manufactured goods, especially of a labor-intensive type, can be exported to the developed world, but there is significant danger that success in exporting makes an

LDC subject to developed-country barriers to trade. Export promotion schemes make sense if they are tailored to present or predicted future comparative advantage. On the contrary, neither general export promotion (with subsidies) nor general import substitution (with quotas and licensing) is sensible if it neglects the underlying comparative advantage of the country concerned. These issues are explored more fully in Chapters 13 to 15.

The importance of foreign trade is supported by empirical evidence. Recent econometric work indicates that increasing the export share in total output by 10 percentage points is associated with an increase in a country's economic growth by 0.6 of a percentage point.[9]

Efficient Resource Allocation

The fourth area that has recently come to be regarded as critical to growth is the ability to allocate resources efficiently. If government-administered prices fail to reflect opportunity costs, growth is hindered. The use of market prices more proportional to social marginal costs than controlled government prices is seen to be a "cheap" mechanism for allocation. A free-market price mechanism involves low administrative costs, high transmission of incentives, and rapid signaling of scarcity and glut. Corruption costs are likely to be low because so much corruption is based on the ability to exploit the difference between an artificial price established by government and a free-market price based on marginal costs.

True, monopoly influence and small markets make the market system less than perfect. Growing evidence indicates, however, that even an imperfect market is better than the controlled price structure so long used by many governments. The LDCs have passed through a lengthy era of high tariffs and restrictive quotas on their imports, low government-set producer prices for agricultural commodities, widespread price controls on foodstuffs and transport, artificially low interest rates, and measures that raise labor costs. Often the foreign exchange rate has been sharply overvalued by government action, with one unit of local currency then buying more dollars or other foreign money than it could in a free market.

Each of these policies has its justifications. Protection against imports was and is popular among export pessimists—those who fear exports are subject to low growth in demand, high fluctuations in price, and economic "dependency." Low producer prices in agriculture are justified on the grounds that supply is not very responsive to price, that larger farmers benefit from high prices more than smaller farmers, that these same high prices hurt low-income consumers, and that industrialization requires a transfer of income from agriculture to manufacturing. Price controls are rationalized as protection for the poor. Low interest rates are said to encourage investment and keep down the burden of the public debt. Minimum-wage laws and pro-union legislation are advocated as means to bring adequate income to the workers. Overvalued exchange rates are said to ease the burden of importing costly capital goods; with an overvalued rate, the foreign exchange to purchase such imports appears cheaper.

There was always a large element of doubt in each one of these propositions, doubts that are carefully examined in the chapters to come. Nowadays there is less doubt that the country with large distortions (divergence from market prices) in its price system pays a penalty in reduced growth, whatever the reason the distortions were adopted in the first place. The World Bank has constructed index numbers indicating the extent of distortion in a country's price system. When it compared the extent of distortion to the rate of economic growth, it found a strong correlation between high distortion and slow growth in the sample of 31 countries it studied.[10]

Moreover, it has become clear that efficient resource allocation involves not just microeconomics, but also governments' macroeconomic policies. The overly great creation of money by the central bank and large government budget deficits cause inflation, which, in turn, interferes with price signals, increases uncertainty, and causes capital flight to other countries with more stable policies. The resulting decline in the level of investment and the efficiency of investment is very likely to reduce growth. Governments have a duty to contribute macroeconomic stability to the development process, but many do not do so.

Research Findings Concerning Efficient Allocation The connection between economic distortions and growth in output has been investigated econometrically. Recent findings indicate that an increase in the overvaluation of the foreign exchange rate (as measured by the difference between the black market premium over the official rate) of 10 percentage points will lower economic growth by 0.4 of a percentage point. Policies that boost average producer input prices by 23 percentage points will lower economic growth by one percentage point. Policies that cause interest rates to be negative also harm economic growth. Moving from a positive to a negative real rate of interest is associated with a decrease in economic growth of 1.5 percentage points.[11]

Human Capital Formation and Resource Development

The fourth area that is critical for development centers on the realization that progress will be difficult unless the quality of human resources is improved directly. Depending solely on growth of income to bring about educational improvement, reduce population pressure, or alter inhibiting cultural and social institutions runs the risk that the growth in income will be slowed and the distribution of its benefits skewed. The need to concentrate directly on qualitative changes is more strongly felt now than it was 20 years ago. There are many considerations concerning this area of human resources. Direct government provision of basic services may raise productivity because a healthier, better-nourished, better-educated labor force works with more efficiency and allows more output from each unit of input. Education and the accompanying increase in literacy and numeracy is particularly important. Recent econometric work indicates that raising primary and secondary school enrollment by 10 percentage points is associated with an increase in economic growth of 0.2 to 0.3 percentage points.[12]

Rapid population growth may, on the contrary, make it more difficult to raise per capita national income and thus make direct action necessary. In some (though not all) LDCs, the population is large and growing relative to the available land and natural resources; the overpopulation contributes to low investment, low labor

THE ROLE OF GOVERNMENT IN EFFICIENT RESOURCE ALLOCATION AND HUMAN DEVELOPMENT

The role of government in development has been undergoing considerable reassessment. Clearly government activity was once too limited. Government interventions in the economy are necessary, especially in such areas as agricultural extension work, bankruptcy law, bond rating, a flow of research information among universities and firms, land titling and surveys, and banking supervision. Public investment in health, education, transport, and communications is often complementary to private investment. Government successes in population control and the encouragement of foreign trade have been frequent. Especially when economies are very poor, with fragmented markets and inadequate infrastructure, government participation in the development process may be indispensable.

But government can also be damaging to growth, as when it becomes too pervasive, allowing its public investment to compete with private investment, or when its rules and regulations cause resources to remain in low-productivity employment rather than transfer to other uses. Government interventions may lead to stagnant bureaucratic structures, the creation of monopolies, and rent-seeking behavior. Such outcomes may exhibit much more of the search for personal gain rather than national gain.

In something of an overreaction to government mistakes, a school of thought called "state minimalism" has arisen, just as an earlier school of thought overemphasized the role government should play. Paul Streeten has noted that in a sense adherents of both camps are partly right. Markets can fail, requiring governments to assist; and governments can fail, with markets able to fill the breach and control government abuses. But the very word *failure* has to be interpreted. Consider that the market's signals may be given in a world of highly unequal ownership of land, other assets, and income, so the signals may be quite accurate (success, not failure), but with government needed to correct the circumstances. Similarly government can be very successful in what it does, but what it does might benefit the rent-seeking few rather than the many. As Streeten suggests, market failure is not necessarily an argument for government intervention—governments might do even worse. Nor is government failure necessarily an argument for the market, as when the market would not do as well. "Only pragmatic experiments can show when and where intervention is the lesser evil." The trick is to discover the approach that does the least harm.[13]

Many observers have come to believe that the extremes of ethnic, cultural, and linguistic diversity in Africa, and the intense struggles of entrenched interests, ruling oligarchies, and landed elites in Latin America, have contributed to weaknesses in the ability to govern in these areas and to pursue a sustained development effort. By contrast, East Asia has been more fortunate in this regard.[14]

Modern development economics has turned strongly to these micro and macro issues concerning improvement in the efficiency with which resources are used and macroeconomic stability. The subject is treated in Chapters 4, 5, and 12.

productivity, unemployment, and a "fouling of the nest" through environmental degradation. Population grows faster because birth rates are high and death rates are rapidly reduced due to advances in public health. Population and human resource development are the central subjects of Chapters 9 and 10.

An important negative factor on the human side is that the social and cultural value systems, including attitudes toward thrift, profits, risks, education, and even the view of work, may present obstacles. The influence of the middle class of managers, technicians, and professional people may be slight and their numbers small. The legal and religious systems—the one often directly related to the other—may have a substantial impact on land tenure, credit and interest rates, taxes, and inheritance. Entrepreneurship may be lacking if a society is immobile, if its institutions do not promote growth, and if tradition hinders the operation of what Oxford's John Hicks calls the "economizing principle," the principle that people will take the opportunity to gain an advantage when it is offered to them. Of course, the barriers to growth often become insuperable in the countries where property ownership or personal safety itself is in doubt. Some LDCs face conditions of civil war or lower-level strife, an army out of control, or an arbitrary and dictatorial government. The implications of these conditions are explored later in the chapter.

The Great Problem of Corruption The suggestion has been made that political organization and the administrative competence of government may be the most important elements in the growth process.[15] Gunnar Myrdal has put it bluntly: He argues that one great difficulty in the process of development is to get the profit motive out of government. Corruption makes daily life and business transactions more cumbersome, whether we speak of a major bribe or just a minor rip-off. Public servants, for example, may slow down or obstruct business in hope of a fee. The widespread use of credit controls, tariffs, foreign exchange controls, and the like makes corruption profitable and leads to illicit gains, which, modest or vast, are ruinous to the morale of the remaining honest public servants. It delays all forms of economic intercourse, thereby boosting costs and diverting energies to the concealment of private gain.[16]

Clifton Barton's research showed how the propensity for power and the potential profit for those government officials who set the prices, allocate the permits, and supply the licenses, can lead to harassment of medium-scale businesses.[17] The smallest firms mostly escaped the harassment because they were insufficiently visible. The largest firms employed specialists for expediting transactions, often with bribes, and had both political connections and clout. In between, there was a middle ground of firms too visible to escape the attention of corrupt officials, but with few skills to deal with them and few good strings to pull. Small firms may thus deliberately choose to remain small. The resulting scarcity of the vulnerable middle-size firms has been termed a "Barton gap."

Numerous vivid examples show how corrosive endemic corruption can be. The work of the Peruvian economist Hernando de Soto has received wide notice.[18] In 1983, de Soto's research institute set up a small garment factory in Peru's capital, Lima. Its "machinery" comprised only two sewing machines. De Soto's confederates set out to obtain the necessary government permits. It took them 289 days and visits to 7 ministries to fulfill 11 requirements. Bureaucrats asked for bribes 10 times. In Tampa, Florida, exactly the same enterprise was given all the necessary permits in three-and-a-half hours.

De Soto's work has led other investigators to focus on such abuses elsewhere. For example, in recent years obtaining all the permits to start a new business in Cameroun took two years even for businesspeople who know the territory, with 24 steps involving 20 different offices.[19] In India, graft and corruption are endemic. The bribe to get a job as assistant engineer on water projects, where contractors pay kickbacks and villages bribe to get a project, is about one-and-a-half times the annual salary; for a senior engineer 10 to 15 times; for a superintending engineer on delta lands, up to 40 times. The government has responded by limiting such postings to just two years, but that merely increases the intensity of the effort. Labor office employees can be bribed to overlook regulations, electrical board officials can be bribed to connect service; government hospitals allocate beds by illegal payment and sell drugs on the black market. The task of a minister, according to Robert Ward, "is not to make policy, but to modify the application of rules and regulations on a particularistic basis, in return for money and/or loyalty."[20] The situation is perhaps at its worst in the administration of the trade barriers. In the Philippines, the Internal Revenue Bureau's posts have rather openly been bought and sold, and the best cars in the country are said to be found parked outside the bureau's offices. Government auditors accepted bribes to overlook bribes.*

The corruption can grow so pervasive that "ghost workers" appear on the civil service roster. These are workers who exist in name only, their salaries pocketed by senior officials. In Uganda, investigation into the affairs of the Ministry of Education revealed not only that many teachers were nonexistant, but so were some entire schools whose funding disappeared into the pockets of the corrupt.[21]

The corruption and incompetence have grown so bad in some countries that they "threaten the basic function of government."[22] Perhaps the most discouraging factor is the temptation all this affords to the yet uncorrupted. A statistic from Nigeria that is full of foreboding is that a majority of new university graduates applying for federal civil service positions want to join the customs and excise department, where the bribes are fattest.[23]

There is a school of thought that corruption does little harm when the demands are predictable, expected, standardized, and noncumulative. It certainly appears that when corruption is institutionalized, with well-known rules and disciplined practitioners as in Japan, the harm is reduced.[24] Moreover, some commentators believe that bribery and corruption serve to introduce a market-pricing system to the provision of public services. In this view, bribes represent the marginal revenue product of government officials' efforts in a kind of auction market. In effect, the payments are a substitute for low wages.[25] There is doubtless some merit in this argument, too, as when payments of "speed money" are effective in

*A 1970s Philippines plan to entrust internal revenue auditing to skilled outsiders working with the most trusted senior people, to monitor on the basis of performance, to dismiss for corruption, to simplify what had to be administered, to introduce control systems, and to recruit on the basis of merit had temporary positive effects. But in the 1980s the agency sank again into corruption. See *WDR 1991*, 132.

the rapid circumvention of unwise regulations. But an overwhelming problem can then develop, with officials motivated to introduce deliberate delays. In that case, government services can be inefficient or nonexistent unless they are paid for by means of bribes.

In any event, bribery hardly seems to resemble an auction market. Information is not at all complete, and fear of detection weighs on some more than others. Kinship and personal ties often provide the access to public officials, a major reason being that this minimizes the risk of detection and exposure by the press. Often the burden is greater on some ethnic or religious groups than on others, as with lower castes in India, ethnic Chinese in Southeast Asia, Indians in East Africa, the black population in the era of South African *apartheid*, and negroid peoples in Sudan and Mauritania, to mention a few cases from a vast array. So bribes often reflect some form of discrimination rather than auctioning, with the winners being the rich and powerful and the losers being the weak and the less-trusted, rather than those who find the service least useful. Generally, corruption, its effects, and the need for new incentives and merit pay to overcome it are even now too little studied by development economists, perhaps because those with the deepest interest and commitment to the peoples of the LDCs feel the most embarrassed by the situation.[26]

Avoidance of Unsustainable Practices

The word *sustainability* as applied to development has been overused, and too loosely used, but it contains a core of good sense. A developing country can find itself in difficulties if it undertakes unsustainable practices. For example, a given rate of economic growth may be unsustainable if the environment degrades catastrophically, or if population growth runs out of control, or if agricultural land is being fragmented, or if warfare sets back growth, or if dictatorial government leads to a populist revolution and bad economic practice.[27] We take up the environment, population pressures, and the fragmentation of land in Chapters 9, 11, and 17. Here, we focus on wars, revolutions, and the question of democracy versus authoritarianism.

It is clear enough that peaceful conditions are essential for long-term growth. Otherwise, investment is not made, foreign capital goes elsewhere, and professionals and entrepreneurs decide to depart. After a period of instability, it can take years for investors, domestic and foreign, to trust the rules, and more time for them to decide on new investments, and more time yet for the investments to bear fruit. At any point, new instability can interrupt the process.[28] The extent to which wars and civil unrest can be damaging is illustrated by the truncated development of Afghanistan, Angola, Cambodia, Haiti, Iraq, Liberia, Mozambique, Rwanda, and Somalia among the more prominent examples.

Democracy Versus Authoritarianism Recent work investigates the relationship between democracy and economic performance. The idea that freedom and liberty enhance the chances for development is debatable, and indeed has been debated for a long time. There is an argument that more discipline is necessary for successful growth than democracies are usually able to muster. Democracies may be open to heavy pressures for immediate consumption and less investment, together with short-run pork-barrel politics. Proper economic policies may have to involve resistance to special interests, for example, in the areas of land reform, racial politics, trade barriers, and capture of the regulators by monopolies. It is argued that an executive stronger than the legislature helped China, South Korea, and Taiwan, which are not very democratic, while lack of a strong hand hindered the progress of more democratic India, the Philippines, and Sri Lanka.* On the opposite side of the debate, some authorities posit a significant positive relationship between political freedom and economic growth, with the causation involving beneficial outlets for dissent, better morale, and less "kleptocratic" exploitation by dictatorial governments.[29] Adherents of this view note that some of the most dictatorial governments have performed very poorly indeed, citing Argentina before its recent free elections, Iraq under Saddam Hussein, Uganda under Idi Amin, Zaire under Mobutu (and the Soviet Union until its breakup).[30]

The middle ground between these two views seems to be the most sensible position. As a recent study suggests, "We do not know whether democracy fosters or hinders economic growth."[31] The World Bank is also cautious. It claims to have detected no systematic link between economic growth and the level of liberty, though it *has* found evidence linking social performance positively to democracy.[32] In support of this conclusion, the United Nations recently asserted its tentative finding that "high levels of human development tend to be achieved within the framework of high levels of human freedom."† Democratic governments can be effective or overwhelmed by political pressures. Authoritarian governments can be interested in growth, or they can be interested in the self-enrichment of the rulers.[33]

Whatever position one takes in this debate, recently there has been some movement toward democracy. In Latin America, the military has been returning to barracks, with important examples including Argentina, Brazil, Chile, and Uruguay. In Africa, democratic governments have recently been elected in Malawi, South Africa, and Zambia. These signs are encouraging for those who consider democracy to be conducive to development, though in special cases many would also agree that there may be a tension between democracy and economic advance.

---

*A study published by the Overseas Development Council presents disquieting evidence that authoritarian regimes performed significantly better in terms of economic growth (1970–1982) than did democratic countries. The sample size of ten countries was small, however, and during the period the democracies accumulated much less foreign debt and achieved more income equality. See Atul Kohli, "Democracy and Development," in John P. Lewis and Valeriana Kallab, eds., *Development Strategy Reconsidered* (Washington, D.C., 1986).

†*HDR 1991*, 3. In connection with this statement, the United Nations published a human freedom index for 88 countries with Sweden ranked first, the United States thirteenth, and South Africa, China, Ethiopia, Romania, Libya, and Iraq occupying the last six places. There was substantial criticism of the index because equal weight was given to petty freedoms (watching an independent TV channel) and major ones (right to travel, unlawful imprisonment, extralegal killings by government), criticism that has caused the index to be withdrawn for the time being.

To say that the six requirements of development discussed so far are "known" does not mean that they are a certainty, but only that there is advancement toward a consensus position among specialists that these requirements are broadly necessary even if not always sufficient. Nor does it mean that these "knowns" are easily quantified. Even in discussing the causes of a growing GNP and national income, it is fascinating and challenging to discover how the most careful studies show that much of growth cannot be attributed to changes in physical inputs such as capital, labor, and natural resources. The attitudes, motivation, and social framework of a people loom much larger in development economics today than they did two decades ago. They are hard to measure, hard to change, and not even easy for economists to discuss. But the attention devoted to them later in this book is an indication of their rising importance for the subject.

IS GROWTH MORE DIFFICULT NOW THAN IT WAS?

Although there are many differences, today's developed countries had to overcome some of the same problems facing today's LDCs. They were poor, they were agricultural, their growth was very slow, and many were historically feudalistic. Significant changes have, however, taken place in the nature of the hurdles; they are not the same now as they were in the eighteenth and nineteenth centuries. In certain respects, today's rich countries appear to have had some advantages at the start of their growth process that are not available to today's LDCs, and initial advantages can be a big asset.[34] In other ways, the prospects for growth are more favorable now. What are these main points of difference?

Disadvantages Facing Today's LDCs

We focus first on the disadvantages from the perspective of today's LDCs.[35]

1. The output and income levels of many low-income LDCs are lower at the present time than the output levels that modern industrial countries possessed even before their industrial revolutions. The average per capita income of the least-developed LDCs in the late twentieth century was in real terms probably about half that of the United States in 1776 or of Britain at the start of its industrialization in the eighteenth century.[36]
2. In a number of LDCs, especially parts of Asia, Central America, and Egypt, there is less land per capita and often less valuable natural resources than there were in the developed countries a hundred or two hundred years ago. There is usually no open frontier and thus no frontier spirit, although Brazil is a notable exception. Population growth is often more rapid, due especially to the sharp decline in death rates. Numerous LDCs are registering population increases of about 3%, and increases in this range can have negative consequences. Europe and North America never had a natural rate of population change (excluding emigration) greater than 2%; vast, underpopulated North America with immigration included did not exceed 3%, even in the years of maximum influx from abroad. Emigration is much too

small to serve as a safety valve for population growth. Only those with training or skills find it legally possible to enter most developed countries, and only a small minority of LDCs welcome unskilled workers.

3. Even though rural development has been a bright chapter in the recent experience of the LDCs, many poor countries face a number of greater barriers to raising agricultural productivity than the rich countries did a century or two ago. Agriculture had a better base during the development of today's developed countries; farming was about 45% more productive, comparing the European average in 1840 to agriculture in much of Asia and Africa in the late twentieth century.[37] Numerous social factors, including land ownership, tenure patterns, and perhaps the extended family system, can retard rural progress. The climate and the soil can be enemies. The combination of low government procurement prices and, sometimes, narrow and undeveloped markets on which surplus produce can be sold constrains growth and inhibits change. Levels of capital, education, nutrition, and health may be very low. General underdevelopment may mean less overall effectiveness in mobilizing agricultural resources. Finally, even if agriculture is successfully mobilized, there is evidence that primary product exports are a less certain path to development now than was true a century ago.

4. Nineteenth-century entrepreneurs were for the most part free to save and invest within a system of market prices, low taxation, and little direct production by government or government-controlled firms. In many of today's LDCs, private entrepreneurs face a more hostile climate. Frequently enough, three-quarters or more of all industrial assets are owned by nationalized firms. The management of such state firms is usually marked by conservative practices; in most cases, the public enterprises are simply not allowed to fail. Private competition may not be permitted or operates under severe restraint. Prices, including exchange rates, may be influenced by government action—in a way that reduces their value as indicators of scarcity—to a far greater degree than in the nineteenth century. Taxes, including foreign trade restraints and the costs of other government intrusions in the economy, can be high, and the greatest financial rewards may go to the corrupt or those who can wield influence in the public sector. In many LDCs, entrepreneurs have little opportunity to borrow in world capital markets; the sale of bonds and shares by firms in poor countries to tap the capital of rich countries is proportionately less important now than it was before World War I. Not only capital flows but also currency movements were freer then than now. In the latter part of the nineteenth century only a very few countries regulated the exchange of their currency, whereas now many do. There are certainly some countries where the supply of private entrepreneurship is low and some sectors where free markets are limited. Government programs under such conditions may be welcomed even when they fall. Yet when government impedes entrepreneurs and itself restricts the market, the climate becomes worse than it was in the nineteenth century.

5. It is probably fair to say that the stability of government institutions and legal systems was greater a hundred years ago in what became today's developed countries than it is today in many LDCs. In the former, enforceable contracts involving land, labor, and business affairs have permeated economic relationships and have been standard for a long time. In today's LDCs, this is too often not the case. The benefits of stability and consistency are difficult to measure but are surely large.
6. Finally, very rich and very poor countries must now coexist, where one hundred or two hundred years ago the gap between the richest and the poorest countries was not nearly so great as it is today. On a broad reckoning, in 1850 per capita income in the developed countries of the day was no more than 70% above that of the less developed. Today the gap is more like 1000%. For one carefully studied example, Dahomey in West Africa, now called the Republic of Bénin, had a national income estimated to be about one-third of Great Britain's during the period of the Atlantic slave trade; this has sunk to only one-thirtieth now.[38] Modern communications make the great disparity very obvious, and the poor feel their plight all the more. The resulting sense of confrontation has embittered relations between the LDCs and developed countries and contributes to an understandable mood of hurry. "Haste makes waste" is an apt phrase whenever inflated ambitions lead to premature steps and careless execution. (Other arguments based on the existence of rich and poor together are far more controversial. These "dependency" arguments hold the developed countries responsible to some degree for the poverty of the LDCs, either through the adverse effects of international trade or the exploitative investment strategies of multinational firms and lending institutions. Unlike the six disadvantages discussed above, these charges are much more debatable. They are treated in Chapters 6 to 8 and 13 to 15.)

Advantages Facing Today's LDCs

There are, fortunately, substantial offsetting advantages for a country undertaking its growth now. For many, these advantages probably outweigh the difficulties, as demonstrated by the unexpectedly strong growth of numerous LDCs over the past 25 years—though there are never any guarantees.

1. Knowledge about what causes development has multiplied, from the accumulation of decades of experience with the development process and research into its causes. There are specialized international institutions for conveying useful advice and for financing development, and foreign aid to stimulate economic growth was a thing unheard of a hundred years ago. The dollar amounts of all these activities are indeed limited, and the record of accomplishment certainly could be better, but the knowledge and the money can be of strategic importance.
2. Late developers have access to new technology in a quantity far greater and a quality immensely superior to that of past centuries. In spite of debates on

the appropriateness of much of this to conditions in the LDCs and even though acquaintance with many new techniques may be difficult to acquire, the consequences are highly positive.

3. Orthodox colonialism is largely a thing of the past. Many LDCs are for the most part free to consider their own economic interests and usually even to put them uppermost in their policy making and diplomacy.
4. World trade is certainly more open today than it was in the eighteenth century. Even the nineteenth century, especially after the 1870s, was an age of high protection except in Britain. The United States raised tariffs sharply after the Civil War; following a period of free trade, protection emerged strongly in Germany in 1879 and in France shortly thereafter. Today, however, an LDC without a large home market can take advantage of specialization through trade, and this appears a strong and largely uniform element in the recent growth of the most successful LDCs. Continuation of this favorable prospect for foreign trade is by no means assured. As exporting by LDCs increases, interest groups in the developed world arise with a strong desire to protect their high wages and profits. Through their lobbying, free trade is attacked with tariffs, quotas, voluntary restraints, and the like. Thus far, though, the damage has been relatively limited, and opportunities for trade remain a major path to growth.

Whatever the obstacles today—and in spite of the sometimes angry rhetoric emanating both from the LDCs and from the developed countries—on balance the barriers to economic advance are probably no greater than they were in the past, and for some they are surely lower. This is reassuring, even given the absence of a guarantee.

The Experience of the Late Starters

There is much to be learned from the experience of the developed countries.* Most apt are the lessons of the two developmental late starters, Germany and Japan. Germany was a relatively poor country well into the nineteenth century, eclipsed economically by Britain, France, and the Netherlands among others. Until past the middle of that century, Japan was one of the world's most isolated countries, feudal, with primitive transport and communications and economically stagnant for centuries past. Their experience stands out.[39] In both there was a

*Though not so much as was once believed, during the height of popularity for a theory known as the "stages of growth." Walt W. Rostow's well-known 1960 book *The Stages of Economic Growth: A Non-Communist Manifesto* (Cambridge, 1960) posited that the historical evidence from the now-developed countries proved that these moved through five stages of growth: (1) traditional society, (2) preconditions for takeoff, (3) takeoff, (4) drive to maturity, and (5) era of high consumption. Much attention was given to the idea of a takeoff, and much criticism centered on it. Scholars eventually shifted their focus to evidence of the gradualness and long continuity of growth rather than its sharp steps, and later studies indicated that any sudden takeoff is difficult to identify in most of the developed countries. The phrase caught attention and is still heard, but it raised false hopes that there exists a master key always able to open the development door. Unfortunately, there was and is no such key.

national push for development, with a pronounced emphasis on education, heavy capital investment, imported technology (often improved upon), and intensive effort by labor and management. The individual details and emphases were, however, somewhat different, as we shall see.

Germany The key to German development, which achieved startling success in the last half of the nineteenth century, was the combination of science and education with new investment. Universal primary education was achieved early, science was emphasized in the curriculum, and technical schools sprouted. The government subsidized research in the universities, leading most importantly to great advances in the chemical and electrical industries. Germany started as a borrower of technology—the borrowing encouraged by government policy—improved upon it, and put it in the hands of an educated workforce. Simultaneously, the government encouraged scientific education and encouraged liaison between university professors and industry.* In short, Germany was the country that did the most with human capital during its development.

Japan Among today's developed countries, Japan was a hundred years ago the most underdeveloped and most akin to a present-day low-income LDC. It was backward and isolated, had a large population for its meagre land area, and had a small stock of natural resources. Japan began by lifting many of the restrictions on free movement of people and goods, including internal tolls, export bans on silk and other products, and widespread prohibition of imports that had marked the rule of the feudal shoguns. Tariffs were kept low for a long while; the clauses covering trade in the treaty signed with Commodore Perry included a limit on tariffs of 5%. There was an awareness that agriculture was the foundation of economic strength. Land was turned over to the peasants, and even though the land tax used to finance substantial government participation in investment was high, it was paid at fixed rates on assessed valuation rather than on the size of the harvest as had been the case. Thus farmers could keep the profits from any increments to production.

Japan encouraged agriculture and labor-intensive manufactures for export, in the beginning particularly silk (which made up 99% of the country's textile and clothing exports in 1880–1882, and still 88% in 1900–1902) and low-cost dishware and trinkets.[40] It thus thoroughly grounded its foreign trade on a comparative advantage determined by factor proportions. As late as 1890, 68% of investment was still in agriculture and labor-intensive light industry. The figure remained as high as 32% in 1917. In particular, Japan imported old textile machinery from Britain and lavished labor on its service and repair. Through these machines ran

*The German government also promoted advances in the organization of financial markets or at the very least, did not impede them. For example, joint-stock and investment banking were innovations in which Germany played a major part.

cheaper cotton than through those used by producers in other countries. Therefore more labor was required to repair the broken threads—another example of the close attention paid to comparative advantage. The major shift to capital-intensive heavy industry did not take place until after World War II.

Japan studied and imported foreign technology, welcomed but carefully policed private foreign investment, and searched for lines of production that might become more capital-intensive over time. The Japanese government was development-minded. It successfully encouraged saving and investment, engaged in public entrepreneurship while encouraging private entrepreneurs, and funneled its relatively high tax collections into development expenditures. Japan's government, institutions, and social framework all combined to generate high levels of saving and investment. Saving, for example, came to be promoted by the light taxation of interest income, by the poorly developed market for consumer credit, and by the not-very-generous social security system, all reinforcing the tradition of very high saving by entrepreneurs.

Education was promoted, and as early as the 1870s, Japan had literacy rates almost as high as those in Europe. At first wages were quite low, unions were suppressed, and labor conditions were poor. Few would recommend emulating these aspects of the Japanese development experience. By 1911, however, the Factory Act, which regulated hours and working conditions, surprised even antagonistic employers by leading to higher labor productivity. Eventually, income became quite equally distributed—according to the latest figures somewhat more so than in the United States. The Japanese were fortunate that so much went right in the process. Even the loss of a disastrous war—in 1952, seven years after the war's end, per capita income was still below that of Chile, Brazil, and Malaysia—proved to be only a temporary setback. Japan's income figures are now 10 times higher than Brazil's, the richest of those three countries. Per capita income ($28,190 in 1992) is now well above that of the United States ($23,240), and Japan's score on the human development index is third highest in the world, 0.929 out of a perfect 1.0, compared to 0.925 in the United States, which is in eighth place.

THE GREAT SUCCESS OF THE HPAEs

A quarter-century ago, Germany and especially Japan were the main examples of development by late starters. Today the list can be expanded, and with it, new insights can be gained into a range of potentially successful development strategies. It is generally acknowledged that the greatest modern development successes have been registered by a number of high-performing Asian economies (HPAEs); an alternative term is newly industrializing countries (NICs). The HPAEs illustrate how powerful a strategy of industrialization through trade can be.[41]

The HPAEs consist of seven Asian LDCs: the four "Tigers" that made up the initial wave of high performance (Hong Kong, South Korea, Singapore, and Taiwan), and three additional countries that all show the potential to perform on the level of the Tigers (Indonesia, Malaysia, and Thailand).[42] Table 3.1 shows their

TABLE 3.1 HPAE's AVERAGE ANNUAL PERCENTAGE GROWTH, GNP PER CAPITA 1980–1992

Hong Kong	5.5	Indonesia	4.0
Singapore	5.3	Malaysia	3.2
South Korea	8.5	Thailand	6.0
Taiwan	6.7[a]	All LDCs	0.9

Source: WDR 1994, 162–163.

[a]Statistics for Taiwan are not published separately by the World Bank because of its breakaway status. The figure for Taiwan is for 1965–1990, and is from the World Bank's *The East Asian Miracle: Economic Growth and Public Policy* (New York, 1993).

average growth in GNP per capita, 1980 to 1992. The figures contrast to the 0.9% per capita annual growth in GNP in the remainder of the LDCs during the same period.

The success of these countries is shocking by historical standards. For example, the four Tigers together account for about 10% of world exports, just two percentage points less than the 12% of the United States, which is the world's largest exporter. The Tigers were responsible for only about 5% of all exports by the LDCs in 1960, but the figure is about one-third now.[43] Presumably, it will not be long before the Tigers are thought of as developed economies and not as LDCs. (If they can just keep growing at present rates until the year 2000, Taiwan will have surpassed New Zealand, and Hong Kong and Singapore will have passed Great Britain.) Nonetheless, they will have a place in development economics for a long time to come because of the lessons they convey about "how to do it."

Explaining the Success

Why have the HPAEs been so remarkably successful? The most obvious similarity, that they are all Asian, has led some to conclude that there may be a "racial" component to development. It is probably true that these Asian countries have more cultural, ethnic, and linguistic homogeneity than do many other LDCs, so modern state-building has been somewhat easier than elsewhere.[44] Yet those who point to Asian intelligence, discipline, and energy as the source of success face the difficult task of explaining why, as recently as just 40 years ago, these countries were extremely poor, had been so for centuries, and being "Asian" did not seem to have helped.[45]

In the past there have been two distinct schools of thought concerning the HPAEs' achievements. The neoclassical economic view is that stable macroeconomies, strong legal systems, an absence of distortions ("getting the prices right"), considerable investment in education and health, and a strong focus on international trade have been telling. A revisionist view contends that state-led development has been important, with significant government intervention in industrial policy and financial markets ("fiddling with the prices"). The World Bank's new study takes a middle position, a "market-friendly view" suggesting that important parts of both arguments are correct. Market-based incentives were utilized, but with helpful state intervention that does not interfere in a damaging way with the market signals.

The study concluded that the principal causes of the HPAEs' success were high levels of private domestic investment, fueled by high saving, and rapid growth in human capital. The investment, almost twice as high as in the world's other LDCs, was promoted by subsidized interest rates; artificially low capital goods prices; risk limits for private investors; and well-crafted tax, tariff, and exchange rate policies. Local stock and bond markets were not a cause of initial growth, but they developed because of the growth and now contribute to it.

Macroeconomic stability has been good, due to well-designed macro policy. Fiscal deficits have been controlled, and major macro imbalances have been rapidly addressed. In most of the HPAEs, government intervened systematically to encourage saving, keep interest rates low to borrowers (and sometimes to lenders, though only temporarily and with controls on capital movements), information-sharing between the government and the private sector, subsidies to targeted industries, and protection of certain sectors using an infant-industry strategy. Government intervention has been selective and generally performance-based, with clear criteria that firms are expected to meet and close monitoring of firms' performance. Fiscal overextension has rarely been allowed, and price distortions have not been carried to extremes.

In South Korea and Taiwan, which were first-generation HPAEs, there was more state intervention to promote industrialization, including guidance and directed credit, by comparison to the second-generation HPAEs, Indonesia, Malaysia, and Thailand, where there has been less government intervention. Indeed, there may have been less capacity for it. A greater stock of natural resources in these second-generation high performers allowed for more gradual industrialization. Export promotion and policy fundamentals have still been adhered to, and the competence of the bureaucracy has improved greatly, especially in Malaysia. Most of these countries took steps to share the fruits of growth, steps such as rural sector development including land reform, public housing, and programs to assist small and medium enterprises. But in general they did not utilize direct income transfers or subsidies.

According to the World Bank's studies, about two-thirds of the HPAEs' growth seems to have been due to capital investment and human capital formation, while another third was due to an increase in productivity not directly connected to the increased capital formation. In terms of human capital, the HPAEs actually do not spend much more on education than other LDCs (Africa, 4.1% of GNP; East Asia, 3.7%; all LDC average, 3.6%). But the HPAEs have concentrated heavily on primary education, allocating far less of their education budgets to higher education. One of the major distinctions among the HPAEs at present is that the early successes have had an extremely good record in education, whereas the latecomers have not been so effective. For example, a Taiwanese student is twice as likely to go to university, where there are 42, than is a British student, and a Korean student is more likely to go to a university than is a Japanese student. These institutions are in general rather better than the less highly regarded schools of Thailand and Malaysia, where educational deficiencies are among the last hurdles to cross before these countries can emulate the economic success of South Korea and Taiwan.[46]

Export promotion has been pronounced, with export targets common. The HPAEs did use moderate import protection in the 1960s and 1970s especially, to establish potential exporters.[47] Whether steps would help or hinder export competitiveness was always a central question for policy. Unlike the older HPAEs, the newer ones have relied less on specific measures and more on gradual reductions in protection combined with institutional support of exports and assurance that inputs would be duty-free. Key measures have been ability to buy imported inputs at world prices, plenty of financing for firms that export, often including subsidized credit, international trading companies, and income tax incentives for exporting. Exchange rate overvaluation has generally been avoided.

In particular, these economies' policies have been flexible, with cross-fertilization of ideas commonplace. The deliberation councils in Malaysia that do an excellent job of maintaining government–business liaison are closely related to the same idea in South Korea (the Export Promotion Council), which in turn appears to be descended from similar activities undertaken by Japan's famous Ministry of Trade and Industry (MITI). Some of the HPAE governments created "contests" that allowed for considerable cooperation among firms and the government, but also rewarded the most successful firms, that is, the ones that exported the most, with access to credit, foreign exchange, and sometimes licensing of capacity. When voluntary export restraints are met with in developed countries, the HPAEs often allocate shares to producers on the basis of their success in exporting to other unrestricted markets. Governments refereed the contests fairly and with competence. Contests become more difficult to carry out, however, as firms become more powerful, so the more developed the economy, the less successful the contest. With all of these, a process of trial and error was used, with ineffective or damaging policies rapidly abandoned. Exports are in fact an appropriate test of business performance, because export markets are usually highly competitive, standards must be high, and new production processes and higher efficiency often emerge from exporting firms.

Explicit government intervention to support specific sectors did occur from time to time, but did not always work very well. Certain differences appeared even in the four original Tigers. South Korea's government interventions were at their maximum during the 1970s, while at other times, rough neutrality among sectors was maintained. Taiwan was less interventionist than Korea, and achieved considerable neutrality. Hong Kong was laissez-faire, with no government encouragement of industry, while Singapore indulged in the greatest amount of intervention among the Tigers.*

*The two city-states Hong Kong ($15,360 per capita GNP in 1992) and Singapore ($15,730) are the outstanding examples of LDCs that have now achieved output levels greater than those of some developed countries (Ireland, New Zealand, Spain). Average annual real per capita growth in GNP during the period 1980–1992 was 5.5% for Hong Kong and 5.3% for Singapore. These are world-class results. Both Hong Kong and Singapore are very small, but this was once considered by economists to be a substantial disadvantage. They are also very much free traders: Singapore has a liberal policy of letting the market separate winners and losers and of substantially free trade, whereas Hong Kong is the only one of the Tigers to pursue a strategy of virtually *complete* free trade. That, too, was once thought to be a disadvantage.

A CLOSER LOOK AT SOUTH KOREA

South Korea is one of the world's best examples of a recent transformation almost to developed-country status, with per capita GNP and human development indexes similar to those of European Union members Greece and Portugal. As such, that country should and does command wide attention among those who study economic development. Korea benefited from early events. It had some advantages from Japanese colonization in the first part of this century. There was a manufacturing sector even before World War I, and although the nascent industries were ruined by World War II and the Korean War, much industrial experience and acquired skill survived. Korea obtained confiscated Japanese land and property and followed that with pervasive land reforms.

About the time the Korean War ended in 1953, South Korea had fewer resources and a higher population density than the crowded Netherlands. Manufactured goods made up less than 10% of all output. Exports were still only a very small 3.5% of national product at the start fo the 1960s, and per capita income in 1961 was only $80. Growth in that measure had been less than 1% per year since the end of World War II. There was a balance of trade deficit, and 43% of GNP came from farming. Added to that, Korea had a low rate of saving. Anyone suggesting that it would be a development success ran the risk of ridicule. India, with an income per capita now only one-ninth of Korea's, looked to be the better prospect on several counts. Even Ghana, Sudan, and Zaire, three African LDCs that have had major economic problems, were wealthier countries than South Korea at the start of the 1960s.[48]

Aid from the United States mostly offset the country's high defense costs plus the costs of rebuilding its shattered economy after the Korean War. Some of the aid was intelligently used to assist with the establishment of an infrastructure of roads, railways, ports, communications, electricity generation, and a power grid. Korea emphasized education on its own; a literacy rate of 30% in the mid–1950s reached 93% by 1980, and more students are now in high school as a proportion of the population than in the developed countries. Repressive labor laws did not prevent wages from rapidly reflecting the increased demand for labor. Land reform and rural manufacturing enterprise contributed to keeping income distribution more equal than in most LDCs.

Export-led development was a key. Korea's early policy included the manufacture and export of labor-intensive products and did not include the export of primary products. It allowed exporters to import duty-free as long as the imports were reexported within a year. It was a follower in technology and marketing; it used Japanese-style policies, and it benefited from the reputation of goods from Asia first established by Japan. The foreign exchange rate was kept from becoming overvalued. (Chapter 14 discusses the adverse effects of overvaluation and its frequent occurrence in the LDCs.) The price system was freed so that prices reflected real costs and guided entrepreneurs toward labor-intensive manufacturing activities that had a comparative advantage. According to one recent study, "the allocation of factors has not been very different, at least since 1965, than it would have been under a free-trade regime."[49] To overcome infant industry problems, government promoted exports with subsidies and tax reductions and actively, though selectively, intervened in investment decisions. The reward was good performance in output, exports, and, later, progress in research and development. Korea also utilized protective quotas against imports to develop the home market, especially in the 1950s and 1960s; even in 1970 quota restrictions still applied to about 40% of basic imports, and for 25 years no foreign cars were allowed in. From about 1960, however, export promotion was increasingly emphasized, and by 1985 protection of manufactured goods by quotas had largely been superseded by sweeping import liberalization. Tariffs are coming down rapidly, though they remain steep in agriculture and on some manufactured goods. Foreign investment, initially very difficult, was eventually made much easier.

The government's basic rules were as follows: (1) achieve efficient production, (2) gather all relevant information about exports, including from critics and industries themselves, (3) continuously reevaluate ideas in the light of experience instead of sticking to a fixed plan, (4) target only a few industries at one time, and (5) refrain from interfering with the comparative advantage of already established firms.[50]

The result was real per capita growth of 8.5% per year from 1980 to 1992, reaching 12% in some years. Saving was 37% of national product in 1991, investment was 39%, and 1992 per capita GNP was $6790. Exports, mostly manufactured goods, at $76 billion make Korea the world's twelfth largest exporter, ranking ahead of countries such as Sweden and Spain.[51] About a quarter of these exports are now heavy manufactured goods, including steel, ships, and cars. Policy, in particular a low interest-rate strategy, for a long time favored larger firms because the government directed bank lending to those firms. This is one reason why the ten largest *chaebols,* as Koreans call their large conglomerate companies, account for about one-third of all manufacturing and export about one-half of their output.* In many ways, the Korean economy resembles Japan's in the late 1960s.

The picture has its darker side. Large firms will probably be a clumsier, less nimble tool in the future than they have been in the past. The *chaebol* are

---

*One of the most important differences in the development of South Korea and otherwise similar Taiwan is that Taiwan adopted a policy of allowing real interest rates to find a market level, whereas Korea imposed artificially low rates. Taiwan's relatively high rates were helpful. They simulated domestic saving and thus limited the need for foreign borrowing. They resulted in an industrial sector composed of generally smaller firms than in Korea, because large firms usually are the main beneficiaries of low interest rates. Investment had to be more efficient in Taiwan if there was to be a payoff from loans taken out at the high rates. There was also less inflation than in Korea. The predominance of small firms contributes to Taiwan's low Gini coefficient of 0.29, which gives it the most equal income distribution of any capitalist country. Still, questions surround Taiwan's structure of small firms. Its research and development effort is fragmented, raising doubts as to whether such firms can keep up with the competition abroad. Attempts to coordinate research and development by means of cooperative research institutes may or may not succeed.

very big, and they compete with each other a lot—five of them make cars, and a sixth wants to.[52] Probably the government should work to ensure that they pay market interest rates, which would reduce the allure of the large size. There is overconcentration in shipbuilding, textiles, and shoes; the government's support of industry has recently had some mixed results; and there have been policy mistakes in agriculture. Hours worked are still long, and wages are low. Even so, living conditions are changing for the better. Korea's boys are now 4.5 inches taller than they were in 1965; nearly all households have TV sets; 70% have telephones; about half have refrigerators. Its Gini coefficient of 0.36 is low, reflecting a substantial degree of income equality. Its technical progress has been rapid: Samsung's 4 megabyte computer chip was on the market only six months after Japan's first 4 megabyte chip. Undeniably, Korea's growth has been a remarkable feat, no doubt shocking to development pessimists.

Can Other NICs Emulate the Asian High-Achievers?

There are other newly industrializing countries—Brazil, Chile, Mexico, the Philippines, and Israel among them. Vigorous debate now centers on whether these NICs and other poorer, aspiring ones can emulate the spectacular East Asian successes with export-led growth.[53] A great hope of lower-income LDCs is that as the NICs grow richer, labor-intensive manufacturing in them will become increasingly more costly. That would cause the comparative advantage in labor-intensive goods to shift to the lower-income economies, with the NICs providing new markets for the very goods they once produced before moving on to more capital-intensive items.

One element in the debate concerns whether latecomer NICs will be able to utilize the tools of the Tigers. Three such tools are in doubt: (1) The globalization of finance means the capital controls that must be in place to keep interest rates low are difficult to use. (2) Using tariffs to protect the domestic market is more difficult because of the worldwide pressure to lower trade barriers. (3) Export subsidies are increasingly subject to retaliation.

The debate also concerns the degree to which exports of manufactures by NICs would also impinge on developed-country markets and the extent to which protectionist trade barriers would be stimulated by the impact. As a value judgment, it is probably correct to believe, as the protagonists in the debate generally seem to agree, that the 30% annual real growth in exports achieved over long time periods by South Korea and Taiwan will be difficult to generalize. If this figure were achieved by many countries in the long run, it probably would stimulate industrial-country trade barriers under modern political conditions. But William Cline, a major skeptic on the possibility of generalizing a 30% growth rate in exports, nonetheless believes a "brisk" 10% to 15% growth rate should be possible for the LDCs over a long time period. The crucial point will presumably be the extent to which the political influence of industrial-country exporters will grow as their exports to LDCs grow, offsetting the protectionist lobbying of the affected industries. Another possibility that would reduce the pressure would be rapid expansion in trade among the LDCs themselves. We return to this important subject in Chapter 15.

DEVELOPMENT FAILURES

Often as much or more can be learned from failure as from success. To illustrate the failures that lie in wait, there are numerous cases where, without fighting a war or undergoing some natural calamity, income and output have fallen far in the long run. Africa is home to most of the countries in this situation, and development economists are urgently trying to explain why.[54]

The inferior performance is not a long-standing feature. Sub-Saharan Africa experienced good growth in the 1960s and early 1970s, but then its output fell by 15% between 1977 and 1986, and the contraction has unfortunately continued in many countries. The point receives emphasis because one African country, Botswana, employing alternative policies, has recorded some of the world's fastest growth (6.1% annual average increase in GNP, 1980–1992). This is a standout in a continent where the annual average growth during the period was –0.8%. The region with the lowest income and which is most in need of growth has had the least.[55]

Evidence of Africa's lagging development can be found in numerous areas.[56] Though that continent's GDP per capita is actually about the same as in China and India, life expectancy is some 20% lower. In general, there has been no great revolution in agriculture, as has been true of Asia. The share of Africa in world trade is now only a quarter of its 1960 level. Unlike elsewhere in the LDCs, Africa's exports are still almost wholly primary products rather than manufactured goods. Primary product exports were 93% of sub-Saharan Africa's total exports in 1965, and still 92% in 1990. In the same time period, Latin America's figures went from 93% to 67% and East Asia's from 69% to 31%. Population growth in Africa has frequently been over 3% per year in some countries. It was 2.1% per year in the 1960s, 2.8% in the 1970s, and 3.1% in the 1980s. In Somalia, for example, population growth of about 3.2% per year for three decades has raised the total size of the population from 2.9 to 7.5 million people—contributing to the famine conditions and political instability in that country.

Explaining the Failure

How can the poor performance be explained? One explanation is that government policies have been worse in Africa. Typically governments have employed severely overvalued exchange rates, with black market premiums far larger than in most other LDCs. Considerable use has been made of import substitution policies, with high trade barriers in manufacturing. Public sector enterprises have been extended during commodity booms and could not be cut back in slumps. Taxation of agriculture has been much higher (about 70% more on average) than in other areas.[57]

Why policy has been worse in Africa is a more complex question. Probably the most important reason is that weak governments and institutions have been unable to bridge the gap of ethnic, cultural, and linguistic diversity. Poorly drawn colonial boundaries did not help. Ruling elites, their power based on force and patronage, have used the tools of price fixing, state enterprises, exchange rate policy, trade barriers, and heavy taxes on agriculture and mining to feather their nests. These elites have been inclined to use tools such as subsidies, licenses, and price controls to reward specific firms and individuals. Rural resistance is suppressed. State enterprises and government bureaucracies stay bloated because employment can be used as a reward for loyalty. Because the beneficiaries are influential, and the urban proletariat favored by cheap food can be volatile and dangerous for politicians if its benefits are lost, it becomes difficult to dismantle the system.[58]

In the 1960s and 1970s, when world growth was good, the effects of these policies were somewhat hidden. But it became very visible in the lower-growth 1980s, and in some countries became a collapse of governance. It is noteworthy that some of the worst performers (such as Ghana, Nigeria, Sudan, Uganda, Zaire, Zambia) have some of the best resource endowments and that the level of skills and education was relatively high at independence in a number of these (including Ghana, Sudan, Uganda). In effect, the ability to administer has declined even as governments have undertaken more tasks. Capable, honest, and accountable administrators will be needed in quantity before the situation can be turned around. Progress will also depend on the willingness of governments to reduce the compass of their efforts, eschewing unnecessary and counterproductive interventions and allowing more scope for market forces.[59]

The problems extend beyond mistakes of economic policy. Other explanations for Africa's lagging performance include high dependence on primary product exports, and the declining demand for these has led to an adverse shift in the relative prices (terms of trade) of these items. Drought and famine, and limited attention to education until recently, all play a role. So does weaknesses in the framework of land ownership, which is often communal rather than private.

Reform Can Help In some African countries, economic reform has helped. For example, the countries that engaged in extensive macroeconomic reform during the period from 1981 to 1991 saw a median increase in GDP per capita of 2 percentage points, while those that didn't saw a median decline of 2.6 percentage points. Those that reduced taxation of major export crops saw a rise of 2 percentage points in agricultural value added, while those that didn't saw a decline of 2.6 percentage points. Thirteen out of the 15 countries that had major restrictions on private trading of food crops have now turned marketing over to private enterprise rather than utilizing state boards or agencies. The countries with overvalued exchange rates that allowed these rates to fall in real terms by 40 percent or more had a median increase in GDP per capita growth of 2.3 percentage points, while those with fixed exchange rates that appreciated suffered a decline of 1.7 percentage points. In countries classified as having adequate or fair macroeconomic policies, growth in GDP per capita was positive (though low), while growth in those classified as having poor or very poor macroeconomic policies was negative. Countries with limited government intervention in markets had a median growth rate of almost 2% per capita in 1987 to 1991, while those with extensive government intervention suffered from median negative growth of over 1%.[60]

A CLOSER LOOK AT GHANA

An outstanding example of the temporary ruination of development prospects by poor economic policies is Ghana, in West Africa.[61] Once a leading light for Africa and the other LDCs, blessed with a number of advantages, in the 1970s and 1980s it ran aground in a shipwreck of its economy. Only recently have salvage operations begun to succeed.

Historically, Ghana had an advantageous position. Its precolonial Ashanti Kingdom was politically sophisticated. Its gold exports were famous and lucrative in a day when slaves were the only export from most of West Africa. After Britain's colonial conquest, the area was the pioneer in the cocoa industry, quickly rising to the position of the world's foremost exporter. Ghana was the first country in sub-Saharan Africa to receive its independence from a colonial power (in 1957); at that time and for several years thereafter it was a showpiece of development. With its strong currency fully backed by British pounds, good growth in real per capita GDP that averaged about 4% annually from independence to 1960, a comparatively capable civil service, relatively good transport and communications compared to its neighbors, and an electricity supply said to be the best in sub-Saharan Africa with the exception of South Africa, Ghana seemed set to maintain its good showing in per capita income, which was about double South Korea's at the time.

The wreck of Ghana's economy in the 1970s and 1980s would have astounded anyone who visited the country during its first years of independence. It was foreshadowed during the 1960s when real per capita GDP fell in three different years. Performance worsened in the 1970s with falls in five of the ten years, and it reached bottom in the early 1980s with an unbroken streak of annual losses that lasted until 1984. The decline in output was not inconsequential: –1.4% in 1980, –6.5% in 1981, –9.3% in 1982, and –7.0% in 1983. Real per capita GDP in 1983 was less than two-thirds what it had been in 1960. At bottom in the early 1980s compared with 1970, the volume of imports had fallen by about one-third, and exports from 21% to 4% of GDP. During the same period, domestic savings as a proportion of GDP fell from 12% to 3%, and investment from 14% to 2%—both representing a move from respectable to among the world's lowest figures. The government's budget deficit rose from 0.4% of GDP to 14.6%; real wages plunged by 80%. The proportion of children in school dropped by 9%, and the daily calorie supply per person by 10%. Many Ghanians who were able to do so returned to the subsistence production of their own food. Serious academic authors could not resist using words like *appalling* and *nightmare*; these words seemed appropriate.

For the wreck to be this complete without any physical damage from war or earthquake or anything else, the economic policies adopted by the government of Ghana had to be damaging to an unprecedented degree. What were these policies? Basically there were three. First, the chief aim of the government's economic program as put in place during and after the 1960s was industrialization of the country by means of import substitution, that is, attempting to produce at home what was being imported. That policy was promoted by extensive foreign exchange control and licensing of imports. Second, the policy was financed primarily in two damaging ways: taxation of agriculture, in particular cocoa, the major export; and by fiscal budget deficits funded by money creation that proved inflationary. This led to a long period of widespread price controls and an ill-managed system of rationing. Third, many of the new industries were state owned and operated and frequently proved to be inefficient lossmakers. It is hardly a surprise, given the economic collapse, that there was instability in government, with several coups by the military. The change in governments did not, however, alter the basic reasons underlying the chosen economic policies. These damaging policies were used to reward the government's supporters, who thus became dependent on continuation of the system, and to penalize its opponents.

Industrialization by means of import substitution was broad in scale. In 1960, only 11 of Ghana's 43 most important import items were being produced in Ghana, whereas by 1970, that number had risen to 33. To make production profitable, imports were rigorously controlled by means of tariffs and quotas, and the currency was kept overvalued by foreign exchange controls—in 1983, dollars were 26 times more expensive to buy on the black market than at the controlled price. The taxation of the cocoa farmers, who grew the country's main export, reached the point that they were being allowed to keep only 41% of what their crop was worth in 1965, 37% in 1970, and 34% in 1983 to 1984. Money creation to finance budget deficits was being used to cover nearly 60% of government spending in the early 1980s.

The new industries so financed were mostly state owned and operated, but they were poorly managed and inadequately supervised, the prices they charged were kept below costs, they used expensive imported capital, they were not allowed to fail, their level of capacity utilization was almost always low, and they were frequently overmanned with unneeded labor (though it was needed from a political point of view). Only about 5% of these enterprises were able to make a profit, and they often utilized little of their capacity—on average only about one-third of it. They created jobs for political supporters and those leaving school, so that eventually nearly three-fourths of all those formally employed and over 10% of the working population had jobs in these new state-operated firms. It was a particularly expensive way for providing what amounted to unemployment benefits.

Meanwhile, price controls were introduced to control the inflation generated by the money creation and budget deficits. It soon became apparent that the price control inspectors were open to bribes, so the inspectorate was abolished. The policy became one of comprehensive price control enforced haphazardly through the strict and often brutal offices of the army and police.

The predictable shortages of goods at the controlled prices were met with an ad hoc rationing system in which supplies were turned over to large organizations for distribution to their members. At one point, the distribution of 15 "essential commodities" in short supply was entrusted to the Ghana Trades Union Congress, the Civil Servants' Association, the National Association of Teachers, the universities, the police, the Farmers' Council, the Cocoa Marketing Board, the Food Distribution Corporation, and the ministries of defense, education, and health. Only their own personnel and clientele received the scarce goods, of course. It was alleged (by the newspaper *West Africa*) that 8% of available supplies remained for everyone else.[62] Surveys in the early 1980s indicated that nearly two-thirds of Ghana's population simply had no access to the price-controlled goods, with the lowest availability in villages and the countryside. Whatever these controls accomplished, it can hardly be claimed that they helped the poor. Extraordinary amounts of time and energy were expended by consumers in searching for available supplies.*

When the World Bank published an index of price distortions in 1983, taking into account foreign exchange pricing, factor pricing, and product pricing, Ghana was named as the most distorted economy, at the bottom of a 31-country list.[63] This was no mean feat, and the damage inflicted by the policies was overwhelming. The highly taxed cocoa crop fell from a high of 566,000 tonnes in 1964/1965 to 159,000 tonnes in 1983/1984. Other exports collapsed, too. Real wages in the formal economy fell sharply, at one point in the early 1980s to about 16% of the figure in 1970, and the decline pushed even salaried professionals into the underground economy to feed their families. Eventually, a month's salary for a university teacher did not cover even a week's supply of food.[64] The effect on living standards was pronounced. Two revealing examples were a decline during the 1970s of nearly 40% in newspaper circulation and a decline of 82% in cinema attendance.[65] Not surprisingly, the urge to emigrate was strong among professionals and unskilled workers alike. By 1985, it was estimated that one-half to two-thirds of Ghana's skilled and qualified managers had been lost to other countries.[66]

Finally, virtually all aspects of the economic infrastructure decayed. Schools without books, streetlights without bulbs, telephones permanently out of order, shrinking availability of pumped water and electricity, highway surfaces so broken up that it was advisable to drive on a dirt track instead—all became the order of the day. In 1983, it was estimated that 70% of the country's buses and trucks were idle, mainly because of the unavailability of tires and batteries. According to the IMF, the Ghana western railway had "stopped operating because of severe deterioration of the wooden sleepers [ties] that hold rails in place." Even if repair had been possible, about 80% of the country's locomotives were out of service due to a lack of spares.[67] The post office, once a model for Africa, went derelict, moving just 44 million items in 1981 compared to five times that quantity a decade before.

Far too late, so it would seem, one of Ghana's military governments at last abandoned the damaging policies that had been in place for 20 years, called for worldwide assistance, and with the help received, put in place an economic recovery program. Ghana engaged in sweeping reforms, with great support both from the government and the population.

It tackled price distortions, the deficit, and money creation first. Many subsidies were eliminated. The foreign exchange rate reform together with other

---

*The author, giving a guest lecture at the University of Ghana, Legon, was asked by a group of economics faculty to cut the lecture short because a supply of light bulbs had suddenly come on sale in a local store. His hotel in Accra, at which a night's lodging cost over $100 at the overvalued official rate of exchange, apparently got the same news and also acted quickly—a bulb appeared that night to illuminate his dark room.

reforms almost doubled exports between 1984 and 1990. Import barriers were lowered. A stock market was established in 1990. Ghana's cocoa farmer snow get about 60% of the world price for their cocoa. Eleven thousand ghost workers were eliminated from the civil service. GDP is growing again, and inflation has been much reduced. Yet the ground gained is basically nothing more than what was lost in the shipwreck, and unfavorable legacies remain. Many people still hold their savings in foreign currency or outside the banking system, credit is hard to obtain, investment is low, aid from abroad is of considerable importance, and the government's hand is still heavy on the economy.

Ghana thus stands as a powerful example of what bad economic policies can do to an otherwise favored country, but it also serves to show that policy reforms can be effective.

The Devastating Results of State Failure: The Recent Experience of Zaire

Catastrophic implications for economic development follow from state failure. When a government cannot govern effectively any longer, development efforts are doomed and economic and social collapse become real possibilities. This phenomenon, relatively rare since World War II until recently, is becoming more common. In the growing list of examples are Haiti in the Americas, Burma (Myanmar) and Cambodia in Asia, Yemen in the Middle East, and, in Africa, Liberia, Siera Leone, Somalia, Rwanda, and Zaire. It is abundantly clear that a breakdown in the ability to govern is devastating for an economy. In what follows, we emphasize Zaire in west-central Africa as an outstanding example of state collapse.

That country has been under the iron hand of Mobutu Sese Seko for about thirty years, since he seized power in 1965 with backing from the U.S. CIA. As a Cold War measure, Mobutu's government received considerable amounts of foreign aid—over a billion dollars during the 1970s and 1980s. Even without aid, prospects were excellent because Zaire is rich in natural resources. Indeed, it is one of the world's best endowed countries, with enough arable land to feed all of Africa, enough hydroelectric power to supply all of Africa's demand, as well as being rich in copper, cobalt, and diamonds. In spite of all this, during the period 1965 to 1990 its economy contracted at about –2.2% per year. The decline is apparently accelerating—though the international agencies no longer publish output statistics for Zaire.[68]

Zaire's government and economy are presently in a state of virtual collapse. Many factories built by the Mobutu government lie abandoned. Gecamines (formerly Union Minière), once one of the world's largest and most lucrative copper and cobalt mining operations, has been virtually abandoned to scavengers since 1991 when disgruntled army units smashed up its facilities. Expatriate mining engineers, merchants, and technical experts have fled the country.

Defaults on most loans made to the government caused the World Bank to break off contacts in 1993 and the IMF to suspend Zaire's membership in 1994. Most aid from the developed countries has been halted. (This has made little difference to most of the population, however, because a high proportion of the aid that had gone to Zaire was stolen by government officials—just as they steal much of the government's budget by collecting the salaries of ghost workers, thought to make up two-thirds of the people on the civil service roster.)

In some parts of the country ethnic cleansing is going on. Wild inflation, recently running at 9000% per year, slows down inexplicably for weeks at a time, perhaps because the government temporarily cannot afford to import new currency notes. Zaire's banks are often closed because of shortages of currency. In 1993, with the "zaire" nearly worthless—the largest note, for 5 million zaire, was worth less than two dollars—the printing of ever larger notes provoked riots and several hundred deaths.

In the capital, Kinshasa, public transport has largely broken down. As of 1994 there had been no fuel deliveries in months. The bankrupt army looted the capital in 1991 and 1993; these events plus other rounds of pillaging by disgruntled soldiers have led to closed businesses everywhere. Not one cinema remains in the city. Rubbish piles up in the streets and malnutrition is rising rapidly. Bribery and corruption are rampant, with military officers running protection rackets and police arresting hapless citizens in order to extort fines or bail from them. Schoolteachers demand a payment before releasing grades. Hospital guards demand a cut before letting people into hospitals. It would seem wholly credible to be told that revolution is just around the corner, but informed observers doubt it. As *The Economist* of London has reported, "Zaireans are just too exhausted . . . by the daily struggle to survive."[69]

Nonetheless, people do have to survive somehow, and they do it by a combination of subsistence production and by participating in the illegal underground activity. These two economies now dominate most parts of the country. The underground economy is surprisingly organized, given the chaos of the official economy and government. It features a relatively fixed scale of bribes (in real terms) for many transactions, standard equivalences in barter transactions, well-understood obligations, and personal ties to powerful people, smuggling, and theft. The profits from the underground economy are used to provide unofficial health care, schools, and the maintenance of roads, but sporadically so that the degree of deprivation is great. There are informal business tribunals as substitutes for the corrupt courts when property rights and contracts fail to be enforced by the regular courts. With loans through banks having broken down, credit is provided by unofficial rotating credit societies.

In official jobs, wage are very low. Employees are expected to make a living from under-the-table payments, bribes, or activity in the underground economy, where prices are high because of risks and numerous intermediaries. Transport problems keep imports from being supplied in central areas, broken-up roads cause broken-down trucks. Massive outflows of plantation labor have occurred, and neither teachers nor students will stay in the schools, as people seek to make a living in the underground economy. In some areas, large numbers of people dig for gold, diamonds, and copper in the abandoned works of the old state mining corporations. Food rots (in some areas, as much as half of it) because farmers choose to market it through the underground economy, where the obstacles of cost and risk are great. The fuel for the transport of much of the underground economy's production is stolen, often by workers in the state corporations who sell it to corrupt soldiers who then market it unofficially to truckers. The same soldiers often hire themselves out as bodyguards or watchmen for those who can afford it. Some call the government mercantilist, its main motive to redistribute wealth to its members. Others choose to call it a *kleptocracy*, a government based on theft.

Conclusion

Readers of this chapter will hardly doubt that the gap between the LDCs that have performed well and those that have performed poorly has been vast. A common thread appears to link the experience of these countries, however. When government intervention in the economy has been carried out judiciously and effectively, it has paid off. When it has been misconceived and carried to extremes, it has been damaging. Neglect of agriculture and high taxation of farmers is seen to be an unpromising path. The foreign trade strategy of actively promoting exports by paying close attention to existing or potential comparative advantage and rarely promoting anything obviously disadvantageous appears to be effective policy, whereas a policy of overly broad general import substitution appears costly and very damaging. In the best performing countries, government policies involve fairly uniform incentives and do not discriminate to any great degree against any existing sector. The countries with excellent records successfully manage to keep their price structures, including the foreign exchange rate, free from serious distortions; whereas the poor performers' economies are highly distorted by controls of all kinds that reduce efficiency. Arguing that widespread controls help the poorest portion of the population is not very convincing when these same controls are doing significant damage to an economy or even bringing it to a state of collapse. These are, presumably, useful lessons.

The Road Ahead

At this point in the text, we turn to specific topics concerning growth and development. The broad framework has been sketched in this chapter: Growth is not the result of any one factor but of a whole constellation of economic and social determinants. These include the availability of capital; labor (including human resource considerations such as education, health and nutrition, and the influence of income distribution); land and natural resource endowment; entrepreneurship and management ability; technical improvement in all its forms; and the psychological, cultural, and social differences (including government and attitudes toward foreign trade) that inhibit or promote growth.

This rather long accounting is worlds apart from models that seek to identify some paramount cause of growth. Even at the introductory level, to consider the individual components requires a book-length study. It clearly gives no easy description or prediction of growth, and because some of its components are inherently difficult to measure with precision, constructing a mathematical model of the growth process defined in this way is not very practical. The experience of the last two decades shows, however, that this is exactly the problem. The causes of growth are complex, more so than was believed by the earlier generation of development economists who searched for single explanations with a notable lack of success.

And so to work.

NOTES

1. The major works of synthesis depended on for this chapter were cited in the first endnote to Chapter 1.
2. For a recent mathematical model incorporating several of the factors discussed in this section, see Ichiro Otani and Delano Villanueva, "Long-Term Growth in Developing Countries and Its Determinants: An Empirical Analysis," *World Development* 18, no. 6 (June 1990): 769–783. A recent book is Elisabeth Sadoulet, *Quantitative Development Policy Analysis* (Baltimore, 1994).
3. William Easterly and Lant Pritchett, "The Determinants of Economic Success: Luck and Policy," *Finance and Development* 30, no. 4 (December 1993): 40.
4. See J. Bradford DeLong and Lawrence H. Summers, *How Strongly Do Developing Economies Benefit from Equipment Investment*? (Washington, D.C., 1993); the same authors' "Equipment Investment and Economic Growth," *Quarterly Journal of Economics* 106 (May 1991): 445–502; and Easterly and Pritchett, "The Determinants of Economic Success: Luck and Policy," 40.
5. IMF, *World Economic Outlook 1993* (Washington, D.C., 1993), 47.
6. For thorough analysis of the issue, see Hollis B. Chenery, Sherman Robinson, and Moshe Syrquin, *Industrialization and Growth: A Comparative Study* (Washington, D.C., 1986); and Moshe Syrquin, "Patterns of Structural Change," in Hollis Chenery and T. N. Srinivasan, eds., *Handbook of Development Economics,* vol. 1 (Amsterdam, 1988), 203–273.
7. *WDR 1994* and *WDR 1992*, table 3.
8. Calculated from Subrata Ghatak, *Development Economics* (London, 1978), 7.
9. Easterly and Pritchett, "The Determinants of Economic Success: Luck and Policy," 40.
10. *WDR 1983*, 57–63. See this book's Chapter 12 for details.
11. Easterly and Pritchett, "The Determinants of Economic Success: Luck and Policy," 40.
12. Easterly and Pritchett, "The Determinants of Economic Success: Luck and Policy," 40.
13. Paul Streeten, "Markets and States: Against Minimalism," *World Development* 21, no. 8 (August 1993): 1281–1298.
14. Michael T. Rock, " 'Twenty-five Years of Economic Development' Revisited," *World Development* 21, no. 11 (November 1993): 1796–1797.
15. By Lloyd G. Reynolds, "The Spread of Economic Growth to the Third World, 1850–1980," *Journal of Economic Literature* 21 (1983): 976. This branch of development economics has been mushrooming. Among the sources that have informed my work, in alphabetical order, are a special issue of *World Development* 17, no. 9 (September 1989) edited by Irma Adelman and Erik Thorbecke, "The Role of Institutions in Economic Development"; Robert H. Bates, ed., *Political and Economic Interactions in Economic Policy Reform: Evidence from Eight Countries* (Oxford, 1993); Partha Dasgupta, *An Inquiry into Well-Being and Destitution* (Oxford, 1993), especially chapters 2 and 5; Cynthia Morris and Irma Adelman, *Comparative Patterns of Economic Develop-*

ment, 1850–1914 (Baltimore, 1988); Douglass C. North, *Institutions, Institutional Change and Economic Performance* (New York, 1991), which points to the importance of proper institutions (laws, courts) and how they may be subject to increasing returns; Eberhard Scholing and Vincenz Timmermann, "Why LDC Growth Rates Differ: Measuring 'Unmeasurable' Influences," *World Development* 16, no. 11 (November 1988): 1271–1294; Robin Theobold, *Corruption, Development and Underdevelopment* (Durham, N.C., 1990); and Gustav Ranis, *The Political Economy of Development Policy Change* (Cambridge, 1992).

16. Myrdal's views are in "Need for Reforms in Underdeveloped Countries," in Sven Grassman and Erik Lundberg, *The World Economic Order: Past and Prospects* (New York, 1981), especially 518–525.
17. Clifton Barton, *Problems and Prospects of Small Industries in the Republic of Vietnam* (Saigon, 1974).
18. See Hernando de Soto, *The Other Path: The Invisible Revolution in the Third World* (New York, 1989). Robert Klitgaard, *Tropical Gangsters* (New York, 1990), the personal reminiscences of a development economist working in Equatorial Guinea and the best of its genre, is a very readable account of what it is like to work and advise in such a setting.
19. *WDR 1991*, 132.
20. *The Economist*, May 4, 1991.
21. *WDR 1991*, 132, 140.
22. Robert Klitgaard, "Incentive Myopia," *World Development* 17, no. 4 (April 1989): 447–459.
23. See *The Economist*, May 7, 1983.
24. Andrei Shleifer and Robert Vishny, "Corruption," *Quarterly Journal of Economics* 108, no. 3 (August 1993): 599–617.
25. See Klitgaard, "Incentive Myopia"; and M. S. Alam, "Some Economic Costs of Corruption in LDCs," *Journal of Development Studies* 27, no. 1 (October 1990): 89–97.
26. Myrdal, "Need for Reforms," 523.
27. *HDR 1994*, 13.
28. Michael T. Rock, "'Twenty-five Years of Economic Development' Revisited," 1796–1797.
29. *WDR 1991*, 50. For a survey, see Larry Sirowi and Alex Inkeles, "The Effects of Democracy on Economic Growth and Inequality: A Review," *Studies in Comparative International Development* 25, no. 1 (Spring 1990): 126–157. There is a special issue of *World Development* 21, no. 8 (August 1993) on the topic. Edited by Laurence Whitehead, its title is "Economic Liberalization and Democratization."
30. Pranab Bardhan, "Symposium on Democracy and Development," *Journal of Economic Perspectives* 7, no. 3 (Summer 1993): 45–49.
31. Adam Przeworski and Fernando Limongi, "Political Regimes and Economic Growth," *Journal of Economic Perspectives* 7, no. 3 (Summer 1993): 51–69.
32. Lawrence H. Summers and Vinod Thomas, "Recent Lessons of Development," *World Bank Research Observer* 8, no. 2 (July 1993): 245–246.
33. See George Sorensen, *Democracy, Dictatorship, and Development: Economic Development in Selected Regimes of the Third World* (New York, 1990); and also *The Economist*, August 27, 1994.
34. Gustav Ranis and John C. H. Fei, "Development Economics: What Next?" in Gustav Ranis and T. Paul Schultz, eds., *The State of Development Economics* (Oxford, 1988), 100–101.

35. An insightful discussion of why the presently developed countries had historical advantages over the LDCs that promoted their growth is Nathan Rosenberg and L. E. Birdzell, Jr., *How the West Grew Rich* (New York, 1985). The work of Angus Maddison is informative. See his *Dynamic Forces in Capitalist Development* (Oxford, 1991). This section also utilizes the views of Gerald Meier in various editions of *Leading Issues in Development Economics* (Oxford) and the contributions of Simon Kuznets and Alexander Gerschenkron reprinted there.
36. John W. Sewell et al., *The United States and World Development Agenda 1980* (New York, 1980), 99.
37. See P. Bairoch, *The Economic Development of the Third World Since 1900* (Berkeley, 1975), 40–41.
38. The broad estimate is cited by Hans W. Singer and Javed A. Ansari, *Rich and Poor Countries* (Baltimore, 1977); and see William W. Murdoch, *The Poverty of Nations* (Baltimore, 1980), 246. For the Dahomean data see Patrick Manning, *Slavery, Colonialism and Economic Growth in Dahomey, 1640–1960* (Cambridge, 1982), 224–225.
39. My general background on these countries has been informed over the years by Gustav Stolper, Karl Hauser, and Knut Borchardt, *The German Economy, 1870 to the Present* (New York, 1967); Kunio Yoshihara, *Japanese Economic Development* (Oxford, 1994); Kazushi Ohkawa and Miyohei Shinohara, eds., *Patterns of Japanese Economic Development* (New Haven, 1979); Lawrence Klein and Kazushi Ohkawa, eds., *Economic Growth: The Japanese Experience Since the Meiji Era* (Homewood, Ill., 1968); and William W. Lockwood, *The Economic Development of Japan: Growth and Structural Change* (Princeton, N.J., 1968).
40. See Young-Il Park and Kym Anderson, "The Rise and Demise of Textiles and Clothing in Economic Development: The Case of Japan," *Economic Development and Cultural Change* 39, no. 3 (April 1991): 531–548.
41. The original idea for this section comes from Gerald M. Meier, *Emerging from Poverty: The Economics That Really Matters* (New York, 1984), 57–65.
42. The World Bank has made a major study of the HPAEs, entitled, *The East Asian Miracle: Economic Growth and Public Policy* (New York, 1993). Japan is included in the study. Other works on the HPAEs depended on here, listed alphabetically, include Shirley W. Y. Kuo, *The Taiwan Economy in Transition* (Boulder, Colo., 1983); Lawrence J. Lau, ed., *Models of Development: A Comparative Study of Economic Growth in South Korea and Taiwan* (San Francisco, 1986); David Lim, "Explaining the Growth Performances of Asian Developing Economies," *Economic Development and Cultural Change* 42, no. 4 (July 1994): 829–844; Edward S. Mason et al., *The Economic and Social Modernization of the Republic of Korea* (Cambridge, Mass., 1980); Harry T. Oshima, "The Transition from an Agricultural to an Industrial Economy in East Asia," *Economic Development and Cultural Change* 34, no. 6 (1986): 783–809 (which gives details of Korea's policy mistakes in agriculture); Peter A. Petri, "Korea's Export Niche: Origins and Prospects," *World Development* 16, no. 1 (January 1988): 47–63; Anthony M. Tang and James S. Worley, eds., "Why Does Overcrowded, Resource-Poor East Asia Succeed—Lessons for the LDCs?" a special issue of *Economic Development and Cultural Change* 36, no. 3 (April 1988) that includes a useful article by Paul W. Kuznets, "An East Asian Model of Economic Development: Japan, Taiwan, and South Korea," S11–S43; Yung Whee Rhee, Bruce Ross-Larson, and Gary Pursell, *Korea's Competitive Edge: Managing the Entry into World Markets* (Baltimore, 1984); Ezra Vogel, *The Four Little Dragons: The Spread of Industrialization in East Asia* (Cambridge, Mass., 1991); Robert Wade, *Governing the Market: Economic Theory and the Role of Government in East Asian Industrialization* (Princeton, 1991); and Peter G. Warr, ed., *The Thai Econ-*

omy in Transition (Cambridge, 1993). I also utilized the frequent articles in *The Economist*, including special sections in the issues of November 16, 1991, and October 10, 1992.

43. *The Economist*, June 1, 1991; Anne O. Krueger, *Economic Policies at Cross-Purposes: the United States and the Developing Countries* (Washington, D.C., 1993), 105.
44. Rock, " 'Twenty-five Years of Economic Development' Revisited," 1795.
45. Following Helen Hughes, *Policy Lessons of the Development Experience*, Group of 30 Occasional Paper No. 16 (1985), 14.
46. *The Economist*, November 16, 1991, and August 13, 1994.
47. Danny M. Leipziger and Vinod Thomas, "Roots of East Asia's Success," *Finance and Development* 32, no. 1 (March 1994): 6–9.
48. *The Economist*, June 1, 1991.
49. Mason et at., *Republic of Korea*, 6.
50. From Larry Westphal, "Industrial Policy in an Export-Propelled Economy: Lessons from South Korea's Experience," *Economic Perspectives* 4, no. 3 (Summer 1990): 41–59.
51. The information is from *WDR 1994* and *HDR 1994*.
52. *The Economist*, June 8, 1991.
53. The debate is nicely captured in William R. Cline, "Can the East Asian Model of Development be Generalized?" *World Development* 10, no. 2 (1982): 81–90; Gustav Ranis, "Can the East Asian Model Be Generalized? A Comment," *World Development* 13, no. 4 (1985): 543–545; and William R. Cline, "Reply," *World Development* 13, no. 4 (1985): 547–548. There is a comparison of various authors' lists of which countries deserve the label NIC in Helen O'Neill, "HICs, NICs, and LICs: Some Elements in the Political Economy of Gradation and Differentiation," *World Development* 12, no. 7 (1984): 711–712.
54. For comprehensive surveys, see World Bank, *Adjustment in Africa: Reforms, Results, and the Road Ahead* (New York, 1994); and World Bank, *Sub-Saharan Africa: From Crisis to Sustainable Growth* (Washington, D.C., 1989). A recent volume addressing the subject is Thomas M. Callaghy, ed., *Hemmed In: Responses to Africa's Economic Decline* (New York, 1993).
55. Christine Jones and Miguel A. Kiguel, "Africa's Quest for Prosperity: Has Adjustment Helped?" *Finance and Development* 31, no. 2 (June 1994): 2–5.
56. Rock, " 'Twenty-five Years of Economic Development' Revisited," 1790–1791; *HDR 1992*, 4.
57. Christine Jones and Miguel A. Kiguel, "Africa's Quest for Prosperity: Has Adjustment Helped?" *Finance and Development* 31, no. 2 (June 1994): 2–5.
58. D. K. Fieldhouse, *Black Africa 1945–1980* (London, 1986), 94–97.
59. Nurul Islam, "Comment on 'Economic Regress: Concepts and Features,' " *Proceedings of the World Bank Annual Conference on Development Economics 1993* (Washington, D.C., 1994): 346.
60. The figures in this paragraph are presented and discussed in Ishrat Husain and Rashid Faruquee, eds., *Adjustment in Africa: Lessons from Country Case Studies* (Washington, D.C., 1994).
61. The details in this section are from Jan Hogendorn and Robert Christiansen, "Perspectives on the Economic Experience of Two Countries of Sub-Saharan Africa: Ghana and Malawi" (paper presented at Stanford University, 1990). Also see Douglas Rimmer, *Staying Poor: Ghana's Political Economy, 1950–1990* (Oxford, 1992).
62. *West Africa* (April 20, May 18, and June 15, 1981).
63. *WDR 1983*, 60–63.
64. M. M. Huq, *The Economy of Ghana: The First 25 Years* (New York, 1989), 231.

65. World Bank, *Ghana: Policies and Program for Adjustment* (Washington, D.C., 1984), xii.
66. From E. R. Rado, "Notes Toward a Political Economy of Ghana Today," *African Affairs* 85, No. 341 (October 1986): 563.
67. *IMF Survey,* November 12, 1984, 340.
68. For this section I have relied on two works by Janet MacGaffey, *The Real Economy of Zaire: The Contribution of Smuggling and Other Unofficial Activities to National Wealth* (Philadelphia, 1991), and *Entrepreneurs and Parasites: the Struggle for Indigenous Capitalism in Zaire* (Cambridge, 1987); Stephen C. Smith, *Case Studies in Economic Development* (New York, 1994), 14–19; *New York Times*, February 21 and 26, 1993; and *The Economist*, April 16, 1994, and December 17, 1994.
69. *The Economist*, April 16, 1994.

Chapter 4

Financing Development I

The Role of Capital, Domestic Saving

This chapter begins our consideration of the first key element in the development process: capital formation through saving and investment. The early generation of development economists thought capital was the most critical factor in the development process, and the legacy of this belief has lasted to this day. Although the evidence has not confirmed their view that capital is the only key, it is certainly important. Additions to capital have the capacity to raise the productivity of labor and hence the demand for labor. In the long run, that higher demand can raise the real wage and cause yet more investment in a "virtuous circle." A balanced perspective is much needed after a long period of overly great attention to capital in development, followed by what now appears an overly great reaction against it.

In the early days of the specialty, just after World War II and in the 1950s, W. Arthur Lewis, Walt Rostow, and others established the position that a stagnant economy normally saves and invests about five cents out of every dollar of national income, a savings ratio of 5%, whereas a growing economy manages to save and invest 12% to 15% of its income. They saw in that difference the essential strategy for any country desiring to develop.[1]

The theoretical linchpin connecting capital formation to economic growth was the capital-output ratio. This appealing concept of a relatively stable ratio between capital as an input and a growing output (GNP) as a result became a fixture in the literature on economic development, as we shall see in Chapter 12.

CAPITAL IN THE LDCS

In any discussion of the connection between capital formation and growth, there immediately arises a problem of definition. What is capital? We mean, of course, the accumulated stock of material resources that contributes through time to a larger flow of goods and services. Items fitting this definition in one country may not, however, fit it in another. Any observer would surely agree that expenditures classed as consumption in North America or Europe may form capital in Asia or Africa. Take, for example, the hand tools of a household or a farm—the hammers, hoes, sickles, and so forth. These are treated as consumption goods in the national accounts of a developed country, but they serve as capital in many LDCs. The bicycle, considered a consumption good in developed countries, is an important contributor to production in many LDCs. Bicycles are used to transport goods to market or as taxis. They are like very small trucks, except that they are able to go where the trucks cannot. They can carry a large load, easily over 500 pounds, if they are wheeled along. Bicycles carry cocoa and peanuts in bags, cotton in bales, rubber in sheets, palm oil in drums, or imported commodities in boxes.

Improved agricultural land provides a similar definitional problem. By conventional practice, the clearing and improving of land and the planting of tree crops that take a long time to bear are not counted as capital formation. What if, however, much time and effort is devoted to clearing and planting as opposed to other types of capital formation? What if the agricultural sector is very large? A serious omission in the measurement of capital can result if these are overlooked, as ordinarily they are.

"Human Capital"

It is frequently recognized that output of some goods classified as consumption has a capital aspect. Examples include education and health measures, which are commonly called "human capital," and increases in spending on them, "human investment." If education is counted as (human) capital formation, in LDCs it could easily be as much as one-third to one-half of all capital formation as conventionally defined.[2] In agriculture, inputs with capital characteristics, such as pesticides, fertilizers, and improved seeds, have had an extremely important role in the "green revolution." Often their cumulative effect on yields has far outweighed the impact of physical capital as conventionally defined.

One can go a long step further, as did Gunnar Myrdal, and claim that the distinction between investment and consumption is not justified in an LDC even when speaking of consumer goods with no obvious capital characteristics. Myrdal argues that higher consumption of goods in a low-income LDC ordinarily raises production as a direct result. So consumption acts as investment, even though for definitional purposes it remains consumption. The clearest example is food. Observers of the LDCs do not doubt that in many of them, larger supplies and better quality would, by improving nutrition, cause an increase in worker productivity and hence output. To turn the example around, cutting the consumption of food would surely reduce output, perhaps substantially. Clothing shares this property to a lesser extent. (Housing does, too, but this is everywhere classified as capital.) Even more broadly, any new consumer goods (including imports), if made available, may have a capital aspect if they act on consumers as an inducement to better economic performance.

As Andrew Kamarck has argued convincingly,

> it is now time for economists working on problems of developing countries to accept fully the Fisherian definition of investment [from Irving Fisher's 1927 book, *The Nature of Capital and Investment*]: . . . any outlay made today for the purpose of increasing future income—whatever the asset (tangible or intangible, a piece of machinery or a piece of productive knowledge, a passable road or a functioning family planning organization) that is purchased with the outlay. . . . The whole apparatus of investment decision can be applied to this as it is applied now to the purchase of durable goods. The figures and calculations will be less precise, but the analysis and conclusions will be more correct.[3]

All of these difficulties of definition must be kept in mind by the experienced development economist. They mean that comparisons of the size of the capital stock among countries, especially the lowest-income ones with the better off, may contain intrinsic inaccuracies. This lessens confidence in the exactness of mathematical relationships between growth in a country's capital stock and growth in its output.

ASSESSING THE CONTRIBUTION OF CAPITAL

For a long period, the crucial role of physical capital formation in the development process was more or less taken for granted—osmosis, so it seems, from the idea that low-income countries are capital-short, while rich countries are capital-abundant.

Research in the Developed Countries Downplayed the Role of Physical Capital

The pioneering attempts at "growth accounting" in the developed countries, rough-and-ready econometrics at the start but becoming increasingly more sophisticated, gave surprising results. Respected investigators who focused on the United States in the 1950s and 1960s included Moses Abramovitz, Alec Cairncross, John Kendrick, Benton Massell, and especially Robert Solow, who won the 1987 Nobel Prize largely for his earlier work on economic growth. Later, Edward Denison became prominent among the economists who continued these studies. These scholars were united in their conclusion that the physical quantity of capital itself (and of other physical inputs such as labor and raw materials) was less important than the productivity or efficiency of the inputs.[4] This became the accepted view of economic growth in the developed countries.

Economists dealing with growth accounting began to speak of the importance of total factor productivity (TFP)—the part of any increase in output not due to the increased quantity of inputs. This "residual" of growth due to the changing quality, rather than quantity, of inputs began a long search for what actually comprised the residual. The residual was originally believed to represent the importance of technical change. Further research refined the evidence with growing confidence that the residual, which explained the bulk of the increases in real income, consisted of (1) the quality of labor, as affected by education, experience, on-the-job training, and an increase in the quality of each hour worked due to a reduction in number of hours worked; (2) a reallocation of resources from uses with lower productivity to those with higher productivity, including the employment of unused resources and a reduction of the distortions due to government policy; (3) economies of scale; and (4) improved ways to produce goods due to technical progress.[5] This line of research suggested strongly that much of developed-country growth stemmed not from more inputs but from better quality inputs.

Development economists rapidly became aware of this research, which introduced a note of skepticism about capital. The skepticism eventually grew into a great reaction against the belief that the sheer quantity of capital is central to development. For a time, these models made explanations of growth based on capital distinctly passé.

The Importance of Physical Capital for LDCs

The reaction against capital was pushed too far and led to some underestimation of the role of physical capital investment in the growth of the LDCs. The problem was that findings from U.S. and European historical experience could not be transferred unaltered to today's LDCs. The United States always, even in the early nineteenth century, had relatively capital-intensive factor proportions. In more labor-intensive countries, capital would be predictably more effective per unit because it is scarce.

Starting in the 1980s, important studies began to revive the conclusion that capital per se is very important to the economic growth of the LDCs. There is, for example, a noticeable statistical correlation between today's LDCs with the highest output growth and LDCs with the highest rate of capital accumulation. World Bank data indicate that on average a one percentage point increase in the ratio of investment to GDP raises the rate of growth by about 0.1 to 0.2 of 1 percentage point.[6] Similarly, low growth and a low rate of capital formation are also correlated.

A widely publicized study of 1986 yielded the results shown in Table 4.1. The study concluded that the contribution of capital, about 40% of growth, exceeded that of total factor productivity. This was a result far in excess of that reported for the developed countries.

Later refinements indicated that in general, when total output growth is slow, the contribution of total factor productivity increases is negligible. When growth is high, however, as in Taiwan, South Korea, and Japan, the contribution of increased total factor productivity is considerable.[7]

Data presented by the World Bank in its 1991 Development Report (see Table 4.2) tend to confirm how the physical accumulation of factors, particularly capital,

TABLE 4.1 THE SOURCES OF ECONOMIC GROWTH IN LDCS, SAMPLE OF 20 COUNTRIES (AVERAGE ANNUAL RATE OF GROWTH, PERCENT)

Growth in value added	6.3
Contribution of total factor input of which	4.3
Labor	1.8
Capital	2.5
Contribution of total factor productivity	2.0

Source: Hollis Chenery, Sherman Robinson, and Moshe Syrquin, *Industrialization and Growth: A Comparative Study* (New York, 1986), table 2-2.

TABLE 4.2 PERCENTAGE SHARE OF GROWTH IN OUTPUT ACCOUNTED FOR BY CAPITAL INPUT, LABOR INPUT, AND TOTAL FACTOR PRODUCTIVITY, 1960–1987

	Capital	Labor	TFP
Africa	73	28	0
East Asia	57	16	28
Latin America	67	30	0
South Asia	67	20	14
Total (including other LDC areas)	65	23	14
France	27	–5	78
Germany	23	–10	87
Japan	36	5	59
United Kingdom	27	–5	78
United States	23	27	50

Note: The LDC figures are from a sample of 68 countries. See the technical note, 158–159 of *WDR 1991*, and sources cited there, for why the numbers sometimes do not add to 100.

Source: WDR 1991, 45.

counts for more in LDCs' growth than it does in developed countries. The wealthier a country becomes, the less important is its physical capital formation and the more important is its increase in the efficiency of inputs (that is, increase in total factor productivity).

A consensus view now seems to have emerged. Physical capital on average in the LDCs is more important for growth than it is in the developed countries. As growth occurs, however, physical accumulation of capital tends to fade in importance. For example, the World Bank study of the HPAEs notes that in these (South Korea, Taiwan, etc.), improvement in total factor productivity growth has become the most important contributor to growth, even though this is not typical of most of the other LDCs.[8]

Why is capital of greater importance to growth in the LDCs than it is to growth in the developed countries? [9] There appear to be two main reasons: (1) capital scarcity could be making the return to capital greater, on the principle that the scarce factors are more productive. This is the famous idea of diminishing returns to a factor. It may explain why as a country grows richer, knowledge and technology become more important and sheer accumulation of capital becomes less so;* (2) perhaps at lower levels of development, inadequate education means that the best technologies cannot be adopted so more physical capital must be employed. (But the wide technological gap between the LDCs and the developed countries presents an opportunity to the LDCs. As the gap is closed in a catching-up process, the LDCs can acquire *better* capital as well as more of it.)†

The Efficiency of Investment

The controversy over the role of capital has had another aspect. Almost all economists would now agree that changes in the quality of capital—its productivity or efficiency—and not simply the quantity of it, are vital in the growth of the LDCs. This is perhaps rather obvious; if it were not so, the scarcity of capital in the LDCs would cause returns to capital to be higher, capital would flow from rich countries to poor ones, and LDCs would catch up to the rich countries almost automatically. Joseph Stiglitz has calculated that on the basis of capital shortage alone, it would be plausible to say capital may be about 60 times more productive in the LDCs than in the developed countries.[10] Everything else being equal, capital would flow abundantly to the LDCs and economic growth would be faster there. This is obviously not so for many countries. Therefore, the productivity or efficiency of investment must be playing a major role, with capital having less effect in the LDCs than it does in the developed countries. It appears that in many cases returns on new investment may be *higher* when the existing capital stock is large. In short, one possible reason why the significance of capital investment has historically been

*But note that in the developed countries, new growth theories propounded by such scholars as Paul Romer, Maurice Scott, Moses Abramovitz, Robert Lucas, Robert Barro, and others downplay diminishing returns to capital. The argument is generally that knowledge and technology can raise the return on investment. Romer was a leader with his "Increasing Returns and Long-Run Growth," *Journal of Political Economy* 94 (1986): 1002–1037. Scott's theory emphasizes externalities of new investment, as the investment creates and reveals opportunities for further investment. See M. F. G. Scott, *A New View of Economic Growth* (Oxford, 1989), and his "Policy Implications of 'A New View of Economic Growth,'" *Economic Journal* 102, no. 412 (May 1992): 622–632. Abramovitz notes that the accumulation of physical capital and the advance of knowledge interact with one another to produce joint effects. See his article "The Search for the Sources of Growth: Areas of Ignorance, Old and New," *Journal of Economic History* 53, no. 2 (June 1993): 217–243.

†Compare Dennis Anderson, "Economic Growth and the Returns to Investment," *World Bank Discussion Paper No. 12* (1987), 17. Anderson makes the point that calling technical progress a "residual" fails to show how, in the absence of investment, LDCs can incorporate that technical progress. Technical progress embodied in capital can clearly take effect only if the investment itself takes place. He also asks how a more educated labor force can be more productive unless physical capital is in place; and how reallocation from one sector to another—said to be a source of growth—can occur unless capital has been put in place.

underestimated in the LDCs is that its use in many of these same countries has been less efficient than in most developed countries.

Unfortunately efficiency questions have a disturbing aspect because economists know considerably less about the efficiency of capital use than they do about quantitative applications of capital. This is due to the great variety of elements that lead to productivity change—education and the acquisition of skills, the research and development effort leading to technical progress, internal and external economies of scale, and improved management and organization, among others. Yet it is clear that much investment in LDCs is of low productivity and low efficiency because of poor management, underdeveloped conditions in domestic markets, and inadequate maintenance. When the infrastructure of the economy—its schools, roads, bridges, communications, electrical power, and the like—is inadequate and neglected, results are even worse. Finally, a negative setting for how business is done, including much bureaucratic red tape, crime, corruption, and inadequate property rights may also contribute to the low efficiency with which capital is used.[11] The difference in the efficiency of investment among countries has become a central issue of economic development, though admittedly the question is difficult to investigate.[12]

Data on the Differences

Wide divergences exist in the effectiveness of capital investment among LDCs. If we define such effectiveness as a ratio between growth in GNP and the proportion of GNP invested ($\Delta Y/\Delta K$), we find some LDCs investing a given proportion of their output obtain a considerably greater rise in output than some other countries investing the same amount. For example, South Korea's efficiency of investment has been high for many years. From 1980 to 1987, its rate of income growth averaged 7% per year, and the proportion of its GDP invested was 31%. Thus, its efficiency of investment, $\Delta Y/\Delta K$, was ${}^{.07}/_{.31}$, or 23%. With that high figure, well above the LDC average of 16% during this period, it obtained greater returns from its investment and grew faster than, say, India, even though at first India saved and invested a greater proportion of its GDP.[13] Often enough, one country will have an efficiency of investment four times higher than another, and on average, the one-third of the LDCs that are growing fastest have an efficiency of investment a little more than twice as great as the one-third of the LDCs that are growing slowest.

Taking the LDCs together, their efficiency of investment is in decline. In all LDCs during the period from 1978 to 1980, the figure averaged 18%; it fell to 16% for the period 1983 to 1986.[14] Unfortunately, there are some countries where the efficiency of investment is actually negative, a situation that arises when investment is positive but income declines. This has been true of a dozen or so countries in the quarter-century after 1965. Obviously, if the LDCs' existing investment could be made more productve, their development prospects could be greatly improved. Making their capital just 10% more efficient would bring greater benefit than if capital inflows to the LDCs from the rich countries, including foreign aid and foreign investment, were to grow by 10 times.[15]

THE DISTRIBUTION OF INVESTMENT

One aspect of capital formation is highly visible in many LDCs. Problems arise when insufficient attention is given to the distribution of investment. In the popular mind, investment is often equated with the establishment of industry and mechanized agriculture, especially the machinery associated with these activities. Indeed investment of this type is very important to development, and investment in equipment is believed to contribute as much as two to three times as much to growth as investment defined broadly.[16]

Yet the usual figures for capital formation over long time periods in the developed Western countries show only about 40% of all investment going to machinery and equipment. Experience shows that the country devoting most of its investment funds to the machinery of industry and agriculture, as compared to other types of investment, is certain to pay a serious penalty of popular discontent and lopsided, inefficient development. In a working free market, scarcity of capital in any given sector will be reflected by a high rate of return to investment in that sector, and capital will flow to it. If markets are working poorly, however, or if governments override their signals, then serious problems of misallocation may result. Both the LDC that plans its investment through the government and the LDC that channels private investment through government influence, advice, controls, and subsidized credit must be aware of this penalty.

The sectors that are neglected include housing; the infrastructure of transport, communications, other utilities, and social services; the stock of inventories; and construction.[17]

Housing

The country that does not channel at least 20% of its investment into housing is vulnerable to some serious social consequences. Perhaps even more of such investment will be needed in an LDC suffering from rapid population growth and a shift in population from rural to urban living, for example, Brazil, where the population has gone from 45% urban to 75% in thirty years.

Failure in this regard is familiar everywhere, and shantytown slums have become a standard feature of urban life. New words find their way into many languages to describe these slum conditions: the *bustees* of Calcutta, the *gece kondu* of Istanbul, the *colonias proletarias* of Mexico City, the *poblaciones calampas* of Santiago de Chile, the *favelas* of Rio de Janeiro, and the *barriadas* of Lima. (The literal meaning of the first five of these names is, respectively, "registered slum," "put up in the night," "poor people's colonies," "population mushrooms," and a type of prolific flowering fruit tree.) Slums and uncontrolled settlements of squatters make up about 43% on average of urban population in the LDCs. In many cities, the proportion is over half.[18] Table 4.3 shows recent figures.

In many of these slums, tens of thousands of street children survive anyway they can—including participation in crime.[19] Large-scale public housing has been a solution only in a few cases, especially in the high-performing Asian economies, where relatively high incomes, good administrative skills, and social acceptability

TABLE 4.3 PERCENTAGE OF POPULATION LIVING IN SLUMS

City	%	City	%
Bogota, Colombia	60	Mexico City, Mexico	46
Calcutta, India	67	Nairobi, Kenya	70
Colombo, Sri Lanka	44	Recife, Brazil	50
Dakar, Senegal	60	Tunis, Tunisia	43
Dar es Salaam, Tanzania	50		

Source: UNESCO, *New Book of World Rankings.*

are the rule. Otherwise, public housing on a national scale has simply been too expensive for most LDCs to manage.

Public Works and Utilities

Transport and communications systems, power plants, water works, schools, and hospitals are the so-called infrastructure or social overhead capital of an economy. They take up about 40% of total capital formation in the developed world. There is no reason to expect that LDCs can avoid spending at least this percentage without suffering severely from inadequate capacity. The results of deficiencies in these areas are both predictable and highly visible.

The Electricity Supply Insufficient investment in a country's electrical system has vivid consequences. Run-down electric power plants gasp and die at peak power load (usually when the lights are turned on at dusk). Sometimes the lights come on again after a few minutes; sometimes the wait can be for hours. A blown fuse in a transformer may mean days before overworked maintenance crews fix the problem. A fractured bearing somewhere in a hydroelectric installation may mean no electricity for weeks or months. On average in the LDCs, the on-line availability for power plants is less than 60% compared to over 80% under international best practice. In many low-income countries, power plants are out of service half to two-thirds of the time.[20]

Even when the current stays on, large voltage swings cause appliances to burn out with some frequency. One reason Japanese electronic goods and appliances have established an advantage over similar U.S. products in the Third World is that they often contain built-in voltage regulators. Extension of the power grid is also slow and often long delayed. Electricity use is often subsidized by government, costing customers about half of what it does in developed countries, while the cost of providing electricity averages 40% more than the price. (Costs are high because old power plants consume from 18% to 44% more fuel per kilowatt-hour than is the case in best-practice plants.)[21] The low price raises demand, perhaps by 10% to 20% compared to the case if prices reflected costs.[22] Much waste also occurs because of the leakage from old-style long-distance transmission lines, and the problem is getting worse—a World Bank survey of the electric systems of 51 LDCs reports that on the whole technical efficiency has declined over the past 20 years.[23] Transmission losses are only 7% of the current generated in Japan and 8% in the

United States, but 18% in Thailand and the Philippines, 22% in India, 28% in Pakistan, and 31% in Bangladesh.[24] In some African countries, $1 million spent on reducing transmission losses could save $12 million in new generating capacity.*

The effects on an economy can be severe.[25] It is estimated that India currently loses an amount equivalent to 1% to 3.5% of its GDP from electric energy losses. In Nigeria, the unreliability of public electricity means that firms with more than 50 employees have invested an average $130,000 in private power supplies. Ninety-two percent of the firms sampled have done so. In Indonesia, almost two-thirds of manufacturers maintain their own generators, and the practice is also very common in India.† Regulations prevent firms from selling any of this excess capacity, so these private facilities on average are utilized at about a quarter of their capacity. Everywhere, when firms are too small to obtain this private capacity, they are subject to frequent debilitating interruptions in service. It needs to be said that, even so, those with electricity are the lucky ones. Four-fifths of the population of the LDCs has no access to electricity at all, and per capita consumption is only 10% that of the United States.

The Telephone System The telephone system may be in even worse condition than the power grid. According to the World Bank, in the Third World over half the local telephone calls and nearly nine out of ten long-distance calls simply do not go through. Some firms may hold phone lines open all day long to raise the likelihood of a connection when it is needed. In a sample of 95 LDCs, the waiting period to have a phone installed was six years or more in one-third of the countries, and more than nine years in over 20 of them, compared to under a month in most developed countries.[26]

Water and Sanitation Water shortages are especially common in drier areas, with water often available only a few hours a day.[27] One-fourth to one-third of urban dwellers in LDCs have no regular supply, and the World Health Organization (WHO) estimates that 1.2 billion people are without access to clean water. A separate estimate by the World Bank is that 23% of the urban population in LDC cities has no drinking water within 200 meters.

Buying water from vendors who deliver it by truck, cart, or hand is at least two to four times more expensive than the marginal cost of piped water. The actual price charged is often much more than that, with multiples of 15 or 30 times reported in some areas. The cost in lost time is also high when family members, often women and girls, have to walk to a public tap or well. In the latter case, they

---

*A considerable amount of outright theft in the form of unauthorized hookups goes on as well. When the author moved into his new quarters while teaching in Nigeria, he found that his house's electric meter had been wired by someone from a nearby trailer park. All the current going to the trailer park was being charged to the author's house, and the first month's bill was over $600. (The bill was settled amicably, by the way.)

†LDCs with efficient services escape these heavy penalties. In Thailand, for example, only 6% of firms felt they needed auxiliary generators.

may have to crank or lift the water up in a bucket. Low-income families are the ones most affected. For example, in Peru, only 31% of the poorest fifth of households are connected to public water systems, well below the 82% for the top fifth of households. Piped water is often subsidized, however, and in that case the cost to consumers is *low*, not high. The low cost causes waste and presents the government with a budgetary problem that may keep the water system from being extended. Much water that is put into the pipes—up to 30%—never arrives at its destination because of leaks. There is considerable scope for capital saving in the provision of water. For example, standpipes cost only one-eighth as much as house connections to piped water.[28]

In the absence of a water supply there can be no effective sewage system either. According to the World Health Organization, 1.8 billion people have to live without proper sanitation.* Often sanitation is not readily available even in the capital city. For example, in Manila, capital of the Philippines, only about a third of all residents have access to proper sanitary facilities.[29] When there is no sewage system, the expenses for sanitation can be surprisingly large. Payment at public latrines absorbs more than 2% of annual household income in some localities, while disposing of waste from bucket latrines can cost 1% of income. Even when public sewer systems exist, the sewage often receives no treatment at all, for example, just 2% of it in Latin America.[30] Here, too, there is scope for considerable economies if governments make different choices, For example, well-maintained community pit latrines cost only one-fifth to one-eighth as much as waterborne sewage systems.[31]

Transport Ill-kept highway surfaces can develop enormous potholes. It is hardly noteworthy to find holes in roads that could swallow a car, and some are truck-size, which can add considerable excitement to night-time journeys. Unpaved surfaces develop corrugations, which are hard ridges that build up laterally across the road. This washboard effect is caused by heavy traffic moving at high speeds over roads that are given little or no maintenance. The results can be devastating to motor vehicles. On a one-day trip on corrugation in West Africa, the author's Volkswagon bus was shaken severely. Several nuts came loose in the transmission, and oil streamed from the apertures. A headlight was dislodged from its bracket, leaving it dangling from its wires at bumper level. The World Bank's research indicates that rates of return on road maintenance programs in the LDCs are almost twice as high as those on new road construction. Proper maintenance of African roads would have cost $12 billion but would have saved $45 billion in road reconstruction over the past decade, and the ratio is approximately the same in Latin America. In Africa, one-third of the roads built in the past two decades have eroded because of inadequate maintenance, and sometimes the deterioration goes so far that the whole road has to be replaced. In Cameroun, which has by no means

*Of all Tunisian dwellings, 76% have no plumbing; the figure is 70% in Nepal, 67% in Bolivia, 42% in Colombia, 41% in Mexico, and 0.1% in West Germany.

the worst road system in Africa, about 80% of the unpaved roads have deteriorated to the point of requiring considerable repair or complete rebuilding.[32] (The effect of poor maintenance of roads is, by the way, usually not that severe for the poorest part of the population, which usually walks.)[33]

Railway lines are often single-track, with so much congestion that crops awaiting export may rot in storage. Bridges wash out and are not replaced for months or years; rolling stock deteriorates, and locomotives go out of service. North America has 90% of its railway locomotives available at a given time compared to about 70% in the LDCs as a whole (and 35% in Colombia).[34] Sudan Railways carried 3.5 million tonnes annually in the early 1970s but only 600,000 tonnes in the late 1980s while employing about the same-size workforce.[35] Sometimes these infrastructure difficulties are self-reinforcing. In China, railway bottlenecks are the main reason for the short supplies of coal that adversely affect the supply of electricity.[36]

At the ports, ships anchor for days at overcrowded ports, waiting for berthing space and charging the "demurrage" (waiting time in port) that runs up shipping bills to sometimes spectacular levels in the LDCs. Dockworkers, even though often redundant—up to 80% in some areas have little to do—still move cargo at an average speed of only about 40% of the speed at best-practice ports.[37]

What To Do? All these costs are obviously high in inconvenience, in shutdowns or slowdowns, in time lost, and in damage to equipment. In Nigeria, the cost of firms providing themselves with generators, wells for water, radios and motorcycles for communications, and so forth, makes up between 10% and 25% of the value of all firms' equipment. In Indonesia, 18% of firms' capital consists of this private infrastructure.[38]

These costs, however, are sometimes little considered by the country concentrating its efforts on "directly productive" manufacturing or agriculture rather than on the neglected, underfinanced public works and utilities of the economy. The imbalance is clear; the penalty large. It is inescapable that LDC governments must heed the research that commonly shows high rates of return for investment in infrastructure in the LDCs—research such as a 1993 study by David Canning and Marianne Fay that shows a rate of return on investment in transportation five times greater for LDCs than for developed countries, or World Bank calculations that show the rate of return on all its projects was 15% in 1983 to 1992, but 19% for telecommunications, 23% for urban development, and 29% for highways.[39]

What can be done? First, the LDCs must realize that subsidies to bring down the price of these services typically carry major administrative difficulties and usually do not much aid the poor because better-off people end up gleaning most of the advantages.[40] Beyond that, increasing efficiency in government operations and privatization of these services are being advocated around the world. Leases, concessions, and management contracts that import foreign assistance to improve management have recently been adopted for railways in Argentina; water in Buenos Aires, Côte d'Ivoire, Guinea, and Guinea-Bissau; the ports in Colombia, Ghana, and the Philippines; the power plants in Colombia, Guatemala, and Sri Lanka; water and sanitation in Chile, Malaysia, and Mexico; and telephones in

Indonesia, Sri Lanka, and Thailand. In Latin America, a wave of privatization has recently affected telephone networks.*

But it is also fair to issue the warning that regulatory capability for private utilities is quite limited in many LDCs. Government regulation of monopoly power may not keep up with the privatizing, and if it does not, markets may fail to give fully satisfactory results.

Inventories

A third area of potential neglect in allocating investment funds is inventories. In a developed country, inventories comprise 10% or more of net investment (12% is the usual benchmark), and shortchanging here either through planning or through policies to protect the balance of payments can lead to extensive difficulties. The main symptom will be breakdowns in the supply of raw materials, spare parts, and final goods as wholesalers and retailers find that their backlogs are easily exhausted.

In the underdeveloped world, it is common to see a motorcycle or car temporarily off the road because some minor part cannot be obtained. The little things of life taken for granted in a developed country, for example, the tiny starter for a fluorescent lamp without which the lamp will not turn on, may be next to impossible to obtain. In Zambia at one point in the 1980s, the copper mines could not get spare parts, soft drinks were not being bottled because there were no caps, and flour was not being shipped from local mills because there were no sacks.

Construction

It is a common misconception that investment in manufacturing industry involves mostly machinery and equipment. On the contrary, in both developed countries and LDCs, from half to two-thirds of gross fixed capital formation in manufacturing is in construction. The very fact that the magnitude of building activity comes as something of a surprise indicates that a shortage of construction capacity can be an unexpected bottleneck in the development process and that the human instruments of such activity—architects, builders, and trained construction workers, for example—are also likely to be scarce.

Under such circumstances, the profits of contractors are likely to be larger than they would be otherwise, and the shortage of trained supervisors too often results in bad designs and poor workmanship. The most visible aspect of construction shortages is, without doubt, the unfinished project, just started or perhaps half completed, standing in what amounts to a state of suspended animation for months or years, waiting for the next stage of construction to begin.

---

*With good results so far. Telephone networks were expanded by 35% in Venezuela in the first two years after privatization; Chile's has been expanding by 25% per year, Argentina's by 13% per year, Mexico's by 12% per year. See *WDR 1994*, 9.

FINANCING CAPITAL FORMATION

Where can an LDC obtain the capital it needs for development? How does it finance its capital formation? The answers to these important questions always involve either domestic saving or flows from abroad. A little simple algebra from the principles of economics course shows why and gives us our lead in addressing these issues in the next three chapters.[41]

Take the fundamental proposition of national accounting that a country's total spending equals its total output. Letting Y stand for total spending, then

$$Y = C + I + (X - M)$$

with C = consumption, I = investment, X = exports of goods and services, and M = imports of goods and services. Both government and private consumption and investment are included in $C + I$.

An economy's total output at equilibrium is equal to its total spending, so we can use Y to stand for output as well. Because every dollar of output generates a dollar of income, then a country's total output must also equal its total income. Of all income, some is consumed (C) and some is saved (S). So,

$$Y = C + S$$

(Again, government consumption and saving is included in $C + S$.) Then, because total spending equals total output and income, by substitution

$$C + I + (X - M) = C + S$$

We can easily discover the essential constraints on capital formation by simple manipulation of this equation. Cancel C on both sides. Then move $(X - M)$ to the right-hand side, reversing its sign. The result is

$$I = S + (M - X)$$

The algebra is significant. A country's investment opportunities are determined by its potential for domestic saving (S) plus any net capital inflows from abroad, $M > X$. A country's net capital inflows have to equal $M > X$, because the only way a country can import more than it exports is for it to obtain the financing from abroad. $M > X$ is thus equivalent to an inward movement of capital, which must have originated as the saving of foreigners.

The domestic saving can be (1) private and voluntary, which can then be loaned to businesses or the government by banks or other financial intermediaries, or (2) government saving, when taxes exceed expenditures, so making funds available for investment. This latter case includes the forced saving of inflation, whereby central bank creation of new money allows the government to bid resources away from the rest of the economy.

As the algebra demonstrates, the only way a country's investment can exceed its domestic saving is if capital flows in from abroad. That capital, which is ultimately derived from the saving of foreigners, may come in a number of forms. It can be (1) foreign private investment, called direct when it involves a controlling interest in a factory or mine (hence, usually involving the activities of multinational firms) or portfolio when, as with the purchase of a bond, it does not; (2) medium- or short-term loans from commercial banks; (3) official development assistance (foreign aid) from governments abroad; (4) long-term international loans, as from the World Bank; or (5) medium- and short-term loans from the IMF. The domestic alternatives will be discussed in the remainder of this chapter and the next, and the foreign capital flows in Chapters 6 and 7.

Three major considerations concerning saving are significant.

1. In modern economic theory, the level of saving within a country is closely correlated with the level of disposable income. So a low-income country will ordinarily mobilize less savings than a middle-income or rich one, both in total amount and percent of income saved. Indeed, the least developed LDCs save on average only 2% of their GDP (1991 figure), with ten of them saving nothing, whereas the LDCs as a whole save 25% of their GDP.[42] Obviously, growth itself helps to alleviate the shortage of savings because the ability to save rises with income. Econometric studies from some Asian countries show nearly 83% of the total variation in saving per person is explained by the value of income per person.[43] On the grounds of income alone, therefore, the LDC starts at a disadvantage. The poorer the country, the greater the difficulty. One implication is that well-developed credit markets may be more a consequence of development than its cause.[44]
2. The ability to generate domestic saving is much more significant for most countries than is the ability to attract capital flows from abroad. The first is overwhelmingly greater in amount than the second. One result is that a strong cross-country correlation exists between domestic saving in an economy and the amount of investment that takes place there.
3. In most LDCs, the largest part of domestic saving that flows into a country's capital markets is the private saving of households. A sample survey of 14 countries shows the average gross saving of households to be 12.9% of GDP, with 6.0% of GDP invested directly and the remainder (+6.9%) placed in the financial sector. Businesses invested more (15.6% of GDP) than they saved (8.6%), so the business sector caused a net drain on the financial sector of −7.0%. These are the major net influences on the credit markets. Government saving was 4.8% of GDP, and government investment was 6.7%, resulting in a small net drain on the credit markets of −1.9%, while foreign inflows (aid and private capital) resulted in a relatively modest addition of +2.0% of GDP. Notice particularly from this analysis that household saving dominates the net inflows to the credit

market and that domestic saving is on average much greater than any foreign contribution.[45]

Private Domestic Saving (Households and Firms)

Household saving, including the saving of small family businesses, usually predominates, most frequently making up 60% to 70% of domestic saving.[46] Even in the LDCs with the lowest income, household saving does take place and is important for development. Much of the saving does not enter the financial system. Some does not do so because the saving is in real terms, involve real saving and real investment combined in the same act. For example, peasant farmers contribute to saving by giving up leisure, by clearing land, by retaining seed for output growth, and by putting in commercially valuable trees such as cocoa and rubber that take a long time to mature. Other household saving represents a flow of finance, but the flow is kept outside of financial institutions. Small, family-owned businesses in both urban and rural areas save part of their earnings and reinvest a substantial portion of them in low-technology pursuits, such as making cement blocks, thatching roofs, constructing irrigation facilities, making tools, milling rice, processing food, and the like. As a country grows richer, this sort of saving is likely to rise significantly, and in fact has done so in the last two decades.

An important debate on saving behavior concerns the question whether greater income inequality increases saving. If the wealthy save more, then allowing a more unequal income distribution through measures such as abolishing the progressive income tax would increase saving and therefore promote investment. Generally, however, the statistics do not support the contention, there being no noticeable correlation between high income inequality and high saving. As the World Bank states, "there is no evidence that saving is positively related to income inequality or that income inequality leads to higher growth. If anything, it seems that inequality is associated with slower growth."[47] Some of the LDCs' biggest savers (Algeria, China, Singapore, South Korea, Taiwan) are among the countries with the greatest income equality.

The Extended Family and Saving Some factors affecting household saving are socioeconomic in nature. One such is the well-known extended-family system wherein parents, children, grandparents, aunts, uncles, and cousins are closely tied and perhaps live together in the same family compound. Each member is under an obligation to help the others. In some cases, the impact on saving is negative. With the extended family acting as a social security system (relatives caring for the elderly), saving for retirement is less necessary. Additionally, should a member of the family succeed in accumulating a significant increase in wealth, the relatives are there to claim their share. In response to the situation, the successful family member might be likely to reduce the amount saved. The extended family may thus be seen as a form of insurance, with the near-compulsory participation an implicit high tax on those who save.

In some ways, however, the extended family may encourage saving, working virtually as an internal capital market by pooling funds to promote a business venture or the education of a talented family member. Cases in point are the Chinese, many Indian and Philippine families, and the Igbo (Ibo) of Nigeria. Family members may be a better risk as borrowers because knowledge about them is more complete and pressure for repayment can be applied more directly. With the social security aspect noted above, the extended family may be rather more workable than is usually appreciated by economists. The criticism of this institution as an obstacle to development has probably been overdone.

A Stratified Society and Saving One inhibiting factor that may reduce the level of domestic household saving, again socioeconomic in nature, can be detected in many LDCs. If society is highly stratified so that accumulated savings are of little help in advancing socially (India is a pertinent example), then an important incentive to save is destroyed. For this reason, an overly large share of income may be expended on fancy clothing, extravagant ceremonial expenditures, and other conspicuous consumption rather than going for saving. Even in the absence of social stratification, customs involving conspicuous consumption may permeate social relationships. The extravagance is sometimes competitive, as in the size and value of gifts exchanged on ceremonial occasions.

Religion and Saving The effect of religion on saving is a mixed case. Scholars such as R. J. Tawney and Max Weber have advanced famous theses on the contribution of Protestant theology to the rise of capitalism by means of a "savings ethic." A similar argument emphasizing religion has been made for Japan. There are, however, also religious factors that retard saving. Religious scruples against receiving a rate of interest are especially strong (and growing) in Islamic countries. The Quran states, Chapter 2, verses 278–279, "O you who believe! Observe your duty to Allah and give up what remains from Riba [interest] if you are believers."[48]

The prohibition against interest payments to bank depositors or interest charges to borrowers has been strictly enforced in Iran since the fall of the shah. Other Muslim countries have followed suit, and about 45 countries have some type of Islamic banking. Banks stopped paying interest in Sudan in 1984 and in Pakistan in 1985. In 1991, Pakistan's Islamic court ruled that interest paid or demanded was against Islamic law. Islamic law does allow for administrative charges and service fees, though these are considerably lower than interest would be. Banks also often give prizes and provide "free" services. Where these rules are in effect, depositors subsidize investment and returns to saving are low.

Recently, major innovations have affected Islamic banking in such a way that the results for saving and investment have not been nearly as bad as might be expected. In some countries, a firm that wants new capital equipment can, instead of borrowing the money to buy it, get its bank to buy the equipment and retain ownership for a time. The firm then buys the equipment from the bank at a higher price than the bank paid. The bank takes the risk of holding the equipment, and so is entitled to a payment for risk. This is called *murabaha*. This idea has been pressed forward to the point where the bank may retain ownership for a few minutes or just seconds, which troubles more conservative theologians.

The basic idea that the sharing of risks is permissible, while payment of interest is not, has led to further innovation in Islamic banking. In 1977 Prince Faisal of Saudi Arabia took part in establishing national bank profit sharing with borrowers and lenders. Banking subject to that law works something like a mutual fund in the stock market. Under this system, known as *mudarabah*, banks in effect share in the profits of borrowers and must share in the risk, while depositors share in the profits of the banks.

A case can be made that profit-and-loss-sharing has the potential to enhance capital investment if it improves information about a project. It forces banks to have a direct stake in how well the economy performs, thereby requiring them to pay more attention to potential profitability than they would under a system of contractual interest payments. It is argued that this leads to more careful supervision of loan applications.[49] (It also presumably encourages the sale of stock in place of borrowing from banks.) Depositors find that it is more difficult for them to judge the security of their banks. Their returns on deposits subject to profit-and-loss sharing are often higher in amount than interest would have been, but there is also much greater risk because losses are possible.

Critics note that Islamic banking practices mean that monetary policy working through interest rates cannot be used (although the money supply can still be constricted or expanded by means of reserve requirements). Sale of bonds abroad is difficult. Loans become shorter in term because the service fee for longer-term loans would be high, and because profitsharing is not very attractive to banks. Generally, banks subject to Islamic law have been less successful than previously, and this could have led to a large decline in saving and investment—except that these laws are often not enforced very rigorously. It is fair to say that those who predicted that a banking collapse would follow from the imposition of Islamic banking practices have been wrong. As *The Economist* magazine rightly states, Islamic banking "does not deserve the usually rather ignorant sneer it gets from many non-Muslims."[50]

Even without the dictates of religion, countries may still have stiff anti-usury laws that reduce interest receipts and stiff bank-reserve requirements that have the same effect.

Inflation, Taxes, and Saving Saving may also be inhibited by inflation. Inflation is often a more serious problem in LDCs than it is in the developed world. A normal response is to avoid its effects by buying and hoarding tangible goods, by purchasing land and buildings, or by any other purchase that will act as a hedge against rising prices. (It is said that India has the world's largest collection of gold in private hands, estimated at more than 7000 tonnes.)[51] Similarly, governments may inhibit saving because the interest on accounts is easy to tax as are the accounts themselves by means of a wealth tax. Households might then shun saving in bank accounts as overly risky.

Can Household Saving Be Enhanced? In spite of these inhibiting factors, household saving can still be enhanced by well-designed government policies. Governments have the power to attack inflation, restore incentives to save including reducting the taxation of saving, and undertake pro-saving campaigns. A major area where governments could contribute is to find a solution to the problem that banks find it expensive to manage small accounts. Banks do not like low-volume savers because it is hard to supervise their accounts. One estimate from Africa is that noncorporate lending by a bank would require 2500 accounts to cover the cost of a single employee for a year.[52] Stimulation to save can come from new institutions, such as credit cooperatives, which can build on traditional structures such as the *esusu* credit societies of Ghana, the *tontine* in Niger, the *hui* in China, and many others, in which funds are pooled by a small group of people and lent to one of them at a time, in rotation.[53] Governments can also combine plans for insurance and saving (as in Egypt) and establish pension funds and post-office savings accounts to tap small depositors. In many countries, banks have an urban bias. To counter this, governments can encourage branch banking outside major urban centers. The response is not likely to be overwhelming, but every little bit helps.

Corporate Saving

In net terms, corporations borrow from financial institutions for investment more than they bring to these institutions as saving. Corporate saving in the form of retained earnings is of importance in the excellent saving performance of the middle-income LDC, where such saving often involves foreign multinational firms as well as domestic ones. (The activities of multinational firms are discussed in Chapter 6.) In the lower-income LDCs, less corporate saving through reinvestment of earnings takes place, and so the demand for loans from domestic financial institutions is proportionally greater than it would otherwise be.

Domestic stock and bond markets are also rudimentary in many LDCs—though they are very important in some, as we will see in Chapter 6. Even though a few LDC stock markets have recently grown large, raising equity capital through share issues is not very practical in many LDCs because there is still no easy way to sell the shares. The indigenous stock market is often very small even where one exists. For example, among the dozens of LDCs that now have stock markets, in some only 10 or 20 companies may be listed (four in Swaziland), the turnover of shares is tiny, and the trading facilities may be so poor that on the trading floor share prices are chalked up on blackboards and walls.

There are various reasons why many LDC stock markets are small. Some of them are closed to foreigners and others restrict them to mutual funds. More could certainly be accomplished in improving access to these markets. Even if shares can be widely sold, it is quite characteristic in most LDCs for the shares of a firm to be closely held by a founding family or group of families, with no real desire to dilute the ownership. So even where there is an active market, prices are volatile because only a smallish proportion of a company's shares are ever traded. Imperfect information means that it is difficult to screen new issues and to differentiate good from bad risks.[54] Minority shareholders under such circumstances can be taken for a ride as the majority shareholders pay each other high salaries and otherwise divert the profits to themselves, engage in insider trading, and easily avoid weak government regulation. The element of gambling is not conducive to the sale of shares. Where these markets are limited or nonexistent, firms that cannot rely on their own internal savings in the form of reinvested profits for their expansion will have to depend on banks and similar financial institutions.

Lending Institutions

Everywhere, but especially where stock markets are undeveloped, the commercial banking system has particular significance for investment in the LDCs. Unfortunately, there are reasons to expect that rates of interest will be high. The high rates are readily explicable. Loanable funds are usually in short supply. Household saving is inadequately tapped by the banking system, as we have seen. Governments, rather than supplying funds to the credit market, are often found in that same market trying to borrow for their own purposes. Business corporations will usually either do their own investing or pay dividends. All of these limit the supply of funds available for lending.

The risks of banking also inhibit its growth. The absence of credit bureaus (like Moody's) and the scarcity of national business publications and industrial newsletters mean that information is limited and risks are harder to assess than in the developed countries. The ability to enforce contracts by seizing assets or garnisheeing wages may be circumscribed by the institutional setting. Small borrowers may vanish without a trace; large ones protected by friends in high places may thumb their noses and refuse to repay. The general lack of information is a major impediment to lending, thereby raising the cost of credit. This may also explain why membership in an extended family or ethnic group often serves as a proxy for credit worthiness.

Additionally, commercial banks may find themselves required to lend to the government to finance the government's programs. Preferential and penalty discount rates may be imposed on lending in certain sectors. In the 1980s, for example, Turkey had 30 categories of discount rates, with interest rates in the preferred sectors averaging 36 percentage points lower than those in the nonpriority sectors.[55] Reserve requirements are often high anyway, but differential reserve requirements may also be put in place. These have been most used in Latin America. In India, 40% of all bank deposits have to be held as required reserves in one form or another, including government bonds.[56]

Lending targets may also be enforced for priority industries. Pakistan's national banks were required to target 70% of their new loans by sector until the late 1980s, when the figure was somewhat reduced. In India, 40% of what banks have available for lending must be loaned to priority sectors at controlled rates. India along with Thailand require that 60% of the loans of rural banks must be in agriculture or related activities. Together with the high reserve requirements discussed above, this means that Indian banks can freely lend only 36% of their deposits.[57] In Turkey, a surcharge on loans to the nonpreferred sectors has at times raised real interest rates there to a punishing 30% to 50%. Targeting sectors increases risks for the lender because loans will be less diversified, will decrease banking profits if the targeted sector does not perform well, and will raise costs for nonpriority borrowers who find the rates on their loans marked up to cover the cost of the targeting. Subsidies to cheapen loans in priority sectors could be used rather than surcharges on nonpreferred sectors, but these are so expensive—recently sopping up 3% to 8% of GDP in Brazil, Costa Rica, and Mexico—that they are used less often. Moreover, few LDCs have deposit insurance, with Colombia, India, Kenya, the Philippines, Thailand, Trinidad, Turkey, and Venezuela on the short list of those that do. All of these inhibit the development of private banking, especially because informal credit markets, including money-lending, pawnbroking, and so forth, are subject to none of these limitations. The supply of credit from the banking system is yet further restricted.

The result is a supply curve for loanable funds positioned inward to the left, as in Figure 4.1. Meanwhile, underdeveloped economies are typically short of capital, and there are many profitable opportunities for its employment. So the demand curve for loanable funds is located to the right. The combination of low supply and high demand results in a relatively high market rate of interest, shown at the equilibrium, r_e. Various barriers, including imperfect knowledge, risk, expectations of a currency devaluation, and pervasive government controls on capital movements keep international flows of capital from equalizing interest rates across

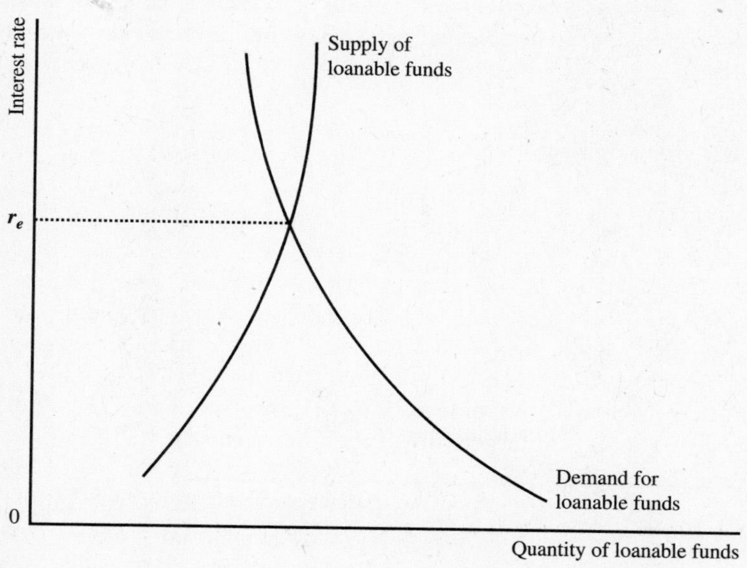

Figure 4.1 Low supply and high demand for loanable funds lead to a high market rate of interest.

countries. Not only will the rates be high, but they may be highly variable as well. Often, advantageous rates are granted to trusted borrowers while strangers face much higher charges, so that over a wide range of credit markets there is no single rate of interest.

Financial Repression

In some countries, this description of conditions in LDCs must be modified to take account of a strange fact. In the organized, relatively developed sectors of the economy, businesses often have had access to local capital, both short-term and long-term, at quite low nominal interest rates, sometimes only 3% to 4%. In many cases, real interest rates are lower yet.

How can interest rates in capital-short countries ever be lower than in the developed world, conflicting as that does with the clear-cut prediction of Figure 4.1? One answer lies in government interference with capital markets through the use of controls that affect both saving and investment. Especially important are the selective credit controls used to repress the financial markets by allocating funds into specific types of capital formation and also directing them toward specific firms. This is often combined with prohibitions on certain types of investment.

Figure 4.2 shows a fixed interest rate, r_f, below equilibrium. Rationing will have to occur, allocating a quantity *A* among borrowers who would like to have *B*. Risk taking by lenders is discouraged because a risk premium cannot be charged.

A little financial repression may not do much harm. But more severe repression may be damaging. Small firms are penalized in contrast to established large-scale enterprises, which are usually the ones to benefit from the controls on interest rates. Transactions costs are commonly lower when borrowing is large, so banks will generally choose to lend to established firms when interest rates are kept at

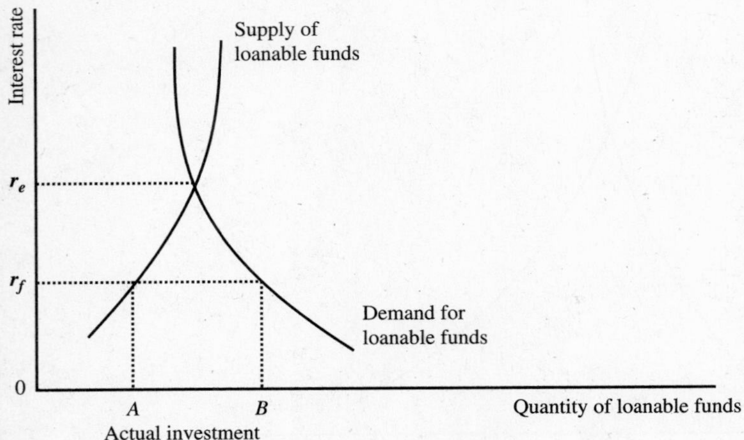

Figure 4.2 Financial repression involves the control of interest rates. A below-market interest rate leads to an excess demand for loanable funds, that is, a shortage, equal to *AB* in the figure.

below-market levels. Such enterprises are frequently found leading the defense against any suggestion that capital be priced competitively. The main manifestation of the controls is ordinarily a tendency toward investment in projects where the marginal return to capital is low, toward overly high capital intensity, and toward overcapacity. The completion of projects slows down because, with interest rates low, a delayed project costs its investors little.

Below-market nominal interest rates can be pushed even lower in real terms if unanticipated inflation sets in. Such unanticipated inflation often causes *negative* real interest rates, sometimes strongly so. The mechanism is as follows: If borrowers' and lenders' expectations of inflation lag behind the actual rate of price increase, then the inflation premium built into the interest rate will not, at least temporarily, be sufficiently large to compensate for it. Thus real rates are pushed below nominal rates. This is the main reason why real interest rates could be below –10% at various times in Bolivia, Brazil, Côte d'Ivoire, Nigeria, Peru, and Uruguay; as low as –40% and –50%, as they were in Ghana, Mozambique and Uganda in the 1980s; or even –70% (Argentina) to almost –120% (Chile).[58] Whatever the reason, when real rates are very low or negative for long periods, they have an inhibiting effect on saving and growth.

Whether real interest rates are positive but below market rates, or whether they are actually negative, they contribute to a low efficiency of capital. Uses of funds that would be uneconomic at market rates of interest now appear to be profitable. Raising the interest rate would eliminate some of the investments that are low yielding; a rise in the efficiency of investment would occur along with a rise in saving. On this reading, an adequate real rate of interest will have a positive effect on saving, investment, and economic growth. (The contention that higher interest rates for savers will lead to higher levels of investment is sometimes called the "McKinnon-Shaw hypothesis," after its formulators, Ronald McKinnon and Edward Shaw.)[59]

The Effect of Real Interest Rates on Growth Table 4.4 shows the relationship between positive real interest rates and GDP growth for a sample of 80 countries. The interest rates in parentheses are the averages for the countries in the group. Table 4.5 presents another view of the same question. The worst growth performance is found in the countries with the most negative real interest rates.

TABLE 4.4 REAL INTEREST RATES AND GROWTH 1965–1985, 80-COUNTRY SAMPLE (IN PERCENT)

	1965–1973			1974–1985		
Real interest rate	Positive (3.7%)	Moderately negative (–1.7%)	Strongly negative (–13.7%)	Positive (3.0%)	Moderately negative (–2.4%)	Strongly negative (–13.0%)
GDP growth	7.3	5.5	4.6	5.6	3.8	1.9

Source: WDR 1987, 31.

TABLE 4.5 REAL INTEREST RATE AND GROWTH, 1971–1985, 31 COUNTRIES (IN PERCENT)

Real interest rate (range)	Average real interest rate	Average GDP growth	Average industrial growth
–60 to –10	–21.1	2.3	1.1
–10 to –5	–7.8	3.0	3.3
–5 to 5	–1.4	5.5	7.2

Source: WDR 1987, 118.

An updating of these statistics covering the years 1984 to 1993 shows the relationship remained basically the same. In those years the median real interest rate for all LDCs was 0.02%, but +2.89% for high-growth LDCs and –2.81% for low-growth LDCs.[60]

A major reason why growth is affected by low real interest rates has to do with the efficiency with which investment is used. In the group of countries with positive real interest rates, the output from a given amount of investment was four times greater than in the group with strongly negative rates. This is not surprising; when saving flows into the financial system, it is likely to be allocated more efficiently than when households and businesses do the investing themselves. Ronald McKinnon now believes that the mechanism tying higher real rates of interest to higher rates of economic growth works more through increasing the efficiency of investment rather than by raising the level of saving.[61] Another adverse effect of low or negative real interest rates on growth is that people will hold their savings outside the domestic financial system, in turn encouraging credit rationing and slowing the development of financial institutions. Moreover, capital flight will occur. People with savings transfer them abroad where they can earn market rates of interest.

Econometric evidence confirms that the level of real interest rates has a clear effect on the form of saving. Research on 81 countries using 1985 data show that higher real interest rates of one percentage point lead to a rise in bank deposits of all kinds of 0.75 percentage points.[62] Priority in restoring positive rates of return to saving would clearly seem called for.

Financial Reform Must Be Undertaken With Care Nowadays, the advice to undertake financial reform is being heeded by more and more countries where financial repression was at one time severe. Among the LDCs that have now shifted largely to free-market finance are Argentina, Chile, Malaysia, Mexico, the Philippines, Thailand, Turkey, most of francophone Africa, and Uruguay.[63] But experience has been rather chastening, and it is apparent that the ending of financial repression must be undertaken with care.[64] If a country liberalizes its financial sector by freeing interest rates while macroeconomic conditions are unstable, banking supervision is lax, and banks have some monopoly power, it may find that the result is sky-high real rates of interest. This was the experience of Argentina, Chile, the Philippines, Turkey, Uruguay, and Venezuela.

In particular, lenders will demand and borrowers will pay high real rates of interest to guard against future inflation. Without proper supervision, new banks will spring up, and these might not initially be very accomplished at screening out bad credit risks. Dishonest practice might prevail. The lack of regulation of banks in Chile at the time financial repression was ended was especially damaging. Wildcat banking practices led to many bad loans eventually amounting to almost one-fifth of GDP in the late 1980s. It is much more advantageous to free interest rates at the same time that macroeconomic stability is achieved and proper banking supervision is established. Ghana, South Korea, Malaysia, and Tunisia have done it this way, without having to endure the negative side effects.

FINANCING GOVERNMENT INVESTMENT: BORROWING AND TAXATION

The discussion to this point amounts to saying that private saving and the capital formation generated from it are likely to be deficient in low-income LDCs, with the deficiency correctable as growth takes place. This deficiency leads us to consider the government as saver and investor. In the developing world, government saving and investing averages about a quarter of the total of such activity.

A government can finance investment by its own saving. Government saves by taxing more than it spends on current economic activity. If the government did no investing itself, this would cause a surplus in the budget. The surplus could be used to finance private investment if the government placed the funds in private capital markets. Economists see much to recommend in such a policy. It could potentially increase the level of saving, encourage the efficient allocation of investment, and build the capacity of the private sector, which is otherwise inhibited by lack of credit.[65] Only rarely, however, have LDCs used a budget surplus on any scale to mobilize funds for lending to the private sector on a competitive and neutral basis. Much more commonly, the government does the investing itself. Government investment can also be accomplished by borrowing from the private sector or by running a budget deficit, as we shall see.

Financing Government Investment by Borrowing from the Private Sector

Government domestic borrowing potential, exercised through the sale of government bonds to its own public and business firms, is usually strictly limited in the low-income LDCs. Most LDCs nowadays have one or more development banks that attract interest-bearing deposits from the public and lend the funds for development projects. They are intended to correct for imperfect capital markets, to provide a substitute for raising capital through the sale of bonds, and to motivate firms to retain and reinvest their profits. Such banks often have the additional task of improving project appraisal, undertaking some equity investment themselves, and perhaps pushing funding toward the neglected agricultural sector. In the low-income LDCs, they may receive foreign aid. Well-known institutions of this sort are the Industrial Credit and Investment Corporation of India, the Korean Development Finance Corporation, and the similar development banks of Taiwan and Indonesia. In general, however, LDC development banks have not been nearly so successful in many other countries, and they performed poorly in the world economic downturn of the 1980s and early 1990s.

We have already noted the shortage of investable funds that afflicts most LDCs, and even payment of a high rate of interest on government bonds may be ineffectual in attracting funds because of alternatives elsewhere in the economy. Commercial banks may consider government bonds to be a poor place to hold funds, and in the early days of independence for the LDCs, when such banks were largely foreign owned, this was especially a problem. At times, some governments have lessened the attractiveness of their own bonds by arbitrarily altering their terms of issue or calling them back. Furthermore, an increase in government bond sales at any given time and given level of national income must imply either a matching reduction in funds available to the private sector (so that the total does not increase) or a voluntary reduction in private consumption. Reductions in consumption are clearly more difficult to achieve the poorer the country is. Development, then, means that domestic borrowing will become easier as income rises, but little is to be expected from domestic borrowing in the earlier stages of the process.

A number of countries have at times required the compulsory purchase of government bonds out of wage and salary payments, an idea initiated by the Soviet Union. This practice has always been much the same as taxation, however, as shown by the Soviet Union itself, where interest on the bonds was first reduced and then eliminated and where repayments of principal were not made on numerous categories of the compulsorily purchased bonds. That such bonds have never been popular is an understatement. There were riots in Ghana and Guyana when similar schemes were introduced, and the author's own Turkish bonds, purchased with part of his salary in compliance with Turkish law when he was teaching in that country a number of years ago, have now lost almost all of their value due to inflation.

Financing Government Investment Through Taxation

If borrowing is largely ineffective at low levels of development, financing government investment then becomes a problem in taxation.[66] Direct transfers of goods and physical controls on the movements of productive factors could be used instead, but these are less efficient mechanisms and often generate more public resentment. A typical LDC at once runs into policy problems in its tax decisions. Any kind of tax is almost certain to apply inequitably, affecting some of the population more than others, for the simple reason that most forms of modern taxation will not cover a very wide range of economic activity in the average LDC.

Another concern is that growth may be a tender shoot, easily discouraged by high taxation.* A 20-country study by the World Bank comparing low-tax and high-tax nations at approximately the same level of development concluded that there is some correlation between low taxes and rapid growth.[67] Low taxes might be expected to increase private investment (both domestically and by foreigners) and to raise returns both to work and to innovation, augmenting the supply of all of these. The study warns, however, against any simplistic notion that cutting taxes is an automatic path to faster growth. Low taxes might still be very complex or poorly administered. World recession, high interest rates caused by heavy government borrowing—made necessary by the slimness of tax revenues and causing a crowding-out of private investment—or overvalued foreign exchange rates all might swamp the positive effect of the lower taxes. In any case, the positive effects are unlikely to occur in the short run. It will take time for the low taxes to bring about the changes in attitudes that may lead to more work effort, more innovation, and more investment.

Effective collection of taxes is typically an arduous task for an LDC, usually more difficult than in a developed country. The problem of how a government is successfully going to collect the revenue it needs tends to submerge consideration of whether the means of collection is fair.[68] There is often far less public discussion and debate in poor countries concerning tax incidence (progressivity versus regressivity) than in the rich countries. The result is often a quite regressive tax system, as in Mexico, for example, where in the 1980s the proportion of income paid in tax by highest income taxpayers was 14.9% while the lowest paid 40.2%.[69] (Major reforms were implemented from 1990 to 1991, however.)

Collection, then, is the crux of the matter. Income, output, and sales are by definition all low in a low-income LDC. It follows that any form of tax tied to these will collect little. So it is not surprising that total central government tax proceeds as a percent of GNP were much lower in LDCs than in developed countries. In 1991, the figures averaged 24% for the developed countries, ranging from 18% to 34% for the United States, Great Britain, and Germany, with the Netherlands higher at 45% and Japan lower at 14%. The proportion was only 5% to 14% for most low-income LDCs, with an average of 16% for all LDCs.[70] The figure has even fallen below 1% at times, for example, in troubled Uganda during the early 1980s. There are, however, exceptions. Tanzania for a time raised its tax take as a percentage of GNP to 30%, but at the cost of serious disincentive effects on its entrepreneurs and farmers; a retreat ensued. Large exporters of minerals can also raise their tax collections, as in Zimbabwe, 29% of GNP; South Africa, 30%; and Botswana and Namibia, 34%. Even these figures, very high for LDCs, are below the figures for many developed countries.

---

*Stanley Please has questioned whether governments that increase the effectiveness of their tax collection would not just end up indulging in more extravagant spending. This became known as the Please effect. See Stanley Please, "Saving Through Taxation: Reality or Mirage," *Finance and Development* 4, no. 1 (1967): 24–32.

Understandably, all LDCs search for types of taxes that collect more as national income rises. Technically, the responsiveness of the tax take to income increases is known as the income elasticity of tax revenue. This figure can be derived from the so-called tax ratios: If T = tax collections and Y = GNP, then T/Y is defined as the average tax ratio, and $\Delta T/\Delta Y$ is the marginal tax ratio. Expressed as a percentage, the amount by which tax revenues increase, $\Delta T/T$, divided by the increase in income, $\Delta Y/Y$, is the elasticity of tax revenue.

$$\frac{\Delta T/T}{\Delta Y/Y} = \textit{elasticity of tax revenue}$$

Typically, this tax elasticity tends to be highest for excise and sales taxes, not as one might expect for income taxes, as we shall see. Taxes on foreign trade tend to be the lowest, ranking behind income taxes. Rarely is tax elasticity above one, however.[71]

Income, Property, and Inheritance Taxes

The personal income (and social security) tax, heart of the revenue system in the developed world, collects about 56% of government revenue in the developed countries. Income taxes are, however, particularly hard to collect in the LDCs. There, they are of relatively minor importance, responsible for only about 17% of total tax revenues.[72] In many countries, income tax is collected from less than 15% of the population, less than 5% in South Asia and sub-Saharan Africa.[73] In some countries, this low importance is due to the realization that income taxes may discourage the profit-making entrepreneur from saving and investing. (That has led to interesting proposals for taxes on expenditure rather than income, but with little practical effect thus far as discussed in the accompanying box.) Many countries for a long time apparently had little concern for disincentives; the marginal rates of income tax on the largest incomes were often set very high. For example, Burma/Myanmar, Ethiopia, Niger, and Tanzania recently had marginal rates of 72% to 95%, the highest in the LDCs. (India's highest rate once reached 97.75%.*) When income tax rates are over about 50%, they probably distort behavior and usually collect little revenue because of legal and illegal tax avoidance.

A more significant reason why the income tax is of limited importance in most developing countries, however, is the fact that such a tax is difficult to operate in conditions of underdevelopment. The difficulties arise for the following reasons:[74]

1. There must be measurable income to tax. Where subsistence output is common, or where barter is carried on, there are serious problems of determining how much income is subject to tax.

*Recently, however, many countries have cut their income tax rates. Indonesia's top rate has been moved from 55% to 35%, Egypt's from 95% to 65%, Jamaica's from 57.5% to 33.3%, Singapore's from 55% to 33%, and India's from 97.75% to 40%. See Gerardo P. Sicat and Arvind Virmani, "Personal Income Taxes in Developing Countries," *World Bank Economic Review* 2, no. 1 (January 1988): 8–23.

AN EXPENDITURE TAX?

Realizing that income taxes could discourage saving and investment, Nicholas Kaldor proposed a tax reform for India that would reduce the disincentive effects on saving and investment brought by an income tax. He suggested an expenditure levy—that is, a tax applied only to expenditure—defined as the difference between income and saving ($Y - S = E$). Such a tax on spending would tend to restrict consumption and increase saving. The idea has its attractions and it has advocates in the United States and Western Europe, but to date only India and Sri Lanka have actually employed it.[75] It proved difficult to administer in these two LDCs. A major complication is that it requires taxpayers to calculate changes in their total net worth because drawing down past saving in any form can contribute to expenditure. India adopted an expenditure tax, repealed it because of these problems, readopted it, and finally re-repealed it. Sri Lanka repealed its expenditure tax as well.

2. An extremely low rate of literacy—46% of the population in the least developed countries, and frequently below 30%—means limited ability to understand and to fill out income tax forms.
3. A shortage of suitable clerical skills in the business sector means that record keeping will be lax.
4. Where the notion becomes popular that the government is there to be cheated and that such cheating is socially acceptable, the income tax will yield a low return. A 1978 study of the income tax in Argentina found that 80% of income was not reported, while in Indonesia, tax evasion was 84% to 94% of tax due on personal income according to a 1980 study. Similarly, evasion in Jamaica has resulted in loss of revenue amounting to 84% of the actual tax collected. Large-scale evasion is reported from other countries as well.[76] One reason is that enforcement may be very lax, with punishment for tax avoiders hardly ever meted out. In India in a recent year there were just 16 convictions for tax avoidance, while in Mexico between 1921 and 1988, only two tax evaders served prison sentences.[77] Governments in this situation may be virtually powerless to increase income tax revenues. (Of course, taxpayers may be fully justified in their tax avoidance if the tax revenues they pay just disappear into the pockets of corrupt officials, including tax officials.)
5. Many LDCs have undemocratic political structures run by wealthy merchants or landowners who themselves would be most affected by a progressive income tax, and their opposition is often adamant. Gunnar Myrdal wrote that the question of the income tax is "drenched in hypocrisy."[78] Proposals for an income tax in Guatemala were more than once officially termed a Communist plot inspired by agents of Cuba's Castro, and although an income tax was finally adopted in 1987, it is low and narrow in its coverage. The system may even become a mockery, with low budgets

and corresponding low levels of personnel and low pay in the taxing authority. The end result is that elites often escape income taxation even when it is otherwise feasible.

6. An income tax requires an able and honest group of administrators. In many parts of the underdeveloped world there are deficiencies in accounting skills. In parts of Latin America, the response to the low level of skills has been some privatization involving receipt of tax payments and processing of tax returns.[79] More damaging for income tax collection are the many opportunities for bribery and corruption, both all too welcome to tax officials because of the low salaries noted above. The lack of skills and frequent dishonesty can breed a reaction in the form of massive red tape and formal procedures to ensure that taxes are paid, making the tax collection system even more difficult to administer. Many an airplane flight out of a country has been delayed when some traveler finds a required tax form is missing. Some countries, Turkey for one, have felt it necessary to adopt presumptive rules based on occupation or living standard. (Do you have a car, a house, servants? Do you travel abroad?) The income tax is then levied on your declared income or your presumed income, whichever is greater, with a probable gain in accuracy but at a cost of much more complexity.
7. Withholding of taxes from wages and salaries is central to income tax collection in the United States, Great Britain, and many other developed countries. It was introduced in 1943 in the United States. With surprising candor the British call it PAYE for "pay as you earn." In the poorest LDCs, however, withholding often will affect only government employees and a small group of workers and managers in private industries. The chances for tax avoidance are therefore increased.

All these reasons mean that the income tax in LDCs is likely to bring in less per dollar spent on administering the tax system than the same dollar will when used to support other types of tax collection. To be sure, such criticisms have not stopped LDCs from trying to obtain some income tax revenue from the well-to-do, especially when the wealthy are foreigners or some immigrant group lacking in political power. Even if the amount in money terms is not very significant, collection from the well-off gives an appearance of equity and has good propaganda value. Yet on the whole, the lower a country's income, the less success is to be expected from an income tax.

Corporation Taxes As a proportion of government revenues, corporate profits taxes collect more than in the developed countries, 18% compared to 8%, a figure slightly higher than that for personal income taxes in the LDCs. The reason for the greater importance is that large corporations, especially the foreign ones, are very visible. Also, certain corporate profits such as those from natural resource exports are rather easy to ascertain.[80] The statutory rate can vary greatly from the rate actually charged because complicated investment incentives, including many deductions from revenue, often coexist with the corporate tax. These were adopted to attract foreign capital and promote domestic investment. The complexity makes these taxes hard to administer, while the investment incentives often seriously erode the tax base. Avoidance is a serious problem for corporate taxes as well as for income taxes: in Indonesia, tax evasion according to a recent study was 76% to 93% of the corporate income taxes that should have been collected.[81]

Property and Inheritance Taxes Another possibility is taxes based on property, which would seem relatively simple and efficient. It is difficult to conceal land, which cannot be moved around like other assets. A land tax could be graduated by size or value of plot, and could encourage cultivation and a move into the cash economy. It has the potential to broaden widely the tax base in the poorest countries, and it could be rather neatly tied to the provision of rural services. It promotes the sale of property by very large landowners and may thus encourage productivity.[82]

In spite of these arguments, which for the most part are sound, the land tax has traditionally been even less successful than the income tax. The difficulty in some LDCs is that land tenure does not involve private ownership of land. Instead, ownership may be vested in an ethnic community, village, or extended family. The land in such cases is held in common, with no identifiable single owner. Individuals and families possess use rights, with the farmland reallocated from time to time so that no one has permanent control over the best land. This situation is not very conducive to the usual form of property tax. Although it is theoretically possible for collection to be made by village elders on the basis of the entire community's holding, with each individual's share determined by the elders, it is rarely carried out in practice. (Uganda and Burma/Myanmar are countries with such a system.) Even where land is held individually, parcels may be fragmented, or ownership records may be badly outdated, making administration difficult.

Another problem involves assessment, which can be ticklish. Will the land's value be judged by its actual output or its potential output? Nicaragua now relates its land tax to soil fertility, and in neighboring Honduras and Guatemala, taxes rise when land is kept unused. A land tax based on potential output may face a problem of elasticity. Unlike land itself, the supply of which is inelastic, the supply of *improved* land must be elastic. In that case, a land tax would decrease the amount of land improvement. Another difficulty with a land tax based on potential rather than actual potential output is that landowners lose the coinsurance with government that sets in when output falls because of weather or other natural causes. When actual output is taxed, a fall in that output causes the tax bill to fall as well.

Given that the disadvantages of land taxes are relatively slight, the fierce opposition to them has to be explained mostly on political grounds. The political power of the landholders of large estates (or *latifundia* in the literature) is such, particularly in parts of Latin America and Asia that they are able to resist the tax completely or adapt it to their advantage. This is undoubtedly the major explanation why property taxes on average collect only some 3.5% of all tax revenue in the

LDCs, a figure that has fallen slightly in recent years. (But as in the developed countries, many LDC local governments—cities in particular—often do rely on property taxes.)

Another tax, that on inheritances, is even rarer and more limited in scope in almost all LDCs. Here again, the low occurrence of such taxes seems to reflect the balance of political power, with wealthy merchants and landowners allied in resisting such levies.

Consumption Taxes

For want of more effective taxes, many LDCs are forced to fall back on the taxation of local consumption, foreign trade, individuals on a "per head" basis, and on such eccentricities as a national lottery. These together often account for the lion's share of government revenue in the LDCs. Domestic excise (sales) taxes plus taxes on imports and exports frequently comprise 65% or more of that revenue. In the lower-income LDCs, taxes on foreign trade alone may make up over 40% of government revenue; the average for all LDCs is about 29% as against only 2.8% in the developed countries and below 2% in the United States.[83] The justification in every case is not that these taxes are fair or efficient but that they collect revenue.

Local consumption taxes of the excise and sales types are collected at the wholesale point of production or at the retail level. They collect about 28% of government revenue in the LDCs, about the same as in the developed countries.[84] But their importance varies greatly, from small to quite large, 40% to 60% of revenue in Chile, Haiti, India, Kenya, Morocco, Peru, the Philippines, Tanzania, Thailand, Uruguay, and Zambia, and reaching 65% in Mexico. Their collection must be at individual factories or stores and hence is often spotty by comparison to import duties, which are collected at more easily policed ports of entry. Excise and sales taxes are most effective when applied to goods produced by a small number of firms and sold through a limited number of outlets that can be supervised by the tax authorities. They are almost impossible to collect—often the attempt is not even made—when production is widespread and sale is in local markets.

A value-added tax (VAT) is a type of sales tax collected on each stage of production; it is central to the tax systems of Europe. VAT is too complex for many low income LDCs because of its dependence on good record keeping, but it is growing rapidly in favor. Brazil imposed the first comprehensive VAT in the LDCs in 1967. Only 17 LDCs were using this method in 1983, but 44 had a VAT by 1990.[85]

A VAT is easier to administer than an income tax, and it has the splendid advantage over most other taxes of being in part self-policing. Those who pay the tax at each stage of production pay only on the value they add. For example, the firm that manufactures the paper on which a magazine is printed pays the tax on the value it added when the paper is sold to a magazine publisher. Hence, the firm that publishes the magazine will want to ensure that the proper VAT receipt is sent along with every paper delivery from a supplier so that it does not get saddled with the payment itself. Evasion needs to involve many people. (Even so, evasion of VAT is said to be widespread in Latin America.) Along with this remarkable element of self-policing is the further advantage that value-added taxes are collected only on spending and not on saving.

The rate of VAT in LDCs has ranged from 5% in Taiwan to 30% in Chile (which was so high it promoted evasion, so the tax was reduced), with about 20% to 25% the highest rates found in practice. If VAT is too difficult to collect at the retail level, as in Africa where much retailing is in informal open-air markets, it can be applied anyway to the manufacturer, importer, or wholesaler at earlier stages. (In 1990, 20 of the 44 LDCs with a VAT did not extend them to the retail stage.) When this is done, however, it narrows the tax base so that the rate must be higher to collect the same amount of revenue. Even so, plenty of experience indicates that a VAT is feasible under a wide variety of conditions.

VATs do contribute to higher prices, but only in a one-time event, and there is little evidence that they are a cause of inflation. They are not in themselves progressive, although this may not be very important because even if they replace more progressive taxes, the rest of the budget can make up for it with transfers and programs directed toward the poor. In any case, a VAT can involve several different rates, lower on necessities, higher on luxuries. (About half of the LDCs' VATs involve more than one rate, with the range being from two to five.)[86] However, multiple rates increase complexity, are more difficult to administer, and are harder to enforce.

It is significant that no country having once passed a VAT has ever repealed it with the single exception of South Korea in the early 1970s.[87] All in all, there seems to be a bright future for VATs in the LDCs, and their increasing use has been the most important tax development of recent years in these countries.

Taxes on Foreign Trade

Taxes on foreign trade are ordinarily easier to collect than either a sales or income tax. It is much easier to police a country's ports of entry and even its borders than it is to collect taxes in all local markets or implement an income tax. Hence the administrative costs of trade taxes are estimated to be only 1% to 3% of the revenue collected by such taxes, compared to up to 5% for a VAT and reaching 10% for an income tax. This consideration can be important where tax-management skills are low and staff is short.[88]

Import Taxes Import duties are the most important example of taxes on foreign trade. All LDCs have them with the single exception of Hong Kong, and on average they currently collect about a quarter of all government revenue. Import duties are at least a partial substitute for a corporate income tax on multinational firms whenever the full burden of the tax cannot be passed on to consumers. It has been said in criticism that import duties are not progressive, weighing on rich and poor alike, but this is not necessarily so. Luxury consumer imports can easily be taxed at higher rates than necessities, as is done in Indonesia and Tanzania. Alas, the tactic may backfire: There will then be a stronger incentive to produce the luxuries at home in the LDC. Countries where import duties are important but inflation is present will want to make sure that their tariffs are *ad valorem*, collected as a percentage of value, rather than specific or flat rate, for if they are not, the revenue collected from this source will fall.

In a wide range of LDCs, import duties have been applied extensively in support of an import substitution policy designed to promote the domestic economy. When generalized import substitution is encountered, our topic turns from revenue collection to the nationwide effects on economic efficiency caused by the protection. This broad issue is central to Chapter 14.

Export Taxes Export taxes are also common, used in 53 of 74 LDCs studied by the World Bank in 1987. In numerous countries, they collect over 10% of tax revenue, and over 20% in some, though on average in the LDCs they collect only 4%.[89] (This compares to only 0.02% in the developed countries. Indeed, they are prohibited in the United States by Article I of the Constitution.) They have certainly been much in the limelight because of the OPEC oil cartel, which essentially involves export restriction that acts as a tax. Export taxes are often levied on agricultural and mineral products but hardly ever on manufactures because the average LDC wants to encourage their sales. Export taxes are most effective revenue collectors when a country or group of countries has some monopoly power over the production of an essential item—oil, for example, or possibly copper, tin, uranium, and the like.

Elasticity and Export Taxes From the point of view of the LDC using export taxes, their success or failure depends largely on the elasticity of demand and supply. Beginning with demand, the tax collects most when the foreign demand curve for the export being taxed is highly inelastic, as shown in Figure 4.3. In this case, a country has some monopoly power, and export taxes can be passed on to consumers abroad. OPEC's oil, Brazilian coffee before World War II, Ghanaian cocoa and Pakistani jute to some degree in the 1950s, and Chilean nitrates in the early part of this century are all examples.

Placing a per-unit (per-ton, per-barrel, etc.) tax on the product is tantamount to shifting its supply curve upward, from S to S_t. This is because domestic producers willing to supply a given quantity at some given price will not be willing to do so after a tax unless they receive the previous amount plus the tax. The vertical distance AB in Figure 4.3 is the dollar amount of the tax and is also the distance by which the supply curve is shifted upward. Note that the tax will, in this case, lower the quantity sold only slightly from Q to Q_1, will raise substantially the price the producer can charge from P to P_1, and will result in a large increase in total revenue earned from the sale of the product from $0PEQ$ to $0P_1E_1Q_1$. As will be seen in later chapters, OPEC is the outstanding example of success for countries employing export taxation as a method of generating government revenue.

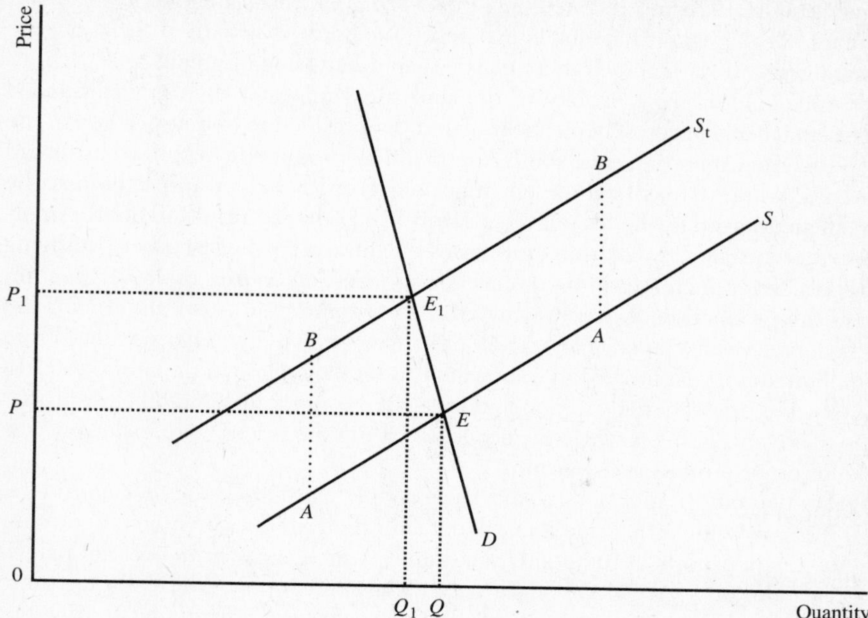

Figure 4.3 The effect of an export tax *AB* on a product with an inelastic foreign demand curve. Price rises from *P* to P_1, but quantity falls only slightly, from *Q* to Q_1. So total revenue earned from the sale of the product increases from 0*PEQ* to $0P_1E_1Q_1$.

There are, however, a host of difficulties in using an export tax even when demand is inelastic. The risk is that the monopoly position will be lost, as new sources of supply emerge and as consumers learn to economize. OPEC's petroleum is an object lesson. High prices, reaching well above $30 per barrel at the start of the 1980s, stimulated new production in areas such as Alaska, Mexico, and the North Sea. They also led consumers to switch to alternative sources of energy, to turn down the thermostat, and to buy smaller, more efficient autos. The elasticity of demand turned out to be much higher than it was originally.

The most vivid case of a producer squandering a monopoly position is that of Chile's nitrates. In the first decade of this century, the rich nitrate deposits in the Atacama Desert were essential both for fertilizer and the manufacture of explosives. The latter use meant that the war machines of Europe and the United States were to a significant extent dependent on imports of the Chilean natural resource; 65% of the nitrate market was under that country's control just before the outbreak of World War I, even more when neighboring Peru (with its bird guano islands) is included. Chile's very high export taxes backfired, however, because they encouraged technical research into synthetics. At the Oppau plant of the German firm Badische Anilin und Sodafabrik (BASF), a technical breakthrough by Carl Bosch led to the availability of synthetic nitrates drawn from nitrogen in the air. Chile was left with untold stocks of much-depreciated nitrates, its share of the market down to only 25% in 1928 and retained only by severe price cutting. By better tax management, all this might have been avoided.* Technically, as with OPEC's oil, the demand curve became much more elastic than it had been originally.

Similar increasing elasticity of demand was the result of high tax-induced prices for Ghanaian cocoa, which stimulated the production of that product in the Côte d'Ivoire, Cameroun, and South America. The production of coffee has spread in Africa, where it has become an important crop in Kenya and Ethiopia, the spread encouraged by the tax policies of Brazil and other Central and South American coffee producers. Pakistan's jute taxes encouraged a shift to other packaging materials. Steep increases in the Jamaican export tax on bauxite in the 1970s stimulated the production of that raw material for aluminum in Australia, Brazil, and Guinea. As a result, Jamaica lost much of its market share; its sales declined from 15 million tons a year in 1974 to somewhat less than 6 million in the mid–1980s. In all cases, the price elasticity of demand facing the country imposing the tax proved to be relatively elastic: A single country's efforts to raise prices were making it possible for other producers to expand.

For a country imposing an export tax, supply elasticity is another consideration. If supply is inelastic, suppliers will not alter their production much. For example, the copra exports of the South Sea islands (which come from coconut palms) and the palm oil of West Africa are very inelastic in supply. The palm trees are long-lived, so that production from existing groves takes the form of gathering but need not require planting for many years. Whatever the price, the fruit is there for the taking. A tax per unit of output on these crops is safe in that it will not lower quantity significantly, as seen in Figure 4.4, where Q_1 is only slightly lower than Q. Similarly, supply elasticity will be low for any crop where opportunities for substitution in production are limited. Similarly, within a wide range the supply of minerals from mining operations might be relatively inelastic.

But supply may instead be elastic. Taxing an export crop may mean that marketing food domestically and even subsistence food production look more attractive. Exports may decline, and very high taxation may even lead producers to withdraw effort from the money economy. Steep taxes on rubber output in colonial days had this effect in Indonesia, Sabah, and Sarawak. They caused substantial cuts in production for export and increased effort in the subsistence sector. With minerals there is the danger that costs of production including the tax will be forced too high for profitable operation. A first symptom is that low-grade ore will cease to be mined, as has happened from time to time with Bolivian tin.

An elastic supply curve appears in Figure 4.5. With elastic supply, a $0.20 tax per pound of rubber exports cuts production seriously. Before the tax, price is P, and the quantity produced is Q. A tax equal to AB raises the supply curve to S_t. For any given elasticity of demand, an elastic supply curve means a large cutback in

---

*The episode was perhaps even more upsetting to Allied war strategy in World War I. With German artillery firing more shells during the Battle of the Marne in September 1914 than in the whole of the Franco-Prussian War of 1870–1871, it was expected that the Wehrmacht would run out of ammunition by the start of 1915 because the naval blockade had cut off the supply of Chilean nitrates. For details, see Gerd Hardach, *The First World War, 1914–1918* (Berkeley, Calif., 1977): 31, 59, 266, 268–271.

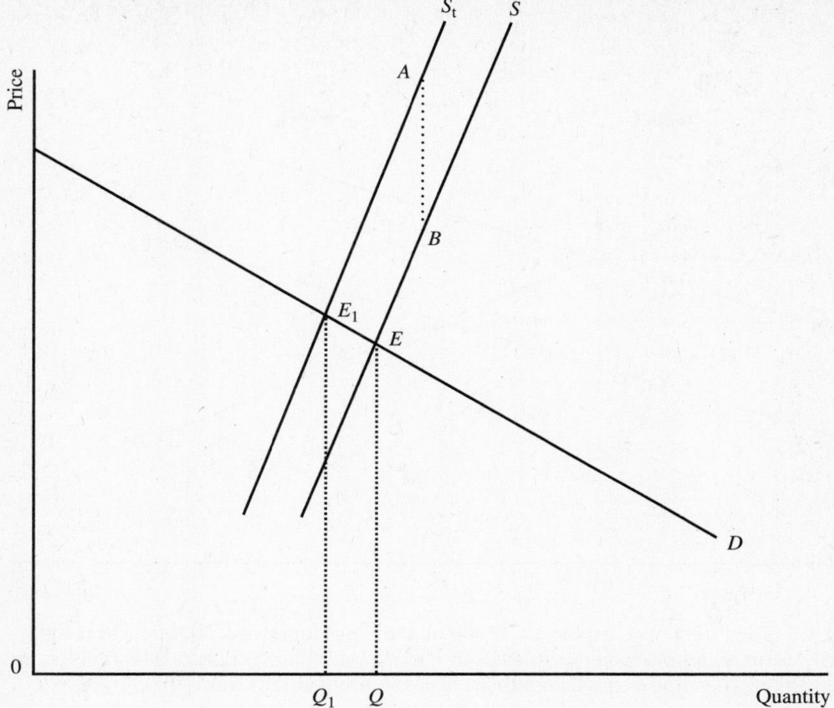

Figure 4.4 The effect of an export tax on the quantity produced of a product with an inelastic supply curve. Because of that inelasticity, quantity falls only a little, from Q to Q_1.

output to Q_1 and a reduction of total revenue earned from the production of the commodity from $0PEQ$ to $0P_1E_1Q_1$.

A general problem with the taxation of commodity exports is that they do not ordinarily grow as fast as national product. (Manufactured exports often do grow as fast or faster than GNP.) Too much dependence on taxing such exports may mean that the government captures a declining share of national product. Further, such taxes make a country fiscally dependent on changeable foreign demand in the developed world, subject as it is to the recurring ups and downs of the business cycle.

In short, it seems reasonable to suppose that each individual export will require careful study to determine whether it should be taxed, with duties on some clearly causing more difficulties than duties on others. Lumping them together, although common, is unwise. Such levies will, however, continue to be popular in any case because they are easy to collect, hard to evade, and often fall on well-off foreign-owned enterprises such as plantations, mining firms, and oil companies. There is a darker side, however. The duties are often heaviest on the politically

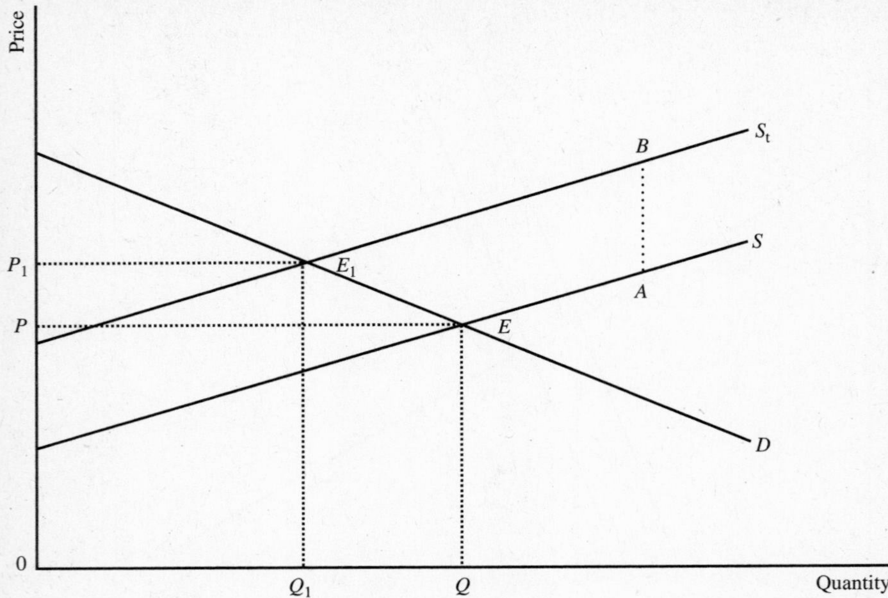

Figure 4.5 The effect of an export tax on the quantity produced of a product with an elastic supply curve. Price rises only a little, from P to P_1, but quantity falls substantially, from Q to Q_1. So total revenue earned from the sale of the product falls from $0PEQ$ to $0P_1E_1Q_1$.

powerless and poor peasant producers of agricultural exports, even though in theory the duties could be graduated to take account of the wealth and income of those taxed, this is seldom done.

Multiple Exchange Rates Taxation of imports and exports need not be direct. Much the same effect can be achieved by a system of multiple exchange rates used as a revenue-earning device equivalent to taxation. (More often, they are used as a substitute for devaluing the currency.) For example, take a mythical country, Penuristan, and its dual rate. All exporters who earn foreign exchange, say, dollars, must sell these to the government at a cheap price, perhaps $1 = 20 penuris. Meanwhile, the only legal way to obtain foreign exchange for imports, tourism, investment abroad, and the like is to buy the exchange from the government at an expensive rate, say, $1 = 30 penuris. The Penuristan government therefore obtains a revenue, akin to a tax, of 10 penuris on every dollar bought and sold. The real effect is a combined tax on exporters, who have to sell their dollar earnings at a penuri price that is overvalued, and on importers, who have to buy their dollars at a price that undervalues the penuri. The economic effects are similar to direct taxation. Peru's long-overvalued currency caused a dramatic reduction in that country's exports of copper, lead, zinc, and silver, all of which boomed when the controls were removed. After a decline in the use of multiple exchange rates during the 1970s, there was a resurgence in the 1980s, when about 25 countries were using them, some with as many as five different rates.

The Poll Tax

Historically, one of the most common and effective forms of taxation was the poll tax, sometimes called the head or capitation tax. It was once used almost universally, but its importance is now dramatically lower. It is levied on some basis such as $5 per person per year. Of course such a tax is extremely regressive, but it takes little paperwork and administrative skill. A policeman does not even need to be literate to check whether a suspect is carrying his official, stamped tax receipt. Some economists, such as P. T. Bauer of the London School of Economics, support the poll tax for another reason. It is not likely to reduce the supply of effort to the money sector or to agricultural exports as may well happen with a tax on money income or a tax on exported commodities. The poll tax is in fact likely to cause an increase in the supply of effort to the money economy. The reason is that it is a lump-sum tax, raising the marginal utility of income by reducing that income but not altering the reward for marginal effort. The result will ordinarily be more work to pay the tax, with leisure being sacrificed.

Unfortunately, in the hands of an authoritarian government, an overly high poll tax may have the effect of lowering nutritional levels to the point where effort is reduced. Further, it has been used as a device to compel labor to enter the money economy—sometimes harshly, as in the former Belgian Congo, Northern and Southern Rhodesia, and in South Africa. Among its side effects may be a disruption of local community life and the forcing of large-scale migration to the cities. These are reasons for the great decline in its use.*

The National Lottery

An often-used method of revenue collection in LDCs is the national lottery, whose legions of ticket sellers throng the streets and marketplaces. Although they are popular with the government (which likes the revenue) and the public (which hopes for a chance to get rich quick), it is possible to have an especial antipathy for lotteries in low-income countries. Cash is extracted from people far less able to pay than their counterparts in rich countries. This might be harmless enough if the voluntary purchase reduced the consumption of no one but the ticket buyer, no matter how unfavorable the odds, but a large and dependent family may have no voice in the matter. A penny spent on the lottery by a poor man is all too conceivably a

*The much more sophisticated lump-sum taxes adjusted for income and/or wealth, often supported by economists as promoting both effort and equity, have had virtually no trial in the LDCs, nor in the developed countries for that matter. These lump-sum taxes would bring some difficulties of their own if they were tried. For example, they cease to be lump-sum when people realize their basis, and tax differentials of this type would surely prove a field day for special interests. See Stern, "The Economics of Development: A Survey," 653. Perhaps economists should show more favor to land taxes differing by quality, because as opposed to taxes on output, these are close to lump sum taxes. Valuation is difficult, however. For this point, see Joseph E. Stiglitz, "Some Theoretical Aspects of Agricultural Policies," *World Bank Research Observer* 2, no. 1 (January 1987): 47. For an understandable discussion of lump-sum taxes, see Edmund S. Phelps, *Political Economy* (New York, 1985): 316–323. 340.

penny less food for wife and children. True, people will gamble anyway, but governments are uniquely able to lend legitimacy to the activity and advertise it widely. Such reasoning has, however, not been at all persuasive to LDC governments.*

Taxation of Agriculture

Because of the difficulties in revenue collection, any alternative taxes with any promise of easy collection are sure to be welcomed. One such alternative, little emphasized in the rich countries, is taxing agriculture. Because poverty and a dominance of agriculture are virtually synonymous, LDC governments early in the game turned their attention to agricultural taxation. This would have been true even if revenue collection were the only aim. Many countries have in addition attempted to transfer food output to the cities at below-market prices in often ill-advised attempts to promote the growth of manufacturing or to placate the politically more powerful and potentially troublesome urban populations.

There are many examples of agricultural taxation to finance growth outside of agriculture, either in cash (thus forcing the farmer to sell food or some crops for export in order to pay the tax) or in kind (collection of food that is taken to the cities). Probably the best-known example of deliberately depressing agriculture was the Soviet Union, where explicit taxes plus forced deliveries at low compulsory purchase prices for farm produce were the major tools. The taxation was accompanied by the mechanization of farming and large shifts of labor to the cities. Less harsh but equally effective in encouraging a shift were the high exactions on Japanese farmers after the Meiji Restoration of 1867/1868. It is said that farm productivity doubled in the 30 years before World War I but that little increase in farmers' net real income occurred. Taxes on farming accounted for about 80% of total Japanese tax revenue from 1893 to 1897 and were still about 50% from 1913 to 1917.[90]

Agricultural Marketing Boards A familiar, more recent device for taxation in the agricultural sector is the agricultural, or produce, marketing board set up during and after World War II in countries that were formerly British colonies.[91] Various government organizations with similar titles serve the same function in the

---

*The most studied case is the United States, which, though not an LDC, has many poor people who buy lottery tickets. U.S. lottery ticket sales to the 5% for adults who buy the largest number of tickets (these heavy players bet about $1,200 per year) account for about half of total sales. Lottery sales increase as education decreases. There is little relation between lottery sales and household income—hence the tax element in lotteries is highly regressive. Expenditures are not very sensitive to odds and depend on the size of the jackpot. Data from New Jersey indicate that one out of three families earning incomes under $10,000 spend a fifth of their income on lottery tickets. U.S. state lotteries keep 37% of the take and pay only 48% to winners. Operating costs, including advertising, make up the remaining 15%. The advertising for lottering does not say this, nor does it give the much lower real present value of a "million-dollar" winning ticket or the tremendous odds against winning, in some cases worse than being struck and killed by lightning three times over. For details, see Charles T. Clotfelter and Philip J. Cook, *Selling Hope* (Cambridge, Mass., 1989); and the same authors' "Implicit Taxation in Lottery Finance," NBER Working Paper No. 2246 (May 1987).

French sphere of influence and in parts of Latin America. Among the best known of the marketing boards in the developing world are or were those of Ghana, Nigeria, Sierra Leone, Kenya, Uganda, Argentina, and the rather notorious one in Burma/Myanmar.* These boards generally follow the same line of action. They are established with the seemingly sensible claim that they will buy the entire output of some particular export crop and pay a fixed price for it all season long. Such policy ensures against cheating by middlemen because the marketing board price can always be received just by carrying produce to the nearest official buying station, of which there will be many. A second publicized advantage is the elimination of price variation during a season and the security provided thereby. There is none of the old uncertainty as to whether today's prices will collapse tomorrow or be higher.

In almost every instance, however, the marketing boards in the LDCs became devices for heavy taxation. Their technique is simple. If cocoa is selling on the world market for $10,000 a ton, the Ghana cocoa marketing board might announce an official price of $8,000 a ton for the following year. It intends not to change that price even if the bottom drops out of the world market, and indeed the cash reserves of the various boards have been called upon to support above-market prices a fair number of times. (Boards in this circumstance, however, have been known to stop buying, as recently happened in Kenya.) In normal circumstances the gap between the marketing board producer price and the higher world market price can be skimmed off and used for government development expenditure. Very large sums have been acquired in this manner. (The export marketing boards must be distinguished from domestic food marketing boards common in East Africa, which by "selling cheap," are a means for subsidizing consumers.[92] Food boards that act in this way are a drain on public revenue rather than an addition to it.)†

Political objections on the part of the peasant producers can be intense on the grounds that one of the poorer sectors of the economy is being singled out for heavy taxation. The objections can be forestalled by keeping all the revenues thus acquired in a reserve fund earmarked for "price stabilization." Then the cash can be used as interest-free or low-interest long-term loans for development projects or for subsidizing inputs such as fertilizer and machinery, especially for the large farmers whose political protests might be effective. In Nigeria, for example, during the first decade of its marketing board operations, 36% of the accumulated stabilization reserve was distributed as development grants and 21% as development loans. In some countries, the whole concept of a reserve was eventually lost, and taxation became the only function. The Ghana marketing board, for example, was not permitted to keep reserves after 1965.

---

*There are also marketing boards in the developed world, including Great Britain, New Zealand, and the Canadian provinces. One was recently established in Hungary as well. These boards differ from those in the LDCs in that they are generally designed to raise farmers' income rather than to tax them, which as we shall see became the chief purpose of the LDC boards.

†The food boards in Africa have been much criticized for their sometimes extraordinary inefficiencies. In some countries, they "buy dear" to subsidize farm output in addition to "selling cheap," so increasing the drain on the budget.

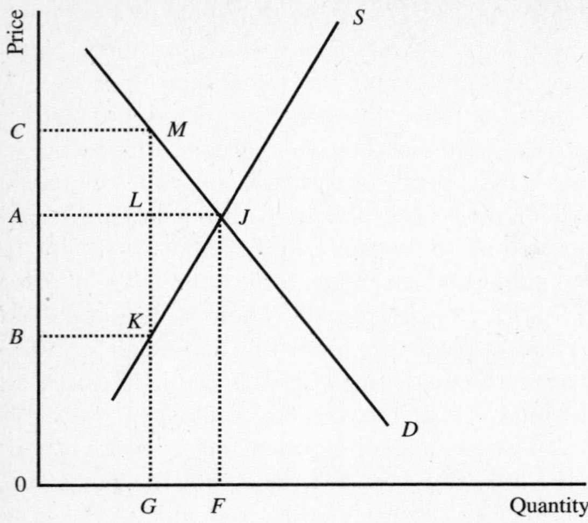

Figure 4.6 Agricultural marketing boards set a below-equilibrium price such as *B*, reducing quantity supplied to *G*. They then sell on the world market for what that market will bear, in this case *C*. The marketing board surplus is *BCMK*.

Analytically, marketing boards can be viewed as in Figure 4.6, where *S* and *D* are the supply and demand curves for a commodity in a free market, and proceeds to the producer at the equilibrium price are 0*AJF*. If the marketing board sets a below-equilibrium price *B*, quantity supplied will fall to *G*. Producers earn 0*BKG*; their loss from taxation is *BALK* plus the loss because their output is reduced by *GF*. At first glance this appears to be *GLJF*, but the resources freed from not producing the quantity *GF* will be available for other presumably less useful purposes. In the diagram, these alternative uses would yield producers *GKJF*, leaving a net loss of *KLJ*. The marketing board surplus is *BCMK*, of which *ACML* came from supply reduction that raised the sale price of the commodity to *C*, while *BALK* is a transfer from producers.

The greater the elasticity of supply, the greater the shift by farmers to other products. The more elastic demand is, the smaller the gain to the marketing board. Thus the longer the period of marketing board operations (allowing time for farmers to substitute untaxed crops) and the less the importance of the covered crop on world markets (so that no price increase can be passed on to foreign consumers), the less effective the marketing board will be as an instrument of taxation.

Tax Reform

What can be said to summarize this section on taxation? In general, the tax system ought to yield more revenue as income grows, should not be too complex, should not penalize saving, and should avoid massive distortions in production, such as can happen in taxing agriculture and foreign trade. This is no doubt tantamount to saying

THE NEGATIVE RESULTS OF MARKETING BOARDS

Marketing boards certainly can mobilize financing for development purposes, but the adverse economic repercussions can be substantial. In Ghana, for example, implicit taxation by means of a marketing board reduced the real cocoa price by 44% between 1967 to 1968 and 1977 to 1978. The government, which had been taking only 3% of sales revenue in 1947 to 1948, obtained nearly 30% in 1953 to 1954, and 60% in 1978 to 1979. Across the borders in neighboring Côte d'Ivoire and Togo, prices were much higher. There were three predictable effects: less work expended on cocoa, more on other crops, and extensive smuggling. Official marketing board exports fell from an average 430,000 metric tonnes per year from 1964 to 1966 to an average 202,000 tonnes from 1979 to 1981. During the same time period, the Côte d'Ivoire's cocoa exports rose from 84,000 to 298,000 tonnes per year. Rice and maize prices were not controlled by a marketing board. There was much shifting to these untaxed crops, which gave a net return of about double that of cocoa. The estimate of cocoa smuggling in the late 1970s was a minimum of 10,000 tonnes; the actual amount may well have been about 45,000 tonnes. That amount would represent 15% of the value of Ghana's total exports of all products. The Ghanaian cocoa industry was left in economic shambles, contributing to that once fortunate country's political turmoil.[93]

Other marketing boards have also become highly politicized. A rice price unchanged for a decade by the Burma State Marketing Board was said to have been instrumental in the downfall of a Burmese government.

Of all the domestic measures to raise investment, the marketing boards are high on the list of those with unfavorable side effects. Recently, reform has set in. In the mid-1980s, Ghana almost tripled the fixed cocoa price (though this did no more than offset the real decline since about 1975). Further increases have followed, and the situation is improving. Nigeria abolished its marketing boards in 1986. Production responded favorably, with cocoa output up by 50% and rubber and cotton by over 400%. Economists regularly recommend that if these boards are retained, they should pay farmers higher prices for their crops.

that designing appropriate taxes for LDCs is a difficult task. The author would recommend phasing in value-added taxes as soon as possible, eventually putting major emphasis on them, and perhaps exempting small firms and traders to reduce the administrative burden. Withholding could be introduced into the income tax system whenever feasible. In the long term, it is crucially important to lower dependence on taxes directed at production, especially agriculture, and international trade. It is unlikely, however, that progress in reforming taxes will be either easy or rapid.

NOTES

1. W. Arthur Lewis, *The Theory of Economic Growth* (London, 1955), 201–303.

2. Mark Gersowitz, "Saving and Investment," in Hollis Chenery and T. N. Srinivasan, eds., *Handbook of Development Economics*, vol. 1 (Amsterdam, 1988), 394–395.
3. Andrew M. Kamarck, *Economics and the Real World* (Philadelphia, 1983), 113. The chapter in which the quotation is contained, " 'Capital' and 'Investment' in LDCs," 106–115, makes numerous valuable points.
4. For a recent work by one of these respected scholars, see Moses Abramovitz, *Thinking About Growth and Other Essays of Economic Growth* (Cambridge, 1989). Denison's much-quoted research includes *The Sources of Economic Growth in the United States and the Alternatives Before Us* (New York, 1962); *Why Growth Rates Differ* (Washington, D.C., 1967); *Accounting for United States Economic Growth, 1929–1969* (Washington, D.C., 1974); and *Trends in American Economic Growth, 1929–1982* (Washington, D.C., 1985).
5. See Arnold C. Harberger, "The Cost-Benefit Approach to Development Economics," *World Development* 11, no. 10 (1983): 864–866.
6. See William Easterly and Lant Pritchett, "The Determinants of Economic Success: Luck and Policy," *Finance and Development* 30, no. 4 (December 1993): 40.
7. Robert Evenson, "Technology, Growth, and Development," in Gustav Ranis and T. Paul Schultz, eds., *The State of Development Economics* (Oxford, 1988), 490. The importance of growing total factor productivity in the HPAEs is emphasized in World Bank, *The East Asian Miracle: Economic Growth and Public Policy* (New York, 1993). See especially Appendix 1.1, 60–69.
8. See World Bank, *The East Asian Miracle: Economic Growth and Public Policy*.
9. For a review of studies showing capital accumulation is more important for the LDCs than for developed countries, see Oli Havrylyshyn, "Trade Policies and Productivity Gains in Developing Countries: A Survey of the Literature," *World Bank Research Observer* 5, no. 1 (January 1990): 4. Nicholas Stern in his authoritative survey stated that capital accumulation is "rather more important than for more advanced countries." See Stern, "The Economics of Development: A Survey," *Economic Journal* 99, no. 397 (September 1989): 627.
10. Joseph Stiglitz, "Economic Organization, Information, and Development," in Hollis Chenery and T. N. Srinivasan,. eds., *Handbook of Development Economics*, vol. 1 (Amsterdam, 1988), 143.
11. Dennis Anderson, "Economic Growth and the Returns to Investment," 13; and the continuation of Anderson's work in "Investment and Economic Growth," *World Development* 18, no. 8 (August 1990): 1057–1079.
12. See in particular R. J. Barro, "Economic Growth in a Cross Section of Countries," NBER Working Paper No. 3120 (1989).
13. The example stems from two articles in *The Economist*, September 3, 1988, and September 23, 1989. The LDC average is from IMF, *World Economic Outlook 1987*, 79.
14. See Gerald M. Meier, *Leading Issues in Economic Development*, 5th ed. (New York, 1989), 177; IMF, *World Economic Outlook 1987*, 79.
15. *The Economist*, September 23, 1989.
16. See J. Bradford DeLong and Lawrence H. Summers, *How Strongly Do Developing Economies Benefit from Equipment Investment*? (Washington, D.C., 1993); the same authors' "Equipment Investment and Economic Growth," *Quarterly Journal of Economics* 106 (May 1991): 445–502; and Easterly and Pritchett, "The Determinants of Economic Success: Luck and Policy," 40.
17. This method of approach came originally from Lewis, *Theory of Economic Growth*, 209–213. The distribution of investment figures in this section are mostly from *WDR 1994* and *WDR 1989*.
18. For the figure of 43%, see Jeffrey G. Williamson, "Migration and Urbanization," in Chenery and Srinivasan, eds., *Handbook of Development Economics*, vol. 1, 428. For a

study of the topic, see Peter Lloyd, *Slums of Hope: Shanty Towns of the Third World* (New York, 1979).

19. *HDR 1993*, 24.
20. *WDR 1994*, 29; *The Economist*, May 7, 1988.
21. *WDR 1994*, 5.
22. *WDR 1992*, 117, says 20%; *The Economist*, August 31, 1991, says 10% to 20%.
23. *WDR 1994*, 4.
24. From *WDR 1994*, 27, and *The Economist*, August 31, 1991.
25. For the information in this paragraph, see Arun P. Sanghvi, "Power Shortages in Developing Countries," *Energy Policy* (June 1991); Lawrence H. Summers and Vinod Thomas, "Recent Lessons of Development," *World Bank Research Observer* 8, no. 2 (July 1993): 245–246; *WDR 1994*, 27–31; *WDR 1992*, 117; *WDR 1991*, 85; and *The Economist*, June 18, 1994, August 31, 1991, May 7, 1988, and January 12, 1985.
26. *WDR 1994*, 6, 30–31.
27. The data in this paragraph are from *WDR 1994*, 4, 29–31; *WDR 1988*, 146–149; *WDR 1987*, 65; and UNESCO's *New Book of World Rankings*.
28. *WDR 1979*, 82.
29. *HDR 1993*, 24.
30. *WDR 1992*, 47, 106.
31. *WDR 1979*, 82.
32. *WDR 1994*, 4, 27, 29.
33. *WDR 1994*, 31–33.
34. *WDR 1994*, 6, 29.
35. For these examples, see *WDR 1987*, 65.
36. *WDR 1994*, 18.
37. *WDR 1994*, 5, 27.
38. *WDR 1991*, 85; *WDR 1994*, 30–31.
39. *WDR 1994*, 15, citing a Columbia University working paper by Canning and Fay, and 17.
40. *WDR 1994*, 80–81.
41. This section and others in this book showing the algebra of capital financing draw on Eprime Eshag, *Fiscal and Monetary Policies and Problems in Developing Countries* (Cambridge, 1983), especially chaps. 3 and 4. See also Alan R. Prest, *Public Finance in Developing Countries* (New York, 1985).
42. The figures are from *HDR 1994*, 178.
43. *WDR 1990*, 194–195; and Subrata Ghatak, *Development Economics* (London, 1978), 77, reporting work by Jeffrey Williamson.
44. Clive Bell, "Credit Markets and Interlinked Transactions," in Chenery and Srinivasan, eds., *Handbook of Development Economics*, vol. 1, 826.
45. *The Economist*, September 25, 1993. The data are from the 1970s and 1980s.
46. V. V. Bhatt, "Improving the Financial Structure in Developing Countries," *Finance and Development* 23, no. 2 (1986): 20.
47. *WDR 1991*, 137.
48. For a discussion, see (in alphabetical order) Ziauddin Ahmad, Munawar Iqbal, and M. Fahin Khan, eds., *Money and Banking in Islam* (Islamabad, 1983); Masudul Alam Choudhury, *The Principles of Islamic Political Economy: A Methodological Enquiry* (London, 1992); Ali F. Darrat, "The Islamic Interest-Free Banking System: Some Empirical Evidence," *Applied Economics* 20 (1988): 417–425; Zubair Iqbal and Abbas Mirakhor, "Islamic Banking," IMF Occasional Paper No. 49 (1987); Moshin S. Khan and Abbas Mirakhor, "The Framework and Practice of Islamic Banking," *Finance and Development* 23, no. 3 (September 1986): 32–36; Moshin S. Khan and

Abbas Mirakhor, "Islamic Banking: Experiences in the Islamic Republic of Iran and in Pakistan," *Economic Development and Cultural Change* 38, no. 2 (January 1990): 353–375; Moshin S. Khan, "Islamic Interest-Free Banking: A Theoretical Analysis," *IMF Staff Papers* 33, no. 1 (1986): 1–27; John R. Presley and John G. Sessions, "Islamic Economics: The Emergence of a New Paradigm," *Economic Journal* 104, no. 424 (May 1994): 584–596; and the survey of "Islam and the West" in *The Economist*, August 6, 1994.

49. Presley and Sessions, "Islamic Economics: The Emergence of a New Paradigm," 584–596.
50. *The Economist*, August 6, 1994.
51. *South*, February 1988.
52. *WDR 1989*, 112.
53. *WDR 1989*, 116.
54. Stiglitz, "Economic Organization, Information, and Development," in Chenery and Srinivasan, eds., *Handbook of Development Economics*, vol. 1, 144–145.
55. *WDR 1989*, 55–56, 59, 76, and 129, which gives the details in this and the next paragraph, is thorough on priority sectors and requirements for bank loans.
56. Jack Glen and Brian Pinto, "Debt or Equity? How Firms in Developing Countries Choose," IFC Discussion Paper No. 22 (1994), 3.
57. Glen and Pinto, "Debt or Equity? How Firms in Developing Countries Choose," 3.
58. For most of these, see Deena R. Khatkhate, "Estimating Real Interest Rates in LDCs," *Finance and Development* 23, no. 2 (1986): 48.
59. Among their seminal works are Ronald McKinnon, *Money and Capital in Economic Development* (Washington, D.C., 1973); and Edward Shaw, *Financial Deepening in Economic Development* (New York, 1973). For a generally sympathetic view of their work, see Lazaros E. Molho, "Interest Rates, Saving, and Investment in Developing Countries: A Re-examination of the McKinnon-Shaw Hypothesis," *IMF Staff Papers* 33, no. 1 (1986): 90–116. Also see Maxwell J. Fry, *Money, Interest, and Banking in Economic Development* (Baltimore, 1988); *WDR 1987*, 118; and *The Economist*, September 5, 1993.
60. IMF, *World Economic Outlook 1994*, 57.
61. Ronald McKinnon, *The Order of Economic Liberalization* (Baltimore, 1991).
62. *WDR 1989*, 27.
63. *WDR 1989*, 122, 131.
64. For this and the next paragraph, see Ronald McKinnon, *The Order of Economic Liberalization* (Baltimore, 1991); IMF, *World Economic Outlook 1992*, 28; *The Economist*, December 11, 1993, citing work by Palle Andersen; and World Bank, *The East Asian Miracle: Economic Growth and Public Policy* (New York, 1993), 250.
65. Mario I. Blejer and Adrienne Cheasty, "Using Fiscal Measures to Stimulate Savings in Developing Countries," *Finance and Development* 23, no. 2 (1986): 19.
66. For thorough treatments, see (in alphabetical order): Ehtisham Ahmad and Nicholas Stern, *The Theory and Practice of Tax Reform in Developing Countries* (Cambridge, 1991); Ehtisham Ahmad and Nicholas Stern, "Taxation for Developing Countries," in Chenery and Srinivasan, eds., *Handbook of Development Economics*, vol. 2, 1005–1092; Richard M. Bird, *Tax Policy and Economic Development* (Baltimore, 1991); Richard M. Bird and Milka Casanegra de Jantscher, *Improving Tax Administration in Developing Countries* (Washington, D.C., 1993); Robin Burgess and Nicholas Stern, "Taxation and Development," *Journal of Economic Literature* 31, no. 2 (June 1993): 762–830; John F. Due, *Indirect Taxation in Developing Economies* (Baltimore, 1988); Malcolm Gillis, *Tax Reform in Developing Countries* (Durham, N.C., 1989); Richard Goode, *Government*

Finance in Developing Countries (Washington, D.C., 1984); Arnold C. Harberger, ed., *Economic Policy and Economic Growth* (San Francisco, 1984); Chad Leechor, *Tax Policy and Tax Reform in Semi-Industrial Countries* (Washington, D.C., 1986); Stephen R. Lewis, Jr., *Taxation for Development* (Oxford, 1984); Richard A. Musgrave, *Taxation and Economic Development Among Pacific Asian Countries* (Boulder, 1994); and D. M. G. Newbery and N. H. Stern, eds., *The Theory of Taxation for Developing Countries* (Oxford, 1987), including especially Richard A. Musgrave, "Tax Reform in Developing Countries," and Vito Tanzi, "Quantitative Characteristics of the Tax Systems of Developing Countries."

67. See Keith Marsden, "Links Between Taxes and Growth: Some Empirical Evidence," World Bank Staff Working Paper No. 605 (1983).
68. Richard Goode, "Tax Advice to Developing Countries: An Historical Survey," *World Development* 21, no. 1 (January 1993): 37–53.
69. See A. J. Mann, "The Mexican Tax Burden by Family Income Class," *Public Finance Quarterly* 10, no. 3 (1982): 305–331.
70. Figures in this paragraph are calculated by the author from *HDR 1994*, 180–181 and 205.
71. See Richard Goode, "Tax Advice to Developing Countries: An Historical Survey," *World Development* 21, no. 1 (January 1993): 37–53; and Michael Roemer and Joseph J. Stern, *Cases in Economic Development: Projects, Policies, and Strategies* (London, 1981), 218, citing work of R. J. Chelliah.
72. Robin Burgess and Nicholas Stern, "Taxation and Development," *Journal of Economic Literature* 31, no. 2 (June 1993): 762–830.
73. *WDR 1988*, 117.
74. Drawing on the work of Richard Goode and Walter Heller reprinted in Gerald M. Meier, *Leading Issues in Development Economics*, 1st ed. (New York, 1964), 115–127, and on *WDR 1988*, which contains much useful information on LDC income taxes.
75. For a review of the expenditure tax, see Robert Tannewald, "Should We Adopt an Expenditure Tax?" *New England Economic Review* (March/April 1984), 29–39.
76. *WDR 1988*, 85, 100.
77. *The Economist*, October 6, 1990.
78. Gunnar Myrdal, "Need for Reforms in Underdeveloped Countries," in Sven Grassman and Erik Lundberg, eds., *The World Economic Order: Past and Prospects* (New York, 1981), 521.
79. See Bird and Casanegra de Jantscher, *Improving Tax Administration in Developing Countries*.
80. Most LDCs collect *ad valorem* royalties on natural resources. The rates of royalties and differing methods employed in collecting them are discussed in David C. L. Nellor, "Sovereignty and Natural Resource Taxation in Developing Countries," *Economic Development and Cultural Change* 35, no. 2 (January 1987): 367–392.
81. *WDR 1988*, 91, 100.
82. For this section, see the analysis in Burgess and Stern, "Taxation and Development"; Stephen R. Lewis, *Taxation for Development*, chap. 7; Goode, "Tax Advice to Developing Countries: An Historical Survey"; and *WDR 1988*, 160.
83. Burgess and Stern, "Taxation and Development," 773.
84. Burgess and Stern, "Taxation and Development," 773.
85. Goode, "Tax Advice to Developing Countries: An Historical Survey"; *IMF Survey*, February 8, 1988; Malcolm Gillis, "Micro and Macroeconomics of Tax Reform: Indonesia," *Journal of Development Economics* 19, no. 3 (1986): 241. A comprehensive study is Alan A. Tait, *Value-Added Tax: International Practice and Problems* (Washington, D.C.,

1988). I also drew from Carl Shoup, "The Value Added Tax and Developing Countries," *World Bank Economic Review* 2, no. 2 (July 1988): 139–156.

86. Goode, "Tax Advice to Developing Countries: An Historical Survey."
87. Shoup, "The Value Added Tax and Developing Countries," 149.
88. *WDR 1988*, 85.
89. *WDR 1988*, 91.
90. Subrata Ghatak, *Development Economics* (London, 1978): 98, citing B.F. Johnston and J. Mellor.
91. This section draws heavily on Douglas Rimmer's analysis of marketing boards in "The Economic Legacy of Colonialism in British Tropical Africa" (paper presented at a UNESCO conference, Lake Naivasha, Kenya, June, 1981), which contains the diagram used in the text, and in his *Economies of West Africa* (New York, 1984): 164–173. The boards are surveyed in Kwame Arhin, Paul Hesp, and Laurens van der Laan, eds., *Marketing Boards in Tropical Africa* (London, 1985). Another good treatment of the boards (and of export taxation as well) is George S. Tolley et al., *Agricultural Price Policies and the Developing Countries* (Baltimore, 1982).
92. See Arhin, Hesp, and van der Laan, *Marketing Boards in Tropical Africa*, and William O. Jones, "Economic Tasks for Food Marketing Boards in Tropical Africa," *Food Research Institute Studies* 19, no. 2 (1984): 113–138.
93. See especially *WDR 1983*, 77.

Chapter 5

Financing Development II

Cutting Current Spending, Macro Imbalances

In the previous chapter, we discussed how finance for development could be obtained from domestic saving, either in the private sector or through the government's taxation and domestic borrowing. In this chapter we move on to consider further financial opportunities from government budget cuts in areas that contribute little to development or are detrimental to it. Then we conclude by reviewing how difficult political and economic choices have had to be made by LDC governments, choices that have frequently involved macroeconomic imbalances with inflationary results.

CUTTING CURRENT SPENDING

Are there items in the government budget that represent waste, extravagance, or inefficient use of public funds? Undoubtedly such is the case in many LDCs. Could such expenditure be reduced and the resources made available for investment purposes so as to increase the stock of physical and human capital? Surely, but with great difficulty because wasteful extravagance in an LDC is often the outcome of a political process wherein a government utilizes public resources to reward its loyal supporters, to buy off its potential opposition, and to purchase protection by means of the defense budget.[1] This politicization of economics is often highly visible, taking the form of (1) overstaffing of government and state-operated enterprises (parastatals), (2) subsidies that mainly affect certain favored groups, (3) government projects selected for political return rather than economic effects, and (4) surprisingly high spending on defense.

A well-managed development strategy will require substantial participation by government, but participation can translate into gross overstaffing in the government sector. Such overstaffing is rampant in many LDCs, a well-developed "spoils system," so to speak, in otherwise less-developed lands. According to a 1980s study, the share of central government salaried jobs as a percentage of all salaried jobs was only 9% in the industrialized countries, whereas it was 23% in the LDCs.[2] In some areas, the figure was far higher: India 54%, Liberia 53%, Bénin 50%, Tanzania 46%. In Brazil, rampant overstaffing in state enterprises has been reported, with four times as many employees as necessary on the government railways and five times as many in government-operated shipping and the Coffee Institute's warehousing.[3] In many countries, the opportunity to use employment as a perquisite for supporters of a particular government has proved irresistible.

Cutting Subsidies

Subsidies for foodstuffs, manufacturing, credit, seed, fertilizer, farm machinery, rural water supplies, electrification, and the like also have a strong political side to them. Frequently they go to the middle classes and urban dwellers rather than the poor, especially the rural poor. The subsidies can be substantial: bread in Egypt priced at one-tenth the price in the United States, cheap gasoline and kerosene for cooking and heating (Bolivia, Venezuela, Sri Lanka), and electricity at a third or a quarter of the U.S. price (Brazil, Colombia, Ecuador).* Public spending on transport may focus on urban roadways, amounting to a subsidy to the car-owning middle class, while rural roads are neglected.

The poor do not have cars, often do not live in cities, and are not connected to electricity or running water, but it is these items that receive the government's attention. Politically well-organized urban workers benefit from the food subsidies; allied industrialists and merchants can be granted production subsidies and cheap credit. Large and thus influential farmers can receive the subsidies in rural areas. Poor rural labor is rarely covered by social security schemes of any kind, whereas urban workers often are.† The poor usually benefit little from the educational subsidies for university education and high schools.

---

*Energy subsidies in Egypt have at times totaled nearly 90% of the country's export earnings. Not surprisingly given these prices, petroleum demand has grown at 10% to 12% per year. See *WDR 1988*, 119.

†Only 8% of Brazil's rural labor benefits from that country's otherwise broad social security schemes. In the richest sector (transport and communications), 80% are covered. See *The Economist*, September 23, 1989.

Cutting Spending on Politicized Projects

Another form of politicization of economics is the selection of government projects to reward loyal supporters. The authority to decide where to locate a project and who is to staff it gives politicians an instrument of political power. Government money therefore often goes to regions, castes, industries, unions, and occupations whose support is politically important to the government in many LDCs (with India representing a prime case). Politicians regularly announce the establishment of new government projects just before an election. The presence in a country of many inefficient projects underway, each with a large staff sporting the ruling party's colors on a sleeve, cap, or collar, becomes more understandable when viewed in terms of their political implications.

Broadly, the budgetary losses of many sorts of state enterprises, ranging from telephones and electricity to transportation and many sorts of manufacturing, are often covered by subsidies. These amounted to about 4% of GNP on average for the seven largest economies of Latin America in the 1980s and at least that high in many other LDCs. Often these state enterprises produce goods or services consumed by the middle classes and rich rather than the poor and serve as a major source of employment for political supporters, including many in the middle class.

As we shall see later in the chapter, in a reaction to the situation, comprehensive moves toward ending price controls and subsidies, together with privatization of state enterprises, have become common, especially in Latin America where Argentina, Brazil, Mexico, Peru, and Venezuela have done so. Elsewhere, the trend has been more limited, but it has been worldwide and includes even such countries as Algeria, China, India, Laos, Pakistan, and Vietnam where the practices have been entrenched. In spite of that, the problem remains serious.

Cutting Defense Spending

High defense budgets can be seen to serve a political purpose in the same way that subsidies do. A well-equipped military can reinforce the police in suppressing political opposition, and military adventures may provide a distraction from a government's problems. Modern arms may deliver prestige to the government of the day. Whatever the reason, defense spending is surprisingly high in many LDCs. It rose by five times in real terms from 1960 to 1988, twice as fast as per capita income, to a figure of about $170 billion per year.[4] Most of this goes for personnel, not equipment. In any case, foreign aid pays for many of the weapons.

Nonetheless the outlays involve expensive missiles, high-tech aircraft, submarines, and even aircraft carriers (Argentina, Brazil, India, and with China attempting to acquire one). Almost all of these are imported; arms make up about 5% of the LDCs' total imports, and nearly three-quarters of the world's armament exports are to the LDCs.[5] Several LDCs (China, Brazil, Israel, and Egypt) are big arms exporters themselves, and so profit from the trade. China, whose exports of arms are five times greater than Brazil's, is the fifth largest in the world, while Brazil is eleventh. LDC arms exporters have held as much as 15% of the world market.

TABLE 5.1 AVERAGE PERCENT OF GDP AND CENTRAL GOVERNMENT SPENDING ON THE MILITARY, 1972–1988

	Percent of GDP	Percent of Central Government Spending
Developed countries	3.8	14.3
LDCs	5.9	20.0
Asia	6.3	27.2
Middle East	11.6	23.1
Sub-Saharan Africa	3.7	12.8
Latin America	2.3	8.6

Source: Daniel P. Hewitt, "Military Expenditures in the Developing World," *Finance and Development* 28, no. 3 (September 1991): 23.

Defense spending in the LDCs often represents more than their governments spend on either health or education and almost as much as is spent on both combined. Table 5.1 shows the percentage of GNP devoted to defense and defense as a percentage of all central government expenditures for the developed countries and the LDCs. (It should be noted that many governments do not like to admit to their high figures for military outlays, which, it is believed, are sometimes concealed.)

Spending on the armed forces is highly concentrated in certain countries. In the late 1980s, only 12 of them accounted for two-thirds of LDC military spending. (In order, they were Iraq, India, Saudi Arabia, Afghanistan, Iran, Israel, Cuba, Angola, Vietnam, Syria, Taiwan, and North Korea.) Some of these have been spending more than 20% of their GDPs on the militaries.[6] But *low* spending does not necessarily mean the military is unimportant. In the following list of the LDCs where military spending was less than 1.6% of GDP during 1972 to 1988, the armed forces played an important role in government in the ones marked with an asterisk: Bangladesh, Brazil,* Costa Rica (which, uniquely, has no army at all), Côte d'Ivoire, Dominican Republic,* Fiji,* Ghana,* Haiti,* Jamaica, Mauritius, Mexico, Nepal, Niger,* Panama,* Paraguay,* Sierra Leone.*

Research on what influences LDC military spending as a percentage of GDP points to the following factors: the danger or actuality of wars (obviously), high income, large inflows of capital, a military government, and long borders. One factor that tends to reduce such spending is a heavy existing burden of debt. It follows that the military must be something of a luxury item. Otherwise very poor countries would spend a *greater* proportion of their GDP on the military, which typically they do not do.[7]

Military spending clearly competes with other uses for the funds. Table 5.2 presents recent data on military spending as a percentage of the social spending on education and health in the countries concerned.

Of course, defenders of military spending would point out that a strong military can be an advantage in a disturbed world. There were 82 armed conflicts just in the four years 1989 to 1992, all but three of which were domestic in nature rather than international. Most of these were in the LDCs.[8] When the military is

TABLE 5.2 MILITARY SPENDING AS PERCENTAGE OF SOCIAL SPENDING, 1990–1991

Syria	373
Oman	293
Iraq	271
Burma (Myanmar)	222
Angola	208
Somalia	200
Yemen	197
Ethiopia	190
Saudi Arabia	151
Jordan	138

Source: HDR 1994, 34. Social spending is defined as the combined government spending on education and health.

used to promote law and order, the effect can undoubtedly be beneficial. All too often, however, a strong military is used to enforce repression.[9] And unfortunately, aggressive or pugnacious countries such as Iraq and Iran are often willing to incur the highest costs to support their militaries, forcing hitherto peaceful neighbors to become more belligerent as well.[10]

In any case, Tables 5.1 and 5.2 give some idea of the potential for raising development expenditures if defense costs could be reduced. Many countries could double their spending on health care or infrastructure with the money they spend on the military. Some progress has already been made, with military spending by the LDCs starting to decline in the mid-1980s, the fall mostly due to cuts in Syria, Egypt, and Latin America.[11] (That decline has mostly been on outlays for heavy weapons, and not for small arms or personnel expenditures.)[12] The decline has also been less than for most other government outlays; the military is often protected from spending cuts. The United Nations estimates that during the period 1987 to 1994, the "peace dividend" to LDCs that reduced their military spending was $125 billion, equal to about three years of foreign aid from the developed countries. UN sources suggest that in the near future (to the year 2000), continued annual defense spending cuts of 3% would be fully feasible.[13]

The Cuts Can Be Harmful

Certainly there are some forms of government spending that, if cut, would free resources for activities that would do more to promote economic development. Every example discussed in this section represents an opportunity to increase productive investment spending on physical and human capital. Whether the opportunity will soon be seized is a difficult matter of politics and social psychology. It must be emphasized that the seeming irrationality of some types of government spending is in the eye of the beholder. From the point of view of the ruling party, the spending on state enterprises, subsidies, and the military is rational and perhaps even necessary if the government is to stay in office. The dilemma of a politicized economy looms ever more important as an obstacle to development, and the dilemma is not easily escaped.

THE DEBATE ON MILITARY SPENDING AND GROWTH

A debate exists on the impact of military spending. An earlier view was that defense spending is positively correlated to growth.[14] It is undoubtedly true that military spending can bring technical innovation (though the technology is often too advanced for use in the civilian sector), provide training, and contribute to institution building and industrialization. The question is not that, but whether spending for the military detracts from the other forms of government spending that would have contributed even more. The balance of scholarly opinion has now tipped toward a recognition that the economic impact on growth of maintaining a strong military is a negative one, with a higher proportion of defense spending correlated with lower economic growth. Among the reasons underlying this conclusion are that military spending can distort labor markets, displace other production and imports, reduce social expenditures, and create macroeconomic instability through budget deficits.[15] The reduction in private investment and absorption of scarce human capital can be especially serious. Even the idea that military aid allows for greater spending in other sectors runs up against the problem that military aid often leads to *more* local defense spending, not less.

Essentially, the economic benefits of a reduction in military spending do not emerge from what happens to GDP in the short run, but from the change in the composition of output toward items that increase people's welfare.[16]

All this being said about government spending, it is necessary to remain cautious. The criticisms can be overdone. In the developed countries, the tide in the 1980s ran strongly against government involvement in the economy, especially in the United States and Great Britain. This view had a substantial influence on aid-giving institutions and on economists generally. But it must be remembered that in LDCs the infrastructure of transport, communications, credit, and public goods such as education and health must involve government participation and investment to some significant degree. Any recommendation to cut bloated government spending, to reduce the crowding out of private investment, and to decrease the politicization of economics presumably reflects a desire to increase the efficiency of an economy and further its development prospects. If it carries beyond this so that desirable government investment in infrastructure is not undertaken or is cut back, and public goods are not provided in sufficient quantity and quality, then an economy will be less efficient, not more so.

So it is rather alarming to find that when Mexico decided to cut spending in the 1980s, it cut its public investment as a percentage of GDP by nearly a half, and its public outlays for education by about one-third.[17] Spending cuts lay behind Costa Rica's reductions of its health and education budgets by about a quarter. In a sample of 15 countries encountering serious debt problems during the 1980s, spending cutbacks caused a decline in real total government expenditure of nearly one-fifth, with *capital* spending falling by more than a third, while these governments chose to cut their *current* spending by only 7.8%. Outlays on these economies' infrastructures fell about a quarter, social spending about 15%, and defense by only about 5%. To avoid problems with health, nutrition, housing, and so forth, it is much preferable to curtail services to the middle class and shift the spending to the poor. These choices are critically important, and the methods for making informed judgments are explored in Chapter 12.

MACRO IMBALANCES: INFLATION AND THE LDCS

The combination of difficulties in raising sufficient government revenues and cutting unnecessary government spending leads to a rather obvious conclusion. The government may end up with a budget deficit. Considerable evidence exists that the financing of deficits by monetary expansion will cause an inflation. Or, if the deficit financing is carried on by the sale of bonds to the public, higher real rates of interest or increased financial repression will be the result. Higher interest rates cut private investment, and so does increased financial repression.[18]

LDC governments have often chosen the alternative of financing the deficit through the creation of new money. As a result, inflation is a frequent problem. Adding to the danger, governments may believe that deliberate inflation can even be desirable, for reasons explored below. The question of adequate finance for development is therefore always close to the question of whether the macroeconomy will be a stable one. This section explores the issue.

The Prevalence of Inflation in the LDCs

Undoubtedly inflation has become a serious disease in the LDCs, reaching average levels never seen before. In these countries, the average rate of inflation was only 10% between 1965 and 1973. But it was 71% from 1980 to 1991.[19] Table 5.3 shows the wide gap in inflation between the developed countries and the LDCs. The usual technical reason for the greater inflation was the financing of budget deficits by new money creation. According to the World Bank, nearly 47% of the government deficits have recently been financed by borrowing from central banks, which is the fastest method for creating new money.[20] Immediately the question arises as

TABLE 5.3 ANNUAL INFLATION IN CONSUMER PRICES, PERCENTAGE

	1992	1993
Developed countries	3.3	2.9
All LDCs	38.8	45.9
Africa	40.6	31.7
Asia	7.4	9.5
Latin America, Caribbean	165.8	236.5

Source: IMF, *World Economic Outlook 1994*, 13, 22.

to why a central bank would permit these tactics. The answer is that most LDC central banks are not as independent of government as is, say, the U.S. Federal Reserve System. According to a World Bank index of central bank independence, only one LDC bank, that of Egypt, has as much independence as the U.S. Fed.[21]

The inflation is not at all uniform, however, as the Table 5.3 indicates. Latin America exhibits much the greatest degree of inflation; Asia the least.

In the countries where macroeconomic instability is at its worst, the government, unable to raise its revenues or cut its spending, has probably come to depend on what economists call the *seigniorage* from new money issues.[22] Seigniorage is the principle that new money is cheap to create (a currency note costs only a few U.S. cents to print, and a government's bank deposits can be added to by a simple bookkeeping entry), whereas the new money can be spent at its face value. Thus it might cost the Poverian government only 30 povos to print 1000 in new povos, which could then be spent at their full face value by the government to buy goods and services. Seigniorage in the late 1980s was 4% or more of GDP in Argentina, Peru, and Zaire, among others.[23] At times the figure has been over 6% in Argentina and Bolivia.[24] Seigniorage is estimated to have reached as much as 70% of government revenue in a number of countries, though figures in the range of 20% have been more common.[25]

The reputation of inflation is sufficiently bad, and the damage it has done when it is severe is so well-known, that it comes as something of a surprise to find that there once was some optimism that inflation could be used successfully as a tool of development finance. That is where we shall begin our analysis.

Forced Saving: Inflationary Finance as a Tool of Development

A government may attempt to fund development expenditure by means of forced saving through inflation. Forced saving works as follows: The government runs an inflationary budget deficit financed by the creation of new money. Assuming full employment, the new government spending associated with this deficit will bid away output from private consumption. In real terms, the private sector must consume less because the government consumes more. If the private sector consumes less, it must save more. It thus endures "forced saving," which is akin to a tax.* Another element in the forced saving is that government's tax revenue may rise

*The enthusiasm once felt for forced saving as a tool of growth strategy stemmed from the observation of economists that inflationary government spending might lead to a larger stock of capital goods and hence to eventual further output. Deficit spending used for financing capital formation could directly increase productive capacity, leading to a stream of new output. When the output is sold on the market, it could dampen the inflationary consequences of the deficit. Because the effect of the deficit-financed spending is to increase supply, it will thus restrain inflation. In the long run, the inflation might thus be a limited one, "self-destructive," so to speak. How self-destuctive it is depends on how quickly the new output is forthcoming and how large it is. (It was agreed by all that a budget deficit used to finance a war, to pay the government's wage bill, or to construct public monuments or government buildings would have a more violent inflationary impact because these forms of government spending will not eventually increase the stock of consumer goods.)

more than proportionately because the tax system is progressive. The rise in government tax collection is also a reduction in private consumption, hence forced saving. Often, however, it is the other way round. Government tax collection is unable to keep pace with inflation if the tax system depends heavily on excise and sales taxes and if there is a lag in tax collections. This will especially be the case if price controls are utilized. In these cases, taxes may fall as a percent of GNP and even more deficit spending will have to be engaged in than otherwise.*

As John Maynard Keynes said of forced saving,

> The method is condemned, but its efficacy, up to a point, must be admitted. A government can live by this means when it can live by no other. It is the form of taxation which the public finds hardest to evade and even the weakest government can enforce, when it can enforce nothing else.[26]

Recent analysis suggests strongly that the decision to force saving through the inflation tax is correlated with political instability in the country using the tactic.[27]

A Monetary View of Forced Saving It enhances understanding to look at forced saving in monetary terms. If government printing of money is financing the budget deficit and is causing the inflation, then the real value of the already existing money stock held as transactions balances will decline. To restore the real value of the money stock, holders will have to reduce their consumption to acquire the larger balances—this is the forced saving. Intriguingly, within narrow limits the process would not be inflationary. For example, if real GDP growth is 4%, then on a broad average the demand for real money holdings to restore the value of transactions balances will rise from + 0.6% to + 1.2% of GDP. (The figures differ from country to country; careful study is needed for individual cases.) New money growth within that range would then not be inflationary because people would add the money to their transactions holdings. The government could purchase real goods with the newly created money, their value deflated by whatever price increase has occurred.

This process of forced saving could conceivably work until inflation reached the point where people cut their real money holdings, that is, until velocity increases. That point is thought to be at an inflation rate between perhaps 33% and 200%. Thus, the maximum likely yield from inflationary finance is perhaps 2% to 11% of GDP, but this is uncertain, and many economists would argue that the higher side of this scale is far *too* high.[28] Eventually, because of the inflation, people would not be willing to increase their real holdings of money and would simply make their existing stock of money work harder. In that case, velocity increases and inflation outruns the annual change in the money supply.

A serious obstacle to intelligent use of inflationary finance is that the information needed to determine exactly the degree of permissible stimulus is difficult to

---

*The lag problem is often a serious one. If there is a lag in tax collections, say of three months, inflation of 1% per month lowers the real value of taxes collected by 3%; a six-months' delay lowers it almost 6%. At 5% per month inflation, the figures are 13.6% and 25.4%, respectively. See Richard Goode, *Government Finance in Developing Countries* (Washington, D.C., 1984), 212–227.

ascertain. Worse, government willpower to avoid further damaging inflation may be lacking. Wishful thinking may all too easily overtake rational economic analysis. For example, Peru's planning commission has used a dangerously inaccurate argument that budget deficits lead to increased consumption, which thus lowers average costs of production, and accordingly means the deficits are not inflationary; Uganda at one point in the 1980s issued new money to finance its budget deficit and at the same time revalued its currency upward by three times with a hang-the-consequences spirit that defied reason.[29] Although these are egregious cases, use of moderate inflation as a tool of development most often does seem to run out of control.

Other Arguments for Inflationary Finance There might be other situations, usually more debatable, when a case might be made for inflationary finance. In countries where prices have been relatively stable (and there are still some), there may be significant "money illusion" for labor, landlords, and capitalists. All may decide to work harder or allow the factors they own to work more intensely in order to obtain a higher money income, even if real income does not increase. Because goods prices may rise faster than costs, inflation could also redistribute income to profit-earning entrepreneurs, thus possibly promoting the prospects for development as the entrepreneurs increase their saving and investment. Simultaneously, inflation may raise the rate of return on investment relative to general interest rates. This would be true whenever the inflation premium in interest rates underestimates the degree of actual price increases. Investment is thus stimulated. Unfortunately, any possible advantage is likely to accrue to a government only in the very short run; behavior will change as inflation comes to be anticipated, as we examine later. In particular, inflation will not lead to a higher reward for investment if interest rates rise fully to take account of the inflationary expectations of bondholders and other lenders. Predictably, this will happen after the elapse of only a short period of time.

Suppressing Inflation with Controls A last possibility for deficit financing without apparent inflation is to suppress the inflation with controls. Price fixing, rationing, licensing of investment, exchange control, government propaganda, and dozens of other measures may play a part in such "disequilibrium systems." The widespread use of these tools in wartime has led to an alternative name, the "war finance approach." In essence, this approach worked reasonably well in most major countries during World Wars I and II. It certainly can work when there is sufficient popular enthusiasm for some cause so that the public accepts the inflation-suppressing measures.

More commonly, however, insoluble problems erupt. Lack of public support leads to the growth of large black markets, controllable only with an extensive police-state apparatus. LDCs employing a disequilibrium system often lack the able and honest administrators needed to make the mechanism work. In fact, of the countries that could use a disequilibrium system, it would appear that LDCs as a group would be least able to do so for this reason. Finally, economic theory reminds us that the supporting price controls, rationing, and other tools had better be very short term in nature or else serious economic distortions will arise as the price system fails to give adequate signals.

The Adverse Consequences of Inflation

Advocates of inflation as a tool of development must consider a number of detrimental consequences. Against any possible advantages, there will be the likelihood of the following economic distortions, all of which could occur at the same time and each of which could be potentially serious.

1. The impact on saving and investment may be adverse. Productive saving will be reduced if people put their income into assets considered to be hedges, such as land, buildings, gold, silver, jewelry, or stocks of goods that people believe will advance in value with the inflation. Banks, suffering an outflow of deposits, may find themselves in distress, possibly increasing their lending to less-solvent borrowers to keep them alive. For such reasons, during Argentina's early-1980s inflation, approximately 15% of that country's banks failed.[30] Inflation, especially when it is not fully predictable, can also hinder investment plans. Firms will try to find hedges rather than investing. In the face of uncertainty, it is often very easy to postpone or cancel investment plans.
2. Inflation obscures signals about relative prices, especially when it is unsteady. It punishes people who simply guess less well than others and can result in large transfers from lenders to debtors. These losers may instigate political upheaval.[31]
3. Groups with political or economic power will attempt to defend themselves. Those with political influence push for government subsidies, supplements, and price floors. Those with economic power use the strike. Groups with this sort of leverage may well keep up with the inflation, and their success may even fuel it. In the LDCs, this leaves only a few groups within society whose consumption can be squeezed by the inflation. Professional people, government employees, unorganized industrial workers, and landless laborers are the most vulnerable, and it is difficult to justify treading on these classes, some of which are small and important for development and one of which (landless laborers) is very large and very poor.
4. Inflation may have serious effects on income distribution. It may frighten people who have just entered or are on the margin of the cash economy and drive them back to subsistence production because of their growing distrust of money. The poor may have few opportunities for hedging. Large firms with access to government-supported low-interest loans prosper in comparison with small firms.
5. If inflation is faster than it is in a country's trading partners, imported goods become relatively cheaper, while exports become more expensive. There is a rise in the value of the former, a fall in the latter. As a result, the foreign exchange rate will depreciate if the rate is floating, or the balance of trade will move adversely if the rate is fixed. Currency depreciation, by boosting

the price of imports, feeds back on the rate of inflation when domestic substitutes are unavailable or high in price. Governments may impose trade barriers against imports to halt the slide of the foreign exchange rate under floating rates or the increasing balance of trade deficit under fixed rates.

6. Foreign capital is repelled, while domestic savers attempt to invest abroad (capital flight). In the late 1980s, it was believed that about two-thirds of the private foreign assets owned by residents of LDCs was the result of these residents exporting their capital. It was common to find that capital held abroad amounted to as much as a third of all the foreign debt a country had run up.[32] The capital flight from Argentina, Mexico, and Brazil was especially large. The outflow raises real interest rates because the supply of loanable funds is lower than it otherwise would be, so investment falls. The foreign exchange rate depreciates because people are using the domestic currency to purchase foreign currencies such as the dollar. Tax collections decline because capital held abroad is much harder for the tax authorities to detect.

Structural Arguments That Inflation Is Likely to Be More Serious in LDCs

There is a justified fear that the political and economic structure of many LDCs may make inflation less easy to control in these countries. The political economy of the question is broad and does not admit of easy solutions. The demand for modern, up-to-date social welfare programs in education, social security, and health care, among others, may be the cause of a country's inflationary spending in the first place. Public provision of food and transport may swell budgets, and subsidies in these sectors may go far beyond the ability of the public to pay for them in prices, rates, fares, and fees. Commonly, public enterprises have been run at a loss and have suffered from swollen employment figures because of over hiring and the difficulty of firing or laying off employees. Almost all LDCs with high rates of inflation have large public-sector deficits as a percent of their GNPs, and these deficits mean the country is spending more than it can afford. Meanwhile, as we have already seen, tax yields may not rise in proportion to the inflation if income and corporate taxes are unimportant or are not progressive. With tax revenues not keeping pace, inflation is further fueled. Populist governments may raise wages and other spending without a tax increase, financing their programs by borrowing from a pliable central bank. The resulting inflation is often countered by freezing the prices of basic goods, which results in shortages and inefficiencies.

Disturbingly, the economic structure of many LDCs, as well as the political structure, may be especially conducive to the transmission of the inflation. Bottlenecks caused by shortages of skilled labor and certain indispensable types of capital equipment may always be close to the surface. Such bottlenecks may arise long before full employment is reached in LDCs that are attempting to utilize deficit financing. In addition, resource immobility, itself a symptom of underdevelopment, means that transfers of resources into bottleneck areas may be slow. Lack of information and good economic data, high risk, and long-established traditional patterns of production all contribute to the immobility. These factors lead to the conclusion that the basic structure of many LDCs could be more conducive to inflation than the more flexible structure of the developed economies.

This structuralist view of inflation was pioneered in South American, particularly Chilean, academic circles.[33] It suggests that the pure inflationary effect of money supply increases will, all things equal, set in earlier in an LDC because of the structural and institutional blockages. This conclusion is presented in Figure 5.1. In Panel b, notice how the aggregate supply curve in LDCs may start to turn upward at a point below the output level where the curve would begin its upward turn in a more flexible, developed economy (shown in Panel a). In the language of a macroeconomics course, the potential level of output may be lower in LDCs than in developed countries (and the associated natural rate of unemployment below which inflation will break out would therefore be higher). Moreover, bottlenecks and inflexibilities may also mean that an LDC's aggregate supply curve goes vertical at an output level lower than in a comparable developed country.

To trace the argument, assume that aggregate demand expands from AD_1 to AD_2, say because of money creation to finance a budget deficit. In that case, the flexibility of resources in a developed country (Panel a) would prevent inflation from breaking out and the price level would remain at P_1. In an LDC subject to

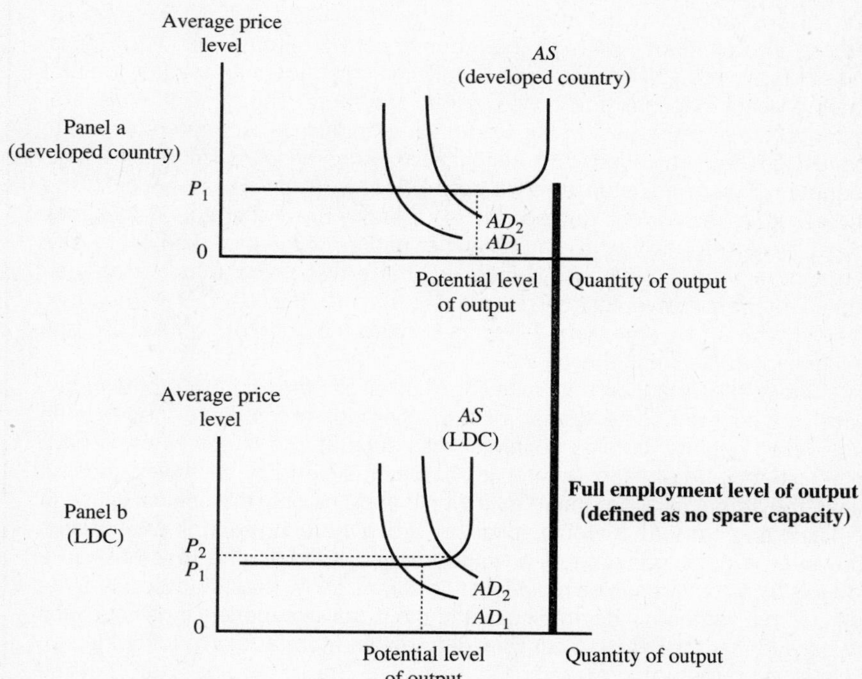

Figure 5.1 The aggregate supply curve of an LDC, subject to structural bottlenecks and rigidities, may turn upward and then vertical below the levels of output where this would happen in a developed country. LDCs in this situation are susceptible to structural inflation; a rise in aggregate demand from AD_1 to AD_2 would cause prices to rise in (b) but not in (a).

inflexibility (Panel b), inflation *would* break out, however, with the price level rising from P_1 to P_2.

The upshot is that an LDC's structural considerations may be such that inflation is generated even without serious budget deficits and monetary overheating. In such a case, supply-side reforms to lend greater flexibility to the economy would clearly be called for.

INDEXING

In reaction to what it saw as structural problems difficult to solve with conventional tools, Brazil pioneered indexing in the mid-1960s. Indexing is a system wherein the effects of inflation are assimilated without attacking the causes. (The first country to use the idea was Iceland, which is a very small economy, in 1939. Finland followed in 1944, and Israel was also an early convert, adopting indexing shortly after its independence. But Brazil was the first large economy to employ this policy on a wide scale.) With Brazilian inflation running at over 90% in 1964, economists there, led by the influential finance minister Roberto Campos, felt that standard monetary and fiscal solutions would reduce growth too drastically. Their solution was to incorporate escalator clauses (known in the United States as COLA or Cost of Living Adjustments) into almost all phases of economic activity. From small beginnings, these clauses by 1967 covered cost of living adjustments for wages, interest rates on bank deposits and bonds, taxes, and rents. The principle was later extended to asset values. In the full flower of indexing, corporate stocks and bonds, government bonds and securities, savings accounts, and even legal judgments were adjusted upward according to the latest price index. The increases in value were not subject to taxation. Brazilians argued that they could live comfortably with a much higher degree of inflation than could, say, Americans, where much less is indexed. There was some evidence on their side. The Brazilian average real growth rate from 1970 to 1977, 9.8% per year, ranked with a few other world leaders despite the country's annual average inflation of 29% during this period.

Today, the enthusiasm for indexing in Brazil and the numerous other countries that adopted some version of the scheme is much diminished.[34] In an unindexed country, outside supply shocks such as the OPEC oil crisis have only a temporary inflationary impact before their effects die away. Indeed, even the structuralist argument as a whole explains only the original cause of inflation and not why it would spiral upward. Where indexing is widespread, however, a price rise triggers a wage rise and then another price rise in a vicious circle. The resulting rapid inflation carries costs even if adverse effects on income distribution do not occur, and the Brazilian experience gives reason to believe that the indexing has been somewhat more effective for holders of capital than for wage earners. For example, Brazil's original plan indexed according to an expected rate of inflation, but the estimates were often too low, so some groups fell behind the inflation. At other times, Brazil did not index all wages fully. Current checking accounts were not indexed either. The poor have a special problem: Any assets they hold will likely be in cash, which is never indexed.[35]

One major cost of serious inflation appears to be the rapid obsolescence of knowledge concerning prices. Studies showed that during the mid-1980s inflations in fully indexed Israel and equally indexed Argentina, annual price rises of about 400% in the former and 1000% in the latter discouraged people from shopping around. With such rapid changes, consumers lost track of how prices compare at different stores. Israelis asked to state a price for the same type and brand of shoes gave answers varying by as much as 20 times. In Argentina, supermarket managers in one chain were getting new price lists from headquarters on average once every 1.3 days.[36] Understandably, the term *menu cost* is used to describe this situation of outdated information. There are also so-called shoe-leather costs, the expenditure of time and money to move out of cash balances and low-interest deposits into higher yields. With real rates of return of, say, 3% or 4% completely submerged by the wave of inflation, people search for assets where indexing works more quickly and avoid investing in physical capital where the return is in the future. A vivid example of shoe-leather costs in countries suffering from heavy inflation is the rush to sell the local currency for dollars or other foreign exchange as soon as any balances are obtained.

Indexing is now seen as abandonment of the fight against inflation. In a reaction against this psychological surrender, numerous governments have pulled back from the idea. In the developed countries, beginning in 1983, Iceland suspended its almost total index system as a major contributor to inflation, and Belgium, Finland, and Italy have retreated as well. Chile deindexed in 1982. Even in Brazil, the scheme's major proponent, the government lost its enthusiasm, first reducing the degree of indexing and ending it altogether in 1994. (Though there is strong resistance to such steps from organized labor and firms desirous of protecting their flow of cheap credit.) All in all, it is now far more common to find *deindexing* proposed as a solution to inflation than the reverse.

The Relationship Between Inflation and Growth

The actual statistics on inflation in the LDCs reveal a mixed case. We have already seen that inflation is somewhat more prevalent in the less developed world than in the developed countries. The median rate in the LDCs was about 10% from 1980 to 1991 compared to about 4% in the developed countries. (Using median instead of mean prevents the hyperinflations in several countries—five had inflations averaging over 100% from 1980 to 1991—from skewing the results. The mean for the LDCs in 1991 was 71.0%.)[37] There is, however, no persuasive evidence that slightly higher rates of inflation or even rather rapid ones do anything significant to discourage reasonable growth in real terms. Table 5.4 gives examples of both moderately high inflation accompanied by good growth performance (but fewer than before—the previous edition of this book listed six countries in this category compared to two in this one) and moderately high inflation accompanied by poor growth. Similarly, the table also presents examples of both low inflation and good growth, and low inflation and poor growth.

It is reasonably clear that some degree of inflation, if that inflation remains stable and is anticipated, *may* possibly do little damage to economic growth. As seen in Table 5.4, Chile is a good example of a country that has maintained excellent growth for some time, even with inflation staying in the 20% range. A number of authorities conclude that even inflation running up to 50% or so per year can be compatible with reasonable growth.

Yet an expanding amount of research makes the case that high inflation, even when it is anticipated, is harmful to economic growth. The findings have come both from empirical work[38] and from theoretical models and simulations.[39] For example, evidence from a sample of 50 LDCs indicates that an increase in inflation of 10 percentage points a year cuts the growth in the capital stock by about 0.30 of a percentage point and reduces the growth of productivity by about 0.15 of a percentage point.[40] According to Stanley Fischer, a country with an inflation rate 100 percentage points higher than another country (for example, 110% per year compared to 10%) will have a growth rate of GDP lower by 3.9 percentage points.[41] One of the greatest problems with even moderate inflation in the range of 15% to 20% is the risk that the rate will accelerate. If that risk of acceleration is widely feared, then an economy will suffer from uncertainty and reduced investment.

Hyperinflations Harm Growth Hyperinflations are quite another thing. They are clearly inimical to growth. As with any major bout of inflation, the proximate cause is money creation to fund government spending in excess of revenues. The government may have decided to do so in order to maintain spending in response to some supply shock such as an oil crisis or an embargo on foreign trade, or union pressures for higher wages, or an inability to restrain high-spending politicians. When moderate inflations turn into hyperinflations, it is usually because central banks and treasuries lose track of where the spending is going. Politicians want subsidies to protect their constituents against the effects of the inflation. Similarly ministries want to protect their budgets. Officials who hold back on their demands will find their interests have been ruined. A free-for-all develops with a compliant central bank providing new money to meet the requests.[42]

In Figure 5.2, fiscal deficits and money creation push aggregate demand even further into inflationary territory (from AD_1 to AD_2). In response to increasing prices, unions fight for wage increases while government and private firms raise the prices of the production inputs that they produce. Inflationary expectations become entrenched among all economic actors. As a result of the increases in the costs of production and the expectation of more of the same, the aggregate supply curve rises from AS_1 to AS_2. The new money to support these increases is then poured into the system by the central bank, raising aggregate demand again to AD_3. That causes more inflation, more cost increases, further upward shifts in aggregate supply, more money creation, and a hyperinflationary spiral.

TABLE 5.4 ANNUAL AVERAGE RATES OF INFLATION AND GROWTH, 1980–1992

	Inflation (percent)	Growth (percent)
	Moderately High Inflation, Good Growth	
Chile	20.5	3.7
Turkey	46.3	2.9
	Moderately High Inflation, Low Growth	
Sierra Leone	60.8	–1.4
Uruguay	66.2	–1.0
Venezuela	22.7	–0.8
Paraguay	25.2	–0.7
Nigeria	19.4	–0.4
Mexico	62.4	–0.2
Ghana	38.7	–0.1
	Low Inflation, High Growth	
South Korea	5.9	8.5
China	6.5	7.6
Thailand	4.2	6.0
Singapore	2.0	5.3
Chad	0.9	3.4
Pakistan	7.1	3.1
	Low Inflation, Low Growth	
Niger	1.7	–4.3
Ethiopia	2.8	–1.9
Panama	2.1	–1.2
Congo	0.5	–0.8
Bénin	1.7	–0.7

Note: Growth is change in real GNP per capita.

Source: WDR 1994, 162–163.

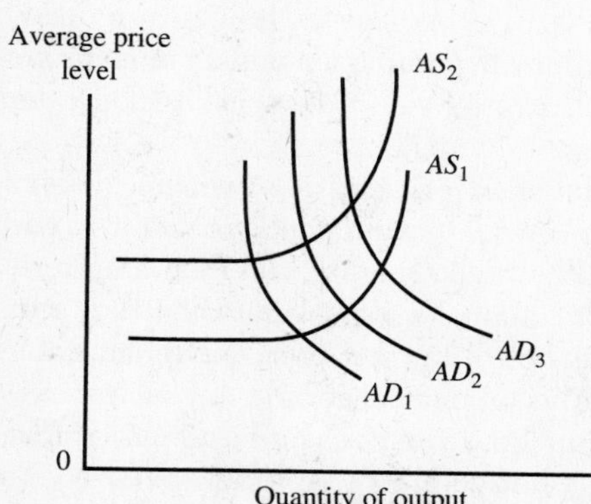

Figure 5.2 A hyperinflationary spiral often involves initial increases in aggregate demand, triggering cost increases and expectations of more of the same. This, in turn, causes the government to create new money to finance its increasing budget deficit, which further serves to raise the rate of inflation.

TABLE 5.5 HYPERINFLATION AND GROWTH (ANNUAL AVERAGE RATES, 1980–1992)

Country	Annual Rate of Inflation (percent)	Growth of GDP (percent)
Argentina	402.3	–0.9
Bolivia	220.9	–1.5
Brazil	370.2	0.4
Nicaragua	656.2	–5.3
Peru	311.7	–2.8

Note: The maximum monthly inflation rates in four of these were Peru, 396% in August 1990; Argentina, 197% in July 1989; Bolivia, 182% in February 1985; and Brazil, 81.3% in March 1990. See Zarazaga, "How a Little Inflation Can Lead to a Lot," 3.

Source: WDR 1994, 162–163.

There have not been many hyperinflations, but even though the sample size is small, it does appear to convey a lesson, as shown in Table 5.5. Growth in all these economies was poor and mostly negative. Notice that the definition of hyperinflation employed here—"very bad," over 200% or so—is less rigorous than that of Philip Cagan, who set the original bounds for the term.[43] Cagan defined hyperinflation as setting in when the inflation rate reaches 50% per month, corresponding to an annual rate of 12,800%. (At that rate, money loses over 99% of its purchasing power within a year.) Many students of hyperinflation also add to the definition the proviso that the inflation is accelerating.

In hyperinflations, "dollarization" becomes prevalent: People rush to exchange any domestic money they receive into dollars or other hard foreign currencies, and actual transactions are increasingly made in the foreign moneys. For example, in 1982 Bolivians were holding in value about 50% again more dollars than pesos in their bank accounts, compared with only 10% ten years before. In some Latin America countries, dollarization has reached as much as 80% of the total money supply. Governments sometimes attempt to prohibit this (such as Bolivia in 1982 and Peru in 1985). But the prohibition typically just drives the dollarized economy underground. In that case, dollarization means a given government budget deficit will be more inflationary than it would be otherwise, because the tax base is reduced as people conceal their transactions. Even after a hyperinflation ends, a momentum to further dollarization may still exist as risk-averse holders of money seek greater security for their assets.[44]

The wrenching experience of hyperinflation provides a convincing lesson: Hyperinflations may in the end be easier to control than mild inflations. Firms and banks can live with the mild sort of, say, 50%, by allowing for it in their long-term contracts. But inflations of 500% or 1000% annually, especially when they vary unpredictably, will cause contracts to break down. Furthermore, moderate stable inflation is sufficiently tolerable so that expectations concerning a government's behavior are difficult to alter. Hyperinflation, however, ends up being intolerable, so when governments decide to take steps, they will be more widely believed. So

A LOOK AT BOLIVIA'S HYPERINFLATION

The effects of Bolivia's hyperinflation and its sudden end have been carefully studied.[45] From 329% in 1982, that country's inflation rose to 2700% in 1984. Nicely printed bank notes became the country's third-largest import, after wheat and mining equipment. They soon became torn and tattered because coins disappeared, their value having vanished, and bank notes served as the fractional currency. (These wear out even faster than they would otherwise because of the tendency for the velocity of circulation to increase during a hyperinflation.) At one point in 1985, the most common bill of 1000 would buy one bag of tea; 68 pounds of the notes were needed to buy a television set. But the set and the tea would soon be even more expensive, for in that year inflation was running at an annual rate of about 12,000%. Real growth was negative, –5.8% annually from 1980 to 1984, and it was believed that the economy was working at only about 80% of its potential.*

the end to hyperinflations can appear almost miraculous. They can die away in a month or a week. How can it be done?

Controlling a Hyperinflation: Orthodox Measures

Let us address the issue of what might be done if a country finds itself in growth-inhibiting hyperinflation and attempts to bring it to an end.

A Currency Reform A typical cosmetic first step will be to make the currency more convenient by withdrawing the old money and replacing it with a new one that lops off a certain percent of the nominal value. Frequently the ratio selected is one of the new currency to 1000 of the old. Argentina, Brazil, Israel, and Mexico have done so. Sometimes, though, the situation is so far gone that the rate chosen is a million or 100 million to one, or even more. The inconvenience of writing so many zeroes on bills and checks ends, the ugly stickers with extra zeroes on gas pumps and cash registers disappear, and eight-digit calculators, once thoroughly clogged, become useful once again.

*A worse case can be found in wartime Yugoslavia (Serbia and Montenegro). Yugoslav inflation in August 1993 was 1,880%, which at an annualized rate is 363 quadrillion percent. In November it reached 20,190%, an annualized rate of 45 octillion percent and not far from the highest monthly rate in the famous 1923 German hyperinflation. Toward the end of its inflation, Yugoslavia printed 500 billion dinar currency notes. A currency-stabilization program in January–February 1994 put an end to the money creation and the hyperinflation, though whether temporarily or permanently was not clear at the time of writing.

Monetary Stabilization A new currency, however, will be merely window dressing unless monetary and fiscal policies to halt the inflation are implemented.[46] On the monetary side, orthodox stabilization programs usually include a drastic initial cut in the money supply through a currency reform, as previously discussed, together with a great subsequent reduction in the rate of growth of the new money supply. The reduction in the money supply is crucial. With a rather strong correlation between money supply growth and rates of change in prices, the reduction will attack directly the main underlying cause of the hyperinflation.*

Figure 5.3 shows how a fall in the money supply will reduce aggregate demand from AD_1 to AD_2, leading to a decline in the average price level from P_2 to P_1.

Perhaps the government will limit its future monetary growth by law, and perhaps it will bolster this move by tying the foreign exchange rate to that of a low-inflation country. For example, Argentine legislation in 1991 prohibited the central bank from printing new money to finance deficits in the government budget unless

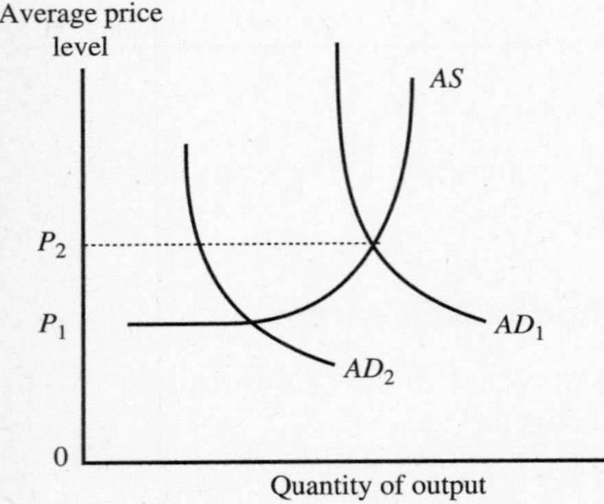

Figure 5.3 Orthodox stabilization involves reducing the money supply to decrease aggregate demand and hence the price level.

*Very generally over a large sample of LDCs, a one percentage point increase per year in the rate of growth of the money supply is associated with roughly a one percentage point per year increase in the rate of inflation. The relationship is strongest when money supply growth is high (over 15% per year) or low (under 5% per year). The relationship is even stronger when changing demand for money as reflected by growth rates of output, interest rates, and financial innovation is allowed for. See Robert Barro, *Macroeconomics* (New York, 1984), 152–158. Some countries are so distrustful of their ability to control their money supply that they actually issue no currency of their own and use foreign bank notes as their circulating medium. These must be acquired by the export of goods and services, so representing a high-cost money. The countries doing so must give up an independent monetary policy. Inflation will, however, be unlikely to exceed the rate in the issuing country, and exchange rate risks and currency conversion costs are reduced. Panama and Liberia, which use the U.S. dollar, are cases in point. Several Pacific island nations use the Australian dollar; much of former French West and French Equatorial Africa use a CFA franc (CFA being the French initials for French African Community) tied tightly to the French franc. No country in modern times went so far, however, as Cambodia under the Pol Pot regime. It abolished money. The Cambodian economy was already in ruins, so less harm ensued than might have been expected. Money was officially restored when Pol Pot was overthrown in 1979. In the late 1980s, Burma/Myanmar canceled all notes above 15 kyats, about $0.10 at the black market rate of exchange, to hit at currency speculators. Such notes made up about 80% of the money supply, so Burma found itself moving rapidly to an economy based on barter.

the money is backed by gold, foreign exchange, or certain "hard" government bonds. The Argentine currency is not only pegged to the U.S. dollar, but it must be backed by actual dollar assets. As a result of this strong medicine, inflation plummeted from over 3000% in 1989 and over 2000% in 1992 to 21% in the months following the reform.[47]

Fiscal Stabilization and Liberalization Cuts in government expenditure and higher taxes on the fiscal side will usually be required as well. The public sector deficit, doubtlessly huge and financed by money creation, will be sharply cut at the same time. Many superfluous government workers may be laid off, wage increases for the remaining workers will be limited, state enterprises will be required to balance their budgets, and expensive subsidies will be cut back. The macroeconomic effect will be similar to what happens when the money supply is cut. Aggregate demand will decrease, as in Figure 5.3, and the average price level will decline.

At the same time, liberalization of the economy may be considered. Liberalization involves lifting price controls, freeing interest rates, and ending other government controls on the economy. To control price increases, tariffs on imports may be reduced and quotas augmented, thereby providing more competition in the private sector. Sharp reductions in export taxation will have the same effect. The private sector may be enlarged substantially by the sale into private hands of state-owned enterprises. Many restrictions on financial flows may be relaxed; the exchange rate may be floated. Indexing of wages may be ended.

Liberalization is supply side policy. Its purpose is to move the position of the aggregate supply curve. Perhaps the liberalizing measures increase efficiency, allowing a greater amount to be produced at the same cost as before. That would mean a movement of AS to the right in Figure 5.4 with the economy now able to produce more (Q_2 instead of Q_1) at any given price level such as P_1. Or perhaps the

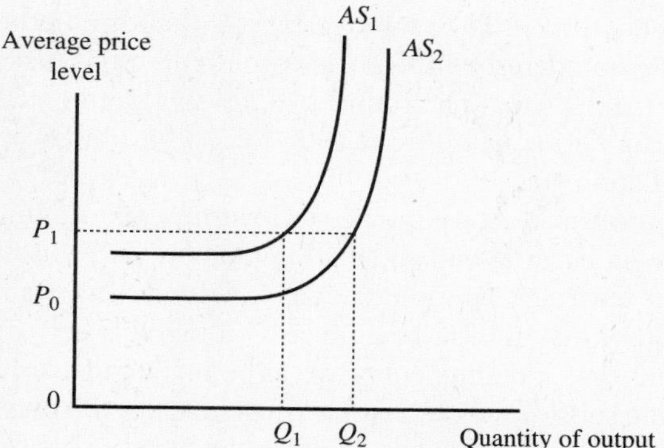

Figure 5.4 Liberalization is designed to make the economy operate more efficiently. It may allow more output at a given price level, thereby shifting the aggregate supply curve to the right. Or, it may cause a decline in the cost of a given quantity of output, shifting AS downward.

liberalizing measures lower the cost of producing a given quantity of output. That could be seen as a downward movement of AS, where a quantity of output Q_1 can now be produced at an average price P_0 instead of the previous average price P_1. Whether characterized as a rightward movement or a downward movement, aggregate supply shifts from AS_1 to AS_2.

Stabilizing and liberalizing simultaneously is debatable policy, however. Many economists would recommend that stabilization and liberalization not be undertaken at the same time because of the danger of damage from the two together. Stabilization, which is deflationary, squeezes the whole economy. Liberalization is expected eventually to make the economy more efficient, but this may not happen right away. Firms that have been protected from imports by trade barriers may be hard hit by liberalization, as may firms that have been receiving cheap loans. Too many of these firms may fail. If inflation is running at more than some mild figure such as 25%, stabilization before liberalization may be the preferred path. Advocates of this approach argue that high inflation must be stopped as the first priority so that prices accurately reflect scarcities. Only then should liberalization be embarked upon. (If inflation is below about 25%, however, then it may be possible to stabilize and liberalize at the same time.)

The Potential Damage from Orthodox Measures Even if well-designed, such orthodox programs are likely to carry a significant adverse side effect.[48] Restraining the budget deficit can reduce real spending and hence aggregate demand. This could cause a recession, perhaps a sharp one, with a steep decline in output and rise in unemployment. Liberalization takes time to have an effect. Since investors may wait for some time to see what happens, recovery may be slow. Capital that has flowed abroad may not flow back right away because its holders take a cautious approach.

Chile, for example, defeated an inflation running at 500% in 1975 (down to 90% in 1981), but part of the cost of this victory was a slump that hit bottom in 1982 with an unemployment rate for a time as high as 20% and a temporary decline in output that was also about 20%.[49] The main reason was that during the hyperinflation, investment was disrupted and inefficiencies proliferated.* It takes time as well as proper policy to turn the situation around. (To a lesser degree, the United States encountered the same costs when from 1980 to 1983 it employed tight money to control its own inflation.)

A deep recession can have unfortunate consequences. Governments running short of tax revenue might decide on harmful cuts in health, nutrition, and education programs, all of which might have serious ramifications for its citizens' well-being.[50] The politics of the situation may therefore be nearly intolerable for the government. It frequently happens that spending cuts have to be made in government employees' wages, in gasoline subsidies that make driving cheap for the owners of cars, in electricity and running water subsidies, in educational subsidies for universities and high schools, or in the social security programs that affect a

*In Chile's case, the unemployment was made more intractable by high minimum wages plus wage inflexibility caused by union power. See *WDR 1991*, 80.

favored few. Such attacks on the living standards of the middle class will probably be resisted with a fervor and an effectiveness that the poor would not be able to approach. Rather than cut the consumption of this middle class, the government might even prefer to cut public investment. In fact, it is not unusual to find substantial declines in the range of 30% or more in investment as a percentage of GDP in countries forced to cut their government spending.[51] Economic growth can certainly be affected negatively by zealous cutbacks in public investment that is complementary to private investment.[52]

Even in the long run, there is no guarantee that an orthodox program will succeed because such programs run the great risk of lacking credibility.[53] Commonly, stabilization is implemented too little and too late, with the inflationary fires not adequately damped at the point where the government loses its will to continue the battle. Next time around, control measures will be viewed even more skeptically than before. In some countries, a cycle of populist policies has arisen where a new government abandons orthodox anti-inflation programs in order to rescue the poor with new programs whose subsidies rekindle the inflation.[54]

In the end, the political difficulties even of well-managed stabilization and liberalization can be daunting. Success may have to be measured by the government's ability to fend off the political opposition. So the structure of government, including the ability of the opposition to obstruct, may hold special importance.[55]

Controlling a Hyperinflation with Heterodox Measures

The discomfort of orthodox policies against inflation led to a long popularity for what is called "heterodox" measures. A heterodox approach holds that direct government controls—in particular the sudden shock of wage-price freezes and a general deindexing of the economy—will remove inflationary expectations and in turn dampen the inflation itself. Proponents of such policies suggest that inflation has an inertia of its own that will continue because businesses find it too risky not to raise prices. Believers in the heterodox tactics contend further that the government's budget deficit is usually the result of inflation (because tax revenues have been reduced and interest rates raised) rather than the cause of it. Therefore, they believe that suppressing the inflation with controls will automatically improve the budget deficit. In effect, heterodox measures involving controls try to halt the cost increases that follow from a bout of inflation. Instead of allowing the upward movement in aggregate supply in Figure 5.4, they attempt to lock the *AS* curve in place, halting the inflationary spiral.

Undoubtedly, heterodox measures of control can catch the public imagination and mobilize public support, but they also carry economic costs of disequilibrium, shortage, and inefficiency (already discussed earlier in the chapter). The standard result appears to be poor long-run growth. It is thus probably fair to say that most development economists have been convinced by recent experience that heterodox policies are not a substitute for proper orthodox macroeconomic policy, including contractionary fiscal and monetary policies.[56] Often the controls lead to complacency, and may disguise, although only temporarily, the need for strong monetary and fiscal measures. Cutting inflation may indeed reduce the budget deficit, but if the lower deficit still delivers inflationary pressure, then problems remain.

Argentina's Austral Plan of 1985 took an inertial view of inflation, implying that price and wage controls were needed, but that fiscal and monetary changes were not. The Austral Plan's controls failed largely for two reasons. First, because the budgets of state corporations were not reduced, resulting in the continuation of a huge budget deficit equal to 7% of GDP in 1987 and creation of money to fund it. Second, because militant trade unions caused the wage controls to be relaxed in their favor.

Brazil's original Cruzado Plan of 1986 also took an inertial view of inflation. It consisted mostly of price controls and did not cut the federal budget or the budgets of state enterprises, nor did it halt indexing.[57] Government spending soared. A wage increase was allowed just at the start of the price-wage freeze, which was harmful because it increased demand. The Cruzado Plan failed even faster than Argentina's Austral Plan. Later, Brazil's Summer Plan of 1989 also used a price freeze along with various orthodox measures. But Brazil's government continued to create more money to pay the bills, the government was unwilling to give strong enforcement to the price controls, and so it was unable to halt the resulting inflation. Like the Cruzado Plan, the Summer Plan also collapsed.

In technical terms, the continuing budget deficits and money creation to finance them caused the aggregate demand curve to move out further even in the presence of controls over wages and some input prices. The impossibility of enforcing general economy-wide price controls, together with the vast increase in *AD*, brought hyperinflation in both countries.

Combining Heterodox and Orthodox Policies

Experience indicates that whatever the real impulse to an economy that starts the inflationary process, inflation cannot proceed without money creation involving the finance of government budget deficits. That being the case, control of inflation will require orthodox contractionary monetary and fiscal policy. But where inflation has lasted a long time, the public's expectations of further inflation are likely to have become entrenched. The orthodox measures of monetary and fiscal policy will be more successful if the inflationary expectations can be broken. A short episode of heterodox controls on wages and prices may be able to deliver the shock that weakens the expectations built up by chronic inflation. Such controls cannot succeed without orthodox monetary and fiscal measures to reduce or remove the inflationary pressures, as the experience of Brazil and Argentina vividly demonstrates. But they may be able to help.

The key is to use the heterodox controls to provide a powerful announcement effect that the government means business, and to allow a breathing space during which the orthodox measures can be introduced. After a few weeks, they should be removed. If they are not, damaging distortions to the price system are the likely result. Sadly, many governments have shown themselves quite unwilling to lift such controls within a short period of time. Yet a government that wants to implement an *optimal* policy may well want to find room for a short period of temporary controls that make a strong statement at the same time that they provide some room for orthodox maneuver. As we shall see in the next section, Israel's combination of orthodox and heterodox measures in 1985 is an outstanding example of successful use of this one-two punch to inflation.

Inflation and Growth: A Conclusion

All in all, the acute distress caused by hyperinflation and the difficulties of stabilizing an economy in its grip have made this a condition to be dreaded. Governments that attempt to use moderate inflation to promote growth may be unwilling or unable to keep this genie under control. The risk that inflation will escalate has considerably diminished the enthusiasm once felt for it as a tool of development finance. The best advice is to keep it firmly inside the bottle. If it escapes, then stabilization and liberalization will be required, and a short heterodox wage-price freeze may help to dampen inflationary expectations. Unfortunately, a short-run side effect of recession and unemployment is likely. But confidence in macroeconomic management must be restored if economic growth is to resume. The recession is a price that must be paid.

Recent Examples of Macroeconomic Reform

Several recent efforts at macroeconomic reform have commanded international attention. Five such attempts, which differ considerably in their details, are addressed here.

Argentina: Stern Stabilization, Wide-Ranging Liberalization[58] The main problem with Argentine reform before 1990 was that it employed wage and price controls without reducing the budget deficit, it was not believable, and it did little to spur greater efficiency. In 1990, Argentina's President Menem began the stabilization and liberalization by converting all seven-day time deposits over one million Australs ($560) into ten-year dollar bonds paying interest. The stroke removed from the economy 70% of all local currency, though the effect was somewhat limited because so much dollarization had already occurred. All tariffs were reduced from an average of 28% in 1989 to 18% in 1990, with many food product tariffs reduced to just 5%. Export taxation (imposed on many agricultural exports) has been ended. The foreign exchange market has been freed and more foreign investment has been permitted. Government approval is no longer needed for new investment, and performance requirements have been dropped. Indexing has been abolished as well, and subsidies to private industries have been removed. Substantial privatization is being achieved, with Aerolineas Argentinas sold to Iberia; the telephone system (Entel) privatized; and the water, electricity, and gas industries soon to follow.

Predictably, high unemployment (over 10%) followed as the economy adjusted to these reforms after many years of distortion. Argentina offers high hopes for good economic growth, but in that country there is no guarantee that populist politicians, or the obstreperous trade unions, or the army, will stay out of the arena.

Bolivia: Comprehensive Stabilization and Liberalization Bolivia's reform of 1985 was a comprehensive case of stabilization and liberalization. At the same time that Bolivia slashed the money supply and cut the government budget deficit, it moved to broad liberalization. It also cut many tariff rates to a single one of 10%, held a daily foreign exchange auction, freed interest rates, allowed banks to take deposits denominated in foreign currencies, made the central bank more independent of political pressures, dismissed many public employees, and repealed several restrictive labor laws that had established special holidays and prevented layoffs. Bolivia's combination of stabilization and liberalization was an exemplar of simultaneous use of these policies to end a hyperinflation.

Brazil: Many Tries, but Stabilization Still Not Certain[59] In 1990, Brazil decided to "eat up money." President Fernando Collor de Mello closed the banks, then froze the most common type of demand deposit for 18 months. Savings deposits were also frozen, except for the first $1,000. The government promised to impose large tax increases, scrap all its remaining subsidies, sell its state enterprises, and lay off 80,000 government workers. But the task was extremely difficult. Federal and state legislators sabotaged the effort by voting themselves high salaries, establishing more holidays for workers and one-third more pay than they would usually get, and providing 120 days of maternity leave for women and retirement with full pay after 35 years of work. (Many Brazilians had started work at age 14). They made it unconstitutional to fire civil servants and mandated that 44% of federal tax revenue must be devoted to revenue sharing with states and localities. At the same time the states borrowed heavily from state banks, which have the power to create money, in order to accommodate these deficits.

A new finance minister, Fernando Henrique Cardoso, took strong measures. Indexing was halted. Much progress has been made in reducing trade barriers. The threadbare former policy of unsustainable heterodox wage-price freezes was avoided. Brazil adopted a new currency, the *real*, which was linked to the dollar. (That was the country's fifth currency in ten years, following the new cruzado, the new cruzeiro, the old cruzado, and the old cruzeiro.) Inflation dropped from 50% per month in June 1994 (an annualized rate of almost 13,000%) to 2% per month in September (an annualized rate of 27%). It was undoubtedly an encouraging sign when, in October 1994, Brazil rewarded Cardoso by electing him as the country's new president. Whether the government would at last have the courage to keep the budget deficit and money creation under control is still an open question, however. Unions are calling for a return to indexing

Mexico: Major Attention to Liberalization Following Earlier Stabilization[60] Mexico's bad inflation of the late 1980s was controlled mainly by orthodox stabilization policies, which were then followed by wide-ranging liberalization. The centerpiece of Mexico's policy was the reform of international trade, culminating in the formation with Canada and the United States in the North American Free Trade Agreement (NAFTA) to reduce trade barriers. Mexico privatization has been rapid and extensive. Subsidies to state-owned enterprises were 2.9% of GDP in 1982, but fell below 1.5% in 1991. The Banco Nacional de Mexico, one of the three largest banks in Latin America, and Teléfonos de Mexico, the national telephone company, have been privatized. By February 1992, the number of state enterprises was down to only 234, compared to 1,155 in 1982. Among the important state enterprises, only the railways, electricity, oil (PEMEX), and the postal service will remain in the government sector.

India: Major Liberalization, Stabilization Not Needed[61] India needed little stabilization because its macro policies had not generated runaway inflation. But that country's punishing taxes, inconvertible currency, high trade barriers, restrictions on foreign ownership, and host of other pervasive government controls on business activity were damaging to economic growth. India has recently become a major example of liberalization, although much remains to be done. In 1992 to 1993, the Indian government under Prime Minister P. V. Rao cut the highest rate of income tax from 50% to 40%, floated the rupee and made it fully convertible, cut the percentage of nonconsumer goods covered by quotas from 40% to 5%, and reduced the compulsory channeling of imports through public sector agencies by 28 items to just eight. His government also cut the maximum tariff from 150% to 80%, although tariffs are still among the highest in the LDCs. India reduced export restraints by 80% (62 items are still restricted, seven are banned, ten channeled through government), allowed foreigners to enter stock markets, and permitted foreign investment in more sectors. The maximum permitted ownership by foreigners went from 40% to 51%, or 100% in certain high-tech or export-oriented industries and in tourism. One reason for the liberalization has been concern with China's great economic success, success that India has not emulated.

Israel: A Successful Combination of Orthodox and Heterodox Measures[62] Israel's Stabilization Plan of 1985 is perhaps the best example of a combined orthodox and heterodox effort, with macro stabilization achieved by contractionary monetary and fiscal means, but bolstered by temporary wage-price controls. A tight monetary policy was put in place, the budget deficit was reduced by 7 percentage points of GNP mostly by means of cuts in subsidies, and big boosts were made in the price of subsidized goods. Indexing was suspended. All of this was orthodox policy. At the same time, a wage-price freeze was imposed. This was heterodox. The effort to stabilize the inflation was largely successful, with Israel's inflation down to about 15% between 1987 and 1988.

Recent Reforms: A Conclusion Stabilizing and liberalizing the macroeconomy is a key element in increasing the financial flows necessary for economic development in the LDCs. Without a sound macroeconomy, these flows are likely to be inadequate. Not only will that be true of domestic finance, but of the foreign flows as well, as we address in the next two chapters.

NOTES

1. For surveys of the subject, listed alphabetically, see B. B. Bhattacharya, *Public Expenditure, Inflation, and Growth* (New York, 1985); Michael Bruno, Stanley Fischer, Elhanan Helpman, and Nissan Liviatan, with Leora Meridor, eds., *Lessons of Economic Stabilization and Its Aftermath* (Cambridge, Mass., 1991); Rudiger Dornbusch, *Stabilization, Debt, and Reform: Policy Analysis for Developing Countries* (Englewood Cliffs, N.J., 1993); Rudiger Dornbusch and Sebastian Edwards, eds., *The Macroeconomics of Populism in Latin America* (Chicago, 1992); Riccardo Faini, ed., *Fiscal Issues in Adjustment in Developing Countries* (New York, 1993); Stephan Haggard, Chung H.

Lee and Sylvia Maxfield, *The Politics of Finance in Developing Countries* (Ithaca, N.Y., 1994); Anne O. Krueger, *Political Economy of Policy Reform in Developing Countries* (Cambridge Mass., 1993); Gustav Ranis and Syed Mahmood, *The Political Economy of Development Policy Change* (Cambridge, Mass., 1992); and Lance Taylor, ed., *The Rocky Road to Reform: Adjustment, Income Distribution, and Growth in the Developing World* (Cambridge Mass., 1993).

2. The figures here and to follow are from Peter S. Heller and Alan A. Tait, "Government Employment and Pay: Some International Comparisons," IMF, quoted in *WDR 1983*, 102. A comprehensive account of state-operated enterprises is Leroy P. Jones, *Public Enterprise in Less Developed Countries* (Cambridge, 1982).
3. Benjamin Higgins and Jean Downing Higgins, *Economic Development of a Small Planet* (New York, 1979), 241; and *Wall Street Journal*, December 5, 1985.
4. Robert S. McNamara, "The Post-Cold War World: Implications for Military Expenditure in the Developing Countries," World Bank, *Proceedings of the World Bank Annual Conference on Development Economics 1991* (Washington, D.C., 1992), 95–125; *WDR 1991*, 140.
5. *IMF Survey*, May 30, 1994.
6. Jurgen Brauer, "Military Investments and Economic Growth in Developing Nations," *Economic Development and Cultural Change* 39, no. 4 (July 1991): 873–884; and Brauer, "Perilous Information Gap: Third World Military Expenditures," *Challenge* 34, no. 3 (May/June 1991): 54–58.
7. See Daniel P. Hewitt, "What Determines Military Expenditures," *Finance and Development* 28, no. 4 (December 1991): 22–25.
8. *HDR 1994*, 47.
9. See Brauer, "Military Investments and Economic Growth in Developing Nations," and Brauer, "Perilous Information Gap: Third World Military Expenditures."
10. Saadet Deger and Somnath Sen, "Military Expenditure, Aid, and Economic Development," World Bank, *Proceedings of the World Bank Annual Conference on Development Economics 1991* (Washington, D.C., 1992), 159–186.
11. *WDR 1991*, 142.
12. *The Economist*, June 4, 1994.
13. *HDR 1994*, 59.
14. See Emile Benoit, *Defense and Economic Growth in Developing Countries* (Lexington, Mass., 1973).
15. See, in alphabetical order, Saadet Deger, "Economic Development and Defense Expenditure," *Economic Development and Cultural Change* 35, no. 1 (October 1986): 179–196; Saadet Deger, *Military Expenditure in Third World Countries: The Economic Effects* (Henley-on-Thames, 1986); Saadet Deger and Somnath Sen, "Military Expenditure, Aid, and Economic Development," World Bank, *Proceedings of the World Bank Annual Conference on Development Economics 1991* (Washington, D.C., 1992): 159–186; Saadet Deger and Somnath Sen, "Military Expenditure, Spin-Off, and Economic Development," *Journal of Development Economics* 13, no. 1 (1983): 67–83; David Lim, "Another Look at Growth and Defense in Less Developed Countries" *Economic Development and Cultural Change* 31, no. 2 (1983): 377–384; and Alfred Maizels and Machiko K. Nissanke, "The Determinants of Military Expenditures in Developing Countries," *World Development* 14, no. 9 (September 1986): 1125–1140.
16. See Tamim Bayoumi, Daniel Hewitt, and Steven Symansky, "The Impact of Worldwide Military Spending Cuts on Developing Countries," IMF Working Paper 93/86 (1994).
17. For this paragraph, see *WDR 1988*, 108, 110, 113; Norman R. Hicks, "Expenditure Reductions in High-Debt Countries," *Finance and Development* 26, no. 1 (March 1989): 35–37; and *World Bank Research News* 7, no. 3 (Spring 1987).

18. See William Easterly and Klaus Schmidt-Hebbel, "Fiscal Deficits and Macroeconomic Performance in Developing Countries," *World Bank Research Observer* 8, no. 2 (July 1993): 211–237.
19. *HDR 1994*, 183.
20. *WDR 1989*, 61.
21. See the rankings in the *World Bank Policy Research Bulletin* 3, no. 5 (November/December 1992): 4.
22. See Stanley Fischer, "Seigniorage and the Case for a National Money," *Journal of Political Economy* 90, no. 2 (1982): table A2.
23. *WDR 1989*, 63.
24. Robin Burgess and Nicholas Stern, "Taxation and Development," *Journal of Economic Literature* 31, no. 2 (June 1993): 762–830; *WDR 1988*, 61.
25. See Alex Cukierman, Sebastian Edwards, and Guido Tabellini, "Seigniorage and Political Instability," *American Economic Review* 82, no. 3 (June 1992): 537–555.
26. John Maynard Keynes, *A Tract on Monetary Reform* (London, 1923), 41. Also see Easterly and Schmidt-Hebbel, "Fiscal Deficits and Macroeconomic Performance in Developing Countries."
27. See Sebastian Edwards, "The Political Economy of Inflation and Stabilization in Developing Countries," *Economic Development and Cultural Change* 42, no. 2 (January 1994): 235–266.
28. Goode, *Government Finance in Developing Countries*, 212–227
29. Rudiger Dornbusch, "Peru on the Brink," *Challenge* 31, no. 6 (November/December 1988): 31–37, citing the Peruvian planning document, *El Peru Heterodoxo: Un Modelo Economico* (July 1987); *The Economist*, June 20, 1987.
30. *WDR 1989*, 71.
31. Arnold C. Harberger, ed., *Economic Policy and Economic Growth* (San Francisco, 1984), 9–16.
32. See IMF, *World Economic Outlook 1987*, 82.
33. For a study, see Osvaldo Sunkel, *Development from Within: Toward a Neostructuralist Approach for Latin America* (Boulder, Colo., 1993).
34. See John Williamson, ed., *Inflation and Indexation: Argentina, Brazil, and Israel* (Cambridge, Mass., 1985), for a collection of papers on the subject.
35. *The Economist*, July 9, 1994.
36. *The Economist*, May 28, 1983; *The Manchester Guardian Weekly*, September 16, 1984, 17.
37. The figures are calculated from *HDR 1994*, 182–183, 206. A few other countries for which data are not published in this source also had bad inflations during the period.
38. An empirical study of growth and inflation in 47 countries is Roger Kormendi and Philip G. Meguire, "Macroeconomic Determinants of Growth: Cross Country Evidence," *Journal of Monetary Economics* 16, no. 2 (September 1985): 141–163.
39. See Robert Barro, "A Capital Market in an Equilibrium Business Cycle Model," *Econometrica* 48, no. 6 (September 1980): 1393–1417; Angelo Mascaro and Allan H. Meltzer, "Long and Short-term Interest Rates in a Risky World," *Journal of Monetary Economics* 12, no. 4 (November 1983): 485–518; and Alan C. Stockman, "Anticipated Inflation and the Capital Stock in a Cash-In-Advance Economy," *Journal of Monetary Economics* 8, no. 3 (November 1981): 387–393.
40. World Bank, *World Economic Outlook 1993*, 49.
41. Stanley Fischer, "The Role of Macroeconomic Factors in Growth," *NBER Working Paper No. 4565*, 1993.
42. See Carlos Zarazaga, "How a Little Inflation Can Lead to a Lot," Federal Reserve Bank of Philadelphia, *Business Review* (September/October 1994): 3–13.

43. In his classic essay, "The Monetary Dynamics of Hyperinflation," in Milton Friedman, ed., *Studies in the Quantity Theory of Money* (Chicago, 1956).
44. Guillermo A. Calvo and Carlos A. Végh, "Currency Substitution in High Inflation Countries," *Finance and Development* 30, no. 1 (March 1993): 34–37; Benedict Clements and Gerd Schwartz, "Currency Substitution: The Recent Experience of Bolivia," *World Development* 21, no. 11 (November 1993): 1883–1893.
45. See especially Jeffrey Sachs, "The Bolivian Hyperinflation and Stabilization," NBER Working Paper No. 2073 (1986). A gripping newspaper account is Sonia L. Nazario, "When Inflation Rate Is 116,000%, Prices Change by the Hour," *Wall Street Journal*, February 7, 1985.
46. For surveys of the subject, see (in alphabetical order): B. B. Bhattacharya, *Public Expenditure, Inflation, and Growth* (New York, 1985); Michael Bruno, *Inflation Stabilization: The Experience of Israel, Argentina, Brazil, Bolivia, and Mexico* (Cambridge, Mass., 1988); Michael Bruno, Stanley Fischer, Elhanan Helpman, and Nissan Liviatan, with Leora Meridor, eds., *Lessons of Economic Stabilization and Its Aftermath* (Cambridge, Mass., 1991); William R. Cline and Sidney Weintraub, eds., *Economic Stabilization in Developing Countries* (Washington, D.C., 1981); Vittorio Corbo and Jaime de Melo, "Lessons from the Southern Cone Policy Reforms," *World Bank Research Observer* 2, no. 2 (July 1987): 111–142; W. Max Corden, "Macroeconomic Adjustment in Developing Countries," *World Bank Research Observer* 4, no. 1 (January 1989): 51–64; W. Max Corden, "Protection and Liberalization: A Review of Analytical Issues," IMF Occasional Paper No. 54 (1987); Rudiger Dornbusch and Sebastian Edwards, eds., *The Macroeconomics of Populism in Latin America* (Chicago, 1992); Riccardo Faini, ed., *Fiscal Issues in Adjustment in Developing Countries* (New York, 1993); Moshin S. Khan, "Macroeconomic Adjustment in Developing Countries: A Policy Perspective," *World Bank Research Observer* 2, no. 1 (January 1987): 23–42; Anne O. Krueger, *Political Economy of Policy Reform in Developing Countries* (Cambridge, Mass., 1993); Sheila Page, ed., *Monetary Policy in Developing Countries* (London, 1993); and Lance Taylor, ed., *The Rocky Road to Reform: Adjustment, Income Distribution, and Growth in the Developing World* (Cambridge, Mass., 1993). A special issue of *World Development* 19, no. 11 (November 1991) edited by François Bourguignon, Jaime de Melo, and Christian Morrisson is entitled "Adjustment with Growth and Equity." For general modeling of macroeconomic reforms not otherwise referred to in this section, see J. Neary and S. van Wijnbergen, *Natural Resources and Macroeconomy* (Cambridge, Mass., 1986); Sebastian Edwards and L. Ahamed, eds., *Economic Adjustment and Exchange Rates in Developing Countries* (Chicago, 1986); and Lance Taylor, *Varieties of Stabilization Experience* (New York, 1988).
47. *International Economic Review*, February 1992.
48. The problem is considered in most of the works cited at the start of this section (see note 46). In addition, I used Eliana Cardoso, "Hyperinflation in Latin America," *Challenge* 32, no. 1 (January/February, 1989): 11–19; Rudiger Dornbusch, "Policies to Move from Stabilization to Growth," World Bank, *Proceedings of the World Bank Annual Conference on Development Economics 1990* (Washington, D.C., 1991); Andres Solimano, "Inflation and the Costs of Stabilization," *World Bank Research Observer* 5, no. 2 (July 1990): 167–186; Liaquat Ahamed, "Stabilization Policies in Developing Countries," *World Bank Research Observer* 1, no. 1 (1986): 99–105; a special issue of *World Development* 13, no. 8 (1985) entitled "Liberalization with Stabilization in the Southern Cone of Latin America"; a special issue of *Economic Development and Cultural Change* 34, no. 3 (1986), "Growth, Reform, and Adjustment: Latin America's Trade and Macroeconomic Policies in the 1970s and 1980s"; and Leland B. Yeager et al., *Experiences with Stopping Inflation* (Washington, D.C., 1981).

49. I used the following on Chilean experience during this period: Barry P. Bosworth, Rudiger Dornbusch, and Raúl Labán, eds., *The Chilean Economy: Policy Lessons and Challenges* (Washington, D.C., 1994); Arnold C. Harberger, "Observations on the Chilean Economy, 1973–1983," *Economic Development and Cultural Change* 33, no. 3 (1985): 451–462; Sebastian Edwards, "Stabilization with Liberalization: An Evaluation of Ten Years of Chile's Experiment with Free-Market Policies, 1973–1983," *Economic Development and Cultural Change* 33, no. 2 (1985): 223–254; Sebastian Edwards, "Monetarism in Chile, 1973–1983: Some Economic Puzzles," *Economic Development and Cultural Change* 34, no. 3 (1986): 535–559; Ricardo Ffrench-Davis, "The Monetarist Experiment in Chile: A Critical Survey," *World Development* 11, no. 11 (1983): 905–926; and various articles in *The Economist*.
50. For a discussion, see G. Cornia, R. Jolly, and F. Stewart, eds., *Adjustment with a Human Face* (Oxford, 1987); and Sebastian Edwards, "Structural Adjustment Policies in Highly Indebted Countries," NBER Working Paper No. 2502 (1988).
51. IMF, *World Economic Outlook 1988*, 77.
52. IMF, *World Economic Outlook 1993*, 49.
53. See Vittorio Corbo, Jaime de Melo, and James Tybout, "What Went Wrong with the Recent Reforms in the Southern Cone," *Economic Development and Cultural Change* 34, no. 3 (1986): 607–640.
54. See Rudiger Dornbusch and Sebastian Edwards, eds., *The Macroeconomics of Populism in Latin America* (Chicago, 1992); and Jeffrey D. Sachs, "Social Conflict and Populist Policies in Latin America," NBER Working Paper No. 2897 (1989).
55. Stephan Haggard and Steven B. Webb, "What Do We Know About the Political Economy of Economic Policy Reform," *World Bank Research Observer* 8, no. 2 (July 1993): 143–168.
56. Miguel A. Kiguel and Nissan Liviatan, "When Do Heterodox Stabilization Programs Work?" *World Bank Research Observer* 7, no. 1 (January 1992): 35–57; and Mario I. Blejer and Adrienne Cheasty, "High Inflation, Heterodox Stabilization, and Fiscal Policy," *World Development* 16, no. 8 (August 1988): 67–81.
57. See Werner Baer, *The Brazilian Economy* (New York, 1988).
58. See the special section on Argentina in *The Economist*, November 26, 1994.
59. See *International Economic Review*, November 1994; *The Economist*, December 7, 1991, July 2, 1994, July 9, 1994, and October 8, 1994; *Wall Street Journal*, October 14, 1994; *New York Times*, July 30, 1993.
60. See Pedro Aspe, *Economic Transformation the Mexican Way* (Cambridge, Mass., 1993); and Nora Lustig, *Mexico: The Remaking of an Economy* (Washington, D.C., 1993).
61. *International Economic Review*, June, 1992; *The Economist*, March 7, 1992 and March 6, 1993.
62. For a thorough recent study, see Leonardo Leiderman, *Inflation and Disinflation: the Israeli Experiment* (Chicago, 1993)

Chapter 6

Financing Development III

Inflows of Private Foreign Capital

This chapter begins a two-part consideration of the foreign alternatives for a country that wishes to invest more than it is willing or able to save domestically. The basic proposition is as before: A country can consume and invest no more than it can produce at home, plus any deficit in the current account balance ($M - X$) financed by financial inflows. Because of these flows of foreign finance, many LDCs do indeed invest far more than they save at home. In 1991, on average the least-developed LDCs saved only 2% of their GDP but were able to invest a much greater sum equal to 15% of their GDP because foreigners provided the additional saving making it possible. For all LDCs, the figures are much closer, 25% domestic saving and 26% investment—the middle-income LDCs are in general high savers domestically.[1]

Flows from abroad can be private or official, as seen in Table 6.1, which shows the situation in 1981 and 1991. In 1991, about 42% of the $205.3 billion total was in the form of private inflows, including purchases of stocks and bonds, foreign direct investment (FDI) in the branches of multinational firms, and bank loans. About 45% of the total flow was from public institutions such as national governments, the World Bank, and the International Monetary Fund, in the form of grants and loans. The remainder was export credits for the short-term financing of foreign trade. The private flows, which were growing rapidly in 1993–1994, are considered in this chapter. The official flows, which were fairly stable in 1993–1994, are treated in the following one.

TABLE 6.1 EXTERNAL GROSS FINANCIAL FLOWS TO LDCS, PERCENTAGE OF THE TOTAL (GROSS, PERCENT)

Year	Total	Bank loans	Equity (stocks)	Bonds	FDI	Public grants	Public loans	Export credits
1981	($156.9 bn.)	46.1	0.1	1.2	8.3	7.3	26.0	11.0
1991	($205.3 bn.)	17.4	3.7	4.8	16.5	14.5	30.8	16.5

Source: World Bank, *Global Economic Prospects and the Developing Countries* (Washington, D.C., 1993).

These flows have been quite volatile in recent years. In the early 1980s, they started to fall, mostly because bank loans collapsed as part of the so-called "debt crisis" that occurred during this period. They only started to rise again in 1987.[2] The rise in equity, bonds, and foreign direct investment to over 25% of the total in 1991 compared to only 9.6% in 1981 has been a remarkable development. Even more remarkable, the flow of private investment to the LDCs increased by about an additional 60% in 1993–1994, to a figure about three times more than all foreign aid from governments. Other major changes in the flows include their much greater concentration on a few favored LDCs, the considerably smaller amount coming in loans from banks, and the fact that the flows now go much more to private firms rather than to government or state enterprises.[3]

Foreign Capital Flows for Development Make Good Economic Sense

In general, a flow of finance from the developed countries to the LDCs makes good economic sense. In effect, the rich world does not absorb all its own output and is using some either for gifts and loans to or purchases of equity in poor countries. Rich countries are able to generate income over and above the desired domestic uses for these funds, whereas poor countries cannot. Financial capital is abundant in the developed world and scarce in the LDCs; there are many favorable opportunities for profitable investment in the latter.

As capital flows in from abroad, an LDC could finance investment for development purposes. In essence, the LDC incurs debt to the developed world and repays out of the higher national product made possible by the new investment. As long as the investments are profitable enough to allow payment of the interest on the loans and yield a further net return, the process is a sensible one, filling a savings gap between what can be saved at home and profitable investment opportunities. The majority of today's LDCs do just this, and indeed, so did many now-developed countries, especially the United States, which for most of the first 125 years after independence ran a current account deficit, importing foreign capital (much of it from London) to finance its expansion. Current account deficits (with imports greater than exports) involving capital inflows from abroad are quite normal and desirable in the development process. But it is also possible that things will temporarily go wrong, as they did in the debt crisis. That episode was terribly damaging to the LDCs' prospects of developing through capital flows from abroad, because bank loans to these countries collapsed.

FOREIGN PRIVATE INVESTMENT

Investment from private sources abroad is an important alternative for LDCs that wish to invest more domestically than they are able to save. Such private investment may be portfolio, that is, the purchase by foreigners of stocks or bonds but not involving a controlling ownership. It may also be direct, meaning the creation or acquisition of capital assets that are owned fully or in amounts large enough to imply control. The dividing line between the two is not always very clear. Australia has a 25% minimum figure of equity ownership for the term direct investment to apply. France uses 20%; the United States, Germany, and Sweden each use 10%. Great Britain and Japan make a value judgment and do not employ a fixed dividing line.

Portfolio Investment

In the nineteenth century, private, nonbank portfolio investment was important, with investors in Europe actively buying the shares and bonds of firms in the United States, Canada, Australia, New Zealand, Argentina, Chile, and others, especially in Latin America.[4] Britain was the chief source of the flows, investing 5% of its GNP abroad from 1870 to 1913. The funds, representing over one-quarter of all British saving, were used especially for railways and utilities (nearly two-thirds of the total) and for many types of heavy industry. There was also a vigorous government bond market involving the securities of national and regional governments. Both for private and government borrowing, the interest rates on the bonds were generally fixed and the maturities very long: 99-year bonds were not uncommon. After World War I, the balance swung to borrowing by governments, and the United States emerged as the major source of long-term capital.

There had been some troubles in this market for a long time.[5] All but one of the newly independent Latin American countries defaulted in the 1820s, and there were some further defaults in Latin America as well as in Egypt and Turkey in the 1870s and in Argentina and Brazil in the 1880s and 1890s. The financial disasters of the 1930s were much more general. After Germany's default in 1932, many LDCs followed suit. In all of Latin America, only Argentina continued to service its debt during the Great Depression. The result was severe restriction of this market, and for many years after World War II, private investors understandably considered portfolio investment in the LDCs a highly risky proposition. There are few recourses for a private holder of an LDC government bond if default occurs because the principle of sovereign risk permits a government to disallow suits against itself within its own borders. Neither were the LDCs very receptive to portfolio investment, which was discouraged with high taxation, foreign exchange restriction, and limits on the types of shares that could be held by foreigners. As a result, such flows were only half a billion dollars or less annually in the 1960s and early 1970s, often as little as one-tenth the figure for direct investment.

Now, however, in a 1990s phenomenon, portfolio investment flows to the LDCs are increasing rapidly. The total, only $7.5 billion in 1989, had reached $36.7 billion in 1992 and preliminary figures indicate a further large rise to $55.8 billion in 1993. In 1992, portfolio investment was over one-fifth of all capital flows to the LDCs. The investment, which involves either stock equity or debt instruments, is made in international securities markets or through direct purchase in LDC stock markets, as seen in Table 6.2.[6]

Some of the institutional arrangements in Table 6.2 are new. Country funds are mutual funds that sell shares in the fund to investors in developed countries and use the proceeds to buy stocks in LDC stock markets. For a few years, these country funds were the only form of investment permitted by some LDCs. But now that the rules have been liberalized, investors have shown that they prefer to pick their stocks. So country funds have fallen in popularity. Depository receipts are American or global. American depository receipts (ADRs) are negotiable equity-based instruments issued by U.S. banks which hold underlying stock in non-U.S. corporations. They are priced in dollars and pay dividends in dollars. (ADRs have become Mexico's largest source of portfolio capital.) Global depository receipts are the same thing, but are issued simultaneously in securities markets around the world. Direct equity purchase is less often permitted. All these forms of portfolio investment have been a means for developed-country investors to participate in the recent wave of privatization of state-owned enterprises, particularly in Latin America. The debt instruments in the table are more familiar. They include international bond issues, which are medium or long-term, and much smaller amounts of short-term commercial paper (CP) and certificates of deposit (CDs).[7]

Some of the portfolio investment is being made through an agency of the World Bank, the International Finance Corporation. In 1986, this agency announced an Emerging Markets Growth Fund (EMGF), which is investing $50 million in the stock markets of nine LDCs, while selling its own EMGF shares in

Table 6.2 Gross Portfolio Investment Flows to LDCs (billions of U.S. dollars)

	1989	1992
Portfolio equity investment of which	3.5	13.0
country funds	2.2	1.3
depository receipts	0.0	5.9
direct equity investment	1.3	5.8
Debt instruments (bonds, CP, and CDs)	4.0	23.7
Total	7.5	36.7

Note: The preliminary figures for 1993 presented in this source indicate a further large rise to a total of $55.8 billion, almost all of the rise in the form of debt instruments.

Source: Stijn Claessens and Sudarshan Gooptu, "Can Developing Countries Keep Foreign Capital Flowing In?" *Finance and Development* 31, no. 3 (September 1994): 62–65.

developed-country securities markets. The EMGF does not put more than 20% of its assets into any one country or over 5% in any one company.

Does Portfolio Investment Have Disadvantages? The dramatic increase in portfolio investment, most of it going to blue-chip private borrowers in the LDCs, is a welcome addition to financing in these areas. Are there disadvantages? Some, no doubt.[8] The volatility of the investment has been pronounced, and critics call attention to a casino mentality in some of these markets. A herd instinct seemed to be part of the sudden sell-off by investors that roiled Latin American, and especially Mexican, markets in early 1995. Changes in interest rates in developed countries often drive changes in the portfolio capital flows to the LDCs. The time horizon of this investment is largely medium-term, with the maturity of the bond issues (which make up most of it) averaging only about five years, much shorter than the long-term horizon for most development projects. Finally, and most importantly, the lending is very heavily concentrated in a few countries, mostly in Latin America. These received about half the 1993 total for portfolio investment; earlier, in 1989 to 1992, Argentina, Brazil, Mexico, South Korea, and Turkey received over two-thirds of it. Africa received virtually nothing from this source.

LDC Stock Markets For firms in the LDCs, sale of stock has certain advantages over loans. Loans must be serviced even when business conditions turn down, whereas dividends on stocks are paid only if there are profits. So more emphasis on stocks would have helped the LDCs during the worldwide recession of the 1980s and 1990s.

The success of some LDC stock markets has been a remarkable story.[9] The largest LDC market is currently Hong Kong's ($296 billion in 1994), followed by South Africa's and Taiwan's. Other large ones in order of their 1994 size are Malaysia, Mexico, South Korea, Singapore, India, Thailand, Brazil, and Chile. These countries list considerably over half of all the companies listed on all LDC markets, which numbered 13,000 in 1992 compared to 7,000 in 1983. Turnover in the 20 largest LDC stock markets rose by nearly 40 times in the 1980s, and by 35% in 1991 alone; over a decade, share values in these markets ($635 billion in 1991) increased by seven times. The total value of the stock in these markets, only about 6% of their nations' GDP in 1980, rose to 32% in 1990 (though that is still considerably short of the 60% in the developed countries).

In 1991, eight of the world's top ten stock markets in terms of price increases were in the LDCs, with Argentina, Colombia, Pakistan, Brazil, and Mexico making up the top five. Returns in these markets have been consistently higher on average than in developed-country stock markets.* The shares in these markets are what the private mutual funds in the developed countries buy, along with the resi-

*The International Finance Corporation calculated that the average return in 20 LDC stock markets was 148% during the period 1987 to 1992 (Latin America 321%, Asia 153%). That exceeded the return in the U.S. market of 119%. But it is also true that in 1991 6 of the 10 worst-performing markets were in the LDCs. Zimbabwe's shares fell by 55% in that year.

dents of the LDC themselves. The diversification of holdings will be especially helpful to the overseas purchasers whenever the swings in developed-country stock markets do not match the swings in the LDCs. Research indicates that though the LDC markets are more volatile than those of developed countries, their movements are not correlated with the movements in the developed countries or with each other.[10] (But LDC markets did undergo a fall along with those of the developed countries in the early 1990s recession, and major declines followed Mexico's problems in early 1995.)

The amount of investment in the securities markets of the developed countries is extremely large, now over $7 trillion. Developed-country pension funds, insurance companies, investment trusts, and the like have about $300 billion in new money to invest every year. A trend toward the purchase of LDC stocks might have a substantial impact. This route is now perhaps the LDC's best hope for obtaining new capital.

Generally, portfolio investment in the LDCs has risen in the countries with better macro policies, more liberal trade rules, more open foreign investment, and a better record of repaying debt. The process may be self-reinforcing in that the financing raises growth, which attracts more financing. Recently the portfolio inflows have included considerable stock and bond purchases by the LDCs' *own* citizens, who transferred their assets abroad as "flight capital" during the financially disturbed 1980s. Since 1989, some of this flight capital has been flowing back to the LDCs, helping to fuel the rise of these markets.[11]

DIRECT INVESTMENT: THE MULTINATIONALS

Private foreign direct investment (FDI) in the LDCs, $40 billion in 1992, has for many years been much larger than portfolio investment, though that relationship is now changing. The share of the world's foreign direct investment flows going to the LDCs fell during the financially troubled 1980s, but it rose again during the early 1990s. This investment has always attracted controversy because it involves the activities of the so-called multinationals. The common abbreviations for these are MNE for multinational enterprise, MNF for multinational firm, and MNC for multinational corporation.[12] Such enterprises usually have a home base with operations abroad.* The United Nations and many scholars argue that because the

*There are now about 35,000 MNEs controlling about 170,000 foreign affiliates. The top ten firms in 1993 by assets, not including banks and utilities, are Royal Dutch/Shell (British-Dutch), Ford (U.S.), General Motors (U.S.), Exxon (U.S.), IBM (U.S.), British Petroleum (British), Nestlé (Swiss), Unilever (British-Dutch), Asea Brown Boveri (Swiss-Swedish), and Philips Electronics (Dutch). The United States, Japan, and the EC account for 81% of total outward foreign direct investment. (The United States, with 31% of the total, Britain 21%, Japan 20%, Germany 8%, and France 6%, are the largest investors.) The United States dominates investment in Latin America, the Philippines, and Saudi Arabia; Japan leads in East Asia; and the EC is preeminent in Eastern Europe and Brazil. (But multinationals still employ less than 1% of the economically active population of the LDCs.) The figures are from "Recent Trends in FDI for the Developing World," *Finance and Development* 29, no. 1 (March 1992): 50–51, except for the last sentence, which is from *HDR 1992,* 52.

firms have a home base, the word *multinational* is not fully appropriate. They prefer the term *transnational corporation* (TNC).*

The Reasons Why Multinational Firms Engage in FDI

Multinational firms emerged in the middle of the nineteenth century, though their greatest growth did not come until a century later. They arose mostly because of the advantages in cost and convenience in dealing with foreign branches of the same firm, rather than independent firms in the host country. Transactions costs could be kept low by keeping as many decisions as possible within the multinational. Commercial secrecy involving technology was easier to police. There was far less risk that technology transferred to a foreign branch would leak to others than if the technology was sold or licensed. Servicing of a product could be supervised, an important means to keep the good reputation associated with a brand name. Economies of scale in management, inventory stocking, advertising, and other activities were other potential sources of gain. A multinational firm could deliberately locate its production facilities in a manner that would minimize labor, transport, and raw materials costs; and it could diffuse risk by spreading its operations among many countries. So business declines or political unrest that might be damaging to a firm operating in just one country might be little noticed by a multinational firm operating in many.[13]

The investment of multinational firms in developing countries has most often followed the growth of new markets in these countries for goods where the firms' superior technology and popular brand names lend advantages over domestic firms. MNEs are likely to be attracted by strong economic growth in the host country. MNEs are also lured by the existence of a large domestic market, macroeconomic stability, a good credit record, liberal trade policies including easy conversion of foreign exchange and profit repatriation, duty-free inputs, and tax breaks. Some firms stress that operations in LDCs can give them a strategic regional position.[14] Rather commonly, they seek to establish operations inside the protectionist trade barriers of an LDC pursuing an import substitution strategy. This is called *tariff jumping.* Generally, they prefer investing where markets are relatively similar to those at home or where the combination of factor inputs is comparable to those the firm is already skilled at handling. MNEs have no special advantage in designing products or marketing goods in environments far different from those they face at home, nor in organizing and managing factors of produc-

---

*Though developed countries are overwhelmingly the main source of FDI, some multinational investment flows from one LDC to another. Examples of moderately large investors are Brazil (active in the Middle East and West Africa), India (active in Indonesia and Malaysia), Hong Kong, Singapore, and South Korea. Brazil and Hong Kong are in the top 15 providers of multinational investment. LDC multinationals are said sometimes to provide more labor-intensive technologies and to be politically more acceptable than their developed-country brethren. See Louis T. Wells, Jr., *Third World Multinationals: The Rise of Foreign Investment from Developing Countries* (Cambridge, Mass., 1983). A skeptical view of the supposed advantages is Sanjaya Lall et al., *The New Multionationls: The Spread of Third World Enterprises* (Chichester, 1984). Singapore has even invested in the United States in electronics and South Korea in semiconductors.

tion when the mix and qualities are far different from what they are used to. That is one important reason why such firms either avoid the lowest-income countries or address themselves in these countries only to the middle- and upper-class markets familiar to them from their home operation.

Less frequently, though more in the news, MNEs have sought new sources of inputs. Examples include minerals and oil to offset declining reserves at home and to capture part of the rents on especially valuable deposits. Labor also can be an attraction, as when a multinational moves an operation overseas in search of cheaper wages, thereafter exporting the product back to the home market and elsewhere. (The proportion of MNE investment that shifts work to cheap labor is actually rather small, however.) As a company's multinational operations proliferate, the knowledge available to it about other markets increases, as does its confidence in that knowledge, which now comes at low cost. This is one reason why MNE reactions to changing economic conditions are both more rapid and more finely tuned than they were two decades ago.

Most MNE investment has traditionally been in manufacturing and primary products, but the most rapid growth is now in the service sector. Services have grown important because they cannot be so easily traded as goods. Many LDCs still do not welcome MNE operations in services, but such operations can be helpful to a country's export and general development effort if they increase efficiency, as, for example, when the telephone system works.

Given the capital shortage in the LDCs, these countries attract less of the world's FDI than might be expected.* In general, the least private investment flows to the lowest-income countries that have the smallest domestic markets, the least adequate infrastructure, the lowest stock of skilled labor, the lowest standards in education, health, and nutrition, the least commitment to private enterprise, the least stability in their political-economic environment, and the most damaging economic policies. Indeed, problems of this sort mean that the average return to capital investment is actually greater in the developed countries than in the LDCs. For U.S. foreign investors, returns averaged 14.1% for the LDCs in 1985 to 1989, compared to a return of 16.9% in the industrial countries. In a sample of 200 investments studied by the International Finance Corporation, investors considerably overestimated the real rates of return in the LDCs, expecting 21% but actually receiving only 12%. The lowest returns, which are only half of what they have been in Asia, have been in Africa because of the problems mentioned above.[15]

MNEs' intense interest in judging the riskiness of their overseas investment has led to a new growth industry: risk evaluation by specialized consulting firms. For example, the Economist Intelligence Unit in London gives A, B, C, D, and E ratings in three categories: lending and debt, politics and policies, and quality of economic management. The International Country Risk Guide ranks by political, financial, economic, and composite standards. In 1991, the highest LDC on this list was Singapore (ninth), which ranked just ahead of the United States (tenth).

*Though before World War II, when many of today's LDCs were colonies, about two-thirds of all foreign direct investment went to them.

Taiwan, at fourteenth, was ahead of France (eighteenth). South Korea was twenty-seventh. (The ten lowest-ranking countries in descending order were Guinea-Bissau [120th], and Zaire, Haiti, Ethiopia, Uganda, Burma/Myanmar, Iraq, Sudan, Somalia, and Liberia [129th].)[16]

The Investment Is Heavily Concentrated Of the FDI flowing to the LDCs, less than one-half of 1% goes to the least developed low-income countries. Just 11% goes to Africa, compared to 34% going to Latin America, and 52% to Asia. Most foreign direct investment is heavily concentrated in countries that have promoted export-led growth. The ten biggest recipients in 1991 were, in order by amount of investment, Mexico, China, Brazil, Malaysia, Argentina, Thailand, Indonesia, South Korea, Venezuela, and Turkey. The first five of these received almost exactly half of all FDI going to the LDCs.[17] Although the information is fragmentary and the range of data is wide, the share of exports accounted for by foreign majority-owned affiliates in many of these countries is about 20% to 30%, though it is much higher in some (for example, Singapore, where it has been as large as four-fifths.)[18]

Benefits to the LDCs from Foreign Direct Investment

Contrary to the early work on the subject, the most important benefits brought to the LDCs by the multinationals are not directly associated with the capital transfer itself. These benefits are wide in scope. Consumers gain because the investment may make available in larger quantity and better quality goods and services formerly high in price. The government may garner extra tax revenue from the expanded operations of foreign firms. Additional domestic investment may be stimulated because the new foreign operations open up profitable opportunities for supplying them with components or raw materials. The multinational may reduce production costs through its coordination of marketing and its ability in planning. MNEs may bring nonmarket, cost-reducing externalities to their hosts, including the technical knowledge that flows to the branches of MNEs, managerial ability, organizational competence, and the capacity to avoid the waste and inefficiency that might be present if the project were forced to depend on indigenous talent alone. These nonmarket advantages, especially the transfer of knowledge in all its forms, are now emphasized by most scholars as the key explanation as to why multinationals prefer to operate in LDCs themselves rather than to license production to local firms. Evidence from country studies in Côte d'Ivoire and Venezuela suggests that on average foreign-owned manufacturing firms are more productive than local firms.[19]

Some of these advantages will, of course, accrue as profit repatriated abroad by the MNE, but some will be reinvested or will be paid to local factors of production. Even when profit is repatriated, it must be kept in mind that no outflow will occur unless a profit is actually earned by the MNE, unlike debt where the outflow of interest and repayment of principal will occur in good times or bad. So countries hosting MNEs are less vulnerable to economic shocks than they would be if all capital were obtained from debt financing. Finally, MNEs can often export more easily from the LDCs because of their distribution and marketing networks. If they wish to export some of their production, they may become influential lobbyists for world free trade because tariffs and quotas in developed-country markets would otherwise interfere with these plans. When it pushes for free trade, a country with little clout in the U.S. Congress or EC parliaments may find it has puissant allies in its corps of multinationals.

Even the role of the multinationals in investment itself does not primarily involve the direct transfer of capital into an LDC. A large amount of capital is transferred by means of commercial bank loans to LDC subsidiaries of MNEs. To a significant degree, often more so than the direct and indirect capital transfers, MNEs also add to saving by building retained earnings, which may be reinvested in the operation. Much of this saving is still foreign, done by the corporate shareholders in the parent country, who receive lower dividends than they would have otherwise. (In the figures for foreign direct investment, these reinvested earnings are included. They generally make up about half the total.) To the degree that multinationals serve to raise local income, they also play a part in stimulating domestic saving, as already noted in Chapter 4.

Assessing the Benefits and Costs of Multinationals

Ownership by foreign firms is much more visible both physically and politically than are stock and bond holdings and bank loans. This makes the operations of multinationals a highly controversial topic, involving a wide variety of issues, some of which are only vaguely related to saving, investment, management, and technology. Yet a country cannot have these inflows without facing the other issues as well, so it is convenient to take them up here. LDCs have gone through a long stage of learning how to deal with multinationals. The early "acceptance" school of thought gave way to "rejection" in many countries. Nowadays an "assertive pragmatism" marks policy in many LDCs, with these countries now actively seeking FDI. Rejection, although still found, is sinking in importance.[20]

MULTINATIONAL ACTIVITIES ARE SAID TO "FILL GAPS"

Economists sometimes speak of multinationals "filling gaps" in economic development. Their gap models usually emphasize the role of foreign companies in (1) bringing saving from abroad so that domestic investment can be larger than domestic saving; (2) generating foreign exchange receipts and so filling a gap between the desired earnings of foreign exchange and what a country could otherwise acquire through exports, aid, and so forth in the absence of the multinationals; (3) alleviating the shortage of managerial and technical skills; and (4) mobilizing new government revenue through taxation of the multinationals, so filling a gap between the revenues a government wants to expend and what it can acquire through local taxation.

Economic Analysis Suggests Benefits for Both the MNEs and the LDCs Concerning the transfer of capital into a recipient LDC, the standard microeconomic argument in favor of foreign direct investment is that the investment benefits both parties to the transaction. For the LDCs, the rise in real income is greater than the profits earned by the investor and repatriated to the foreign country. The argument is presented in simple diagrammatic form in Figure 6.1.[21] A rich and capital-abundant country's marginal product of capital (*MP* of *K*) is shown by the downward-sloping line relating to origin 0 on the left side of the diagram; a poor and capital-short country's *MP* of *K* is drawn relating to origin 0′ on the right. Assume a large stock of capital (0*K*) in the rich country. If profits per unit (0*A*) are equal to the marginal product of capital (*KB* = 0*A*), then total returns to domestic capital are 0*ABK*. Assume that the quantity of capital (0′*K*) in the LDC is small. Then the marginal product of capital there is *KC* = 0′*D*, and total returns to domestic capital in the LDC are thus 0′*KCD*. Because the area under an *MP* curve is the return to all factors, then 0′*KCJ* is the total income earned, and this minus the return to capital is the return to other factors, 0′*KCJ* – 0′*KCD* = *CJD*. This return will be wages if the model is limited to just the two factors, capital and labor.

Now consider what happens if rich country owners of capital seek out the higher per unit returns in the LDC by making a transfer *KK*′ of capital to the poor country, either by lending or direct investment (including reinvested earnings). Transferring that amount will equalize the return on capital in the two countries because the two *MP* curves cross there at *E*.

First, note the advantage to the rich country. Consider just the transferred capital *KK*′. Profits earned on that capital when it was in the rich country, *K′FBK*,

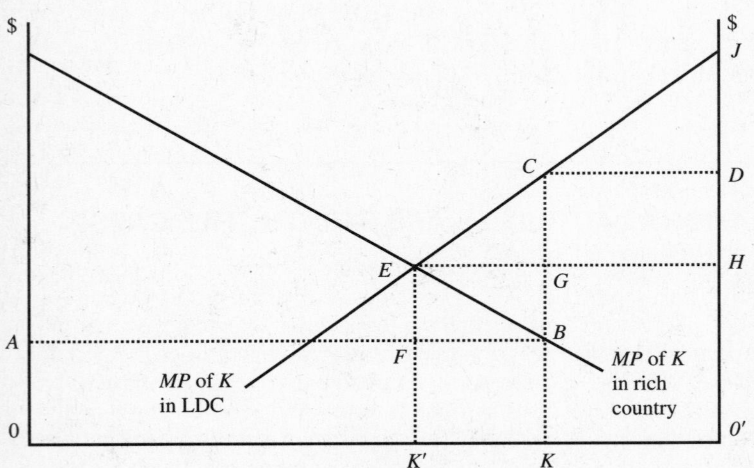

Figure 6.1 In the standard neoclassical economic argument, both the multinational firms that invest in an LDC and the LDC gain from the investment.

is now lost, and total incomes earned at home in the rich country fall by *K'EBK*. But the additional returns from the new investment in the LDC are *K'EGK*. There is a clear gain to the developed country of *BEG*, so providing the motive for the transfer from the investor's point of view. This mirrors logic based on the theory of diminishing returns, that the return to capital will be greater where capital is less abundant. (The risk on an individual investment in an LDC is higher, of course, but the investors who transferred the capital must have thought that it was to their advantage to do so.)

Now consider the advantage to the LDC. It loses *K'EGK* as profit repatriation on direct investment, but it gains *K'ECK* in greater total income, so increasing its total income by *ECG*. The world is ahead by $BEG + ECG = ECB$.

The transfer of capital will have an effect on income distribution that can be traced in the diagram. In the LDC, domestic capitalists find their returns reduced from *KCD*0′ to *KGH*0′. The real income of labor rises from *CJD* to *EJH*, an increase of *ECDH*. Much of this rise is a transfer away from domestic capitalists to labor in the amount *GCDH*, but the rest of the rise (*ECG*) is a net addition to the incomes earned in the country receiving the capital.

The model portrayed here is within a framework of competition and full employment and ignores possible monopolistic or oligopolistic behavior of MNEs, as is discussed later. Yet it does make a salient point that on occasion is forgotten: Adding to capital where capital is scarce is likely to bring benefits.

Costs to the LDCs Against these benefits must be weighed the costs—both economic and political. There is an active mythology concerning the multinationals, much of which, both pro and con, is politically motivated and has a strong emotional content that must be recognized. Hard-line defenders of free enterprise may see nary a negative, pointing to the overwhelming advantages of competition in free markets. The opposition, which sometimes comprises xenophobes with a "blame the foreigner" attitude, deplores foreign control over a country's resources and may see nefarious exploiters wherever it looks. Indeed, foreign firms can often make convenient scapegoats. Other opposition can come from local firms who fear the competition and trade unions in the MNE's home country who claim that jobs are exported. Here we shall attempt to confine the discussion to economic analysis and forgo the rhetoric.

The major economic complaints are (1) excessive repatriation of profits and dependence on imported inputs, with associated balance of payments problems and crowding out of domestic firms in local capital markets; (2) the high cost of enticing the MNEs through tax reduction or other means; (3) MNEs' monopolistic behavior, with overpricing, stultifying effects on domestic entrepreneurship and management that blunts local initiatives and displaces local firms, and political meddling that undermines sovereignty; (4) their overcharges for patents and technical knowledge through the use of an internal price system for transfers between branches of the same firm; (5) their marketing of inappropriate goods; and (6) their use of inappropriate technology. Next we expand on these accusations, weigh them, and allow the multinationals an opportunity for rebuttal.

Repatriation of Profits, Balance of Payments Problems Repatriation of profits has been criticized for leading to lower levels of reinvestment in the country concerned, with an attendant greater dependence on local capital markets and the crowding out of local borrowers. The repatriation involves foreign exchange, which has to be generated somehow. In an efficient economy with market-determined exchange rates and that follows the dictates of comparative advantage, this may not be a serious problem. Widespread trade barriers plus artificial exchange rates in the LDCs defended by controls on currency movements may, however, mean that obtaining the necessary foreign exchange is not so easy. Moreover, to avoid technical disappointments and to maintain product quality, MNEs may decide to import a large proportion of their inputs.

A defender of the MNEs would argue that the fault lies with the controls and the trade barriers rather than with the multinationals. If the MNE's investment is otherwise beneficial, then it makes much more sense to attack the controls and barriers directly. The defender would also point out that the sheer size of repatriated profits is not necessarily evidence of wrongdoing. All things being equal, one would expect profits to be higher where capital is in short supply, and indeed, predicted high returns should actually increase an LDC's leverage during the bargaining over entry by an MNE. A common measure of high profits—comparing repatriated earnings to new investment by a single MNE or by the multinationals as a group in a given year—is illegitimate, or so the defender would argue. Although this information is easily obtained from the balance of payments data, the comparison should instead be between repatriated earnings and the stock of capital accumulated from previous investment and on which the returns have been earned.

Another consideration is that the reinvested earnings of the multinational provides low-cost improvement for the balance of payments if the funds would otherwise have been borrowed abroad. In any case, these flows are not the only influence on the balance of payments as the positive increase in exports and decrease in imports caused by the MNE would also have to be considered. Moreover, after MNEs acquire more local knowledge and confidence concerning their ability to employ and manage local factors of production, they tend to increase their purchases in the host country.

As for the argument that crowding out of local investment will occur, MNEs and their supporters maintain that if the investment is otherwise beneficial, then it should be pursued. Any crowding out would be of investment with lower rates of return.

Cost of Attracting Multinationals There is a cost to be considered whenever tax reductions, rebates, concessions, large investment allowances, low interest rates, cheap locations for factories, tariff protection, and public subsidies are granted to attract multinational companies to a particular LDC. For most MNEs, such breaks do not appear to provide the major lure. A large domestic market, cheap labor and raw materials, low inflation, steady growth, and market pricing are all more important. Yet given the intense competition among LDCs for MNE investment, it is conceivable that in the short run the costs of subsidies and tax breaks could be larger than the economic benefits provided by the firms' operations, with resources shifted from more to less efficient uses. Consumers and taxpayers from LDCs would thus subsidize firms from rich countries. Even though LDCs would learn from the experience, the dimension and longevity of the losses might be great. For LDCs, regional agreements to limit tax and subsidy competition to attract MNEs would be advantageous.

Monopolistic Behavior If there is price competition in world markets, we can define overpricing as

$$P_o = \frac{P_m - P_w}{P_w}$$

where $P_m =$ the price charged by the MNE, $P_w =$ the world price, and $P_o =$ the percentage of overpricing.[22] There is no doubt that price discrimination of this sort is frequently found. It is, however, usually based on protectionist trade barriers, as otherwise the price differential could not be maintained. The defender of the MNEs would note that purely domestic firms (as opposed to multinationals) would also overprice if given the chance. In this sense, the LDC's own high trade barriers lead to the exercise of market power. The multinational might, of course, lobby to this end, especially when negotiating its initial entry to a country.

Worldwide monopoly overpricing is much rarer than domestic overpricing because an aspiring monopolist must face the potential competition from all countries, not just one. It is clear that the oligopolistic behavior of numerous industries in a national market (including such industries as the manufacture of steel, autos, aircraft, ships, and electronic goods) is very much less so when the firms face competition from other countries in LDC markets.

Some MNEs do, however, appear to operate in a worldwide oligopolistic structure where they are able to utilize price discrimination based on product differentiation, proprietary technology, or some other secure asset. Different prices can be charged in different countries simply by ordering branch managers not to engage in unauthorized international trade. A case in point is the behavior of pharmaceutical multinationals, which sometimes charge high prices for brand-name drugs that could be purchased for one-tenth as much under a generic label. Drugs are big business in the LDCs, which spend 50% to 60% of their health care budgets on them as opposed to only 15% to 20% in developed countries. Doctors in LDCs often own their own pharmacies. Lack of competition sometimes leads to big markups above the world price and much market segmentation. For example, streptomycin has been sold in Guinea at a price 12 times higher than in Egypt. In retaliation against this behavior, Bangladesh has banned 1700 drugs, India has used unpopular price controls, and Sri Lanka has a state marketing agency that buys pharmaceuticals at world prices.

Some lessons from the past warn that LDC governments had better be vigilant and that, where it exists, uncontrolled behavior by a large and monopolistic MNE can be far from benevolent. Multinationals might attempt to bribe public officials for their benefit, lobby for low taxes, or meddle in domestic politics. Yet a wide range of examples, including the breaking of the power of the Western oil companies in most LDCs, the exposure of bribery and political meddling by ITT in Chile, and the eventual defanging of the United Fruit Company in Central America all demonstrate that MNE behavior can be effectively policed by LDCs that decide they want to do so.* Further extensions to the argument that monopsonistic MNEs underpay for hastily extracted natural resources, usually process them outside of the LDCs in the developed countries, and pollute the environment of their host, are considered later in the book.

Overcharging for Patents and Technical Knowledge The world trade in know-how is large, and most of this trade is contained within the developed world. The 10% or so of the trade that is between the developed countries and the LDCs can, however, be a substantial percentage of the latter's export earnings and is a greater proportion of income than was spent by Europe, the United States, and Japan for imported technology during their periods of development. To take an example from a recent year, over 11% of Mexico's export revenues was paid out in royalties and fees for patents and technologies. Because the amounts involved are large, any potential for manipulation can be magnified in its effect.

Manipulation can arise because the payments often represent a transaction between a branch of a multinational firm in an LDC and another branch of the same firm somewhere abroad. Because the transaction is not on an open market, the real value is not easy to establish. The payment of whatever transfer price is chosen obviously boosts the year's profits for the branch doing the selling and reduces it in the branch doing the buying. Often enough, the transfer price will be an honest one because it is in the MNE's interests to have an accurate profit yardstick to measure the success of its branches. A canny corporate treasurer can, however, try to achieve larger profits in countries with less-stringent tax laws and lower profits where taxes are high through careful juggling of the transfer price. Many LDCs actually tax corporations at a lower rate than do developed countries, but the motive is still there if the shift avoids legal limits on profit repatriation, refutes charges by politicians and trade unions that high profits are being earned, or conceals these profits so as not to encourage competitors. Perhaps holdings of a weak currency can be minimized. Finally, if the government bases price controls on costs of production, then the transfer price can be used to raise costs and hence permit higher prices.

The transfer price issue also arises in the allocation of overhead expenditures within the firm. There is, however, less chance that it will arise in connection with the shipment of goods between branches of a multinational firm or, for that matter,

---

*Often the political pressures are the other way around, as demonstrated by the attempts by Arab states to persuade the MNEs they host to embargo trade with Israel or moves by the United states to alter its firms' behavior in South Africa.

between any indigenous firm and a foreign one. In these cases, the price could be set with an eye on tariffs and other taxes, but overcharges for goods are usually more visible to the tax authorities than are inaccurate values for patents and technology and improper allocation of overhead.

From the early 1980s, national tax inspectors have tried to cope with the MNE transfer price problem using four primary methods. They try to apply a "comparable uncontrolled price," at which technology has been transferred after an arm's-length bargain. This is, however, often hard to find. They attempt to calculate a "resale price," finding a price at which some technology left the group and applying that price when possible. They use "cost-plus," attempting to establish costs and then apply a markup. Finally, they fall back on negotiations with the MNE to see if the firm will accept a compromise solution. Large-scale simultaneous audits by two or more national tax authorities would help to cope with the problem and a number of these have been conducted.

Inappropriate Goods Charges have been made against some multinationals that they market inappropriate products in the LDCs. This argument occupies a spectrum. On one end are charges that MNEs cater to the demands of local elites rather than to the needs of the common people; that they transmit an undesirable home country ("Coca-Cola") culture; and that their advertising leads and shapes demand in undesirable ways.[23] These critics point to the trend to bottled soft drinks instead of fruit drinks and detergents instead of soap. They cite dramatic cases such as a survey showing Samoans (in American Samoa) to be tremendously high per capita consumers of much-advertised Pepto-Bismol in a society where no incidence of intestinal or digestive ailments had previously been reported.[24] Yet examples such as these seldom make much of an impression on economists, who generally believe consumers are better off when free to choose and that prohibitions and controls to enforce someone else's preferences would be much worse than doing nothing. (And it should also be remembered that no charge of inappropriateness is made against a wide range of MNE production.)

Further along the spectrum, however, more serious problems emerge. What about advertising that persuades Third World mothers to use infant formula rather than breast feeding, as in the celebrated Nestlé case? What if products are demonstrably unsafe, as with inflammable pajamas and questionable pesticides? What about the efforts of MNEs to promote the consumption of cigarettes with higher levels of nicotine and tar content than in the developed countries, with no health warnings, and with no restraints on their advertising? Although the market for cigarettes is shrinking in the United States, smoking is sharply on the increase in the LDCs. Former U.S. Surgeon General C. Everett Koop has made the charge that MNE involvement with tobacco products is an "export of death and disease."[25]

Moreover, what if pharmaceutical multinationals sometimes allow unrestricted sale of drugs that require prescriptions in the United States or Europe?[26] The United Nations has singled out Parke Davis's Chloramphenicol, which is severely restricted in the United States because it can cause blood disease problems, but which is sold over the counter without prescription in many LDCs. Dipyrone, a painkiller that can cause fatal blood disease (the AMA says its "only justified use is as a last resort to reduce fever when safer measures have failed"), is severely limited in the United States but sold over the counter in some LDCs.*

Where the consequences of the overseas action of MNEs are sufficiently negative to the public's welfare in the importing LDC, preventive action by the government of the MNE's home country would arguably be justified on ethical grounds even if the importing LDC is unable or unwilling to take any steps.

Inappropriate Technology It is said that multinationals tend to favor capital-intensive production rather than the labor-intensive production that is often more in line with LDC factor proportions. There are thus unfavorable repercussions for employment. Economists certainly agree that the choice of technology involving appropriate factor proportions is an important issue, and it will be considered at length in Chapter 8. But recent research does not indicate any general choice by MNEs of overly great capital intensity. Because the information available to MNEs is often good, these firms can frequently find capital equipment on world markets that have the right level of technical sophistication for their hosts' factor proportions. They may even have established a factory in a labor-abundant LDC to utilize labor-intensive equipment that has become obsolete elsewhere. Often the firms with unwarranted high capital intensity are the state-owned ones, not the MNEs.[27]

The Change in View Toward the Multinationals

Controlling the conduct of foreign firms was much emphasized by LDCs in the 1960s and most of the 1970s. As countries weighed the costs and benefits discussed above, they frequently decided against allowing unfettered operation by the multinationals. Many steps were taken. Whole industries were declared off-limits to the MNEs and reserved for local (often state-owned) enterprise. Controls took the form of maximum allowable ownership and profit repatriation. Strict rules on local participation in the investment and management of the firm became commonplace. Countries often required that any expansion of an enterprise be accomplished through domestic participation, and a steady rise in the proportion of local stockholding often was mandated by law. In some instances, joint ventures were mandated from the time a firm was first established, and foreign shareholders were

*The United States bans the export of drugs not approved by the Food and Drug Administration (FDA). It may seem reasonable to ban such exports, but there is another side to the issue. The World Health Organization has noted that the export ban may keep efficacious medicines from being used to fight diseases that do not occur in North America and may discourage the use of some cheap, although possibly more toxic, drugs because they have not been approved in the United States. The drug companies say regulation should be the responsibility of the importing nation. Critics point to the expense and technical barriers of having the LDCs do the testing. An economic office in the FDA to speed the obvious cases along may seem sensible, but there is no such thing.

under a legal obligation to sell out within a certain time period. Several South American countries (Bolivia, Colombia, Ecuador, Peru, and Venezuela) operated under a 15- to 20-year provision that outside ownership be reduced to a 49% maximum.

Quota targets akin to equal opportunity guidelines in the United States became widespread. Countries mandated a certain percentage of local managers at junior and senior levels, the target number growing larger as time passed. "Local content" requirements, prescribing the use of domestically produced inputs and similar in their economic effects to import quotas, also became common, as did export requirements for some of the MNEs' final output. Many governments restricted royalties and fees to some fixed percentage of total sales in the country. At the United Nations a move was made to adopt a code of conduct establishing strict behavioral rules for multinationals operating in LDCs.

The Turnabout in Attitudes A remarkable turnabout in attitudes took place, however, during the 1980s. The realization spread that the LDCs were being penalized by the lack of foreign capital inflows, which were being discouraged by the controls. Attracting direct investment turned out to be a highly competitive undertaking. Moreover, the debt crisis in bank lending during the 1980s led to more appreciation of direct investment, in which no outflow occurs unless a profit is being made as compared with the debt on which interest and principal must be paid. More equity financing and less contractual lending would obviously have been advantageous during the crisis. The foreign investor, not the LDC, would bear the risk of recessions, major shifts in the exchange rate, and so forth.

The countries with the toughest rules on foreign investment often found that they were experiencing the most serious depression in foreign capital inflows, which, in turn, inhibited transfers of confidential technology. The countries that had gone the furthest—prohibiting foreign ownership (equity holdings) altogether—found the MNEs were extremely reluctant to reveal technology and management methods over which they wished to retain complete control. In many instances, MNEs simply packed up and left, and they were not replaced either by foreign competitors or by viable domestic enterprises. Perhaps most tellingly, there was new demand for MNE investment. The LDCs realized, with some disquiet, that a major increase in hospitality toward the MNEs was taking place in Eastern Europe, Russia, and other parts of the old Soviet Union.

The result has been considerably more agreement on the advantages of MNEs and a lessening of the fear of domination by MNEs. Some countries, once quite hostile to foreign investment, began actively to court it. This group includes Argentina, Chile, China, Egypt, India, Jamaica, Mexico, Pakistan, the Philippines, South Korea, and Turkey, all of which for years were among the most bitter foes of the MNEs. Many limits on repatriated profits, requirements for reinvestment, and limits on sectors where investment was permitted were unceremoniously dropped. In the 35 countries that made changes in investment policy during 1991, 82 steps were taken, out of which 80 represented liberalization of the rules while only two involved tightening them.[28]

Debate over a UN code of conduct was eventually shouldered out of the way by a new set of negotiations at Geneva, undertaken as part of the Uruguay Round of trade talks that concluded in a 1994 agreement. The Uruguay Round was carried on within the GATT (General Agreement on Tariffs and Trade). It was so named because it was begun in 1986 at Punta del Este, Uruguay, before being moved to Geneva. Part of the negotiations involved TRIMs, or trade-related investment measures. Pushed especially by the United States and Japan, the TRIM talks resulted in an agreement with the LDCs to phase out all remaining local content, production, sales, export, and technology requirements over a period of five years, or seven years for the least developed countries.

The upshot for today's multinationals with branches in the LDCs is a major decrease in regulations and performance requirements. For the host governments, the realization grew that controlling the multinationals is a contest that must be closely calculated. Strict regulation cut capital inflows substantially and curtailed access to the latest research and technological developments. The economic penalties from the strictness appeared to be greater than the benefits from the regulation. That explains why host governments are providing a more welcoming environment. Whatever the problems that multinationals bring, many LDCs have now decided that the advantages of their presence outweigh the costs.

Confiscation

It follows that nationalization of MNE assets without adequate compensation, called confiscation or expropriation, has become rare. From the point of view of a capital-hungry LDC, there was always the alternative of seizing assets. Yet doing so has been shown to be devastating for future private capital inflows, not only from the affected firm but also from other foreign firms as well. In such a scenario, U.S. foreign aid must stop by law. Where wrangles over ownership and compensation are likely, commercial bank and World Bank loans will be less forthcoming. Foreign managers and technicians may depart. In technical terms, the present discounted value of the expropriated property would have to be balanced against the present discounted value of the reduced inflows and then weighed for political impact. The tactic always has a high degree of political and emotional content. The fear of nationalization may be an important matter even in a country with no history of such events, especially when politicians put their rhetoric into high gear. Fear, even when largely groundless, can quickly result in big cuts in private foreign investment.

Expropriation was at one time particularly pronounced among plantations, mines, oil companies, banks, utilities, and transportation facilities. But self-interest has led to a massive retreat by the LDCs from outright expropriation. Some countries have passed laws prohibiting the tactic, a number have even put the prohibition into their constitutions, and there are currently about 260 treaties involving the protection of investment, some of them part of the U.S. Bilateral Investment

Treaty (BIT) Program.* When disagreements arise, many are now negotiated in the World Bank's International Center for the Settlement of Investment Disputes (ICSID). Nowadays expropriations are rare.

OFFICIAL INSURANCE FOR FOREIGN DIRECT INVESTMENT

In order to maintain business confidence, several relatively small official insurance plans have recently been established. These are the Overseas Private Investment Corporation (OPIC) in the United States, similar European and Japanese agencies, and the Multilateral Investment Guarantee Agency (MIGA) of the World Bank.

OPIC was founded in 1969. It insures about 20% of U.S. investment in the LDCs.[29] Studies show that OPIC's insurance does raise the amount of U.S. capital flowing to the LDCs. Although there is plenty of private insurance available (pioneered by Lloyd's of London), premiums are frequently about five times higher than the rates charged by OPIC. Also, OPIC's policies are usually for 20 years, far longer than presently available private insurance, and they also usually cover "civil strife."[30] Criticism of this otherwise sensible-sounding idea has centered on the favoritism shown to relatively well-off LDCs and to large projects (recently 83% of OPIC's newly insured commitments was to just 13 large projects valued at over $10 million each). Congress eventually mandated that OPIC turn more toward lower-income countries and small businesses, and some movement has been made in this direction. The AFL/CIO opposes OPIC on the grounds that it fails to promote growth abroad and causes the export of jobs from the United States.

The World Bank's MIGA also insures private-sector loans to LDCs. It started operations in 1988 with a rather small capital of $1 billion. Governments paid in 10% of the capital and gave promissory notes for another 10%, while the remaining 80% was callable on demand. Annual premiums range from 0.50% to 1.25% of the amount insured, slightly more than commercial insurers in national markets because the premiums must support the agency, and because war losses are insured. Under MIGA's rules, member governments agree to pay compensation for loss if expropriations or repudiations of contracts take place. Only 15 insurance contracts supporting

*The U.S. BIT program dates from 1981. It seeks to obtain agreements with LDCs guaranteeing certain rights and safeguards. A "model treaty" revised in 1984 is the basis for the negotiations and contains the following provisions: (1) equal treatment of nationals of the host country and foreigners, including the choice of manager who is wanted rather than one of the correct nationality; (2) unrestricted repatriation of profit and capital; (3) expropriation to be recompensed at fair market value; and (4) binding arbitration of disputes. The United States has discussed BIT treaties with over 40 countries, and 16 such treaties had been signed by 1992. The reports of the U.S. ITC, *The Year in Trade,* present annual updates of the BIT program.

investment of $2 billion were arranged in the first two years of MIGA's operations, but recently applications have increased. By the start of 1992, there were 58 LDC members with 37 more in the process of joining.[31]

PRIVATE BANK LENDING AND ITS COLLAPSE DURING THE DEBT CRISIS

The transfer of foreign resources to the LDCs also includes commercial bank loans. When an LDC borrows from private banks, all can go well. It can use the foreign exchange made available to finance imports of capital goods and materials necessary to build new roads, port facilities, or factories. If the interest payments on the loans are moderate and do not change much, and if the income generated by the new projects is rapidly realized, then the greater economic strength allows the debt to be financed in timely fashion, and the strategy is successful. In this view, the actual size of a debt is much less important than a country's ability to service it by making prompt payments of interest and repayments of principal. The assets acquired through debt finance can make that possible. But as the debt crisis of the 1980s plainly demonstrates, such loans carry considerable risk for the LDCs (and for the banks as well).

Bank lending to countries that need financing is an old idea dating back to the Renaissance in Europe when private banks such as the House of Medici extended loans directly to governments. During the nineteenth and much of the twentieth centuries, bank loans became rarer and capital was transferred mostly by means of bond sales. During the 1970s, bank loans to LDCs became first a phenomenon, and then in the 1980s, a near catastrophe, as this section explores. Curiously, the debt crisis came about 50 years after the great wave of bond defaults during the 1930s, which, in turn, was about 50 years after the first wave of bond defaults in the 1870s to 1890s. Some have suggested a lesson in this: that in time borrowers, lenders, and economists tend to forget the important lessons of the past.[32]

The nature of private bank lending contained its own seeds of disaster. What if the interest charged on the loans is variable and rises? Perhaps banks refuse to renew old loans, so no new flows come in to help fund the repayment of the old. Instead of using the foreign exchange to finance productive investments providing the future means to repay, a country might choose to consume beyond its means while it can, invest inefficiently, or use the funds for political or military purposes. In that case, the economy may grow too slowly to service the required transfers of interest and repayments of principal.

If all of these eventualities were to happen at the same time, there would be a crisis. That was what happened in the early 1980s. By the end of a decade of crisis, it was clear that the world (including many of its economists) had grown somewhat bored, or at least fatigued, with this issue. But it is essential that it be understood, and, this time, remembered.

The Eruption of the Debt Crisis[33]

The crisis, at its worst from 1982 to 1984 and continuing into the 1990s, grew slowly from roots put down in the middle and late 1970s. When commercial banks in developed countries and the LDCs first began the rapid expansion in their relationship, initially most observers applauded. The relationship brought profit to the banks, or so it was believed. It brought no political difficulties, as foreign aid sometimes did. Plenty of funds were available because of the early 1970s' increase in world oil prices, when the OPEC countries deposited their continuing windfalls largely with developed-country commercial banks. Supporters of aid approved because the banks transferred resources to the LDCs on a scale beyond what was politically possible otherwise. Western governments in general were enthusiastic; the transfers cut the need for foreign aid and were a stopgap that avoided emergency responses to OPEC.

The banks, lacking perfect foresight, had little reason to question the developments. For many years, their losses on international loans had been proportionately less than on domestic loans, and numerous LDCs boasted better records of economic growth than did the industrial countries over a period of several years leading up to the lending boom. Lending reached vast proportions, until by the end of 1982 total LDC debt to commercial banks was just over $354 billion, representing growth of about seven times since 1971 and amounting to about half of all financial flows to the LDCs. Debt, only 14% of developing-country GNP in 1970, was nearly 34% in 1984.

Very poor LDCs were never able to borrow much from commercial banks because of their unfavorable economic prospects. Most of the commercial bank loans (about two-thirds) were to 13 relatively well-off LDCs. Slightly over 50% of the total debt was run up by Argentina, Brazil, Mexico, and South Korea. (Korea's rapid adjustment to the economic conditions that brought near catastrophe to so many others was remarkable, though little noticed at the time.)

The crisis erupted with Mexico's announcement in August 1982 that it could not meet its obligations. Among the 32 countries that were in arrears on their international bank loans during that year, Mexico, Brazil, and Argentina presented by far the greatest difficulties. Mexico's announcement, followed by others, brought a high risk of general default, a danger of insolvency for major banks unable to collect principal and interest payments, and concern that banking collapses like those during the Great Depression of the 1930s were in prospect. Paul Volcker, chairman of the U.S. Federal Reserve System, called the potential threat to the international financial system essentially unparalleled in postwar history.[34]

The Causes of the Crisis

The debt crisis had two major causes: (1) the world recession of the early 1980s, and (2) the sharp increase in interest rates starting in 1978.

The World Recession of the Early 1980s The world recession of the early 1980s cut developed-country imports thereby reduced the exports of the LDCs.

The usual estimates of the relation (elasticity) between developed-country growth and the imports into these countries is that a 1% change in the rate of growth causes a change in imports ranging from about 1.2% to 2.2%. Imports from the LDCs are even more sensitive because the demand for many industrial raw materials produced by these countries shifts rapidly with the business cycle. Not only was the world recession deep, but it also was severely underestimated by most forecasters. There was therefore a sharp decline in LDC export performance. The recession in the developed countries also helped to generate intensified pressures for trade barriers in the industrial countries (and in the LDCs as well), which also had an impact on LDC exports.

The Interest Rate Shock The second cause of the debt crisis was the sharp increase in interest rates starting in 1978. Interest payments on LDC debt had been only 0.5% of the LDCs' GNP in 1970 but had reached 2.8% by 1984. Interest rates rose because the developed countries tightened their monetary policies in the late 1970s to fight the inflation stemming from the second OPEC oil crisis. The higher rates were damaging to the LDCs because they had contracted most of their loans at variable interest rates that extended over the entire life of the loans. No particular blame attaches to the banks for floating the rates. Earlier in the 1970s, during a previous bout of inflation in the developed countries, they had frequently been locked in to fixed low or negative real rates of return at great expense to them. Learning from that experience, they had protected themselves by insisting on variable rates that would reflect any future inflation. Unfortunately, although the shift by banks to variable interest rates decreased their risk of loss if interest rates rose, it raised the risk that the loans might not be paid off.

The variable rates were typically adjusted every six months. From 1979, world interest rates rose sharply, carrying upward with them the variable rates paid by LDCs on their existing bank loans. The U.S. prime rate, often used for loans to Latin America, eventually peaked in 1981 at 20.50%. Another much-used rate for LDC loans, the London Interbank Offered Rate (LIBOR), averaged 18% in 1981 with fees and risk premia included. When adjusted for inflation, the resulting real rates on dollar loans were about 11%, the highest peacetime figure for over a century.

Even after the oil crisis passed, macroeconomic conditions in the developed countries conspired to keep real interest rates high. Governments chose to run large fiscal deficits, and these deficits absorbed very large quantities of loanable funds. In effect, through interest rates, developed-country governments were competing with the LDCs for borrowed funds and were winning. In the meantime they contained the expansionary macroeconomic effects of these deficits with tight money. Real interest rates were 6% to 8% from 1981 to 1983, compared with about 0.5% from 1974 to 1978 and 2% in 1980. In 1977 and 1978, most real short-term rates had been negative—no wonder the LDCs had flocked to borrow. Interest costs rapidly doubled from what they had been in the mid-1970s, following the rough rule of thumb that a rise of one percentage point in market interest rates raises the flow of interest payments from the LDCs after about a year by approximately $2 billion. The major losers were the three dominant borrowers, Argentina, Brazil, and Mexico.

The high real rates on the variable-rate loans need not in themselves have caused a crisis if export earnings had also strengthened, providing the means to repay. But as we have seen, these earnings were instead weakening. The outcome was that the debt service ratio (payments of interest and amortization as a percent of export revenue) rose for LDCs from 15% or less from 1973 to 1977 to 24.6% in 1982, the rise almost entirely due to the higher interest payments. Debt service had cost the LDCs $9 billion in 1970 and $100 billion in 1984.

The higher interest rates in the developed countries had another damaging effect for the LDCs. They persuaded holders of assets all over the world to buy the currencies of the countries where the rates were highest. In particular, this meant buying the U.S. dollar. The purchases caused the dollar to rise in value (appreciate) while the currencies of the LDCs sank (depreciated). To make payments on their debts, which were frequently denominated in dollars, the LDCs had to earn larger amounts of their own currencies to make the payments.

To What Extent Did Policy Mistakes Contribute to the Crisis?

Did the commercial banks and the LDCs contribute to their own difficulties by reckless mistakes of policy? To some degree, yes.

The Banks' Errors In hindsight, the banks lent too much and lent without sufficient care. They had too little experience assessing risks in circumstances very different from their usual business and relied on overly simple tests that were not good leading indicators of trouble ahead. They believed they had spread their risks across a wide range of LDCs, but it turned out that the LDCs as a whole were subject to many of the same problems.

Judged by the information available at the time, however, the conclusion that the banks were reckless is less firm. The officially published statistics for credit worthiness did not show cause for alarm until 1981 at the earliest and not clearly until 1982. The private bond markets showed little concern; interest rates on Mexican bonds did not rise until a matter of weeks before the dramatic Mexican announcement of August 1982 that it could not meet its obligations.[35] Even after that, the higher spreads over LIBOR to reflect risk proved to be a poor predictor of difficulty. By the time the banks recognized that there was a crisis, stopping loans would have been too late to stave it off and, by virtually ensuring default, would have been counterproductive.

One major criticism of bank behavior can be called the "small bank problem." Small banks, which joined LDC lending late in the game, soon reduced their lending the most and presented the greatest difficulties in renegotiating the obligations. The large number of banks involved (560 lent to Mexico) and the inexperience of the small ones with such transactions initially made the negotiations very cumbersome. Some of these banks, as well as some of the big ones, had a lesser share of the loans and, with less to lose, they apparently felt they could hold out for stiffer terms. Because in a syndicated loan each participant has to approve if the terms are changed, the negotiations were usually difficult. Advisory committees were eventually pieced together; these, with some arm-twisting by governments, reduced, but did not eliminate, the problem.

The banks, especially those of the United States, were also too quick in reducing the maturity of new loans. They may have hoped to increase their influence on economic policies, or they may have been using shorter maturities as a substitute for reducing loans outright. They certainly wanted to lower their own long-term exposure. But they did not see the extent to which the shortened maturities could cause a liquidity crisis if unexpected shocks had to be faced just when the shorter terms of the loans were increasing the debt service payments coming due.

Policy Mistakes by the LDCs To what extent did LDC policies contribute to the crisis? There seems little doubt that in an understandable attempt to ward off the effects of the deepening recession, prolonged heavy borrowing was continued past the point of prudence. Some LDCs deliberately chose the troublesome short-term loans to avoid the higher spreads on the already costly medium- and long-term loans. Domestic fiscal deficits in the LDCs were allowed to expand, partly financed by the borrowing but in large part by creating domestic money, which was inflationary. The large deficits were often permitted because of the politics of budgeting in the LDCs, as discussed in Chapter 5. The leadership in many countries was unwilling to cut the flows to the urban workers, which benefit from low-cost food and subsidized public services, to the business sector in the form of cheap credit and subsidies, to the military, to the government's supporters in the form of government jobs and large projects, and (sometimes) to the leaders personally. The difficulties of restraining this spending as long as foreign bank loans were still available proved insurmountable. The shortened maturity of the loans did not stop the borrowing, as a number of LDC governments demonstrated they had a short time horizon. "Keep up the spending now; don't worry about whether it is making the economy more productive; let a future generation deal with the problem" seemed to be the motto for some.* The idea that borrowing ought to result in a buildup of assets tended to get lost.

As the crisis deepened, enormous capital flight developed from the indebted LDCs. Many of these were maintaining overvalued foreign exchange rates, which meant that exchanging local currency for dollars was a good bargain. The high real interest rates abroad made it an even better one. The $84 billion in capital flight from Mexico was equal to four-fifths of that country's debt, and the $46 billion from Argentina was three-fourths of its debt. Economists estimated that

*Two studies conclude that until about 1979–1980 the great preponderance of debt was used to finance capital formation and not consumption in the debtor LDCs for which the statistics are good enough to analyze. After 1979, far less debt financing was used for productive investment, so the contribution of debt to growth was diminished. See Iqbal Mehdi Zaidi, "Saving, Investment, Fiscal Deficits, and the External Indebtedness of Developing Countries," *World Development* 13, no. 5 (1985): 573–588; and *WDR 1985*, 46–51.

TABLE 6.3 FLIGHT CAPITAL HELD ABROAD AS A PERCENTAGE OF LONG-TERM GOVERNMENT DEBT, END OF 1988

Argentina	111
Bolivia	178
Brazil	46
Colombia	103
Ecuador	115
Mexico	114
Philippines	188
Venezuela	240

Source: Jeremy Bulow and Kenneth Rogoff, "Cleaning Up Third World Debt Without Getting Taken to the Cleaners," *Journal of Economic Perspectives* 4, no. 1 (Winter, 1990): 37, citing Morgan Stanley.

the private citizens of 15 major debtors stashed $300 billion abroad. The capital flight was particularly large from Latin America. As Table 6.3 shows, at the end of 1988 the foreign currency holdings of depositors from indebted LDCs were often as large or larger than government or government-guaranteed bank debt. So the overhang of LDC debt had a blameworthy counterpart in the overhang of capital held abroad. Its existence, and the fact that most of these deposits belonged to the upper, richer classes, did not make the debt crisis easier to solve.

The Crisis Peaks

The worst part of the crisis was eventually contained during 1983–1984, but not without cliff-hanging negotiations constantly in the news. A process called *rescheduling* was entered into, with the negotiations carried on by teams from the banks, the debtor LDC, government officials, and the International Monetary Fund.[36] Since the teams often met in London, the term *London Club* was used to describe the negotiations. The banks and the LDCs had clear reasons to avoid a default, and they were eventually able to bargain a series of country-by-country rescheduling agreements, almost always involving a postponement of principal repayments but not of interest payments, and with no reduction in the debt.

In the frenetic years from 1983 to 1985 there were 83 rescheduling agreements, of which Brazil's in 1983 was the first of the giant ones, followed by agreements with Argentina and Mexico. Multiyear restructurings were very infrequent at first. The agreements with the smaller borrowers were generally on a year-by-year basis, and it took time for even the largest borrowers to obtain more favorable multiyear agreements. (Long-term rescheduling, as with Mexico in 1984, made much more sense than did year-to-year agreements because the process of arriving at several short-term agreements was repetitious and time consuming, and the time span involved was not long enough to allow a focus on needed policy reforms.) The loans were repackaged with a new schedule of interest rates and fees, in the earlier agreements sometimes higher than the original ones but later lower, with longer maturities, and with "humps" of repayment smoothed over. The negotiations were always hard because so many banks were involved. The results of all the reschedulings in these years meant that eventually higher repayments in total would have to be made, with less at the time and more later.

Soon after the first reschedulings, developed-country government aid was utilized in many cases to prevent immediate defaults, and to give time to work out an acceptable agreement. Frequently, policy changes in the debtor were required and monitored by the International Monetary Fund. This "conditionality" became one of the most controversial aspects of the debt crisis.

Among the private banks, a predictable repercussion of the unwelcome rescheduling was a drastic cut in their willingness to lend outside the agreements to countries perceived as high risks or, indeed, to any LDC borrower at all. Bankers' confidence concerning lending to the LDCs was destroyed (and it has yet to be restored). Table 6.4 shows how bank lending dried up during the crisis years, reaching its lowest point in 1988. Most of the little lending that remained was intended to keep a borrower from defaulting, and in that sense, was not voluntary on the part of the banks.

In the mid-1980s, the debtor countries of Latin America, where the problem was always worst, found that the outflows to service the debt were draining about 4% of total output, or a quarter of domestic saving, from the region. That compared to only 2.5% of Germany's output after World War I in what was then (and now) thought to be an insupportable burden flowing from the Versailles Treaty.

Evidence of economic damage began to mount. The need to service the debt caused governments to transfer their spending toward debt repayment even when that meant cutting productive investment and so hurting development prospects. Governments preferred to squeeze investment rather than undertake the politically difficult task of squeezing consumption, and there may even have been a partial loss of incentives to invest when it was realized that some of the returns from better economic performance would be absorbed by greater repayment of debt. The tendency appears clearly in Table 6.5. (By contrast, in LDCs with no debt problem, investment during the same period fell very little.)

The lower investment also brought reduced domestic spending, which propelled numerous LDCs into recession. Additionally, the investment that did occur was becoming less productive. This was partly because restricting demand meant that some industrial capacity was underutilized because of recession, and partly because the debtors distorted their market signals with controls on prices, interest rates, and the like.

TABLE 6.4 INTERNATIONAL BANK LENDING TO THE LDCs, 1981–1988 (BILLIONS OF U.S. DOLLARS)

1981	$52.3 billion
1983	$35.0 billion
1985	$15.2 billion
1987	$7.0 billion
1988	$5.8 billion (the low)

Source: OECD data, *IMF Survey,* February 18, 1991.

TABLE 6.5 SHARES OF GOVERNMENT SPENDING, 11 HIGHLY INDEBTED COUNTRIES (IN PERCENT)

	1978	1981	1984
Interest	7.0	8.5	13.9
Capital formation	20.2	17.2	12.1

Source: Calculated from *WDR*, various issues.

It seemed a shame that bankruptcy, which within countries has long since provided a way out for insolvent debtors, had no counterpart in the dealings between banks and governments.[37] Within a country, the debt crisis would have led to bankruptcy with debtors protected from creditors while they reorganized. A onetime equivalent to bankruptcy might have been a great advantage in the debt crisis.* Because this was not possible, partial defaults in the form of payments limitations affecting interest, principal, or both, became commonplace, and the mood turned more hostile, with general default in the air.† The atmosphere put the finishing touches to any willingness by the banks to extend new loans. (Though it must be said that the debtor countries engaged in little movement toward a debtors' cartel to coordinate polices. Such a cartel could have led to even worse relations with the developed countries.)

A Turn for the Better

By the late 1980s, many signs were more favorable than most informed observers had thought imaginable a few years before.[38] Some economic recovery from the world recession of the early 1980s boosted developed-country imports and hence LDC exports. Oil prices fell, which helped the non-oil LDCs at the same time that it improved economic growth in the developed countries. Interest rates fell as budget deficits and inflation came more under control, and because U.S. interest rates eased more than those of Germany and Japan, the dollar started to weaken (from 1985).

So-called "conditionality" agreements supervised by the International Monetary Fund, together with many LDCs' own sense that reforms in their policies were needed, caused them to limit government borrowing and coordinate the borrowing by state corporations and the military that had run up the size of debt. Together with stabilization and structural adjustment in some countries, this also

*Jonathan Eaton, "Debt Relief and the International Enforcement of Loan Contracts," *Journal of Economic Perspectives* 4, no. 1 (Winter 1990): 43–56. The U.S. Foreign Sovereign Immunities Act of 1976, and similar measures passed in other countries at about the same time, reduced the ability of governments to claim sovereign immunity from debt collection. Creditors had significantly more latitude to seize assets held abroad.

†For example, Brazil stonewalled for a long time, insisting that it would limit itself by a "capacity to pay" concept which put debt repayment at the end of a long list of priorities for government spending.

led to better export performance. As conditions improved, capital flight from the LDCs declined sharply.

The Baker Plan A "Baker Plan," named for U.S. Treasury Secretary James Baker, was launched in October 1985. It envisaged policy adjustments in the LDCs and new loans from the banks to finance them, both leading to renewed growth. Specifically, the plan advocated comprehensive economic policy reform, a central role for the IMF, and increased loans ($20 billion) by the banks in proportion to their existing loans to the 15 biggest borrowers. Also included were increased World Bank and regional development bank lending ($9 billion) and more IMF assistance in return for a greater commitment by the LDCs to economic reform. The Baker Plan recognized that funds had to be recycled back to the LDCs from the banks, and that meeting the crisis by simply contracting the economies of the debtor LDCs was neither good economics nor pragmatic foreign policy. Under the Baker Plan as well as independent of it, considerable debt restructuring occurred from 1986 to 1988.

That was the period when the private banks began to build up their capital against bad loans, reducing the risk of a major bank collapse. The process had been started by the U.S. International Lending Supervision Act of 1983, which instituted new requirements on the matter—requirements that in any case would have been prudent for the banks to have implemented voluntarily. The loan-loss reserves against LDC debt rose substantially, from virtually nothing at the time the crisis erupted to 5% in 1986 to an average of 50% in June 1990. Reserves were generally higher yet in Britain, France, and Germany. Every percentage-point increase in such reserves lessened the risk of a banking collapse in case of further defaults, and lowered the urgency of the crisis for the developed countries.[39]

Nonetheless, by 1988–1989, it was clear that the Baker Plan had failed, first because it did not allow for any *reduction* in LDC debt, and second, because new bank loans for adjustment were either not forthcoming from the banks or turned out to be considerably less than the return flow of interest payments from the LDCs.

The Brady Plan The Baker Plan was followed by the Brady Plan, named for Nicholas B. Brady, Baker's successor as U.S. treasury secretary. It was unveiled in March 1989, and it represented a breakthrough in that it offered reductions in the burden of the debt as well as restructuring.[40] Under the Brady Plan, banks must advance new loans while accepting a reduction either in the value of the old loans or a reduction in the interest rate they receive. Bankers have been very critical of the plan, as might be expected, because they lose either some of their interest or some of their principal. But developed-country governments put considerable pressure on the banks to accede, and in the end they did so. Because the financial press has emphasized the benefits of debt relief, the Brady Plan has helped greatly to improve the financial climate. The debt relief, together with the economic reforms that have been attractive to investors, played a major part in the 1990s resurgence of capital inflows into the LDCs, particularly into Latin America.

BRADY PLAN DETAILS

Major Brady Plan arrangements have been reached with Argentina, Brazil, Costa Rica, Mexico, Nigeria, the Philippines, Uruguay, and Venezuela. The first, with Mexico in 1989, can stand as our example of how the burden of the debt has actually been reduced. The arrangement allowed the creditor banks (there were over 500 of them) to select one of two main alternatives. (1) They could swap old loans for 30-year Mexican bonds, discounted at 35% below their face value. These bonds pay the same interest rate as the old loans, thirteen-sixteenths above LIBOR; that is, they still bear a flexible rate but on a reduced sum. About 40% of the lenders chose this option. (2) They could swap old loans for 30-year Mexican bonds with no discount, the bonds paying a fixed interest rate of 6.25%; that is, they could opt to keep the principal of the loan as before, but accept a moderate, fixed interest rate; 47% of the lenders chose this option. All the bonds are to be paid off in one lump sum at the end of the year 2019. The agreement with Mexico reduced the country's net capital transfers abroad by about $4 billion a year during the period 1989 to 1994.[41] As a part of it, the banks undertook to extend some new loans ($1.1 billion) to bolster the Mexican economy.

Agreements with other countries sometimes differ in detail, but they generally achieve the same end of a substitution of government bonds for bank debt, and a reduction in principal or interest or both. In some cases, the negotiations have taken years. For example, Brazil's Brady Plan arrangement was not agreed on until 1994.

Other Debt-Reduction Plans

Many dozens of other ideas for partial debt forgiveness emerged during the crisis, and some have been implemented at least to a small degree. We discuss the most important proposals.[42]

A Taxpayer Bailout of the Banks A taxpayer bailout of the banks was a proposal that no doubt had considerable quiet support from both the banks and the LDCs. This would have involved developed-country governments picking up the risks from the commercial banks. But a bailout was never very likely. It would have involved higher taxes and resistance from the taxpaying public. The banks had a major role in initiating the debt crisis because their loan contracts were badly designed. What right did they have to public assistance any more than entrepreneurs in other fields who had guessed wrong?[43] In any case, the necessary funding for a taxpayer bailout would undoubtedly have come in large part from aid budgets, so that the low-income LDCs would have suffered to help the middle-income countries that borrowed the most. Why should Argentina, Brazil, and Mexico, all relatively well-off, have received aid that could go to countries much poorer than they, countries so poor that they were unable to borrow from the banks in the first place? A taxpayer bailout would also have sent signals to countries with a debt problem that they could expect continued government intervention whenever they refused to pay, so leading to future difficulties.

Debt Buy-Backs Years ago a secondary market for international debt developed, similar to the market for mortgages on houses. A bank may need immediate funds and can sell its mortgages to another institution. Similarly, banks can be rid of their LDC debt by selling it to someone else. Needless to say, as the prospects that debtors would ever pay in full and on time receded, the price of their debt on the secondary market fell. For some it was a swoon, as Table 6.6 shows. As of 1991, the Côte d'Ivoire was believed to be so unlikely to repay its debt that it could be purchased on the secondary market for just 6 cents on the dollar.

These prices reflected private investors' predictions as to whether the debt would ever be repaid. It should be noted that one reason for the low prices in the secondary market was that banks attempting to increase their reserves against losses sold some of their debt on this market for what it would bring.

The low price of the debt appeared to some debtor LDCs as an opportunity that could be exploited. The price was so low that perhaps some of it could be purchased in a "buy-back," so reducing the overhang. For example, in 1988 to 1989, Bolivia bought back about half of its debt at 11% of its face value. Obvious problems bedevil this approach, however. A country in difficulties has to have a surplus of hard currency to accomplish this, which is rare enough. If it has the funds, its reputation with the banks will be improved if it simply services its debt rather than buying it back. Furthermore, the price of the debt will rise if banks come to expect that a buy-back is about to begin. (The Brady Plan convinced investors that the chances for repayment were improving, and so the secondary market for LDC debt rose considerably as that plan unfolded.)

Debt-Equity Swaps Debt-equity swaps were introduced by Chile in 1985. The method works as follows: In a typical swap arrangement, a private company in a developed country decides it wants to invest in an LDC. It buys a loan from a bank at a discount, then swaps it with the debtor government for local currency, often at a favorable exchange rate. It then uses the local currency to buy a state-owned enterprise or for new investment, which is the reason why the word *equity*

TABLE 6.6 LDC DEBT PRICES IN SECONDARY MARKET, 1991, PERCENTAGE OF FACE VALUE

Chile	89	Nigeria	42
Argentina	79	Ecuador	24
Colombia	78	Panama	18
Philippines	71	Zaire	17
Venezuela	67	Côte d'Ivoire	6
Brazil	54		

Source: Salomon Brothers data cited in *The Economist,* October 12, 1991.

is used. A problem associated with debt-equity swaps is that the debtor government creates local currency to obtain its debt in the swap. The money creation will usually be inflationary. To avoid the inflation, the debtor government must sterilize the swap payment by selling bonds domestically, probably at a high interest rate. Brazil, for example, found that its ability to control inflation from this source was inadequate.

Environmental Swaps Environmental swaps are an exciting idea. Such swaps seek to protect rain forests and other sensitive areas in LDCs in return for hard currency payments from the developed countries that the LDC governments then use to repurchase their own debt. The first of these involved Bolivia and Brazil in 1987. By 1992, 16 more swaps with eight countries had followed, though all have been on a rather small scale.[44] So far they have mainly been instigated by private environmental groups in the rich countries.* That fact restricts their impact because the resources that such groups can command are limited. Also, the environmental protection does involve local currency costs, and money creation for these purposes might be inflationary. However, environmental swaps have a great potential to accomplish three purposes at the same time: debt reduction for the LDCs, payoff for the creditor banks, and reduction in environmental degradation for all of mankind. Such swaps are examined at greater length when we consider economic development and the environment in Chapter 16.

Some debt-for-development swaps have also taken place, with private aid groups or foreign governments buying debt on the secondary market and trading it with a debtor LDC for local currency, which is then donated for development purposes. In other cases, banks have donated debt to private aid groups with a similar understanding that the debt will be converted into local currency and used for development. The amounts involved in these debt-for-development swaps have been small.

Conclusion

Because of reduced borrowing and improved economic performance in the debtor LDCs, various measures of the intensity of the debt crisis have improved. The LDCs' ratio of debt to GDP, 39% in 1986, had fallen to 32% in 1991. For 15 of the most indebted countries, the debt service ratio (which, we recall, is payments of interest and amortization of principal as a percent of export revenue) fell from 45% in 1986 to 31% in 1991. (For LDCs as a whole, including those without a debt problem, the debt service ratio went from 22% to 14% during this period.)[45]

But the burden of debt remains heavy and the Brady Plan debt reductions have been limited. The debt overhang still inhibits capital investment. A major remaining problem is that investors, both domestic and foreign, view the debt as a type of tax on economic development. They reason that debtor governments may

*Some aid agencies (United States, the Netherlands, Sweden) have used environmental swaps for official debt as well.

have to service the debt either through higher taxes in the future, or by the creation of new money. Either way, investment suffers. Needless to say, the crisis virtually eliminated voluntary private bank lending to the LDCs, and a restoration of bank lending to precrisis levels will hardly be possible for a long time. Moreover, danger still exists that international episodes of high interest rates, or slow growth of LDC exports because of poor developed-country economic performance or the erection of trade barriers could again worsen the situation. The consequences for the LDCs would include further falls in investment, more cuts in their imports, and another episode of slower growth.

So, although the crisis has certainly eased, it has not passed. For a time it was the most threatening and portentous issue in all of development economics. It necessitated painful adjustments in the debtors, it retarded investment and human capital formation, and it basically halted growth for years in the most heavily indebted countries. Yet the crisis *was* successfully contained, and the international efforts to do so showed that the developed countries and the LDCs could cooperate. All in all, it was a close call.

NOTES

1. The figures are from *HDR 1994*, 180–181.
2. Susan M. Collins, "Capital Flows to Developing Countries: Implications from the Economies in Transition?" *Proceedings of the World Bank Annual Conference on Development Economics 1992* (Washington, D.C., 1993), 352.
3. *The Economist*, September 25, 1993.
4. See *WDR 1985*, especially 12–14.
5. Barry Eichengreen, "Historical Research on International Lending and Debt," *Journal of Economic Perspectives* 5, no. 2 (Spring 1991): 149–169; Barry Eichengreen and Richard Portes, "The Interwar Debt Crisis and Its Aftermath," *World Bank Research Observer* 5, no. 1 (January 1990): 69–94.
6. See Stijn Claessens and Sudarshan Gooptu, "Can Developing Countries Keep Foreign Capital Flowing In?" *Finance and Development* 31, no. 3 (September 1994): 62–65.
7. Masood Ahmed and Sudarshan Gooptu, "Portfolio Investment Flows to Developing Countries," *Finance and Development* 30, no. 1 (March 1993): 11. Also see Stijn Claessens, "Alternative Forms of External Finance: A Survey," *World Bank Research Observer* 8, no. 1 (January 1993): 91–117.
8. See Claessens and Gooptu, "Can Developing Countries Keep Foreign Capital Flowing In?" 63; *The Economist*, January 14, 1995.
9. For the details in this paragraph, see Jack Glen and Brian Pinto, "Debt or Equity? How Firms in Developing Countries Choose," IFC Discussion Paper No. 22 (1994), 17–18; *The Economist*, September 17, 1994; *South*, May 1990.
10. Ahmed and Gooptu, "Portfolio Investment Flows to Developing Countries," 11.
11. World Bank, "Rising Portfolio Flows: Short-Lived or Sustainable?" *World Bank Development Brief*, no. 15 (April 1993); *The Economist*, April 24, 1993.
12. For the pros and cons of multinationals, I benefited especially from the comments on this chapter by Wilson B. Brown of the University of Winnipeg, whose own interesting book is entitled *Markets, Organizations and Information* (Toronto, 1992); and the following in alphabetical order: V. N. Balasubramanyam, *Multinational Enterprises in the*

Third World, Thames Essay No. 26 (London, 1980); C. F. Bergsten, T. Horst, and T.H. Moran, eds., *American Multinationals and American Interests* (Washington, D.C., 1978); Thomas N. Gladwin and Ingo Walter, *Multinationals Under Fire* (New York, 1980); Jean-François Hennart, *A Theory of Multinational Enterprise* (Ann Arbor, Mich., 1982); Ian M. D. Little, *Economic Development: Theory, Policy, and International Relations* (New York, 1982), 182–189; Theodore H. Moran, ed., *Multinational Corporations: The Political Economy of Foreign Direct Investment* (Lexington, Mass., 1985); Seymour E. Rubin and Gary C. Hufbauer, eds., *Emerging Standards of International Trade and Investment* (Totowa, N.J., 1984); and A. E. Safarian and Gilles Y. Bertin, *Multinationals, Governments and International Technology Transfer* (New York, 1987). Two modern classics by Raymond Vernon are *Sovereignty at Bay* (New York, 1971) and *Storm Over the Multinationals* (Cambridge, Mass., 1974). *The Economist* publishes many articles on the activities of MNEs, which I utilized.

13. See Wilson B. Brown and Jan S. Hogendorn, *International Economics: Theory and Context* (Reading, Mass., 1994), chapter 19.
14. *The Economist*, September 25, 1993.
15. For the figures, see *HDR 1992*, 53; and *The Economist*, September 25, 1993.
16. *Wall Street Journal*, September 20, 1991.
17. *HDR 1992*, 52; *The Economist*, August 24, 1991, and September 25, 1993; *WDR 1991*, 96. For fuller details see the annual issues of United Nations's, *World Investment Report* (New York).
18. See studies by D. Nayyan and S. Lall cited by Hubert Schmitz, "Industrialization Strategies in Less Developed Countries: Some Lessons of Historical Experience," *Journal of Development Studies* 21, no. 1 (1984): 10–11; and Magnus Blomström, Irving Kravis, and Robert Lipsey, "Multinational Firms and Manufactured Exports from Developing Countries," NBER Working Paper No. 2493 (1988).
19. *WDR 1991*, 94.
20. The terms are used by S. P. Schatz, "Assertive Pragmatism and the Multinational Enterprise," *World Development* 9, no. 1 (1981): 93–105.
21. Illustrating the MacDougall-Kemp model, from G. D. A. MacDougall, "The Benefits and Costs of Private Investment from Abroad: A Theoretical Approach," *Economic Record* 36 (1960): 13–35; and M. C. Kemp, *The Pure Theory of International Trade* (Englewood Cliffs, N.J., 1964). The diagram is adapted from R. J. Ruffin, "International Factor Movements," in Ronald W. Jones and Peter B. Kenen, *Handbook of International Economics*, vol. 1 (Amsterdam, 1984), 255–256.
22. I first saw this formula in the work of Subrata Ghatak.
23. John Kenneth Galbraith has been a leading exponent of this view, especially in *The New Industrial State* (Boston, 1967) and *The Affluent Society* (Boston, 1958).
24. See *The Economist*, June 6, 1981.
25. *Christian Science Monitor*, September 22, 1989.
26. The cases here have been discussed in *The Economist* in recent years.
27. Howard Pack, "Productivity and Industrial Development in Sub-Saharan Africa," *World Development* 21, no. 1 (January 1993): 1–16.
28. *IMF Survey*, July 20, 1992.
29. See Rebecca M. Summary and Larry J. Summary, "The Overseas Private Investment Corporation and Developing Countries," *Economic Development and Cultural Change* 42, no. 4 (July 1994): 817–827.
30. See *WDR 1985*, 131.
31. See "MIGA: Up and Running," *Finance and Development*, 29, no. 1 (March 1992): 48–49.

32. See Barry Eichengreen, "Historical Research on International Lending and Debt," *Journal of Economic Perspectives* 5, no. 2 (Spring 1991): 149–169.
33. There is a large literature. Major recent volumes and articles, arrayed alphabetically, include Masood Ahmed and Lawrence Summers, "A Tenth Anniversary Report on the Debt Crisis," *Finance and Development* 29, no. 3 (September 1992): 2–5; C. Fred Bergsten, William R. Cline, and John Williamson, *Bank Lending to Developing Countries: The Policy Alternatives* (Cambridge Mass., 1985); Michael Claudon, ed., *The World Debt Crisis: International Lending on Trial* (Cambridge, Mass., 1986); Rudiger Dornbusch, *Dollars, Debts, and Deficits* (Cambridge, Mass., 1986); Rudiger Dornbusch, "Our LDC Debts," in Martin Feldstein, ed., *The United States and the World Economy* (Chicago, 1988); Rudiger Dornbusch, *Stabilization, Debt, and Reform: Policy Analysis for Developing Countries* (Englewood Cliffs, N.J., 1993); Jonathan Eaton and Lance Taylor, "Developing Country Finance and Debt," *Journal of Development Economics* 22, no. 1 (June 1986): 209–265, which reviews modeling of debt problems; Norman S. Fieleke, *The International Economy Under Stress* (Cambridge, Mass., 1988); Norman S. Fieleke, "International Lending on Trial," *New England Economic Review* (May/June 1983): 5–13; Jacob A. Frenkel, Michael P. Dooley, and Peter Wickham, eds., *Analytical Issues in Debt* (Washington, D.C., 1989); Stephany Griffith-Jones, *International Finance and Latin America* (New York, 1984); Stephany Griffith-Jones, *Managing World Debt* (New York, 1988); Kenneth Kletzer, "External Borrowing by LDCs: A Survey of Some Theoretical Issues," in Gustav Ranis and T. Paul Schultz, eds., *The State of Development Economics* (Oxford, 1988), 579–612; Donald R. Lessard and John Williamson, *Financial Intermediation Beyond the Debt Crisis* (Cambridge, Mass., 1985); Jeffrey D. Sachs, ed., *Developing Country Debt and Economic Performance*, in three volumes as follows: vol. 1 (Chicago, 1989), vol. 2, *Country Studies—Argentina, Bolivia, Brazil, Mexico* (Chicago, 1990), and vol. 3, *Country Studies—Indonesia, Korea, Philippines, Turkey* (Chicago, 1989); Luis Serven and Andres Solimano, "Debt Crisis, Adjustment Policies and Capital Formation in Developing Countries: Where Do We Stand?" *World Development* 21, no. 1 (January 1993): 127–140; Christian Suter, *Debt Cycles in the World-Economy: Foreign Loans, Financial Crises, and Debt Settlements, 1820–1990* (Boulder, Colo., 1992); Paul Wachtel, ed., *Crises in the Economic and Financial Structure* (Lexington, Mass., 1982); and a symposium on new institutions for developing-country debt published in the *Journal of Economic Perspectives* 4, no. 1 (Winter 1990): 3–56, with articles by Kenneth Rogoff, Peter B. Kenen, Jeffrey D. Sachs, Jeremy Bulow, and Jonathan Eaton. *WDR 1985* addressed the issue. The World Bank's voluminous *World Debt Tables*, annual, contain the raw material for any study. I also made use of material in the *Wall Street Journal*, *The Economist*, and the *IMF Survey*.
34. Statement before the House Banking Committee, February 2, 1983, cited by Fieleke, "International Lending on Trial," 6.
35. See Sebastian Edwards, "The Pricing of Bonds and Bank Loans in International Markets," NBER Working Paper No. 1689 (1985).
36. See Charles Collyns and Mohamed El-Erian, "Restructuring of Commercial Bank Debt by Developing Countries: Lessons from Recent Experience," IMF Paper on Policy Analysis and Assessment (1993); K. Burke Dillon et al., "Recent Developments in External Debt Restructuring," IMF Occasional Paper No. 40 (1985), which is a thorough survey of the early reschedulings with details of the individual agreements; and *The Economist*, September 12, 1992.
37. A. D. Knox in *South*, August 1988.
38. See Collyns and El-Erian, "Restructuring of Commercial Bank Debt by Developing Countries: Lessons from Recent Experience" and *The Economist*, September 12, 1992.

39. Benjamin J. Cohen, "What Ever Happened to the LDC Debt Crisis," *Challenge* 34, no. 3 (May/June 1991): 47–51.
40. See Collyns and El-Erian, "Restructuring of Commercial Bank Debt by Developing Countries"; and Jeffrey Sachs, "Making the Brady Plan Work," *Foreign Affairs* 68 (Summer 1989): 705–713.
41. *WDR 1991*, p. 127.
42. For this section I depended heavily on the "Symposium on New Institutions for Developing Country Debt" in the *Journal of Economic Perspectives* 4, no. 1 (Winter 1990): 3–56, with articles by Kenneth Rogoff, Peter B. Kenen, Jeffrey D. Sachs, Jeremy Bulow, and Jonathan Eaton. I also used C. Fred Bergsten, William R. Cline, and John Williamson, *Bank Lending to Developing Countries: The Policy Alternatives* (Washington, D.C., 1985); Frances Stewart, "The International Debt Situation and North–South Relations," *World Development* 13, no. 2 (1985): 197–200; and many articles in *The Economist*.
43. Jonathan Eaton, "Debt Relief and the International Enforcement of Loan Contracts," *Journal of Economic Perspectives* 4, no. 1 (Winter 1990): 43–56.
44. *WDR 1992*, 169.
45. IMF, *World Economic Outlook 1992*, 22–23.

Chapter 7

Financing Development IV

Foreign Aid, the World Bank, The IMF

This chapter completes the discussion of financing development by considering the flows from governments and international institutions, comprising foreign aid and lending from the World Bank and the International Monetary Fund.

FOREIGN AID (OFFICIAL DEVELOPMENT ASSISTANCE)

Government-to-government foreign aid (often called ODA for official development assistance), often serves political rather than strictly economic purposes. But it is important for the lowest-income LDCs which are least able to attract private foreign capital. In 1992, aid amounted to about one-fifth of all the capital flows to the LDCs, and double that for the low-income LDCs. Aid currently amounts to over 20% of GNP in a number of countries, including Burundi, Chad, Equatorial Guinea, Gambia, Guyana, Malawi, Mozambique (116%!), Nicaragua, Tanzania, Uganda, and Zambia. The average for all low-income LDCs is 13.6%, though when the middle-income LDCs are included in the figure, it falls to only 1.3%.[1]

Proving that aid is correlated with faster and better economic development is not an easy task. In general, countries with the largest receipts of aid have not registered the best performance. There are several reasons why. Aid is relatively small in amount, and, as we shall see, a great deal of it does not go to the lowest-income countries that could use it most. Much foreign exchange comes from other sources, and a country's own policies are extremely important. With proper policies, a low-income country can achieve strong growth with little or no aid, as China clearly demonstrates. With poor policies, large amounts of foreign aid may still not do much good.

Yet aid serves several very useful purposes. It may give a chance to buy off with better-designed alternative programs those who gain from such policies as protectionist trade barriers and cheap urban food. In the sense that it can finance policy improvements, government aid may be a catalyst for development by means of private enterprise. It can also finance health and education programs, agricultural research, roads, ports, power stations, and other infrastructure that may not pay off for 30 or 40 years. Even if the return is high in the long run, delays this extensive make such programs unsuitable for financing in the current private market for lending.[2] Because aid is usually either in the form of grants or concessional loans with an interest rate below the market rate, any problems of servicing a large debt are muted when such assistance is the vehicle for the transfer. (Nonetheless, for some countries there has been an ongoing debt crisis in the repayment of government-to-government loans, as described in a subsequent box.) Finally, aid is often packaged with good technical advice, help with management, and institution building, all less feasible with private lending. About a third of all aid has been free for use as the recipient LDC chooses, while the rest has been designated for specific projects. The most important project areas have been electricity, water, and sewage schemes; education, including some 100,000 students from LDCs attending universities and technical schools in developed countries; and agriculture. Investigations show that, broadly, about a third of foreign-aid-funded capital projects are highly successful, a third are satisfactory, and a third are a disappointment. Of the disappointments, about a tenth are a total loss.[3]

The position of foreign aid in the present political climate is much more a pragmatic than an idealistic one. Some countries, mostly small (including all of Scandinavia, Belgium, the Netherlands, and Canada), appear to act from principles of ethics, accepting that the present world distribution of income ought to be rectified and perhaps even accepting that there is a right or entitlement for poor people to receive aid. But most do not. Such moral arguments as debated by scholars who work on the ethics of economics—Amartya Sen, John Rawls, and Robert Nozick, among others—appear to have little impact on many major aid givers.[4] Among these nations, including the United States, foreign policy goals have a decided edge over moral arguments, though the collapse of communism and the virtual end to the Cold War mean that this situation may change.

In 1993, the official development assistance from the developed countries, including both grants (which predominate) and low-interest loans, amounted to about $67 billion. Significant amounts used to come from the Arab members of OPEC and Communist countries, but Arab aid has recently dropped sharply and aid from the former Communist countries has collapsed. (Most Arab aid goes to

Egypt, Jordan, Turkey, Morocco, and Syria.)* Corrected for inflation, aid has grown by only about one-third in the quarter of a century since 1965. In that year, the developed nations had been giving 0.48% of their combined GNP to the LDCs, but by 1992 the figure had fallen back to 0.33%.

For years, the United Nations has applied pressure for an aid target, 0.7% of rich-country GNP. (Notice that this figure is not graduated by ability to pay.)[5] Only a very few developed countries—Denmark, the Netherlands, Norway, which leads with 1.12%, and Sweden—have reached that goal. Japan, formerly the least-generous developed country, is now the largest giver of foreign aid ($11.3 billion in 1993, 0.30% of GNP), while the United States, at $9.0 billion, is the second-largest. But U.S. aid as a proportion of GNP has fallen steadily, from about 2% of GNP during the Marshall Plan after World War II to 0.27% in 1980 and to 0.14% in 1993, which is lowest among the developed countries. In real terms, U.S. aid in 1993 was 25% lower than the year before.

Contrary to public opinion on the subject, U.S. aid is a small part of the federal budget, making up only about 1% of the total. The public's reluctance to support foreign aid is partly based on misinformation. Sometimes pollsters find that people believe a country is giving ten times more in aid than it actually is.[6] Whatever the facts, opinion polls that ask what budget item should be cut first if cutting is to be done find the public gives the spot of honor overwhelmingly to foreign aid. A Clements Poll in 1992 showed 80% of U.S. voters wanted to cut foreign aid, compared to just over 40% each for space activities and the military.

Developments in Foreign Aid Programs

Recent years have seen both favorable and unfavorable developments in the foreign aid picture. On the plus side for aid proponents, the end of the Cold War has meant somewhat less politicization of aid. The important decision has been taken by the developed countries that all aid to the lowest-income LDCs (34 at the time) would be grants, not loans. This was followed by a decision to write off the loans made earlier to this group, ending the burdensome flow of interest and principal from the poorest to the rich.

Even for the better-off LDCs, there has been a similar tendency to replace loans with grants; about two-thirds of all aid is now in the form of grants. Repayment of principal and interest on foreign aid debt is thus steadily shrinking and, at the start of the debt crisis, was well below 5% of that on other foreign debt owed by the LDCs.

In any case, a grant element is often present even in official loans to LDCs. This is true when the interest rate is below that available on the open market, when

*There is even a little aid from the LDCs themselves but less than a billion dollars total. India and China have been significant contributors, mostly in the form of technical assistance. Others who give some aid include Argentina, Brazil, Colombia, Israel, Mexico, South Korea, and Venezuela. It does seem entirely reasonable that countries receiving aid in the past should, as they develop, give aid themselves. In time, this would mean a sizable augmentation of the amount of aid available.

longer repayment periods are allowed (the average maturity is now a long 30 years), or when there is a grace period with no repayment required (seven years is average). If this grant element is at least 25% of the value of a loan, the aid is considered "concessional." Technically, the concessional element in loan aid is the difference between the amount of the loan and the present discounted value of the stream of repayments. This concessional element also grows if aid is disbursed quickly as opposed to a lengthy gestation period of disbursements.

Outpayments that take a long time can easily cut the concessionary element in half. There is often some trade-off between the total volume of aid a donor provides and how concessional that aid is. Concessional aid is particularly apt when a long-term activity generates little immediate revenue with which to repay loans and where charging for a loan-financed service would cut its use by the poor—for example, immunization or clean water supplies.[7]

THE "PARIS CLUB" FOR OFFICIAL DEBT

Even though official loans are often concessional, there has been an ongoing crisis in the repayment of these loans. Rescheduling of this debt is done within the so-called *Paris Club*, staffed by French Treasury officials. There creditor nations negotiate the rescheduling of official debt with debtor countries. Between 1980 and mid-1992, there were 183 Paris Club reschedulings with 55 countries. The Paris Club negotiations have had the most importance for Africa, where debt is mostly (72%) official. Yet only five out of 50 Paris Club countries had reached normal debtor–credit relationships by 1990.[8] Many are not likely to make it anytime soon.

Developed-country governments eventually decided in the Toronto Agreement of 1988 to allow reschedulings more liberal than those for private loans. The Toronto terms allowed a lengthening to 25 years for all ODA debt, with a 14-year grace period.[9] Through 1991, 20 debtors had been granted 28 reschedulings under the Toronto terms.

Even after the Toronto terms reschedulings, official debt still represented a burden on the lowest-income countries. As in the debt crisis concerning bank loans, reschedulings were not enough. There had to be debt forgiveness as well. In 1990, at the behest of John Major (then British chancellor the exchequer), the Toronto terms were amended by the "Trinidad terms." Under the Trinidad terms, half the bilateral official debt ($3 billion) of the low-income LDCs with a good repayment record was cancelled. (The United States did so in 1993 for 18 low-income African countries.) Repayment on the remaining official debt was extended over 25 years with a five-year grace period.[10] Clearly, some African countries such as Ethiopia, Mozambique, Somalia, and Sudan, were unable to meet even the Trinidad terms. In that continent, *all* government-to-government debt to governments will probably have to be written off. Critics worry that writing off loans would not result in the debt service being used for useful purposes such as education or health, but would result instead in just more leakages into waste and corruption.[11] Yet the African situation is serious, with interest payments claiming four times more than the total spending on health. Burundi's debt service is 30% of its government budget, while Uganda spends about two-thirds of its foreign exchange earnings on debt service. (The sub-Saharan African average is 20%.) It should be noted that about 28% of Africa's debt is to the World Bank and the International Monetary Fund, organizations considered later in the chapter. Under the current rules of these organizations, their loans cannot be reduced or written off.

More aid from developed-country governments is now being channeled through international agencies such as the World Bank. Multilateral aid, as this is called, has reduced charges of political meddling, has often brought good advice, has delivered more assistance to the very poor, and has cut the duplication of effort that sometimes occurs among many individual donors.* Such aid more than doubled in the 1970s, and in 1991–1992 it made up 29% of the total.

Criticisms of Aid

Foreign aid programs involve some controversial features that have been criticized by recipients and by many in donor countries as well.

Tied Aid One problem is that bilateral aid is so often "tied"; that is, the recipient is required to spend the funds received on goods produced in the donor country.[12] The United States was tying over 80% of its bilateral aid in the 1970s, and most Japanese and British aid was tied as well.[13] Some aid was "double-tied"; that is, it had to be spent on a specific project and on goods supplied by the donor.

Donors like tying because every dollar of aid automatically means a dollar of exports, which is important if balance of payments problems are present or if exporters have a strong lobby. Moreover, tied aid often must be shipped in the vessels of the contributing country, at a cost half again to more than double the cost of shipping with the cheapest carrier.[14] (Seventy-five percent of U.S. agricultural aid must go in U.S. ships, approximately doubling the transport cost.)[15]

Recipients do not like tying because the donor may not be the world's cheapest producer, sheltering its high-priced production behind protectionist trade barriers. Businesspeople facing a certain sale will raise their prices in any case. Tying may also mean accepting lower quality goods. Current estimates are that 15% to 20% of

*In the early 1980s, 60 donors were trying to administer 600 separate projects in Kenya. As one example of the results, donors had given the country 18 different models of water pumps. A wide variety of the same medical equipment had also been donated, some of it soon out of service because maintenance is so difficult. (See *WDR 1985*, 107, and *The Economist*, May 7, 1994.) Also in the 1980s, there were 188 projects from 50 donors in Malawi, 321 from 61 in Lesotho, and 614 from 69 in Zambia. "In such numbers, the effectiveness of aid can be severely reduced," according to the World Bank (*WDR 1985*, 107). Some coordination has been achieved under World Bank and UN auspices, however, by aid groups ("consortia") and round tables. In these groups, donors consult on joint approaches. There are currently about 20 active consortia.

the money value of aid to the LDCs is lost because of tying; in some individual cases, the loss is much higher. Clearly, tying also means aid is limited to covering foreign exchange costs and not local costs of projects, and so the tied aid is much more concentrated on capital outlays than on day-to-day recurrent spending. Actually, only some 8% of all aid, tied or untied, is used for this latter purpose. Big dams and superhighways and big hospitals are all an outcome of tying.[16] The concentration on capital may contribute to overly high capital intensity in aid-financed projects.

Undoubtedly the situation is improving, however. Donor governments reached agreement in 1991 to bar tied aid to the upper-middle-income LDCs (those with per capita GNPs above $2450). The low-income LDCs (below $610) will continue to receive tied aid, while the in-betweens will do so when market loans are not available and when projects cannot generate enough income to cover repayment. By the end of 1991, the United States was tying only about 20% of its aid compared to 57% in 1986 and 80% in the previous decade. The U.S. figure is currently lowest among the developed countries. (Forty percent or more is representative of the developed countries as a whole).[17]

The Politics of Aid That aid is permeated with politics is widely apparent. For example, the former colonial powers still have a few colonies that in some cases receive huge amounts of money that is counted in the ODA totals. France, for example, gives its South American colony of French Guiana over 700 times more aid per capita than India receives in aid from all sources. The little French island of Réunion in the Indian Ocean is the world's fifteenth largest aid recipient. Of all foreign aid given by the European Community, over 50% goes to the African-Caribbean-Pacific (ACP) states that, although they have only about a tenth of the Third World's population, are almost all former colonies of the EC members. Most Japanese aid goes to Asian countries.

Foreign aid has become a tool of domestic and foreign politics to be doled out to friends and clients or cut off with dramatic suddenness when differences arise. Political exigencies and economic need are far from the same thing, explaining why over 40% the world's bilateral foreign aid goes to middle-income LDCs that contain only some 20% of the world's absolute poor.[18] The politics of the situation are obvious. *Almost half* of U.S. aid goes to Israel and Egypt. Aid per person to Israel is about $400, while to Egypt it is $280. Neither is among the truly needy. By contrast, sub-Saharan Africa gets $35 per person and India only $3. The richest 40% of the LDCs receive about twice as much aid per capita as the poorest 40%; only a quarter of all aid goes to the ten countries that contain three-quarters of the world's poor.[19] As a vivid example, El Salvador receives five times as much aid as Bangladesh, even though Bangladesh has 24 times more people and only one-fifth of the income.[20]

Politics also play a role in the type of aid, which is subject to swings of political opinion. In the 1980s, with the greater conservatism among developed-country electorates and governments, aid shifted heavily toward helping private enterprise rather than government programs and projects.[21] Much aid goes for military purposes or indirectly supports the military because aid is fungible. Give a dollar to a country to finance health care, and a dollar of its own is freed up to fund its military.

Twice as much aid goes to countries that are big spenders on their militaries compared to those that are not.*

In addition, aid budgets are now being divided with the former Communist countries at the very time that the end of the Cold War has eliminated one of the motives for giving aid. The problem is greatest with concessional aid. Of course, self-interest does seem to militate that the former Communist countries be granted aid, but it seems likely that this will detract from aid to the LDCs. All these political considerations make it probable that aid will be of major importance for only a few of the countries that need it most.

A Critique of the Effects of Aid in the LDCs

Many economists, including both radicals and conservatives, argue that over time aid is certain to involve adverse effects on the recipient country. Such effects might include the politicization of domestic economic policy as effort and trained personnel are thrown into the search for grants rather than into the battle for development. They might include a damaging loss of self-reliance as countries become dependent on aid and as aid strengthens the government sector at the expense of the private sector. One recent line of thought is that aid may reduce the necessity for an LDC government to negotiate with its people concerning the allocation of a country's resources, and leads to increased corruption. Though arguably donor governments ought to take some responsibility for assuring that recipient governments' accountability is not reduced—perhaps by means of incentive mechanisms—they seldom do.[22]

The criticism of aid extends to what it finances.[23] Aid may have little impact on growth if the proceeds do not go for additional physical and human capital formation but rather to finance further consumption. It is noteworthy that only 7% of all aid goes for human welfare purposes, such as education, health, and the reduction of population growth.[24] Aid may also substitute for domestic saving. The programs may largely benefit politicians, large landholders, the educated elite, the civil service, the military, the owners of factories protected by trade barriers, and, more generally, urban areas as opposed to rural.

Aid givers may prefer monuments to their own generosity (with the aid tied so donor countries can get the orders and contracts) to projects with a high rate of economic return. Examples of large showcase projects that are not the most helpful are abundant. Aid might build hospitals and so divert medical staff away from

*Of U.S. foreign aid, about a quarter is military assistance. (Reliable data on security assistance are not widely available; the United States is one of the few countries that provides such data.) The three main components of U.S. security assistance are the Military Assistance Program (MAP), which provides grants; the Economic Support Fund (ESF), which provides balance of payments help and finances commodity import programs, increasingly on a grant basis; and the Foreign Military Sales (FMS) program, which enables countries to purchase military hardware and services on credit. Israel and Egypt dominate the MAP, ESF, and FMS programs. ESF money, which is generally a nationwide subsidy and is seldom targeted specifically toward the poor, is a major reason why an LDC's military can be supported even without loans and grants. It frees a country's own funds for financing its armed forces, as described in the text.

rural areas (in 1988–89, 33% of the foreign aid for health in Jamaica went for hospitals). It might finance machinery to mechanize tasks that could be done by cheap labor. It might result in new universities when what is truly needed is more primary schools. (In sub-Saharan Africa during the 1980s, each primary school student on average received $1 in foreign aid, each secondary school student $11, and each university student $575.) When aid is misconceived, its positive effect on growth may be small.

The point can even be made that aid could conceivably be regressive for donors. The tax systems that finance the foreign aid of the donors may have many loopholes for the rich and a heavier relative burden on the middle classes. Meanwhile, the benefits of aid transferred through these tax systems may go to a favored elite. If foreign aid is to improve the world distribution of income, as Robert Lekachman of the City University of New York has pointed out, then taxing low- or middle-income American workers to support and enrich the entourage of some Third World leader does not seem the appropriate way to go about it.

The Special Problems of Food Aid Food aid is the focus of particular controversy. In 1992, about one-sixth of the least developed LDCs' food imports came as a gift.[25] Such aid seems the essence of humane dealing with the Third World. In cases of famine (discussed in Chapter 10), it can represent the difference between life and death and is the most immediately vital form of all aid. A little surprisingly, given these obvious merits, even this type of aid is controversial, with serious issues of long-term strategy. We should insist at once that modest short-term food aid is unlikely to cause serious harm as an offset to its obvious benefits. If it did, then it would presumably be good practice to reverse the policy by destroying a little food now and then, which would be absurd.

Yet food aid has usually involved the disposal of surplus agricultural commodities put into stock in the developed countries because of their price support programs. Surplus disposal may lead to large quantities of food depressing free-market food prices, and so ruining local incentives to produce. For example, thousands of Indian farmers were bankrupted by U.S. wheat giveaways in the 1950s and 1960s. Food aid after the 1976 earthquake in Guatemala came on the heels of one of that country's largest wheat harvests; prices plummeted and made it harder for farming villages to recover. In the 1984–1985 famine in East Africa, food aid began to reach remote areas such as Darfur in western Sudan and Wollo in northern Ethiopia just as harvests were being collected. Local farmers and traders were ruined.[26]

Much has been learned concerning what not to do. A considerable amount of food aid is now sold on markets, with the local government using the revenue for seed and fertilizer (though also sometimes for higher salaries and more armaments). The U.S. Food for Progress Plan instituted in 1986 uses food aid to promote agricultural reform. The proceeds from sales of the food are used to ease the removal of subsidies. India has a similar scheme. It sells the free food coming as aid, then puts the revenue into agricultural inputs such as cattle, improved processing, and better marketing. Improvements in the planning and coordination of a sometimes haphazard effort have also been added by the valuable, though little-known, U.N. World Food Program. It now handles some 20% of the world's emergency food distributions.

When food aid is given, however, it is still not easy to encourage local production and to keep in repair age-old famine defenses. The aid can interfere with the sale of substitute foods produced by farmers in other, less affected parts of the country, and the migration of pastoralists to better pastures. It is difficult to prevent inappropriate consumption habits—say, a shift from local millet to imported wheat—from spreading. It is also hard to guard against corrupt practices, political manipulation by both donors and recipients, and the solidifying of government agricultural policies that depress farm prices. High taxation of farmers is obviously more feasible if large-scale food aid is being received.

The Reform of Foreign Aid

Such complaints point to the need for reform in both donor and recipient countries. Reform is certainly possible. Aid could be awarded only in response to a recipient's performance, according to such tests as raising saving; increasing the efficiency of investment; improving the infrastructure of transport, communication, power, and human capital; improving the equity of taxation; and adopting economic and political reforms. Such tests are relatively rare. Aid could also be used as a lever for the control of illegal migration, pollution, nuclear proliferation, terrorism, the drug trade, and the like, but this, too, is rare.[27] Yet all these tests would probably favor LDCs that need aid less than others that would come apart without support from this source. Cutting off aid to those that need it most, even if they do not use it best, would be a difficult decision to take.[28]

The United Nations is currently seeking to forge a human development compact called 20–20 that would rectify some of these imbalances. Under 20–20, LDCs would budget at least 20% of their government spending for human welfare spending (compared to 13% now) while developed countries would allocate 20% of their foreign aid for the same purpose (7% now). The LDCs would have to find the funds by reducing military spending, and cutting out loss-making public enterprises and wasteful showcase projects, while donors would have to do the same. That such a reasonable suggestion is everywhere treated as a pipe dream shows how far the world still has to go to achieve economic rationality in its management of foreign aid.[29]

Aid once seemed the central topic in development. Not so now. In the Third World attention has, understandably given its record, swung away from it. The exceptions are the countries with the lowest income, which have little other choice than to pursue aid, and in the favored few, such as Israel and Egypt, whose political clout ensures a continued or increased flow. The old slogan "trade not aid" is obviously winning out. In 1992, the LDCs earned $763 billion in foreign exchange from their combined merchandise exports, which was about 16 times the aid they received. The trade–aid ratio had been only four in the early 1960s. Whatever the value of aid—and it remains crucial for the LDCs with the lowest income—"trade not aid" appears to be both slogan and prophecy.

Private Aid One last, perhaps unexpected footnote. As aid has become more politicized, there has been a surge in effort from private nongovernmental organizations (NGOs), or voluntary organizations (PVOs) or voluntary agencies (Volags) as they are sometimes called. In the developed countries, there are now about 2500 NGOs that deal with the LDCs.[30] Some of the names are familiar everywhere, whereas some are less well known: the Red Cross and Red Crescent, Oxfam, CARE, Caritas, Catholic Relief Services, Save the Children, Interaction, World Vision, Misereor (Germany), Mani Tese (Italy), Maisons Familiales Rurales (France), the Aga Khan Foundation, and many others. The private aid groups are philanthropic, often more trusted than governments, often free from political entanglements, and usually interested in helping those who need the help the most, especially through the development of local self-reliance. Most frequently, they assist local branches of the organization in the LDCs, or transfer their aid to the many independent NGOs that have sprung up in the LDCs themselves. (Some countries have thousands, though too often a proportion of these are really commercial operations in disguise or under the thumb of governments.)[31]

Flows of aid from developed-country governments and NGOs to NGOs in the LDCs is currently about 13% of net official aid. About 11% of U.S. governmental aid in the 1980s was so channeled.[32] Most of the aid originates with governments; assistance from the developed-country NGOs is only about 4% of all aid flows. Though NGOs are only a small part of the aid scene at present, they are growing and morally influential. If a normative statement may be permitted, the effort is altogether laudable.[33] Is such voluntarism the shape of things to come? Will government see merit in transferring more of their aid money to private voluntary organizations to capitalize on the latter's growing reputation? Perhaps.

BORROWING FROM THE WORLD BANK

Governments often have to borrow to create infrastructure, but the long nature of the investment means that funding from private capital markets may be inadequate. Long-term capital flows to the LDCs are available from the International Bank for Reconstruction and Development (IBRD), universally known as the World Bank. A product of the 1944 Bretton Woods Conference at the Mt. Washington Hotel in New Hampshire, the World Bank is actually a family of three related institutions that administer three different sorts of lending to the LDCs. The parent World Bank itself, located in Washington, D.C., by tradition has an American president (James D. Wolfensohn from 1995). A European always heads another product of Bretton Woods, the International Monetary Fund discussed later in the chapter. This clubby arrangement has not delighted the LDCs. Voting power on the Bank's board of directors is allocated according to a country's financial contribution to the Bank. The board has the power to reject staff decisions on lending, but to date it has never done so. Most of the Bank's staff (6800) are based at the Washington, D.C., headquarters. Only about 300 professional staff members are based in the field.[34]

The Bank's influence extends far beyond its capacity to make loans because the publications of its research departments are read avidly by development economists everywhere. This book's endnotes fairly reflect the influence this research has on scholarship. Financial capital for development loans is raised in some small part from the "capitalization" of the Bank, consisting of contributions from its member governments, which now number over 170 countries.* Primarily, however, the Bank's loans are funded by the sale of bonds on the world's capital markets, where the Bank is the single largest borrower. It is also the world's largest lender. It lends on regular commercial terms only to less-developed countries, and even among these, it "graduates" its borrowers when per capita income reaches $4080 in 1989 dollars. Almost all the authorized amount is usually loaned out at a given time; its outstanding loans totaled about $17 billion in 1993. Interest on its loans are at a variable rate set for six months at a time, the rate determined by adding a spread of one-half of 1% on top of what the Bank must pay to borrow in credit markets. (Governments have made much use of the Bank's expertise by putting a part of their foreign aid into projects cofinanced with the Bank.)

Because the Bank basically recycles its loans, making new ones when the old ones are paid off, defaults by borrowers would be painful. In the past the Bank carried virtually no bad debts, even after several years of debt crisis during the 1980s. Its policy is not to reschedule, as that would harm the Bank's AAA bond rating. Even so, problems have developed, with several countries recently in arrears for at least six months or more.

In lending for development projects in LDCs, the Bank estimates a likely rate of return. This must be above a minimum 10% for the project to go forward. Actual rates of return have exceeded this figure in about four-fifths of a sample of 236 projects studied. Only 14% of the Bank's projects were judged to have had an unsatisfactory outcome.[35] About 15% of the Bank's loans are in energy, 15% in transportation and communications, 14% in agriculture and rural development, and 8% in urban development. Another 22% of the lending is for education, control of population size, health, nutrition, water supply, and sewage treatment. Only 5% currently goes for industrial development.[36] (The highest average rate of return among all categories of World Bank lending has been in education, with the lowest in manufacturing.)

During the debt crisis, the Bank became involved in structural adjustment lending to help debtor LDCs eliminate damaging economic policies such as budget deficits, high subsidies, trade barriers, and overvalued exchange rates.[37] As we shall see, such lending reached nearly a third of the total in the late 1980s, though it has now sunk back to 17%.

International Development Association

The second of the Bank's agencies, dating from the late 1950s, is the International Development Association (IDA). The IDA is a major source of scarce concession-

*Traditionally, only 7.5% of the Bank's capitalization is actually paid in; the rest is "callable," to be paid only in case of need. Up to the present, no call on capital has ever been made. Alone of the major World Bank members, the United States has decided what the whole of any increase in capital has to be approved by Congress as new spending in the budget, even though at most only 7.5% actually has to be paid. It is not very likely that any call will be made in the foreseeable future unless the world financial situation worsens dramatically.

ary or "soft" finance, which means loans with very low interest rates and long maturities, for the lowest-income LDCs. Its budget is about a third the size of the parent World Bank. (Its outstanding loans totaled $6.8 billion in 1993.) The IDA obtains its funds not from capital markets but wholly from grants replenished every three years by the rich or better-off governments (32 at present). The terms, recently tightened, are still very soft: Loans have long 40-year maturities (lowered from 50 years in 1987). They are interest free except for a 0.75% service fee and have a grace period of ten years before repayment of the principal begins. Eligibility for IDA loans is effectively limited to the 40-odd low-income countries with per capita incomes of $805 or less. Numerous other LDCs have now been graduated because their incomes are above the cutoff figure; others have never been eligible because they were never in the low-income group. (Three former IDA recipients—Colombia, South Korea, and Turkey—are now IDA donors. A reasonable question is why IDA credits should not be paid back early by countries that have achieved development success, such as South Korea.) The fact that countries can be ineligible for IDA credits even though their per capita incomes are low, but not low enough, has led to the suggestion that an intermediate level be established between IDA credits and regular World Bank lending—but funds are always short, and so far the idea has gone nowhere.

The same standards for expected performance of projects are used for IDA credits as for parent World Bank loans, but far more of the loans (amounting to nearly half) are in agriculture. They are usually paid out over a four- to ten-year period. Recent rates of return, although more variable than the World Bank's, are on average the same or slightly better, reflecting the great capital shortages in the low-income LDCs. In spite of this good performance, there have been failures: In total, about a fifth of IDA loans have not managed an economic rate of return of 10% or more, and nearly 9% of IDA's loans have had a negative rate of return. A few of the failures have been monumental.

By far the biggest recipients of IDA loans have been India and China, but because funds are limited, it has proved necessary to put a ceiling on loans to them and their share has dropped. Sub-Saharan Africa now receives about half of all IDA loans. The agency brings significant amounts of investment to the poorest countries on much easier terms than would otherwise be obtainable. Importantly, it also serves to separate out the worst risks, protecting the World Bank's treasured AAA bond rating and so allowing it to borrow in world credit markets on the most favorable terms.

The funding of the IDA has not been easy. Because the moneys come not from the capital markets but from donor governments at three-year intervals, legislative approval often presents obstacles. Several times the U.S. Congress has delayed and stretched out the U.S. contribution, leaving the IDA on the verge of a temporary shutdown and reducing its funding substantially. For example, the funding for IDA–7 (the seventh replenishment) of 1984 to 1986 was a quarter below that of IDA–6 (1981 to 1983), and financing at the start of the 1990s was lower in real terms than the figure from a decade before. In the most recent replenishment (IDA–10, 1994 to 1996), the U.S. Congress voted its share for only two of the three years, with the third year's funding to be made available only if "the World Bank becomes more open in its decision making."[38]

As with the World Bank itself, one response to IDA funding difficulties has been the syndication of loans with private lenders and governments. The cofinancing to supplement IDA credits with bilateral loans has been as much as half or more of the IDA's own funds.

The International Finance Corporation

The third World Bank agency, dating from 1956, is the International Finance Corporation (IFC).[39] The IFC is even smaller than the IDA. In 1993 it lent $3.9 billion of its own funds to 185 firms. The IFC lends only for investments in the private sectors of its 161 member countries, borrowing for this purpose from the World Bank and also floating its own bonds on world capital markets. When private investors buy 10- to 20-year IFC bonds, the IFC invests the proceeds in LDC firms, receiving stock in return that is the backing for its dollar-denominated debt obligations.

Much cofinancing occurs with governments and entrepreneurs in the host country, so the actual investment is usually multiplied by three or four times the stated value of IFC loans. In any given project, the IFC is always the minority partner. Latin America receives the most IFC money, Asia is second, and Africa is last. Additionally, the IFC's Emerging Markets Growth Fund (discussed in Chapter 6) is aiding LDC stock markets.

Due to the fact that the IFC lends only in the private sector and advises on ways to improve local capital markets, it has been much preferred to both the IDA and the World Bank by those who support development through private enterprise and not government. Many mainstream development economists, reflecting on the mixed record of public enterprise in the LDCs, also see some advantage in the IFC's approach. These same economists are, however, less comfortable with any assumption that the private sector alone is necessarily a better milieu for development than an appropriate public-private mix. Private entrepreneurs, however talented and hardworking, face great barriers in the low-income LDCs that loans, even generous ones, are unlikely to overcome fully. They must cope with an inadequate infrastructure of transport and communication, limited education, overly rapid population growth, and poorly developed institutions for money and credit management and marketing. All are areas that may not respond rapidly to individual entrepreneurial effort in the private sector and all have the potential to block that effort. It seems fair to suggest that only in a country already approaching developed status are these problems likely to be inconsequential.

For some, even the private-enterprise orientation of the IFC has not been enough. In 1991, the United States stopped a capital increase for the IFC as a protest against the parent World Bank's alleged favoritism toward large government programs. One wonders about the good sense of this, seeing that the IFC is the private lending arm of the World Bank, but so it transpired.

Criticisms of the World Bank

The new prominence of the IFC and the debates concerning it fully reflect the politicization of other Bank activities. Some critics wish to impose a human-rights

THE REGIONAL DEVELOPMENT BANKS

In addition to the World Bank family, there are three other smaller international lending agencies that operate only in specific geographical areas but are run on lines similar to the World Bank. The Asian Development Bank, founded in 1964, had loans of $9 billion in 1991 and is the largest of the three, with Japan as its most important contributor. It is not very active in the field and follows the older World Bank "large projects" strategy. The African Development Bank, founded in 1966 and the smallest at $4 billion, is too much under the control of African governments. It has sometimes made loans to governments before an adjustment program could be worked out with the World Bank, causing considerable friction with the Bank. The Inter-American Development Bank, (IDB), founded in 1959, has loans of about $5 billion. It is the least-criticized of the group, though Latin American countries frequently squabble over who will get its loans.

Each of the regional banks borrows on world capital markets and lends mostly for projects on near-commercial terms. Each has a soft-loan affiliate, a fund resembling the IDA, established with rich-country contributions. In addition, the Inter-American Development Bank has an IFC-like agency lending to private enterprise. The argument has been made that the regional development banks should undertake more of the World Bank's project loans and leave the macro stabilization and adjustment programs to the World Bank.

Rates of return have been similar to those of the World Bank. The Asian Development Bank and the IDB concluded recently that 60% of their sample entirely met their lending objectives, 30% partially did so, and 10% were marginal or unsatisfactory.[40]

test on lending, but the World Bank group's various charters permit no discrimination among members in lending. Other critics attack loans for projects such as textile mills, iron ore, copper mining (to Chile), and steel manufacture (to India and Pakistan)—the output from which would compete with developed-country producers. Conservatives criticize what they see as an overemphasis on government projects generally, rather than on private enterprise, hence their preference for the IFC. (By way of rebuttal, defenders of the Bank reply that no more than about 15% of World Bank aid actually competes with the private sector, the rest going for infrastructure development and to finance activity in the private sector.)[41]

Projects or Programs? The LDCs have their own criticisms of the World Bank family. The main one is that for a long time the loans of the Bank, the IDA, and the IFC were for specific projects only—for example, factories, railways, or port facilities. Because of the gestation period for any project, one result was that the Bank's annual disbursements were usually below half the sums approved for lending. LDCs' governments, and many economists as well, often contended also that capital needs could not easily be identified on a specific project-by-project basis. LDCs preferred more latitude to use Bank funding generally to support current spending programs connected with capital projects. Teachers' pay is every bit as much a drain on a government budget as the capital cost of school buildings. Further, it was difficult to support positive policy changes and economic reforms with project loans alone, and a project is not attractive if the economic environment surrounding it is unsound.

Project lending does have certain advantages from the Bank's point of view: Loans not specifically allocated to a project might end up being used for arms purchases, or be wasted or misused. Of course, if the LDC does not use its own funds for a project because the Bank finances it, then the loan is fungible—the resources freed by the loan could in any case be used to buy arms, or be wasted or misused.

Other criticisms concerning projects are that small ones are less favored than large because monitoring the small ones is administratively expensive for the Bank. It is charged that new investment gets priority over improvement in the efficiency of old investment because working capital balances covering labor costs and raw materials procurement are generally not eligible for financing. There is also a suspicion that capital-intensive projects are preferred to those that are labor-intensive because the capital-intensive type of technology is more readily available in the developed world.[42]

Adjustment Lending

The Bank finally recognized that the arguments against loans for projects alone had merit, and that good projects were not enough where the underlying economic policies were flawed. Loans for policy adjustments surged during the debt crisis, reaching 29% of the whole in 1989.[43] The Bank's adjustment loans for stabilizing economies and improving them structurally still make up about 17% of its lending. This financing often aims to assist in the dismantling of controls and to increase the influence of free market pricing, including trade policy reform, tax and financial reform, foreign exchange reform, and the revitalization of state-operated enterprises. Released in installments, the money can be dispensed far more rapidly than project assistance. Sectoral adjustment loans (SECALs) are directed toward the problems in some given sector, whereas structural adjustment loans (SALs) are for the economy as a whole; however, often their prescriptions are much the same. The Bank imposes conditions when it makes adjustment loans, with a wide variety of results from almost complete compliance to very little.[44] (The IDA has followed much the same path in these matters as that of the parent World Bank. Recently over a quarter of IDA's loans have been for adjustment rather than for projects.)

Adjustment lending has its critics. Investment fell in the adjusting countries, presumably because of the contractionary effects of the policy prescriptions. (Though how previous levels of investment could have been maintained during the debt crisis even if there had been no World Bank at all is a question that gives the critics difficulties. LDCs had no choice but to respond to the crisis in *some* manner. Business as usual was impossible.)[45] Some have charged that SALs are used to pay the debts of state enterprises and that to tinker with them without effecting an increase in their efficiency is wasteful. Some SAL funds have been used to perpetuate export subsidies, and the insistence on policy changes has not been strict enough. For example, neither SECALs nor SALs involve controls on capital flight or corruption. Even without such measures, adjustment has proved difficult. It means changes in incomes, benefits, rents, costs, and working conditions, and such changes may bring disappointment to powerful special interests.

Yet the Bank's studies of rates of return on its *projects* give a strong indication that they do better when the underlying macro policies are more positive. Table 7.1 shows the average rate of return on World Bank and IFC projects under different macro conditions.

A variety of effects from the Bank's adjustment lending have been identified.[46] The Bank's research indicates that countries that undertook adjustment early in the debt crisis did better than those that adjusted late or not at all. If dedicated and competent local bureaucracies are already in place, then adjustment is easier. A policy of promoting exports works much better if an economy's industries are strong enough to give up protective trade barriers, but lowering these barriers before industries are securely established may be damaging. One negative result of the Bank's adjustment lending is apparently that some of the funding has been diverted from loans to agriculture. Agricultural lending in general requires more staff resources to plan and carry out, and so funds were transferred to adjustment. In consequence, loans to agriculture have fallen from 39% of total loans in 1978 to 14% in 1993, a worrisome development.[47]

The World Bank's program lending clearly has similarities to the International Monetary Fund activities discussed in the next section and may suggest, as some have argued for years, that a union of the two Bretton Woods organizations might be pursued as a long-term goal. Certainly, better coordination between these organizations is called for. There is still no "cross-conditionality" (that is, need for approval from both bodies) for loans given by one of them.[48]

TABLE 7.1 AVERAGE RATE OF RETURN ON WORLD BANK AND IFC PROJECTS, 1968–1989 (IN PERCENT)

Trade restrictiveness	
High	13.2
Low	19.0
Foreign exchange overvaluation	
High (200% or more)	8.2
Low (less than 20%)	17.7
Real interest rate	
Negative	15.0
Positive	17.3
Fiscal deficit as % of GDP	
High (8% or greater)	13.4
Low (less than 4%)	17.8

Source: World Bank data for 1200 projects, from *WDR 1991*, 82.

People and the Environment Another criticism of the Bank involves what has been seen as its lack of concern for people and the environment. Undoubtedly the Bank's lending was not specifically targeted at the poor part of the population until recently. It has now adopted a Program of Targeted Interventions under which some of its loans must be directed generally at improving the lot of the poor. In 1992, 14% of the Bank's lending qualified. A similar criticism involves the lack of lending to improve the position of women. Here, too, there has been a response, with a Women in Development Division established in 1987. After this date, the situation appears to have improved. The proportion of agricultural lending that reaches women went from 9% before the division was established to 30% afterward. Women's share moved from 22% to 33% in education, while for population, health, and nutrition the figure is now 75%. But more remains to be done in a wide range of project lending.[49]

Some of the Bank's lending in the 1980s was for projects with negative results for people and the environment. The lending that resulted in cutting down parts of the Brazilian and Indonesian rain forests has achieved notoriety. The Brazilian Polonoreste project that drove roads for loggers into the rain forest, and the Indonesian transmigration scheme to shift population to less-densely populated areas where they engaged in intensive land clearing are cases in point.

The massive population resettlement (two million people in eight years) made necessary by some projects has also attracted unfavorable attention.[50] In India, the Upper Krishna II dam resulted in resettlement of 220,000 people, while the Maharashtra Composite Irrigation III scheme meant moving 168,000 more. Projects that displace large numbers of people have proved embarrassing for the Bank. It has withdrawn from some of them, and for others it has imposed rules requiring better compensation to those displaced and higher standards for resettlement. Large mining, power, and industrial projects raised similar concerns. Nowadays the annual meetings of the Bank are regularly picketed by environmentalists. In response, in 1993 the chastened Bank decided to set up an inspection panel to investigate complaints about its projects. It will now compensate people who are evicted by Bank projects, engage in consultation with indigenous peoples before projects are begun, and require environmental-impact statements for its new lending. These environmental issues are returned to in Chapter 16.

The World Bank Family: A Conclusion

The lending of the World Bank family and the regional development banks is important in total, about the same as foreign direct investment and not far below the figure for government-to-government foreign aid. Its capital flows together with the cofinancing it manages and the research expertise it brings to development issues give the Bank family a unique place in promoting economic change in the LDCs.

THE INTERNATIONAL MONETARY FUND

The International Monetary Fund (IMF) is another product, along with the World Bank, of the Bretton Woods Conference of 1944. Its headquarters are also in Washington, D.C. During the debt crisis, the IMF was the first international institution to be involved, and its lending and the conditions of its loans were essential in meeting the crisis and a focus of criticism as well. The Fund, traditionally headed by a European (and since 1987 by Michel Camdessus of France), is a fascinating institution. It employs about 1700 staff, far below the 6800 at the World Bank. The vigorous debates over its role are more comprehensible when one understands something of its mechanics, which is where we shall commence.

From the beginning, countries have joined the IMF by initially paying a subscription fee, or quota, made up of 75% of their own national currency and 25% in hard currencies, mainly the dollar or, nowadays, the special drawing rights (SDRs) of the IMF (which are considered later). Portugal, for example, paid $18.8 million worth of hard currency and $56.2 million worth of its own escudos as its membership fee. The quotas are determined somewhat obscurely by a formula, last modified in 1982–1983, that is based mostly on a country's GDP, its foreign exchange reserves, and several aspects of its foreign trade. Broadly, the formula establishes a country's relative place in the world economy.[51] Nowadays, when quotas are increased (usually every five years), selective adjustments are often made to reflect changes in the world economy. For example, in the 1990 quota increase (the ninth), 60% of the increase was in proportion to the previous quotas while 40% was in the form of special adjustments, the most important being an increase for Japan's to the level of Germany's. It is the sum total of these quota inpayments from its 178 members that furnishes most of the cash that the IMF has available to lend to those in need. The principle resembles that of a neighborhood credit union, but on a giant scale.

The IMF's ninth review of quotas in 1990 raised them 50% to about $193 billion.* It took a long time for member governments to ratify this increase (the United States ratified only after many delays in 1992), and so the tenth review has been postponed. Quotas range from very large (the United States at about $38 billion) to tiny (Marshall Islands, $3.5 million). The quota size determines the number of votes a country has in the Fund's decision-making process. In IMF voting, each member has 250 votes plus one more for each 100,000 SDRs of quota. The five members with the largest quotas each appoint an executive director. The United States, with about 18% of the voting power, is well above the 15% needed under the IMF's bylaws to veto any key issue. If the LDCs vote together, they also have a veto, with about 30% of the votes.[52] Reform of voting has been sought by many LDCs, who would like to see an expansion of the basic voting power and to have population size taken explicitly into account.

The IMF's quotas make up the largest portion of what that organization has available to lend. However, only about half of the listed amount is really usable

*The subsequent admission of new countries has raised the total of all quotas to about $209 billion. The dollar amounts here and in other cases later in the chapter are conversions from the IMF's special drawing rights, or SDRs, which are explained later. The actual amount of the IMFs quotas after the ninth review was 135 billion SDRs, up from the previous figure of 90 billion SDRs. Quotas now stand at 146 billion SDRs. One SDR originally equaled one U.S. dollar, but the value of the SDR now floats, and when expressed in dollars its value can vary. In recent years, one SDR has equaled a little more than $1.40. From 1985 to 1989, when the SDR ranged from SDR 1 = $0.96 to 1 = $1.21, the dollar figures were lower. To obtain exact dollar amounts for a given date, the figures in SDRs must be converted into dollars at the dollar–SDR exchange rate on that date.

because many countries, especially LDCs, have inconvertible currencies surrounded by exchange controls, so that no one would want to borrow them. The billions of "soft" Nigerian naira, Nicaraguan cordobas, Burmese kyats, and the like held on the books of the Fund are, for any practical purpose, virtually useless. Even a relatively hard currency, such as the Paraguayan guarani, might be traded only in thin markets with high exchange costs and would be lent infrequently and only to a neighboring trading partner, such as Argentina, Brazil, or Uruguay. For this reason, the IMF's lending is always far less than its total of quotas.

Working in the other direction, the total available for lending is increased by another $24 billion made available from a group of developed countries united in the so-called General Arrangements to Borrow (GAB).* Some economists argue that the funding from the GAB is less appropriate than are quota increases because in the GAB the major developed countries and not the IMF retain ultimate control over the funds. The IMF also has the authority to borrow from private sources, but it does not do so.

Financing from the IMF

For each country its quota is the primary determinant of how much it is able to obtain from the IMF. A first drawing of funds is virtually automatic, available at any time and without strings. A country simply exchanges its own currency for its original 25% share (called the *reserve tranche*, *tranche* being French for "slice"), which it paid in the form of hard currency. After that, the *first credit tranche* allows a country to use its own currency to purchase hard currency equal in value to another 25% of its quota, also with virtually no strings. Three further credit tranches may be exchanged in each of three subsequent years, each amounting to 25% of the original quota. The first credit tranche requires a "reasonable effort" to meet the problems that caused the exchange of currencies to take place, whereas the upper credit tranches require a "substantial and viable program." The exchanges involved in the credit tranches must be reversed over three-and-a-quarter to five years, with hard currency paid back into the IMF in exchange for the country's own currency. No charge is made on the reserve tranche, while the charge is 6.50% per year on the credit tranches. Standby arrangements can be made in advance, allowing an LDC to go through the formalities before financing is needed. In 1994, 16 countries had IMF standby arrangements.

The IMF's "Facilities" During the debt crisis, the IMF established several special "facilities," which involve loans rather than exchanges of currency. These loans have a longer duration than the exchanges, and they carry low interest rates. The facilities have a strong resemblance to the World Bank's IDA. These facilities were

*The GAB was established in 1962 and originally included ten countries (hence the much-used name "Group of 10"): the United States, Germany, Japan, Britain, France, Italy, Canada, the Netherlands, Belgium, and Sweden. Switzerland was formally added in 1983 after many years of association. Saudi Arabia, though not a GAB member, has also added to the total since 1983. Small amounts have also been borrowed from the Bank for International Settlements.

basically ad hoc responses to the worsening of the crisis, explaining why several separate facilities were established. Most of the funds for these come from loans made by central banks to the IMF, together with some grants. A member that utilizes the facilities can therefore borrow more than would be permitted under normal IMF lending. To undertake such borrowing, a member's plans for economic reform must be approved by the IMF; the loans are "conditional." The existing IMF facilities are summarized in Table 7.2

TABLE 7.2 IMF LENDING FACILITIES, 1994

Name	Comments
Extended Fund Facility (EFF, 1974)	Loans for three years, up to 68% of quota annually and 300% cumulative, payable over 4.5–10 years. In 1994, there were six outstanding EFFs totaling about $6.5 billion. Finances structural adjustment.
Enhanced Structural Adjustment Facility (ESAF, 1987 and 1994)	Replaces Structural Adjustment Facility of 1986 and earlier ESAF of 1987. 78 low-income countries are eligible to borrow up to 190% of their quotas. Repayments begin in five-and-one-half years and end in ten. Financed by extra grants from 43 IMF members, including 24 LDCs, which allow a low interest rate of 0.5%. Target amount about $10 billion. Borrowers must have three-year restructuring program. 29 arrangements made so far, including outstanding ones from the earlier Structural Adjustment Facility (SAF). Often include matching foreign aid and World Bank loans.
Systemic Transformation Facility (STF, 1993–1994 only, but may be extended)	Mostly for Eastern Europe and the old Soviet Union, but also for Mongolia, former Indochina, etc. Cambodia and Vietnam have loans now. Loans up to 50% of quota, about $3.9 billion available.
Compensatory and Contingency Financing Facility (CCFF, 1963)	The compensatory part allows borrowing of another 30% of quota when total earnings from primary product exports fall short of their average over a recent period of years. More can be borrowed (15% of quota) if cereal (grain) imports rise abnormally in price. The contingency part allows borrowing of another 30% of quota to cover the negative results of interest rate movements or key export or import prices. An optional tranche of 20% of quota is allowable with IMF approval for any of these purposes. The total for all these combined is 95% of quota. Repayment in three-and-one-half to five years. (The United Nations suggests that the CCFF be divorced from quotas and that repay ments be delayed until the contingency ends.)
Global Environmental Facility (GEF, 1993)	A new facility that will provide some lending for environmental purposes. Funding of $2 billion, mostly contributed by European countries.

Source: IMF Survey, August 1994 Supplement and March 7, 1994.

These facilities give the IMF much more flexibility than it had formerly to make terms easier or harder for a given member, a departure from past practice in which each country received the same treatment. The IMF holds a considerable amount of gold, and discussions are being carried on as to whether some of this can be sold to finance further facilities to finance adjustment.*

IMF Conditionality

Obtaining the second, third, and fourth credit tranches and money from the various facilities usually involves an ever-greater degree of IMF supervision, including substantial consultation with the officials of the Fund and a visit by an IMF financial team. As prerequisites for borrowing, the IMF will typically require orthodox measures for stabilization and liberalization. The aim is both to reduce expenditure and to switch it to more efficient uses. Cutbacks in budget deficits, which include subsidies to various sectors of the economy, and reduction in the rate of monetary expansion are part of the conditionality in over 90% of all IMF programs, while measures to restrain wages and prices by orthodox means almost reach that figure. Devaluation of an overvalued exchange rate and some dismantling of protectionist trade barriers are usually included as well. The IMF will also often require government action to make the price system reflect true costs more accurately, and some turn toward the encouragement of exports. Well over 100 such programs have recently been in effect, compared with an average of only eight in the years 1971 to 1973.

The conditionality of IMF lending has been by far the most controversial aspect of that organization's operations in recent years, when well over three-quarters of the Fund's loans were on conditional terms.[53] The LDCs have raised a chorus of complaint against IMF conditionality, urging that it be scrapped. Their arguments are usually that the conditions have become tougher, with stiffer terms toward borrowers' domestic policies, and that low-income groups within a country bear the brunt of the adjustment. They say the deflationary policies required by the IMF are one-sided in that the painful contraction of employment and consumption are borne by the LDCs alone and not by the countries whose oil price policies (for example, OPEC) or interest rate policies (for example, the United States) certainly contributed to the underlying problem. The deflation spreads, according to the critics, because the deflating countries import less. So exports are reduced everywhere, even in countries that were not previously in difficulty.

The IMF's position has been that the terms did not become more severe than they were, but that the underlying economic conditions became much worse. During the debt crisis, the IMF had to do far more to ensure that credit was advanced from private sources (the banks) along with aid from developed-country governments.

*Under earlier rules the IMF required payment of gold to cover the first 25% of a country's quota. This was called the "gold tranche." (Nowadays this has become the "reserve tranche," payable in hard currency or SDRs, as we saw earlier.) In 1976 the IMF decided to return one-sixth of its gold to its members, and to sell another one-sixth of its total holding of 25 million ounces to finance loans to developing countries. It still has two-thirds of its original holdings.

Without conditionality, so it is claimed, there would have been far less of both. The Fund notes that indeed each new dollar of IMF loans brings additional finance from governments and the private sector.

Most trenchantly, the Fund also argues that painful adjustment is inescapable anyway. Countries cannot continue policies that cause spending to exceed resources, and no country can choose whether to adjust, just how. "Non-adjustment," states the IMF, is really adjustment in a different way. Even those countries that are considered to be non-adjusting have had to raise real interest rates and agricultural prices for farmers, allow their exchange rates to depreciate, and reduce their public subsidies. In particular, a hyperinflating country is in an unsustainable position. Critics of conditionality must be asked what they would do about the hyperinflation if not stabilize it.[54]

It is certainly arguable that without the IMF, adjustment would be far more disorderly, perhaps with high inflation and severe import restrictions causing reduced growth and more unemployment, which, in turn, would make foreign funds even more difficult to obtain. The proper question, says the Fund, is not whether adjustment is painful but what the situation would have been without that organization's lending. It adds that harm to lower-income groups is a result of a country's own political choice. A country could maintain or increase its social spending even in a period of austerity if it cut the perquisites of the urban elite and the military. A floor for primary school enrollment, nutrition, and health spending could be established and defended with savings taken from elsewhere in the budget or from higher tax revenue extracted from those who could afford to pay. Land reform and irrigation improvement could be a part of structural adjustment. Agricultural exports could be stimulated. All of this would increase the income of the poor. Government policies could aid agriculture and the small-scale sector and provide credit. Resources could be targeted specifically toward food subsidies for the poor instead of toward everyone, including those who are better-off in urban areas; subsidies toward gasoline and other products used by the middle and upper classes could be eliminated. The Fund is undoubtedly correct when it writes, "Any furor over Fund-supported programs . . . may be more directly related to who is being affected than to the burden of adjustment which is imposed."[55]

A good case in point, though perhaps an extreme one, is Peru. That country did not adopt an IMF structural reform plan in the 1980s, deciding instead to employ fiscal expansion and price controls. Inflation by 1987 was very high, reaching nearly 3000% per year in 1990. Loans from international sources dried up. Exports slumped. So did national income. In the capital, Lima, living standards plummeted, with an average decline in consumption of over 50% between 1985 and 1990. The poor were the most affected, their consumption falling 62% in the period, and so income inequality increased. By avoiding macroeconomic stabilization, Peru's government made the crisis worse and made life more difficult, especially for the poor.[56]

The IMF also argues vigorously that the supposed deflationary consequences are not as severe as the critics imply.[57] The usual view of the deflationary bias is, according to the IMF, the short-term result of the restrictive monetary and fiscal policies without consideration of the medium-term stimulation given by the supply-side reforms that reduce the distortions in the economy. The time path, the IMF suggests, is often a deflation followed by a beneficial impact on growth as the supply-side reforms take hold.

Be that as it may, following the imposition of IMF conditions, the recession, even if temporary, can be severe and cause political problems. The political situation deteriorated in some countries to the point of street fighting and mob violence. "IMF riots" occurred in the 1980s in Bolivia, Brazil, the Dominican Republic, Ecuador, Egypt, Ghana, Kenya, Nigeria, Peru, Tunisia, and Zambia among other countries. Governments have even been overturned. Often the condition causing the most political turmoil is the scaling back or elimination of food subsidies in urban areas. The rioting sometimes forced the complete abandonment by governments of their reform programs. Much of this hostility still survives. In 1993, Kenya's President Moi called the IMF dictatorial and its conditions suicidal. Countries regularly renege on their promised reforms; IMF officials are rather routinely booed when they lecture before audiences, especially in Africa. The riots continue.[58]

Economists are often willing to agree that the Fund's teams of experts can be somewhat insensitive to the demands of domestic politics. The public requirement of an immediate devaluation and severe cuts in consumer subsidies before new IMF loans are made can be bitter medicine for the government in power. Presumably, there have been times when with judicious management the conditions could have been made to emerge from a country's own deliberations, or at least have had that appearance to the public. More circumspection and "face-saving" could cost the IMF little but make negotiations easier. If imposed with inadequate political preparation, tough IMF conditions certainly have the capacity to destroy potentially good governments.

The Effects of IMF Conditionality on the Poor The effects of stabilization policies on the poor and on income distribution are complex and uncertain, and the greatest care will have to be exercised to see that the poor do not bear the brunt of an IMF program. It is obvious that, all things being equal, the poorer the country, the more people are pushed over the poverty line by an economic contraction. Adjustment programs certainly can reduce employment in the short run. The firms forced by the initial recession to close their doors may often do so before the new economic incentives lead other firms to open theirs. If the lost jobs could have been preserved, then arguably the poor would have been better off. It may be sensible to establish emergency employment schemes or put the unemployed in school or in training. A special difficulty arises if the spending cuts are extended to capital improvements generally, and even to the maintenance of existing capital, as a country strains to meet its conditions. In that case, deteriorating roads, worsening communications, intermittent electric power and water availability, and the like may all become part of the economic scene.

Yet it is also true that the poor suffer in the absence of adjustment. The poor are usually hard hit by inflation, against which they have less opportunity to protect themselves. Monetary and credit adjustment and fiscal policy adjustment help the poor by halting the inflation. They often do not have access to the price-controlled products; freeing prices may mean greater access to goods than before, even if the price is higher. Because the poor are often rural, holding down agricultural prices is harmful to them, and reforming these prices can encourage exports from rural areas and wages in these areas. If adjustment does not take place, the reduction in public investment and the resulting decline in public services and lower productivity in these services is likely to hit rural areas especially hard as roads deteriorate and the railway system decays. Unfortunately, the rural infrastructure often suffers the biggest losses. The removal of import-substitution incentives that favor capital-intensive industries can lead to more labor intensity, and hence more employment opportunities and higher wages for unskilled labor. The loss of subsidies often has little effect on the poor because the middle classes and the rich elite actually garner the greater part of the benefits from subsidies.[59]

Conclusion on Conditionality

The Fund's economic prescriptions for budgeting, money creation, and foreign trade appear generally sensible. Its insistence that ill-advised government policy is as important an obstacle to development as inadequate resources is a valuable contribution. The conditions can be remarkably useful to a government that wants to take painful economic action but finds it difficult to do so unaided because the political repercussions would be intense. The blame for taking the action can in this view be transferred abroad, useful policies can after all be implemented, and the loud protests from the government are more smoke than fire. To a degree, the Fund's conditions can take a collective view, discouraging beggar-thy-neighbor policies that promote recovery in one member at the expense of others. A final consideration is that if the IMF were to become more lenient in its conditions, it would no longer serve as a de facto guarantee to lenders and investors that reasonable economic policies were being implemented by an LDC in difficulty. Without that guarantee, foreign capital of any sort might be far harder to obtain.[60]

If the IMF's conditionality is actually beneficial for the LDCs, then it is fair to ask why these conditions are not welcomed, even if surreptitiously.[61] One answer is that perhaps they are, and that recently some countries have independently begun to reform policies in ways not dissimilar to what happens with IMF conditionality. When the conditions are not welcomed, various reasons account for their unpopularity. These include ignorance among politicians of the economic principles involved, honest differences concerning the analyses and forecasts, different estimates of the amount of foreign aid and private finance likely to be available, and different assessments of the ability to implement controls. At heart, the real problem may be harder to solve. That problem often appears to be the politicized nature of many LDC economies, with politicians more concerned with distributional issues than with efficiency and confident that controls will benefit those in power and their supporters more than will a free market. The government may assess the costs of adjustment as politically too high to tolerate.

In the final analysis, it is fair to say that compliance with the IMF's conditions has been declining, and also that the compliance record has been less satisfactory than that of the World Bank. Whereas in 1969 to 1978 credit expansion limits were met 55% of the time and fiscal deficit limits 62% of the time, by 1983 these percentages had fallen to 44% and 36% respectively, with little improvement since.[62] In a number of countries, IMF adjustment programs have not succeeded in restoring growth, partly because the group included LDCs that received adjustment loans but did not adjust much, and partly because establishing macroeconomic stability does not *guarantee* successful development.* In essence, poor progress in development is not due to just to bad government policies, but to many other sorts of disadvantages, some of which are structural.[63]

In particular, conditions have had less success in Africa than elsewhere. In that continent, effective policy coordination and the complementarity of adjustment policies seem particularly important. If these are not present, structural adjustment funding may not do much good, leaving a country with a larger debt and a more open, more vulnerable economy, subject to a cycle of liberalization, protests, reimposed controls, and new financial difficulties.[64]

Defaults That conditionality has not always succeeded is reflected by the recent rise in the number of defaults on IMF loans, a thing previously unheard of. The IMF opposes rescheduling of its own loans because that interferes with the short-term, revolving-door nature of its funding. Until 1985, all loans were repaid, but in that year and the next several countries fell far behind in their repayments. New rules were rapidly forthcoming. Now if a loan is overdue for a month, the case goes to an IMF board, with a full cutoff of additional lending six months later. Countries that have been cut off at one time or another include Cambodia, Guyana, Honduras, Liberia, Panama, Peru, Sierra Leone, Somalia, Sudan, Vietnam, Zaire, and Zambia. (A number of these were also cut off by the World Bank.) Most have been reinstated, but further steps were taken against two (Sudan and Zaire), which were suspended from the IMF in 1993–1994. The total arrears to the IMF amounted to about $4 billion in 1994, and it has been necessary to impose special charges to cover these costs.

The Future for the IMF

The IMF, along with the World Bank, was central in containment of the debt crisis. But it could have done better in several respects.

One problem is that as the debt crisis cooled, there was a reversal of financial flows from the IMF and the World Bank. By 1986 to 1990, repayment of IMF loans was removing about $6 billion per year from the economies of the LDCs, compared to the large net additions that reached an annual figure of almost +$8

---

*Some academic studies that purport to compare the average performance of LDCs that have not agreed to IMF conditions with those that have are flawed, because the first group includes countries that did not need IMF assistance to adjust successfully, such as Malaysia and Botswana. The proper comparison is between those that accepted the conditions, and those that should have but didn't, such as Burma/Myanmar and Peru. See Summers and Pritchett, "The Structural-Adjustment Debate," 383–389.

billion during the crisis. The net flow from the IMF in 1991 was positive for the first time in six years, but it turned negative again in 1992. (World Bank net transfers stayed positive for longer, until 1991, but they too have turned negative.) The reversal of the flows from these institutions posed difficulties for the LDCs. To be sure, some of the repayments were made by countries that had successfully adjusted to their difficulties, but for many nations in need, the necessary adjustment had not taken place.[65]

For a long time, lending by the IMF had a time horizon that was too short, and much of the problem still remains in spite of efforts to solve it. When loans extend for only three or four years, or even just 18 months or so as was sometimes true before 1988, the conditions have to focus too much on demand restraint rather than on supply-side adjustments. The LDCs argue that less attention should be given to public-sector budget deficits because these deficits may be the major form of finance for growth-inducing education and human capital development. As we have seen, these objections have been addressed with the various new facilities that do make some loans available on a longer-term basis (up to ten years) to aid in structural adjustments in production, trade, and prices. The amounts available for all the new facilities are, however, smaller than for normal lending.

Perhaps the greatest weakness in the present structure of the IMF is that organization's inability to influence the countries that contribute to economic malaise because of their policies but do not need to borrow. So there is no conditionality for OPEC when it administers oil shocks, nor for governments (including that of the United States) that run up interest rates through budget deficits and tight money, nor for protectionist governments that put trade barriers in place. By its rules, the IMF can require adjustments only among its borrowers, the unfortunate LDCs who, not blameless themselves, are also victims of these policies. Ideally, perhaps, the IMF should have more ability to influence the actions of its members when their actions cause global damage among its other members. Now all it can do is issue rather muted criticisms of developed-country policies and hope for the best.

Some argue that the mission of the IMF now overlaps considerably with the mission of the World Bank, which has also moved substantially toward conditionality in its lending. Should the two organizations be merged? Probably they should be. Economies of scale would result as duplication of programs and staff was ended. A more unified focus would be helpful as well. Combining and cutting the two bureaucracies would undoubtedly be difficult, however, and a merger is not now in sight.

In spite of the criticisms, the IMF was a major factor in the world's response to the debt crisis. On balance it is hard to see how the massive debt reschedulings and the fiscal, monetary, trade, and price reforms could have been accomplished without that organization.

Special Drawing Rights

A last activity of the IMF, interesting and controversial, has the potential to increase long-term capital formation in the LDCs. This activity is the issuance of special drawing rights (SDRs), international reserves created by the IMF and distributed to its members in accordance with the size of their quotas.[66] Six creations of SDRs took place between 1970 and 1978. The last new allocation of SDRs (12 billion) was from 1979 to 1981, bringing the total in existence to 21.4 billion. The value of the SDR fluctuates: Each SDR was worth a little less than one U.S. dollar in early 1985, whereas in August 1995 the figure was $1.49. Its value is determined by a weighted average of five major currencies, the weights of which are established by the share of the currencies in world trade and in reserves held by central banks. Currently (from January 1991), the SDR's value is calculated on the basis of a basket consisting of the dollar (40%), German mark (21%), Japanese yen (17%), French franc (11%), and British pound (11%). Because the SDR's value is based on a market basket, it does not run as much risk of exchange rate changes as any individual currency, which enhances its usefulness. The market basket is adjusted every five years, with the next alteration scheduled for 1996. It is unlikely that the currencies presently employed will change because there is such a large gap between these currencies and the sixth most important one.

SDRs may be transferred between governments in settlement of balance of payments deficits.* Countries holding more than their allocation receive a rate of interest from the IMF; countries that have "spent" their SDRs pay the same rate. These rates, 4.33% as of August 15, 1994, are fixed weekly and are made up of the weighted average short-term interest rates in the money markets of the five countries whose currencies determine the value of the SDR. Because the interest payments and charges balance out, a small charge of about one-half of 1% on all allocations is levied to cover the expenses of running the system.

An SDR Link? Up to now, the LDCs have benefited little from SDR creation because collectively their quotas are small. Innovative ideas are abroad to combine SDR creation with more financing for the LDCs in what has come to be called the SDR link. The link is an old idea, dating back to an earlier scheme called the *Stamp Plan*, devised by the British economist Sir Maxwell Stamp. The Stamp Plan was to introduce something like the SDR as a way of distributing new purchasing power to the needy. Instead of distribution according to quota, the plan envisaged the new credits as aid to LDCs, allowing countries to make purchases internationally with the credits and repay the IMF for these credits many years hence on easy terms.

With the coming of the SDR, the idea surfaced again.[67] Some proponents favor an "organic link" in which the IMF articles would be amended to raise the quotas of the LDCs. They would thus receive a greater proportion of newly created SDRs. The realization that this would be time consuming and involve much infighting over quota sizes gave rise to the "inorganic link" proposal of voluntary contributions of developed-country SDRs to the LDCs with no change in quotas. Such a plan could be more rapidly adopted, but, obviously, there would be doubts

*The IMF can designate countries with strong balance of payments, requiring them to accept SDRs from countries with payments problems. No transactions by designation have been made since 1987.

as to whether all developed countries could always be relied upon to make their voluntary contributions. Only the French gave any support to the "reverse link," which would have excluded LDCs altogether from receiving any of the newly created SDRs. In Peter Kenen's version, countries borrowing from the IMF might receive newly created SDRs instead of dollars or other hard currency in exchange for their own currency. Those in greatest need would thus be the recipients of the assistance. A recent French position taken by President Mitterand involved issuance of SDRs to back guarantees for bonds issued by the debtor countries.

The SDR link proposals have the advantage of avoiding any repugnant political strings attached to "normal" foreign aid. If the decision were taken to transfer resources by means of SDRs, however, a new problem would arise. Under present rules LDCs would have to pay interest charges if they use their new and larger allocations. To counter this flow, either the interest paid on the use of SDRs would have to be lowered below that paid on accumulations, preferential rates for LDCs would have to be negotiated, or new SDRs might have to be available to the World Bank, UN agencies, or national governments as a basis for development grants.

A major objection to the SDR link, as to the original Stamp Plan, is its inflationary potential. The need for development funds is much higher than the optimal need for international reserves, so it is said. But there are arguments on the other side. As world trade grows (and presuming a need for reserves even under floating rates as major nations manage their floating and smaller countries continue to fix their rates), the need for reserves grows also. The result of an SDR link would be inflationary only if the newly created reserves outran the growing liquidity demand for them. To be sure, if the LDCs themselves determined the amount to be created, the charge of inflationary potential would undoubtedly carry great weight. The LDCs did not abate their calls for new SDR issues even when world inflation was high. Yet because it now takes an 85% vote of the IMF to create new SDRs and LDCs have only about 30% of the votes, the volume of SDRs will remain under developed-country supervision unless arrangements are changed very drastically. So there is little likelihood of the money creation running out of control.

Even if through some unknown means the LDCs should seize the decision-making process, the goods furnished in exchange for the SDRs would still come from the developed countries, which always have the option to pull out of the scheme. It is, however, doubtlessly true that an SDR link would have greater first-round multiplier effects than the present system of SDR creation because all the new SDRs would surely be spent. (Under today's system, many countries hold their SDRs without spending them.) SDR creation under a link plan would have to be correspondingly less than otherwise to avoid inflationary repercussions. (The upside of the concerns about inflation is that SDRs would be an appropriate tool for offsetting an international recession. They could be issued when economies are contracting, and they could thereafter be canceled when economies are expanding.)

Other objections have been raised against an SDR link. One is that while new reserves can buy time for transition and adjustment, they can also cause a postponement of necessary economic reforms. So, if they are used to promote adjustment, it might be sensible to limit their duration, requiring them to be bought back and retired in some period of time. The most persuasive objection, perhaps, is that under the present arrangement they cannot be used selectively for the countries that need them most. Employing an SDR link implies that all LDCs would receive the newly created assets. Many ask whether this is sensible when, during the debt crisis, some debtors made painful efforts to implement more reasonable economic policies, while others failed to implement policy reforms and did not repay. Would the well-off LDCs receive far larger amounts than the poorest, who need assistance the most? Would the valuable economic restructuring required when a country borrows from the IMF accompany the new SDRs?

The question was in abeyance for years, but as time passed SDRs slipped as a proportion of world reserves from 6% in 1972 to only half that in 1994. The nagging continuation of high interest rates on long-term loans in the world's capital markets, plus the fall in the importance of SDRs, finally convinced the developed countries that a new distribution of SDRs was justified. But in 1994 the negotiations to do so erupted into sudden conflict.[68] The IMF's head, Michel Camdessus, proposed a new creation of 36 billion SDRs, a figure backed by the LDCs' Group of 24. Camdessus argued that with world inflation relatively low, the time was ripe, and that the many new IMF members joining since 1981 have never received an allocation of SDRs. The developed countries refused to countenance the figure of 36 billion, which would have nearly tripled the old total of 21.4 billion. But they did agree to a new creation of 16 billion. The catch was that half would go to the developed countries, a quarter to the former Communist countries, leaving only a quarter for the LDCs.

The LDCs objected strenuously, voted together in protest, and stunned the developed countries by blocking an extension of the IMF's Systemic Transformation Facility for the former Communist countries. For the moment, the new creation of SDRs is in limbo.

Conclusion

This chapter and the three that came before it have assessed the financing of economic development. Without the domestic and foreign saving that funds the LDCs' investment in physical and human capital, there could be little improvement in levels of living. But the valuable foreign flows backfired in the early 1980s when bank lending led to the debt crisis. With considerable economic cooperation among the World Bank, the IMF, developed-country governments, and reforming LDCs, the crisis has largely been surmounted and large-scale flows of foreign finance have resumed. The foreign flows now seem set to continue their substantial increase of recent years, one of the most encouraging aspects of modern economic development.

NOTES

1. *HDR 1994*, 166–167. The figures for aid as a percentage of GNP are for 1992. Sources used for this section include Robert Cassen et al., *Does Aid Work*? (Oxford, 1986); Saadet Deger and Somnath Sen, *The Political Economy of International Security*

(Oxford, 1990); A. Jennings, Hans Singer, and J. Wood, *Food Aid: The Challenge and the Opportunity* (Oxford, 1987); Uma Lele, ed., *Aid to African Agriculture* (Baltimore, 1992); P. Mosley, *Aid and Power: The World Bank and Policy-Based Lending*, vol. 1, *Analysis and Policy Proposals* (London, 1991); P. Mosley, *Overseas Aid: Its Defense and Reform* (Brighton, 1987); Roger C. Riddell, *Foreign Aid Reconsidered* (Baltimore, 1987); and Vernon W. Ruttan, "Why Foreign Economic Assistance?" *Economic Development and Cultural Change* 37, no. 2 (January 1989): 411–424.

2. See Anne O. Krueger, "Aid in the Development Process," *World Bank Research Observer* 1, no. 1 (1986): 57–58, for a survey of the positive economic effects. Also see Gerald M. Meier, *Emerging from Poverty: The Economics That Really Matters* (New York, 1984), 230–231; and *WDR 1985*, 99–100.
3. The figures are estimates by the OECD.
4. See A. K. Sen, *On Economic Inequality* (Oxford, 1973); "Ethical Issues in Income Distribution," in Sven Grassman and Erik Lundberg, eds., *The World Economic Order: Past and Prospects* (New York, 1981), 464–494; Ian M. D. Little, "Distributive Justice and the New International Order," in Peter Oppenheimer, ed., *Issues in International Economics* (London, 1980), 37–53; John Rawls, *A Theory of Justice* (Cambridge, Mass., 1971); and Robert Nozick, *Anarchy, State, and Utopia* (Oxford, 1974).
5. *HDR 1992*, 43.
6. *HDR 1994*, 71.
7. See Danny P. Leipziger, "The Concessionality of Foreign Assistance," *Finance and Development* 21, no. 1 (1984): 44–46.
8. John Clark and Eliot Kalter, "Recent Innovations in Debt Restructuring," *Finance and Development* 29, no. 3 (September 1992): and 6–8; Benjamin J. Cohen, "What Ever Happened to the LDC Debt Crisis," *Challenge* 34, no. 3 (May/June 1991): 47–51.
9. Thomas Klein, "Innovations in Debt Relief," *Finance and Development* 29, no. 1 (March 1992): 42–43.
10. See Klein, "Innovations in Debt Relief," 42–43; and Clark and Kalter, "Recent Innovations in Debt Restructuring," 6–8.
11. *The Economist*, May 22, 1993.
12. Some data in this section are from *WDR 1985*, 101, and *WDR 1990*, 128.
13. Anne O. Krueger, *Economic Policy at Cross-Purposes: The United States and Developing Countries* (Washington, D.C., 1993), 57.
14. *WDR 1991*, 48.
15. Brian Hindley, "Economic Development and Services," in V. N. Balasubramanyam and Sanjaya Lall, eds., *Current Issues in Development Economics* (New York, 1991), 201.
16. *The Economist*, May 7, 1994.
17. *The Economist*, April 2, 1994.
18. *WDR 1990*, 4.
19. *HDR 1994*, 166–167, 197; *HDR 1993*, 7; *The Economist*, May 7, 1994.
20. *The Economist*, May 7, 1994.
21. John Toye, *Dilemmas of Development* (Oxford, 2nd edition, 1993), 192.
22. See Carlo Pietrobello and Carlo Scarpa, "Inducing Efficiency in the Use of Foreign Aid: The Case for Incentive Mechanisms," *Journal of Development Studies* 29, no. 1 (October 1992): 72–92.
23. See Keith Griffin and John Gurley, "Radical Analyses of Imperialism, The Third World, and the Transition to Socialism: A Survey Article," *Journal of Economic Literature* 23 (September 1985): 1116–1117; and the various articles on aid by Lord Bauer of the London School of Economics, for evidence of some convergence of the critiques by radicals and conservatives. Several studies of the problem conclude that in general aid with all its problems has been beneficial to growth. See Anne O. Krueger, Constantine

Michalopoulos, and Vernon W. Ruttan, *Aid and Development* (Baltimore, 1989); and Anne O. Krueger and Vernon W. Ruttan, *The Development Impact of Economic Assistance to LDCs* (Washington, D.C., 1983).

24. *HDR 1993*, 7–8.
25. *HDR 1994*, 155.
26. For a discussion of adverse effects, see Cassen et al., *Does Aid Work?;* S. J. Maxwell and H. W. Singer, "Food Aid to Developing Countries: A Survey," in Paul Streeten and Richard Jolly, eds., *Recent Issues in World Development* (Oxford, 1981), 219–240; and *The Economist*, April 10, 1993.
27. *HDR 1993*, 8.
28. *WDR 1990*, 4.
29. *HDR 1994*, 77–78.
30. *The Economist*, May 7, 1994.
31. *HDR 1993*, 88, 92.
32. *HDR 1993*, 89, 93.
33. See Robert F. Gorman, ed., *Private Voluntary Organizations as Agents of Development* (Boulder, Colo., 1984); and *WDR 1990*, 129.
34. Hilary F. French, "Rebuilding the World Bank," in Lester R. Brown et al., eds., *State of the World 1994* (New York, 1994), 159.
35. An account of the Bank's record, published by the Bank itself, is Warren C. Baum and Stokes M. Tolbert, *Investing in Development: Lessons of World Bank Experience* (Washington, D.C., 1985). Also see *WDR 1985*, 103.
36. French, "Rebuilding the World Bank," 158.
37. French, "Rebuilding the World Bank," 158.
38. *The Economist*, October 2, 1993.
39. See the *IFC Annual Report, 1994* (Washington, D.C., 1994).
40. For this statistic, see Meier, *Leading Issues*, 5th ed., 234.
41. John Toye, *Dilemmas of Development*, 2nd ed. (Oxford, 1993), 191.
42. These were complaints made by the 1980 Brandt Commission, an international body chaired by former West German Chancellor Willy Brandt. See *North–South: A Programme for Survival* (London, 1980), especially Chapter 15.
43. French, "Rebuilding the World Bank," 158. Early in the Bank's history, just after World War II when the "Reconstruction" in its official title, IBRD, had some meaning, program loans accounted for nearly three-fourths of all lending. But by the 1960s and 1970s, they had dropped virtually out of sight.
44. Paul Mosley, Jane Harrigan, and John Toye, *Aid and Power: The World Bank and Policy-Based Lending*, vol. 1, *Analysis and Policy Proposals*, and vol. 2, *Case Studies* (London, 1991); and see *The Economist*, October 12, 1991.
45. Paul Mosley, "Structural Adjustment: A General Overview, 1980–9," in V. N. Balasubramanyam and Sanjaya Lall, eds., *Current Issues in Development Economics* (New York, 1991), 225.
46. World Bank, "Adjustment Lending Policies for Sustainable Growth," World Bank Policy and Research Series No. 14 (1990); Mosley, Harrigan, and Toye, *Aid and Power: The World Bank and Policy-Based Lending*, vol. 1, *Analysis and Policy Proposals*, and vol. 2, *Case Studies*; Mosley, "Structural Adjustment: A General Overview, 1980–9," 242; and see *The Economist*, October 12, 1991.
47. French, "Rebuilding the World Bank," 167–168.
48. Sidney Dell, "The Question of Cross-Conditionality," *World Development* 16, no. 5 (May 1988): 557–568.
49. See French, "Rebuilding the World Bank," 173.

50. See Michael M. Cernea, "Population Resettlement and Development," *Finance and Development* 31, no. 3 (September 1994): 46–49, and the more detailed "Resettlement and Development: The Bankwide Review of Projects Involving Involuntary Resettlement 1986–1993," World Bank Environmental Department (April 1994).
51. The formula, which is rather lengthy, can be found in Orlando Roncesvalles and Andrew Tweedie, "Augmenting the IMF's Resources," *Finance and Development* 28, no. 4 (December 1991): 26–29.
52. The annual supplement to the *IMF Survey*, issued in August or September, is a convenient introduction to the rules. The IMF's *Annual Report* gives the details on that institution's lending.
53. The literature on conditionality is large. In addition to the specific citations, I utilized Lionel Demery and Tony Addison, "Stabilization Policy and Income Distribution in Developing Countries," Gerald K. Helleiner, "Stabilization, Adjustment, and the Poor," and Paul Streeten, "Structural Adjustment: A Survey of the Issues and Options," all in *World Development* 15, no. 12 (December 1987): 1469–1482, 1483–1498, 1499–1513; Peter Heller, Lans Bovenberg, Thanos Catsambas, Ke-young Chu, and Parthasarathi Shome, "The Implications of Fund-Supported Adjustment Programs for Poverty: Experiences in Selected Countries," IMF Occasional Paper No. 58 (May, 1988); Tony Addison and Lionel Demery, "Alleviating Poverty Under Structural Adjustment," *Finance and Development* 24, no. 4 (December 1987): 41–43; and the survey of the subject by John Williamson, ed., *IMF Conditionality* (Washington, D.C., 1983). A trenchant critique of the conditions for Brazil that focuses on the deflationary aspects is Celso Furtado, *No to Recession and Unemployment: An Examination of the Brazilian Economic Crisis* (London, 1984). For figures on the number of programs see Morris Goldstein, "Global Effects of Fund-Supported Programs," IMF Occasional Paper No. 42 (1985). Goldstein also provides the information from which the percentages used in the previous paragraph were calculated; see p. 9 for the data.
54. Paul Mosley, "Structural Adjustment: A General Overview, 1980–9," in Balasubramanyam and Lall, eds., *Current Issues in Development Economics*, 225–226.
55. *IMF Survey*, November 17, 1986.
56. See Paul Glewwe and Gillette Hall, "Poverty and Inequality During Unorthodox Adjustment: The Case of Peru, 1985–90," World Bank Living Standards Measurement Working Paper No. 86 (1992).
57. See Moshin S. Khan and Malcolm D. Knight, "Fund-Supported Adjustment Programs and Economic Growth," IMF Occasional Paper No. 41 (1985).
58. *The Economist*, May 1, 1993.
59. Lawrence H. Summers and Lant H. Pritchett, "The Structural-Adjustment Debate," *American Economic Review* 83, no. 2 (May 1993): 383–389.
60. *The Economist*, May 1, 1993.
61. So asks Streeten, "Structural Adjustment: A Survey of the Issues and Options," 1480.
62. Jacques Polak, *The Changing Nature of IMF Conditionality* (Paris, OECD, 1991).
63. See Summers and Pritchett, "The Structural-Adjustment Debate," 388–389; Khosrow Doroodian, "Macroeconomic Performance and Adjustment under Policies Commonly Supported by the International Monetary Fund," *Economic Development and Cultural Change* 41, no. 4 (July 1993): 849–864; and John Toye, *Dilemmas of Development*, 2nd ed. (Oxford, 1993), 198–199.
64. Paul Mosley and John Weeks, "Has Recovery Begun? 'Africa's Adjustment in the 1980s' Revisited," *World Development* 21, no. 10 (October 1993): 1583–1606.
65. *HDR 1992*, 51.

66. See Michael Dooley et al., "The Role of the SDR in the International Monetary System," IMF Occasional Paper No. 51 (1987); Graham Bird, "The Benefits of Special Drawing Rights for Less Developed Countries," *World Development* 7, no. 3 (1979): 281–290; Geoffrey Maynard, "Special Drawing Rights and Development Aid," *Journal of Development Studies* 9, no. 4 (1973): 518–543; Geoffrey Maynard and Graham Bird, "International Monetary Issues and the Developing Countries: A Survey," and "Postscript," in Paul Streeten and Richard Jolly, eds., *Recent Issues in World Development* (Oxford, 1981), 343–373; Gerald K. Helleiner, "The Less Developed Countries and the International Monetary System," in Helleiner, *International Economic Disorder: Essays in North–South Relations* (Toronto, 1981), 130–165, especially 153–161; Y. S. Park, "The Link Between Special Drawing Rights and Development Finance," Princeton Essays in International Finance No. 100 (1973); and John Williamson, "SDRs: The Link," in Jagdish N. Bhagwati, ed., *The New International Economic Order: The North–South Debate* (Cambridge, Mass., 1977).
67. For a review of the question, see John Williamson, *A New SDR Allocation* (Washington, D.C., 1984). An article advocating a new issue of SDRs is Arjun Sengupta, "Allocation of SDRs Linked to Reserve Needs," *Finance and Development* 23, no. 3 (September 1986): 18–21.
68. *Wall Street Journal*, October 3 and October 4, 1994; *The Economist*, July 23, 1994.

Chapter 8

Technology, Factor Proportions, and Dualism

We turn now to the question of appropriate technologies for the LDCs.[1] *Techno* in Greek means "art," "craft," or "skill." Technology is the application of art, craft, or skill to a product or a process. Improvements in technique are a key factor in productivity increase. Technical change applies to far more than the improvements in physical capital usually associated with the term. It can occur in the seeds and methods of agriculture, in the organization of markets and marketing, in the control of population, and in virtually any economic endeavor, large or small. (Some authorities prefer to use the term *technological change* to describe the discovery of new production techniques that are useful to producers and the term *technical change* to refer to the actual use of new techniques by producers.)

We are perhaps used to thinking of grand leaps in technology—industrial revolutions, agricultural revolutions, major transformations in transport (sail to steam, propeller to jet), communication (pencil and paper to typewriter, adding machine to computer), and energy (wood to coal to oil). Any item of physical capital, however, no matter how simple it is, always embodies a technology. A humble screw in a machine can be made of iron, steel, steel alloy, aluminum, or other material; it can be manufactured by numerous different methods; it can be inserted by hand or by robot; it can have a metric pitch or one in inches; a slotted head or a Phillips, Robinson, or Allen head; a flat or round top. At some point in the development of the screw each of these characteristics represented, on a small scale, a technical change with implications for the usefulness of that little artifact.

Small or large, whenever we speak of an economic activity, we also speak of the technology bound up with it. The topic actually applies so widely that it is convenient to divide it. The remainder of this chapter concentrates largely on technical change in industry. Technology in agriculture, in forming "human capital," in the establishment of markets, and in relation to economies of scale is considered in the four chapters that follow this one.

The rapid worldwide spread of technical knowledge has been an obvious feature of development in the last half of the twentieth century, and it seems certain that it will increase. Many economists claim (though the view has its critics) that technical change is the most powerful and most dependable engine of economic growth in the developed countries, and is also very important in the performance of the most successful LDCs. Technical improvement, they argue, is a major cause of higher productivity, which in turn is the key to income growth. Applied widely in many areas of output, with one innovation often leading to another, technology is a major defense against diminishing returns to capital accumulation.*

ALTERNATIVE TECHNOLOGIES

How does a country decide what factor proportions to employ as its economy grows, and how are such decisions made? Does it aim for capital-intensive methods that embody the most modern techniques found in the developed countries? Or does it strive to acquire labor-intensive technologies that conserve scarce capital and utilize the country's large labor force, at the expense of appearing less up-to-date? Perhaps some activities in an economy are found to be highly capital-intensive, while others are highly labor-intensive. Such a situation is commonly called a "dual economy."

The question for this chapter is whether a country undergoing economic development should use a capital–labor ratio tailored to its factor proportions or whether it should adopt "modern" technologies fitted to the capital–labor ratios of developed countries. In coping with the question, it is always necessary to ask another: What is the intended outcome of the choice? Maximizing output per person is the most familiar goal, no doubt, but a country's leaders may choose to maximize future as opposed to current output. They may also believe that the choice of technologies can play a part in social reform, in promoting social cohesion, or in lowering class barriers, and so forth.† The effects of technology on saving and

---

*Edward Denison has suggested that unless a country spends something on the order of 1.5% to 2% of its national product (some 10% of total investment) on research and development, not counting education, it will be unlikely to maintain its productivity. The point about diminishing returns was made originally by Alfred Marshall. See Simon James, *A Dictionary of Economic Quotations* (London, 1984), 34.

†So, for long periods of time, the Soviet Union favored factor proportions in industry partly aimed at long-term rather than short-term development, while the production decisions in Communist LDCs around the globe from Cuba to Angola to Vietnam were made in part because of their social effects, rather than aiming at a maximum of present output.

investment (hence on future income) and on income distribution are not considered in this chapter; we will return to these topics in Chapter 12.

The Neoclassical Model

Assume for now that the intent is to maximize present output. What then does economics have to say about the choice of technologies? The traditional argument of neoclassical microeconomic theory is clear and relatively simple. Standard theory suggests that the factors of production should be so allocated that the marginal physical product (MPP) per dollar spent on some given factor is equal to the MPP per dollar spent on any other factor. In the symbols of a first-year economics textbook, this is written:

$$\frac{MPP_L}{P_L} = \frac{MPP_K}{P_K}$$

This formula's ordinary meaning is that if the price of labor (L) is extremely low relative to capital (K), then output per dollar spent is maximized when the MPP of labor is very low and the MPP of capital is very high. For some actual enterprise, in a typical LDC heavily endowed with labor, this means the employment of a great deal of labor and a relatively small amount of capital. For any given dollar outlay on labor and capital, output is the highest that can be achieved. Said another way, for any given output, the dollar outlay on labor and capital is minimized.

In Figure 8.1, a set of production isoquants based on this logic shows diagrammatically the sacrifice of output when a capital-intensive technique is chosen in an economy with abundant labor and scarce capital.[2] The quantity of capital is shown on the vertical axis, and the quantity of labor is on the horizontal. CI_1, CI_2, CI_3, and CI_4 are isoquants showing production levels using a capital-intensive process, with the level of output increasing from CI_1 to CI_4. These isoquants show high capital intensity (a high capital–labor ratio) relative to the isoquants labeled LI, which show high labor intensity. Notice how along CI_4, factor proportions can be altered to include a little more capital and a little less labor, as at A and B, or a little less capital and a little more labor, as at C and D, while still producing the same quantity of output, as shown by the height of the isoquant CI_4. Here the technique itself is capital-intensive. Any combination along the CI isoquants requires more capital than labor relative to a labor-intensive technique such as shown by isoquants LI_1, LI_2, LI_3, and LI_4. Along the LI isoquants, the capital–labor ratio is always lower.

If an economy possesses limited capital (K) but a large quantity of labor (L_2), and if maximum output is the goal, it is clearly a mistake to use capital-intensive technology. That method would allow an output level equal only to CI_1; a shortage of capital precludes reaching a higher isoquant using this technique. A further disadvantage is that much available labor cannot be used in this sector: L_1L_2 labor will not find employment there. Consider, however, adoption of a labor-intensive technique. Then K capital in combination with L_2 labor is sufficient to allow a much higher output level, as at isoquant LI_4. (The "wrong" factor proportions will also cause a further sacrifice than this: Exports with the greatest potential comparative

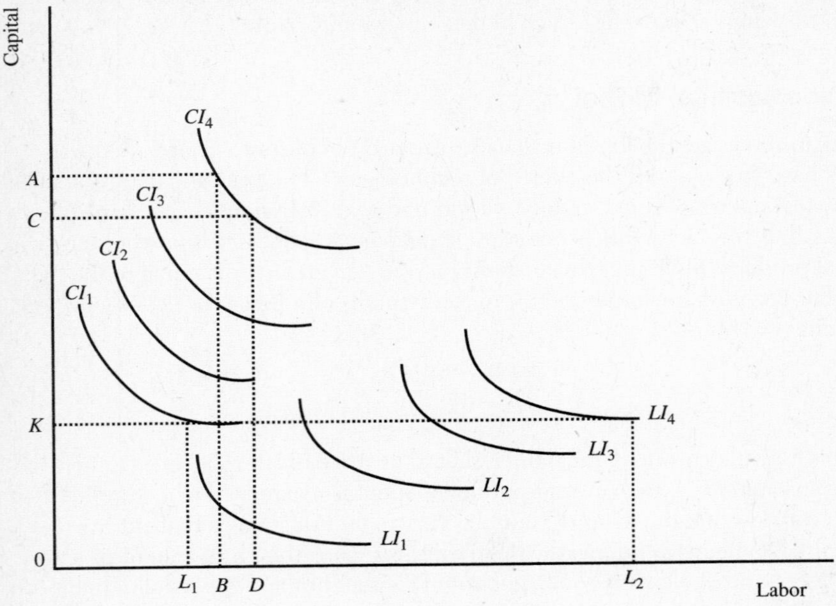

Figure 8.1 Production isoquants for capital-intensive and labor-intensive techniques.

advantage will be penalized, with a resulting reduction in the ability to acquire imports.)[3]

In short, standard neoclassical theory suggests that the availability of factors will determine the appropriate technology. Indeed, much economic behavior reflects just this, with studies usually indicating a rather wide scope for substituting labor-intensive techniques when desired.[4] Certainly, the difference in employment can be large, depending on the technique used. A survey of plants in Indonesia showed labor-intensive techniques resulted in 13 times more employment than capital-intensive techniques for an equal output of cigarettes, 12 times more for flashlight batteries, six times more for tires, and 23 times more for the production of soft drinks. Evidence from Colombia indicates that investment of over $100 million in the capital-intensive petrochemical industry caused a decrease in employment of 290 people and a gain of less than 1000 jobs from the multiplier process in other industries. Analysis showed the same amount of investment in labor-intensive industries such as shoes, furniture, and clothing could have expanded employment by 47,500 jobs, over 20% of all industrial employment at the time, which would have led to 207,000 more jobs from the multiplier effect.[5]

Employment generation through labor intensity may be favored for another reason as well. If a value judgment is made that government is not up to coping with the possible unemployment and income redistribution aspects of capital intensity, then that, too, might point to the adoption of labor-intensive methods.

The argument that labor-intensive technologies generate employment is controversial, however, because of the possibility of an adverse trade-off. The economist must be on guard when government promotes labor intensity as a tactic to increase employment when the combination of factors is not the most efficient one and therefore sacrifices output. For example, one worker with a bulldozer might move the same amount of earth as 200 workers with shovels or 2,000 with trowels or 10,000 using their fingers. A thousand people using trowels or 5,000 using their fingers would surely represent a great deal of employment in earth moving, but notice that the employment would be at the sacrifice of half the output. A severe trade-off between more employment and less GNP would have to receive intense scrutiny. Perhaps markets are poorly developed, so that the absorption of unemployed labor is long delayed and painful. Perhaps the government is incapable of capturing any part of the increased output, so unemployment compensation and training schemes are not feasible and the social consequences of the unemployment are too great to be borne. Yet perhaps the proper policy would be to work on the inadequacies of markets, taxes, and transfer systems rather than sacrifice the output. Chapter 12 returns to this issue.

JUSTIFICATIONS FOR CAPITAL-INTENSIVE TECHNOLOGY

In the past—often it seems without much debate and contrary to all the above—LDCs have tended to deal with this important issue by adopting the latest available technology, a sort of "international demonstration effect" at work, whereby satisfaction comes from obtaining the most modern available techniques. Unfortunately, the most modern techniques may have been adopted in the developed countries because they are "factor biased." That is, they allow a shift away from expensive labor toward cheaper capital. Frequently, the LDCs' foreign consultants, whose culture-bound experience is mainly with capital-intensive technology, will advocate its adoption. For other reasons as well, there may be a bureaucratic bias toward capital-intensive techniques in an LDC. Foreign contractors may be considered more dependable and more likely to produce on schedule. The bureaucrats in charge may view their local poor and uneducated labor force with mistrust or even contempt. Managers may find it more comfortable to cope with fewer workers and deal primarily with trained engineers, so avoiding many problems in human relations. Finally, a government may be locked into an initial choice of capital intensity by fear of appearing wasteful and indecisive if the choice is changed.[6]

Indeed, the latest available technology *is* usually capital intensive, tailored to the labor-scarce factor proportions of the developed world where most of the research has been done. The LDCs currently hold only about a 3% share in the world's annual spending on science and technology.[7]

Several arguments justify the use of capital-intensive techniques even when labor is the most abundant factor. The arguments must be studied with care because they are often used to rubber-stamp a decision already taken to opt for the most modern technique, based not on economic reasons but on demonstration effects. Five economic arguments used to justify high capital intensity are considered below.

Low Labor Productivity

The marginal physical product of labor (MPP_L) may be so low on some particular project that the labor price cannot fall far enough to offset the low productivity. Wages for full-time labor are limited on the downside by the expenses of subsistence, and because a firm cannot pay less than that, it might find capital a preferable substitute because of its high productivity.

A major reason for very low labor productivity is malnutrition and illness in the work force, leading to tiredness, sickness, and general inability to stand up to the required working conditions. Calorie deficiencies have been reported from many parts of the Third World. Disease brings absenteeism and causes low productivity among workers who are on the job.

Cases in point are abundant and dramatic.[8] An average worker in Peru misses about one day of work per month due to sickness; in Ghana 1.3 days; but in the United States, only about a quarter of a day. The World Bank reports that in Côte d'Ivoire, wages are 19% lower among men who lose a day per month to illness compared to those who do not.[9] A study in Indonesia found that 85% of the workers in the construction and rubber industries were infected with hookworm, and 45% of these had the associated iron-deficiency anemia. This anemia, usually caused by inadequate absorbable iron in the diet, saps strength and leaves workers weak and listless. It is thought to affect between one-third and two-thirds of the population in many tropical LDCs, with the figure reaching 80% and more in India. In Indonesia, the productivity of workers who were given iron supplements for two months rose in the range of 15% to 25%.

A growing body of evidence points to direct positive effects of better nutrition on labor productivity among low-income workers in LDCs. (The positive effects on productivity also work indirectly, through better performance in school and through cognitive achievement.) In Africa, mining companies often make a regular practice of feeding new recruits a nutritious diet for several weeks before putting the men into the mines. They reap a substantial reward in increased output per hour worked from this "investment." When Sierra Leonese farmworkers received 10% more calories atop the low 1500 they were consuming, their productivity rose 5%. Firms building the Pan-American Highway found that it was possible to raise labor productivity 200% by providing three balanced meals a day to the work force. Further empirical evidence on the role of health and nutrition in productivity is reviewed in Chapter 10.

Workers might also not be used to factory methods, might be illiterate and uneducated, and might even have only a passing attachment to their jobs, with high turnover and many missed days. All these are symptoms of what Harvey Leibenstein has called *X-inefficiency,* the inefficiency displayed when a firm has average costs higher than necessary for a given quantity and quality of output. Put another way, the firm produces less than could be produced given its inputs. (Leibenstein has also argued that X-inefficiency may prevent the adoption of technologies requiring more intensive effort, higher literacy, and so forth. Here a country may be forced to continue to use an inferior technology by its underlying inefficiencies.) All this amounts to saying that low wages may not after all be a good bargain for an employer if they do not compensate for even lower efficiency.

These considerations suggest that it is necessary to distinguish between countries that did not have early experience with industry and countries that did. In the first group, the supply of managers and skilled workers may be in such short supply that diminishing returns are close to the surface. Countries that did have a significant amount of early experience with industry include Argentina, Brazil, Egypt, India, South Korea, and Taiwan (the last obtained 20% of its GNP in manufacturing in the 1930s, mostly from food processing but also from some heavy industry installed by the Japanese). Except for South Africa, sub-Saharan Africa had no remotely similar experience. True, there is little correlation between early industrialization and the present efficiency of investment, which is high in South Korea and Taiwan but low in Argentina, Egypt, and India. Even so, it is surely better to have had some industrial experience than not to have had any.

Artificially High Prices for Labor or Low Prices for Capital

A complication intrudes if the price of labor is kept artificially high, resulting in a kind of "wage dualism," with wages not reflecting labor's true abundance.[10] Urban wages are often two or three times higher than the income that can be earned in the farm sector, and much higher than would occur in any competitive structure, even if there are large costs of job search and moving. What are the reasons for the large differential?

First, government salaries may still be paid according to wage scales set in the colonial period or just after independence when skills and education were more scarce. Second, the legal minimum wage may be high and sternly enforced. This is especially true in urban areas. In Tanzania, for example, the legal minimum is three times that of India, even though Tanzania has the lower per capita income.[11] Such laws may have originally been aimed at relatively vulnerable foreign firms, but political forces sometimes then spread their effects more widely. Although minimum wages receded somewhat in many LDCs during the 1980s (by 35% in real terms in Latin America between 1980 and 1991), they are still a force to reckon with.[12]

Third, strong trade unions (especially in mining, oil production, and in state enterprises), may lead to a dualistic wage structure.[13] Unions are stronger in Latin America and the Caribbean than elsewhere, with union membership about a third of the labor force in Argentina and Venezuela, a quarter in Jamaica, and a fifth in Mexico. Unions are also important in Bolivia, Brazil and Chile. Elsewhere, union membership is especially important in Mauritius, Sri Lanka, Tunisia, and Turkey, in some cases with a third or more of the labor force unionized. The public sector workers in Africa and India are in general highly organized and militant. In some countries, certain union members—copper miners in Zambia and Chile, tin miners in Bolivia, oil workers in Mexico, Nigeria, and Venezuela—at times have had a virtual lock on policy.* (The Asian Tigers have all to some degree repressed unions, however.)

Fourth, large foreign firms may pay higher-than-market wages to protect and promote their corporate image, to ensure against public hostility, to exhibit social conscience, or to guard against high turnover. If training costs are relatively substantial, the modern-sector employer may be able to minimize unit costs by cutting turnover, and above-market wages are one way to do so. The term *efficiency wage* is used by economists to refer to wages higher than the minimum at which labor is available because higher productivity offsets the higher cost.

Fifth, expensive social programs, such as pensions, compulsory health and safety measures in plants, family allowances, and fringe benefits may raise labor costs by as much as 30% to 40% of the nominal wage bill.† Although few workers in agriculture may be covered by social security, a large proportion of those employed by large firms or in government may participate—for example, in Brazil, 83% of those in public administration. Antilayoff and job security laws may be passed, such as Panama's 1972 statute restricting the layoff of workers with more than two years of service and Brazil's similar protection for public employees.

All this means dualism in the labor market, with wages artificially boosted in the modern sector and still low in the traditional sector. The high wages of the urban centers, which have often grown as fast as or faster than in the developed world and sometimes three or four times faster than the growth of real per capita national income, have been a great attraction to labor. This wage differential is a main cause of the recent heavy migration from rural to urban areas. Historically, over 30% of the addition to urban population in the LDCs has been people from the farms. The figure has been over 60% in Ghana, South Korea, and Tanzania, and over 70% in Côte d'Ivoire and Uganda.[14] Urban population was only about 22% of the whole for the LDCs of 1960, but it was 35% by 1992, with estimated growth of 4.3% between those years, as opposed to only 1.2% in the urban centers of the developed world.[15]

The dual wage structure may also promote the spread of urban unemployment. High wages enhance the supply of labor relative to the demand; so many migrants to the cities may remain jobless. Severe urban unemployment rates of over 20% have sometimes been reported for the age group 15 to 24 in Colombia, Kenya, the Philippines, and Sri Lanka, among others, although many economists believe that such figures are sometimes overstated and are relatively rare. This position that high open unemployment typifies the cities of the LDCs has become controversial, and we return to the subject in Chapter 11.

---

*It might be noted that in recent years there has been a strong correlation between the percentage of the labor force that is unionized and the degree of protests against macroeconomic reform measures involving austerity. Another aspect of strong unions can be seen in the experience of Chile. There during the 1980s, inflexible union demands in combination with high legal minimum wages were responsible for some of the heavy unemployment when government policy turned toward stabilization by reducing aggregate demand. See *WDR 1991*, 80.

†In much of Latin America, social programs are financed by a payroll tax. The employer's contribution (10% of the wage bill is not unusual) represents a direct increase in labor costs. Sri Lanka and Malaysia are notable examples of countries outside Latin America with these programs.

Artificially Low Prices for Capital

The dualism can also be promoted from the capital side if there are special stimuli for the use of capital in a kind of "financial dualism." Examples have already been discussed in earlier chapters and include financial repression, the subsidization of interest rates, and negative real rates of interest on loans. Because banks in effect have to ration credit under these conditions, it is likely that large firms will have the easiest access to the cheap loans. That means a greater expansion of the modern sector than is justified, and more capital-intensity than otherwise.*

The tying of aid from developed countries may have similar effects, as may imports of capital encouraged by overvalued exchange rates or forgiveness of tariffs. In particular, state corporations may be called upon to pay only a small return on capital, or perhaps nothing at all. This is almost certain to ensure that they will end up highly capital intensive and use too much capital in total in an organizational structure that is often overly expanded. Again, labor will appear expensive relative to capital even though it is the abundant factor; there will be far less incentive to search out new technologies that use labor. Whatever the reason, be it artificially high prices for labor or artificially low ones for capital, the result is the same. The demand for labor is reduced and for capital increased in any sector where policy alters prices. Technological dualism sets in.

Analyzing High Labor and Low Capital Costs

Actual data showing the degree to which labor and capital costs are distorted are somewhat scarce. Even where data exist, there is a strong suspicion that the worst cases are not included. Table 8.1, taken from the work of Anne Krueger, shows the estimated percentage distortion in labor and capital costs for a selected group of countries at various time periods. Economists are not certain how large these distortions have to be before they become significant. Krueger's simulations suggest that for a given unit of capital, removing the price distortions would have increased labor use by 10% in Argentina, 15% in Brazil, and 271% in Pakistan.

The expected effect of a combined artificially high price for labor and artificially low price for capital can be seen diagrammatically in Figure 8.2a, which uses a production isoquant similar to those in Figure 8.1. Given any choice between labor intensity and capital intensity, along the single isoquant shown in Figure 8.2a, artificially altering the prices of labor and capital will alter the technology adopted. The line *PP* is a price line showing a small amount of scarce capital exchanging for a larger amount of abundant labor. Production is labor intensive, with L labor and K capital being employed. If, however, the price of labor is boosted and the price of capital subsidized, as shown by price line P_1P_1, then managers choose different factor proportions. More capital is employed (K_1) and less labor (L_1). The type of

---

*Note that high modern-sector wages have the opposite effect on expansion (less of it) but the same effect on factor proportions (more capital intensity than otherwise). See I. M. D. Little, "Small Manufacturing Enterprises in Developing Countries," *World Bank Economic Review* 1, no. 2 (July 1987): 203–235.

TABLE 8.1 DISTORTION IN LABOR AND CAPITAL COSTS

Country	Year(s)	Change in Labor Cost (percent)	Change in Capital Cost (percent)
Argentina	1973	+15	–17
Brazil	1968	+27	– 4
Chile	1966–1968	na	–37
Hong Kong	1973	0	0
Côte d'Ivoire	1971	+23	–15
Pakistan	1961–1964	0	–76
South Korea	1969	0	–10
Tunisia	1972	+20	–36

Source: adapted from Anne O. Krueger, *Trade Strategies and Employment,* vol. 3, *Synthesis and Conclusions* (Chicago, 1983), table 7.1.

technology in use and the resulting employment of capital and labor are here closely related to the price of these factors, even if artificial. Diminished employment possibilities for labor follow directly. Notice in Figure 8.2a how only L_1 labor finds employment on this project because of the choice of a capital-intensive technique, whereas with a labor-intensive technique L labor was at work.

Alternatively, one could show relative prices, if artificially established at P_1P_1, causing a shift to a different (capital-intensive) type of technology as with the *CI* isoquants in Figure 8.2b. This is completely rational from the point of view of the firm making the decision, but it does not reflect the actual scarcity of the factors of production.

Numerous LDCs have recently come to recognize the difficulties for development when technological dualism becomes pronounced. In response, planners have frequently used a device called a *shadow price,* which estimates what the price would have been in the absence of the distortion. Low shadow prices for abundant labor and high shadow prices for scarce capital can be used to guide decision makers in their choice of factor proportions. The topic is discussed in Chapter 12.

Another fairly common reaction has been the attempt to lessen the urban–rural wage gap. Singapore, South Korea, and Taiwan have tried to do so by curtailing the strength of the urban-based trade union movement. A number of other nations, including Ghana, Sudan, and others in Africa, and Indonesia and Thailand in Asia, have reduced their emphasis on minimum wage laws. Other LDCs that have such laws (such as Brazil and Mexico) have set the legal minimum so close to the going wage that the laws have little effect, while others (including India) have used the more direct tools of labor courts, tribunals, and boards to enforce more moderate wage claims. There has also been a slowdown in the spread of expensive social security programs.[16]

Factor Substitution Difficult

A third reason why capital intensity may occur in the modern sector of a labor-abundant country—why technological dualism may be found—is a matter of

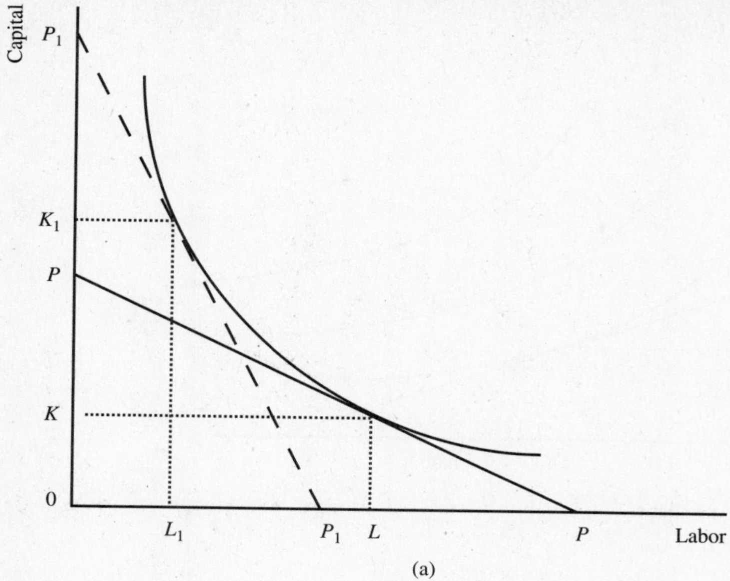

(a)

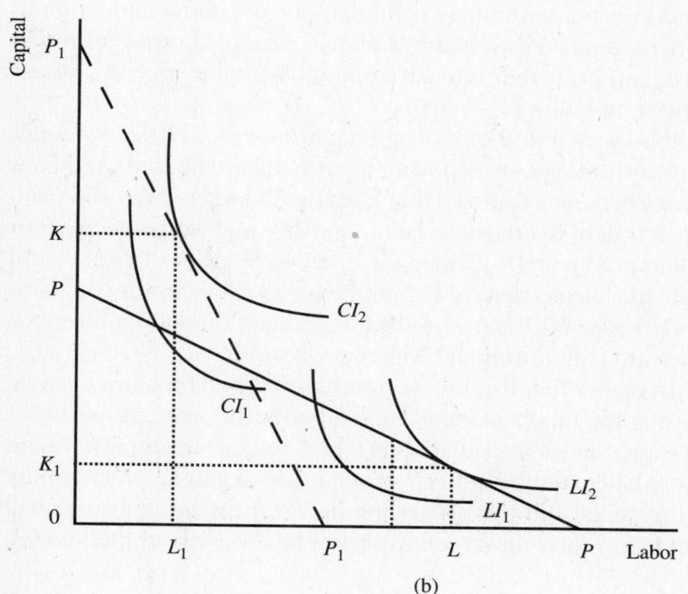

(b)

Figure 8.2 The effect of combining an artificially high price for labor and an artificially low price for capital is to increase the use of capital and decrease the use of labor.

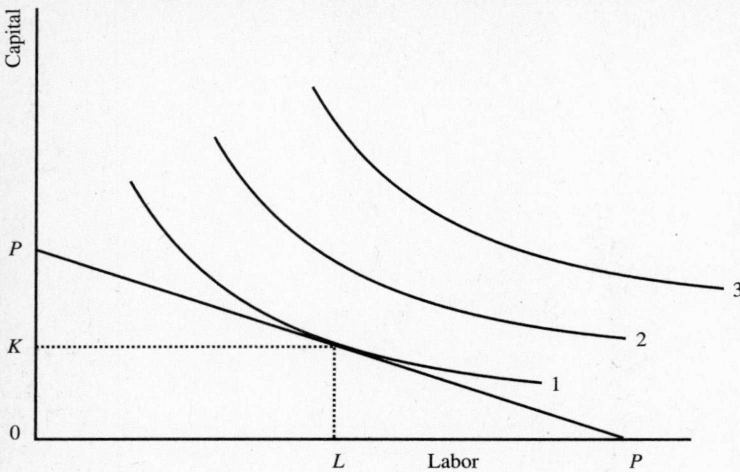

Figure 8.3 Factor substitution in labor-intensive production with smooth production isoquants.

engineering. Here the argument is made that factor substitution is easy in the traditional, largely agricultural sector. This is illustrated in Figure 8.3, where production can be undertaken with many combinations of capital and labor, as shown by the smooth slope of the isoquant. Labor is cheap, shown by the flat price line *PP*, and production is labor intensive, only *K* capital being used alongside the large quantity *L* of labor.

The situation will be very different if, in the modern sector of the economy, the opportunities for substituting between labor and capital are limited. Arguably, some modern industries present a capital–labor ratio that is largely fixed and unalterable. For example, it is hard to imagine a labor-intensive nuclear power plant or labor-intensive gasoline production.* (Though it is fair to point out that much of the construction of the nuclear power plant or petroleum cracking tower could utilize labor-intensive methods, and Biafra produced gasoline, though inefficiently, from crude oil in backyard stills during the Nigerian Civil War.)

If factor proportions are often fixed for technical reasons, then output can be increased only by raising the inputs of capital and labor in the same proportion.† Figure 8.4a shows a capital-intensive situation in which the factor proportions are fixed. There is no possibility of substituting between capital and labor, shown by the L-shape of the isoquants, and the proportion between these two factors will thus remain constant at any level of output, as shown by the slope of the line *0Z*.

---

*The following have nuclear reactors either operating (marked *) or under construction (†): Argentina*, Brazil,* China,† Cuba,† India*† (seven operating, seven planned), Iran,† Mexico,* Pakistan,* South Africa,* and South Korea* (nine operating).

†This assumes that the capital is being operated at full capacity. If the capital is idle part of the time (say, at night), then of course multishift working could change the capital–labor ratio.

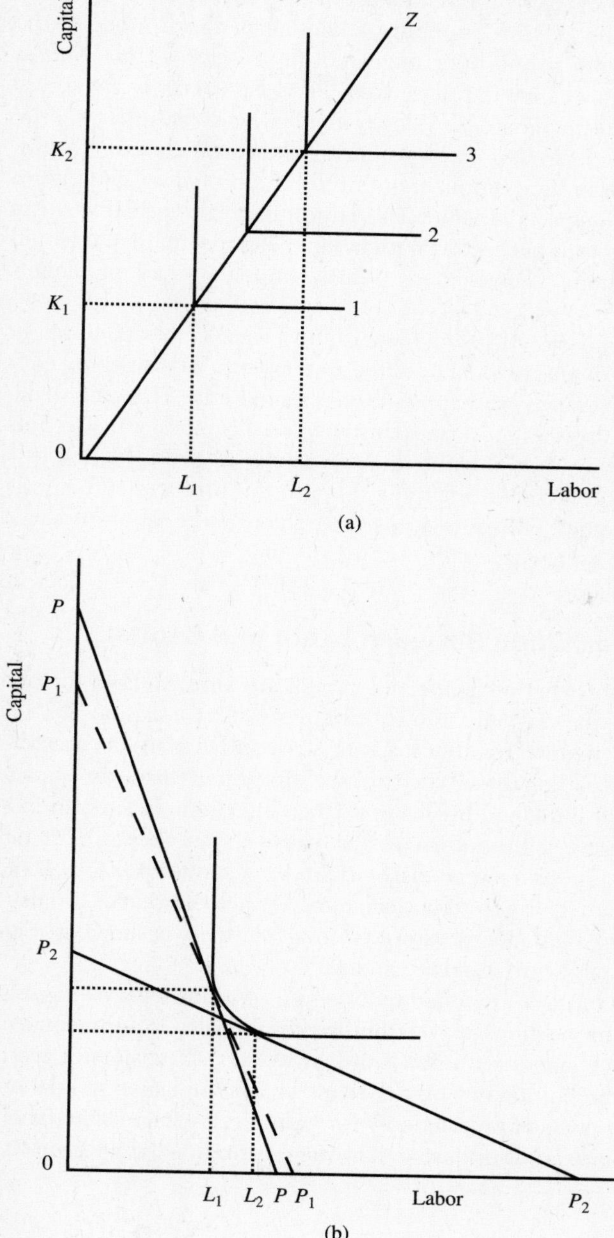

Figure 8.4 Fixed factor proportions in capital-intensive production, shown by the L-shape of the production isoquant.

Notice that large quantities of available labor (L_2) will not alter the outcome; at output level 1, L_1L_2 will simply remain unemployed in this sector. Only the availability of additional capital, K_2, for example, would allow more labor to be employed. Alternatively, factor proportions might not be as fixed as this, but, as shown in Figure 8.4b, a large change in prices (from *PP* to P_2P_2) may be necessary for any shift to occur; a small change (to P_1P_1) leads to no factor substitution. In the modern sector, the outcome is limited employment of labor for technical reasons. The excess labor can, however, find employment in the traditional sector (Figure 8.3), where factor proportions are variable. The large quantities available put a downward pressure on wages in that sector. With labor cheaper even than it would otherwise be in the traditional sector, there is little impetus to adopt higher-productivity methods.

The issue is an important one. If only a few products were involved, all might be innocent enough. What, however, if LDC elites are drawn to sophisticated consumer goods that must be produced by capital-intensive methods? Then the structure of consumer demand itself might push industry toward capital intensity. This particular technological bind would thus be due to a choice of products, not to a choice of technology. The government of India thought the problem sufficiently serious to use the law to require entrepreneurs to search out more labor-intensive methods, with, apparently, some success.[17]

The Elasticity of Substitution Between Labor and Capital

Technically, the question of whether labor and capital are substitutable for one another is one of elasticity, the elasticity of substitution of labor for capital. If a 1% rise in the price of capital relative to labor leads to a rise in labor use so that the labor–capital ratio grows 2%, then the elasticity of substitution in that industry is 2. A study cited by the World Bank and involving a 70-country sample showed that when wages rose 10% relative to the return on capital, there was about a 10% fall in the labor–capital ratio, for an average elasticity of 1. (A range of 6% to 20%, meaning elasticities of 0.6 to 2, was cited in that study.)[18] Such elasticities are usually lower in manufacturing than in agriculture.* A high elasticity is shown in Figure 8.3, a low one in 8.4b, and zero elasticity in 8.4a.

The entire argument must be qualified to a degree. Within limits even great apparent fixity of factor proportions may be indirectly flexible. Equipment can sometimes be run faster or longer with new shifts of workers. Transfers of input and output to and from the equipment may perhaps be accomplished in a labor-intensive manner. Some aspects of production—for example, packaging and labeling a product—may be more labor-intensive than some central activity within the

*If the elasticity of substitution is in fact lower in manufacturing, then problems of flexibility in labor absorption could potentially worsen as development proceeds.

operation, so making the whole operation less capital-intensive than it would otherwise be.[19]

A further problem with factor proportions appears when technical improvements take place. Such changes are more likely to occur in modern capital-intensive industry than they are in traditional farming or small business. In the traditional sector, there is less emphasis on research, there are fewer inputs of complementary capital, and often production is on a very small scale. Technical improvements may therefore have considerably less effect in the traditional sector than they do in the modern one, thereby perpetuating the technological dualism, the low wages, and the low productivity growth in much of the economy.

The model of fixed capital–labor ratios leads to some pessimistic predictions in countries with rapid population growth. In these countries, fixed capital–labor ratios in the advanced sector, or a belief by entrepreneurs that the ratios are fixed even if they are not, will mean that employment in the modern sector will not be encouraged by the tendency toward lower wages as population grows. Unless new investment occurs at a rate fast enough to absorb the large numbers, the growing work force has to find employment in the traditional sector. There is an ever lower capital–labor ratio in that sector and ever less land per unit of labor. The resulting fall in the marginal product of labor lessens any tendency to adopt labor-saving innovation in agriculture. Why bother if the labor is so cheap? Hence there may be a cut in the incentive to invest in agriculture. Labor-using innovation can, of course, be profitable under these circumstances and can drive up rural wages.

Designing and Servicing Labor-Intensive Equipment

A fourth reason why capital intensity may be favored in the modern sector even in the face of high labor availability has to do with the design and servicing of machinery and equipment. The initial design of more labor-intensive alternative machinery calls for entrepreneurial ability, for fresh insights, and for research that costs money—all scarce in the LDCs. Firms may resist undertaking the development of new labor-intensive technologies because other firms borrow the technology and profit from it. Typically, even multinational firms clever enough to manipulate transfer prices to maximize profits do not appear to do much research into the development of new labor-intensive processes.[20] They usually prefer to shift older equipment, which is ordinarily less capital-intensive, to their branches in the LDCs. Perhaps this is because they have the ability to seek out and find equipment of this sort all over the world, perhaps because they can obtain it at good prices because it is being discarded in a developed country and because of their good bargaining position, or perhaps because they already own surplus stocks that might be easily shifted. (It should be added that banks frequently will not lend to finance the purchase of secondhand machinery.)

Even when labor-intensive equipment is available for purchase from LDC manufacturers, it is frequently found that the capital-intensive machines and equipment from the industrial countries can be more quickly serviced by trained personnel and are better provided with spare parts. Say a firm purchases labor-intensive machinery from India or Brazil or from a local manufacturer. It runs the risk that a repair crew, perhaps only days away if the machine were made in Germany or the United States, will take weeks or months to arrive from a manufacturer that produces on a much smaller scale and is far less experienced in such matters. It amounts to a question of risk. This problem has received less attention than it deserves.

Technology as a Competitive Device

Finally, capital intensity may be favored for competitive reasons. A country may conclude that the advantages conferred through "learning-by-doing" may point to adopting newer rather than older technologies. On the micro level, firms may believe that they will capture and keep higher returns when they employ sophisticated, hard-to-copy technology.[21] Competition can be kept at bay longer and more profitably when technology provides a barrier to entry, especially if the barrier survives the expiration of patent protection. Predictably, this behavior will be more likely among multinational firms, with their easier access to advanced technology. It should be noted, however, that MNEs are not generally more capital-intensive than domestic competitors in the same industry.[22] Their reputation for emphasizing capital is instead due to their tendency to concentrate on industries that are themselves capital-intensive and where their experience has given them advantages.

Labor Intensity: A Conclusion

It is a basic neoclassical presumption that relatively labor-intensive technologies are appropriate for countries where labor is abundant, but there are a number of significant impediments, from the point of view of a private decision maker, to adopting labor-intensive methods. The result is that no general rule is likely to be applicable to every private firm. A specific investigation will be necessary to ascertain whether, in any particular industry, the impediments will overcome the basic presumption. There is little reason to expect any great similarity in the decisions between countries or between industries in the same country because of the diversity involved. Short-run decisions for capital intensity, appropriate on a private basis where alternatives are not available or where servicing is poor, may be quite inappropriate in the long run when these problems have been overcome. From a social point of view, ensuring that a country's factors are combined in an efficient way will involve attention to basic human services when labor productivity is so low that it offsets low wages; to government policy on wages and interest rates when these are the causes of the dualism; to the development of alternative technologies when appropriate substitutes are unobtainable; and to the provision of better servicing for these technologies when they do become available. It is also fair to warn that the beneficial effects of the "right" technology can easily be overpowered if a country's macroeconomic policies are poorly designed.

There seems no question that in the years to come, research on alternative technologies will be an exciting part of development economics. Even if progress is slow, however, there is no need to despair. The fastest growers of recent years have been countries with (initially) very cheap labor, including South Korea, Taiwan, Hong Kong, Singapore, and Japan. These have been successful far beyond expectation without much development of new labor-intensive methods beyond what could be achieved through management and organization.[23]

GROWTH THROUGH TECHNICAL CHANGE

To this point, we have addressed the issue of technology as it relates to a country's factor proportions. Now we move to the prospects for growth through the adoption of more productive technology that would raise the productivity of capital

THE APPROPRIATE TECHNOLOGY CONTROVERSY

The appropriate technology (AT) debate dates from the publication of E. F. Schumacher's famous book, *Small Is Beautiful*, in 1973. Some proponents of AT believe that traditional labor-intensive methods are best because of their ability to raise employment in the countryside.[24] India has been a major protagonist in the debate; Mahatma Gandhi and the Congress Party were believers in small-scale enterprises and traditional methods. (The Congress Party's flag sports a traditional spinning wheel, and the emblem in the center of India's national flag is a stylized wheel.) In that country in 1950, more than 800 products were restricted by law to production by small firms. Textile mills were suppressed, and cloth was produced on power looms that did indeed employ three times more labor per unit of cloth than the mills did—but exports declined and jobs were lost. Analysis showed that preserving employment by these means in textiles was high in cost. The same was true of sugar production, where large mills were discouraged and small village mills were favored. Again, analysis showed that the large mills were economically superior. (Research by Ian M.D. Little, who studied industries in India, Korea, and Colombia, has shown that, contrary to intuition, firm size is a poor indicator of whether production is labor-intensive or not. Little found that the degree of labor intensity depends much more on the nature of the industry. Proponents of small-scale industries also believe that capital is more productive in small firms. That belief was not verified by Little.)[25]

The debate over AT turns on this implied trade-off. Is a technology more "appropriate" if it provides a little more employment but a little less income?[26] What if a less-traditional technology creates sufficient new income and higher labor productivity so that the total demand for labor rises? What if the traditional technique would miss out on economies of scale, provide much less output than the more modern technique, and therefore furnish less employment? There are existing traditional technologies that are labor intensive and could also lower costs and give higher output, but the concern is that not all of them will do so. That is the crux of the debate.

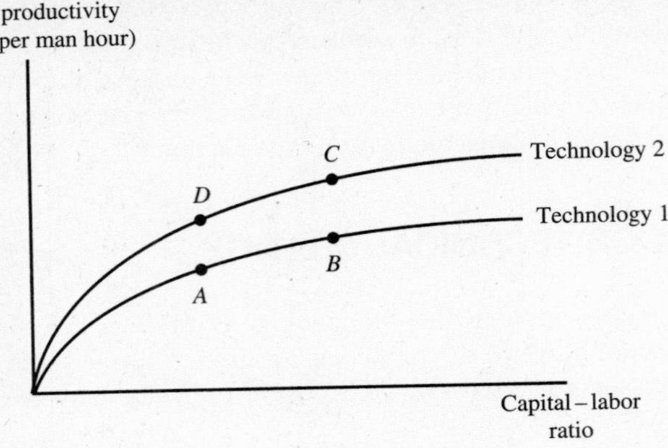

Figure 8.5 Acquisition of capital raises labor productivity, but the increase can be accelerated if the capital embodies improved technology.

and labor. Consider Figure 8.5. Here more capital investment but without a change in technology will raise the ratio of capital to labor and so increase output per man hour, moving a country from point A to point *B*, significantly increasing productivity. But an improvement in technology from the less-effective Technology 1 to the more-effective Technology 2 can move the country from *A* to *C*. Howard Pack concludes that the ability of the high-performing Asian economies to acquire improved technologies by borrowing it, buying it, or otherwise obtaining it, together with the provision of enough technical education to support it, have been the main factors promoting these countries from moderate growth to superior growth.[27]

A major problem is that below a certain level of development, LDCs may not have an adequate educational base to support technological improvement because the skills to support new technology are in very short supply.[28] For example, recently in Tanzania there were just six trained textile engineers working in the country's eight large textile plants; 160 would have been a more reasonable figure. Limits on the ability to sustain technological improvements are most pronounced in Africa, though they exist in every country where prior industrial experience is lacking and investment in education has been low. Where that is the case, reliance on other domestic suppliers may be harder, and rapid responses to changing demand may be more difficult. Such countries may have to eschew trying to acquire electronic, biotechnological, or chemical technologies, and stick to elementary manufacturing technologies that can often be acquired with lower levels of education and technical competence.

For LDCs in this position, simple technologies with simple equipment may be the order of the day. These can often be improved upon by suggestions at the blue-collar level, as was true in the initial development experience of South Korea and Taiwan. Only later did these countries move to acquire higher-level technologies. For a few years it may be necessary to make do by hiring skilled foreigners, perhaps in connection with the activities of multinational enterprises. The foreigners know where to find the needed information and how to incorporate it into manufacturing.[29] Overall, lower income countries are better advised to focus on general education rather than basic research and applied research in universities. These countries simply do not have a comparative advantage in pioneering technical change, which is better left to the best-performing LDCs and the developed countries.

Government and the Acquisition of Technology

The more advanced LDCs have assimilated the lesson that technical change can be spurred by official action and that the potential for growth through this means is high in the LDCs because so much remains undone. Government encouragement of manufactured exports often means that the firms involved will have a vested interest in acquiring information about technology. New technology requires investment in both physical and human capital, and there is a strong link between these forms of investment and technical change.

A number of countries, including Brazil, Ghana, India, Indonesia, South Korea, Taiwan, and Mexico, have established institutes for research and for the spread of information on research. The expectation is that the institutes will advertise, and perhaps develop, alternative labor-intensive technologies. For a salient case, Taiwan's Industrial Technology Research Institute at Hsinchu studies mainly electronics technology. It seems patterned after Japanese examples. Its research, mainly designed to foster catch-up with the developed countries, is rapidly communicated to the firms that cluster around it. These clustered firms are attracted not just by the access to technology, but by tax exemptions, duty-fee imports of inputs, innovation prizes, and even prefabricated factories into which new enterprises can move. South Korea's Taeduck Science City is similar, though much more lavish.[30] The other side of this coin is that some countries may push most avidly in industries protected by trade barriers, which could not compete without the barriers. Where this is so, the resources may be "wasted" from a social point of view.

In the lowest-income countries, there is a growing realization that an important source of useful technological improvement is local farmers and artisans. The "interactive research" enabling ideas to work up from below has already brought improvements to charcoal production and in the design of charcoal stoves.[31] The idea of change from below is a good one that deserves encouragement.

On a small scale there is now some export of technology from one LDC to another, the major producers being Argentina (plants for fruit processing and meat refrigeration), Brazil (steel), Mexico (steel), India (textiles, sugar processing, solar-powered irrigation pumps, and cement), and South Korea and Taiwan (electronics and light manufacturing). Except for India, these are all relatively high-wage LDCs, however, with their contributions of limited significance where labor is even cheaper. A story reported in the press shows how difficult things can be sometimes. India's sale to Tanzania of a "technically appropriate" system for turning waste into combustible gas backfired when it was found that Tanzania's wages (the legal minimum three times higher than India's) were too high to justify the labor-intensive Indian technology. A little developing-country technology has even flowed to the North, particularly in energy. Brazil is a gasohol pioneer; India and China are leaders in the development of biodigesters that convert garbage to power.[32]

The LDCs have become more discriminating in their purchases of foreign technology. Sometimes in the past, several local firms have each contracted to buy exactly the same imported technology from some foreign firm, the negotiations kept secret, of course, for commercial reasons. To economize on these costs, national registers of imported technology have been established by, among others, Argentina, Colombia, India, South Korea, and Mexico. The agencies in charge of the registers work to ensure that expensive duplication of technology imports is avoided. The World Bank has singled out the programs of Colombia and Mexico for favorable mention, noting their "significant success in reducing costs and acquainting domestic entrepreneurs with cheaper alternative technologies."[33] In Colombia, the government's examination and appraisal of contracts involving technology led to a reduction in royalties paid of some 40% and also to a cutback on the restrictions for exporting goods produced with the new technologies. In the first year after Mexico's new technology law, 36% of all contracts registered with the government were rejected and thereafter renegotiated. Of these, 81% were objected to on the basis of excessive cost. Other reasons included limits on the volume of production and restrictions on export of the finished product.[34]

For years there was discussion of a "technology code" to control restrictive practices by developed-country providers of technology, though such practices have proved difficult to define. Recently, however, the better-off LDCs' eagerness to acquire advanced technology has rather muted the calls for this sort of supervision.

TECHNOLOGICAL PROPERTY AND THE LDCs

Technology can often be property in the sense that someone or some firm controls its use through patents or copyrights (particularly on computer programs). The property aspect of technology has led to long-standing disputes between the LDCs and the developed countries.[35] The latter have consistently argued that patents serve the very useful purpose of increasing the flow of new products and new technologies by rewarding their developers. They argue that encouraging research by granting a temporary exclusive right to the inventor is fully as beneficial to a low-income country as to a rich one.

LDCs reply that the monopoly aspects of patents can be manipulated to their disadvantage. They claim that the benefits accrue mainly to firms in the developed nations, which typically hold 80% to over 90% of the patents taken out in the LDCs. Even the residual of patents held domestically may include citizens acting as a front for foreigners, and a good portion of the remaining patents have little importance. The chief criticism is that often the patents are taken out as a competitive tool to prevent the use of an invention by competitors, so protecting imports of products embodying the patents. The statistics seem to confirm this: Only 10% of patents issued in LDCs are actually being used; 90% are not. A suspicion arises that the present state of patent law does not tend to encourage the spread of new technologies to industries in the developing countries.

For years the LDCs advocated the compulsory licensing of patents to prospective users after, say, five years of non-use. (Under the Paris Convention of 1883, to which most countries adhere and which governs international patent law, compulsory licensing is legal and so is complete revocation if the licensing arrangements do not work out. But the international rules are very stringent, compulsory licensing is rare, and revocation is even rarer. The process is long and costly, and usually seems not worth the trouble.) Another idea for reform advocated by the LDCs was shorter terms for patents than the 17 to 20 years in the United States and other developed countries. They argued that this was overly long for protecting a monopoly position, and many adopted shorter limits, so that the average for 45 of these countries fell to just 11 years. More radically, some LDCs suggested replacing patents altogether in favor of a system of government prizes for new technology, followed by free public use of the knowledge. Others argued that patents should apply more favorably to, or perhaps only to, locally developed technologies, and not to imports.

A conference to reform the Paris Convention (called WIPO for World Intellectual Property Organization) met first in 1980 and continued for some years. It eventually made several recommendations involving compulsory licensing after a period (30 months) of non-use, and revocation of patents after five years of non-use.

But many developed countries were implacably opposed, insisting that such changes in the Paris Convention would certainly reduce the flow of technology to the LDCs. The question was eventually folded into the Uruguay Round of trade negotiations negotiated within GATT. An agreement on trade-related aspects of intellectual property rights (TRIPS) was included in the final Uruguay Round document. The LDCs gave some ground in this area in return for considerable reductions in the trade barriers facing their goods in international trade. The TRIPS agreement expands copyrights to computer software, which will receive the 50-year protection already accorded to literary works and music. Patent protection will be standardized at 20 years. Compulsory licensing was strictly limited—mainly to government use—with little change from the original Paris Convention rules. A transition period is permitted to bring national laws into accord with the TRIPS agreement, one year for the developed countries, five years for the LDCs, except 11 years for the least-developed countries.

Conclusion

Finding technologies that provide a better fit to factor availability without sacrificing output is a major task for the low-income LDCs. Then, as economic growth propels countries to middle-income levels, technologies that can promote and expand that growth take center stage. Unlike physical capital acquisition, the influence of technology actually grows as an economy matures. In the final analysis, technology change is the ultimate line of defense against diminishing returns to capital investment.

NOTES

1. Standard works, listed in alphabetical order, include Edwin Mansfield, *The Economics of Technological Change* (New York, 1968); Howard Pack, *Productivity, Technology, and Industrial Development* (New York, 1987); Hubert Schmitz, *Technology and Employment Practices in Developing Countries* (London, 1985); A. K. Sen, *Choice of Techniques: An Aspect of the Theory of Planned Economic Development* (Oxford, 1960) and *Employment, Technology, and Development* (Oxford, 1975); and Frances Stewart, *Technology and Underdevelopment* (London, 1977) and "International Technology Transfer: Issues and

Policy Options," in Paul Streeten and Richard Jolly, eds., *Recent Issues in World Development* (Oxford, 1981), 67–110. A good introduction to the economic history of technology is Charles Singer et al., eds., *A History of Technology* (London, 1958). Informative essays from a symposium on technological change and industrial development were published in the *Journal of Development Economics* 16, nos. 1 and 2 (September/October 1984). I also benefited from Thomas R. Degregori, *The Theory of Technology* (Ames, Iowa, 1985); Howard Pack and Larry E. Westphal, "Industrial Strategy and Technological Change," *Journal of Development Economics* 22, no. 1 (June 1986): 87–128; Howard Pack, "Industrialization and Trade," in Hollis Chenery and T. N. Srinivasan, eds., *Handbook of Development Economics*, vol. 1 (Amsterdam, 1988), 333–380, especially 337–340; Martin Fransman, "Conceptualising Technical Change in the Third World in the 1980s: An Interpretive Survey," *Journal of Development Studies* 21, no. 4 (1985): 572–652; and Ian M. D. Little's unorthodox critique in *Economic Development: Theory, Policy, and International Relations* (New York, 1982), 176–181.

2. Some of the diagrams in this chapter either appear in or were suggested to me by the Bruce Herrick-Charles Kindleberger texts. I also was informed by the insights of Gerald M. Meier in his *Leading Issues in Economic Development*, various editions (New York).
3. For evidence that the penalties for using the latest technology can be significant, see Howard Pack, *Productivity, Technology, and Industrial Development: A Case Study of Textiles* (New York, 1987).
4. See the discussion by Fransman, "Conceptualising Technical Change," 583–584.
5. For the Indonesian evidence, see Theodore Morgan, *Economic Development: Concept and Strategy* (New York, 1975), citing work of L. T. Wells, Jr. For the Colombian examples, see William Loehr and John P. Powelson, *The Economics of Development and Distribution* (New York, 1981); 162–163, quoting a study by D. Morawetz.
6. For a discussion of locking in to a particular technology, see Harvey Leibenstein, *General X-Efficiency and Economic Development* (London, 1978), 113–122. In this section I also utilized Loehr and Powelson, *The Economics of Development and Distribution*, 179–183; and Michael Roemer and Joseph J. Stern, *Cases in Economic Development: Projects, Policies, and Strategies* (London, 1981), 13.
7. Research in the LDCs is becoming increasingly important, however. See Fransman, "Conceptualising Technical Change," 584–589.
8. For the following data, see Jere R. Behrman, "The Economic Rationale for Investing in Nutrition in Developing Countries," *World Development* 21, no. 11 (November 1993): 1749–1771; Henry M. Levin, "A Benefit-Cost Analysis of Nutritional Programs for Anemia Reduction," *World Bank Research Observer* 1, no. 2 (1986): 219–245; *WDR 1990*, 81; *WDR 1991*, 54; *WDR 1993*, 18; Loehr and Powelson, *The Economics of Development and Distribution*, 225; and Andrew M. Kamarck, *Economics and the Real World* (Philadelphia, 1983), 75.
9. *WDR 1993*, 18.
10. A discussion can be found in *WDR 1987*, 123–129.
11. *The Economist*, April 30, 1983, 100.
12. For minimum wages see Richard B. Freeman, "Labor Market Institutions and Policies: Help or Hindrance to Economic Development?" *Proceedings of the World Bank Annual Conference on Development Economics 1992* (Washington, D.C., 1993), 117–144, especially 130–131; the comments on that paper by Victor E. Tokman, 145; *WDR 1991*, 80; and Carlos E. Santiago, "The Dynamics of Minimum Wage Policy in Economic Development: A Multiple Time-Series Approach," *Economic Development and Cultural Change* 38, no. 1 (October 1989): 1–30.

13. See Joan M. Nelson, "Organized Labor, Politics, and Labor Market Flexibility in Developing Countries," *World Bank Research Observer* 6, no. 1 (January 1991): 37–56.
14. See *WDR 1979*, 55.
15. *HDR 1994*, 173.
16. See *WDR 1979*, 54–55.
17. Indian employment strategies have been innovative and are surveyed at length in Austin Robinson, P. R. Bhramananda, and L. K. Deshpande, eds., *Employment Policy in a Developing Country*, 2 vols. (London, 1983).
18. See *WDR 1987*, 123–129.
19. See Little, *Economic Development*, 178–179.
20. The statement is made by Howard Pack in Meier, *Leading Issues*, 4th ed., 355. This section reflects Pack's work.
21. See Stephen P. Magee, "Information and the Multinational Corporation: An Appropriability Theory of Direct Foreign Investment," in Jagdish N. Bhagwati, ed., *The New International Economic Order: The North–South Debate* (Cambridge, Mass., 1977), 327–328. A general view of the multinationals and technology is J. Davidson Frame, *International Business and Global Technology* (Lexington, Mass., 1983).
22. See Howard Pack, "Industrialization and Trade," in Hollis Chenery and T. N. Srinivasan, eds., *Handbook of Development Economics*, vol. 1 (Amsterdam, 1988), 369.
23. Compare Little, *Economic Development*, 181. Little has examined the technological choices of these countries in "The Experience and Causes of Rapid Labour-Intensive Development in Korea, Taiwan Province, Hong Kong, and Singapore, and the Possibilities of Emulation," in Eddy Lee, ed., *Export-Led Industrialisation and Development* (International Labour Office, 1981).
24. Analysis of the issue is found in Frances Stewart, ed., *Macro-Policies for Appropriate Technology in Developing Countries* (Boulder, Colo., 1987); Howard Pack, "Aggregate Implications of Factor Substitution in Industrial Processes," *Journal of Development Economics* 11, no. 1 (1982): 1–37; Howard Pack, *Productivity, Technology, and Industrial Development* (New York, 1987); James C. W. Ahiakpor, "Do Firms Choose Inappropriate Technology in LDCs?" *Economic Development and Cultural Change* 37, no. 3 (April 1989): 557–572; and Bela Balassa, "The Interaction of Factor and Product Market Distortions in Developing Countries," *World Development* 16, no. 4 (April 1988): 449–463.
25. See I. M. D. Little, "Small Manufacturing Enterprises in Developing Countries," *World Bank Economic Review* 1, no. 2 (July 1987): 203–235.
26. The debate can be traced in R. S. Eckaus, "Appropriate Technology: The Movement Has Only a Few Clothes On," *Issues in Science and Technology* (Winter 1987): 62–71; and Frances Stewart, "The Case for Appropriate Technology: A Reply to R. S. Eckaus," *Issues in Science and Technology* (Summer 1987): 101–109.
27. Howard Pack, "Technology Gaps between Industrial and Developing Countries: Are There Dividends for Latecomers," *Proceedings of the World Bank Annual Conference on Development Economics 1992* (Washington, D.C., 1993), 283–302. For the diagram, see p. 286.
28. For material in this paragraph, see Howard Pack, "Productivity and Industrial Development in Sub-Saharan Africa," *World Development* 21, no. 1 (January 1993): 1–16.
29. Howard Pack, "Technology Gaps between Industrial and Developing Countries, 296–299.
30. *The Economist*, May 21, 1994.
31. See Matthew S. Gamser, "Innovation, Technical Assistance, and Development: The Importance of Technology Users," *World Development* 16, no. 6 (June 1988): 711–721.

32. *The Economist*, March 24, 1979, 122.
33. *WDR 1979*, 66.
34. Gerald K. Helleiner, *International Economic Disorder: Essays in North–South Relations* (Toronto, 1981), 52.
35. In this section I used Peter O'Brien, "Developing Countries and the Patent System: An Economic Appraisal," *World Development* 2, no. 9 (1974): 27–36; Gerald K. Helleiner, "International Technology Issues: Southern Needs and Northern Responses," S. P. Magee, "Information and the Multinational Corporation," and Charles P. Kindleberger, "Response," all in Bhagwati, *New International Economic Order*, 295–343; Constantine V. Vaitsos, "The Revision of the International Patent System: Legal Considerations for a Third World Position," *World Development* 4, no. 2 (1976): 85–102; Pedro Roffe, "Abuses of Patent Monopoly: A Legal Appraisal," *World Development* 2, no. 9 (1974): 15–26; and Edith Penrose, "International Patenting and the Less Developed Countries," *Economic Journal* 83, no. 331 (1973): 768–786.

Chapter 9

The Population Problem

On rough estimate, it took perhaps four million years for the earth to reach its first billion of population in about 1800, 130 years to reach the second billion in 1930, 30 years to reach the third billion in 1960, 15 years to reach the fourth billion in 1975, and just 11 or 12 years to reach the fifth billion in 1986 or 1987. The growth rate of the world's population was virtually nil (0.03%) between A.D. 1000 and 1750, approximately 0.5% in 1900, 1% in 1930, and 1.8% between 1960 and 1992. In 34 countries, population growth from 1960 to 1992 exceeded 3% per year.[1] Remember the Rule of 72. If population growth is 2% per year, then 72 ÷ 2 = 36 and the doubling time for population is 36 years.

Every hour more than 10,000 people are added to the world's population. Every week the increase is equal to another city the size of Philadelphia; every year, another entire Mexico. Most of the additions are in the LDCs, where in the next three to four decades it is expected that 95 to 97 out of 100 births will occur. In 1950, two out of three people lived in LDCs, whereas by 2025 the proportion will be five out of six. Nigeria by 2050 will have as many people as all of Africa does today. In the year 2000, all but three of the world's top ten cities will be in the LDCs; Mexico City at 26 million will be as large as New York plus London were in 1985.

World population is currently about 5.3 billion. This figure is likely to increase for a long time even if people and governments decide to do more to control population, because half of the world's population is under 24 years of age. World Bank demographers present three scenarios based on various projected paths of population growth. Because there are so many young people in the population, even if people decide at once to have fewer children and this has a rapid effect on family size, cessation of growth will not occur until a total of about 10 billion people is reached late in the 21st century (in 2085 to be precise). If an overall decision to have fewer children is not taken until the year 2005 and the decline in family size is slower, then population would reach about 13 billion in the year 2110. Or if the decline begins only in 2020 and is slow, then population will continue to grow until about 2135 and will reach 23 billion.[2]

This chapter considers whether and how this "population explosion" affects economic development.[3] Though demographers are cautious in their conclusions, a large and rapidly growing population influences economic development in several ways and arguably accounts to a significant extent for the low per capita incomes and slow growth of poor countries. In no other area of development economics has there been a more dramatic change in attitudes and prospects. Whereas in the 1960s and 1970s pessimism ruled—and justified pessimism at that, given the available information that population growth was not slowing down—today, more rapidly than was once thought possible, there is progress to report. It now appears that the world's population growth rate peaked around the year 1970 and that fertility has fallen faster than had been foreseen. The negative side is that fertility has not fallen fast enough, so pressures on land and the prospects for the environment continue to worsen.

INCREASING OR DIMINISHING RETURNS TO POPULATION?

People are an input into production. Why should more people not be considered an augmentation of inputs that will increase economic growth, rather than a problem?[4] There are indeed arguments favoring population growth in certain circumstances. Population size can be so small in relation to land area that there are severe diseconomies of scale in transport, utilities, other public services, and the production of goods. Roads and railroads improve with greater population density, as do other areas of the infrastructure such as health, education, irrigation, extension services, communications, and markets—at least until a certain size is reached. A larger population can allow greater specialization; economies of scale in production and marketing; and economies in providing transport, communications, irrigation, and the like. Scholars—Ester Boserup prominent among them—suggested that increased population density could be the catalyst for productive innovation and new methods of organization. North America in the nineteenth century and Australia earlier in the twentieth century were both areas where a large and growing population allowed more efficient use of natural resource endowments, the development of larger markets with the attendant realization of scale economies, all of which served to enhance technological change. The higher demand meant that the risks associated with investment were reduced.*

But a cardinal rule of economics is diminishing returns to a factor—in this case, people. The standard expectation is that, all other things being equal, additional increments to population will result in smaller and smaller marginal increases in the amount of output. It appears that areas of low population density were able to escape diminishing returns because these areas had abundant resources and a well-developed public and private infrastructure of transport, communications, storage, and power. They also had stable governments able to cope administratively with a rapid increase in population. Their high incomes enabled them to afford good education and public health, which were not only well-developed but improving. A growing population therefore brought a flexible, qualitatively better labor force, and greater investment, land improvement, better education, and the spread of more productive technology all served to raise labor productivity.[5] The positive changes in the quantity and quality of the other factors of production, and the rising quality of the population itself, appeared to offset the diminishing returns of standard theory.† For a time, it seemed reasonable to suggest that perhaps today's LDCs could escape diminishing returns to population in the same way. Remarkably few problems were encountered from the rapid population growth of the 1950s and 1960s.

Presently, many scholars have less hope that most of today's LDCs can escape from diminishing returns to population. With their low levels of capital and their masses of unskilled, uneducated labor, it is doubtful what obvious economic gains would flow from rapid population growth even in areas of low density such as Brazil or parts of West Africa. It is doubly difficult to see any advantage in countries (Egypt, Bangladesh, and China, probably) where population per acre of cropland is already higher than that of the Netherlands, the developed country with the densest population.[6] Even where more people might eventually be advantageous, as they were in North America during the frontier era, the immediate costs of rapid population increase may submerge the eventual benefits for years, long delaying any positive effects. Africa is a region where on the whole population densities are not especially high, but where there is convincing logic that further rapid population growth is harmful because complementary resources are limited by poverty.

---

*Note that domestic scale economies are certainly not crucial to growth. Economies can export to the world and so can thrive without a large national market, as shown vividly by Belgium, Denmark, Luxembourg, and Switzerland in Europe, and by even smaller Hong Kong and Singapore in Asia.

†Technical note for readers who are conversant with intermediate microeconomics: When population size is sufficiently small, there may be increasing returns to labor. Population growth will cause the average product of labor to rise as long as the marginal product of another worker is above the average product. When population passes a certain size, however, all things being equal the marginal product of labor will fall below the average product of labor, and the average product will fall.

AN OPTIMUM POPULATION SIZE?

For over a century, economists have debated the concept of an optimum population—the idea that a population size can be identified where output is maximized. According to this concept, the addition of people to a population below the optimum would allow greater division of labor and economies of scale, so raising the average product of labor. Additions to a population above the optimum would, however, involve diminishing returns given the stock of resources, so lowering the average product of labor. The idea of an optimum population size fell into disrepute when it was realized that other factors were not staying equal. Additions to the physical or human capital stock, changes in technology, and changes in the quantity or quality of the other factors of production meant that the optimum population size at any given moment would soon not be the optimum at all. Nowadays, it is understood that a low-income country may be vastly overpopulated in relation to its factors of production even if its population density per square mile is much under that of, say, the Netherlands, where the quantity and quality of most other factors is high.

Noneconomic Arguments Against Limiting Population Growth

There are a number of noneconomic arguments that look with disfavor on controlling population increase, or even favor rapid growth. These arguments are religious, social, and political in nature.[7] The religious beliefs of several groups lead them to the position of opposing population control. The hierarchy of the Roman Catholic church, many conservative Muslim malams (Saudi Arabia bans all contraception) and Hindu priests, and lately some fundamentalist Christians, are opposed on moral grounds to birth control by artificial means.* This is not necessarily a pronatalist position, because one can certainly oppose rapid population growth but at the same time find artificial means for slowing the growth unacceptable. Even so, it would seem that rejection of major means for controlling population increase would inevitably have the result of larger numbers.

It is perhaps somewhat surprising, therefore, that there is little correlation between national religions and the birth rate, and with the lack of correlation pronounced for some Catholic countries. Birth rates in the United States, for example, are above those of Catholic Belgium, France, and Italy, all of which rank well above the developed-country average for the use of contraceptives.[8] Indeed, Catholic France was historically the pioneer in fertility decline in the nineteenth century. It had a devout, predominantly peasant population and a rather slow pace

*These views are generally not held by mainstream Protestant Christians, Buddhists, Taoists, Confucianists, practitioners of Shinto, liberal Muslims, or secularists.

of development, but its fertility decline far outpaced that of richer, Protestant, modernizing, urbanizing England until late in that century.[9] In Canada, the image of Catholic Québec as extremely conservative is shaken by the statistic that birth rates are lower there than in any other Canadian province. In addition, by the 1970s, government-supported family planning was already in place in Catholic Guatemala, El Salvador, Peru, Honduras, Bolivia, and Colombia. The large decreases in birth rates in all these Catholic countries and areas suggest strongly that religion has less influence on this vital matter than was once supposed.

Right-wing nationalists and conservatives often take a position in favor of population growth for a different reason, namely, that military as well as economic power depend on population size. There is sometimes an anticolonial aspect to the argument: The mother country had a period of rapid population growth, and therefore so should the independent nation. The implication is that population control entails an attempt to maintain an inferior and racist status quo. This pronatalist position emphasizes not only economies of scale and an augmentation of labor supply, but also protection of currently underpopulated areas from covetous neighbors. It sees military power, political power, and the "vitality" of a younger age structure all arising from population growth. These arguments are heard in Latin America, especially Argentina and Chile, and in Israel, but nowhere more so than in the former French colonies, especially in West Africa. About half of the LDCs without any public support of family planning were formerly French.*

The argument that military power is enhanced by the availability of conscript soldiers is certainly persistent. It seems seriously flawed, however. One would have thought that the history of war from the days of Alexander the Great to the era of nuclear weapons shows conclusively that it is technology, good management, and national product, not sheer manpower—especially when that manpower is undereducated and malnourished—that strengthens military capacity. How else can one explain Alexander's victories over the masses of Asia, or British power in the nineteenth century, or the well-oiled Israeli military machine in a country with a small population (in spite of that country's pronatalist policies)? Or, conversely, why is Bangladesh not a great power or India a juggernaut?†

*For the numbers, see *WDR 1984*, 127. As might be suspected from the references in the text to former French colonies, France has a very long tradition of boosting the population. French leaders have considered the birth rate low since early in the nineteenth century, and for years births have been encouraged by financial means. Cash loans are made to married couples, and the debt is reduced by 15% if a child is born before the end of an eight-year period and 25% further for each additional child until the debt is canceled on the birth of a fourth child.

†The military argument played an important role in the decisions of many of the former Communist countries to encourage population growth by means of cash grants, a birth bonus, additional paid holidays, loans for apartments, long paid maternity leaves, tenured jobs for mothers, the discouragement or abolition of abortion, and the putting of difficulties in the way of divorces. Nazi Germany followed many of the same policies and is the best historical example of emphasis on the military side of the argument. The Nazis used a system of honors and awards for fecund females to boost the birth rate. The Kreuz Deutsche Mutter, first class, in gold, was awarded to mothers of six or more children. A silver cross for four or five children and a bronze cross for three or four feted lesser feats of fecundity.

THE COSTS OF RAPID POPULATION GROWTH

By what reasoning might one conclude that rapid population growth is detrimental to economic development? The first well-known idea, very influential in its time and even today, was contributed by the "gloomy parson," T. R. Malthus, in the early part of the nineteenth century. Malthus argued that unrestrained population growth would keep per capita incomes limited to a subsistence level. Whenever income rises above subsistence, procreation would increase, and the greater numbers would cause deprivation and famines that would push income per capita down again. Income is thus "trapped," unable to expand because of population pressure.

Although once the centerpiece of population economics, the Malthusian trap models have been found to apply poorly to the underdeveloped countries of the twentieth century, or of the nineteenth for that matter.[10] As we shall see, for many years cross-section analysis among countries actually revealed quite poor correlation between faster population growth and lower growth of per capita income.[11] The increase in the world's productivity was great enough to counter the effects of the increase in fertility.

Malthus's vision was apocalyptic. Economists and demographers today do not as a rule speak of apocalypse and catastrophe in their discussions of rapid population increase, rather of lower quality of life and less opportunity for improvement. They emphasize how, if neglected, the problem will be ever harder to solve because a bigger population base today provides the potential for an even greater increase tomorrow. That does not mean, however, that Malthus was entirely wrong, as we explore below.

The Burden of Dependency

The modern critique of rapid population growth suggests that a negative effect on development arises because of the resulting adverse changes in the age composition of the population. In a country where population is growing slowly, no particular age group predominates, and there are far more people of working age (15 to 65) than there are children or elderly. The effect of rapid population growth is to increase sharply the percentage of children in the population; the effect is intensified by the LDCs' concentration on infant and child mortality reduction. Typically, 40% of the population in the LDCs is less than 15 years old or 65 and over, a figure that increased by 5 to 15 percentage points between the 1940s and the 1960s. The normal figure in rich countries is a little over 30%.

These dependents, contributing relatively little in labor power but making heavy demands on food, shelter, clothing, and education, are an extra burden on an LDC's resources. The term *burden of dependency* has been coined to describe the situation. The percentage of dependents in LDCs is not as high as would be true if the over-65 age group were as large as it is in the developed world, but the problem is serious nonetheless. Table 9.1 shows the percentage of dependent population of selected countries in 1991. It points to a sharp contrast

TABLE 9.1 THE BURDEN OF DEPENDENCY: PERCENT OF POPULATION IN AGE GROUPS 0–14 AND 65+, 1991

Canada	33	Egypt	43
France	34	India	40
Germany	32	Kenya	51
Italy	31	Mexico	40
Japan	30	Nigeria	48
United Kingdom	35	Pakistan	47
United States	34	Sudan	48
All developed countries	33	Syria	51
		Tanzania	51
		All LDCs	
		Low income	45
		Middle income	40

Source: WDR 1993, 288–289. An alternative method of expressing the burden is the "dependency ratio," the number of people under 15 and 65 and over for every 100 people between 15 and 64. That ratio is over 80 for the LDCs, compared to a little over 50 for the developed countries.

between the poor and the rich. Notice that a figure of 50% in a low-income country translates into about one dependent for each worker, whereas the rich-country average of 33% means one dependent for every two workers. Within the LDCs themselves, this distinction can be important. Each Ethiopian of working age has to support more than twice as many dependents (1.04) as does each Korean (0.44).[12]

The result is that even if economic conditions were exactly the same in every way between the countries on the left and those on the right of Table 9.1 except for the dependency burden, the burdened nations would suffer lower growth of per capita income because of having to divert a substantial amount of their resources to meet the needs (food, housing, education, and so forth) of their young. In the countries with really rapid population growth, in the 3% to 4% range (as in Kenya and Malawi, among others), it is estimated that education costs could be cut sharply—by as much as 50% to 60% over 30 years—if the increase could be slowed to a more moderate rate.* The funds would be freed for other uses, improving the quality of education, for example, or for other investment or consumption. The dependency argument alone is therefore a powerful incentive to limit population growth. The problem is ultimately self-correcting after population increase is brought under control. Taiwan's dependency burden, for example, fell from 45.1% in 1960 to 35.7% in 1975. This is little consolation in the short run, however,

*See *WDR 1984,* 86. The suggested large cost decrease would occur if there were "rapid fertility decline" compared to standard fertility assumptions, as calculated by the World Bank.

because the problem generally worsens with some development as a greater proportion of children enter school.

Capital Widening Versus Capital Deepening

With rapid growth of the labor force, a given stock of capital has to be expanded (capital widening) or the productivity of labor will fall, causing wage incomes to decrease as well. Current projections suggest that in the next 20 years, 95% to 97% of the world's population growth will be in the LDCs but only 15% of the world's capital investment. All other things being equal, that would mean a fall in the capital that is available per worker in the LDCs with high population growth, and thus a further fall behind the developed countries in their productivity. To avoid this outcome of diminishing returns to labor, either huge capital formation in the LDCs will have to occur, or migrants will have to be accepted by the developed countries in unprecedented numbers.[13] Neither outcome is very likely in the immediate future.

If, however, population growth is limited, the new investment that does occur will allow a greater quantity of capital per worker (capital deepening), resulting in higher productivity and growing wage income.[14] The infrastructure of an economy—its railways, highways, ports, electric power grid, telecommunications, and so on—will be harder to provide and harder to improve if substantial saving must be devoted to capital widening. The country that cannot keep up will suffer from "capital shallowing."[*]

Economic Consequences for the Young

Several adverse consequences for children can result from rapid population growth. On a national level, the greater the drain of keeping pace with the burden of dependency and the need to widen capital, the less the potential for spending on improved health care, better schools, and higher nutritional standards. Indeed, the greatest of the ill effects from fast population growth is likely to be the high cost of proper education for children and ultimately the inability to provide it.

On the family level, more of current income must go for the children's consumption, which worsens educational prospects and the security of the family. The dilution of family resources as income is spread among larger numbers can contribute to malnutrition in children; it seems obvious that parents who have a sixth child will usually not be able to spend as much on that child as they did on their first, even if their income has been rising. Such children pay a penalty. There was

---

*See Nancy Birdsall, "Economic Analyses of Rapid Population Growth," 23–50; and Angus Denton, "Saving in Developing Countries: Theory and Review," *Proceedings of the World Bank Conference on Development Economics 1989* (Washington, D.C., 1990), 61–96.

THE DEBATABLE EFFECTS ON SAVING

Sometimes it is argued that the burden of dependency will result in a lower level of saving (and hence investment). But a long-standing finding is that there is little relation between population growth (and hence dependency) and saving, with any such effect at most very mild. "The empirical evidence does not support strong generalizations concerning the relationship between population dependency and savings rates," according to a recent study.[15] Much saving by business and government would not be affected, and the poor save little anyway. Better-off families may actually increase their saving to finance education for their children. Also, the young save more than the old. Recent use of life cycle models leads to a different conclusion, however. The newer research indicates that saving is adversely affected by population growth. One reason, perhaps, is that it may be difficult to find prudent ways to save over long time periods in the LDCs. The effect is significant, with a fall in population growth from 2.40% to 2.16% per year associated with an increase in the percent of income saved of 18%, from 15.6% to 18.4%.[16] The new evidence of a decline in saving associated with population growth may be sufficient to explain at least part of the growing negative correlation between population growth and economic growth between the 1960s and 1970s and the 1980s, as described later.

a 16% greater probability of malnourishment in Colombian families with five or more children than in families with four or fewer, and 38% in Thailand when comparing four or more to three or fewer. The result is more sickness and, hence, a much higher risk of infant mortality. Birth control will therefore arguably raise the average levels of education, health, and nutrition.[17]

A large number of closely spaced young children contributes to a weakened mother, premature weaning, and hence a much higher risk of infant mortality. Demographers estimate that an average decline in infant mortality of 10%—or as much as 30% in some countries (Pakistan, for example)—would be registered if the time interval between births were increased beyond three years.[18]

Children are likely to have lower birth weights, be physically smaller, and have higher incidences of infectious diseases more than twice as often in families of eight than in families of three, according to one study.[19] There is possibly even an adverse effect on intelligence, according to some reports. The children of large families also tend to perpetuate the cycle by having more children themselves.

The much larger numbers of young people contribute to the growing numbers of homeless "street children," recently estimated at 75,000 in Manila; 100,000 each in Bombay, Calcutta, and New Delhi; and 25,000 in Nairobi. Many of these children have living parents, but contact with them is infrequent.[20] As these and other children grow older, they become inexperienced, low-productivity workers with relatively poor prospects for modern-sector jobs. They may have to be absorbed into the rural labor force or take informal-sector city jobs such as porterage, shining shoes, hawking small quantities of merchandise, or producing cheap handicrafts, with their accompanying depression of wage levels.

Richard Easterlin of the University of Southern California suggests that negative economic and social consequences will flow from the overcrowding of the poor into great cities. His Easterlin Hypothesis points in particular to a high supply of unskilled low-productivity labor, which causes a surge of new entrants into the schools that increases the number of students per teacher, reduces space in the schools, and likely lowers academic attainment. The crowding in these cities can mean bitter people and disappointed hopes, more drug use, greater alcoholism, more mental depression, more crime, and a severe increase in political tension.*

Environmental Consequences

Beyond the congested and inadequate health and educational facilities and the impact on wages, these young people may face an ever-deteriorating environment. Population growth shrinks the amount of land available per person. In rural areas, the result can be subdivision of land as inheritances are divided among heirs, with resulting parcels too small to achieve minimum efficient scale. So the plots are sold and the dispossessed end up as additional landless labor. Bangladesh is a prime example of decreasing access to land.[21]

Rural population pressure on land (for farming) and forests (firewood for cooking) leads to erosion, silted rivers and dams, encroachment by deserts, and the like.[22] It is therefore plausible to conjure up a bleak picture of deteriorating soils and declining availability of fuel and fresh water. Deforestation by the year 2010 is expected to reduce the per capita availability of forest land by 30%. In Brazil the loss of forests is believed to be in the range of 0.5% to 2.3% per year, while in Côte d'Ivoire it is running at 6% to 16%, with less than 20 years remaining for that country's forests. The ramifications can spread wide. The cutting down of Nepal's forests by people seeking firewood led to more silting in rivers running down through overpopulated Bangladesh to the Bay of Bengal. In turn, that brought the formation of islands in the estuaries of those rivers, the occupation of those islands by Bangladeshis seeking farms, and many disasters from the cyclones (as hurricanes are called in that region) that sweep these islands almost every year. To be sure, such consequences have other causes as well, including inadequate definition of property rights and government policy errors, such as subsidies to the timbering industry. It is also true that much of the evidence on the environmental costs of an

*The study of "territorial imperatives" among animals show animal behavior can become much more belligerent under crowded conditions. Though there is probably less similarity with human behavior, the examples of Hun, Goth, Vandal, and Viking do indicate that when population is thought to be intolerably high in relation to resources, people can become ill-tempered and acquisitive in their relations with their neighbors.

expanding population is limited.[23] To exclude overpopulation from any of the blame seems, however, to go too far.

Even if damaging environmental consequences can be avoided, there will be adverse effects from the overcrowding. The costs of obtaining quiet and privacy; of escaping congestion; of access to wilderness and unspoiled streams, meadows, and woodland; and of uncrowded housing will rise because of the "social scarcity" of these amenities, and a much smaller proportion of the population will be able to enjoy them. It is common in some quarters to ignore these concerns and to say they do not matter, but to do so is to dismiss the importance of the quality of life, which you and I in the developed world would certainly not abide if it were our lives thus blighted.

THE STATISTICAL RESULTS

We have seen reasons to believe that population growth may foster economic growth. These include the size effects of larger domestic markets and economies of scale, specialization, economies in providing infrastructure, and technological improvement of the Boserup type. There are other reasons to believe that population growth may *diminish* economic growth, as with the burden of dependency, a decline in saving because of that burden, a diminishing returns argument that capital has to be spread among more people as population grows, crowding and congestion costs, and negative consequences for children and the environment.

The effect of population growth on economic growth is thus a net effect, with some factors encouraging better economic performance and some discouraging it. What does statistical analysis contribute to the question? In fact, the statistics are mixed. In the 1960s and 1970s, the standard finding was that population growth rates were not correlated with growth rates in output. This lack of correlation was used to suggest that arguments concerning the ill effects of population growth were exaggerated.[24]

Information covering the 1980s forces a reconsideration of this view, with population growth now clearly correlated negatively with economic growth. The correlation is stronger in the late 1980s than in the earlier part of that decade.[25] In the period from 1984 to 1993, LDCs with "high growth" (that is, with growth in per capita GDP above the 2.02% average for developed countries) exhibited population growth of 1.7% a year; LDCs with low GDP growth (under 2.02% per year) had population growth of 2.5% a year; while LDCs with negative GDP growth had population growth of 2.7% a year. The figures were not much different whether the country concerned was a high-income, middle-income, or low-income LDC.[26] Work by Allen Kelley and Robert Schmidt indicates that a fall in population growth from approximately 2.5% per year to 2.3% is correlated with a rise in the growth rate of output per capita from 2% to 2.4%, a significant rise of 20%.[27] This effect is largest in the lowest-income LDCs. It must be remembered that statistical correlation is not the same as proof, and that the statistics that now point to serious damage from population growth did not do so only a few years ago. Yet the data do now

EXTRAPOLATIONS CAN BE STARTLING

Sensationally gloomy predictions, though tongue-in-cheek because they could not occur in actual fact, can be made by extrapolating forward from recent population growth rates. Ansley Cole noted in the 1970s that at the growth rate then being registered, six-and-a-half centuries in the future there would be only one square meter of land per human being. Or, if population grew at the same rate for 12 centuries, the weight of the people would exceed the weight of the earth. Or, in 6000 years the earth would be at the center of a sphere of human bodies expanding at the speed of light![28] Argument from compound growth rates and their effects centuries hence is not meant to be taken very seriously, but it does serve to warn vividly that one way or another high rates of population growth must come down.

It should be noted that those who do not fear rapid population growth make startling statements of their own. One such recently in the news is that "there is plenty of room—the entire population of the earth would fit into the city limits of Jacksonville, Florida." Perhaps so, but would you want to be one of Jacksonville's five billion residents?

suggest that negative consequences have been building up, outweighed for many years by the positives, but with the negatives now predominating.

Might Malthus Be Right in the Long Run? A Shortage of Food[29]

As we have seen, T. R. Malthus took the position that unrestrained population growth would result in a negative check on population in the form of famines and starvation. Up to now, increases in world food supply have kept pace with population growth, so that Malthus's prediction of calamity have in general not been borne out. But some authorities take a neo-Malthusian position that food shortages will eventually result from rapid population growth.

In support of a pessimistic view, cropland has virtually ceased to expand and the needs for housing and businesses encroach on what exists, overgrazing hurts grasslands, and many fisheries are on the way to exhaustion. Population continues to expand, but these resources essential to food production do not. If population grows as projected to the year 2010, the per capita availability of cropland will drop by 21% and grazing land by 22%. The results could potentially include not only food shortages and hunger, but also mass migration that spreads the problem to other less-populated countries, and conflicts spawned by the shortages.

Technical change that raises output from the available resources (described in Chapter 11) may allow food production to keep up with population growth.[30] But it is sobering to realize that if technology change had *not* raised yields of food per acre above the 1950s yield, then today's world would need at least twice as much cropland for food production. From 1950 to 1989, the world fish catch expanded by nearly five times, and the world's rangelands by 2.6 times, rates that seem unlikely to be sustained. Since the mid-1980s the increase in world grain production has plateaued, with growth of less than 1% per year between 1984 and 1993 compared to more than double that in the preceding three-and-a-half decades. Even if the expansion in food supplies *does* continue, that expansion would have to be much greater to raise the per capita consumption of food rather than simply keeping pace with the growth of population.

John Maynard Keynes was premature, but perhaps prophetic, when he wrote that

> Malthus disclosed a Devil. For half a century all serious economical writings held that Devil in clear prospect. For the next half century he was chained up and out of sight. Now perhaps we have loosed him again.[31]

It is true that the Malthusian Devil stayed in chains for a longer time yet. But is it wise to depend on technology always keeping pace? Does prudence suggest that population be controlled as a matter of insurance? Can we risk the Devil loosed? These are questions that humanity must answer.

THE CAUSES OF RAPID POPULATION GROWTH

To this point we have discussed the consequences of rapid population growth. Let us now turn to the causes that underlie the so-called population explosion. This and the following section discuss the substantial changes in both birth rates and mortality that have occurred historically in the LDCs, especially over the past three decades.

Why Birth Rates Are High

Central to demographic detail is the fact that human beings have the ability to achieve very high birth rates, usually fully adequate to offset high death rates even under primitive conditions. Table 9.2 shows some current birth rates, calculated as the number of live births per thousand of population and called the "crude birth rate." Although the statistics are subject to a wide margin for error, they do show dramatically that some countries have birth rates at just about the natural maximum—a rate of 50 per 1000 is extremely high and is seldom exceeded.* The highest national birth rate in 1992 was 55 in Malawi.[32] That the situation can be changed is shown by the rates for Hong Kong, Singapore, South Korea, and Taiwan, where rates have been reduced to almost the low levels found in the developed countries. In these countries, rates of 10 to 16 are typical. For example, the

*The highest birth rates ever recorded in modern times are among the Hutterite religious sect, many members of which live in Canada. A religious duty to bear children has led the Hutterites to an average of 11 children per woman, 400 births per 1000 women per year in the age group 25 to 29, and a crude birth rate on the order of 85 per 1000. See Don E. Dumond, "The Limitation of Human Population: A Natural History," *Science* 187 (February 28, 1975): 713–721.

TABLE 9.2 CRUDE BIRTH RATE (LIVE BIRTHS PER THOUSAND OF POPULATION), 1992

Country	Rate
Bolivia	36
Ethiopia	51
Iran	37
Kenya	37
Mexico	28
Nigeria	43
Pakistan	40
Tanzania	45
Yemen	50
Hong Kong	12
Singapore	16
South Korea	16
Germany	10
Great Britain	14
Japan	11
United States	16

Source: WDR 1994, 212–213.

birth rate in the United States is 16, and in Britain it is 14.* The average for all low-income LDCs excluding China and India has slowly come down from 47 in 1960 to 45 in 1970 to 37 in 1992, though it remains at 44 in sub-Saharan Africa.[33]

Micro Reasons Underlying High Population Growth In spite of some decline in recent years, birth rates in many LDCs remain high. We have already seen several macro reasons that influence attitudes toward population. Here we focus on the very important micro reasons that encourage the production of children, based on what is perceived as social and economic necessity at the family level.

The social milieu may be an incentive for large families. The concept of "machismo" or manliness in Latin America leads to a high personal value put on family size as evidence of virility. In Africa, a desire for large families is a result of a family structure based on lineages (descent groups) or clans, with loyalty, support, and veneration after death frequently a cultural norm. The wives of polygamous husbands may depend in part for their economic advancement on the immediate control of numerous children of their own. In any case, men generally want

*Japan's reduction from earlier high levels was the most rapid ever recorded until quite recently. From 35 between 1920 and 1924, and still high at 30 between 1940 and 1944, the figure fell to 19 in the mid-1960s and 11 in 1988, where it remained in 1992.

more children than their wives do, and women accede to these demands.* Moreover, childlessness may be treated as a taint.[34] In prerevolutionary China, traditions of ancestor worship meant more benefits to the departed when the descendants were large in number, and this social norm survived for a long time. There may be a bias in favor of sons (especially strong in China and Korea), which encourages trying again. With child mortality high, parents might decide to have as many as five offspring simply to ensure that one boy will survive.[35] (Evidence of the preference for boys in Asia is provided by the widespread practice, among those that can afford it, of amniocentesis leading to abortion of females.)

Large numbers of children may be thought to guarantee an adequate labor supply for farming. Some useful work can be obtained from about the age of 7, and with wages low, any lost income to the mother may be minimal compared to the later economic returns from the children. Perhaps half the costs of a child (goods and services, mothers' lost wages) may be offset by these early earnings, based on a rural study in the Philippines.[36] Numerous children also serve to ensure that this labor supply will be available in spite of the high child mortality characteristic of less-developed rural areas. There is both a replacement effect as parents attempt to have another child to offset a death and a hoarding effect as parents hedge against mortality by having more children.[37] One reason why sub-Saharan Africans continue to want more children than elsewhere is that children are relatively more productive there. When resources are held in common with access open to all, a frequent practice in Africa, more children are desired because they give a greater chance for increasing a family's share of such resources as firewood (used for 80% of energy needs), the grazing of animals, and fishing. Land, often held in the name of descent groups, is often allocated in larger amounts to families with more children. Children can help in gathering firewood and brush, in tending cattle and goats (and the family's babies too), in carrying water, and in similar work.[38] In many parts of the world, families still appear to act on these premises, and birth rates often are a quarter more in rural regions than in urban surroundings.

Similarly, numerous children act as insurance against the parents' old age or disability. The offspring serve as a social security system for their mother and father. In Indonesia, the Philippines, South Korea, Thailand, Turkey, and other countries, surveys find 80% to 90% of parents intend to rely on this form of old age insurance.[39] The children in turn count on the grandchildren for the same service a generation hence. The greater the numbers, the less the burden on each individual. In numerous cultures, boys are looked upon as likely to produce higher incomes than girls, so adding to the preference for male children.

These microeconomic influences on procreative decision making help to explain why many parents in the LDCs desire large families. Surveys asking "what

*Calling attention to the often-overlooked point that husbands and wives can have conflicting preferences concerning fertility. See Robert A. Pollak and Susan Cotts Watkins, "Cultural and Economic Approaches to Fertility: Proper Marriage or Mésalliance?" *Population and Economic Development Review* 19, no. 3 (September 1993): 467–496.

number of children do you desire?" often report replies of four or more, and sometimes as many as six. Obviously, the mere availability of modern and effective means of contraception will not solve a population problem if families are large because parents desire them to be large.

Why Death Rates Have Declined

At the same time that birth rates have stayed high for various economic and social reasons, death rates have fallen sharply. Representative crude death rates (deaths per thousand of population), shown in Table 9.3, reveal spectacular declines from the 30 or so that was typical prior to World War II. The world's highest death rate in 1960 was 35 in Guinea. The highest in 1992 were far below that: 25 in neighboring Guinea-Bissau, and 22 in Sierra Leone and Uganda. (It should be noted that many African countries still do not have a comprehensive system of death registration, so their mortality statistics are imperfect and subject to error.)[40] For the LDCs as a whole, death rates averaged 24 per 1000 in 1960 and 12 per 1000 in 1992 in low-income countries. In middle-income countries, the figure was 17 in 1960 and 8 in 1992. The low-income countries are approaching and the middle-income countries have actually gone below the 9 per 1000 that is the average for the developed countries.[41]

Crude death rates in the LDCs that are actually below those of the United States (9), Britain (11), and Germany (11) are at first mystifying. How can the citizens of Costa Rica (4), Jordan (5), Malaysia (5), Mexico (5), Panama (5), and Venezuela (5) be dying at only half the rate of the population of the developed countries? Have these countries outdone Ponce de León and found an elixir of

TABLE 9.3 CRUDE DEATH RATE (DEATHS PER THOUSAND OF POPULATION), 1992

Country	Rate
Bolivia	10
Ethiopia	18
Iran	7
Kenya	10
Mexico	5
Nigeria	14
Pakistan	10
Tanzania	15
Yemen	15
Hong Kong	6
Singapore	6
South Korea	6
Germany	11
Great Britain	11
Japan	7
United States	9

Source: WDR 1994, 212–213.

life? No, more prosaically it has to do with the age distribution of the population. There are simply so many young people due to earlier rapid growth that fewer deaths occur in the population as a whole. For example, in 1991, over 40% of the population was younger than age 15 in 55 of the LDCs, compared to 16% to 20% in the developed countries.[42]

The Stages of Mortality Decline In all the LDCs, death rates have dropped dramatically, in a process of change with three identifiable stages. In the first stage, usually occurring earlier in this century, the imposition of law and order (often by colonial rulers) plus the provision of better transport meant that food production and distribution improved markedly. As a result, the periodic famines of an earlier period became much rarer. In India, for example, the construction of a railway system made it possible to ship food from regions of relative plenty to those of scarcity, and famines in that country became considerably less severe than those of earlier centuries. Areas where long-distance commerce in bulky items was once difficult (such as Mali, Ethiopia, Cambodia) have had serious food shortages in recent years, but these shortages have not caused anywhere near the number of deaths that would have resulted in the days before the paved highway, the airstrip, and the modern port.*

The second stage began with the introduction of public health programs. These involved water supplies and sanitation in many towns and vaccines against the great killer diseases—typhus, typhoid, cholera, and yellow fever. Smallpox has been eliminated; the last case outside a laboratory occurred in 1979. Plague, which is thought to have killed more than 10 million people in the LDCs from 1900 to 1920, appears only rarely. (There was, however, an outbreak in India in 1994.) Most important of all was the development of DDT to kill the anopheles mosquito and hence to halt the transmission of malaria. Malaria is not particularly fatal per se, but a body weakened by it is often easy prey to some normally mild ailment. It was really the biggest killer. When DDT was introduced, its effect was immediate and stunning. Thirty-nine countries wiped out the disease, for the time being at any rate; the number of new cases reported fell to less than 1% of the old level. In Ceylon (now Sri Lanka) the first big antimalaria campaign

*In an earlier time period (eighteenth and nineteenth centuries) there was another large improvement in food supplies stemming from a green revolution in which North and South American crops spread to Europe, Asia, and Africa, bringing especially potatoes and corn (maize) to many millions of new consumers. The better nutrition that accompanied the new crops meant that a considerably larger population could be supported, a fact dramatized by the famine in Ireland when that country's potatoes were severely damaged by blight in the 1840s. The much larger Irish population made possible by the potato could not be maintained without it. Hence the "great hunger" and the mass emigration off the island. A similar, though less obvious, role in African population increase has been played by maize and manioc. Better nutrition is credited with about 40% of the decline in death rates during the development of the now-developed countries, with the impact almost totally on infant mortality. See *WDR 1991*, 53.

in 1946 brought the crude death rate down from 20 in that year to 14 in 1947. Spending to control mosquitoes had a remarkable payoff: the ratio of the benefits to costs of malaria control in Sri Lanka, 1947 to 1977, is estimated to be 140 times.[43] (A revisionist literature notes that mortality also declined in areas not affected by malaria, and that some important share of the decline was due to higher income and more equal distribution of it.)[44] The chemical also gets the major credit for raising life expectancy from 36 to 60 years in Mexico between 1930 and 1964, from 38 to 58 in Mauritius between 1940 and 1960, and from 45 to 65 in Taiwan in the same years.*

The third stage, achieved by all the developed countries and by a few LDCs, involves the provision of widely available intensive medical care through hospitals and clinics. In the underdeveloped world, reasonable care along such lines can usually be found only in some South and Central American countries (Argentina, Chile, Costa Rica, Panama, Trinidad, and Venezuela, for example) and occasionally in Asia (Hong Kong, Malaysia, Sri Lanka, Singapore, South Korea, and Taiwan). Most other countries are just embarking on the third stage, and their death rates still show the effects of high child mortality, largely due to diarrheal disease and gastroenteritis, flu, and pneumonia, which at present are not easy to combat outside the confines of a modern clinic or hospital. Many LDCs have age-specific death rates (that is, death rates within age categories) similar to those of the developed countries for the adult years; their crude death rate is "spoiled" by high infant mortality. In some countries, over 50% of all deaths are among children under five,

*The celebration of the victory over malaria was premature, however. By the 1990s it was again a serious disease, with the number of deaths per year doubling to 2.5 million in the decade up to 1990. About three-quarters of these deaths were in Africa. All told, about eighty percent of the 200 or so million people with the disease are African. In Asia, Sri Lanka now reports two million cases a year after nearly eliminating the disease. Malaria has even reappeared in Europe, with 10,000 cases diagnosed there in 1991. Partly the recurrence was due to overconfidence as the human population expanded in mosquito-infested areas. If people are not bitten, they lose their immunity in less than three years. So resistance was lost when mosquitoes were eradicated by DDT. Spraying and drainage were sometimes neglected, and governments failed to maintain the intensity of their programs. DDT-resistant strains of mosquitoes were reported from India in the early 1970s, so more of that ecology-damaging chemical had to be used. Now DDT will not kill resistant anopheles mosquitoes. The best substitute, malathion, works well, but it must be spread more often and costs more; the end results is six times more expensive than DDT. Meanwhile, the World Health Organization is moving back from a strategy of mosquito elimination to the earlier strategy of treating malaria when it occurs. Discouragingly, however, the malaria parasite has developed new resistance to antimalarial drugs such as Chloroquine, which has lost substantial effectiveness. The search for effective substitutes is a first priority. Several new techniques are becoming available. These include impregnating bednets with environmentally safe insecticides and the use of polystyrene beads in pit latrines to cover the waste. The first has been successfully tested in China, the second in Tanzania. Attention now focuses on a vaccine that will prevent the disease, but development has proved to be difficult. Trials of an experimental vaccine, SPf66, have recently been promising, however, with reductions in infection of nearly 40% among volunteers in Latin America and 31% in Africa, where malaria is much more intense. Details of malaria's comeback and the renewed struggle against it may be found in Robert S. Desowitz, *The Malaria Capers* (New York, 1991); *WDR 1993*, 34, 94; *South*, August 1991; *The Economist*, October 31, 1992, August 21, 1993, and March 12, 1994; and Everett G. Martin, "Resurgent Use of DDT in World's Malaria War is Worrying Ecologists," *Wall Street Journal*, May 17, 1985.

and over 30% are among children less than one. Even so, life expectancy at birth has shown remarkable improvement, as shown in Table 9.4.

Population Growth Rates

The slow decline in birth rates in combination with the rapid decline in mortality is the main reason for the population explosion. On occasion, a high rate of immigration also contributes. The rate of growth of population is calculated by subtracting the crude death rate (CDR) from the crude birth rate (CBR) and then moving the decimal point one place to the left to express the rate of growth as a percentage (number per hundred, instead of per thousand). For example, using the data from Tables 9.2 and 9.3, for Bolivia CBR – CDR = 36 – 10 = 26, an increase of 26 per 1000 per year, or 2.6%. Selected rates of growth are given in Table 9.5.

TABLE 9.4 LIFE EXPECTANCY AT BIRTH (IN YEARS)

	1950	1992	Percent Increase
Developed countries	68	77	13
Low-income LDCs	41	62	51
Middle-income LDCs	46	68	48

Note: It should be noted that only 30 LDCs out of 117 have reliable data on life expectancy at birth for the period after 1980 and only 15 more for the 1970s. Of 50 African countries, before 1975 nine had acceptable data, but currently only three do. For many countries, the figures involve estimation subject to a substantial degree of error. See *WDR 1991*, 44.

Source: Calculated from *WDR*, various issues, table 1. The 1992 data is in *WDR 1994*, 162–163.

TABLE 9.5 ANNUAL GROWTH RATE OF POPULATION (CRUDE BIRTH RATE–CRUDE DEATH RATE, EXPRESSED AS PERCENT), 1992

Bolivia	2.6
Ethiopia	3.3
Iran	3.0
Kenya	2.7
Mexico	2.3
Nigeria	2.9
Pakistan	3.0
Tanzania	3.0
Hong Kong	0.6
Singapore	1.0
South Korea	1.0
Germany	–0.1
Great Britain	0.3
Japan	0.4
United States	0.7

Source: Calculated from data in Tables 9.2 and 9.3.

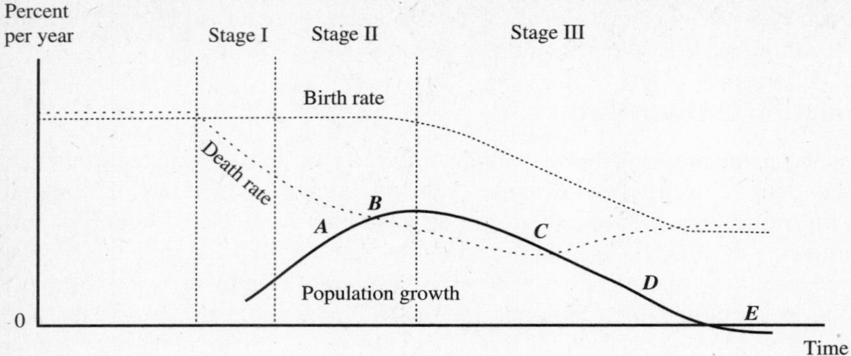

Figure 9.1 A stylized representation of birth rates, death rates, and population growth. Death rates fall long before birth rates do, leading to a substantial rise in population growth that, although temporary, can boost the size of the population substantially.

The data in Table 9.5 can be illuminated by looking back at the birth rates and death rates of Tables 9.2 and 9.3. They permit a stylized representation, shown in Figure 9.1. The figure shows birth and death rates at their original highs. Then death rates fall in the three-stage process discussed above, sometimes to unusually low levels because of the superfluity of young people in the population. Later, birth rates decline because of the changing desire to bear children. Eventually death rates rise somewhat as the age distribution becomes more normal; birth and death rates are again similar. Population growth is the difference between the birth rate and the death rate, and over time it follows the shape of an inverted U.

There are several considerations here: (1) The countries with large population increases are those where birth rates have fallen little, while death rates are sharply down (Nigeria, Pakistan, Tanzania, and Yemen, for example, represented at point *B* in Figure 9.1), or those where birth rates have fallen, but previous population growth has left the country with numerous young people and an especially low death rate (Bolivia, Iran, Kenya, and Mexico, for example, represented by point *C*). (2) In some countries, the recorded increase would be even greater but for the fact that the first or second stage of mortality decline is not yet complete. Thus death rates still have some distance to fall (Ethiopia, for example, represented by point *A*). (3) Some LDCs have registered remarkable success in controlling their birth rates and hence their population growth (Hong Kong, Singapore, South Korea, and a few others, represented by point *D*). (4) The developed countries have in recent years reduced their birth rates so substantially that population growth is often virtually nil or even negative (represented by point *E*). In recent years, no developed country has had a population growth rate of as much as 1%.

The population gap between rich and poor is amply demonstrated by the average figures for 1980 to 1992. In that period, the annual growth rate was 2.6% for the world's poorest 42 countries (excluding China and India), 1.8% for 66 middle-income LDCs, and only 0.5% for the developed countries. (Historically, natural population increase did not exceed 2% in any presently developed European or North American country, as noted in Chapter 3.)

WHY BIRTH RATES DECLINE

With this background, we must ask why birth rates decline, as inexorably, sooner or later, they seem to do in countries undergoing development.[45] An ongoing debate involves whether private decisions at the microeconomic level must always precede a decline in population growth, or whether efforts by government including greater availability of contraceptives, propaganda, the education of women, or even coercion (as in the case of China and at one time of India) can lead the process.[46]

Most authorities argue that income growth causes demographic change on the level of the family, with a new appreciation of the costs and benefits of children leading to a decision to produce fewer children. This, it is argued, is the main reason why birth rates are now declining substantially everywhere except in Africa, and why even there some significant reductions can be reported. But it is also possible that demographic change leads precedes growth, and is perhaps a precondition for it. Or perhaps the most partisan advocates fail to realize that income growth and a decline in population growth are part of the same process.

The crux of the argument is whether organized family planning has led to a demographic transition earlier than would have otherwise occurred. Observers who conclude that it does not highlight historical experience indicating that the techniques of contraception are less important than the incentive and desire to use them. France, for example, realized a substantial decline in its birth rate in the nineteenth century, long before the arrival of safe, effective methods. For that matter, the primitive contraceptive methods of the later Roman empire, involving a number of antisperm chemicals, were reasonably effective more than a millennium before. Other observers counter by arguing that cheap and effective modern methods of contraception can be pushed by peer pressure and propaganda, so that family planning programs have an independent effect. They posit that the widespread availability of effective contraception is a major reason for the faster fall in fertility rates in the LDCs than in Europe during the last century.[47] A middle ground between these two extremes seems logical. Family planning efforts do have an independent effect, but that effect is stronger when other economic and social factors encourage lower fertility.[48]

Costs and Benefits: A Changing Desire to Bear Children

The argument that changes in the costs and benefits of children alters the desire to bear them is traced in this section. The monetary and nonmonetary costs of having many children rise with economic progress, while at the same time, a number of economic benefits tend to decline. The "taste" (or desire) for children changes as a result. The main considerations follow.

1. Many children bring nervous strain in modern housing, where the units are often small. The modern family in a developed country is much more mobile, moving from place to place and job to job more than in the past. The ensuing mental stress is higher as a result. Modern societies thus have something in common with the hunter-gatherer peoples of prehistoric times who had to carry their children around with them.* Moreover, the steady decline of the prevalence of living together in extended families means that low-cost child care by many "mother substitutes" becomes less possible.[49] The costs of children under these conditions is raised.
2. There are many substitutes for children (and sex?) as a source of pleasure, with travel, music, film, television, and consumer goods generally, all serving as alternatives to parenthood. In general, there is a much closer correlation between low literacy and a high birth rate than there is between low per capita GNP and the birth rate.
3. Children lose their role as a built-in system of social security when, with economic progress, the state takes over this function. A benefit of numerous children is thus reduced. To show what happens with development, in Japan in 1950, 55% of those polled answered "yes" to the question "do you expect to depend on your children in old age?" But by 1961, the yes answers had declined to only 27%.[50] Some LDCs, especially the high-performing Asian ones and a number of Latin American ones, are even now developing systems of social security. Public action need not always mean state action. Chile actually uses Individual Retirement Accounts in which employees pay into a fund, and no money comes either from government or from employers. Other Latin American countries are also considering the idea.[51] But for most LDCs, the tax and administrative mechanisms for social security programs, especially in rural areas, are still years in the future. Even if parents continue to see security in old age as an important benefit from children, higher survival rates among children mean that fewer need be born in order to ensure that this function is fulfilled. Preventing ten deaths among infants yields one to five fewer births, depending on local circum-

---

*The hunter-gatherers were able to achieve lower population growth by three main means. First, sexual abstinence could be practiced for a year or as much as two after the birth of a child. Second, breast-feeding suppresses ovulation somewhat, so extended nursing, for 2.5 to 3.5 years, could delay the conception of the next child an average of 2 to 10 months. Third, infanticide is another method. It was said to have occurred in possibly 15% to 50% of all births among Australian aborigines. Infanticide played a major part in the early decline of population growth in Japan; the practice, once applied especially to female babies, is now universally illegal. A fourth reason, malnutrition, has now been shown to apply only weakly. Until a short time ago it was believed that malnutrition induces intermittent female sterility, delaying menarche (first menstruation) and hastening menopause. Careful work now indicates, however, only a slightly longer delay in having another child. Famine *does* reduce fertility, because under these conditions there may be less intercourse and more fetal loss. It is also now known, contrary to another theory, that malnutrition does not *increase* fertility in a kind of Darwinian defense mechanism. See T. Paul Schultz, *Economics of Population*, 123, citing sources; and Birdsall, "Economic Approaches to Population Growth," 516.

stances.[52] Higher life expectancy also correlates more closely with reduced birth rates than does higher GNP.

4. The net money costs of raising children increase with development, an effect that is strong. Higher education becomes the norm as parents emphasize quality in a few healthy, better-educated children rather than quantity. Families do not live on subsistence farms, so the opportunity costs for food, shelter, and clothing are higher. There is less or no income from child labor to offset the increase in expense, whereas sedentary agriculturalists in their extended family structure have fewer of such costs and more benefits.
5. The changing status of women has an especially large impact. With development, opportunities widen for women to become part of the paid labor force and to receive an education. They are much less likely than before to think of themselves primarily as mothers, and the price of their time rises. Education of the mother, much more than the father, is especially important in reducing the desire to bear children. It brings better knowledge of contraceptive methods, a higher age of marriage, and greater opportunity costs of childbearing because the potential mother is more employable. Employability in turn brings less need for support from the children in old age. Educated mothers also tend to desire more education for their children, which raises their costs. Education of the mother is also correlated with reduced infant mortality, and hence the motive to bear more children to ensure the survival of some is reduced. One year of education for a mother is associated with a 9% decrease in the mortality of children under five; in Latin America, infant mortality is often three to four times greater among the children of mothers with no schooling than among children of those with six or more years of education.[53] World Bank evidence suggests that in places where women do not attend secondary school, the average number of children per woman is seven, but in places where 40% of women go to secondary school, the average falls to three. Other World Bank data indicate that raising the level of women's education from zero to seven years is associated with a rise in the average age of marriage from three to five years and increases the use of contraceptives by 20 to 29 percentage points, depending on the continent.[54] T. Paul Schultz states that an increase in women's education is the *best* predictor of a decline in the desire to have children.[55]

Demographers therefore almost universally recommend that programs to further the education and employability of women be part of official population control policy. Such policies are far less successful when the level of female education is low. (For example, in Africa, the low level of education is blamed for the unawareness of modern contraceptives, with only about half of all women aware of them compared to 85% to 95% in other less developed regions.)[56] The other side of the coin is that the effect of educating females is much reduced where no official program is operating, and that increasing the education of girls cannot have an impact on fertility for some considerable time.[57]

6. Demographers note that greater equality of income distribution also serves to lessen the desire to produce children among the poorer portion of the population where fertility is high for economic reasons.[58] As discussed above, with more adequate income the economic benefits of offspring decline and the costs rise. Greater productivity in the rural sector and government programs to redistribute income can raise the levels of living of the poor, thereby spurring a decline in birth rates.

In short, the changing balance of costs and benefits leads to a lessened desire to produce children, a sort of reduction in the "demand for fertility." In fact, fertility has fallen faster than was foreseen 20 years ago. But differences in the speed with which all these economic factors operate are pronounced and explain why fertility adjustments are so variable among countries. In one society the interval between the decline in death rates and the decline in birth rates may be short; in another it may be long.

Evidence of a Changing Desire to Bear Children

In the developed countries this higher net opportunity cost for children, including especially a mother's time and the costs of education, led to a great decline in the desire to bear children. A similar effect is being felt in the LDCs, in a reflection sometimes pale but, when buttressed by the propaganda, peer pressure, and economic incentives and penalties of official family planning programs, sometimes strong. There is now substantial evidence to support the claim that desires are changing.

The declining desire is evident in the demographers' measure called the total fertility rate (TFR). The TFR is an age-specific measure that is obtained by adding the average number of children born alive to a woman in each age group to arrive at the average number of live births per woman at the end of her child bearing period (ages 15 to 44). For the low-income LDCs, the TFR was 6.0 in 1970 and 3.4 in 1992, though if population-conscious China and India are excluded from the data, the decline in the desire for children in the low-income countries has been less, from 6.3 to 4.9.[59] The decline in sub-Saharan Africa has been small, from 6.5 to 6.1.* For the middle-income LDCs, the figures were 4.6 and 3.0 in the same years. (There remains a large gap between the LDCs and the rich: The developed-country figures went from 2.4 to 1.7.) Crucially, the TFR figures are not affected by the skewed age distribution of the population. They therefore show a much better correlation between rising income and reduced births than does the crude birth rate.

*Though here, too, there are some encouraging statistics. Botswana went from a TFR of 6.9 in 1970 to 4.7 in 1992, Zimbabwe from 7.7 to 4.6, Kenya from 8.0 to 5.4. See *WDR 1992*, 26.

MORE ADVANCED ANALYSIS OF THE CHANGING DEMAND FOR CHILDREN

For those with a knowledge of indifference curves, the reduced demand for children can be viewed diagrammatically in Figure 9.2, which shows goods consumed by the parents on the vertical axis and the number of children desired on the horizontal. A set of indifference curves is drawn. *AB* is the original budget line, so that the number of children desired is X_1. An increase in the opportunity cost of children relative to goods shifts the budget line to *AD* and lowers the number of children desired to X_2. (If income rises at the same time as the shift in cost, moving the budget line to *C′D′*, then the number of children desired will be X_3.)

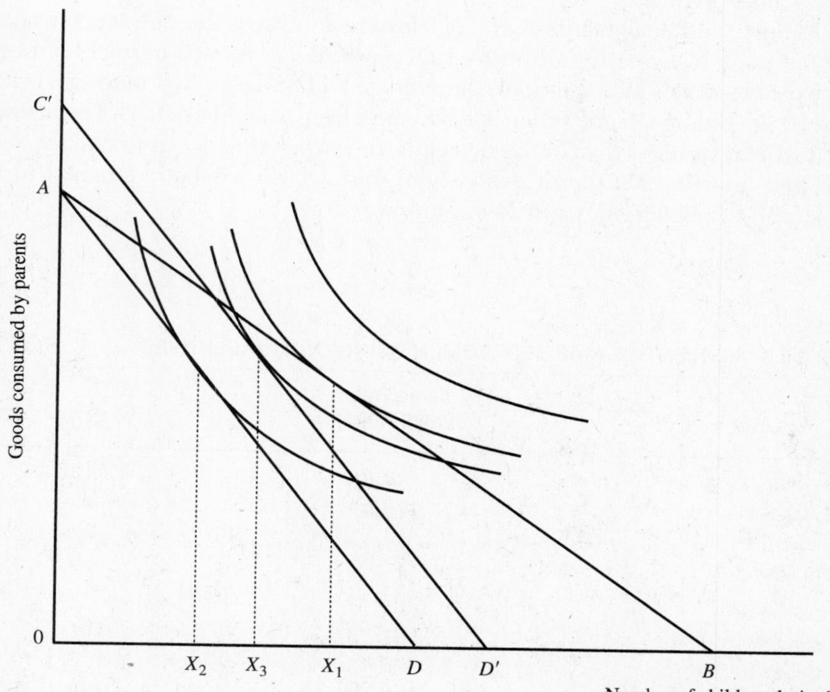

Figure 9.2 The choice of family size can be analyzed by means of indifference curves relating goods consumed to the number of children desired. A rise in the opportunity cost of children relative to goods that shifts the budget line from *AB* to *AD* will lower the number of children desired from X_1 to X_2.

A mirror image of the decline in the total fertility rate is the increase in the percentage of the married female population using contraceptives. In some cases that increase has been substantial, as shown in Table 9.6.

Where contraceptive use is high, the TFR has typically fallen much more rapidly than the crude birth rate. The larger number of women of childbearing age serves to prop up the birth rate long after the desire to bear children starts to decline.

In numerous countries, however, the declining desire for children is far less evident. Average contraceptive use among married women in sub-Saharan Africa is only 15%, and in some (low-income) countries the figures are lower yet, as shown in Table 9.7.[60]

Even when contraceptive use has risen greatly, however, the absolute number of women *not* practicing birth control has fallen little, because there are so many more women in total.

A fourth and final manifestation of a lessened desire is that the average age at first marriage is increasing. In many LDCs where it was once normal for 14- or 15-year-old females to be married, the average female age at first marriage is now 18 to 20 (including Ghana, Indonesia, Jamaica, Kenya, and Pakistan). The average age is still far younger than in the rich countries, where the age at first marriage is now well into the 20s almost everywhere, but age 25 has been attained in Sri Lanka and the Philippines and 24 in Tunisia.

TABLE 9.6 PERCENT OF MARRIED WOMEN USING CONTRACEPTIVES

	Latest Year (1985–1992)	1970
Egypt	46	10
Guatemala	23	—
India	43	12
Kenya	33	6
Colombia	66	34
Hong Kong	81	42
Malaysia	48	7
Panama	58	44 (1977)
Peru	59	1 (1977)
Singapore	74	60
South Korea	79	25
Sri Lanka	62	6

Note: By comparison, the 1985–1992 figures for developed countries were: United States 74%, Belgium 79%, France 80%, the Netherlands 76%, Japan 64%.

Source: HDR 1994, 174–175, for the latest figures, and earlier issues of *WDR* for the 1970 figures.

TABLE 9.7 PERCENTAGE OF MARRIED WOMEN USING CONTRACEPTIVES, SUB-SAHARAN AFRICA

	Latest Year (1985–1992)
Afghanistan	2
Côte d'Ivoire	3
Ethiopia	4
Liberia	6
Madagascar	5
Mali	5
Mauritania	3
Niger	4
Nigeria	6
Yemen	7
Sierra Leone	4
Somalia	1
Uganda	5

Source: HDR 1994, 175.

Population Momentum

The higher costs of children and the changing desire to bear them were certainly effective in bringing down birth rates to 10 to 15 per 1000 in most of the Western world. Some of these countries (Austria, Belgium, Great Britain, Luxembourg, Sweden, and Germany) have virtually achieved zero population growth (ZPG) or even a decline. The problem from the perspective of the LDCs is that it took at least half a century for this process to complete itself, and a population explosion did not occur only because death rates also declined slowly.

Arguably, the LDCs do not have the time to allow this process to work itself out unaided. Even under the optimistic assumptions of fertility decline discussed at the beginning of this chapter, the world's total population will not stabilize at ZPG until about the year 2085. By that time, the present five billion people will have multiplied to approximately double that, or ten billion. Under less-optimistic assumptions, ZPG would come at 13 billion in the year 2110, or least optimistically, at 23 billion in the year 2135. The prospect that countries even now considered overpopulated will be burdened with two to four times their present numbers commands attention.

We must ask why the predicted date of stabilization, 2085 at the earliest, is so far in the future when fertility rates have been dropping noticeably. That is because population will still continue to rise even if fertility rates fall to the level where mothers are bearing only enough children to replace the current population. (At that replacement level of fertility, the average mother bears slightly more than two children. The replacement total fertility rate of 2.1 is more than two because a few people die before the end of their childbearing years.) Yet even after the replacement level of fertility (2.1) is reached, the large number of young people in the population will keep crude birth rates above crude death rates for many years. This population momentum will usually double the ultimate number of people over a period of 50 to 75 years between the time when the replacement level of fertility is reached to the time when absolute population growth stops.

Table 9.8 gives population projections for a selected group of LDCs: the population size in 1992; the year in which, if present rates of change are projected forward, the replacement total fertility rate of 2.1 will be reached; population momentum, defined as the multiple by which population will increase between the time when the replacement total fertility rate is attained and the time when zero population growth is reached; and the hypothetical size of the population at the time when population finally ceases to grow.

GOVERNMENT FAMILY PLANNING PROGRAMS

Government-sponsored family planning programs involving widespread distribution of contraceptives are now commonplace. One rationale for these programs is that the negative social consequences of population growth on a nation may not be recognized soon enough at the level of the family, so that government must act. Another is that contraceptive use may be too low because of inadequate supply, so that their cost is high, or inadequately demanded because income is too low, as we

TABLE 9.8 POPULATION PROJECTIONS

	1992 Population (millions)	Year in Which the Replacement Total Fertility Rate of 2.1 Is Reached	Population Momentum	Projected Population When ZPG Is Attained (millions)
Bangladesh	114	2010	1.4	263
China	1,162	2030	1.3	1,680
Ethiopia	55	2050	1.5	370
India	884	2010	1.4	1,888
Indonesia	184	2005	1.4	355
Iran	60	2025	1.7	204
Kenya	26	2015	1.7	75
Malawi	9	2045	1.5	51
Mexico	85	2010	1.6	182
Nigeria	102	2035	1.6	382
Pakistan	119	2030	1.6	400
Tanzania	26	2035	1.5	117

Source: World Bank, *World Population Projections 1994–95* (Baltimore, 1994), Table 12, 38–41. The replacement level is more than 2 because some people die before they reproduce. It should be stressed that any unexpected delay in reducing fertility, which would be reflected in the year the replacement level of population growth is reached, could make a large difference in the projected population size.

discuss later. Only birth control pushed strenuously by government appears to offer much hope of reducing birth rates before long-term economic development brings this about, as it did in the rich countries. Recent experience shows that LDC birth rates can fall *before* improvement in income, the status of women, and living conditions generally. The evidence points to the power of peer pressure and a media effort in bringing fertility control into the realm of conscious choice before that would otherwise happen.[61]

Evidence from most studies supports the position that official family planning programs do reinforce the decline in birth rates caused when improved social and economic conditions lower the benefits and raise the costs of children. Recent attempts to analyze the interplay of official programs and social and material progress show that all these together have a far greater impact than each acting separately. One study suggests that socioeconomic change alone or a family planning program alone on average has only one-eighth or one-ninth as much effect as the two acting jointly.[62] A 63-country survey reported by the World Bank notes that birth rates fell most in countries with official family planning programs and announced objectives, less where there was family planning but no specific objectives, and least where there was no family planning program at all.[63] Because the adoption of objectives and family planning are themselves correlated to the level of social and economic development, including health, education, and other basic human needs as well as industrialization and income growth, this is not surprising. The lesson is that the population battle is easier fought on more than one front. Family planning availability and announced objectives must be pursued simultaneously with measures to raise growth rates of income, to ensure that the very poor share in the gains, and to improve the position of women. Doing these together means that no single policy must be pushed to heroic extremes.

It might fairly be asked why government is needed at all, since family planning could conceivably be wholly provided by the private market. In practice, however, private distribution channels are poorly developed in some rural areas. In a private clinic, the price may be high, the wait long, and travel time tedious. Little private profit (whatever the social gain) may lie in disseminating information. Initially demand may be small or even nil. Information about the availability of family planning may be very limited: Recent survey data from Mexico and Kenya showed over half the married women interviewed did not know where to obtain modern methods of contraception.

Reflecting this situation, surveys in over 40 countries show the number of women of childbearing age who want no more children is greater than the number using some form of contraception. Surveys by continent reveal 28% of sexually active women in Africa do not want another child at the present time but are not using contraceptives; the same is true for 18% in Asia, 21% in Latin America, and 22% in the Middle East and North Africa.[64] The figure is over half in 14 sub-Saharan African countries, and over 80% in Liberia.[65] Some authorities argue that the idea of an unmet need is fallacious because it implies people are too unintelligent to know how to limit the size of their families. They argue that family size falls because people decide they want fewer children, not because they have fewer unwanted children. If this is true, then funding of family planning may be less effective than spending on the education of girls.[66] But the evidence for unmet need is drawn from in-the-field interviews of women in LDCs, and it is not clear that these surveys are necessarily inaccurate. Other critics note, rightly, that the idea of unmet need does not measure the strength of preferences. That is, the figures do not indicate how much people would be willing to pay to prevent a birth. If the net costs of children are low, then the motivation and willingness to prevent births may be low too. To reduce the costs of contraception to the point where people will act may be very difficult. But other people, who consider the net cost of additional children high, might be motivated to act with only a small decline in the price of contraception. The "unmet need" percentages may, or may not, indicate the degree of response to population programs.

Government programs for limiting population growth differ greatly from country to country. The Population Council categorizes such programs as strong in 15 LDCs, moderately strong in 28 others, weak in 38, and very weak or nonexistent in 13 more. Geographically, the experience is diverse. Of the 15 countries classified by the Population Council as having strong programs, nine are in Asia and only two (Tunisia and Botswana) are in Africa. Of the 13 LDCs whose effort is very weak or nonexistent, only three are in Asia (Cambodia, Laos, and Burma/Myanmar) while eight are in Africa.[67] The rapid initiation of family planning programs in Catholic Latin America has been noteworthy.

Government programs generally involve five different avenues of approach, employable in any combination or all together: (1) advocating a goal by skillful propaganda, (2) raising the legal minimum age of marriage, (3) legalizing abortion, (4) promoting contraception, and (5) providing financial incentives for small families and penalties for large ones.

Goals and Propaganda

It is now widely agreed that a national goal advertised by a skillful program of marketing (propaganda) can harness emotions and instill peer pressure that may be able to change attitudes toward family size before economic development and the changing status of women brings this about.[68] The first step is usually to set a target and advertise it widely. Cases in point are Pakistan's national goal of reducing the birth rate from 50 to 36 and India's goal from 40 to 21 by 1996. Both still have a long way to go. Singapore's more dramatic target was a birth rate of 18 by 1975, achieved nearly on time and now below that. Some countries set goals in percentage terms. South Korea aimed at a reduction in growth from 2.9% a year to 1.2% by 1980 (achieved), while Ghana is aiming at 2.0% by 2000. Others aim at ZPG by a target year, such as 2000 as the goal for Bangladesh and Jamaica. Yet others set a target population size, such as China's 1.2 billion in 2000.

After the publication of the target come the "media events." In China, posters, broadcasts, and word of mouth are used to circulate slogans such as "One child best" in a propaganda program that reaches down to the smallest factory and village. India's "No-baby year" used the slogans "Two or three children—and that's all! Listen to your doctor, he knows!" and "When you have two, that will do." The advice was repeated on the radio, on movie screens, on billboards, even on matchbook covers. Numerous Central American radio stations have run soap operas highlighting the trauma of excessive family size. In Bangladesh, singing teams perform in bazaars; in Pakistan, songs in simple language boost family planning; in wealthier Singapore, contraceptive propaganda comes with the utility bills.[69]

The motivation in Indonesia is intense. There, schools have been set up for shadow-play puppeteers, whose traditional art form is then used to broadcast a new message. The army, police, and civil service have been asked to use their influence to further the acceptability of family planning. Persuasion of Muslim religious leaders (malams) was embarked upon, and many became enthusiastic supporters of the program. *Gamelan* orchestras, that all-male Indonesian form of music-making familiar to tourists, were co-opted into the effort, and nowadays some of these orchestras are made up of women committed to the cause. Classical dancers further advertised the goal. The government turned the effort into a sort of serious game, awarding prizes to communities with the best performance in meeting targets. Peer pressure is enlisted. On the island of Bali, each village pavilion displays a map. On that map, the houses of the pill-users are colored red, the houses of the IUD-users are colored green, and those of the condom-users are black. Houses of nonusers are not colored, and the social stigma attached to that is clear enough.[70] (Obviously, Indonesian methods would not work as well in a less cohesive, close-knit, centralized environment.)

In Singapore, motivation focuses on new mothers. "Motivators" interview new mothers in hospitals and attempt to sign them up there and then for family planning. Fifty percent of all those contacted do so. There is then a follow-up home visit by a Post Partum Contact Service (PPCS) to reinforce the decision and give further assistance. The midwives, planning assistants, and social workers who serve as motivators and staff the PPCS are given extensive family planning training. Contraceptives are thereafter made available at a price that includes a large subsidy.

All these campaigns focus on making people aware of the costs to the country of population growth, the costs of large numbers of children to the family and to the children themselves, the benefits of smaller families, and the means for limiting size. Because failure to make this effort successfully means that the resulting effort to plan family size is likely to fail, it is difficult to find a self-respecting program these days that does not boast some similar large-scale advertising effort.

Minimum Age of Marriage

Campaigns to raise the legal age of marriage are often part of the effort. The legal minimum age may be very low by today's Western standards, though not by the standards of yesteryear when Roman Catholic canon law set 12 as the minimum age of marriage for girls. India's campaign to eliminate the child bride is the most well-known. That country has moved the minimum age for females from 16 to 18 and for males from 18 to 21. In some Indian states, until recently half of all marriages involved girls under 15. To be sure, even India's old law was frequently disregarded, but proponents of the legal change nevertheless expect a noticeable effect on birth rates. In China, the legal minimum was moved up to 20 for females and 22 for males in 1980. (But this was less than the 23 and 25 being unofficially enforced already, so marriages and births both "blipped" upward, showing at least that such regulations do have some effect.)*

Abortion

Abortion can certainly play a role in population control, with an estimated 20% of all pregnancies in the LDCs ending in abortion, many of them illegal.[71] The experience of Japan and Singapore is illustrative. Abortion in Japan is credited with two-thirds of the effect in the halving of its birth rate in a ten-year period after World War II. More than half of all Japanese married women have had at least one abortion, and estimates show as many aborted pregnancies as those that come to term. In Singapore during the mid-1980s, abortion halted 36% of all pregnancies. There is also considerable abortion in China, India, Vietnam, and Latin America among others. The poor opinion of the practice held in many countries and cultures will, however, mean that abortion is unlikely to be the main tool of population control in much of the world. Indeed, the practice is illegal in many LDCs.

The abortion issue has been damaging to international funding for population control and to international efforts to coordinate government policies. The Vatican and several Latin American governments that follow the Vatican's lead have allied most unusually with fundamentalist Muslims in countries such as Iran and Egypt and antiabortion forces especially in the United States. These groups have set themselves against the practice. They have often been able to block funding in any way touched by abortion, even if tangentially. For example, in the Reagan and Bush administrations, the United States suspended its financial support of the International Planned Parenthood Federation (largest of the private groups, British, and active in Africa and Asia) and the U.S. grant to the United Nations Fund for Population Activities (UNFPA). The financing did not involve U.S. funds for abortion, by the way, as this has not been permitted since 1973. Nor did it imply direct activity of international agencies in abortion, which these agencies deny vehemently. Instead it involved any indirect connection, for example, helping to fund family planning publicity in a country permitting abortion.†

In the early 1990s, about $5 billion per year was being spent on family planning in the LDCs, of which about $3 billion came from the LDCs themselves, just

*One recent case represented a movement against the trend. In Iran after the Ayatollah Khomeini's revolution of 1979, the government lowered the legal age of marriage from 18 to 9. It also banned contraception and eliminated family planning agencies and facilities. In the 1980s, Iran's population growth reached 3.9% per year, with very serious results for education and housing. (After Khomeini's death in 1988, the government retraced its steps to some extent, and population growth fell to 3.2% in 1992.) See *The Economist*, August 27, 1994.

†U.S. funds had contributed a quarter of UNFPA's budget. When Congress restored UNFPA's money in 1989, the move did not survive President Bush's veto, and further veto threats prevented U.S. funding—in spite of a guarantee from UNFPA that it would abide by a U.S. veto on any use of the funds not approved by the U.S. ambassador to the United Nations. With the election of President Clinton, policy changed. A high-level State Department post (undersecretary for global affairs) was created with population control part of the mission, and the funding was restored.

over $1 billion from donors, mostly as grants, and the rest as payments by users.[72] To get full coverage, that level of funding ought to be doubled according to the United Nations Fund for Population.[73]

The abortion issue caused the partial failure of a major conference on population and development in Cairo, September 1994. (These population conferences are held every ten years. The last one, in Mexico City in 1984, was the venue for the U.S. announcement that it would cease to aid any international organization that provided funds for countries where abortions were permitted.) The aim of the Cairo conference was to adopt a plan to stabilize world population at 7.27 billion in the year 2015. But the deep disagreements over abortion, and among some delegations, the very concept of family planning, meant that a main outcome of the conference was the proof of the deep disagreements on the issue of population control.

Contraception[74]

The use of contraception in the LDCs on average is far below its use in the developed countries: an average of 38% of couples (or 51% if China is included) compared to over 70%.[75] The promotion of contraception has usually taken the form of birth control clinics and the wide distribution, at low cost or free of charge, of contraceptive materials. Clinics have their problems, and they have often been underutilized or even ignored, especially in rural areas. Sometimes only limited propaganda is undertaken in their support for fear of giving offense. Sometimes they are located in urban areas or centrally in rural areas, with little outreach and no fieldworkers. Sometimes there is no follow-up, now known to be a fundamental mistake because repeated contact is of great value when motivation is marginal. Sometimes clinics put a cultured, educated, often male doctor with a poor, shy, uneducated woman. The cultural gap is real, and it takes effort to bridge it. Many countries have successfully done so by utilizing paramedical staff, midwives, and local women already in the program as staff at the clinic.

Even a well-managed clinic will have little impact when the demand for family planning is low. It may take some ingenuity to make a visit more popular, perhaps a literacy or child health program in the same center or even a rural credit scheme.

Another problem is cost. In some low-income LDCs, the cost of proper birth control exceeds 25% of average per capita income. The cost element makes provision of birth control by private enterprise difficult, and even subsidies may not be enough to make modern methods available to the lowest-income group. This is true even of rich countries such as the United States, where economic position and use of birth control are closely correlated. (Ninety percent of women in U.S. higher-income groups use one method or another, but of the lowest fifth in terms of income, 40% did not want their last child and knew very little about family planning.) Free or very low-cost distribution of contraceptives to those with the lowest income is clearly necessary for effective family planning. Even so, experience shows that some cost recovery can be made, say 10% to 60%, from higher-income users through the "social marketing" of contraceptives, with a price being charged even if it is subsidized. Social marketing is now carried out in over 30 countries, although its administrative costs are relatively high.

The available data indicate that of all birth control use worldwide, sterilization accounts for about 33%; the pill, 20%; intra-uterine devices, 15% (though the IUD is the most important method in China); and the condom, 13%.[76] Diaphragms, injections such as Depo-Provera, spermicides, douches, rhythm methods, abstinence, withdrawal, and deliberate prolonged breastfeeding are the other methods. Obviously, when a couple's commitment to lower fertility is only marginal, effectiveness of any given method is likely to be greater when that commitment is not tested with every act of intercourse. For example, even though condoms have been distributed by many governments on a large scale, couples that use them must test their desire to limit births every time. (It is fair to add that the rising danger of AIDS infection in many LDCs is tending to make the condom much more popular, contrary to the pre-AIDS expectations of demographers.) The pill must be taken on a regular schedule, the Depo-Provera injection is effective for only three months, and the IUD must be checked regularly.

Sterilization, in the form of vasectomy for males, requires only one decision and takes less than ten minutes. It is cheap and can be done by a medic using local anesthetic in a room in a railway station or bus depot. For these reasons it has been the central tool of some official programs where overpopulation was an especially serious problem, for example in Bangladesh and India (where it accounts for 70% of all contraception, and where for a time compulsion was employed, with the doleful results discussed below). But vasectomies can be difficult to reverse, and deep-seated fears keep the number of volunteers low. Antipathy toward vasectomies is so pronounced that they are actually illegal in a number of nations, including Burma/Myanmar, Somalia, Spain, and Turkey.

Technical Developments in Population Control Technology has been contributing to the struggle to control population size. Norplant, implanted into the arm, releases its progestogen at a constant rate for five years, with less progestogen in a five-year implant than in a three-months' dose of Depo-Provera. Norplant can be removed at any time, restoring fertility. Its use is spreading rapidly in the LDCs. New IUDs such as Levo-ova also provide for progestogen release. A surge in female sterilization followed the development of laparoscopy and minilaparotomy.* Laparoscopy involves a small incision, electrocautery, and the use of clips or rings on the tubes. Minilaparotomy, or minilap, draws the tubes outside the abdomen for cutting. Both operations can now be accomplished in outpatient facilities, and minilap (but not laparoscopy) can be done by a nonspecialist surgeon. Reversibility is still problematic, but there has nonetheless been a very large shift to female sterilizations, and they are now much more common than vasectomy in China, Malaysia, the Philippines, South Korea, and Thailand among others, sometimes by a margin of eight to one.

---

*The traditional tubectomies on females are rather expensive, somewhat complicated, and relatively hard to reverse, and so they never became especially common.

Menses-inducing pills using hormonal compounds are on the horizon, and vaccines that prevent conception are being investigated. The abortion pill RU486 is not currently being used in any LDC, but if it proves to be as safe as it now appears and if politics allow it, that pill might have an important place in government programs.[77] Up to now, male contraceptive drugs have exhibited too many adverse side effects for general use.

Financial Incentives

The use of taxes and subsidies to promote family planning was once rare. But after the adoption of such tools by the pioneer, Singapore, and their major employment in China and India, they have spread, particularly elsewhere in Asia. At the most elementary level, financial incentives to limit population growth may involve nothing more than ending subsidies for children by limiting tax deductions beyond a certain number. (Ghana, Malaysia, Pakistan, the Philippines, Singapore, South Korea, and Tanzania are among the LDCs that do this.) Countries may also put limits on maternity leave above a certain number of children.

At a greater degree of intensity, the financial incentive may amount to a bribe in cash or kind. About 30 countries use incentive awards of one sort or another.[78] Thailand, for example, increases the willingness of Thais to participate in population planning by offering incentives, often through private groups. Rural credit, lower prices for seed and fertilizer, or a free pig for a woman to rear are all tactics used by these private supporters of family planning. Innovative use of financial incentives can be found in the Ammanpettai Family Welfare Program in India's Tamil Nadu State. Here the incentives are directed at persuading participants to acquire information about contraceptives and move to their trial adoption. Evidence from this scheme indicates that the money was able to change attitudes to some extent: Many women have continued to use contraceptives after the incentive payments lapsed.[79]

To promote sterilization, Indian men are rewarded with the rupee equivalent of more than a month's pay for a farmworker, while women get slightly less. They may also receive travel allowances to the place of operation, free transistor radios, cash bonuses or scholarships for children already born, and gifts of consumer goods. Lump-sum payments for sterilization have been as much as 20% of the Indian government budget for family planning.[80] Large Indian industrial firms often boost the incentives with additional cash payments. Bangladesh, Sri Lanka, and China have also established cash rewards for sterilization. One problem with such rewards is that people may accept sterilization and the accompanying payments even though they intended not to have additional children anyway.

Singapore's Pioneering Effort Singapore has gone much further in its use of financial incentives, and its system of taxes and subsidies deserves careful study. In adopting financial measures, Singapore started with two substantial advantages: no organized opposition to family planning on religious, political, or other grounds (there were antiabortion laws, but these were repealed in 1970) and a booming economy that has destroyed the extended family system and so all but eliminated a major reason for large numbers of children.[81] In that island nation, both taxes and national benefits are altered as a weapon of population control. For example, the law dictates a mandatory end to maternity work leaves and benefits for women delivering their third child. The cost of childbearing is raised immediately. Such costs are also directly affected by the policy of scaling maternity fees. Delivery charges are graduated by the number of children, rising by five times between the delivery of the first child and the fifth for low-income parents. (The fees start at a larger figure, rise less, and reach a maximum at four children for higher-income parents.) The fee for any given child is remitted if one parent presents evidence of sterilization within six months.

In public housing, where much of Singapore's population lives, priorities for large families have been abolished; those with fewer offspring receive more space per person. Families with four or more children get a lower priority in their choice of primary schools, unless the fourth can be proved to be the last because one of the parents has since been sterilized. Top priority of choice in schools goes to the children of sterilized parents. Some studies suggest that these education policies have been the most influential, more so even than the financial disincentives. The potentially damaging effects on children in the "4+" bracket—poorer housing, worse schools, lower income because of the taxes—are not seen much because there are now so few families who qualify for the sanctions. In a less successful program, however, these unfortunate side effects could be severe: The penalties fall on children, who were without fault and who must go uncompensated.[82]

Incentive Payments Could Go Further Neither Singapore nor any other country has used positive economic incentives to the extent that is possible. A nation could in principle go much further in its use of financial tools by employing deferred incentives. It could estimate the eventual budgetary impact of an additional (marginal) child and undertake to make this sum available as a reward for not bearing the child. A recent (1980s) estimate of the reduced budgetary costs of permanently preventing a birth in India was $800. This sum could be paid out to women who have no more than two children, perhaps $1600 for no more than one or $2400 for none at all. The figures represent a large amount of cash for the average villager. It would undoubtedly be an incentive and would be an excellent counterweight to the argument that large families serve as social security.

There are, of course, serious loopholes. First, the sum represents the figure saved over the years, so making the outpayment up front would present budgetary problems. Second, a woman could take the cash but then go ahead and have a child. Both problems could be addressed by paying the money in installments every six months or so into a blocked savings account (one which cannot be drawn upon), with the whole amount forfeited if a child is born. The money would be paid in its entirety to a woman at her menopause. To keep enthusiasm high, interest on the blocked account could be paid out when it is earned. The second problem could also be handled by limiting the program to sterilization, which would be administratively simple. Critics emphasize that fraud might be altogether too easy if such payment programs were adopted widely in the LDCs. Monitoring of births would be necessary, and not easy given the incentive for concealment.

Some critics of incentive payments argue that they are not moral, intruding Mammon into realms where he was not intended to be, and having an impact on the poor much more than on the rich who have less need for the money. Supporters reply that those who accept the incentive payments do so voluntarily, and that the acceptance presumably leaves the family better off or they would not have chosen to participate.

EXPERIMENTS WITH PAYMENTS PLANS

Several small experiments have been instituted along these lines. In south India, three tea estates made payments of blocked savings to women at age 45; in Taiwan a local government unit deposits funds for the education of two children, but the funds are forfeited on the birth of a fourth. There is also some local use in Nepal. The Indian plan started in 1971 and had a positive impact, but it was eventually wound up.[83] There were five reasons why: (1) It had less effect in the earlier years because the dollar payments were less. (2) Administration of the plan was not fully satisfactory. The information flow was limited, and within a few years it was found that only 8% of participating women could name any of the conditions that would result in forfeiture of their payments. (3) The passbooks showing the values involved were not in the women's possession, nor were they seen regularly. (4) No revision was made for inflation. (5) Contraceptives were not easily available and so sterilization was used, thus robbing the scheme of some of its rationale.

Bangladesh is considering two deferred-incentive schemes, one a nonnegotiable bond for sterilized parents, the other a cash certificate for those who delay a first birth after marriage for three years or a second or third birth for five years. The obvious problem is that if such schemes were extended to the country's entire population, they would be very expensive, comprising some 10% of the entire Bangladesh budget.

An Assessment

There are outstanding examples of success in official family planning efforts, with a decline in population growth far faster than ever achieved anywhere in the absence of war or natural calamity.[84] Take the period of sudden progress in the Indonesian program as an example. It focused on densely populated Java and Bali; on those islands, annual population growth in 1970 of 2.5% fell to 1.4% in 1978. The proportion of women aged 15 to 44 using contraceptives was almost zero in 1970 but by 1977 had reached almost 40% in Java and almost 60% in Bali.[85] Indonesia's birth rate had fallen by 1991 to 25 per thousand. Thailand's 7000 urban and rural health centers and its legion of population volunteers have helped to reduce birth rates from 44 in 1960 to 21 in 1991. When the program was adopted in 1970, contraceptive use among Thai women was only 15%; the figure was 66% in 1989. The population control program of

Bangladesh is an outstanding case of contribution to population decline before much was accomplished to raise the position of women, who in that country still suffer discrimination in education and considerable illiteracy.[86] In spite of that, the total fertility rate in Bangladesh fell from 7.0 in 1970 to 4.4 in 1991.

China has attracted more attention than any other country. Its birth rate declined from 39 in 1960 to 22 in 1991; during the period from 1970 to 1975, it registered the largest fall ever recorded anywhere during a five-year period. By 1989, 72% of Chinese married women were practicing contraception, a figure about the same as that of the United States. Unfortunately, as we shall see, the lessons to be learned from China are not all that clear-cut. The emphasis in its program is on community social pressure; the willingness of people to conform to this pressure is in part a product of thousands of years of social history and in part a result of the revolutionary doctrines of the late Chairman Mao. Duplicating the Chinese feat using Chinese methods would doubtless prove difficult in many other LDCs.

COMPULSION

Sometimes the measures discussed previously can cross over a boundary and become coercive.[87] Compulsion has indeed been resorted to at times, both officially and unofficially. The argument in favor is akin to that supporting price controls in wartime. "We face an emergency, so something must be done." But the advisability of outright compulsion is questionable. The two most important cases are China, where the government has somewhat backed away from compulsion though strong pressures persist, and India, where coercion was abandoned after tremendous public outcry and political overturn.

China[88]

In China, coercion ranging from mild to severe was at a high level in the early 1980s, with some backing off of the pressure from about 1984. Nowadays, there is somewhat greater willingness to let a couple have a child without permission if they cannot be persuaded otherwise, but an element of compulsion remains.

From 1979, with the Chinese expressing dissatisfaction with the results of their previous voluntary approach, China introduced penalty fines on unauthorized children. Chinese incentive and disincentive schemes have typically been provincial rather than national. Many Chinese provinces instituted "baby fines" on couples producing more than two children. The fines were in the form of a wage reduction of 5% to 10% for a period of years (often four) after the birth of a second or third child, rising to as high as 15% to 20% over a longer period (as many as 14 years) for subsequent children. In addition to the fines, parents are ineligible for promotions or bonuses for several years. Conversely, rewards include monthly wage bonuses and bigger pensions to those with one child only. The rewards must be paid back if a second child is born. Very generally, the state requires reimbursement for the costs of educating a second child but not a first. Only children also receive job preferences.

Eventually it became apparent that China's one-child campaign was not working as successfully in rural areas as in the cities. Farm families were more and more paying the fines, bribing officials, or circumventing the policy in other ways in order to try to have a boy. These families were apparently voting that, for them, more children (especially males) would bring economic advantage in the form of as social security.[89] One result was that in 1988 the fines were increased, by up to 100%. The second-child fine is now often about $400, although it can range up to $1000. But the one-child program has become decentralized, with provinces establishing their own rather different policies. One reason for the recent flexibility is that the total fertility rate has fallen far. It was only 2.4 in 1991 (very close to the U.S. figure of 2.1) compared to 6.4 in 1965.[90]

A considerable element of compulsion extends beyond China's fines and other tangible costs and benefits, in the form of peer pressure. Although the Chinese insist that this involves "patient persuasion by peers," the pressure can be intense. It is delivered by means of small groups of 10 or 20 couples, organized within a neighborhood, factory, or village, which consider population targets communicated from above. These groups meet once or twice a year. Individual births are then allocated within the small group. One couple may receive permission to pursue conception in the forthcoming few months, another may be told it is next in line. Couples successful in conceiving are, after birth, often advised to turn to sterilization now that their family is complete. (Recall that perhaps 40% of the world's sterilized population is Chinese.) China uses visitations—possibly as many as eight after a birth—and very close intervention into personal lives, including viewing personal records of contraceptive use.

Exactly how this pressure mechanism works is not altogether clear, nor is it always easy to understand the conformity to it. Few countries can show such extensive deference to group opinion, especially when backed by only mild legal sanctions. The unanimity of purpose needed to run a program of this sort must be rare in the LDCs, and, indeed, in the rich countries as well. The lessons from China may thus not be very general ones.

India[91]

The experience of India is probably more indicative of what might happen in most LDCs were coercion to be used broadly. India, the first LDC to have an official family planning program (launched in 1952), was also the first to include some physical compulsion in its programs. The outcome was not favorable.

In the Indian experience we find the outstanding example of resistance to enforced limitations on population, especially the popular revulsion against the mandatory sterilizations carried out in 1976 and 1977. With the hard official attitudes of those years, sterilization was made compulsory for government employees after two children, and some states (such as Maharashtra, West Bengal) established fines or imprisonment if sterilization was not performed after the birth of the third child.

More generally, motivation based on compulsion was employed. Police, teachers, public health workers, and other civil servants were given target figures for the number of people they had to "motivate" for the operation. Teachers often had a quota of four or five. Those who did not meet their motivation targets might have their salaries reduced, be transferred to less pleasant posts, be demoted, or even suffer curtailment of their food ration. The *Manchester Guardian* reported (in November 1976) that

> a 50-year-old schoolteacher, given a quota of four for the year, . . . had been threatened by her superiors with the loss of her house and job unless the numbers were accounted for. A water engineer, given a higher quota, ended up allotting tube wells and irrigated water only to those villagers who would agree to sterilization under his so-called motivation—so that he could claim the numbers.

There were also reports of police roundups to fill their own quotas.

In an atmosphere approaching hysteria, vasectomies reached eight million in 1976 to 1977. The birth rate, 48 per thousand in 1960, was thought to have dropped to 33 in 1976. Population growth fell below 2% for the first time in many years. But the prime minister, Mrs. Gandhi, then near the end of her first term in office, was in political trouble. Thousands rioted against the compulsory rounding up of married men for vasectomies. The police opened fire; dozens were killed.

The bloodshed contributed to Mrs. Gandhi's election defeat, after which family planning fell into disrepute. Even the name was changed, to "family welfare," and vasectomies, voluntary once again, fell to only 800,000 in 1977 to 1978. Other methods did not take up the slack. The succeeding government cut the free condom distribution nearly by half, and it was estimated that yearly IUD insertions fell to only 10% of their former figure. The rural vasectomy camps were abandoned. For some time government officials spoke of compensation to those involuntarily sterilized, but this did not occur. The result was a reversal of the birth rate's downward trend, and population growth rose above the 2% mark once again. In India, coercive measures received a conclusive demonstration, and they failed. As Amartya Sen has commented, compulsion involves "breathless responses that are deeply counterproductive, preventing the development of rational and sustainable family planning."[92]

Since the end of compulsion, there has been some steady progress in bringing down the birth rate, with the 1991 figure of 30 per thousand. But population growth remains high, 2.0% in that year, and India continues to face a major population problem.

THE OUTLOOK?

The good news is the pronounced increase in contraceptive use by married women in LDCs and the associated relatively rapid fall in total fertility rates in numerous countries. The reinforcing effect of economic growth, which cuts the desire for children, programs for better education, health, and nutrition, and programs for family planning is now recognized. Addressing the population issue through a package of all of these has become standard practice, and in many countries the results are impressive. Evidence has not supported the once-common belief in

Malthusian traps. Slowly, the balance between the economic benefits and the costs of more children has been tilting. With development in the LDCs, the benefits fall and the costs rise, just as they did in the now-developed countries in the last century and earlier in this one, and the process can be accelerated by well-designed programs of family planning. These are the reasons why development economists now view the population problem with much less despair than they did two decades ago.

The bad news is that some countries, especially in Africa, have hardly started on their march. Moreover, even when people choose to have fewer children, population will continue to grow for many years as the much larger numbers of young people in the population reach childbearing age. Further growth might be supportable if complementary factors of production, such as physical and human capital and natural resources, were to rise in proportion. But how could this happen in most of today's LDCs? Are we sure that a much larger world population can be adequately fed? Even if we knew that *these* challenges could be met, would not a world with two or three times as many people have to face deteriorating environmental conditions? In the 1960s, world environmental problems were like little clouds on the horizon, but by the 1990s they had grown to great thunderheads portending a storm. And finally, even if we knew that environmental catastrophe could be avoided, would not continued population growth sentence humankind to a rabbit-warren existence of crowded conditions, limited access to nature, and a life less-pleasant than it could be? Prudence would seem to dictate that we not take the chance. That is why many development economists urge rapid action to control population, rather than to leave the matter to the slow outcome of market forces.

NOTES

1. *HDR 1994*, 174–175.
2. *WDR 1992*, 26. In detail, these estimates are obtained by hypothesizing a first case (fast stabilization) where fertility begins to decline immediately in the high-fertility countries where decline has not started and declines by more than half in four decades, and it declines rapidly in countries where it has already started. In the second case (slower stabilization), fertility begins to decline only in 2005 in the high-fertility countries where decline has not started, and it declines only at half the fast-decline rate of the first case. In the third case (slowest stabilization), fertility begins to decline only in 2020 in the high-fertility countries where decline has not started, and declines at only half the base rate in countries where decline is underway.
3. There is an extensive literature. I have used (in alphabetical order) Nancy Birdsall, "Economic Approaches to Population Growth," in Hollis Chenery and T. N. Srinivasan, eds., *Handbook of Development Economics*, vol. 1 (Amsterdam, 1988), 477–542; Nancy Birdsall, "Economic Approaches to Population Growth," *World Bank Research Observer* 4, no. 1 (January 1989): 23–50; John Charles Caldwell, *Causes of Demographic Change* (Madison, 1989); John C. Caldwell, "The Soft Underbelly of Development: Demographic Transition in Conditions of Limited Economic Change," *Proceedings of the World Bank Annual Conference on Development Economics 1990* (Washington, D.C., 1990), 207–253; Robert H. Cassen et al., *Population and Development: Old*

Debates, New Conclusions (New Brunswick, 1994); Robert H. Cassen, "Population and Development: A Survey," in Paul Streeten and Richard Jolly, eds., *Recent Issues in World Development* (Oxford, 1981); Partha Dasgupta, *An Inquiry into Well-Being and Destitution* (Oxford, 1993); Peter N. Hess, *Population Growth and Socioeconomic Progress in Less Developed Countries* (New York, 1988); Paul Ehrlich and Anne H. Ehrlich, *The Population Explosion* (New York, 1990); Allen C. Kelley, "Economic Consequences of Population Change in the Third World," *Journal of Economic Literature* 26, no. 4 (December 1988): 1685–1728; Kerstin Lindahl-Kiessling and Hans Landberg, *Population, Economic Development, and the Environment* (Oxford, 1994); Ozzie G. Simmons, *Perspectives on Development and Population Growth in the Third World* (New York, 1988); D. G. Johnson and R. D. Lee, eds., *Population Growth and Economic Development: Issues and Evidence* (Madison, 1987); Scott Menard, *Perspectives on Population* (New York, 1987); T. Paul Schultz, "Economic Demography and Development: New Directions in an Old Field," in Gustav Ranis and T. Paul Schultz, *The State of Development Economics* (Oxford, 1988); Gita Sen, Adrienne German, and Lincoln Chen, eds., *Population Policies Reconsidered: Health, Empowerment, and Rights* (Cambridge, Mass., 1994); Julian Simon, *Population and Development in Poor Countries* (Princeton, 1992); and the major part of the World Bank's *World Development Report 1984*.

4. This question has been asked particularly by Julian Simon, *The Ultimate Resource* (Princeton, 1982), and his *Population and Development in Poor Countries* (Princeton, 1992).
5. T. Paul Schultz, "Economic Demography and Development: New Directions in an Old Field," 423, 441.
6. *WDR 1980*, 39.
7. The discussion here was informed by Michael S. Teitelbaum, "Population and Development: Is a Consensus Possible?" *Foreign Affairs* 52, no. 4 (1974): 742–760.
8. *HDR 1994*, 201.
9. Teitelbaum, "Population and Development," 745.
10. *WDR 1984*, 57.
11. Birdsall "Economic Approaches to Population Growth," 516.
12. Rodolfo A. Bulatao, "Family Planning: The Unfinished Revolution," *Finance and Development* 29, no. 4 (December 1992): 5.
13. Following Lawrence H. Summers, "Knowledge for Effective Action," *Proceedings of the World Bank Annual Conference on Development Economics 1991* (Washington, D.C., 1992), 13.
14. Among economic demographers, this line of reasoning was first emphasized by A. J. Coale and E. M. Hoover, *Population Growth and Economic Development in Low-Income Countries* (Princeton, 1958).
15. Linda D. Shumaker and Robert L. Clark, "Population Dependency Rates and Savings Rates: Stability of Estimates," *Economic Development and Cultural Change* 40, no. 2 (January 1992): 319–332. Also see Birdsall, "Economic Analyses of Rapid Population Growth," 23–50; and Denton, "Saving in Developing Countries: Theory and Review," 61–96.
16. Kelley and Schmidt, "Population and Income Change: Recent Evidence," 77–78.
17. Work of Susan Horton, "Birth Order and Child Nutritional Status: Evidence from the Philippines," *Economic Development and Cultural Change* 36, no. 2 (January 1988): 341–354; and Joe D. Wray cited by William Loehr and John P. Powelson, *Economics of Development and Distribution* (New York, 1981), 227.
18. *WDR 1984*, Chapter 7, has a thorough discussion.

19. Loehr and Powelson, *Economics of Development and Distribution*, 229. The data apply to a U.S. city (Cleveland).
20. *HDR 1993*, 24.
21. See Azizur Khan in Ronald D. Lee, Arthur W. Brian, and Allen C. Kelley, *Population, Food, and Rural Development* (Oxford, 1991); and Mohammad Alauddin and Clement Tisdell, *The "Green Revolution" and Economic Development* (New York, 1991).
22. See Maureen Cropper and Charles Griffiths, "The Interaction of Population Growth and Environmental Quality," *American Economic Review Papers and Proceedings* 84, no. 2 (May 1994): 250–254.
23. A prominent skeptic is Allen C. Kelley. See his "Population Pressures, Saving, and Investment in the Third World: Some Puzzles," *Economic Development and Cultural Change* 36, no. 3 (April 1988): 449–464.
24. Allen C. Kelley and Robert M. Schmidt, "Population and Income Change: Recent Evidence," World Bank Discussion Paper No. 249 (1994), 33–34.
25. Kelley and Schmidt, "Population and Income Change: Recent Evidence."
26. IMF, *World Economic Outlook 1994*, 56. A study based on a 55-country sample during the years 1970 to 1985 that makes the case that population growth has a negative impact on economic growth is reported by Ichiro Otani and Delano Villanueva, "Major Determinants of Long-Term Growth in LDCs," *Finance and Development* 26, no. 3 (September 1989): 20–23.
27. Kelley and Schmidt, "Population and Income Change: Recent Evidence," 29.
28. Taken from Ansley J. Coale, "Man and His Environment," *Science* 179 (October 9, 1970): 132–136.
29. This section draws on Sandra Patel, "Carrying Capacity: Earth's Bottom Line," and Lester R. Brown, "Facing Food Insecurity," both in Lester R. Brown et al., eds., *State of the World 1994* (New York, 1994), 3–4, 10–11, 13, 179, 184.
30. A study suggesting that it will is Ronald D. Lee et al., *Population, Food and Rural Development* (Oxford, 1988).
31. John Maynard Keynes, *Economic Consequences of the Peace* (London, 1919), 10.
32. *HDR 1994*, 175.
33. *WDR 1994*, 212–213.
34. John C. Caldwell and Pat Caldwell, "High Fertility in Sub-Saharan Africa," *Scientific American* (May 1990): 118–125, especially 118, 120–122. Also see John C. Caldwell and Pat Caldwell, "The Cultural Context of High Fertility in Sub-Saharan Africa, *Population and Development Review* 13, no. 3 (September 1987): 409–437; and John C. Caldwell and Pat Caldwell, "Cultural Forces Tending to Sustain High Fertility in Tropical Africa," in George T. Acsadi and Gwendolyn J. Acsadi, eds., *Population Growth and Reproduction in Sub-Saharan Africa* (Washington, D.C., 1990).
35. *WDR 1984*, 52.
36. *WDR 1984*, 51, 122.
37. Jere R. Behrman and Anil B. Deolalikar, "Health and Nutrition," in Hollis Chenery and T. N. Srinivasan, eds., *Handbook of Development Economics*, vol. 1 (Amsterdam, 1988), 691.
38. For the position that children are economically more advantageous in Africa than elsewhere, see Caldwell and Caldwell, "High Fertility in Sub-Saharan Africa," 120.
39. *WDR 1984*, 52.
40. *WDR 1991*, 44; *Wall Street Journal*, September 17, 1986.
41. For the data see *WDR 1994*, 212–213.
42. *WDR 1993*, 288–289.
43. *WDR 1993*, 19.

44. R. H. Gray, "The Decline of Mortality in Ceylon and the Demographic Effects of Malaria Control," *Population Studies* 28, no. 2 (1974): 205–229; and T. Paul Schultz, *Economics of Population* (Reading, Mass., 1981), 116.
45. See Richard A. Easterlin and Eileen M. Crimmins, *The Fertility Revolution* (Chicago, 1985).
46. See John C. Caldwell, "The Soft Underbelly of Development: Demographic Transition in Conditions of Limited Economic Change," *Proceedings of the World Bank Annual Conference on Development Economics 1990* (Washington, D.C., 1991), 225.
47. Bryant Robey, Shea O. Rutstein, and Leo Morris, "The Fertility Decline in Developing Countries," *Scientific American* (December 1993): 60–67.
48. Following Birdsall, "Economic Approaches to Population Growth," 520.
49. Rebecca Wong and Ruth E. Levine, "The Effect of Household Structure on Women's Economic Activity and Fertility: Evidence from Recent Mothers in Urban Mexico," *Economic Development and Cultural Change* 41, no. 1 (October 1992): 89–102.
50. Ronald Freedman, "Norms for Family Size in Underdeveloped Areas," in Charles B. Nam, ed., *Population and Society* (Boston, 1968), 222.
51. See Ehtisham Ahmad, Jean Drèze, John Hills, and Amartya Sen, *Social Security in Developing Countries* (Oxford, 1991).
52. *WDR 1984*, 108.
53. See Schultz, *Economics of Population*, 119; *WDR 1990*, 81; and T. Paul Schultz, "Human Capital, Family Planning, and Their Effects on Population Growth," *American Economic Review Papers and Proceedings* 84, no. 2 (May 1994): 255.
54. World Fertility Survey data reported in World Bank, *Population and Development* (Washington, D.C., 1994), 53.
55. Schultz, "Human Capital, Family Planning, and Their Effects on Population Growth," 260; *The Economist*, September 3, 1994.
56. Caldwell, "The Soft Underbelly of Development: Demographic Transition in Conditions of Limited Economic Change," 232.
57. Birdsall, "Economic Approaches to Population Growth," 520; *WDR 1984*, 121.
58. Useful studies of this issue include Robert Repetto, *Economic Equality and Fertility in Developing Countries* (Baltimore, 1979); and C. R. Winegarden, "Income Redistribution Versus Accelerated Economic Growth: A Comparison of Demographic Effects," *Oxford Bulletin of Economics and Statistics* (August 1984).
59. The figures are from *WDR 1994*, 212–213.
60. For the African figure, see *HDR 1994*, 175.
61. Robey, Rutstein, and Morris, "The Fertility Decline in Developing Countries," 60; and John W. Bongaarts, W. Parker Mauldin, and James F. Phillips, "The Demographic Impact of Family Planning Programs," *Studies in Family Planning* 21 (1990): 299–310.
62. See the correlations by W. Parker Mauldin and Robert J. Mauldin quoted by Robert Repetto, "Population Policy After Mexico City: Reality vs. Ideology," *Challenge* 28, no. 3 (1985): 43.
63. Roberto Cuca, "Family Planning Programs and Fertility Decline," *Finance and Development* 17, no. 4 (1980): 37–39.
64. World Fertility Survey data reported in World Bank, *Population and Development* (Washington, D.C., 1994), 61.
65. See *WDR 1984*, 196–197, table 3; and Robey, Rutstein, and Morris, "The Fertility Decline in Developing Countries," 67.
66. *The Economist*, May 28, 1994, citing especially Lant Pritchett of the World Bank. Also see C. Peter Timmer, "Population, Poverty, and Policies," *American Economic Review Papers and Proceedings* 84, no. 2 (May 1994): 261–265.

67. Rodolfo A. Bulatao, "Family Planning: The Unfinished Revolution," *Finance and Development* 29, no. 4 (December 1992): 6. The figures exclude the rich oil-producing countries.
68. See Pollak and Watkins, "Cultural and Economic Approaches to Fertility: Proper Marriage or Mésalliance?" citing sources.
69. Some of these are from J. Mayonne Stycos, "Prospects for World Population Control," in Morgan and Betz, eds., *Economic Development*, 321.
70. *WDR 1980*, 80.
71. World Bank, *Population and Development* (Washington, D.C., 1994), 57, 62.
72. World Bank, *Population and Development* (Washington, D.C., 1994), 91.
73. World Bank, *Population and Development*, 97.
74. For this and the following sections, I often relied on articles in the press, including especially *The Economist*, the *Christian Science Monitor,* and the *Wall Street Journal.*
75. Robey, Rutstein, and Morris, "The Fertility Decline in Developing Countries," 62.
76. *WDR 1980*, 69.
77. *The Economist*, January 9, 1993.
78. See *WDR 1984*, 125–126.
79. For a description see Kenneth M. Chomitz and Nancy Birdsall, "Incentives for Small Families: Concepts and Issues," *Proceedings of the World Bank Annual Conference on Development Economics 1990* (Washington, D.C., 1991), 331–336.
80. Chomitz and Birdsall, "Incentives for Small Families: Concepts and Issues," 310.
81. A useful survey article is James T. Fawcett and Siew-Ean Khoo, "Singapore: Rapid Fertility Transition in a Compact Society," *Population and Development Review* 6, no. 4 (1980): 549–579.
82. Birdsall, "Economic Analyses of Rapid Population Growth," 42.
83. See Chomitz and Birdsall, "Incentives for Small Families: Concepts and Issues," 323; and Ronald K. Ridker, "The No-Birth Bonus Scheme: The Use of Savings Accounts for Family Planning in South India," *Population and Development Review* 6, no. 1 (1980): 32–46.
84. For much of the data in this paragraph, see *WDR 1994*, 288–291.
85. See especially *WDR 1980*, 68.
86. See World Bank, *Population and Development*, 64–66.
87. Amartya Sen calls coercion the "override view," that is, the idea that people's voluntary decisions should be overridden by legal or economic compulsion. See Sen's "Population: Delusion and Reality," *The New York Review*, September 22, 1994, 62–71.
88. A book-length study is Judith Banister, *China's Changing Population* (Stanford, 1987).
89. Chomitz and Birdsall, "Incentives for Small Families: Concepts and Issues," 322–324.
90. *WDR 1994*, 290; *Christian Science Monitor*, January 11, 1993.
91. Some of the details in this section are from a series by Carol Honsa in the *Christian Science Monitor*, May to June 1981 (especially June 4), and July 30, 1982. Also, see Jan Stepan et al., "Legal Trends and Issues in Voluntary Sterilization," *Population Reports* 9, no. 2 (1981): E73–E102; and articles in *The Economist* and elsewhere in the press.
92. Amartya Sen, "Population: Delusion and Reality," 71.

Chapter 10

Labor and Human Capital

Preventing excess population was the subject of the last chapter. Making the existing population productive and finding employment for it are the subjects of this one.

THE ECONOMICS OF LOW WAGES

On average, wages are low in the LDCs compared to the developed countries. Figure 10.1 shows how low LDC wages emerge from the operation of demand and supply in labor markets. The basic problem is that because of decades of rapid population growth, the supply of unskilled labor is high in relation to the demand for labor, leading to a low wage W in the figure. For any given population size, the key to increasing wages is to raise the demand for labor. The higher demand for labor, D' instead of D, would lead to a higher wage W'. The main way to raise the demand for labor is to raise its productivity. For any given population, the low productivity of labor is the main reason for the low pay it receives.

There is general agreement that the main way to increase the productivity of labor, and hence the demand for it, is to raise the stock of "human capital" by fostering education, the acquisition of skills, better health, and improved nutrition. Endowing workers with more human capital makes the population more productive and more employable as well.[1] Some countries are rich and some are poor not only because of the disparity in their stock of physical capital, but because of the

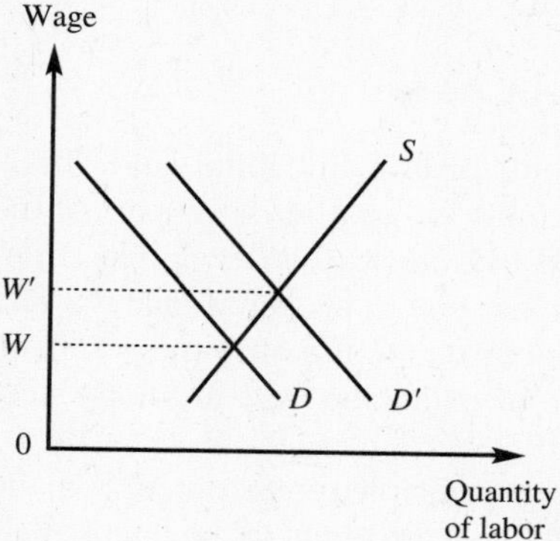

Figure 10.1 Wages are low in LDCs because of demand and supply. A high supply of labor together with low productivity, and thus low demand D, leads to a low wage W. An increase in productivity can raise the demand for labor to D' and increase the wage to W'.

unequal endowment of human capital.[2] The positive effect of investment in human capital goes far beyond the rise in a population's productivity that it causes. By increasing capabilities it widens the range of choice, affects people's perceptions of what they can attain, and thereby raises the value of life itself. Obviously investment that leads to these results is desirable in its own right in addition to what it does for productivity. UN experts believe that if the percentage of a country's total income spent on human capital formation could rise from the present low figure of 2% or so in many LDCs to 5% or 6%, substantial progress could be made.*

People voluntarily acquire human capital all the time by investing in their own education and training and by caring for their own health and nutrition. But human capital is decidedly not the same as physical capital. It does not survive the individual who does the investing. It may take a long time to acquire, increasing the risks of obsolescence if conditions change. It is not easily transferred to other uses; surgeons may have a huge amount tied up in their training, but it will be wasted if they want to switch to designing computers.[3] For these reasons, governments have an important role to play in human capital acquisition, even though government activity and the taxes to support it are undoubtedly unpopular in many quarters.

EDUCATION AND TRAINING

No highly educated and well-trained population is poor, but almost all populations with poor education and limited skills suffer from low income. Gross deficiencies in education and training may have the particularly bad result that they prevent

*A balanced program might involve 0.5% of GNP for food security, 0.2% for nutrition, 1.5% for funding universal primary school education, 0.8% for family planning, 0.5% for water and sanitation, and 2.0% for primary health care. This is the recommendation of Partha Dasgupta, *An Inquiry into Well-Being and Destitution* (Oxford, 1993), 540. Also see *HDR 1991*, 6.

workers and managers from absorbing the technologies that could increase growth. This section explores the issue.

Private and Social Returns to Education

Education is one of the most important elements of human capital, and differences in educational endowments certainly account for a rather large part of the gap in national income per capita between the LDCs and the developed countries.* Education involves two difficult questions, one concerning analysis and one concerning policy. The first is how the economist is to measure the costs and benefits of education. The second is what type of education best promotes economic development.

As for the question of measurement, the basic principle seems simple: expand education until the rising marginal costs of providing it are equal to the falling marginal benefits (due to diminishing returns) accruing to society from it. This is shown diagrammatically in Figure 10.2. Since the slopes of the tangent lines are equal at *E*, marginal costs are equal to marginal benefits at that level of education. Unfortunately, calculation of the costs and benefits is not easy, and measurement is complicated by several valuation problems.

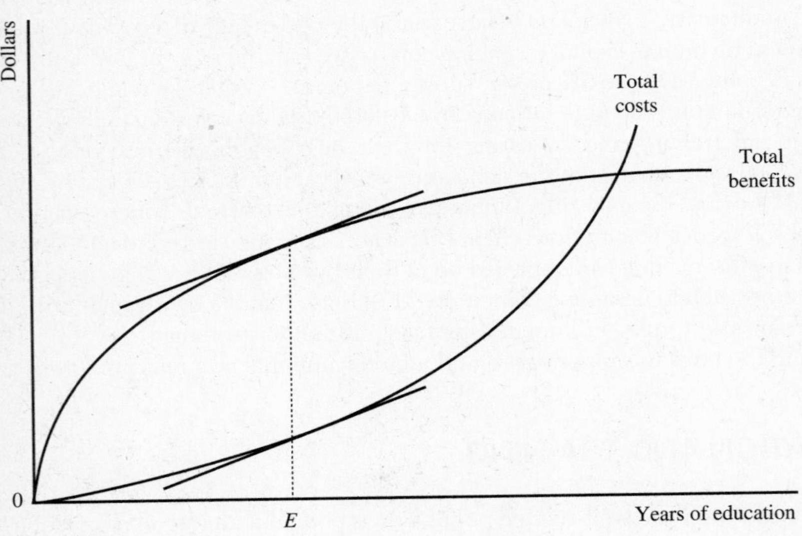

Figure 10.2 The optimal amount of education is that amount where the marginal costs and marginal benefits of the education are equal. That would be where the slopes of the tangent lines in the Figure are the same, at *E* years of education.

*The advanced levels of literacy and numerical facility attained early in their development process appears an especially important cause of the high growth rates attained by some "late developers," such as Germany, Japan, Israel, and all the high-performing Asian economies, such as South Korea and Taiwan.

One such problem is that the private benefits of education may differ substantially from the benefits to society as a whole. Social benefits may rise sharply with primary education because elementary literacy and facility with numbers will make factory workers more productive and because farmers-to-be may gain some knowledge of technical advances in agriculture from their elementary science courses. Child mortality falls, health improves, and efforts to extend family planning are more successful as mothers are more educated, as we shall see. The direct social benefits from secondary and university education will probably not rise as rapidly (as represented in Figure 10.3). Admittedly, it is difficult to take into account the less direct benefits that some have claimed for education, particularly the higher level of decency and morality in society. Additional education arguably brings less crime, more honesty and concern for others, changing attitudes toward tolerance and civic duty, greater openness to new ideas, greater self-confidence, and higher cultural standards, such as more pleasure from music, art, and reading. Indeed, some studies show that voting, savings habits, and attitudes toward work and toward life itself are more influenced by schooling than anything else.[4]

Private benefits, however, may be perceived as increasing rapidly at the secondary or university level in the presence of credentialism and screening. These are the terms used when high educational attainment is required for job procurement and promotion, or when wage and salary scales are geared to educational levels rather than to performance and productivity. George Psacharopoulos has shown that earnings at higher levels of education relative to earnings at lesser levels of education are uniformly greater at every stage in LDCs than in the developed countries. For example, his research revealed private returns to university graduates over 6 times higher than to primary school graduates in Ghana, India,

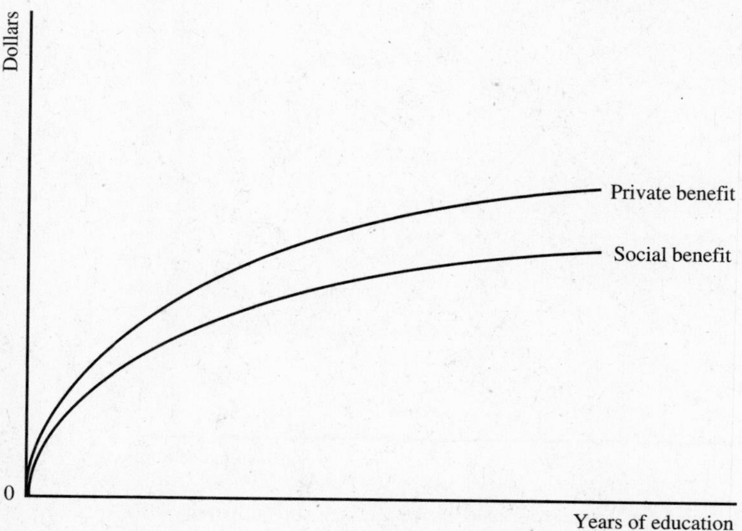

Figure 10.3 Private benefits of education in the LDCs typically exceed social benefits.

Kenya, Malaysia, Nigeria, South Korea, and Uganda, but only 2.4 times higher in Canada, Great Britain, and the United States.[5] (Note that an argument can then be made that education has tended to increase income inequality in LDCs. One study of 49 countries suggests that about a fifth of all income inequality is explained by educational inequality, and that raising education from a very low level can indeed cause a decrease in income equality.)[6]

In such circumstances, the demand for secondary and university education will be artificially inflated as in Figure 10.4. A country may then devote an unjustifiably high amount of money to these activities, shown by the level of education Q_2 rather than Q_1.

The large wage and salary rewards to education may, as we shall see, be due to disequilibrium in the labor market, with resulting heavy unemployment among the more highly educated. This highlights a problem with rate of return calculations for education. As long-term estimates based on past income data, they will be valid predictions of future rates of return only to the extent that future incomes do not greatly change—and heavy unemployment among graduates would certainly represent one such change.[7] Typically, the unemployment is highest among those who have completed some high school or college training but did not graduate.

Another question in valuing the benefits of education is how to treat the "joint product" problem. A graduate engineer will no doubt have a very different level of performance when working with other college graduates as opposed to working with primary school dropouts.

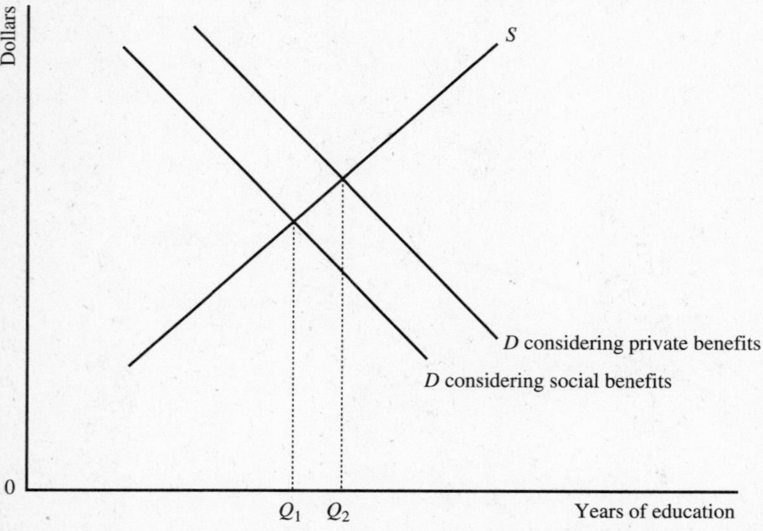

Figure 10.4 Because the private demand for secondary and university education reflects private benefits higher than social benefits, the equilibrium amount desired of these types of education (Q_2) is likely to be above the social optimum (Q_1).

Still another problem for measurement is differing levels of intelligence, as measured by IQ or by other suitable means. Would these not lead to eventual differences in income even if education levels are the same? And are not those who seek more education sometimes more motivated than those who do not?

In spite of the difficulties of measurement, calculation of the costs and benefits of education is now standard practice. The basic task, as illustrated in Figure 10.5, is to calculate the earnings over time of a person who receives more education compared with another person who receives less education. Young person *A*, taking work after leaving high school, will have higher earnings for a time than young person *B* who goes on to university. In time, *B's* earnings will surpass *A's*, as the figure shows. From *B's* point of view, university is economically worthwhile if the pluses, discounted for the passage of time, total a greater amount than the minuses.[8]

The following formula is a standard one for calculating the rate of return for attending university.[9] It divides the increased earnings from university training by the direct cost of the education plus the earnings forgone during the four-year period of education.

$$\begin{array}{l}\textit{Private}\\ \textit{rate of}\\ \textit{return}\end{array} = \frac{\begin{array}{l}\textit{average annual}\\ \textit{after-tax earnings}\\ \textit{of university graduates}\end{array} - \begin{array}{l}\textit{average annual after-}\\ \textit{tax earnings of}\\ \textit{secondary school graduates}\end{array}}{\textit{4 years} \times \left(\begin{array}{l}\textit{average annual}\\ \textit{after-tax earnings}\\ \textit{of secondary}\\ \textit{school graduates}\end{array} + \begin{array}{l}\textit{average annual}\\ \textit{private direct}\\ \textit{cost of university}\\ \textit{study}\end{array}\right)}$$

(To convert this formula to a social rate of return, before-tax earnings would be used, because, from society's point of view, taxes are just a transfer. Additionally, the cost figure must be the full quantity of resources committed, whether included in fees or not.)

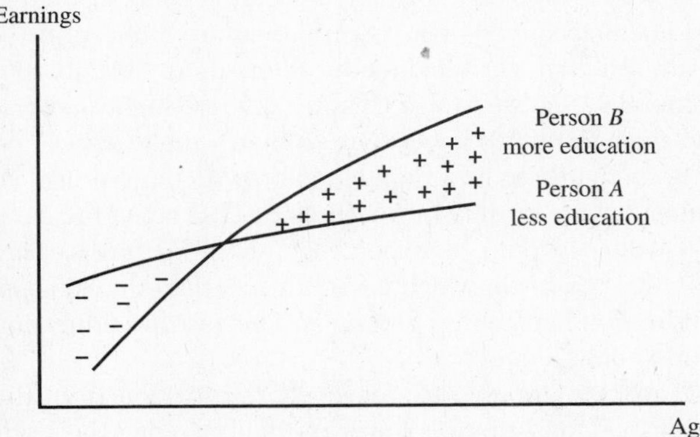

Figure 10.5 Calculating the costs and benefits of education. Education typically involves net costs earlier in life and net benefits later.

TABLE 10.1 SOCIAL RATES OF RETURN TO EDUCATION (PERCENT)

	Primary	Secondary	Higher	Number of Countries
LDC exporters of manufactures	15	13	9	4
Other LDCs	28	17	14	26
Developed countries	15	11	11	10

Note: The period covered is from the 1970s to the early 1980s.

Source: WDR 1987, 64.

The difficulties of measurement aside, various studies by the World Bank reveal social rates of return to education, calculated with formulas similar to that shown above, as in Table 10.1. Notice the 28% return to primary education in low-income LDCs, a figure rarely matched by any capital investment.[10]

The Returns to Educating Farmers and Women Are Particularly High

The returns from educating farmers and women, who are frequently one and the same, are higher yet. For farmers, some elementary competence in arithmetic and science, plus basic literacy, is strongly correlated with agricultural output in most studies of the subject. A study of 88 countries suggests that an increase in literacy from 20% to 30% is associated with an increase in real GDP of 8% to 16%. The social rate of return to the elementary education of farmers is as high as 40%.[11] A main reason for the high return is that farmers can more easily absorb information that can raise their productivity. They can also respond faster and more effectively to changes in their economic environment, such as the availability of better or lower-priced seed and fertilizer. In Thailand, farmers with four years of education were three times more likely to use chemical fertilizers, herbicides, and pesticides than those with one to three years. In Peru, an additional year of schooling raised the probability that farmers would adopt modern technology by 45%.[12] All this is a major reason why in time the wide provision of primary education generally makes income distribution more equal in a country—the poorer areas are often rural.

Social rates of return are also high for female education, about 30% to 40% more than for education generally.[13] As we saw in Chapter 9, more highly educated mothers marry later and their fertility is lower than women with no education or less education, assisting in the battle against population growth. On average, an extra year of educating women lowers fertility by 5% to 10%. That being the case, $3000 spent educating 100 women would be expected to avert 50 births. That amounts to a cost of $60 per averted birth, which is slightly *less* than the $65 cost per averted birth estimated for family planning programs. This justifies education of females on a family planning basis alone.[14]

Furthermore, educated women are able to extract more nutrition from the same level of expenditure on food, and there is lower mortality among their offspring. A more highly educated woman earns higher income. This, too, aids nutrition because on average more of women's income is used to buy food than is the case with men's income. Both quality and quantity of food rise. The effect on nutrition is not nearly so great when the income of *men* increases. There have been cases of rural development projects that led to greater production of cash crops but did not safeguard women's income, leading to adverse nutritional consequences and (in what appeared to be an effort to regain lost status) the birth of more children.[15]

World Bank data indicate that an additional year of education for women is associated with a fall of two percentage points in the rate of infant mortality; some studies indicate that the reduction can be as much as five to ten percentage points.[16] (The figures include the effect of better decision making and the higher incomes earned by the more educated.) Research from Nigeria and the Philippines suggest that the positive effect of mothers' education has sufficient impact on child mortality to make up for the lack of medical facilities.[17] In all these cases, there is significantly less correlation with the educational level of the father.

Returns to Education: A Conclusion The high rates of return will in time decline as diminishing returns to education set in. But they are not apparent yet, especially in the lowest-income LDCs. Until diminishing returns do set in, the formation of human capital through education appears to be one of the most productive investments an LDC can make.

Can Economies Be Made in Education?

Education involves considerable costs. Teachers must be trained, and trained people are much in demand, with other opportunities available to them in business and government. Several possibilities exist for reducing the costs of education, perhaps by as much as a quarter, while retaining most of the benefits.[18] Feasible reform measures might include the following.

1. Economizing on the use of regular teachers, who make up the largest part of a school's budget. Cheaper teaching assistants and helpers, less well-trained regular teachers, and volunteers (parents and the like) could all be utilized. Radio and television projects may help to lower expenditures. The South Korean Air Correspondent High School, for example, is run at a cost of only a fifth of that of traditional schools, and correspondence schools have also had good success in Brazil, Kenya, and the Dominican Republic, among others.
2. Doubling shifts in schools, which brings more effective utilization of personnel and school buildings, and allows class size to be cut. With *triple* shifts, Zambia has cut schooling costs by nearly half. Such steps obviously put more pressure on parents and teachers alike, but the saving may be worth it.
3. Allowing class size to rise. Little harm seems to ensue from raising primary school class size from 25 to 40. If at the same time up-to-date textbooks are substituted for more expensive teachers, the better books help to offset the more crowded classrooms. Nonformal education could receive more emphasis.

4. Reform of university education, which is typically very expensive. It is not unusual to find an LDC's university professors earning 50 times the country's per capita national income, compared to three times or so for a primary school teacher. University buildings are frequently much fancier in comparison to the general architectural standards of an area than is true in the developed countries. In some LDCs, university students may still receive generous grants ("bursaries") over and above the free room, board, and tuition that is often made available. In some low-income African countries, the living allowance for students is half the average public-sector wage in these countries. The bursaries, a leftover from an elitist past, are often paid to all, even to students from well-to-do families. In the 1980s, primary school spending in some countries could have been raised 20% if these bursaries had been eliminated.[19]

Table 10.2 below shows education costs per student in primary, secondary, and higher education if the costs of students in primary school is equal to 100. The differences are extraordinary. Overall, in 1980, primary education received only 22% of all funding for schooling in LDCs, while university education swallowed nearly 40%.

There would seem to be a strong argument for shifting funds away from university education and toward primary schooling, where the social rate of return is much higher. At the least, cost recovery from university students by means of higher fees and reliance on student loans would seem called for. South Korea shows what can be done, having raised 45.9% of the costs of university training from user charges, compared to Papua New Guinea's 0%, Bangladesh's 0.1%, and India's 4.9%.[20]

Needless to say, these moves would be difficult because they would tread on the toes of the urban elites who so often hold political power. But it can be done, as the high-performing Asian economies show. An outstanding feature of education in these economies is not that they spend more as a percentage of GDP—actually they don't—but their concentration of public spending on primary education. For example, recently South Korea has devoted only 10% of its education budget to higher education, compared to 43% in Venezuela. For the HPAEs as a whole, the figure was 15% over the past 30 years, compared to about 24% in Latin America.[21]

TABLE 10.2 EDUCATION COSTS PER STUDENT (PRIMARY SCHOOL = 100)

	Primary	Secondary	Higher
Industrial countries	100	109	223
All LDCs	100	293	413
Sub-Saharan Africa	100	2643	5333

Source: WDR 1988, 135.

The Educational Structure in the LDCs

The burden of dependency with its masses of young people, combined with misallocation of the education budget, has led to serious difficulties in providing both schools and teachers. But there has also been substantial progress, as can be seen in Table 10.3, which shows the numbers enrolled at a given educational level (primary school, secondary school, college and university) as a percent of the relevant age group for that level.

At the top of the table are comparative data for the developed countries. One important result of the high percentages in this part of the table is a corresponding high rate of adult literacy. No developed country has a literacy rate below 98%.* The lower part of the table shows the situation for the low-income and middle-income LDCs.

The data for 40 low-income countries (excluding China and India), in the middle of the table, simultaneously show poor educational opportunities and substantial

TABLE 10.3 PERCENT OF RELEVANT AGE GROUP ENROLLED, 1991, AND LITERACY, 1992 (1970 IN PARENTHESES)

Developed Countries		
Primary school enrollment	104*	(106)*
Secondary school enrollment	93	(73)
College and university enrollment	33†	(36)
Literacy	99	99‡
Low-Income LDCs§		
Primary school enrollment	79	(55)
Secondary school enrollment	28	(13)
College and university enrollment	5	(3)
Literacy	46	(29)
Middle-Income LDCs		
Primary school enrollment	104*	(93)
Secondary school enrollment	55	(32)
College and university enrollment	18	(13)
Literacy	79¶	(60)

Note: *Over 100% because some outside the age group are enrolled. †1990 figure. ‡1975 figure, from *WDR 1979*, 127. §Excludes China and India. ¶Category used is the UN's "medium human development" LDCs.

Source: WDR 1994, 216–217 and *HDR 1994*, 136–137.

*The standard employed in establishing literacy rates is, however, quite low. A higher standard cuts the percentages substantially in both the developed countries and the LDCs. Jonathan Kozol in his book *Illiterate America* (New York, 1985) estimated that 60 million U.S. adults (about one-third of the whole) were unable to read and understand the Bill of Rights.

improvement since 1970. (The 1970 figures are shown in parentheses). The data for the 60-odd middle-income LDCs at the bottom of the table give a more favorable impression; the goal of universal primary education (UPE) has basically been attained by this group. Not surprisingly, there is often a good correlation between increasing primary school enrollment and improvement in literacy.

Much is not revealed by these statistics, however. They fail to make clear that women still have a long way to go before educational equality with men is achieved. Consider Table 10.4, which shows female educational attainment as a percentage of male attainment in three categories: school enrollment, total years of schooling, and literacy. Two-thirds of all illiterates are women.[22] Equality in education is important not only because it is fair to give women an equal chance but also because the education of females carries substantial positive benefits, as we have seen earlier in the chapter. (Then again, the gap was much wider in the past, as Table 10.4 shows.)

The averages do not reflect the very high dropout rates. In the LDCs, about 30% of students who enter primary school fail to finish, and the number is over 40% in many low-income LDCs.[23] The wastage is therefore highest in the countries that can afford it the least. (Dropping out is less common in upper-middle-income countries, where only 15% fail to finish primary school. It is also less prevalent in secondary school everywhere, though the problem is still severe—something under 20% in Asia and Latin America and approximately double that figure in Africa.)

Moreover, the overall averages do not reflect the wide variance in LDCs' recent performance, nor how far some have to go to raise the stock of education in their populations. Primary school enrollment in China is 123% of the relevant age group, 126% in Peru, and 114% in Mexico, compared to 25% in Ethiopia and Mali. Mean years of schooling among people over school age (25 years old or more) is a good indicator of the accumulated education in the adult population. The 1992 figure was over nine years in Argentina, Barbados, and South Korea, but it was below *one* year in Bénin, Bhutan, Burkina Faso, Burundi, Mali, Mauritania, Niger, Senegal, Somalia, Sudan, Oman, Yemen, and several others. In the LDCs with the least accumulated education (Niger and Burkina Faso) the 1992

TABLE 10.4 1990 FEMALE ENROLLMENT, 1992 YEARS OF SCHOOLING, AND 1992 LITERACY AS PERCENT OF MALE ENROLLMENT, YEARS OF SCHOOLING, AND LITERACY (1960 ENROLLMENT AND 1970 LITERACY IN PARENTHESES WHERE AVAILABLE)

	All LDCs	Least-Developed LDCs
Primary school enrollment	91 (61)	80 (44)
Secondary school enrollment	72	60
College and university enrollment	60	30
Total years of schooling	55	42
Literacy	71 (54)	54 (38)

Source: HDR 1994, 147.

average figure was about 2.5 *months* of school education.[24] Though illiteracy has now fallen to about 30% of the population in all LDCs (as of 1992), it remains above 60% in many countries and 75% to 80% in some (Nepal, Somalia, Sierra Leone, and Sudan among others). Heroic efforts will be needed to overcome deficiencies this extreme.

Finally, the figures do not reflect the strong urban bias in some countries. Funding per pupil in rural schools is often much lower than it is in the cities. Moreover, during the debt crisis and Africa's economic travail, education budgets declined in numerous countries. For example, enrollment rates in Tanzania actually fell from 93% in 1980 to 66% in 1987, and from 94% to 76% in Zaire during the same period. Progress may not keep up the rapid pace of recent years, even though populations are rising.[25]

Unemployment Among Graduates, Curricular Relevance, Quality

A serious problem with education in the LDCs is the disillusionment of those who complete their training and develop expectations regarding jobs, income, and prestige based on that training. The expectations may well go unfulfilled. If many wages and salaries are not very flexible in the downward direction, there will be limited capacity to absorb primary and secondary school graduates in jobs outside agriculture.* Those educated in rural schools too often tend to think of farming and life in the village as "bush," to use the piquant word much heard in Africa. There is also little inclination to accept a job as an unskilled laborer in the city. Often only a government clerkship or work in the managerial or sales end of a large firm confers adequate status.

At the same time, pay scales for those with primary or secondary certificates may be relatively high, originally so set because of the scarcity of such graduates. This was especially true of the colonial governments of Asia and Africa. The educational situation has changed substantially, but sometimes pay scales have not. For example, the pay of government bureaucrats expressed as a percentage of per capita GDP is about 200% in the developed countries but about 300% in Latin America and Asia and some 600% in Africa. Some bureaucrats are even higher paid relative to the national income, for example Cameroun 750%, Bénin 1000%, and Burundi 1500%.[26] The resulting disequilibrium wages have frequently meant a surplus of job applicants and inevitable disappointment.†

There are other reasons for the surplus and the disappointment, as we shall see in following chapters when we examine the enormous rural–urban migrations

*Note that this disillusionment ceases to occur after UPE has been achieved for a number of years. School completion then becomes the norm rather than a special accomplishment. Hence the problem is worse for the lower-income countries than it is for the more well-to-do among the LDCs.

†Some countries, Brazil and some of the skill-short oil exporters being notable examples, have an especially low percentage in secondary education and hence a shortage of job applicants with this sort of training.

of recent years in the LDCs. Whatever the cause, open unemployment rates among young people 15 to 24 years of age, many of these being "school-leavers," are often double the national average. For example, Indian government statistics show unemployment among school-leavers averaging 36% in the mid-1980s.[27] It may, of course, be rational for a school-leaver to accept a rather lengthy period of unemployment if the probability of eventually finding a high-paying job is significant. The group of unemployed "turns over" to a degree, some finding jobs as others begin their search. We return to the subject of unemployment in later chapters.

Curricular Relevance and Quality In addition to the problem of finding jobs for graduates, and indeed another cause of the employment difficulty, is lack of relevance in the curriculum. Connecting education with economic development is a task yet incomplete. Only a decade or two ago, however, the situation was much worse. There was little concern for rural needs in rural schools. In former British and French colonies there was an overwhelming emphasis on Western history and literature. Students in Ghana and Nigeria, even after independence, would study William the Conqueror and the Magna Carta, but not the remarkable ruler Mansa Musa or the history of the ancient empires of Ghana or Melli or Songhay. They would learn of the heritage of higher education in Britain, with its historic universities, but not of the great medieval university at Timbuktu. They would read Dickens and Thackeray instead of the indigenous literature.

Training in Western history and literature was eventually replaced almost everywhere by a more indigenous curriculum, but a problem still remains. The traditions of British and French education attached much more prestige to the law and the arts than they did to vocational training in applied science and (especially) agriculture. The same tradition is present in Latin America, which has not been colonized since the early nineteenth century. It is reinforced by religions (Hinduism, Confucianism, Buddhism) that value contemplation or the study of sacred and traditional texts. Whatever the causes, the result can clearly be seen in the statistics. Generally, over 60% of university students in the LDCs study liberal arts subjects. Of students in their final year in India's universities, well over 80% have been in the arts, the law, and the social sciences.* Less than 10% were in science and technology, and only 2% were in agriculture.[28] Even within fields, this symptom shows: Tropical medicine is less prestigious than surgery; architects prefer to

*It is possible to take a more favorable view of the arts. They are much cheaper to teach than the sciences, so even though the benefits are lower the net result may not be so bad—especially since women have historically been attracted to the arts, and the education of women gives such significant residual benefits. Also, in India's case even a small percentage educated in science and technology in time yields large absolute numbers. India's 2.4 million scientists and engineers form the largest pool of technical talent outside the United States and Russia. See Walt W. Rostow, "Economic Growth and the Diffusion of Power," *Challenge* 29, no. 4 (1986): 30. Other LDCs, including China and Mexico, have also undergone a vast expansion of their technical graduates.

design edifices rather than the "standard" sort of building that is usually required; economists gravitate to sophisticated modeling rather than nuts-and-bolts work in the field. All this is a most unfortunate legacy, cultural or colonial, that will not be broken for some time.

Most worrisome has been the deterioration in the quality of education that set in during the debt crisis and the slowdown of growth of the 1980s. Truncated budgets mean worn-out books and obsolete equipment, or none at all. In the 1980s in Brazil, less than a quarter of all first grades had textbooks for that level; in the Central African Republic there were over ten students per textbook; in the Dominican Republic and Botswana over 80% of the students surveyed in various courses such as mathematics and science had no text.[29] It is clear that LDCs have generally made the decision to emphasize the quantity of education rather than its quality. The quality deficiencies raise the likelihood that increased quantity will not be as beneficial to development prospects as might be expected.

Tailoring Education to Job Openings Another discouraging realization is that the labor force in the LDCs has been growing at unprecedented rates, more than double the European experience of the nineteenth century. Whereas Europe in that century could absorb almost half of its growing labor force into industry, recent statistics show that the low-income LDCs are managing to place less than 20% of their additional labor in industrial employment. The figure for the middle-income LDCs is somewhat better at just under 35%.

Vocational training to make labor more productive and more employable has been a popular response. Yet some of these programs have not been overly successful. Training centers outside the regular school system have often proved to be more adaptable and successful than schools, which found it difficult to institute new courses and were forced to adhere to standard school schedules. Sometimes traditional institutions (including, for example, Kenya's secondary technical schools and Colombia's comprehensive schools) were too rigid, failing to alter specialist training rapidly as market conditions changed and suffering from inadequate ties to the labor market. As with the nonvocational schools, inadequate attention was paid to what the job openings actually were.

In response there has been an upsurge in vocational programs to train labor for employment outside of industry or to tailor training specifically for employment in that part of industry where the demand for labor is the largest. An impressive lead in this regard has been taken by Singapore, whose Industrial Training Board conducts courses in which class time is combined with on-the-job training in industries where a need is expressed. By focusing on actual needs, the program tries to avoid the experience of neighboring Thailand, where in the 1970s government support for the training of technicians was overdone, with 40% unemployment among the graduates. Brazil's National Industrial Apprenticeship Agency (SENAI) relies on labor market surveys and detailed analyses of job openings in planning and implementing its training programs. The program is financed by a 1% payroll tax that is not charged if a firm agrees to sponsor on-the-job training. More of this could be done in the lowest-income countries, which might implement strategic training for entry-level manufacturing such as textiles and clothing.[30]

The tying of training to job availability is an idea now spreading widely in both LDCs and developed countries. It has had extensive use in Sweden, Germany, and Japan and has now been adopted in the United States, where it is central to the Jobs Training Partnership Act (JTPA) that dates from the 1980s.

A more general criticism involves the fact that many of the vocationally trained are now taking jobs outside the scope of their training.[31] That being the case, perhaps secondary education should be made more general in nature, increasing the flexibility of graduates, who may end up working in a wide variety of occupations as industrial and commercial occupations change. Some students of the subject now believe that on-the-job training of generally educated people is more beneficial than classroom vocational training. Employers are likely to have more knowledge than schools do about what skills and training are needed, and generally educated students will have the flexibility to absorb this training.

Other possible policy changes could be made so that human capital formation would accord more closely to a country's development needs. In the primary schools, curricula could often be more directed to rural requirements, focusing on basic literacy and numerical facility for illiterate adults as well as for children.* Training in how to improve family life through nutrition, health, child care, and family planning is likely to be extremely useful. The undoubted positive benefits of educating more women, already mentioned, could certainly receive more emphasis in the countries that still neglect this resource. Some nations, for example, continue to count virtually no women among their university graduates.

In addition, job specifications could be redrawn so that high educational attainment is not overemphasized, especially in the government's own civil service. Similarly, the tying of wages and salaries to educational levels could be modified to conform more to market supply and demand. All these steps would reduce the inflated private benefits from higher education and bring them closer to equality with the social benefits.

Some of these proposals would represent a step back from the goal of universal primary education and would thus be both politically charged and highly debatable, but they might also be more cost-effective than the very expensive goal of a standard primary education for everyone. That could allow the attainment of other objectives as well.[32]

---

*However rewarding such a reform might be, it may not always be easy to accomplish, as Mexico discovered long ago. That country in the 1920s and 1930s followed famous educator John Dewey's suggestion that special rural schools be established, but after about a decade faced a reaction in which the rural areas demanded and received the same sort of schools as urban areas. Rural people thought their schools were inferior and that they were being discriminated against. See the work of Donald Keesing, quoted by David Morawetz, *Twenty-five Years of Economic Development, 1950 to 1975* (Baltimore, 1977), 54.

The "Brain Drain"

Another area of concern is the "brain drain"—students who go overseas for their higher education and remain there, and those who are trained at home and then emigrate to the developed countries.[33] Large-scale migration of all types of labor was of course common in the nineteenth century but was much restricted early in the twentieth century. It came to notice once again in the 1960s when the Common Market countries began to welcome large numbers of unskilled or semi-skilled workers. Yugoslavs and Turks toiled on German assembly lines as "guest workers"; Algerians, Moroccans, and other nationalities worked in factories in various Common Market countries. A similar pattern developed in the LDCs, especially where a low-income country had richer neighbors. Pakistanis, Jordanians, Egyptians, and Yemenis augment the labor force in the oil states around the Persian Gulf; Burkina Faso supplies labor to the Côte d'Ivoire; workers from Bangladesh go to India; Botswana, Lesotho, Malawi, Swaziland, Zambia, and others send labor to South Africa. When the labor has not been expensively trained, there may be little loss to the home country and a potential for considerable gain in remittances of hard currency. Remittances from workers abroad, which are usually 10% to 50% of the income they earn, yield almost as much hard currency as do exports in Pakistan and Burkina Faso, and are the chief source of foreign exchange in Egypt. Such remittances are 2.4% of the GNP of the least-developed countries (1991) but as much as 10% of GNP in Jordan, 11% in Egypt, and 12% in Yemen.[34] Migrants everywhere are unusually high savers, building a "nest egg" for their return home.[35]

When the labor is skilled, expensively trained, and perhaps irreplaceable in the short run, the result can be far different, however. Most of the following data are for the United States, but the brain drain also includes Western Europe, Canada, Australia, and New Zealand.[36] A substantial number of professional people, including especially engineers, managers, physicians, and nurses, have been attracted to these countries from the LDCs. Such immigrants to the United States, formerly very small in total number, during 1969 to 1979 comprised three-fourths of the professionally trained entrants to that country. Preponderantly they came from Asia: The number of professionals coming from the Philippines alone in a recent year (over 9,000) nearly equaled those from all Europe (a little over 10,000); in the 1970s, 12% of the qualified professionals in the Philippines emigrated to the United States. By 1987, nearly a third of Africa's skilled professionals had emigrated to Europe.

The drain of doctors from the Third World is the most striking case. Of the annual flow of about 3000 doctors who immigrate into the United States, over 60% are from LDCs. It is said that there are more Haitian physicians practicing in the United States than there are in Haiti. Over 70% of Pakistan's newly trained doctors leave the country, as do about 60% of Ghana's. The figure is between 50% and 67% for the Republic of South Africa. Nearly 45% of Sudan's engineers, scientists, and doctors have emigrated. Many come to the United States.[37]

In all fields of study about two-thirds of the foreign students doing graduate work in the United States stay as immigrants. The numbers are large. Currently about a quarter of all doctoral degrees in the United States are awarded to foreigners; the number of foreign students in U.S. doctoral programs nearly doubled in the 1980s.[38]

All this, of course, brings a large financial transfer. The cost of training is incurred by the LDCs, where funds for education are short, but the benefits are received by the developed world. This "reverse foreign aid" has been estimated for some countries by the World Bank. In 1972 the United States is said to have saved $883 million in education costs, against a loss of $320 million for Third World countries spent on educating those who moved. Canada, Britain, and the United States in the period 1961 to 1972 gained in higher income $44 billion more than the income lost by developing countries.[39] On an annual basis some developed countries receive more from this source than they pay in foreign aid, over twice as much for Canada and about 50% for the United States and Britain.[40]

The real losses to poor countries are, however, higher than this. The emigration of a good professor can cause stagnation in a university department, and some courses may not even be given as a result. A key industry (Guyana's bauxite, Turkey's coal and electricity) may be severely handicapped by the drain of its most skilled engineers and managers.[41] The most spirited people, the most enterprising, and the better-than-average talents are often the ones to join the flow. Measuring the cost of their education and training may not remotely reflect the true costs. A contrary circumstance should, however, be noted. If those who leave would otherwise form a frustrated, festering class of educated unemployed, allowing the drain to continue might be a preferred strategy in the short run for a country that lacks the immediate capability to do much about the oversupply.[42]

Assuming a desire to control the brain drain, what might be done about it? Simply stopping the immigration on the receiving end is one alternative. A number of countries (such as Britain, Denmark, France, Germany, and the Netherlands) have limited the inflow of foreign students and put quotas on individual fields of study. Britain has greatly increased the fees charged to foreign students.[43] Such measures have obvious negative consequences for the recipient country, however, and risk provoking the charge of prejudice, which touches a sensitive chord in the developed countries. Instead, a joint approach involving both the developed countries and Third World governments seems more promising.

The underdeveloped countries have also responded with a range of programs including information, incentives, and service and financial obligations. Kenya, for example, runs a successful recruitment program among its emigrants overseas, based on an original and equally successful British scheme. India sends a weekly list of employment opportunities at home to its students in foreign universities. The science institutes of South Korea and Taiwan, which were discussed in Chapter 8 were established in part to keep the best scientific minds at home; in Taiwan, about 23% of the scientists who go overseas now return. Turkey has a scheme called TOKTEN, assisted by the UN Development Program, that involves the temporary return home of Turks who have achieved prominence abroad in their field of specialization for short technical assignments. The advantages to the emigrant include the fast arrangement of a visit, an easier rapport with colleagues at home than can be managed by a visiting "foreigner," and continuing contact when the Turkish expert returns to the country of residence. Programs similar to TOKTEN have now been established by China, Egypt, Greece, Grenada, India, Pakistan, and Sri Lanka. Finally, developed countries have helped to establish programs and centers such as the International Center for Theoretical Physics in Trieste that gives Third World physicists a chance to keep abreast even if their home institutions are deficient.

Several nations push this thinking further and require a number of years of government service from students educated abroad: three to five years in Tunisia and Colombia; seven years of teaching, research, or administrative work in Egypt for the institution or office that provided the student with a scholarship. Singapore and Tanzania are more stringent, requiring their students studying abroad to post a bond that is forfeited unless they return. Egypt, too, has a bond and a requirement that scholarship aid must be repaid by those choosing to live abroad. (When the bond has cosigners, who may be relatives, severe financial hardship can result when a student "jumps ship.") Pakistan attempts to levy a tax on its expatriate nationals. The least popular financial measure is no doubt the high "exit tax" charged emigrants on their departure. This device, once used by the Soviet Union, is now less common than it was in the LDCs, but here and there it still exists.

There is not likely to be a halt or even a slowdown in the brain drain for years to come. Only stern restrictions, rapid rises in relative income, or the proposed new tax offer much hope. Of these, the first is impalatable, the second is unlikely to be a solution in the short run, and the last is rather radical politics in what, for the developed countries, is a rather conservative era. It is one of those clear situations where an attempt at individual betterment may be detrimental to a country's development prospects. As such, the issue is likely to be with us for a long time.

FORMING HUMAN CAPITAL WITH HEALTH AND NUTRITION

The emphasis on human capital has helped to increase the appeal of a strategy based on providing basic human services in health and nutrition.[44] A human development approach involves an awareness that human capabilities must be maintained before they can be increased, a perception that if economic growth bypasses a large segment of a country's population, then low standards of public health and nutrition will mean inferior human capital. The approach postulates that the poorest may be unable to obtain income transfers from government because of a lack of political power. It suggests that a dangerous psychological dissatisfaction with the relative affluence of others may arise. A human development approach also proposes that living standards of the less-advantaged part of the population

A BRAIN-DRAIN TAX?

An innovative solution to the problem based on some concrete economic analysis has been proposed by Jagdish Bhagwati of Columbia University. Bhagwati suggests that developed countries place a supplementary income tax on the earnings of emigrants from LDCs living in those rich countries and then channel the funds collected via the United Nations back to the LDCs for development spending. The rationale for such a tax is compensation for the losses of all those remaining behind in the LDCs, with revenue collected and transferred from the emigrants who have been able to improve their economic positions through employment in a developed country. In support of the tax a moral principle is invoked: The lucky few from LDCs, trained in their homeland and now earning substantially higher incomes in a developed country, should share their gains with those left behind.

Diagrammatically, the case appears as in Figure 10.6.[45] The marginal revenue product curve of skilled labor for a developed country (MRP_{dev}) is shown running from upper left to lower right. The curve for an LDC (MRP_{ldc}) is shown running from a right-hand vertical axis. Before immigration the quantity of skilled labor employed in the developed country is 0_1A; in the LDC the quantity is 0_2A. The wage, equal to productivity, is *RA* in the LDC and *PA* in the developed country; earnings are much higher in the latter. When migration opens, *AB* skilled labor migrates from the LDC to the developed country, the motive for the migration ceasing when labor productivity in the two countries is equalized at *QB*. National income in the LDC is reduced by the area *ARQB*. A part of this loss is what used to be earned by those who left, *ARTB*. But another part is lost by those who stay behind, *RQT*. The national income of the developed country will rise by *APQB*; of this the migrants themselves get *ASQB* (thus gaining *RSQT* over what they earned in the LDC), while others in the developed country gain *SPQ*. Here, in summary, are the main concerns: the loss to the LDC of *RQT*, the gain to the emigrant of *RSQT*, and the gain to others in the developed country of *SPQ*. These gains and losses are used to justify the tax, which could be applied to either *SPQ* or *RSQT* or both.

The LDC Group of 77 endorsed the Bhagwati proposal, initially in 1978, and recommended changes in national tax laws to bring it into use. The suggestion was not followed up, however, because of some obvious difficulties. One is the reluctance to bend national tax laws for international purposes. Another is unwillingness to tax refugees from a tyrannical administration. Many educated Iranians, Cubans, Vietnamese, and others are working abroad not for the money but out of necessity or conscience. Under the proposal, how would they be treated? Who would distinguish immigrants who came for gain from those who had to come? Yet the idea is still an intriguing one. A World Bank study of some years ago suggests that such a tax would finance about a 13% increment to U.S. foreign aid if it were set at a flat rate of 10% of earned income, if immigrants earned the U.S. average for their occupation, and if 90% of those who came stayed.[46]

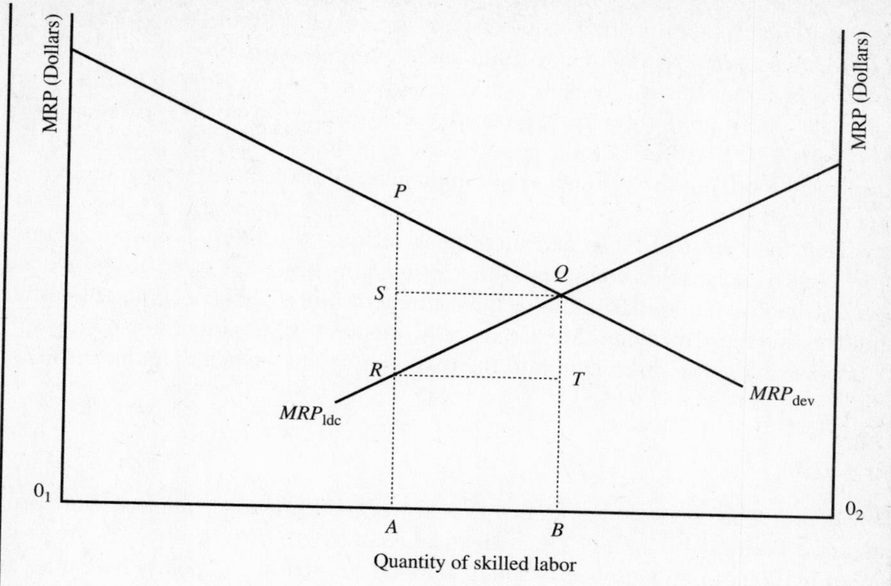

Figure 10.6 Analysis of brain drain tax suggests that losses to an LDC from emigration of *RQT* could be compensated for by a tax on the emigrant to a developed country of *RSQT* and/or a tax on the other factors that gain *SPQ* from the immigration.

may be improvable more rapidly and at a lower cost in resources if the inadequate standards of health, sanitation, and nutrition are attacked directly, rather than waiting for growth in income to bring them about.[47] If labor productivity can be raised by such methods, then an eventual payoff in terms of higher income and output is to be expected. The returns to this form of investment can certainly be tangible as well as raising the quality of life.

Aside from the argument that health and nutrition can be improved more rapidly with a direct approach than through eventual income growth, advocates of programs to improve human capital posit that a direct approach can prevent problems that a market system might not recognize or might not cure for some time. (1) In the absence of a national nutrition strategy, consumers may possibly not optimize their food consumption as income rises. Wheat may be substituted for rice or polished rice for coarse grains because of taste or for reasons of prestige. Tasty and prestigious crops may bring more profits than the more nutritious but less-profitable pulses (legumes) such as chickpeas, lentils, and beans. Nonfood items may be substituted for food. (2) Within households, social strictures may lead to a result where women and children consume less food as a proportion of needs than do men. (3) Health and nutrition may normally be looked after by an extended family of relatives, but an individual without such family ties may be on his or her own unless a program fills the breach. (4) With a market system as long as income is unequally distributed, there is no guarantee that malnutrition and poor health will be eliminated. Because of their poverty, some people will command inadequate supplies of food, impure water, and unsanitary conditions unless government intervenes directly.[48]

That the thrust of these arguments has substantial validity is hard to refute. How else to explain that countries with a strong attachment to basic human development, such as Sri Lanka or China, have attained similar life expectancies to other countries such as Brazil and Mexico on only one-seventh the income per capita?[49] Below we divide the discussion into the two separate areas, health and nutrition.

Health[50]

In Chapter 8 we reviewed evidence that better health leads to higher labor productivity. Poor health in the LDCs causes a loss of two to three times as many work days per 1000 of population as in the developed countries, and nearly five times as many in sub-Saharan Africa.[51] Obviously, improved health leads to a better quality of life as well.

There is little debate that income growth does eventually lead to improvements in public health. In the developed world, for example, rising income levels led to better water supplies and sanitation; the incidence of cholera and typhoid in Britain declined long before effective treatment was available. Tuberculosis in the United States fell from 200 cases per 100,000 people to 70 per 100,000 from 1900 to 1930, and then to 30 in the 1950s, before chemotherapy was available.[52] But there are strong arguments that waiting for income growth to improve health takes too much time. Directly by making people more "able-bodied," and indirectly by bolstering morale, better health will improve labor productivity and the personal sense of well-being (and so the political climate).

The Need for Low-Cost Health Care It is plain that the LDCs will have to go a long way before they are able to match today's level of health care expenditure in the developed countries, with their hospital-based systems and hi-tech methods. The rich countries spend 7% to 14% of GDP for care, compared to only 2% by the LDCs. In 1986, U.S. expenditure per person per year on health was $1926, compared to South Korea's $150, Brazil's $85, China's $11, the LDC average of $6, and $3 each in Ethiopia and Zaire.[53]

Not only is developed-country health care expensive, but it is not the most rapid way to improve conditions of health. The need for LDCs to economize and their need for haste has led to emphasis on universal, basic, low-cost treatment. It should indeed be possible to deliver health care more cheaply in the LDCs. Health care is often labor-intensive, and in the LDCs real opportunity costs are lower than in the developed countries. Low-cost health improvement can have large payoffs. For example, in Bangladesh an inexpensive rural clinic could treat 10,000 people for a sum ($2700) that would only fund the recurrent cost of a single hospital bed serving an average of 27 patients. At the margin, *raising* spending by about the equivalent of half a bed ($1300) would allow attendance at a rural clinic to rise by 7000 to 10000 people.[54] Such clinics in the poor areas of many LDCs have played a major role in the rise of the LDCs' average life expectancy by over a third during the past three decades.[55]

China, with its emphasis on inexpensive disease prevention especially in rural areas, has been the role model for low-cost care. The "barefoot doctors," selected from a local population, trained by the government, and returning to serve that same population, have been most remarked upon. But local public health personnel of all kinds are numerous in proportion to population and work directly to improve water supplies, sanitation, and nutrition.[56] Even by the 1970s, China could boast health levels about the same as the United States had in the 1930s, remarkable for a country with a per capita income only just over $300. Shanghai currently boasts a longer life expectancy and lower infant mortality than New York City.* In many LDCs, however, primary health care is still more a challenge than a reality—in Africa, for example, 70% of the population is out of reach of health workers—but it remains a focus for health policy.

In many countries the World Health Organization and UNICEF are now sponsoring primary health care programs involving universal, low-cost care. The emphasis in these programs is on community health workers (CHW), with limited training, and volunteers who can refer patients to dispensaries and hospitals. The special need for such a new system lies in the scarcity of doctors: one for 19,000 people in the low income LDCs, one for 390 people in the developed countries.[57] Because of the scarcity, waits for health care can be extraordinary: eight hours on average in Nigeria, five hours in Uganda.[58] (It should be noted that doctors sometimes lobby industriously to limit the spread of community health workers, whom they see as providing competition.)

Adding to the scarcity of health care in many areas is the urban bias.[59] Sixty percent to 70% of the doctors in LDCs commonly work in an urban setting. The number is as high as 80% in India, but the cities contain only 26% of the population. In Colombia, 38% of the population is rural but only 19% of the government's

*Northeast Brazil has adopted a version of China's barefoot doctor program. Local people are trained as government paramedics and paid the minimum wage. Their visits to poor families have helped cut the state's infant mortality by 32% in a three-year period. UNICEF has called this program "a model for poor-country child health care." See *The Economist*, December 7, 1991. It should be noted that China's health statistics have been harmed in recent years because of organizational problems having to do with the market reforms in rural areas. Some 16,500 private and collective clinics closed during the year 1991. China has moved far toward private payment for medical services with some government-supported insurance. See *The Economist*, December 14, 1991.

subsidies for health go to them. The bias is largely due to the urban location of heavily subsidized, expensive hospitals. Curative medicine involving hospitals is far more costly, up to ten times as much as preventative medicine. Yet the LDCs spend about the same proportion (about 40% to 50%) of their health budgets on hospitals as developed countries do. Numerous low-income LDCs spend even more, Bangladesh 56%, Brazil 70%, some others 60% to 80%, even though few people will ever find themselves in hospital. There are African countries where a single hospital in the capital city consumes 75% of the government health budget.[60] These percentages should be sharply cut back. The opposite happened during the debt crisis, however. When health budgets were reduced during the debt crisis, the cuts were focused more on disease control than on hospitals.*

A desirable step would seem to be the introduction of user fees, or increases in them.[61] Charges for urban hospital patients who can afford it would seem called for. These fees could be structured so that poor people go first to a free clinic. Modest fees charged at clinics to those that could afford them could be useful in halting malingering. The revenues collected from these fees could be used to extend health coverage for the poor, whether urban or rural. (But Ghana's experience warns that people may use the health services less as a result, turning to medicines and traditional healers.)

Another possible reform is to avoid the serious cost problems caused by a preference for modern techniques. India, for example, attains a 95% cure rate for tuberculosis with modern chemotherapy compared to 85% with cheaper treatment with the drug isoniazid. Yet by using isoniazid it could reach 100 times more people for the same cost. One country asked the WHO for a computer-assisted wholebody scanner when the same amount of money could have immunized all children for 10 years, saving perhaps 500,000 lives.[62] The high cost of brand-name pharmaceutical drugs presents a similar problem. So little is available for spending per person—$7 in China, $3 in India, $2 in Bangladesh and Mozambique, compared to $191 in the United States—that any economies in purchasing are welcome. It has transpired that the cost of drugs can be cut by as much as half or even two-thirds through national purchasing in bulk, and UNICEF now gives assistance to LDCs for this.[63] In addition, the World Health Organization has compiled a list of 220 drugs it considers most essential, helping LDCs to be more selective in their purchasing.

Government budget problems, the debt crisis, and the high costs of health care have led to spending cutbacks in many countries—a fall that was greatest in

*Another cause of the urban bias toward health care is the absence of formal health insurance and social security programs in the countryside. In the LDCs, wide-ranging public or private health insurance is still not common, though they are now found in some countries including Brazil, Chile, China, Costa Rica, South Korea, and a few others. Only about 15% of the world's population is insured for medical expenses.

Africa.[64] Fortunately, however, standards of health in the LDCs have stood up rather well to the spending cutbacks, though for how long still remains to be seen.[65]

Why Death Rates Stay High The main reason why LDC death rates stay high is continuing high mortality among infants and young children under 5 years of age. Though such mortality has been cut by more than half over the last 30 years, it is still 160 per 1000 live births in the 55 LDCs classified by the United Nations as low in human development, and 240 to 270 in the present record holders, Afghanistan, Guinea-Bissau, Mozambique, and Sierra Leone.[66] These figures compare to only 7 to 11 in the developed countries (and Hong Kong and Singapore as well). It is noteworthy that, over time, countries with the worst child mortality have been the least successful in bringing it down, contrary to expectations that the first steps would be the easiest. Wars and famines, together with economic problems that have prevented the deployment of preventative technologies, appear to be the reasons why.[67]

Among young children, the main cause of death, by far—encompassing five to ten million children per year—is the diarrheal condition that can come from cholera but takes many other forms. It is transmitted by human fecal content in soil, food, and water. A new treatment called oral rehydration therapy has replaced the older and much more difficult intravenous drip. It has brought a great advance, saving about a half-million children every year.[68] Influenza and pneumonia types of disease are also big killers of children, affecting four to five million per year. The two together are responsible for about 40% of all deaths from birth to 5 years of age in LDCs; the comparable figure is 2% in the developed countries. We saw in Chapter 9 that malaria, once thought to be under control, is making a comeback.

Improved water supplies and better sanitation would represent a major advance because water and sanitation problems are responsible for about 80% of sickness in LDCs. The associated diseases include cholera, dysentery, typhoid, hookworm, guinea worm, roundworm, river blindness, trachoma, and yaws, among other illnesses.* Currently only 45% of the population of the least developed countries has access to safe water (up, however, from 21% in 1975 to 1980), only 32% has access to proper sanitation.[69] By improving water and sanitation, it is believed that as much as three-quarters of the incidence of some of the tropical diseases

---

*Sometimes, disappointingly, activities that promote economic growth can also bring an increase in diseases associated with water. Schistosomiasis (carried by snail-borne parasites and causing chronic debilitation) and onchocerciasis (more commonly called river blindness) have been spread by new dams and irrigation canals. The rise of schistosomiasis in Egypt and the Sudan is striking; it causes one in five deaths in Egypt and can rarely be cured in rural conditions. See Halfdan Mahler, "People," 68; and Robert P. Ambroggi, "Water," *Scientific American* 243, no. 3 (September 1980): 106.

AIDS IN AFRICA

There is a particularly high level of AIDS in Africa, with a substantial likelihood that this disease poses a very serious long-run threat to economic and social well-being.[70] The World Health Organization estimates that more than 8 million Africans were HIV positive in 1993, amounting to over 60% of all the cases in the world. It estimates that 1.2 million Africans have already died from AIDS. Alarming predictions suggest that after 50 years, national HIV infection might rise to 10% to 20% or in some cases even 50% of the adult population. Already 25% of the population in several African capital cities are HIV positive, and 50% of new hospital admissions are AIDS-related. The prevalence is much greater in urban areas and tends to affect higher-income and higher-skilled men out of proportion, which means that the economic damage will be great. For a vivid example of how serious the situation is thought to be, it is estimated that unless decisive action is taken, Tanzania's GDP could be reduced by 15% to 25% by the year 2010, and its working-age population by 20%. A breakthrough in the treatment of this disease would be a major gain to the LDCs.

could be eliminated.[71] Piped water and system maintenance are expensive, however, and in many countries would cost per person as much as a quarter of annual per capita income.*

Nutrition[72]

Better nutrition is another element in a strategy that emphasizes basic human development. Chronic hunger kills more people than actual famines do.[73] In the 1960s and 1970s, it was believed that malnutrition was mostly a protein (and some vitamins and minerals) shortage, but later research showed that most people obtain sufficient protein from their regular diet. While protein deficiency is still recognized as a problem, attention has shifted to undernourishment—simply a shortage of food.

---

*Even in Latin America, which is relatively well-off, only 2% of sewage receives treatment. *WDR 1992*, 47. On occasion, cultural attitudes can interfere with improvements in water and sanitation. An excellent case in point involves the water supply in a Pathan village of the Northwest Frontier District of India. From time immemorial the village women walked 5 miles each way to a water supply to launder clothes. Then a laundering facility near the village was provided by foreign aid. The women refused to use it. A female anthropologist was hired to investigate. She reported that the women's husbands only rarely allowed them to leave their homes, and the weekly laundry expeditions—which they very much looked forward to—gave them a chance to talk and play for a whole day. The women also assumed that husbands would simply find something else for them to do if their laundering took less time. See Dasgupta, *An Inquiry into Well-Being and Destitution*, 536, citing Andrew Feldman.

Nutritional deficiencies are most common in Africa and Southeast Asia, less so in Latin America and the Middle East. The basic metabolic rate of calorie consumption is about 1300 calories per day. According to one widely quoted estimate, in 86 poor countries 23% of the population, or 436 million people, are thought to receive less than 1600 per day.[74] A level of 1600 calories per day will not allow for much physical activity; it is not sufficient for an active working life. At this level many people exhibit stunted growth and their health is at risk. Because in hard agricultural work calorie consumption can reach 3500 per day without weight gain, it is not surprising that studies indicate malnourished farmers work fewer hours per acre cultivated than do the well fed. There are great difficulties in obtaining accurate measurements of food intake, however, and the estimates of the number of people chronically undernourished vary widely, from 340 million to 730 million, excluding China.*

It appears that better nutritional standards were important in the development of Europe. Robert Fogel provides evidence that increased intake of calories reduced mortality and increased productivity in that region, with the same process likely to be at work in low-income LDCs.[75] Between 1965 and 1990, the number of countries around the world where people received the necessary calorie intake doubled from about 25 to about 50, and the average daily calorie supply in the least developed countries has now reached 2070.[76]

Malnutrition is largely correlated with poverty, so that even relatively rich LDCs, if they have high income inequality, can have serious undernourishment. Malnutrition of children is also correlated (inversely) with the education of the mother, partly due to nutritional information, but no doubt mostly due to the enhanced chances of increasing income through paid work. Inadequacies in nourishment are estimated to contribute to a third or more of infant and child deaths in the LDCs. Girls suffer more than boys, pregnant and nursing mothers more than other women, which exhibits the gender bias that characterizes many parts of the less developed world. Nutritional deficiencies are particularly noticeable in very young children, aged 18 to 24 months, just after nursing stops. Weight at this age is often 25% to 40% less than average for 15% to 25% of the population.[77] Not only may growth be stunted, but there is also the possibility of retardation in mental development when the condition is extreme. The retardation continues on intelligence tests even after the malnutrition is corrected. There are other data, though less confidence can be placed on them, showing that retardation and its continuance can occur even with more mild long-term malnutrition.[78] Immunity processes are also sometimes impaired. One does not often actually die from malnutrition, but it is a serious factor contributing to death from many causes.

*One difficulty is that adaptation can occur; that is, small and lean people may be quite efficient at converting food to work. In the absence of good data, reasonable proxies for nutritional status of children are height-for-age and weight-for-height. Increases in height are closely correlated with the decline in death rates in the now-developed countries. See *WDR 1986*, 7; W. C. Edmundson and P. V. Sukhatme, "Food and Work: Poverty and Hunger?" *Economic Development and Cultural Change* 38, no. 2 (January 1990): 263–280; Dasgupta, *An Inquiry into Well-Being and Destitution*, 82; and *WDR 1991*, 53.

Malnutrition is much cheaper to prevent than to cure.[79] The hospitals in low-income LDCs commonly contain many nutrition cases. In the Caribbean, 20% to 45% of the pediatric beds are taken up with such cases, as are 15% in India and 80% in Guatemala. Even though hospital stays are much less expensive in the LDCs than in the developed countries, a day there still costs at least 200 or 300 times as much as the daily cost of preventing child malnutrition with a small protein and calorie supplement.

Attacking Malnutrition What to do about nutrition problems is a major topic for research. In one sense the solution seems simple. It is thought that only about 2% of world grain output, if placed in the right mouths, would end malnutrition. As we have seen, though, the complication is how to get the food to the poor who need it. Attention has been directed to several new sorts of policy.[80]

1. The level of nutrition among the poor may be improved by raising their income level. In three case studies (carried out in Gambia, Guatemala, and Rwanda), a 10% increase in income from a base level of $100 was correlated with a 3.5% to 4.9% increase in household consumption of calories, and a 1.1% to 2.5% increase in the weight-for-age measurement of children.[81] The correlation between nutrition and poverty clearly points toward the desirability of development targeted toward the lower-income part of the population. It has been widely observed that cash-crop farmers eat better than subsistence food-crop farmers because their incomes are higher. Commercialization of agriculture is usually highly favorable for the nutritional standards of those who are able to accomplish it.[82] Fortunately, there is little evidence to suggest that more work by women in LDCs causes a decline in the nutritional standards of children; the higher income apparently more than offsets any negative effects.[83] A warning should be issued, however: Higher income may not lead to better nutrition if people do not believe they are malnourished or do not pay attention to nutrition, instead searching for more variety in their food when they can afford it. In that case, nutritional standards may not improve as much as might be expected as income increases. Indeed, it does appear that "nutrient elasticities with respect to income" are rather low.[84] In consequence, wide dissemination of information on nutrition is essential.
2. Production of the foods eaten by the poor, such as millet, coarse grains, and root crops, might be boosted. These crops have been neglected by agricultural researchers even though these and other carbohydrate foods provide 75% of the calories consumed in the lowest-income countries, compared with only 30% or so in countries above $3000 in per capita income. Millet and sorghum, for example, do badly in severe drought, and properly directed research might help. (Good work has, however, been done with these foods in several international research centers, including those of India, Colombia, and Nigeria.)
3. Food ration subsidies are effective in improving nutritional standards. Generally, however, they have proved to be very expensive, accounting for 10% to 20% of the government budget in Egypt (where spending on food

subsidies in the 1980s rose ten times in real terms over what it had been in the 1960s), Sri Lanka (where they once about a quarter of the budget), and elsewhere.

The main problem is that much of the food subsidy goes to people who do not need it.[85] Subsidizing foodstuffs such as wheat bread, refined flour, frozen meat, chicken, and vegetable oils are a sure way to channel the benefits to middle- and upper-class consumers who do not need the assistance. For example, in Morocco 80% of the budgetary cost of rural food subsidies did not go to the most needy. Egypt and Brazil are frequently cited as offenders in this regard. In Egypt, wealthy farmers have been known to buy the cheap (subsidized) bread loaves to feed to their donkeys and other livestock. In that country, urban households in the top quarter of the income distribution actually received about 20% more by value from the food subsidies than did households in the lowest quarter. In Sri Lanka, more than half the benefits from food subsidies went to middle- and higher-income families, and only one calorie in 13 was going to the malnourished. Once food subsidies are established, the vested interests make it hard to reduce them.

If an administration is strong-willed, it can use a means test that makes higher-income families ineligible for the aid, as Sri Lanka began to do during the late 1970s. Introducing a means test and ending the subsidies to those who do not need them are, however, always tough politically. Whatever the difficulties, many development economists now recommend some variant of the food stamps distributed to the poor in the United States as a much more economical substitute for across-the-board subsidies. Colombia, Jamaica, and Sri Lanka all have highly regarded food stamp programs that have cut costs. For example, both Jamaica and Sri Lanka were spending 5% to 6% of GDP on general food subsidies in the late 1970s; targeting their food subsidies toward the poor allowed a reduction in costs to about 1% of GDP in the mid-1980s.[86] When Sri Lanka began to use stamps for distributing fuel for cooking (kerosene) in 1979, it issued the stamps only to the poor half of the population, and for the rest it tripled the formerly much-subsidized kerosene price. Kerosene consumption fell almost immediately by 25%. Large economies were also made in food distribution.* Mexico used food coupons for tortillas when phasing out its universal food subsidies in 1985 to 1986, and then in 1990 moved to a sort of credit card

*Problems can develop, however. The poor lost political help when the Sri Lankan subsidies were limited to them, so few steps were taken when the value of these subsidies eroded because of inflation. Inflation halved the real value of the stamps, which were not indexed. Moreover, parliament refused to pass a law allowing the government to check people's declarations of income, and so about 30% of the better-off half of the population continued to get the stamps. Calorie consumption among the poor dropped by 8%, and the proportion of the population in poverty rose from 23% in 1978 to 27% in 1987. See *HDR 1991*, 65; a thorough study by N. Edirisinghe, "The Food Stamp Scheme in Sri Lanka: Costs, Benefits, and Options for Modification," *International Food Policy Research Institute Research Report No. 58* (1987); and Timothy Besley and Ravi Kanbur, "The Principles of Targeting," in V. N. Balasubramanyam and Sanjaya Lall, eds., *Current Issues in Development Economics* (New York, 1991), 69–90.

arrangement for poor recipients. (But as so often happens, the program has much more coverage in urban areas than in rural ones.)[87]

Some countries may simply not be able to manage a food stamp program because income records are weak and administrative costs are high.[88] Zambia, for example, recently informed the World Bank that it lacked the administrative capacity to adopt such a program. In these cases, which sometimes are just a way to say the political will is not there, a number of alternatives are available. For example, subsidies could be directed only toward the foods that the nonpoor do not eat, such as sorghum in Bangladesh and cassava in Brazil. Alternatively, the subsidy program might be established only in the poorest areas, as in projects in Brazil and Colombia, or it might be operated only at certain times of the year.[89]

4. Another possible strategy is to target any vulnerable groups specifically. Food supplements could be made available to pregnant women and young children only, with the distribution undertaken at schools and health clinics. Such programs tend to be much cheaper, but they run the risk that these same vulnerable groups will find their consumption not really increased because of a family decision to cut the amounts made available to them at home.
5. Finally, rather than providing food, a program might concentrate on food additives and fortification during processing. The difficulty here is that the poor buy little processed food in the first place, and even that from small processors, so that such programs can be uneconomically expensive.

Famines

Famines, the extreme of malnourishment, have been the subject of much recent research.[90] They are particularly vicious in that children always make up a disproportionate share of the victims. Many scholars now attribute modern famines not to a fall in the food available to a nation, though this can obviously be a factor, but to local drought leading to a local fall in income, leaving the poor unable to afford adequate food if they cannot grow it themselves. Because the very poor spend such a high proportion of their income on food (83% for the poorest fifth of the population in India, which still provides fewer than 1500 calories per day), a fall in cash availability does have a catastrophic potential. Victims may include small and tenant farmers who cannot find work after their crops fail, as in Ethiopia in 1973. Pastoralists who have to trade their cows for food may also find the consequences of drought severe, as in Africa all across the Sahel in 1973 and again in 1984 to 1987.

The impact is especially hard on the landless, who are mainly casual, unskilled farm laborers. The damage may stem from an employment decline as agricultural output falls. Because of the floods in Bangladesh during 1974, rural landless laborers lost their jobs planting and transplanting rice and so lost their income long before any actual food shortfall showed up.[91] Private food stocks rose following panic buying and hoarding. It appears that traders may have overestimated the damage to future crops; rice prices therefore rose more than was warranted. (But bans on hoarding are not a particularly good idea either, because they are too easy

POLITICS AND FAMINE

In several works, A.K. Sen has called attention to the importance of political pressures in spurring goverments to famine relief measures.[92] Such pressures are powerful in India, where no full-scale famines have occured for many years. But the impulse is less easy to sustain against more mild hunger, which still persists. In China, where grass-roots politics was stifled during the Great Leap Forward, policy mistakes led to what scholars are now calling the greatest famine of modern times during the years 1959 to 1961.[93] Policy problems in Colonel Mengistu's Ethiopia—food distribution not allowed in the rebellious northern provinces, prevention of stockpiling with anti-hoarding laws that also prohibited private road transport of food, a move toward state farms, a low price policy that discouraged private production, and enforced resettlement of hungry refugees in the south—made Ethiopia's experienced with famine in the 1980s worse than it had to be. Somalia is an obvious case of failed entitlements, as warlords and their gangs keep food distribution in their own hands. Some countries (Sudan, for example) partly for political reasons did not ask for food aid until too late. Needless hunger ensued.

to avoid. The government must work to overcome such destabilization by food distribution, imports, and by directing a glare of publicity at big offenders. It may also want to consider temporary price controls.) The Bangladesh famine of 1974 killed perhaps a million people.

Ethiopia in 1973 to 1974 was suffering from serious drought, but the major food problems were localized in areas that were relatively accessible. A major complication was that farmers stopped hiring labor; even though food prices rose only a little, significant numbers of people were less able to buy it. (This was a "slump famine," in the words of Jean Drèze and A. K. Sen.) In Bengal during 1943, a rapid rise in the demand for food caused by the wartime boom in urban incomes and government buying of food to feed war workers, a poor crop year, and poor transport made worse as the government destroyed boats to deny them to the Japanese combined to cause the harm.* The food supply was not the lowest of the decade, but the upshot was India's last great famine.[94] (This was a "boom famine," in the language of Drèze and Sen.)

In an influential argument of A. K. Sen, the entitlement to food is more important than its availability.[95] Entitlement can come from personal income, through membership in an extended family, or through government relief programs. In an unadulterated market system, if entitlements fail among particular classes or occupations, then famines follow. Even the famines caused by the great

*Not infrequently, war can cause a food shortage which is the direct cause of the hunger. Examples include Biafra during the Nigerian Civil War in the late 1960s, Kampuchea in the late 1970s, and Mozambique and Somalia in recent years.

drought in sub-Saharan Africa, at their worst in 1984 and 1987 when they killed half a million to a million people in Ethiopia and Sudan, were not caused by the general unavailability of food. Politics often plays a role, as discussed in the accompanying box.

Famine Relief Foreign aid in the form of food for the starving clearly has more public support in the developed countries than other forms of aid, and these countries now mobilize quickly for famine relief in the LDCs. Their extraordinary efforts, especially during the last decade, meant for the most part that sufficient quantities of food have been made available in countries hit by famine. (In the past it took far longer to mobilize large-scale food aid, five years in the case of the African Sahel during the drought of the late 1960s and early 1970s.)[96] Sometimes, however, the food was not in the right place, and overloaded transport systems and bureaucratic inefficiencies impeded the relief programs.

The experience emphasized that several seemingly simple steps remain to be taken in coping with emergency famine relief. Data collection to give early warning remains poor, though much improved from the days of simply examining crop statistics, which always come in late. LDC governments must do a better job at responding to initial signals, such as wanderers on the roads following a drought, rather than waiting for signs of actual starvation. Some countries have foreign trade policies that impeded food imports and government monopolies that mismanaged food distribution. These policies did not help.

The developed countries had to learn that transport to stricken areas is often more crucial than providing the food itself. These countries have never agreed to establish food buffer stocks in famine-prone zones. Such stocks would seem a good idea. Further, although many organizations both public and private became involved, their efforts were sometimes little coordinated. There is definite scope for improvement on this score. (The UN World Food Program, dating from 1961, is an extremely valuable agency. It serves as an organizer and clearinghouse for information, and has become a major player.)[97]

Above all, it took a long time to learn that food aid may avert starvation for a time in the particular place where the food is distributed, but it will do nothing to change the conditions that caused the famine. This is especially evident when hungry people are collected in unhealthy refugee camps, with nothing to do but wait for better times. As a result, especially in Ethiopia during 1984 through 1987, the World Food Program pushed the new idea of "food for work" projects, which enabled victims of famine to remain in their villages and on their farms so that they could maintain their productive assets, even if small, and some measure of their independence and self-respect. In return for food rations, recipients worked on soil and water conservation schemes that resulted in millions of trees planted and hundreds of thousands of miles of new terracing to control erosion.[98]

Food for work programs are self-selecting because wages are low and the work is hard and manual. The poor and hungry with their low opportunity costs are the only participants.[99] The short-term goals of averting starvation and preserving some of the dignity of recipients were joined to the laudable long-term goal of altering the conditions that caused the famine in the first place.

A further lesson soon emerged, however. It was found preferable to pay cash wages in relief programs, "cash for work," when possible. The cash can be disbursed much more rapidly than emergency food. It raises the demand for food, rather than diminishing it as happens when free food is passed out. The cash when spent will raise food prices, so the private marketing system will add to the quantity of food supplied, mainly through higher imports of food from other areas in the same country or from abroad. If food is donated by aid-givers, it can be sold for money, so financing the cash-for-work plans. Cash for work is an especially good idea if local prices are below world prices or if traders can deliver food more efficiently than aid agencies. The resulting rise in food prices will erode the value of the aid, of course, but recipients will still be better off and there is a greater incentive to bring food to the hungry. (Food for work is preferable to cash for work when corrupt officials find it easier to appropriate the cash than the food, or if a government is prone to inflationary financing, or if markets are very poorly developed or highly regulated. To be sure, developed-country governments often prefer food aid to cash aid because of the surpluses generated by their farm programs and because budget deficits make financial aid difficult.)[100]

Experience with cash for work has been good. It has led to short-term employment and hence food for millions in India's Maharashtra state, and has also been highly successful in several African countries and in parts of Latin America. In some cases, the schemes have been managed by private enterprise, with government paying some or most of the bills.[101] The resulting roads, wells, and the like built by the workers have the beneficial effect of raising income even further, although the initial cash payments are the main object. Needless to say, cash aid will be less successful or fail if it is administered corruptly, if state pricing inhibits supplies, or if a civil war is going on. In that case, direct delivery of food may be necessary, as in Somalia. Obviously, the work provided must not be too hard for the very poor and hungry, so small terraces may be more appropriate than roads or deep wells. Finally, after the end of the drought the lack of seed and breeding animals must not be overlooked. If they are, there may be a long delay in the recovery. These lessons had immediate use, because in 1993 to 1994, drought returned to the horn of East Africa—where because of population growth there were now 20 million more people than during the famine of the 1980s.[102]

Banning Exports? Self-Sufficiency Versus Self-Reliance Should food exports be banned from countries suffering from famine? Certainly a country in this situation must either have a food stockpile, or import more, or export less. But evidently, banning food exports will be damaging if a country is exporting a high-value commodity and can import cheap foodstuffs in return. The question calls attention to the difference in the terms self-sufficiency and self-reliance. *Self-sufficiency* means producing one's own food, whereas *self-reliance* means being able to consume enough food either by producing it, or producing something more valuable and exporting it in order to import cheap food—the price of which on world markets has been declining for years. Self-reliance involves the pursuit of a country's comparative advantage, while self-sufficiency may not.

A RISK IN A HUMAN CAPITAL APPROACH

Few, if any, would disagree with the aims of a human capital or basic human development approach discussed in this section. There are, however, two caveats. First, goals and results involving human capital are hard to quantify (much harder than income growth, for example) and so hard to analyze. How does one go about comparing a program that doubles literacy and lowers the incidence of malaria 10% with another that halves malaria and increases literacy 10%?[103] Because the ramifications are wide and difficult to measure, informed decision-making is not easy. We return to the topic of analyzing and quantifying costs and benefits in Chapter 12.

Second, there is always the risk that a human capital strategy might conflict with some of the means for achieving higher income per person. Any costs of human capital formation may be far more than recompensed by increases in labor productivity, but it is certainly conceivable that this might not be so. The funding for a human capital improvement, if from domestic taxation, might directly reduce saving and investment. The taxes might involve high administrative costs and therefore a deadweight loss; they might discourage work effort and entrepreneurship. In Chapter 1 we encountered evidence that pointed to the reverse being the case—that concentration on basic human development showed significant correlation by country to more rapid income growth. Yet it would be optimistic indeed to forget the possible negative consequences, and the careful development economist will be alert to their appearance.

Whatever the difficulties in finding reasonable solutions, it is beyond dispute that approaches emphasizing human capabilities do have the effect of focusing far more attention on the health and nutrition standards of the poorer part of the population in the LDCs. That effect is likely to be a lasting one.

NOTES

1. For a critical review of the subject, see Mark Blaug, "The Empirical Status of Human Capital Theory: A Slightly Jaundiced Survey," *Journal of Economic Literature* 13, no. 3 (1976): 827–855. All recent issues of the UN's *Human Development Report* treat education, nutrition, and health, and *WDR 1990* and *WDR 1993* also focused on these issues. I have used them frequently.
2. See Mark Gersowitz, "Saving and Investment," in Hollis Chenery and T. N. Srinivasan, eds., *Handbook of Development Economics*, vol. 1 (Amsterdam, 1988), 394–395; and J. B. Knight and R. H. Sabot, "Educational Policy and Labour Productivity: An Output Accounting Exercise," *Economic Journal* 97 (March 1987): 199–214.
3. See Lester C. Thurow, *Dangerous Currents: The State of Economics* (New York, 1983), 178–179.
4. See *WDR 1980*, 47–48; and Pan A. Yotopoulos and Jeffrey B. Nugent, *Economics of Development: Empirical Investigations* (New York, 1976), 186–188.
5. For these data, see George Psacharopoulos, *Returns to Education: An International Comparison* (Amsterdam, 1973), especially table 8.4. For work on education and development, see T. Paul Schultz, "Education Investments and Returns," in Hollis Chenery and T. N. Srinivasan, eds., *Handbook of Development Economics*, vol. 1 (Amsterdam,

1988): 543–630; George Psacharopoulos, "Education and Development: A Review," *World Bank Research Observer* 3, no, 1 (January 1988): 99–116; George Psacharopoulos and Maureen Woodhall, *Education for Development: Analysis of Investment Choices* (Oxford, 1985); and numerous other works by Psacharopoulos, including "Education and Returns to Education: An Updated International Comparison," *Comparative Education* (October 1981); "The Economics of Higher Education in Developing Countries," *Comparative Education Review* (June 1982); and "Education as an Investment," *Finance and Development* 19, no. 3 (1982): 39–42.

6. See *HDR 1992*, 69.
7. See Yotopoulos and Nugent, *Economics of Development*, 195.
8. George Psacharopoulos, "Education and Development: A Review," *World Bank Research Observer* 3, no. 1 (January 1988): 99–116.
9. The formula here is from Psacharopoulos, "Education as an Investment," 40, as amended in *Finance and Development* 19, no. 4 (1982): 49. Psacharopoulos and Woodhall, *Education for Development* (Oxford, 1985), analyzes the issue. T. W. Schultz won a Nobel Prize in economics in part because of work of this type.
10. For further confirmation of high returns to education, see Gregory Mankiw, David Romer, and David Weil, "A Contribution to the Empirics of Economic Growth," *NBER Working Paper No. 3541*, 1991; *WDR 1991*, 43; and Lawrence H. Summers, *Investing in All the People*, World Bank Policy Research Working Paper No. 905, 1992.
11. For this paragraph, see T. Paul Schultz, "Education Investments and Returns," 598; *HDR 1992*, 69; and *WDR 1991*, 57. A book-length study is D. T. Jamison and L. J. Lau, *Farmer Education and Farm Efficiency* (Baltimore, 1981). Productivity increases are higher or lower depending on whether complementary inputs were available or not. See *WDR 1980*, 48.
12. *WDR 1991*, 57, which also cites a variety of other evidence on the subject.
13. For a recent survey, see E. King and M. A. Hill, eds., *Women's Education in Developing Countries* (Baltimore, 1992).
14. Lawrence H. Summers, *Investing in All the People*.
15. See especially Dasgupta, *An Inquiry into Well-Being and Destitution*, 525, citing work by D. R. Gross and B. A. Underwood; T. Paul Schultz, *Economics of Population*, 117–119; Constantina Safilios-Rothschild, "The Role of the Family in Development," *Finance and Development* 17, no. 4 (1980): 44–47; and *WDR 1980*, 50.
16. *WDR 1991*, 49.
17. *WDR 1991*, 56.
18. See *HDR 1991*, 62, 67.
19. *WDR 1988*, 134, 136.
20. For this paragraph see Emmanuel Jimenez, "The Public Subsidization of Education and Health in Developing Countries: A Review of Equity and Efficiency," *World Bank Research Observer* 1, no. 1 (1986): 118, 125, quoting work by Alain Mingat and J. P. Tan; *HDR 1991*, 62, 67; and Douglas Albrecht and Adrian Ziderman, "Student Loans: An Effective Instrument for Cost Recovery in Higher Education?" *World Bank Research Observer* 8, no. 1 (January 1993): 71–90.
21. See World Bank, *The East Asian Miracle* (New York, 1993), Chapter 5.
22. *HDR 1993*, 12.
23. *WDR 1990*, 79.
24. For the figures, see *HDR 1994*, 138–139.
25. This is the conclusion of Adriaan Verspoor, "Educational Development: Priorities for the Nineties," *Finance and Development* 27, no. 1 (March 1990): 20–23. For Tanzania and Zaire, see *WDR 1991*, 56.

26. See *The Economist*, May 25, 1985, 110.
27. *South*, January, 1987.
28. *The Economist*, August 25, 1979, 54.
29. *WDR 1990*, 79.
30. See John Middleton, Adrian Ziderman, and Arvil Adams, "Making Vocational Training Effective," *Finance and Development* 27, no. 1 (March 1990): 30–32; Howard Pack, "Productivity and Industrial Development in Sub-Saharan Africa," *World Development* 21, no. 1 (January 1993): 1–16; *WDR 1979*, 53; and *The Economist*, April 28, 1984.
31. Middleton, Ziderman, and Adams, "Making Vocational Training Effective," 30–32.
32. See *WDR 1980*, 50.
33. A book-length study is William Glaser, *The Brain Drain* (London, 1978). I also utilized *WDR 1983*, 103–106; and *WDR 1984*, 102.
34. *HDR 1994*, 168–169.
35. *WDR 1984*, 101.
36. For the data in this paragraph, see *HDR 1992*, 56–57; *WDR 1984*, 102.
37. *HDR 1994*, 65; *WDR 1984*, 102; *The Economist*, August 18, 1979; and articles in the press.
38. *Statistical Abstract of the United States 1993* (Washington, D.C., 1993), 185; and also see Vinod B. Agarwal and Donald K. Winkler, "Foreign Demand for United States Higher Education: A Study of Developing Countries in the Eastern Hemisphere," *Economic Development and Cultural Change* 33, no. 3 (1985): 623.
39. *WDR 1983*, 105.
40. *WDR 1983*, 105.
41. *WDR 1983*, 105.
42. See the work of Don Patinkin and Harry Johnson in Walter Adams, ed., *The Brain Drain* (New York, 1968).
43. See Alan Smith, Christine Woesler de Panafieu, and Jean-Pierre Jarousse, "Foreign Student Flow and Policies in an International Perspective," and Mark Blaug, "The Economic Costs and Benefits of Overseas Students," both in Peter Williams, ed., *The Overseas Student Question* (London, 1981).
44. For the history of this strategy, see Douglas Rimmer, "Basic Needs and the Origins of the Development Ethos," *Journal of Developing Areas* 15 (January 1981): 215–238.
45. See Koichi Hamada, "Taxing the Brain Drain: A Global Point of View," in Jagdish Bhagwati, ed., *The New International Economic Order: The North–South Debate* (Cambridge, 1977).
46. See *WDR 1984*, 102.
47. See the discussions in *WDR 1990* and Paul Streeten et al., *First Things First* (New York, 1981).
48. See David Colman and Frederick Nixson, *Economics of Change in Less Developed Countries* (Deddington, 1978), 169; and Streeten et al., *First Things First*, 35–37.
49. Compare Amartya K. Sen, "Development: Which Way Now?" *Economic Journal* 93 (December 1983): 753.
50. *WDR 1993* focuses on health. I also drew on all recent issues of the UN's *HDR*.
51. *WDR 1993*, 3.
52. Halfdan Mahler, "People," *Scientific American* 243, no. 3 (September 1980): 69.
53. Charles C. Griffin, "The Need to Change Health Care Priorities in LDCs," *Finance and Development* 28, no. 1 (March 1991): 45–47; and *WDR 1993*, 158.
54. Griffin, "The Need to Change Health Care Priorities in LDCs," 45–47.
55. *HDR 1993*, 12.

56. See Lawrence H. Summers, "Knowledge for Effective Action," *Proceedings of the World Bank Annual Conference on Development Economics 1991* (Washington, D.C., 1992), 11; Morawetz, *Twenty-five Years of Economic Development*, 49; and *WDR 1980*, 74.
57. *HDR 1994*, 153.
58. *WDR 1988*, 135.
59. See Emmanuel Jimenez, "Public Subsidization of Education and Health," 120.
60. Griffin, "The Need to Change Health Care Priorities in LDCs," 45–47.
61. For this paragraph, see *WDR 1993*, 158; *HDR 1991*, 7, 66.
62. These examples are taken from Mahler, "People," 73.
63. *WDR 1993*, 145; *HDR 1991*, 63.
64. Jimenez, "Public Subsidization of Education and Health," 122. The fall in Africa was as much as 20%.
65. Jere R. Behrman and Anil B. Deolalikar, "Health and Nutrition," in Hollis Chenery and T. N. Srinivasan, eds., *Handbook of Development Economics*, vol. 1 (Amsterdam, 1988), 701.
66. See *HDR 1994*, 151; *HDR 1993*, 12.
67. Amartya Sen, "Economic Regress: Concepts and Features," *Proceedings of the World Bank Annual Conference on Development Economics 1993* (Washington, D.C., 1994), 315–333.
68. See *WDR 1980*, 54, 56; *The Economist*, November 3, 1984; and William U. Chandler, "Investing in Children," *Worldwatch Paper No. 64* (June 1985): 21–22.
69. *HDR 1994*, 133, 137.
70. *WDR 1993*, 32; *WDR 1991*, 63; Jill Armstrong, "Socioeconomic Implications of AIDS in Developing Countries," *Finance and Development* 28, no. 4 (December 1991): 14–17; Martha Ainsworth and Mead Over, "AIDS and African Development," *World Bank Research Observer* 9, no. 2 (July 1994): 203–240; and John T. Cuddington, "Modeling the Macroeconomic Effects of AIDS, with an Application to Tanzania," *World Bank Economic Review* 7 (May 1993): 173–189.
71. *WDR 1992*, 49.
72. For research on nutrition, see Dasgupta, *An Inquiry into Well-Being and Destitution*, particularly Chapter 17; Behrman and Deolalikar, "Health and Nutrition"; Jere R. Behrman, Anil B. Deolalikar, and Barbara L. Wolfe, "Nutrients: Impacts and Determinants," *World Bank Economic Review* 2, no. 3 (September 1988): 299–320; Shubh K. Kumar and Michael Lipton, eds., "Current Issues in Food Security," *World Development* 16, no. 9 (September, 1988); Nevin S. Scrimshaw and Lance Taylor, "Food," *Scientific American* 243, no. 3 (September 1980): 78–88; Thomas T. Poleman, "Quantifying the Nutrition Situation in Developing Countries," *Food Research Institute Studies* 18, no. 1 (1981): 1–58; *WDR 1990* and *WDR 1980*; and Morawetz, *Twenty-five Years of Economic Development*, 44–47.
73. See Jean Drèze and Amartya Sen, *Hunger and Public Action* (Oxford, 1990).
74. This is FAO data reported in Scrimshaw and Taylor, "Food," 80.
75. See Robert W. Fogel, "The Conquest of High Mortality and Hunger in Europe and America: Timing and Mechanisms," in Patrice Higonnet, David S. Landes, and Henry Roskovsky, eds., *Favorites of Fortune: Technology, Growth, and Economic Development Since the Industrial Revolution* (Cambridge, Mass., 1991); and also his "Economic Growth, Population Theory, and Physiology: The Bearing of Long-Term Processes on the Making of Economic Policy," *American Economic Review* 84, no. 3 (June 1994): 369–395.

76. *HDR 1994,* 155; *HDR 1993*, 12.
77. Scrimshaw and Taylor, "Food," 81.
78. For a discussion see *WDR 1990*, 81.
79. From the work of Alan Berg, reprinted in Gerald M. Meier, *Leading Issues in Economic Development*, 4th ed. (Oxford, 1984), 592, 595.
80. Material in this section not otherwise cited was taken from Behrman and Deolalikar, "Health and Nutrition;" various issues of the *WDR*, particularly *WDR 1990*, chap. 6, and *WDR 1986*, 90–94; and Alan Berg, "Improving Nutrition: The Bank's Experience," *Finance and Development* 22, no. 2 (1985): 32–35.
81. Hans P. Binswanger and Joachim von Braun, "Technological Change and Commercialization in Agriculture: The Effect on the Poor," *World Bank Research Observer* 6, no. 1 (January 1991): 61–62.
82. See Shubh K. Kumar and Michael Lipton, editors' introduction to "Current Issues in Food Security," *World Development* 16, no. 9 (September 1988): 994.
83. Based on a survey of over 50 studies. See Joanne Leslie, "Women's Work and Child Nutrition in the Third World," *World Development* 16, no. 11 (November 1988): 1341–1362.
84. Behrman and Deolalikar, "Health and Nutrition," 700–701.
85. For the following, see *HDR 1991*, 64; Behrman and Deolalikar, "Health and Nutrition," 693; and *WDR 1986*, 93.
86. *WDR 1990*, 117–118. See Dasgupta, *An Inquiry into Well-Being and Destitution*, Chapter 17, for a good discussion of targeted food subsidies.
87. *The Economist*, December 11, 1993; *WDR 1988*, 119.
88. *HDR 1991*, 64–65.
89. Behrman and Deolalikar, "Health and Nutrition," 694.
90. A major work in three volumes is Jean Drèze and Amartya Sen, eds., *The Political Economy of Hunger*, vol. 1, *Entitlement and Well-Being*, vol. 2, *Famine Prevention*, and vol. 3, *Endemic Hunger* (Oxford, 1990–1991). Also see "Current Issues in Food Security," *World Development* 16, no. 9 (September 1988); Donald Curtis, *Preventing Famine* (Boston, 1988); Drèze and Sen, *Hunger and Public Action*; G. Ainsworth Harrison, ed., *Famine* (New York, 1989); M. J. Mortimore, *Adapting to Drought* (Cambridge, 1989); Shlomo Reutlinger and Jack van Holst Pellekaan, *Ensuring Food Security in the Developing World: Issues and Options* (Washington, D.C., 1986); Michelle McAlpin, *Subject to Famine* (Princeton, N.J., 1983); and *The Economist*, October 20, 1990.
91. For this paragraph, see Drèze and Sen, *Hunger and Public Action*; and Martin Ravallion, "On Hunger and Public Action,' " *World Bank Research Observer* 7, no. 1 (January 1992): 1–16.
92. See"Development: Which Way Now?" 757–759, and the citations there.
93. See Penny Kane, *Famine in China, 1959–61* (New York, 1988).
94. See Alasdair I. MacBean, "Achieving Food Security," in Balasubramanyam and Lall, eds., *Current Issues in Development Economics*, 50–68; and *WDR 1982*, 89.
95. A. K. Sen, *Poverty and Famines: An Essay on Entitlement and Deprivation* (Oxford, 1981).
96. There is a review of international planning for famine relief by Barbara Huddleston et al., *International Finance for Food Security* (Baltimore, 1984); and see *WDR 1986*, 145–148.
97. See Ravallion, "On Hunger and Public Action," 1–16; and *WDR 1986*, 147.
98. Edward J. Clay, "Rural Public Works and Food-For-Work: A Survey," *World Development* 14, no. 10 (October/November 1986): 1237–1252; Chandler, "Investing in Children," 41; *The Economist*, January 12, 1990.

99. See Ehtisham Ahmad, "Social Security and the Poor: Choices for Developing Countries," *World Bank Research Observer* 6, no. 1 (January 1991): 105–127; and Timothy Besley and Ravi Kanbur, "The Principles of Targeting," in Balasubramanyam and Lall, eds., *Current Issues in Development Economics*, 69–90.
100. *The Economist*, April 10, 1993.
101. See *WDR 1990*, 98–100, 118.
102. *The Economist*, November 19, 1994.
103. Compare Gerald M. Meier, *Emerging from Poverty* (New York, 1984), 164.

Chapter 11

Rural Development

Agriculture in the LDCs

Poverty in the LDCs was and still is mainly rural. Whether the rural sector of the LDCs is a trap to be escaped or an opportunity to be exploited is one of the greatest of all the questions in economic development. For many years, until about the 1970s, rural development was widely neglected. After that, a striking change in attitudes set in, with agriculture viewed in a more positive light than before. Nowadays, the structure of rural poverty is changing. Rather than being permanently immersed in a subsistence economy, the rural poor are increasingly dependent on incomes derived from marketing their labor, often in nonagricultural activities. These developments, which are especially powerful in China, stress the need for a more diversified approach to rural development.[1]

URBAN BIAS, RURAL NEGLECT

From time immemorial, the representative farmer in a typical LDC has worked by hand on a small plot, facing a hostile tropical climate, with limited inputs of capital and technologies so elementary that productivity has been very low. Farming was a neglected sector, except by the tax men, whom we last saw in Chapter 4 using their marketing boards and state enterprises to tap this accessible source of government revenue. Official policy was usually marked by an urban bias, wherein funds obtained in part through high taxes on farming were funneled largely to manufacturing and showcase projects designed to benefit urban populations.

Further reflecting the urban bias, food prices in the cities were held down by subsidies and strict price controls. The budget costs of the cheap food were minimized by enforcing low government procurement prices in rural areas.[2]

Agricultural incomes depressed by only a third through these policies would have been thought relatively generous to the rural sector. On average, in LDCs the net effect on agriculture from government policies meant an income transfer out of agriculture of 46% between 1960 and 1984. It was not uncommon to find farmers receiving prices 25% to 30% below market-clearing levels, or even 50% to 75% in some cases.[3] For example, before its reforms of 1984 and 1985 Tanzania was paying its farmers about a fourth to a half the world market price for their main crops; India's farmers in 1989 were receiving 35% of the world price for their rice.[4] Obviously policymakers must have believed that the price elasticities of supply in agriculture were very low, or else they would have been much more concerned about the loss of output that such price reductions would entail.

The favored manufacturing sector was frequently sheltered behind high tariff walls, thus raising the prices paid by rural residents for the goods they produced. The protectionist government policies caused a lower level of imports, thus reducing the demand for foreign currencies and causing an overvalued exchange rate. Overvalued rates were also used to make the importing of necessary capital equipment easy for the manufacturing sector. The overvaluation in turn discouraged agricultural exports and encouraged the import of agricultural commodities. Protection of manufactured goods and overvalued exchange rates is often equivalent to a tax of over 20% on the rural sector.[5]

Table 11.1 shows the combined effect on agriculture of the low prices paid for farmers' output and the further effects of overvalued exchange rates and trade

TABLE 11.1 PENALTY PAID BY AGRICULTURE IN THE LDCs, TAX EQUIVALENT (PERCENT)

Country	Period	Reduced Price	Effect of Exchange Rate Overvaluation and Trade Barriers	Total Penalty
Côte d'Ivoire	1960–1982	25.7	23.3	49.0
Ghana	1958–1976	26.9	32.6	59.5
Zambia	1966–1984	16.4	29.9	46.3
Argentina	1960–1984	17.8	21.3	39.1
Colombia	1960–1983	4.8	25.2	30.0
Egypt	1964–1984	24.8	19.6	44.4
Morocco	1963–1984	15.0	17.4	32.4
Pakistan	1960–1986	6.4	33.1	39.5
Philippines	1960–1986	4.1	23.3	27.4
Sri Lanka	1960–1985	9.0	31.1	40.1
Thailand	1962–1984	25.1	15.0	40.1
Average, 18–Country Sample		7.9	22.5	30.3

Source: Schiff and Valdés, *A Synthesis of the Economics in Developing Countries*, 15.

barriers on manufactured goods. The penalty is expressed as a percentage tax equivalence. That is, the "total penalty" of 30.3% in the last line of the table means that the combination of reduced prices, exchange rate overvaluation, and trade barriers on items farmers buy was equivalent to a 30.3% tax on agriculture. At the top of the table are countries with a strong bias against agriculture, while in the middle are countries with a moderate bias. The last line of the table shows the average for a larger sample, including a few LDCs that encouraged rather than penalized their farmers.

The bias against agriculture might seem highly irrational to a casual observer, but there were reasons much more understandable from the point of view of politicians. They listened to the dubious arguments that rural output is not very responsive to price change, arguments that proved to be incorrect, or correct largely because the infrastructure of storage, transport, and extension services was poorly developed or decayed. (See the box on price elasticities of supply.) They considered that the income elasticity of demand for agricultural commodities was low, so that the importance of agriculture would thus fall with growth. They surmised that high farm prices would chiefly benefit large farmers and hurt the low-income urban poor. They thought that growth required industrialization, which could be financed by taxing agriculture. But they also understood that the support and sympathy of the urban masses are a virtual requirement for staying in office.

Concentrated populations when angry are far more troublesome than scattered peasants, and the nation's capital is always urban. Farmers are usually rather inert politically, with poor communications among them and great difficulties in organizing them. They could in many instances be safely discriminated against, allowing rural schools, health programs, electricity, water, and roads to remain less developed even though agriculture was heavily taxed to pay for these largely urban amenities. Influential farmers could be pacified by cheap credit for machines, fertilizer, wells, and the like. The small farmers who benefited little from these government programs thus lost their potential political leadership.

SUPPLY ELASTICITIES IN AGRICULTURE

The available information on price response in LDC agriculture indicates that supply responses are higher than usually believed, even in Africa where elasticities are supposed to be lowest.[6] Higher farm prices cause greater supplier response when roads are good, irrigation water is available, and active extension services are on the scene. The price elasticity of supply ranges from 0.6 to 0.9 in the more advanced LDCs that have abundant land and a reasonable infrastructure; it is lower, between 0.2 and 0.5, in lower-income countries with a less developed infrastructure. The supply response to price change is stronger when the price change is believed to be permanent as opposed to temporary. Evidence indicates that in countries where the infrastructure is inadequate, the elasticity of agricultural supply to improvements in this government infrastructure is often higher, around 1.0. One reason for the greater response to improved infrastructure is the demonstration to entrepreneurs that official attitudes toward agriculture have changed.

Results of Rural Neglect

Not surprisingly, the dismal outlook for agriculture in many countries was not such as to encourage investment in that sector. The results may have been politically acceptable, but the economic consequences were severe, sometimes even horrific. Three examples will make the point. Burma's attempts to keep rice prices low were devastating for production; its once great rice industry sank into a shambles. Ghana's government used a mixture of high taxes on cocoa producers, through its marketing board, and price controls on food to the point where incentives collapsed. So did production. A proportion of what was produced disappeared over the border into the Côte d'Ivoire, where prices were three to five times higher and did encourage production, or into the thriving black market outside the price control system. These cases were treated in more detail in Chapters 3 and 4. Similarly, Sri Lanka's production of tea, rubber, and coconuts was dislocated by taxes (averaging more than 50% on tea) that curtailed the export of these commodities. All three countries eventually implemented urgent programs to rectify the perverse incentives, Sri Lanka in the late 1970s, Burma and Ghana in the 1980s. But the shift of government attitudes back toward an emphasis on rural development was initially very slow.

An early realization was that neglect of agriculture was likely to cause an unwanted repercussion, with the growth of manufacturing industry curtailed by slow growth in farming. Manufacturing found its potential domestic markets reduced in size because of stagnation in the countryside. Later, optimism increased that rural areas, including agriculture and other rural activities, could provide an economic stimulus toward growth and could even be a "leading sector." Presently, the pendulum has swung very far, with international agencies now giving special attention to rural development. Helping the pendulum along was the knowledge that few countries have achieved satisfactory overall growth without developing their rural areas. The last statement is supported by World Bank analysis of a 56-country sample, shown in Table 11.2, which indicates that GDP growth is closely correlated with agricultural growth.

From the perspective of the 1990s it is not easy to see why there was a spirit of confrontation between agriculture and industry for so long. Agriculture could provide food that would otherwise have to be imported; it could engender exports; rural

TABLE 11.2 AGRICULTURAL GROWTH AND GDP GROWTH (BY NUMBER OF COUNTRIES)

	GDP Growth		
Agricultural Growth	Above 5 Percent	3–5 Percent	Below 3 Percent
Above 3 percent	17	5	3
Below 1 percent	2	1	11

Note: The data are for the fifteen years up to 1984.

Source: WDR 1982, 45, and *WDR 1986*, 80.

areas could provide a market for industrial goods; it was often smaller in scale than manufacturing; and it conserved on management ability. All of these were significant attributes.

The idea that in the short run a growing manufacturing sector could generate sufficient exports to pay for a large portion of a country's food imports was extremely optimistic to say the least, as often the industries involved had to be protected by tariffs for a long period of time. Many still are, as we will see in Chapter 15. This implies that at least in the near future the domestic market has to be depended on for growth. If so, then higher incomes in agriculture would serve to enlarge that market.

There also seemed little realization that promoting domestic sources of food might give greater stability of supply, both because bad crop years for overseas exporters might not be bad years at home and because food shipments can be a means for applying political pressure. Some LDCs would not appear to have a comparative advantage in the production of foodstuffs, and as their manufacturing or natural resource output (and population) increase, it would be sensible for them to import more food, paid for by exports. Many other LDCs would, however, seem to *have* a comparative advantage in producing some foods, even though in a fair number of them, governments have employed policies that discourage rural development. For them, the antagonistic policies plus rapid population growth and occasional crop failures have forced greater imports of food than would otherwise be necessary. The percentage of LDC food coming from imports increased by more than half (from 6.7% to 10.5%) between 1969–1971 and 1988–1990.[7] Some of this was due to a greater desire to consume imports, but some of it was because of counterproductive policies.

It is also difficult to understand the confrontation for reasons of income distribution and employment. Agricultural development is often widely dispersed geographically, helping to even out regional disparities in income. It has many rural linkages, to the supply of fertilizer, construction, small-scale repairs, and basic consumer goods, all of which are likely to be labor-intensive and generators of jobs. Typically, a $1 increase in farm income tends to give a rural multiplier effect of $0.50 to $1.50 additional income.[8]

In many LDCs, the potential for employment in manufacturing is not nearly great enough in the short run to generate sufficient employment to absorb the growing labor force. A calculation takes only a moment and is instructive.[9] Say the labor force equals 1000 workers, and labor-force growth is 3% per year, a fairly common figure in the LDCs. The number of workers to be absorbed every year is therefore 30. Given that the manufacturing sector employs about 20% of all labor on average (and therefore 200 workers in our example), it would have to absorb $^{30}/_{200}$, or 15% more labor every year. Labor-force growth in manufacturing at 15% per year is an exceptional rate, attained at times by some countries, but certainly not by very many. Worse, there is unemployment and underemployment to consider; the two together are often a quarter of the whole labor force. To provide jobs for the new entrants plus absorbing the un- and underemployed, during say a ten-year period, would mean a rise in industrial employment of almost 30% per year, beyond any historical record. It is hardly surprising, therefore, that attention must be directed to agriculture with its demonstrated ability to absorb labor and provide that labor with income. Notice that this is not the same thing as saying development can proceed easily through agriculture alone. Neither the capacity of the rural sector to absorb labor nor the market for agricultural commodities is usually large enough to allow major long-term development without a significant shift to nonfarm activities.[10]

Rural Reform

The case for rural reform is compelling, in particular because the population living in rural areas is huge. In the least developed LDCs, 79% of the 1992 population was rural. The figure was 65% for all LDCs.[11] Largely because of rapid population growth, food production per capita in the least-developed countries in 1991 was only 92% of the figure in 1979 to 1981 (though it was 118% in all LDCs). Discouragingly, the countries with the lowest incomes now produce less food per person than they used to. In addition, rapid population growth and policies involving urban bias have led to considerable rural–urban migration, as discussed in the next chapter. Rural development of agriculture and other activities can be seen as a way to give employment to the growing labor force, increasing the per capita food supply and offsetting the "pull" of urban areas. Since about the mid-1980s, numerous LDCs have been trying to address this issue with policy changes, so that agriculture can once more be a source of growth.

Making agriculture more attractive means raising farm productivity. To accomplish this, a clear priority is the reversal of urban bias by ensuring that farmers are not unduly taxed by low producer prices, hindered by overvalued exchange rates, and penalized by high trade barriers on the items they buy. Beyond this rather obvious need to level the playing field, other areas of rural reform are necessary to cope with problems that remain even when these macro reforms are carried out. The areas most in need of reform include land tenure, farm size, debt, and credit (all discussed in the sections that follow), as well as technological change in agricultural production (which is taken up later in the chapter).[12]

The proper strategy for agricultural development is to maximize the output of the scarce factor of production. At one end of a spectrum of possibilities is an Asian model, where labor is abundant and land is short. Here emphasis is placed on growth in output per acre on small farms. At the other end of the spectrum is a North American–Australian model, with abundant land and scarce labor. Here emphasis is placed on higher output per worker. Land–labor ratios will determine which is the most desirable for a particular LDC; perhaps a middle way will be appropriate, such as that taken by Europe.

Land Tenure

Communal land tenure, in which ownership is vested in a village or local ethnic group, is generally thought to inhibit productivity increases. Undefined land rights are more damaging as population grows because when land is held completely in common, the people who work it often have an attitude of "take out of it what you can get, put in as little as you can."[13] This was seen historically in the overgrazing of the common in Great Britain. It is seen today in the exploitation of the ocean fisheries. To be sure, a judgment of community holding must depend on the alternative types of private ownership that may succeed it. In the Andes countries of Latin America, the large, poorly managed private estates that succeeded the earlier communal holdings were not obviously more productive. In Nigeria, the emergence of huge private farms owned by large commercial firms in replacement of communally held farms seems more a case of powerful interests gaining at the expense of the powerless, rather than a genuine move toward higher-productivity agriculture.

Similar negative circumstances for productivity occur when farm plots are privately managed but are shifted about from time to time. (The Russian *mir* system operated this way until the twentieth century.) Because the farmer will not be using the same plot of land in following years, there is an incentive to fertilize inadequately and to skimp on upkeep.

Even when private occupancy and use is protected, a number of countries still do not allow clear titles to land. Among them are China, Ethiopia, Mauritania, Mexico, Nigeria, Zaire, and Zambia. In many other countries, barriers exist to ownership of land by women. Studies show higher productivity in countries where the private ownership of and title to land is secure.[14] Lack of secure title to land hurts productivity in several ways. Farmers might be evicted without ceremony. Credit is harder to obtain and more expensive when land cannot be offered as collateral. Even when it can be so used, lack of secure title may mean that land prices are lower than they otherwise would be, and the usefulness of land as collateral is reduced. Clearing and upkeep are less careful; in Thailand, the clearing of tree stumps was twice as common when farmers had good title to their land.* Fortunately for farm productivity, economic growth has tended to break down communal land tenure patterns and the practice of shifting cultivation. They still exist, especially in Africa where it is reported that 86% of farms and 59% of the farmland are under a system of communal ownership, but they are much diminished in number compared with 30 years ago.[15]

Tenancy Arrangements (Including Sharecropping) Land tenure also involves the question of tenancy arrangements. Some tenancy arrangements can be seriously detrimental to agricultural improvement. A noteworthy case is that of high marginal rents, rising as production rises, with the landlord under no obligation to participate in capital formation or land improvement. The tenant's incentive to increase output is diminished to the extent that part of the gain must be paid over to the landlord. Landlord behavior is not nearly so detrimental when marginal rent is low, there then being an incentive to land improvement. Even elevated (average) rents appear in a more favorable light when landlords have a high propensity to save, and then use these savings for land improvement

---

*Like reforms of any kind, land titling is open to abuse. Kenya's land titling program has brought allegations that is being used to concentrate land ownership in the hands of the wealthy.

and capital formation. Historically, this resembles the situation in Japan and England.

In many LDCs, there is much sharecropping within a patron–client relationship. Sharecropping is much more common in Asia than elsewhere, with 85% of tenancy arrangements taking this form, compared to 16% in Latin America and virtually nothing in Africa.[16] In sharecropping, the tenant farmer pays some of the output, very often half of it, to the landlord.[17] Why does sharecropping exist? Because it is a mechanism for risk sharing. Farmers pay less in poor years than they would if they paid standard rents, so trading off some of their profit for a reduction in risk. Landlords do not have to supervise sharecroppers as closely as wage labor because sharecroppers do have an incentive to increase output.[18] The system may serve as useful insurance for both the patron-owner and the client-farmer.

Because sharecropping is akin to a tax, it follows that tenants may reduce their work effort. That has been a traditional position in economics. Yet there is substantial evidence that in a sharecropping system, agriculture can be successfully advanced. In India, landlords frequently provide production loans to sharecropper tenants (deducting the cost of the loan from output), share in the cost of seed and fertilizer, participate in decision making, and take significant interest in productive investment. Similar findings that tenancy is not necessarily less efficient than owner cultivation have been reported by M. Ahmad for Pakistan, Vernon Ruttan and Y. Huang for Malaysia, and S. N. Cheung for prerevolutionary China. In Pakistan, "landlords in general specify contract terms that encourage sharecroppers to adopt new techniques of production."[19]

Unfortunately, there have been many other cases, especially in Latin America, where landlord behavior was far less beneficial for growth, the land viewed as conferring social status and political power of a semifeudal nature, and the landlord a rentier, a usurious one at that, making little effort to improve the land.* It is not always easy in these cases to distinguish between the effects of tenancy per se and the monopoly element in landlord behavior, as when large estates are the only sellers of land and the only buyers of labor. Some recent efforts at land reform (Ecuador, Sri Lanka) have focused on this issue and have taken the form of fixing rents and establishing security of tenure.

Inheritance A last, potentially serious problem of tenure is that of inheritance. Where farms are not passed on intact to one heir, as in English primogeniture, they may be split among numerous heirs, resulting in small or dispersed land holdings. The Koran, for example, mandates for Muslims an equal sharing of land among heirs. The resulting small plots may suffer special diseconomies, such as having to bicycle from plot to plot, move tools among them, and the like. In some parts of Sri Lanka this reached the point of time-sharing among heirs, who farm the plot in alternate years. Agreement among the heirs or merger and consolidation through land purchases often rectifies the damage, but not always, with resulting problems

*The situation is sometimes made less tolerable by racist overtones, as when the landlords are white and the tenants mestizo, black, or Indian. Caste in India similarly enters landlord–tenant relations.

of productivity. Rapid population growth in the LDCs has made the problem progressively worse.

Farm Size

The issue of farm size is another area of rural reform. It is clear that in some countries farms are too large for maximum efficiency and that these large estates, if broken up into smaller more productive units, would achieve higher levels of output. On the other hand, there are farms that, if combined to give a larger average size per unit, would lead to higher productivity. Even in the same country, it is not unheard of to find some areas where economists would prescribe amalgamation of plots and others where the advice would be to break up the great estates. It is estimated that food production could rise 10% to 30% in some countries if land ownership were reformed.[20]

Unequal Ownership Often the issue of size is overshadowed by that of distribution. Whether or not a large farm is the most efficient economically becomes rather submerged when one realizes that in India 12% of rural families control half the cultivated land or that in Brazil the figures show 10% control three-fourths of the farming area. The sociopolitical aspects are most marked in Latin America, where *latifundia* (large estates) are common. Here, as late as the 1950s, the 1.5% of all farms that were over 1000 hectares in size made up 64.9% of the farmed area. The counterpart to this figure was the existence of *minifundia*: in Peru, 88% of the farms took up just 7.4% of the land area; in Guatemala, 88.4% of the farms comprised only 14.3% of the land; and in Ecuador, 89.9% made up 16.6%.[21] Table 11.3 shows that the inequality persists, with the high levels of landlessness and near-landlessness in many countries. Permanent landless labor is most common in parts of Asia, and especially in India where a caste system prevents certain people from becoming even tenants, much less owners.[22] Notice that the figures for Africa are for once less disturbing than those of most other areas.

The often-heard litany of a stratified society with no opportunity for peasants to improve themselves, limited capital investment in farming, and the political

TABLE 11.3 LANDLESS AND NEAR-LANDLESS AGRICULTURAL HOUSEHOLDS

	Landless	Near-landless	Combined
Dominican Republic	44	48	92
Guatemala	38	47	85
Peru	46	29	75
Brazil	60	10	70
El Salvador	65	—	65
Bangladesh	29	33	62
India	40	13	53
Mexico	18	33	51
Africa	10	30	40

Source: Alan B. Durning, "Ending Poverty," in Lester R. Brown et al., *State of the World 1990* (New York, 1990), 135–153, citing a range of sources. The data relate to the mid-1970s.

power of large landowners with a vested interest in things as they are is all too familiar. There has been improvement in a good many countries on this score, but the problems are still considerable. In numerous nations it is fair to say that unequal access to land is the single greatest obstacle to economic development and the most important underlying cause of unequal income distribution.

Large farms are usually not appropriate where labor is plentiful and land is scarce; it is more economical to maximize the output of the scarce factor (land) by aiming for the greatest possible yield per acre. Small farms certainly do use more labor per unit of land than do large ones. Figures from Colombia, for example, show farms of less than three hectares using 20 times more labor per hectare than farms of 50 to 500 hectares.[23] Labor, when lavishly applied to a given unit of land, means more care in land preparation; individual attention to the seedling and growing plant, including transplanting from seedbeds; and very careful harvesting. Other things equal, output per acre is higher than in mechanized, large-scale farming. Often the large farm is not a family farm and must utilize hired labor. Without any responsibility and reward of ownership, the work may be both less intense and the workers less attentive.*

Finally, the larger the farm the more managerial skill is required. If such skills are in short supply in the LDCs, then this represents a disadvantage for farms of great size. It should be added that a land reform that breaks up large holdings but leaves the new owners without access to credit, technical advice, and reasonable transport is unlikely to achieve much.

When Large Farms Are More Appropriate Large farms are more appropriate under some different conditions. Where labor is the scarce factor, a more capital-intensive kind of farming is in order. Mechanization of agriculture, irrigation facilities, storage, and so forth may well not be economic on small-size farms. Either amalgamation of small plots or a carefully managed cooperative approach with joint participation will then be necessary.

Mechanization in particular is a problem when farms are small in scale.[24] Machines often cannot be reduced below some minimum size and still perform the required tasks. If irrigation is needed, the tube well must be deep enough to reach the water table and the pump powerful enough to lift the water. Some farm machines cannot be scaled down any further (combine harvesters, several sorts of picking machinery, tractors powerful enough to break soil with heavy crusts). Used on small-scale farms, they would be both clumsy with a turning radius that is too large and employed too little of the time to justify the capital outlay. Even a central depot with machines owned by the government or cooperatively is no perfect solution, because by its nature farming demands inputs of machinery during certain fairly short peak periods. Government tractor-hire schemes failed the test of cost-effectiveness in 20 of 21 cases covered in a recent study. Even yields did not increase in the majority of cases. The expected economies of scale did not

*This element is clearly apparent in modern U.S. farming, where even on heavily mechanized farms, the relatively smaller ones utilizing family labor tend to be more productive than larger ones employing hired labor.

THE MANY VARIETIES OF LAND REFORM

Land reform has historically come in many varieties. It may involve collectivization of privately owned farmland into large units, often much larger than before (Soviet Union, early Communist China). It can lead to farmer cooperatives that necessitate the relocation of former peasant cultivators (Tanzanian *ujamaa* villages, Mexican *ejido* cooperatives). Transfer of ownership may take place from landlords, usually absentee, to tenants who were already there (Japan, Taiwan, Ethiopia, Mexico). Finally, it might see the opening of large estates for new settlement by small cultivators (Kenya, Zimbabwe).[25]

Three national programs for land reform may be mentioned. Taiwan's land for the tiller program was one of the greatest and most successful of all land reforms at its peak in the period 1949 to 1955.[26] On that island, after the arrival of the nationalist Chinese, about 40% of farmers did not own their land. Four major steps were taken as part of the program. (1) Leases were extended to a six-year minimum. (2) A maximum rental value of 37.5% of the crop during the past three years was established. (3) Public land was sold to tenants at a fixed price of 2.5 times the value of the annual crop. (4) A limit to individual land holding was instituted, with landlords reimbursed with bonds. These former landlords entered business, and in the 1980s, only 6% of farm families did not own their land. (Note that the value of compensation by means of bonds can be eroded by the ravages of inflation unless they are indexed.)

Mexico's *ejido* farms were less successful. Early reforms led to about 28,000 *ejidos*. Farmers could not own but could inherit the land, could not borrow using it as collateral, and could not rent it to others. One result was that these farmers had little access to credit. *Ejidos* are becoming progressively smaller because of splitting up among heirs, so making them less viable. A constitutional amendment of December 1991 provided for legal title to these lands, and allowed for merger and joint arrangements—a major change in Mexican policy.[27]

The Philippines exhibits an uglier side to the issue. After 12 years of ostensible land reform under President Marcos, only about 11% of land targeted for redistribution had actually been distributed. The Philippines had neither the money to pay for expropriation nor, apparently, the will to carry it out against the intense opposition of the landowners. Rather often, vested interests are able to halt land reform in its tracks.

develop because demand for the machinery was low during much of the season.[28] If a central depot *had* been advantageous, economists would want to know why private rental did not spring up. They would warn that one reason might be the inadequate payoff. If that is the case, then government schemes will be unlikely to work either.*

*The most well-known failure was the Soviet Union's centralized "Machine Tractor Stations" of Stalin's day. Their machinery was eventually distributed to the collective farms because of the competing demands on the machines at planting and at harvest.

CHINA'S DECISION THAT FARMS WERE TOO SMALL

The recent partial reversal of mainland China's great land reform of 1977 to 1984 was partly due to a conclusion that mechanization had been made too difficult by the small size of the resulting plots. China's reform involved massive land redistribution, sometimes by lottery, the result being many thousands of quite small farms of an acre or less, compared with the 1500-acre farms of the communes that came before. The Chinese leadership decided that machinery and fertilizer could not be used efficiently because size had become too small. A movement to bigger fields is being encouraged, with leasing and subletting from the government the major means for expansion.

Notice that the problem of mechanization is also a reflection of existing technological dualism. Sometimes even oxen can do a better job than tractors. They use more labor, they move more easily around stumps, and they do not require expensive gasoline. Yet often enough the gasoline is subsidized; banks will not advance credit for draft animals, whereas they will for tractors; machinery imports are encouraged by tariff preferences and overvalued foreign exchange rates; and labor use is discouraged by high minimum wage laws.

Until recently, almost all farm machinery was intended to be labor saving. Only within the past few years have certain countries, Japan and Taiwan especially, pioneered the development of cheap mechanized implements such as garden tractors and tillers designed to raise productivity in a labor-intensive setting, increasing output without saving labor. These small machines are now making a substantial contribution.

Another aspect of mechanization is that a good many locations are surprisingly ill-suited to it, even where plenty of land is available. Tropical areas with heavy jungle cover are often highly susceptible to "leaching" when the jungle is cut away and the land is put to farming. Leaching is the process whereby heavy rainfall seeping through the soil removes essential mineral content, leaving a poor and unproductive soil in stark contrast to the previous lush jungle growth. The problem is known across tropical East and West Africa, northern South America, Central America, and Southeast Asia.

Storage and marketing are further problems when farming units are small.[29] For example, drying equipment is sometimes required and is uneconomical below a minimum size. Collection and marketing of produce will be an extra burden where farms proliferate and may necessitate cooperative or state marketing or the presence of a competitive system of middlemen. Inputs in small quantities often cost more per unit because transaction costs are high; here again, unless there is cooperative bulk buying and heavy competition among middlemen, the cost penalty may be difficult to tolerate. Middlemen frequently receive undeserved criticism in the LDCs. Their fees are often thought to represent exploitation, when instead they may exemplify a competitive charge for services made necessary because farm size is small. In spite of fervent beliefs to the contrary, there is little evidence of a monopoly of middlemen in the LDCs.

Finally, small farmers cannot afford to spend as much on investigating and adopting new techniques. Their smaller resources also mean that when shortages of seed, fertilizer, and water strike, they will have less influence on suppliers than large farmers will. In all these cases, an efficient market for credit will be needed, as the high fixed costs for small farmers will have to be met with borrowed funds. The rural credit market is, however, often constrained, as discussed in the next section.

Whatever the disadvantages, the weight of the evidence now indicates that the quality of labor advantage on small farms will in many circumstances offset the obstacles.

RURAL CREDIT

Credit is a major issue in agriculture, and in countries where government policies are otherwise supportive, it may be the *most* important issue. The problem is simple enough to explain. Income is low, so to cover production expenses and any other cash outlay, the demand for loans will be high. Financial capital of all kinds is scarce, with the opportunity cost of funds thus increased. The need for funds often has a marked seasonality, as when farmers must borrow even for next year's seed grain, or, as in India, when smallholders must rent draft animals and plows. At the same time, any extraordinary expense not connected with production, such as marriages and funerals, may also mean more borrowing. Commonly, a third or even more of all loans in rural areas are for social rather than productive purposes.[30]

Interest Rates Are High in Agriculture

Interest rates will reflect a premium for the trouble of administering small short-term loans, and, indeed, a little cash for a few chickens, a new spade, or some seed and fertilizer is often the sort of loan most lacking and most useful to small farmers. There will be a risk premium as well, for several reasons. High default rates of nearly 10% are not exceptional. Approximately 25% of all loan payments were overdue in a 35-country study by U Tun Wai.[31] Collateral is often inadequate, not least because titles to land may be insecure. In India, interest rates charged on loans secured with land are in the range of 8% to 16%, whereas with no land for security the rates are 18% to 37.5%. In Costa Rica, rural credit almost doubled after a land-titling program was introduced.[32] Unless the lenders are local, assessing the degree of risk in lending to farmer X, Y, or Z out in the countryside will be difficult. Finally, a country's own policies, including decisions on keeping interest rates low, on the foreign exchange rate, on price controls, and on subsidizing imports, may bring either a direct reduction in available credit or lower agricultural prices, or both, thereby making it much more difficult for farmers to obtain credit.[33]

As a result of these risks, regular commercial banks may avoid rural areas and rural credit except for large and influential farmers. Only 5% of Africa's farmers and 15% of those in Asia and Latin America have access to formal loans.[34] In the absence of formal credit, noninstitutional private lenders supply much credit and sometimes most of it. U Tun Wai stated that noninstitutional rural credit is 72% of the whole in Africa, 72% in Asia, 63% in the Middle East, and 15% in Latin America.* This is, however, older data, and institutional lending is now gaining.[35]

The Importance of Noninstitutional Credit The noninstitutional credit comes mainly from a varied group of professional village moneylenders, traders, pawnbrokers, shopkeepers, landlords, relatives, and friends. This age-old informal finance survived because it was adapted to rural conditions and could deliver credit on a very small scale. From these lenders a farmer could, and still can, borrow, say, $1 for one day. The loans from relatives or friends might be at a zero rate of interest, but lending from the other sources carry high rates of interest. In the Philippines in a study of rice farmers, 15% of producers were paying over 200% for their loans while 20% were paying a zero interest rate.[36] In 22 countries surveyed by U Tun Wai, the mean annual rate of interest on noninstitutional loans was about 40%, the median 30%.[37] Although these rates were nominal, not real, the countries concerned were not suffering from serious inflation at the time, so they imply very high real rates. Usually the highest levels are found in Africa and the lowest in the Middle East. Exceptionally steep rates are reported from time to time—50%, 60%, or 70%, in countries not suffering from serious inflation. Occasionally they are higher yet: nominal rates of 200%, 300%, or even 500% per annum have been reported (though rarely) in countries with relatively moderate inflation. Interest rates in pawnbroking tend to be lower than for other informal credit because it involves its own collateral.[38] Loans from landlords to sharecropping tenants also carry a somewhat lower risk of default because the landlords find it easy to keep tabs on the borrowers.

There are several repercussions of the high structure of real interest rates for agricultural credit. The high expense may mean little opportunity for productive investment in farming. Often one hears that farmers are conservative, reactionary, even stupid, and unwilling to buy the fertilizer, insecticide, or new seed variety that could double their output in a year. How different it all looks when their indebtedness is considered. The reluctance to adopt new methods may be entirely rational if these new methods mean going yet further into debt at very high rates of interest.

---

*Especially in Africa, access to rural land and credit comes from membership in commercial descent groups rather than through commercial channels. Farmers have to look to status and social identity to ensure their access. But migration and education are changing this situation, which is fluid and is resulting in less confidence that land and credit will be forthcoming. See Sara Berry, *No Condition Is Permanent: The Social Dynamics of Agrarian Change in Sub-Saharan Africa* (Madison, 1993).

The reaction against high interest rates has frequently come in the form of government attacks on moneylenders, either by prohibiting their operations or through passage of antiusury laws establishing maximum permissible interest rates. Governments often argue that moneylenders operate as monopolies, though this case is doubtful because, surely, barriers to entry in this occupation are not that high. (It is true, however, that in some areas such as the Indian Punjab, large-scale land acquisition has been accomplished by lenders.)[39] Whatever the facts, the laws against moneylenders always have wide popular support.

The result of these laws often seems to come as a surprise to politicians, but it is highly predictable. The supply of loanable funds available to farmers is reduced, the more drastically the more draconian the laws and the lower the interest rate ceilings. This makes the moneylenders even more unpopular, of course, yet what are they to do? Often farmers cannot legally pledge their land or livestock as collateral for a loan, nor can they pledge their crops before harvesting them.* (These laws were intended to "protect the farmer.") The result is even less credit available in the agricultural sector, as moneylenders turn to other alternatives for their funds—city property, trucking firms, all the other uses for ready money that are so apparent in the LDCs. Specialist moneylenders have indeed declined in importance, being replaced (when they are replaced) by nonspecialist part-time moneylenders, state institutions, and commercial banks.[40] Recent studies of five Asian countries show professional moneylenders now provide an average of only 6% of rural credit.[41]

Attacking the Shortage of Credit in Agriculture

The shortage of credit in agriculture is one of the most persistent problems in development economics.[42] How can it be solved? Standard commercial banking is an unlikely source of funds because the bankers' knowledge of the risks involved will often be inadequate; they will face some of the serious assessment difficulties referred to earlier.† Also, banks in rural areas are high in cost; each individual's balance is small, there is much traffic in the accounts, and "mobile units" traveling from place to place are expensive. Applications for small loans (banks commonly considering even $30,000 to be small) may receive unsympathetic treatment because of the administrative obstacles.

The failure of markets to provide adequate institutional credit have led to various sorts of government intervention.[43] One possibility is to force banks to lend

*There are exceptions. Botswana, for example, has legalized the use of both crops and livestock as collateral.

†In a few countries (Malaysia, Indonesia), banks have begun to employ local agents, mainly traders but including even moneylenders, in an effort to reduce the risks of inadequate knowledge. See V. V. Bhatt, "Improving the Financial Structure in Developing Countries," *Finance and Development* 23, no. 2 (1986): 21.

anyway by establishing compulsory local credit targets for them. In India and Thailand, 60% of the deposits in rural banks must be used for local loans, and a proportion of these (20% of deposits in Thailand) must go for loans in agriculture. Such a course may work to provide more funds if the banks are otherwise profitable enough to stand the costs, but it may also discourage banks from opening at all in disadvantaged rural areas. Even at best, banks will probably charge their other borrowers more to make up for the costs or pay depositors a lower interest rate, or both.[44] It is also possible, even probable, that the policy will not be very effective; banks often find ways to circumvent the requirements.

Government-sponsored development banks have frequently been established with the aim of making subsidized credit available to farmers. Such institutions have not been overly successful, though there have been exceptions including Kenya, Malawi, Morocco, Thailand, and some others.[45] Some have been too much interested in rapid approval of loans and growth in lending, and too little interested in monitoring repayment. Often they have been overstaffed, expensively administered, and not sufficiently accountable for their funds. Default rates have been high: 50% in some Indian programs, 71% in Bangladesh, 40% in Malaysia and Nepal, and the defaults even weakened the general idea that contracts should be enforced. Losses have been heavy in Brazil and Mexico as well. Usually the subsidized credit has led to political struggles to obtain the funds. Often they are tied to particular crops or to machinery purchases. Neither course is usually very sensible; the first runs the risk of artificially distorting cropping patterns, the second gives a damaging boost to displacement of rural labor. In general, the government-sponsored credit institutions tend to minimize their risk by favoring large borrowers, the wealthy and influential farmers who can pull strings to get subsidized low-interest loans much more effectively than can the poor. Losses among these institutions have been heavy, as for example in Brazil, Mexico, and India. Often enough, because of the heavy losses among these development banks, the subsidies to them have been cut back. Then they tend to fail, with the failure tainting the whole idea of encouraging agricultural credit.

Improving Risk Assessment and Lowering Administrative Costs Two major problems are how to improve the assessment of risk and how to lower the costs of administering many small loans. One innovation has helped in both areas. The rural cooperative credit society, with farmers making up the membership, can help in assessing risks while at the same time lowering administrative costs. Where each farmer knows the next, the risks are more clearly evident, and the knowledge so obtained can keep interest rates down. Such cooperative arrangements often draw on preexisting, traditional mechanisms. Groups called *esusu* in Ghana, *tontine* in Niger, *hui* in China, *cheetu* in Sri Lanka, *samabaya* in Bangladesh, and other names in other countries, have for centuries provided credit to farmers on a revolving basis. The members of these revolving credit societies contribute a small sum, which is then loaned to the member who can make the most persuasive case for using the funds productively. Then after that member makes repayment, the balance is loaned to another member, and so on. Such societies do not collect funds from more than a small group and cannot move the funds over a distance, but the principles of a close-knit group providing the risk assessment and serving to police the repayment with peer pressure are valuable ones.[46] Several innovative rural banks now make use of the underlying idea, as noted in the accompanying box.

INNOVATION IN RURAL BANKING: GRAMEEN BANK IN BANGLADESH; BKK AND BUD IN INDONESIA; BAAC IN THAILAND[47]

Innovative rural banks have recently attracted substantial attention. Grameen Bank in Bangladesh is a government-supported institution that relies on self-policing by its borrowers rather than on their collateral. Grameen Bank (*Grameen* means "rural" in Bengali) grants very small loans (averaging $67 in 1992) to five-person groups, mostly women engaged in very small enterprises.*

Two borrowers get the first loans. They must make their weekly repayments to the bank before loans are made to the other three. The prospect of a new loan is the incentive to pay off the previous one. As repayments are made, the sizes of loans are expanded, though not by much (to about $200). Grameen's "bicycle bankers" cycle around the countryside, talking with peasants about credit and telling interested individuals how, if they find four others and form a "solidarity group," they can receive a loan. By the late 1980s, the bank was serving some 5,400 villages and almost 250,000 borrowers (though still just 5% or so of the target population). A default rate of just 3% after the first year and 1% after two years was reported in 1987.

In Indonesia, Badan Kredit Kecamatan (BKK) for off-farm activities and Bank Rakyat Indonesia Unit Desa (BUD) for all rural activities use the same system of small sums, perhaps as little as $5, lent for a short time, with the small loans (less than $100 in BKK, $300 to $500 in BUD) ratcheted up to bigger ones as old ones are paid off. BKK's employees visit villages on market days to handle loans and take deposits. The bank's staff shares 10% of the profits, which has increased the care devoted to supervising loans.[48] The combination of volunteer workers, profit sharing by the paid staff, and group sanctions on the borrowers has worked to keep costs low. The Indonesian banks are less heavily dependent on subsidies than is Grameen Bank. They finance themselves by charging relatively high interest rates, 7.5% per month on some loans. (That is less than what village moneylenders ordinarily charge, but not necessarily much less. The success of these new rural banks has depended more on the timeliness of their loans and their simple application forms than on interest rates.[49])

---

*The Grameen Bank was begun by an economics professor from Chittagong University, who is said to have started operations with $30, and to have personally guaranteed the first few loans.

The Bank for Agriculture and Agricultural Cooperatives (BAAC) in Thailand is similar except that its borrowing groups are much larger, numbering 30. Its loans are in the same \$300 to \$500 range as BUD's in Indonesia. All these banks boast high repayment rates, and all charge higher interest rates than were formerly permitted because of strict interest rate ceilings that had to be repealed in the countries concerned.

There are now many imitators that do not advance new loans to a small group until old ones are repaid. Ghana, Cameroun, Malawi, Malaysia, the Philippines, and Sri Lanka are among the countries that have recently copied that approach. (The idea is being advanced as a model for U.S. inner cities as well.)[50] Sometimes (as in Sri Lanka) these rural banks have successful pawnbroking facilities. Admittedly, local cultural differences may make rotating small loans less successful in some areas. For example, BKK and BUD use village heads as intermediaries, but where there is a strict caste system, that approach may work poorly. Bicycle banking may also be less effective where population density is low. Corruption might overtake the arrangement in some countries. Above all, the overall importance of these banks is still not very large. Grameen Bank, for example, provides only $\frac{1}{10}$ of 1% of all the lending in Bangladesh.

Cooperative arrangements extending beyond group credit are now rapidly gaining ground virtually everywhere, particularly in Asia and the Middle East.[51] The cooperative members may obtain discounts in the bulk buying of seed, fertilizer, and pesticides, and they may also be able to cut costs by arranging for local processing and marketing. Other goals can be pursued at this micro level: Credit availability has been combined with land reform in Egypt, South Korea, and Taiwan; and combined with technical assistance in Brazil's *Operação Tatu*, Kenya's small farmer credit program, and India's Small Farmer Development Agency.[52] Innovations such as these have greatly increased the flow of formal rural credit as opposed to informal credit. Although government institutions to lend to rural groups are now very popular, it remains to be seen whether this approach will be as successful when a country's laws and traditions are not as favorable to this method as they are in Bangladesh, Indonesia, and Thailand.

How to Obtain Funds Even if government institutions that direct their lending toward rural groups are now popular, another major obstacle still remains. Group lending is perhaps a good method of *distributing* funds, but it does not automatically generate *new* funds. Several sources are possible. An institution such as the Grameen Bank may employ its "bicycle bankers" to visit villages and farms, seeking out small deposits. But they might not necessarily always be small because (as in India) traditional practice may have been to hoard currency and precious metals. Credit might be made available through foreign aid. The governments of the United States, Canada, the Scandinavian countries, as well as the United Nations direct some of their funds to small-scale rural lending, and a quarter of all World Bank lending to agriculture during the 1980s went to agricultural credit. It is always best if some local funds are involved as well, however. One dislikes losing one's own money much more than losing donations.[53] *After* farm income has started to rise significantly, but not before, co-op banks can lend the savings of members to other members, so reducing the credit problem. (This was an important source of funds for Japanese rural development.)[54]

IFAD The innovative International Fund for Agricultural Development (IFAD), established in 1977, although small, has been in the front line of rural lending activity.[55] Financed largely by the developed countries, IFAD provides modest loans for tools, or lending without collateral to landless laborers for the setting up of a tiny business. IFAD has also found ways to channel loans to rural women, who ordinarily have little access to credit. This small agency (employing only about a hundred professionals) brings credit to villages that have never seen any except from the village moneylender, can boast a high 19% median rate of return on its projects, and in its peer group schemes has a 95% rate of full repayment by borrowers.

Obtaining money for IFAD has, however, been very difficult; so much so that it has considered becoming self-financing, just rolling over old loans already made. One obstacle has been the farm lobbies in the developed world, which consistently oppose foreign aid to modernize agriculture when the LDCs might export their output, even though LDC economic growth stimulates developed-country exports of commodities, such as coarse grains and feedstuffs.[56] Perhaps a long-term solution to the budget problems of this extremely useful agency would be to allow it to raise funds on world capital markets, as does the World Bank.

Rural Credit: A Conclusion

There is thus significant progress to report in the area of rural credit. Needless to say, however, even fine institutions such as IFAD and Grameen Bank are not likely to be of much help, nor are any other rural credit measures, in the countries that still maintain a posture of urban bias and rural neglect. In these countries, very heavy taxation of the agricultural sector remains a serious obstacle to rural development. Interest rate ceilings staunch the flow of savings to agriculture; requirements for low-cost loans discourage private institutions from participation because they cannot cover their costs. Development banks often still lend to manufacturing enterprises more than to agriculture, and the funds that *are* available are often distributed very unevenly. The World Bank reports that subsidized loans rarely reach more than 25% of all farmers and that these are usually the larger farmers inclined toward mechanization. The smaller the farm, the less chance that credit will be available to the farmer, who therefore must do without the high-yield seeds, the fertilizer, the pumps and the pesticides that could transform small-scale agriculture. Finally, inappropriate land tenure policies and skewed distribution of land may negate any progress made in providing rural credit.[57]

AGRICULTURAL RESEARCH: THE GREEN REVOLUTION

Research had a greater impact on agriculture in the last thirty years than in any previous period of history, and the rates of return to agricultural research have been high, even spectacularly so.[58] The development of new varieties of plants delivered such an increase in yields that the term *green revolution* came to be used. The rapid adoption of these crops by Third World farmers was a body blow to those who argue that farmers are innately and irrationally conservative and unwilling to change.

For a long period after World War II, however, the results of agricultural research were disappointing. Funds were scarce, and the research that did go on was usually directed to cash crops, often those destined for export, rather than to the crops grown for local consumption. For example, there was historically little research on the yams, cassava, and other tubers that are staples in Africa, on the deepwater rice of the Ganges River or Mekong Delta, or on the beans, lentils, and peas so important for nutrition in India. Research on improving their yields and making them hardier and more drought resistant would have paid dividends.

Often the economics of a crop as opposed to the technical side received too little attention. Much research was focused on West African cotton cultivation even though events showed other crops were economically superior. Shifting cultivation (moving a field every few years, burning off the new plot, leaving the old to a long fallow) was condemned by the experts as technically wasteful, but economists later showed that shifting "slash and burn" techniques may well make sense where labor is scarce and land abundant, as indeed was true in much of Africa where the practice was most used. (Rapid population growth is ending the rationality of long fallow periods over most of its old range.) Too much attention to plants sometimes meant not enough for cheap water catchments, miniponds, or terracing in drought-prone regions.

Among the experts there was often a bias toward working with men instead of with women, who so often have a major role (up to 80% in parts of Africa) in the production of food crops. Simple improvements in buckets and the rigging of wells (for women often fetch the water) or in the design of simple woodstoves (for they also fetch the fuel) would free up time, lessen drudgery, and improve the quality of life. Garden projects for vegetables could improve health and provide some income. Tree planting of nitrogen-fixing acacia in dry climates could bring both higher garden yields and some welcome shade. Projects of this type were much neglected until recently. There was a further bias against working with nomadic pastoralists, with the result that population growth among both people and livestock brought overgrazing and consequent unfavorable effects on soils.

The research often concentrated on capital-using techniques, such as mechanized farming, and tended not to emphasize the questions that arose when farming was on a small scale. Sometimes the suggested "improvements" strained managerial ability, as in the many plans for mixed farming with its combination of cropping and animal husbandry. The animals would provide meat and milk, motive power for plowing, and manure for fertilizer. But with education and literacy lacking, inadequate capacity for informed decision making became an obstacle.

Another of the difficulties was how to disseminate information to producers. The original idea of the demonstration plot often proved inadequate to the task.[59] Farmers suspected an economic barrier. The plots seemed to promote high yields rather than high profits, and many an illiterate peasant appreciated the difference (the highest yields will, of course, involve diminishing returns to factor inputs and so will erode profitability). Needless to say, this economic barrier became even more impenetrable in countries with official low-price policies in agriculture. Farmers also realized they could not operate on the research station's technical plane. They saw excellent land, fine buildings, a first-class irrigation system, special attention to the plots, printed instruction leaflets, and experts whose interests were more with agronomy than economy. Understandably, they ended up ignoring the new techniques as irrelevant to their own circumstances. Meanwhile, the extension workers sent out from the research stations were too often poorly trained and supervised. Sometimes they had numerous other duties to perform, such as collecting production statistics or even census data. Often there was no provision for feedback from farmers to field-workers to the agronomists at the stations.[60]

The greatest of all the problems was the combination of risk and low income. The risks in farming are high anyway. Even in the developed world, a change in the weather can have a devastating effect. Add to that the little-studied plant diseases of the LDCs, the pests, and the intensity of weather changes (monsoon failures or floods, African droughts of long duration). Then add the narrowness of markets caused by poor transport and limited storage. Finally, consider an income so low that a mistake might put the farm family below the subsistence level. There emerges an understandable reluctance to adopt new techniques or to specialize completely in crops for the market. Safety first makes sense.[61]

New varieties of trees, shrubs, or plants, although reported to be higher yielding, may in the farmer's mind be untested for risk. One crop failure might not ruin an American or an Australian farmer, but with no cash reserves the risk may be unbearable in Bangladesh, Ghana, or Paraguay. If a cocoa tree or coffee bush takes more than a year to bear fruit, replanting with new, more productive strains results in a loss in income for a year or two that may be insupportable. Finally, risk of crop failure and a narrow market mean farmers have good reason not to specialize in cash cropping. All over the underdeveloped world, farmers continue to grow a large portion of their own food alongside crops for sale on the market (including for export), often *not* planting the cash crop at the time that would give it maximum yield. In Nigeria's north, for example, farmers would plant long-maturing seed four weeks late in order to make time to put in their subsistence crops, reducing yields by a third as compared with planting on the best date.[62] As long as high risks and low income exist side by side, there is a strong motive against complete specialization. Research could focus on cash crops with less than a maximum yield but a shorter growing season. It could search for fertilizers that in small doses give a significant return and aid in minimizing risk. Ordinarily it has not.

Reluctance to innovate and adopt new varieties is sometimes linked to tradition and conservative tastes. New methods may violate some social custom, as with the introduction of higher-yielding, hardier rice in Nepal. The rice would seem to have been an improvement in every way, but because it clung tenaciously to the stalk, it required a new threshing process. The old threshing process, however, had both social and religious significance to Nepalese farmers. Easily overcome, the foreigner might say, but how easy is it to change the Christian's scruples against bigamy or the Muslim's against eating pork?

New methods may also involve subsidiary technology that leads to complications. Such was the case with the steel plow in several widely separated reports in Africa and Asia. The plow was much more efficient than the wooden plows and "crooked sticks" that it was intended to replace. But it also required two hands to control it, and farmers from time immemorial had been trained to use one hand to guide the bullock. A new method might also render a major tool obsolete, with no easy way to obtain replacements; when advisors in Africa recommended planting close together, the result was that the old hoes were too wide for the gaps between the plants. "Perverse conservatism" thus can have an underlying layer of rationality, to which the agricultural researcher should be ever alert.

Finally, new, cheaper, and more nutritious food varieties have sometimes been rejected by farmers because of their taste. African farmers cling to their favored but high-cost yam; East Asians, to the taste of their old lower-yield rice. Such tastes can be slow to change. Westerners should hardly be surprised, one supposes. The tomato was considered inedible by Europeans for over two centuries after the plant was introduced from the Americas.

The Green Revolution and the HYVs

The early failures of agricultural research should not be forgotten, nor should it be believed that the problems just discussed have been overcome. Research into high-yield variety plants (HYVs) has, however, led to two spectacular breakthroughs in recent years, leading to such an increase in yields that the term "green revolution" was coined. The revolution has not been fully sustained in recent years, and it certainly caused some unanticipated difficulties. Nonetheless, the new technical discoveries and their rapid adoption by farmers are a most encouraging aspect of modern development economics, especially because the response of farmers to the new technology belies the claim of "innate, stultifying conservatism" in agriculture.[63]

The pioneer in the green revolution was the International Rice Research Institute (IRRI), founded in the early 1960s by the Rockefeller and Ford foundations at the University of the Philippines at Los Baños, near Manila. The IRRI began the search for a higher-yielding rice. Traditional rice matured by the sun and hence the calendar; if a new rice could be made to mature by the length of growing time, then its harvest need not occur all at once, and two or three crops might be obtained instead of one or two. The traditional practice of harvesting all at once did reduce the insect population, but it also put heavy demands on hired labor, water buffaloes, machines, and trucks. Maturation by growing time rather than by the sun also improved the prospects for irrigation. For example, if the same water could be trickled down from high field A in June to middle field B in July to low field C in August, then field A could be planted early and would mature early. Most important, the new hybrid had to be a sturdy plant with a short stalk to bear a greater weight of rice. Because the old rice was thin and tall, large applications of fertilizer and ample irrigation produced rice on the end of the stalk so heavy that the plant would dip down into the water, with fatal results.

The solution came in trials managed by Hank Beachell of Beaumont, Texas. A rice called IR-8 was hybridized from Indonesian and Taiwanese stock. It matured by time and not by sun and possessed a strong stalk. The first HYV, IR-8 was released in 1966 with outstanding, even astounding, results. With proper application of water and fertilizer, yields were greater by a factor of three to as much as eight.* Within a few years, IR-8 was followed by an improved descendant, IR-20, and then in 1982 by IR-36, created by Gurdev S. Khush of the IRRI. The plant's height has now been reduced from 5 feet to 3, and its growing season has been shortened from the traditional 160 to 180 days to 110 days, allowing three crops per year.

The effect on production and exports was rapid. From 1967 to 1992, the world rice harvest doubled. Thailand became the world's leading exporter; Vietnam went from shortages to number-three exporter; and Indonesia became self-sufficient in production in 1984, increasing its output by more than three times in 25 years. Many parts of India and Sri Lanka also registered production increases of three to four times. The Philippines itself became a major exporter, shipping rice abroad in 1967 for the first time since 1903. China shifted from being a major importer to producing a surplus in the 1980s, with HYV rice grown on 80% of its cultivated land. Yields there more than doubled. The real price of rice in Asia has declined by about half. These developments represent an enormous return on the IRRI's small annual budget of $15 million.

The second of the HYVs to be developed was wheat. The International Maize and Wheat Improvement Center (known by an acronym of its Spanish name, Centro International de Majoramiento de Maiz y Trigo, as CIMMYT), has been located at El Batan, Mexico, since its foundation as a project of the Rockefeller Foundation. Norman Borlaug of Iowa State University won the Nobel Peace Prize in 1970 for his work there with strains of Mexican short-stemmed wheat that, like the rice discussed above, does not bend over after large applications of fertilizer. The total world estimate for the planting of the new wheat varieties was 200 acres in 1965 and 50.5 million acres in 1971. Under Indian conditions some varieties of the HYV wheat give 2.5 to 3 tons per acre as against the Indian average of 800 pounds per acre for older strains. With more than three-fourths of its wheat acreage planted in the new varieties, India became self-sufficient, whereas a short time before it had been the world's second largest importer. Old cropping customs were broken rapidly as farmers showed themselves to be responsive to change. Indian production grew from 11 million tons in 1966 to 46 million tons in 1984. The new wheat also had an especially strong impact on production in China, where yields per acre tripled, and in Pakistan and Turkey as well, where wheat output grew for years at 8% a year or more.†

*The high-side figures are usually experimental data from demonstration plots rather than actual field data. Production in the field usually went up by three to four times. See Douglas Horton, "Assessing the Impact of International Agricultural Research and Development Programs," *World Development* 14, no. 4 (1986): 453–468, especially p. 465.

†As usual, there is room for skepticism. It is possible to overemphasize the role of the international programs such as IRRI and CIMMYT, relative to the less-known but valuable research and extension programs of the LDCs themselves. See Horton, "Assessing the Impact of International Agricultural Research and Development Programs," 465.

A Dark Side With both rice and wheat, there has been a darker side to the revolution. The new crops require the careful and heavy use of fertilizer. Illiteracy is thus a handicap, and cost an even greater one. The manufacture of artificial fertilizer requires large inputs of petroleum, a problem exacerbated in India because about half of its natural fertilizer (manure) is dried and used for fuel. Fertilizer is the largest single import item for Turkey and its HYV wheat, and for many other countries as well, especially in Southeast Asia, where fertilizer use has grown six to ten times. Petroleum also enters the picture with water, pesticides, and herbicides. The water must often be drawn from tube wells by pumps that run on gasoline or diesel fuel. Some paddy varieties of rice are vulnerable to insects, so pesticides are a requirement for high yields. These, in turn, are frequently petroleum-based, taking as much as a gallon of gasoline per pound of pesticide. Any rise in the price of oil is thus a blow to Third World agricultural output.

The wheat revolution has actually been more successful than that in rice. The spread of the new rice has been slowed by the special need for water as an input. Only 25% to 30% of world rice production is irrigated, meaning that much rice farming has been unable to utilize the new technique. It was possible to enlarge the amount of irrigated land by three times since 1950, but further increases will be much more difficult unless massive irrigation projects are completed. There must not, however, be too much water either. The combination of possible flood and drought explains why only about 40% of South and Southeast Asia's rice acreage is presently planted with the new rice.

Even where irrigation is available, there are complications.[64] Irrigation water from wells contains dissolved salts, which are left behind when the water evaporates. Salinity rises. Already 10% of all irrigated land has been spoiled, with 24% more showing problems (27% in Pakistan, 36% in India). Drainage should be altered so the salty water is flushed away by groundwater, and wells should be dug and pumps installed to pump away the saline top of the water table. But proper drainage can cost five times more than irrigation.

A Slowdown in the Green Revolution? Since the mid-1980s, growth in the world's grain output has slowed noticeably, from 3% per year between 1950 and 1984 to less than 1% between 1984 and 1993.[65] One reason is the unsuitability of much acreage for the new rice and the difficulty of further expanding irrigated land, as discussed above. Another is diminishing returns to more fertilizer use, the diminishment partly due to the inability of plants to respond as favorably past a certain point, and partly because of soil exhaustion. If growth in supply continues at its new lower plateau, then per capita food availability is likely to decline.

Can technical change continue to provide green breakthroughs? The best chances appear to be further genetic work with rice that increases the number of stalks that actually bear rice. IRRI is working on rice where there will be fewer but sturdier stalks per plant, with each stalk producing a panicle (branchlet with seed clusters) instead of 60% to 80% of the stalks of the current varieties. Every panicle will produce 200 to 250 seeds compared to 100 produced now. The improved rice will also require less fertilizer and less water. IRRI announced a breakthrough in October 1994. The publicity claimed a 20% to 25% increase in yield, which would be enough to produce an additional 100 million tons and feed 450 million more people. Resistance to insects and diseases still has to be bred in, followed by further work to adapt the rice to different local conditions, so the rice will not actually be available for five years or so.[66]

In general, it is clear that the HYVs succeed most dramatically when literacy is high so that labels and instructions can be read and understood; when land holding is equitable and income evenly distributed, for then risks are less concentrated and credit is more widely available; when water is available, especially for rice; when the fertilizer supply and price are both reasonable; when an area's climate and soils are particularly suited to an HYV crop to start with; and when farm prices are not depressed by government policy. Most of these conditions are not met, or not fully met, in Africa, where as a result the green revolution has yet to make a great impact.

An agricultural extension service that is available and well run is a great help in spreading the new varieties. The impact of agricultural extension is particularly strong when the underlying level of education is low. The extension services of the past, with their too-frequent irrelevance to farmers' needs, have now been much improved in several countries. India's Training and Visit (T&V) System is a case in point. The T&V technique was originally tested in Turkey during the late 1960s, but since 1977 it has achieved its widest use in India. Regular visits are scheduled by extension workers to farmers in their own fields every two weeks, the workers often drawn from among the most successful of these very farmers. Their advice on spacing, pruning, weeding, and general management has been a productive supplement to the HYVs that they recommend. A study by Gershon Feder and Roger Slade suggests that in India, T&V has been responsible for a 7% yield increase over three years in addition to the effects of the HYVs themselves. Rapidly, with World Bank support, T&V has spread to more than 40 countries.[67]

Are Small Farmers and the Landless Left Out?

A major problem on the level of the individual farmer, one involving equity, was apparent from the earliest days of the HYVs.[68] Numerous observers have thus been critical of the new crops' inability to improve income distribution in agriculture and their capacity to make the distribution even worse. The cost of fertilizer, irrigation, and even new seed was a greater burden on the smaller, poorer farmers, whose fixed costs of locating and developing markets and training hired labor were also higher. The deficiency of agricultural credit made the cost barrier even harder to overcome. So those farm families (or absentee landlords) with relatively high incomes to start with received greater benefits than poor farmers. Poorer farmers also found it more difficult to afford the increased storage, transport, machinery, spare parts, and fuel costs associated with larger quantities. Many landless laborers appeared initially to be passed over entirely. Indeed, the real fall in the price of agricultural commodities must, all other things being equal, have the effect of decreasing the demand for labor and so reducing rural wages.

On the contrary, however, evidence has now accumulated to show that the HYVs exhibit a substantial potential to assist the poor, and in many cases have actually done so.

The HYVs in most countries produce the main food eaten by the urban and rural poor, so the fall in their real prices was a decided benefit to the poor as consumers. In effect, the HYVs have allowed food production to keep pace with population increase. Given the fall of land availability per capita in LDCs, dropping from 0.85 hectares in 1980 to a predicted 0.6 in 2000, *not* having the HYVs would have been very damaging for the poor.

Typically, the HYVs raised labor requirements per acre substantially because of the greater quantities involved, especially for transplanting, weeding, and harvesting.[69] (This higher labor demand is, of course, seasonal.) Greater labor inputs may be easier for small farmers to organize and apply, bringing advantages to them. The higher demand for labor time has been a considerable offset to the downward pressure on wages because of the fall in food prices. One Indian study on rice quoted by Michael Lipton showed 46% more labor income per acre. Landless labor being relatively mobile, it is often able to move to where the jobs are.[70] Finally, as noted in the preceding paragraph, the earnings go further when they can purchase more food. Studies from India suggest that the poor gained in net terms from the lower price of food even in the cases where their labor income fell.[71]

That initial gains accrued to bigger farms appears to some degree associated with greater risk aversion on the part of the poorer farmers. Perhaps not surprisingly, the latter looked longer at the results before adopting the technology, and when they did, the adoption was both slower and less complete; the poorer farmers could not afford to make a mistake. One advantage of the newest HYV rice is that its yield is less variable than the older varieties, reducing the risk that a crop will fall much below some modest target. Knowledge of this reduction in the risk of disaster has helped to spread its use. Although risks remain, adoption continues to advance, and at the present time it is clear that the HYVs have spread widely among small farmers as well as large, and among tenant farmers as well as landowners.

Inasmuch as the HYVs are scale neutral, for the most part, it is arguable that the relative position of many small farmers has even been improved because the size threshold of small-farm viability has been lowered by the new crops. Governments can help. India, for example, has made a point of trying to include small landholders by distributing green revolution kits of HYV seeds, fertilizer, and pesticide, millions of which were made available in the 1980s. The upshot in India was that income distribution, which had initially become less equal, returned to where it had been previously.[72] Still, there is little doubt that problems of income distribution will persist. Better-off farmers will continue to be the first to adopt newer HYVs. Better-off farmers will be able to afford more water control, which is important with rice. (A lesson of this is that subsidized credit co-ops and specialized design of irrigation schemes to make it possible for small farmers to participate are especially important.) Even with landless laborers gaining absolutely, it is very likely that owners of land and capital will profit relatively more, especially because they profit first and so are in a position to acquire yet more land and capital. The disparity shows in regional terms also. Areas suited to the HYVs gained relative to areas less suited; regional gaps in income increased.

More disquieting is evidence that employment creation from the revolution is now falling.[73] Evidently, farmers, especially the larger ones, have seen advantages in adopting labor-saving technology that cuts the demand for new labor. This would give little cause for concern if it were due simply to rising wages as development proceeds, but there appears to be more to it than that. Cheap herbicides have proved to be directly competitive with hand weeding; the use of mechanical threshers from Japan, Taiwan, or local production is increasing rapidly; mechanized land preparation is advancing steadily; and small, inexpensive mechanical reapers and transplanters are in the offing.

Sometimes government policies to subsidize credit or the prices of the new machinery are largely responsible for the lessened effects on employment; these policies are in urgent need of reform if relative prices are accurately to measure scarcities. (Overvalued foreign exchange rates, which have the same effect, are discussed in Chapter 14.) Sometimes large farmers prefer to tend machines rather than deal with what they see as intractable laborers, akin to the problem of industrial bias toward capital discussed in Chapter 8. Sometimes, though, the new technology is simply cheaper even with undistorted prices (herbicides), or can reduce losses by faster processing at harvest (machine threshing).

Should these trends persist, they would put an even greater premium on flexibility in LDCs, with a need for more employment creation in other sectors. At best, the higher incomes to farmers and the lower food prices will lead to a higher demand for goods and services; many of these will be labor-intensive, thus providing the jobs that used to be provided in agriculture. But in the short run, landless laborers may suffer more in the future from the green revolution than they have in the past. The extent of the suffering will depend largely on the ability of an economy to adjust rapidly to changed economic circumstances.

Agronomy in the Future

Hopes for feeding a much larger world population rest on further technological advances in agriculture. Though it would be risky to assume that these advances will come along as needed, a number of breakthroughs might be made in the future, either at one of the 18 international agricultural research centers or from other sources.* At the IRRI, scientists are trying to develop rice capable of being grown from seed rather than from transplants. The labor that must be devoted to transplanting rice seedlings is enormous, forming an important bottleneck to

*These centers include not only the IRRI for rice and CIMMYT for wheat and maize, but others in India for sorghum and millet, Peru for potatoes, and Syria for wheat and barley. They are funded by the Consultative Group on International Agricultural Research (CGIAR). CGIAR is based in Washington, D.C., and is funded by 40 donors including government aid agencies and the World Bank. Unfortunately, funding for CGIAR's research has been falling (by 21% in real terms between 1992 and 1994) as the United States and European governments have cut back their contributions in response to budget deficits. The cuts have caused layoffs of 10% of the senior scientists at the centers, and nearly 20% of their local staffs. See *Christian Science Monitor*, June 29, 1994.

increased production. Developments along these lines could raise output from the present maximum of 8–9 tons per hectare to 13–15 tons.

Beyond these advances, cloning through tissue culture would copy the best characteristics of any plant and thus rapidly increase yields. At CIMMYT, a new maize (corn) with high protein content, drought resistance, less need for fertilizer, and adaptability to acidic soils is being worked on by means of gene copying. The supercorn may be able to increase yields by 10% to 40%. For corn and other plants, if a gene conferring resistance to weed-killing herbicides could be bred in, the herbicides could be administered much more liberally, which would promise great increases in yields. Genetic engineering could also be used as a weapon against the devastating insect pests, such as locusts and grasshoppers. New strains of insect disease, or methods to spread old ones, are being worked on. Gene-splicing might also permit the transfer of the leguminous (nitrogen-adding) properties of peas, beans, or peanuts to nonleguminous plants of all kinds, which would result in enormous self-production of fertilizer. (The nitrogen fixation is actually not due to the plant itself but to the bacteria with which it lives symbiotically.) Wheat is the crop now being focused on for this research.*

Further ideas to increase productivity go beyond plant genetics to include more attention to soil conservation through mulching, contour cultivation, and grass contour hedges that can cut erosion substantially and improve yields.[74]

It is possible that we have only seen the beginnings of technical advances that will occur in the future. But it is also arguable that it would not be prudent to allow levels of living and even survival to depend on unknowable technical change. Land available per capita will continue to fall as population grows, soil nutrients will be lost with more intense cultivation, diminishing returns are likely to affect increased fertilizer use, and erosion will increase as forest and grass cover are removed. Therefore, the consequences of rapid population increase may be much more severe than the optimists believe. Those who count on technical change in agriculture always to bail us out may be proved right, but it is sobering to consider what will happen if they are not right.

THE PAYOFF TO AGRICULTURAL IMPROVEMENT

One of the consequences of the green revolution was to confirm that government policy to speed manufacturing at the expense of agriculture usually dampened, and did not aid, economic development. The countries making the most progress and undergoing the greatest structural change were the ones that were developing their agriculture in step with their manufacturing.

There is by now a wealth of illustrative experience.[75] Côte d'Ivoire, Malaysia, South Korea, Taiwan, and Thailand are five good examples of careful attention to

---

*The other side to this coin is that biotechnological developments are not always equally beneficial to the LDCs. NutraSweet and other artificial sweeteners have already reduced the demand for sugar, and other commodities such as cocoa butter, coconut oil, and palm oil may in the future face biotech competition.

rural areas with resulting highly favorable overall effects. Substantial amounts of public money have gone into rural health and education, land improvement, and irrigation. Agricultural research institutes are well staffed. They all have successful programs of bringing credit to the countryside; the credit is backed by a competent extension service. Improvements in village education, health services, water supplies, farm-to-market roads, electrification, and availability of advice on nutrition and home economics have made the rural landscape more hospitable. All are, incidentally, easier to provide to villages than to scattered farmsteads. Often, national funding is made available to be used at the discretion of local development committees for local projects. All these countries have decentralized decision making to some degree, with good results in improved efficiency. (When decision making is decentralized, it often follows that large, capital-intensive projects fall out of favor to some extent.)

All of the successful countries have been especially diligent in continuing the support of their agricultural initiatives, unlike the many LDCs that are littered with the remains of good projects that failed because the initial effort was not followed up with the less glamorous, but critical, day-to-day support work.[76] The centerpiece of all the programs is an adequate reward for the rural sector through producer prices that are remunerative and provide an incentive for production. These are not the countries with the onerous taxes on agriculture.

Prosperous farming has had important ramifications for the countries that have encouraged, or at least not hindered, their agricultural sector. The higher farm output means more reasonable food prices for consumers and more revenues for farmers. The farmers' new income means a market for additional inputs in farming, raising revenues yet again for those providing the inputs. The higher incomes of farmers and suppliers and the income consumers do not have to spend on high-price imported foods mean a larger market for consumer goods generally. The wood, the rubber, the palm products, the oilseeds, and food for processing all may become direct inputs to domestic manufacturing. Agricultural exports make a contribution to a country's earnings of foreign exchange, which, tapped through judicious taxation, is available for industrial development. Higher saving and higher investment are the result.

The higher incomes have an additional effect. Consumers may now be able to afford imported foods that they prefer, perhaps wheat products, to supplement what is grown at home, say rice and coarse grains. The large grain imports to almost all of the better-off LDCs have raised the LDC share of world wheat consumption to about half the total, reflecting a taste change spurred by higher incomes.[77]

China's Exceptional Success The degree to which China has followed this logic in recent years has rightly attracted intense interest.[78] China is still three-quarters rural, so agriculture and rural development are important. But in the Great Leap Forward of 1958 to 1960, China acquired a rigid system of rural communes, the Chinese equivalent of collective farms (and state farms in the far north). In the 1970s, except for the state farms, all of China's rural land was in 50,000 communes, averaging 13,000 people each, collectively farmed according to a plan. State procurement and pricing were the rule, production was erratic, and perhaps 25 to 30 million starved in a record-breaking famine lasting from 1959 to 1961. A great land reform from 1977 to 1984 involved a massive land redistribution in which farms became quite small, an acre or less, compared with the 1500-acre expanse of the communes.

During the period of the land reform, China turned to much higher and more flexible rewards to farmers who successfully increased production. In 1984, compulsory delivery quotas were replaced by contracts for delivery of crops to the government at set prices. Supply and demand were allowed to affect some of these state-set commodity prices in a limited way beginning in 1988. From 1979, farmers were encouraged to produce crops in addition to their contracts for private sale at market prices on both rural and urban farmers' markets. A doubling of grain prices took place from 1980 to 1985, with the rise lower but still over 50% for all crops. The requirement that local areas had to be self-sufficient in the production of food grains was abandoned, encouraging trade in farm commodities. These changes allowed farmers more freedom to determine how much they would produce and to switch production to crops with higher returns. Land could be "rented" from local governments for this purpose, usually for 15 years after a 3-year start-up and occasionally up to 50 years. This land can be inherited on the death of the original renter. A sort of family farming had emerged.

The response in output because of the policy changes and high-yield varieties (and some good weather, too) provoked admiration, even astonishment. In the 10 years to 1978, China's real agricultural output had grown at 2.1% per year. But in the 10 years to 1988, the figure was 6.2%, the highest in the world. China became the world's largest wheat grower, as well as rice grower, and the country even began to export grain. All this was in spite of the fact that in 1978, output per acre was already among the highest in the world, while in subsequent years technology did not improve much and land and labor use in agriculture declined somewhat as people took jobs in cities or in the rural enterprises considered later in the chapter. (From 1987, rural factories were producing more output than were the country's farms.) The excellent results in agriculture were due instead to more efficient organization and higher motivation.[79]

All this was extremely impressive evidence of the effect of improved policy on agricultural performance. Problems remain. There are very few wholly free markets for grain, these being limited to a few coastal areas and in Sichuan Province. Very small plots inhibit the realization of economies of scale and mechanization. The consumption of food is expensively subsidized by government, and one result is that prices are not as high for farmers as they would otherwise be. State prices for grain in 1990 were less than half the free market price. Government payment for contract deliveries is often in the form of IOUs with actual payment delayed for some time. Communal irrigation facilities have deteriorated to some extent as decision making became concentrated at the household level. These factors, together with less favorable weather in recent years, have caused grain yields to plateau. Yet the progress realized in Chinese agriculture has been one of the remarkable events of the world economy in this century.

Avoid Unwise Subsidization

There is a danger that policymakers, convinced of the wisdom of rural development, may overdo the reforms, unwisely subsidizing the activity on the principle that more is better. The countries with the successful rural development strategies have for the most part avoided using their government funds to subsidize credit, fertilizer, and machinery in unwise ways. In many countries, the first attempts to offset years of rural neglect involved the institution of input subsidies to counter the stringent tax policies.[80] Sometimes these subsidies have been comprehensive, covering seed, fuel, machinery, water, pesticides, and fertilizer. They have been applied especially to fertilizer, usually in the range of 30% to 90% of delivered cost; 50% to 70% subsidies are common. Often there has been little public opposition. In addition to countering the disincentive effects of heavy taxation, such subsidies are justified as an attempt to overcome rural credit constraints, to encourage rapid technical change in agriculture, to raise the income of the poor, and in general as a way to raise output.

The subsidies can take many forms, and their negative ramifications can come in subtle ways.[81] In India, farmers' fertilizer is subsidized. But it is manufactured so inefficiently by local producers that the large subsidy, which is twice what the government spends subsidizing food for the poorest, still leaves farmers paying 10% to 25% more for fertilizer than its price on world markets. Fertilizer manufacturers are the chief beneficiaries. In any case, the lion's share of India's fertilizer subsidies (as well as those of Bangladesh, Brazil, Ecuador, Egypt, and Pakistan among others) are garnered by the better-off farmers. In Brazil, large wheat subsidies meant that small farmers, who grew beans, sold their land to commercial farmers who grew wheat. In Zambia, the state pays a low price to maize farmers, and then pays subsidies to keep the price low for city dwellers. There is much smuggling and black marketing, and food riots have made it difficult to change policy.

There is little doubt that many agricultural subsidies have not worked out as their proponents expected. Machinery subsidies seem particularly unjustified because they usually end up in the hands of the largest farmers with land holdings big enough to accommodate the equipment, and who then use the financing to displace labor with capital. Fertilizer subsidies do not have that problem, but they too often benefit rich farmers more than poor ones. The reason is clear enough. Because the price of fertilizer is kept low, demand is usually higher than supply so that some form of rationing must be adopted. With their greater visibility and political power, better-off farmers are able to shove to the head of the queue. There are other problems as well. Fertilizer subsidies do not encourage the use of manure, and chemical fertilizers alone are usually insufficient to maintain soil fertility. Being distributed by state monopolies in many countries, they may not arrive at the proper time for application and may not be tailored to local conditions. The private competition that could overcome these inefficiencies does not develop because government does not permit it to.

On occasion, where a country can afford the expense, one finds these subsidies carried to irrational extremes. Saudi Arabia pays its farmers a subsidized price for wheat that is almost five times the world price. Saudi wheat growers responded by making the desert bloom with wheat watered from deep wells, evidence that large-enough quantities of cash can boost exports of virtually anything, no matter how hopelessly uneconomic the unsubsidized activity is.

There is now a growing tendency in many countries to cut back on these subsidies.[82] The LDCs with the most successful rural development programs generally avoided the difficulties in the first place. When subsidies have been paid in these countries, they have generally been moderate in amount, applied to the achievement of reasonable goals, and have ended up in hands able to accomplish the designed tasks. The lesson is a valuable one.

Food Self-Sufficiency?

In many LDCs, a movement developed in the 1970s and 1980s to move toward self-sufficiency in food production. Was this a good idea? In a major respect, the movement *was* valuable because urban bias in government policy had in many countries led to the payment of import subsidies to keep imported food cheap for urban consumers. By keeping agricultural prices low, such subsidies reduced food self-sufficiency.

Beyond this justified correction, some concerns arise. Self-sufficiency in food, when it is based on a comparative advantage in food production, is to be valued. Many LDCs undoubtedly do have a comparative advantage in the production of a good many foods. But some countries may *not* have a comparative advantage in food production, in which case producing what they do best and importing their food makes sense. In such cases, falling food imports and rising self-sufficiency are not in themselves a cause for congratulation; the reduction in imports reflects lost gains from trade. If comparative advantage is followed, rising incomes and more foreign exchange mean that a country can afford to enlarge its precautionary stocks of food, imported if necessary—and imported food is currently quite cheap by the standards of the past.

Interference with this process can leave a country worse off than before. In Kenya, for example, government policies to increase self-sufficiency upset a thriving specialized peasant sector, and there is evidence that food marketing actually fell, with an attendant rise in imports.[83] Nigeria banned wheat imports from 1987 because bread had become so popular, and then paid subsidies to encourage local wheat growing. The cost of this policy was much greater than the cost of allowing the imports.*

The argument for self-sufficiency in food is often couched in terms of a defense against famine. Often this argument is grossly exaggerated. The family with cash to spend for food is on the whole safer from famine than the family that grows its own food. The reason is that during droughts food will flow from other parts of a country where conditions are better or from abroad as imports when people have the money to buy it. A drought that knocks out subsistence food production has the potential to be much worse for the families that lose their crops. Of course, drought damages the output of nonfood cash crops too, but the point is that growing the crops with the greatest cash return, whether this is food or something else, allows the accumulation of some cash reserves by private individuals and by government to weather the bad times.[84]

*The Nigerian government also banned imports of rice and maize in 1985 and sugar in 1989, with mostly similar results.

Like most other advice in development economics, this wisdom may not always work at all times and places. Transport to certain rural areas may be so poor that food shipments will not flow in even at a high price; it is too risky to specialize on nonfood crops. If the cash is used improvidently, then no cash reserve will have been accumulated. Concentration on cash crops has sometimes led to more landlessness among farmers when large estates growing tobacco, sugar, and other plantation crops prospered (as in Malawi), or it may lead to neglect of children if mothers spend more time on labor-intensive crops such as vegetables and flowers. Usually, however, an increase in cash cropping brings more, not less, access to food because the family's command over resources grows. For one example among many, in Guatemala growing snow peas for export to the U.S. market yields 14 times more revenue per acre than does growing maize for local consumption, with a rise in costs of 12 times. The end result is a doubled return to farming. Much of the cost rise is in the form of payment to hired labor. Both the farmers and the hired labor have a better defense against famine than they would have in subsistence agriculture.[85] The lesson is that trade, not self-sufficiency, is the best defense against poor crops and famine.

COMMUNITY PARTICIPATION

One major problem with rural development is that rural areas can be unattractive because they lack many services such as acceptable education, health standards, and infrastructure of transport and communication. People often leave the farms and go to the cities, partly in search of these amenities. Making rural areas more attractive can admittedly be very expensive. That obvious constraint has led to the grand idea that rural areas could improve themselves through community participation in their own development efforts, building on a tradition of cooperative self-help in farming that has historically been important in rural areas around the world.[86]

Self-help efforts have undergone considerable vicissitudes. Under the name community development (CD), a movement spread nearly worldwide in the 1950s, and by 1960 over 60 LDCs had CD programs, half of them national in scope. By 1965 the effort had faltered, and foreign aid support was down dramatically. There was disappointment, retrenchment, and considerable assessment of what had gone wrong. Eventually, under other names, grassroots self-help organizations involving community participation recovered almost everywhere. New enthusiasm greets these organizations, many of them nongovernment organizations rather than government ones, which are now larger than ever.

The main approach is to persuade people to work on self-help or "bootstrap" projects at low rates of pay or without pay. The well, the road, the clinic, the school, and the community center are common end results of community participation. Sometimes food and housing for teachers and other sorts of current expenditure are also provided through self-help organizations, but current costs have proven much more difficult to finance in this way than one-time capital projects.

Several sorts of aims intertwine in community participation: the efforts of people to improve their own welfare; the use of a seasonal labor surplus in rural areas during the off-season for farming; the encouragement of local organization, initiative, and mutual self-help with government technical assistance; and the use of community participation to further family planning, local credit groups, and the like.

At the peak period of interest, countries discouraged by the difficulties of capital formation were tempted to view community development schemes as a much easier alternative than the normal process of taxing to finance government spending. In some countries a large scale of self-help effort has been achieved. Sri Lanka's *Sarvodaya Shramadana* movement, beginning in 1958, mounts a full program. It is present in over 8000 villages, a third of those in the country, and involves about 3 million people.* South Korea's *Saemaul Undong*, dating from 1970, is present in over 30,000 communities.[87] Kenya's *Harambee* program (meaning "let's pull together" in Swahili) dates from 1963 and is responsible for almost a third of the labor in that country's rural development program. In Pakistan, since 1982 rural self-help projects have proliferated. In India it is estimated that there are about 12,000 independent development organizations. Bangladesh since 1971 has established about 1200 development groups that are especially active among the landless population. In francophone West Africa, the Six-S Movement (*Se servir de la saison seche en savane et au Sahel*) is the largest community effort in Africa. More than 2000 groups, averaging 50 members each, plant vegetable gardens; build small dams; engage in reforestation; primary health care, and education; and run local credit programs. Mexico's National Solidarity Program dating from the late 1980s is another example, with about 60,000 committees that refurbish schools; pave streets; and support larger projects such as electrification, water, and sanitation. It even boasts a venture capital fund that supports the startup of small businesses. Massive use of self-help schemes also occurs in Brazil, Indonesia, Peru, Tanzania, Zimbabwe, and others. (Rural self-help group projects are, however, still scarce in large parts of China and India, the Middle East, and North and sub-Saharan Africa.)

Typically, local people undertake manual work on community projects during weekends or during periods when agricultural labor is at reduced intensity—times when the opportunity cost of labor is expected to be low. But long, hard experience has made it clear that salutary warnings are in order if such projects are to be effective.

It is often forgotten that community projects are really not free at all and may involve considerable expense to the government. They require administrative personnel for propaganda, organization, and supervision, and such trained staff is a scarce commodity. The programs are often widely scattered, so that the management problems can be intractable, involving sluggish coordination, long delays, and stifling both enthusiasm and initiative. Government has to pay for the specialized

---

Sarvodaya means village awakening; *shramadana* means gift of labor. The organization was initiated to include low-caste families in the development effort. In recent years, the organization has been active in keeping the peace between the feuding Tamils and Sinhalese.

inputs such as cement and reinforcing rods in buildings, skilled labor, and technical assistance when necessary. The wiring for the school or clinic and the drainage engineering for the road, without which it would wash out in the first downpour of the rainy season, are not free either, and costs of this sort appear to run from a minimum of around 30% to about 50% of the money costs of a community project. (Sri Lanka's *Shramadana* movement tries to keep budget costs below $1000 per village, but even that may present a serious fiscal obstacle.) Finally, the fact is sometimes neglected that when a community project is completed, it requires current expenditures financed by the government—doctors, nurses, and medicines in the clinic; teachers and books in the school; and so forth. In remote rural areas, any kind of maintenance may be difficult to arrange and may be expensive. Thus, even on the basic ground of low cost, it is easy to be overoptimistic.

Experience has also made it clear that the benefits of the project have to be largely local if enthusiasm is to be generated. Villagers might happily patch or rebuild their road to market but cannot be depended upon to construct a superhighway with infrequent interchanges, from which they might get little advantage if they can only gain access after a 20 mile drive. Yet the benefits ought not be *too* local, as the Peruvian and Indian governments discovered when favoritism toward certain villages, sometimes simply because they were more accessible, was detected in project planning and was resented.

Moreover, it is important to propose projects where there is a common interest in their adoption. Examples to the contrary are abundant. It is likely that some landowners will benefit more than others from a road or well because their properties are located closer to it. When male farmers work together on projects with landless women, it is all too likely that the men will get the lion's share of the benefits. (This problem has led to the formation of self-help groups for women only, including major efforts in India and the Dominican Republic.) Some programs in India, Indonesia, Nepal, Tanzania, and elsewhere have even been made compulsory rather than voluntary, not a way to boost morale. Moreover, vested interests may oppose certain projects: the area's doctors may not welcome a clinic staffed by paramedics; the owners of four-wheel-drive trucks might not applaud the plans for an improved road. The same adverse features accrue more widely if self-help worsens a country's income distribution. At times, poor areas have fallen behind when self-help community development schemes, say in education, have mobilized less local funding for books and teachers than was the case in more well-to-do regions, particularly urban ones. Northeast Brazil, northern Nigeria, and southern Sudan are cases in point.

Benefits flow from the inclusion of local leaders such as chiefs and village elders in the planning and administration, traditional healers into the rural health system, and so forth. This can be taken too far, however, as when the results of a project improved the position of these elites but did not help the poor masses. It is now clear that within the affected community the benefits of the project have to be widely felt across all income groups or else general community participation will not be forthcoming. For example, basic human services projects such as a water supply or a health clinic are predictably more popular than a leper hospital; a farm-to-market road will be preferred to an airstrip. Projects to raise the local food supply, which could at once have enlisted the poorest, were often neglected. In Sri

Lanka, the Shramadana movement eventually allowed the villagers to choose the projects. Even careful choice often cannot cope with the depressed condition of the village poor or the social tensions of unequal income and land ownership. The basic problems can often be enough to foil the most persuasive project advisors. Even where these problems are overcome, the advisors may not be very well trained in any of the technical aspects of agriculture, engineering, road building, well construction, or the like. Such advisors, stretched too thin, may find after all that they have little to contribute to the village. This has especially been a concern in the most broad-based programs. Worst of all, perhaps, is that community participation by its very nature often raises expectations to a high level only to disappoint. Having captured wide attention, project failure is highly visible and doubly discouraging.

Thus community participation is not a panacea. Because voluntary activity will always be limited, it represents a supplement to government and not a replacement for it. In many cases, it may not even make much of an impression. But such projects at their best may lend an esprit de corps to the development experience, may tap a sense of altruism, and may develop local unity and some identification with the growth process when benefits flow to all. They serve also to give at least a brief period of elementary training in activities beyond the limited horizons of traditional village life. There is at minimum some success in keeping people on farms by bettering their living conditions, rather than further swelling the flow of migrants to the overcrowded cities. Finally (this is a major lesson), abundant and perhaps idle labor can be used to augment the stock of scarce capital with less strain on the financial system than capital investment usually requires.

So there are strong reasons for supporting community participation, but these must be fortified with the knowledge of its past weaknesses. In some cases projects can finance themselves, as when self-help teams organize and construct irrigation facilities, raising money by selling rights to the water and perhaps permission to fish. Others might find more foreign financing than before; a number of governmental aid agencies and nongovernmental organizations have added welcome financial support. Even in the absence of such funding, the advantages of small scale and building the capacity of local people and local leaders are attractive. Indeed, the integrated rural development (IRD) efforts of the 1970s and 1980s, many of which initially concentrated on relatively expensive basic needs provision and large-scale efforts to increase food output, are increasingly turning to self-help projects, realizing perhaps that the decline of community participation was greater than it ought to have been. The new enthusiasm for self-help is laudable, but the chances of a favorable outcome will be improved if these organizations' advisors understand fully the experience of the self-help advisors who came before.

RURAL OPPORTUNITIES

Economists have long understood that abundant labor in rural areas together with unemployment during agriculture's slack season opens an opportunity for rural manufacturing. With enough capital and proper organization, the labor might be utilized in rural-based industry, increasing rural incomes and making life outside the cities more attractive. Such industry, utilizing simple technology and perhaps engaging in processing agricultural commodities, may be able to run at different intensities depending on the demand for labor in the fields. Sometimes this manufacturing already exists, or once did, in the form of village handicrafts such as local weaving, basket making, and so forth. How irrational, in retrospect, that such handicrafts were displaced by urban industries using scarce but subsidized capital to produce what surplus labor could do with low opportunity costs in the farming slack season.

Four countries making use of this rural potential are South Korea, Taiwan, Indonesia, and India.[88] Most successful of all has been China, whose township and village enterprises are discussed in the accompanying box. South Korea and Taiwan have concentrated especially on credit for rural manufacturing and the provision of rural electrical supplies that can be used in the "farm factories." There, farm family members can commute to a rural factory on a schedule that varies with the busy season in farming. The rural factories have had linkages that spur rural small businesses and help to slow migration to the cities; the flow was cut by half between the 1960s and 1970s in Korea, where nearly a thousand such factories have been established. With growth, permanent factories have tended to supersede the temporary or seasonal ones.

Indonesia and India have used their low-cost seasonal surplus of labor for local public works projects managed by government. These have included construction, small-scale irrigation, the digging of drainage channels, and the clearing and preparation of land. The joint results are paid employment during the farming off-season, which serves to increase the demand for unskilled labor and to deal effectively with hunger at that time of year; provides higher income for farmers because of the increased land area and higher yields brought about by the project; and, finally, offers some repayment to the government for its spending because there is now a larger tax base.[89]

In all of these cases, the lack of adequate credit tends to constrain the development of small rural industries. Just as institutions to make small loans to farmers have been deemed important, so attention has focused on the provision of microenterprise credit. Many lessons from farming are applicable: inadequate technical assistance or counterproductive government policies can offset the advantages gained from small loans; keeping interest rates low may discourage lending, especially because transactions costs are high; lending programs that focus on mobilizing deposits have more staying power than those that depend on outside assistance; large loans strain the managerial capacity of the borrower and add to the risk that something will go wrong. Many microenterprise credit schemes will probably collapse unless they learn these appropriate lessons from farming. (Badan Kredit Kecamatan in Indonesia is one of the best known of the microenterprise credit institutions, one of the few to draw on experience with small-scale credit in agriculture.)[90]

Finally, policymakers should be warned that the establishment of rural factories involves a danger that one inefficiency will replace another. It is possible that underemployed capital during the farming peak season will replace labor underemployment during the farming off-season. If the opportunity cost of capital is greater than that of the labor, the policy would not be a good idea. This is an argument for careful economic analysis, for keeping the production labor-intensive, and for the encouragement of labor-saving technical change in agriculture that would free up extra labor for the rural enterprises.

CHINA'S RURAL ENTERPRISES: A REMARKABLE SUCCESS

In China, there has been a remarkable move to the establishment of labor-intensive small industries that can absorb the labor freed by the growth in that country's farm output. These township and village enterprises (TVEs) have appeared in many rural areas and represent one of the most dynamic enterprise sectors in the world.[91] They are often financed in smaller part by villages and in larger part by bank loans. Some of the TVEs are private, some are owned cooperatively by the village, some are worker-owned, and many belong to local governments. Highly competitive and not controlled by the central government, they buy and sell their output, and depend on their profits, which fund bonuses for the workers and managers that are large in relation to wages and salaries. The profits also go to investment, including village infrastructure such as housing, education, health, and roads. The TVEs can lay off workers and they can fail.

TVEs have grown to produce half of China's rural output (53% in 1988) and over a quarter of its total output. They employ about 22% of the rural labor force in some 19 million light industrial enterprises. Their low capital requirements and ability to produce without much of a public infrastructure of services has been a key to their success. They have kept incomes in villages relatively equal, but they have contributed to much greater inequality among villages and among regions. Some areas, particularly in the mountains of the south and southwest, have been little touched while in many others the effects have been pervasive (though China's incomes are still quite equal by the standards of LDCs). Considerable research needs to be done on the incentives involved, which are not the same as under private ownership. Conceivably the TVEs are a low-cost option to early privatization in that they economize on administrative skills that a privatization reform would require. Presumably one reason the TVEs have prospered is that they facilitate cooperation among members of a community who have few alternatives to working together. If so, they will presumably become less important with the passage of time, with a movement toward more orthodox private enterprises.

CONCLUSION

The reasons for involving rural areas in the development process were too long neglected, but as seen here, a salutary reaction has set in with very favorable results that are unlikely to be reversed. The reaction could be even more pronounced, incidentally, if developed-country protection against imports of agricultural commodities that they themselves produce were not so intense. Such protection is generally greater than for manufactured goods, as we shall see in Chapter 15. There is thus a limit on present ability to expand exports of these commodities; a reduction in that protection could help to stimulate further output in the LDCs.

The end result is that city and countryside, manufacturing and agriculture, are now seen more as a partnership than as competing sectors. Most observers now rate the partnership as a central proposition of development economics. This realization took a long time to come about, and the message has still not reached some segments of official opinion, with policy problems perhaps most pronounced in parts of sub-Saharan Africa. In that area, the combination of poor policies, high population growth, and bad weather in some years caused food production per capita to fall between 1979 and 1992 in 24 out of 34 countries for which data is available.[92]

The struggle for rural development is part of the general struggle to increase employment in the LDCs, involving the message of each of the last four chapters.[93] Because population growth is high and because economic growth has not provided sufficient job opportunities for all, economists have come to advocate more direct assaults on the structural causes of the employment problem.

From Chapter 8: Artificial barriers exist, leading to less labor-intensive technology than would result in a free market. The task is to implement these labor-intensive technologies, thereby stimulating growth, attacking poverty, and providing more employment without decreasing output.

From Chapter 9: High population growth can lead to a burden of dependency and hinder capital deepening, thus impeding the growth of productivity and reducing employment opportunities.

From Chapter 10: An inadequately educated and illiterate labor force, malnourished and in poor health, is a low-productivity labor force. Increasing the capacity of labor through the maintenance and improvement of human capital is a key part of the development effort.

From this chapter: Agricultural price and tax policies in many countries are disincentives that limit the absorption of labor. Government public services are often targeted to cities rather than rural areas, reflecting an urban bias. Combined with an urban high-wage structure, the result is a flow of migrants so large that no likely rate of economic growth in the modern sector will be able to absorb it. Hence, the general agreement that if the employment battle is to be won in the LDCs, it will require further reforms in agricultural policies.

NOTES

1. See Alain de Janvry, Elisabeth Sadoulet, and Erik Thorbecke, "Introduction" to a special issue (entitled "State, Market, and Civil Organisations: New Theories, New Practices, and their Implications for Rural Development") of *World Development* 21, no. 4 (April 1993): 565–575 on the changing balance between the state and markets in the LDCs.
2. For reviews of agricultural policies, see (alphabetically) Carl K. Eicher and John M. Staatz, eds., *Agricultural Development in the Third World* (Baltimore, 1984); Frank Ellis, *Agricultural Policies in Developing Countries* (Cambridge, 1992); George Horwich, ed., *Food, Policy, and Politics: A Perspective on Agriculture* (Boulder, Colo., 1989); Bruce F. Johnston and William C. Clark, *Redesigning Rural Development: A*

Strategic Perspective (Baltimore, 1982); Anne O. Krueger, ed., *The Political Economy of Agricultural Pricing Policy*, 5 vols. (Baltimore, 1991–1992), particularly vol. 4, by Maurice Schiff and Alberto Valdés, *A Synthesis of the Economics in Developing Countries* (Baltimore, 1992), and vol. 5 by Anne O. Krueger, *A Synthesis of the Political Economy in Developing Countries* (Baltimore, 1992); Theodore W. Schultz, ed., *Distortions of Agricultural Incentives* (Bloomington, Ind., 1978); Joseph E. Stiglitz, "Some Theoretical Aspects of Agricultural Policies," *World Bank Research Observer* 2, no. 1 (January 1987): 43–60; Paul Streeten, *What Price Food?* (New York, 1988); C. Peter Timmer, "The Agricultural Transformation," in Hollis Chenery and T. N. Srinivasan, eds., *Handbook of Development Economics*, vol. 1 (Amsterdam, 1988), 275–332; C. Peter Timmer, Walter P. Falcon, and Scott R. Pearson, *Food Policy Analysis* (Baltimore, 1983); and George S. Tolley et al., *Agricultural Price Policies and the Developing Countries* (Baltimore, 1982). *WDR 1986* is devoted to policy problems in agriculture. A special issue of the *Journal of Development Studies* 29, no. 4 (July 1993) edited by Ashutosh Varshney is entitled "Beyond Urban Bias." This issue basically argues that the concept of urban bias is somewhat oversimplified and has exceptions. See in particular the synthesis in the first article, Ashutosh Varshney, "Introduction: Urban Bias in Perspective," 3–22, and the article by Robert H. Bates, " 'Urban Bias': A Fresh Look," 219–228. A dependable classic is Bruce F. Johnston and Peter Kilby, *Agriculture and Structural Transformation: Economic Strategies in Late-Developing Countries* (New York, 1975).

3. See Schiff and Valdés, *A Synthesis of the Economics in Developing Countries*, throughout but especially 15, 18–19.
4. *WDR 1986*, 62–65, 74–75; *The Economist*, May 4, 1991.
5. Schiff and Valdés, *A Synthesis of the Economics in Developing Countries*, 15.
6. See Ajay Chhibber, "Raising Agricultural Output: Price and Nonprice Factors," *Finance and Development* 25, no. 2 (June 1988): 44–47; and *WDR 1986*, 68. The elasticity estimates given in *WDR* are from studies by Hossein Askari, J. T. Cummings, Pasquale L. Scandizzo, and Colin Bruce.
7. *HDR 1994*, 155.
8. Partha Dasgupta, *An Inquiry into Well-Being and Destitution* (Oxford, 1993), 525.
9. It is based on Jonathan Power's example, quoted by Meier, *Leading Issues in Economic Development*, 4th ed., 213.
10. Compare the analysis in Michael Lipton, *Why Poor People Stay Poor: A Study of Urban Bias in World Development* (London, 1977). A book-length study of the place of agriculture in providing employment for a rapidly growing labor force is Anne Booth and R. M. Sundrum, *Labour Absorption in Agriculture* (Oxford, 1985).
11. *HDR 1994*, 149.
12. A survey with many references is Vernon W. Ruttan, "Assistance to Expanding Agricultural Production," *World Development* 14, no. 1 (1986): 39–63.
13. For a revisionist approach arguing that traditional land tenure patterns do not impede agricultural development as much as has been assumed, see David A. Atwood, "Land Registration in Africa: The Impact on Agricultural Production," *World Development* 18, no. 5 (May 1990): 659–671; and R. A. Cramb and I. R. Wills, "The Role of Traditional Institutions in Rural Development: Community-Based Land Tenure and Government Land Policy in Sarawak, Malaysia," *World Development* 18, no. 3 (March 1990): 347–360.
14. For this paragraph, see Gershon Feder and Tongroj Onchan cited in "Security Helps Productivity," *World Bank Research News* 7, no. 4 (Spring 1987); Gershon Feder and Raymond Noronha, "Land Rights Systems and Agricultural Development in Sub-Saharan Africa," *World Bank Research Observer* 2, no. 2 (July 1987): 150–158 and Hans P. Binswanger and John McIntire, "Behavioral and Material Determinants of Production

Relations in Land-Abundant Tropical Agriculture," *Economic Development and Cultural Change* 36, no, 1 (October 1987): 73–99.

15. Keijiro Otsuka, Hiroyuki Chuma, and Yujiro Hayami, "Land and Labor Contracts in Agrarian Economies: Theories and Facts," *Journal of Economic Literature* 30, no. 4 (December 1992): 1971, 1973.
16. Otsuka, Chuma, and Hayami, "Land and Labor Contracts in Agrarian Economies: Theories and Facts," 1971, 1973.
17. The curious fact that all over the LDCs the percentage sharing is usually 50–50 is noted by Otsuka, Chuma, and Hayami, "Land and Labor Contracts in Agrarian Economies: Theories and Facts," 1977.
18. A. J. Rayner and K. A. Ingersent, "Institutional and Technical Change in Agriculture," in V. N. Balasubramanyam and Sanjaya Lall, eds., *Current Issues in Development Economics* (New York, 1991), 23–49, especially p. 25; Nicholas Stern, "The Economics of Development: A Survey," *Economic Journal* 99, no. 397 (September 1989): 659–660; Clive Bell, "Credit Markets and Interlinked Transactions," in Hollis Chenery and T. N. Srinivasan, eds., *Handbook of Development Economics*, vol. 1 (Amsterdam, 1988), 768, 801.
19. Much of this research is cited by Hiromitsu Kaneda, "Structural Change and Policy Response in Japanese Agriculture after the Land Reform," *Economic Development and Cultural Change* 28, no. 3 (1982): 485–486. See also I. M. D. Little, *Economic Development: Theory, Policy, and International Relations* (New York, 1982), 174. For the comment on India, see Pranab Bardhan and Ashok Rudra, "Terms and Conditions of Sharecropping Contracts: An Analysis of Village Survey Data in India," *Journal of Development Studies* 16, no. 3 (1980): 287–302; and the work of C. H. H. Rao and C. C. Malone. The quote concerning Pakistan is from Ijaz Nabi, "Contracts, Resource Use and Productivity in Sharecropping," *Journal of Development Studies* 22, no. 2 (1986): 429–442.
20. See R. A. Berry and W. R. Cline, *Agrarian Structure and Productivity in Developing Countries* (Baltimore, 1979); G. A. Cornia, "Farm Size, Land Yields and the Agricultural Production Function: An Analysis for Fifteen Developing Countries," *World Development* 13, no. 4 (1985): 513–534; and Partha Dasgupta, *An Inquiry into Well-Being and Destitution*, 525.
21. See Celso Furtado, *Economic Development in Latin America* (Cambridge, 1970), 54–55.
22. Otsuka, Chuma, and Hayami, "Land and Labor Contracts in Agrarian Economies: Theories and Facts," 2003.
23. *WDR 1979*, 50.
24. See Gershon Feder, Richard Just, and David Silverman, "Adoption of Agricultural Innovations in Developing Countries: A Survey," *Economic Development and Cultural Change* 33, no. 2 (1985): 271.
25. See especially the discussion in P. J. D. Wiles, *Economic Institutions Compared* (Oxford, 1977).
26. *The Economist*, March 5, 1988.
27. *International Economic Review* (June 1992); *Christian Science Monitor*, November 12, 1992.
28. See Prabhu L. Pingali, Yves Bigot, and Hans P. Binswanger, *Agricultural Mechanization and the Evolution of Farming Systems in Sub-Saharan Africa* (Baltimore, 1987); and Hans Binswanger and Prabhu Pingali, "Technological Priorities for Farming in Sub-Saharan Africa," *World Bank Research Observer* 3, no. 1 (January 1988): 81–98.
29. See *WDR 1982*, 81–82, and *WDR 1986*, 85–86.

30. U Tun Wai, "A Revisit to Interest Rates Outside the Organized Money Markets of Underdeveloped Countries," *Banca Nazionale del Lavoro Quarterly Review* 122 (September 1977): 311; and see Dale W. Adams and J. D. von Pischke, "Microenterprise Credit Programs: Déja Vu," *World Development* 20, no. 10 (October 1992): 1466.
31. U Tun Wai, "Interest Rates Outside the Organized Money Markets," 309.
32. See Gershon Feder and Raymond Noronha, "Land Rights Systems and Agricultural Development," 143–169.
33. Dale W. Adams, "The Conundrum of Successful Credit Projects in Floundering Rural Financial Markets," *Economic Development and Cultural Change* 36, no. 2 (January 1988): 355–368.
34. Avishay Braverman and Monika Huppi, "Improving Rural Finance in Developing Countries," *Finance and Development* 28, no. 1 (March 1991): 42–44.
35. U Tun Wai, "Interest Rates Outside the Organized Money Markets," 294.
36. Braverman and Huppi, "Improving Rural Finance in Developing Countries," 42–44.
37. U Tun Wai, "Interest Rates Outside the Organized Money Markets," 302.
38. See F. J. A. Bouman and R. Houtman, "Pawnbroking as an Instrument of Rural Banking in the Third World," *Economic Development and Cultural Change* 37, no. 1 (October 1988): 69–90.
39. See Clive Bell, "Credit Markets and Interlinked Transactions," 768, 801.
40. Clive Bell, "Credit Markets and Interlinked Transactions," 794–795.
41. *WDR 1989*, 112–113.
42. For a study that gives many bibliographical references, see Michael Lipton, "Agricultural Finance and Rural Credit in Poor Countries," in Paul Streeten and Richard Jolly, eds., *Recent Issues in World Development* (Oxford, 1981). The work of Joseph E. Stiglitz has emphasized the importance of imperfect information and the costs of overcoming it. Stiglitz notes in particular how imperfect information has repercussions beyond credit alone, including the link between credit and land tenure arrangements such as sharecropping. His article, "The New Development Economics," *World Development* 14, no. 2 (1986): 257–265, refers to several other important articles written by him, some with D. M. G. Newbery, and a wide selection of other works as well. In their extensive and valuable research, Dale Adams and Richard Meyers of Ohio State have discussed subsidized rural credit programs. "How not to do it" is emphasized in Dale W. Adams, Douglas H. Graham, and John D. von Pischke, eds., *Undermining Rural Development with Cheap Credit* (Boulder, Colo., 1984); and by John D. von Pischke et al., eds., *Rural Financial Markets in Developing Countries: Their Use and Abuse* (Baltimore, 1983).
43. See Timothy Besley, "How Do Market Failures Justify Interventions in Rural Credit Markets?" *World Bank Research Observer* 9, no. 1 (January 1994): 27–47.
44. *WDR 1989*, 55–56; Anand G. Chandavarkar, "The Financial Pull of Urban Areas in LDCs," *Finance and Development* 22, no. 2 (1985): 26; *WDR 1986*, 101.
45. For this paragraph, see Dale W. Adams and J. D. von Pischke, "Microenterprise Credit Programs: Déja Vu," 1463–1470; Braverman and Huppi, "Improving Rural Finance in Developing Countries," 42–44; *WDR 1986*, 100; Avishay Braverman and J. Luis Guasch, "Rural Credit Markets and Institutions in Developing Countries: Lessons for Policy Analysis from Practice and Modern Theory," *World Development* 14, no. 10 (October/November 1986): 1253–1267; Jacob Yaron, "Successful Rural Finance Institutions," *Finance and Development* 31, no. 1 (March 1994): 32–35; and *WDR 1987*, 122.
46. Monika Huppi and Gershon Feder, "The Role of Groups and Credit Cooperatives in Rural Lending," *World Bank Research Observer* 5, no. 2 (July 1990): 187–204; Yaron, "Successful Rural Finance Institutions," 32–35; *HDR 1993*, 85; and *WDR 1989*, 116.

47. See Charles W. Calomiris and Charles P. Himmelberg, "Directed Credit Programs for Agriculture and Industry," *Proceedings of the World Bank Annual Conference on Development Economics 1993* (Washington, D.C., 1994), 119; *HDR 1993*, 6, 95; *WDR 1989*, 117; Stephen C. Smith, *Case Studies in Economic Development* (New York, 1994), 38–43; Jacob Yaron, "Successful Rural Finance Institutions," 32–35; and Jacob Yaron, "What Makes Rural Finance Institutions Successful," *World Bank Research Observer* 9, no. 1 (January 1994): 49–70.
48. Jeffrey M. Riedinger, "Innovation in Rural Finance: Indonesia's Badan Kredit Kecamatan," *World Development* 22, no. 3 (March 1994): 301–313; *WDR 1989*, 119.
49. Braverman and Huppi, "Improving Rural Finance in Developing Countries," 42–44.
50. *HDR 1991*, 72; Smith, *Case Studies in Economic Development*, 44.
51. For some of the institutions and a discussion, see *WDR 1990*, 67–68.
52. From *WDR 1979*, 50.
53. *WDR 1989*, 118.
54. *WDR 1986*, 101.
55. For details and data on IFAD, see Idriss Jazairy, Mohiuddin Alamgir, and Theresa Panuccio, *The State of World Rural Poverty: An Inquiry into Its Causes and Consequences* (New York, 1992); and the reports in various issues of *The Economist*.
56. See Alain de Janvry and Elisabeth Sadoulet, "The Conditions for Compatibility between Aid and Trade in Agriculture," *Economic Development and Cultural Change* 37, no. 1 (October 1988): 1–30.
57. For comments in this vein, see Dale W. Adams and Robert C. Vogel, "Rural Financial Markets in Low-Income Countries: Recent Controversies and Lessons," *World Development* 14, no. 4 (1986): 477–487; Adams and von Pischke, "Microenterprise Credit Programs: Déja Vu," 1463–1470; Adams, Graham, and von Pischke, *Undermining Rural Development with Cheap Credit*; and von Pischke et al., *Rural Financial Markets*.
58. As discussed at length by Dean Birkhaeuser, Robert E. Evenson, and Gershon Feder, "The Economic Impact of Agricultural Extension: A Review," *Economic Development and Cultural Change* 39, no. 3 (April 1991): 607–650; Vernon W. Ruttan, *Agricultural Research Policy* (Minneapolis, 1984); and Robert Picciotto, "National Agricultural Research," *Finance and Development* 22, no. 2 (1985): 45–47. Picciotto notes that rates of return on agricultural research are now commonly over 20%.
59. See *WDR 1982*, 73.
60. From Gershon Feder and Roger Slade, "The Impact of Agricultural Extension: The Training and Visit System in India," *World Bank Research Observer* 1, no. 2 (1986): 139–161, especially 140.
61. *WDR 1982* and *WDR 1983* have material on farmer behavior. For a review of the literature see Timmer, "The Agricultural Transformation"; T. W. Schultz, *Distortions of Agricultural Incentives*; and Robert E. Evenson and Yoav Kislev, "Investment in Agricultural Research and Extension: A Survey of International Data," *Economic Development and Cultural Change* 23, no. 3 (1974): 507–521. Uma Lele, ed., *Aid to African Agriculture: Lessons from Two Decades of Donors' Experience* (Baltimore, 1992) addresses the problems in an African context. *WDR 1986*, 87, discusses risk aversion in farming.
62. John Russell, "Adapting Extension Work to Poorer Agricultural Areas," *Finance and Development* 18, no, 2 (1981): 32.
63. For information on the new agricultural technologies, see Mohammad Alauddin and Clement Tisdell, *The "Green Revolution" and Economic Development* (New York, 1991); Randolph Barker and Robert W. Herdt, *The Rice Economy of Asia* (Baltimore, 1985); T. Bayliss-Smith and S. Wanmali, *Understanding Green Revolutions* (Cam-

bridge, 1986); Peter B. R. Hazell and C. Ramsamy, *The Green Revolution Reconsidered: The Impact of High-Yielding Rice Varieties in South India* (Baltimore, 1991); Ronald D. Lee et al., *Population, Food and Rural Development* (Oxford, 1988); Michael Lipton and Richard Longhurst, *New Seeds and Poor People* (Baltimore, 1989); Prem S. Mann, "Green Revolution Revisited: The Adoption of High Yielding Variety Wheat Seeds in India," *Journal of Development Studies* 26, no. 1 (October 1989): 131–144; and Don Paarlberg, *Toward a Well-Fed World* (Ames, 1988). I also used *WDR 1982*, 69–71, and *WDR 1986*, 78. *The Economist* has published frequently on the subject, and many issues have been consulted, including March 9, 1991, and April 20, 1991. Also see *WDR 1991*, 74; and Peter T. White, "Rice: The Essential Harvest," *National Geographic* 185, no. 5 (May 1994): 48–79.

64. See *The Economist*, June 27, 1992.
65. For this paragraph, see Lester R. Brown, "Facing Food Insecurity," in Lester R. Brown et al., *State of the World 1994* (New York, 1994), 179, 184.
66. *Christian Science Monitor*, October 26, 1994. For a study emphasizing the need to appreciate differing local conditions, see Robert S. Anderson, Edwin Levy, and Barrie Morrison, *Rice Science and Development Politics: Research Strategies and IRRI's Technologies Confront Asian Diversity (1950–1980)* (Oxford, 1991).
67. See Birkhaeuser, Evenson, and Feder, "The Economic Impact of Agricultural Extension: A Review," 607–650, and especially 609, 631 for T&V; and a survey article by Gershon Feder and Roger Slade, "The Impact of Agricultural Extension: The Training and Visit System in India," *World Bank Research Observer* 1, no. 2 (1986): 139–161. Also see the same authors' "A Comparative Analysis of Some Aspects of the Training and Visit System of Agricultural Extension in India," *Journal of Development Studies* 22, no. 2 (1986): 407–428; Gershon Feder, Lawrence J. Lau, and Roger H. Slade, "The Impact of Agricultural Extension: A Case Study of the Training and Visit System in Haryana, India," *World Bank Staff Working Paper No. 756* (Washington, D.C., 1985); and *The Economist*, July 5, 1986.
68. For this section I utilized (in alphabetical order) Alauddin and Tisdell, *The "Green Revolution" and Economic Development*; Hans P. Binswanger and Joachim von Braun, "Technological Change and Commercialization in Agriculture: The Effect on the Poor," *World Bank Research Observer* 6, no. 1 (January 1991): 57–80; George Blyn, "The Green Revolution Revisited," *Economic Development and Cultural Change* 31, no. 4 (1983): 705–725; B. H. Farmer, "The 'Green Revolution' in South Asian Ricefields: Environment and Production," *Journal of Development Studies* 15, no. 3 (1979): 304–319; B. H. Farmer, ed., *Green Revolution?* (London, 1977) and the review of this volume by Michael Lipton in the *Journal of Development Studies* 15, no. 3 (1979): 342–349; Feder, Just, and Silverman, "Adoption of Agricultural Innovations," 255–298; Grace E. Goodell, "Bugs, Bunds, Banks, and Bottlenecks: Organizational Contradictions in the New Rice Technology," *Economic Development and Cultural Change* 33, no. 1 (1984): 23–41; Murray J. Leaf, "The Green Revolution and Cultural Change in a Punjab Village," *Economic Development and Cultural Change* 31, no. 2 (1983): 227–270; Michael Lipton and Richard Longhurst, *New Seeds and Poor People* (Baltimore, 1989); John W. Mellor and Gunvant M. Desai, ed., *Agricultural Change and Rural Poverty* (Baltimore, 1985); M. Prahladachar, "Income Distribution Effects of the Green Revolution in India: A Review of the Empirical Evidence," *World Development* 11, no. 11 (1983): 927–944; A. J. Rayner and K. A. Ingersent, "Institutional and Technical Change in Agriculture," in V. N. Balasubramanyam and Sanjaya Lall, eds., *Current Issues in Development Economics* (New York, 1991): 23–49; and Vernon Ruttan, "The

Green Revolution: Seven Generalizations," *International Development Review* (December 1977): 16–22.

69. The empirical evidence on growing labor use is cited in S. K. Jayasuriya and R. T. Shand, "Technical Change and Labor Absorption in Asian Agriculture: Some Emerging Trends," *World Development* 14, no. 3 (1986): 415–428. See especially 417–420 for this evidence. There were some exceptions to the trend toward increased labor use.
70. For a case in point, see Keijiro Otsuka, Violeta Cordova, and Cristina C. David, "Green Revolution, Land Reform, and Household Income Distribution in the Philippines," *Economic Development and Cultural Change* 40, no. 4 (July 1992): 719–741.
71. See Hans P. Binswanger and Joachim von Braun, "Technological Change and Commercialization in Agriculture: The Effect on the Poor," *World Bank Research Observer* 6, no. 1 (January 1991): 64.
72. Binswanger and Braun, "Technological Change and Commercialization in Agriculture: The Effect on the Poor," 64.
73. See Jayasuriya and Shand, "Technical Change and Labor Absorption in Asian Agriculture: Some Emerging Trends," 420–425; and S. K. Jayasuriya, A. Te, and R. W. Herdt, "Mechanisation and Cropping Intensification: Economics of Machinery Use in Low-Wage Economies," *Journal of Development Studies* 22, no. 2 (1986): 327–335, for details in this and the next two paragraphs.
74. *WDR 1992*, 138–139.
75. Several volumes that discuss this experience include Anne O. Krueger, ed., *The Political Economy of Agricultural Pricing Policy*, 5 vols; George S. Tolley, Vinod Thomas, and Chung Ming Wong, *Agricultural Price Policies and the Developing Countries* (Baltimore, 1982); I. Arnon, *Modernization of Agriculture in Developing Countries* (Chichester, 1981); James A. Lynch, Jr., and Edward B. Tasch, *Food Production and Public Policy in Developing Countries* (New York, 1983); and D. Gale Johnson and G. Edward Schuh, *The Role of Markets in the World Food Economy* (Boulder, Colo., 1983). The comprehensive reforms undertaken by Turkey and Bangladesh have attracted especial attention. See *WDR 1986*, 106–108.
76. From Reginald H. Green, in Meier, *Leading Issues*, 3rd ed., 837.
77. *WDR 1985*, 10.
78. Recent analyses of the reform of Chinese agriculture include (alphabetically) Keith Griffin, ed., *Institutional Reform and Economic Development in the Chinese Countryside* (Armonk, N.Y., 1985); Y. Y. Kueh and Robert F. Ash, eds., *Economic Trends in Chinese Agriculture: The Impact of Post-Mao Reforms* (Oxford, 1993); D. Gale Johnson, "Economic Reforms in the People's Republic of China," *Economic Development and Cultural Change* 36, no. 3, supplement (April 1988): S225–S245; Nicolas Lardy, *Agriculture in China's Modern Economic Development* (Cambridge, 1983); Dwight Perkins, "Reforming China's Economic System," *Journal of Economic Literature* 26, no. 2 (June 1988): 601–645; Dwight Perkins and Shahid Yusuf, *Rural Development in China* (Baltimore, 1984); and Simon G. Powell, *Agricultural Reform in China: From Communes to Commodity Economy, 1978–1990* (Manchester, 1992). See also *WDR 1986*, 105–106, and many issues of *The Economist*.
79. See M. J. Gordon, "China's Path to Market Socialism," *Challenge* 5, no. 1 (January/February 1992): 53–56; Carl Riskin, *China's Political Economy: The Quest for Development Since 1949* (Oxford, 1987); and *WDR 1986*, 105.
80. *WDR 1986*, 95–97.
81. For this and the next paragraph, see *WDR 1991*, 139; and *The Economist*, May 4 and October 5, 1991.
82. *WDR 1986*, 109.

83. See Michael Cowen, "Change in State Power, International Conditions and Peasant Producers: The Case of Kenya," *Journal of Development Studies* 22, no. 2 (1986): 355–384.
84. The argument is traced at length by Jean Drèze and Amartya Sen, *Hunger and Public Action* (Oxford, 1990).
85. See *The Economist*, August 12, 1989.
86. This section builds on what W. Arthur Lewis had to say in *The Theory of Economic Growth* (London, 1955), especially 59–60. I utilized especially Dennis Goulet, "Participation in Development: New Avenues," *World Development* 17, no. 2 (February 1989): 165–178; Alan B. Durning, "Ending Poverty," in Lester R. Brown et al., *State of the World 1990* (New York, 1990), 135–153; Durning, "Action at the Grassroots: Fighting Poverty and Environmental Decline," *Worldwatch Paper No. 88* (January, 1989); Lane E. Holdcroft, "The Rise and Fall of Community Development 1950–65: A Critical Assessment," in Eicher and Staatz, *Agricultural Development in the Third World*, 46–58; Alain de Janvry, Elisabeth Sadoulet, and Erik Thorbecke, eds., "State, Market, and Civil Organisations: New Theories, New Practices, and their Implications for Rural Development," a special issue of *World Development* 21, no. 4 (April 1993), particularly Norman Uphoff, "Grassroots Organizations and NGOs in Rural Development: Opportunities with Diminishing States and Expanding Markets," 607–622; *HDR 1991*, 72; *HDR 1993*, 86–87, 95; and *Wall Street Journal*, January 8, 1992.
87. *WDR 1980*, 75; *Newsweek*, June 23, 1986.
88. See *WDR 1979*, chap. 8, for details, and also *WDR 1982*, 85. There is a useful analysis in Samuel S. P. Ho, "Economic Development and Rural Industry in South Korea and Taiwan," *World Development* 10, no. 11 (1982): 973–990. A recent study of what might be done is C. Peter Timmer, ed., *Agriculture and the State: Growth, Employment, and Poverty in Developing Countries* (Ithaca, 1991).
89. See N. S. S. Narayana, Kirit S. Parikh, and T. N. Srinivasan, "Rural Works Programs in India: Costs and Benefits," *Journal of Development Economics* 29, no. 2 (September 1988): 131–156; and I. Singh, Small Farmers and the Landless in South Asia, *World Bank Staff Working Paper No. 320* (1979).
90. Adams and von Pischke, "Microenterprise Credit Programs: Déja Vu," 1463–1470; Riedinger, "Innovation in Rural Finance: Indonesia's Badan Kredit Kecamatan," 301–313.
91. See W. A. Byrd and Lin Qinsong, eds., *China's Rural Industry: Structure Development and Reform* (Oxford, 1990), which is thorough on the TVEs; M. J. Gordon, "China's Path to Market Socialism," *Challenge* 35, no. 1 (January/February 1992): 53–56; Barry Naughton, *Growing Out of the Plan: Chinese Economic Reform, 1978–1993* (Cambridge, 1994); Barry Naughton, "Chinese Institutional Innovation and Privatization from Below," *American Economic Review Papers and Proceedings* 84, no. 2 (May 1994): 266–270; Powell, *Agricultural Reform in China: From Communes to Commodity Economy, 1978–1990*; *The Economist*, November 28, 1992; the *Christian Science Monitor*, May 25, 1993; and *WDR 1986*, 106.
92. *WDR 1994*, 168–169; and see Shahid Javed Burki and Robert L. Ayres, "A Fresh Look at Development Aid," *Finance and Development* 23, no. 1 (1986): 7.
93. Students could continue their study of employment problems with Lyn Squire, *Employment Policy in Developing Countries: A Survey of Issues and Evidence* (New York, 1981); and Kanhaya L. Gupta, *Industrialization and Employment in Developing Countries* (London, 1989).

Chapter 12

Industrialization

Manufacturing and Urban Development in the LDCs

Given the recent experience of the LDCs, and the historical record of today's developed countries, it is clear that improvements in levels of living have been most rapid in countries where the industrial sector has grown. Because industrialization on a large scale requires a concentrated labor force, it typically has been associated with growing urbanization.

Successful industrialization is a complex operation that cannot be explained simplistically.[1] The removal of bad government policies and the implementation of good ones are decidedly not always sufficient to bring it about. At the level of the firm, industrialization involves the adoption of new technologies, the acquisition of new skills, the development of a network of complementary activities and skills, and experience in how to handle risk and uncertainty. At the level of the nation, industrialization requires the establishment of rules on property, the fostering of incentives, the amassing of human capital through education, health, and nutrition, efforts to acquire and disseminate technology, and institutional development. Differences in all of these lead to vastly different degrees of industrial performance.

Experience demonstrates that there is no single optimal path to industrialization. Success will depend on several factors. If the size of a country's market is large enough to generate scale economies, then some protection of infant industries by means of tariffs may allow them to become established and prosper as they learn the ropes and build their capabilities, and as complementary suppliers become established. But this approach must be used selectively, because many industries will never be able to develop a comparative advantage. A strong resource base points to the possibility of industrialization through processing these resources, though some of the most flourishing industrial performers—South Korea, Taiwan, Hong Kong, Singapore, and, before them, Japan, have few or no natural resources.

THE ROLE OF GOVERNMENT IN INDUSTRIALIZATION: MARKET FAILURE IN THE LDCS

In general, government intervention to facilitate the operation of the market mechanism is necessary. Few doubt that government must act in certain ways to promote development. At minimum it must provide a legal framework, including criminal, contract, property, corporation, bankruptcy, and liability (tort) law, and the policing of them; public health measures and safety standards; regulation of the banking system, monopolies, and pollution; the provision of education; infrastructure improvement when the private market does not supply an adequate quantity, including roads, ports, water supplies, and irrigation; management of common property such as rivers, forests, and grazing lands; and measures to improve the position of the poor such as land reform, targeted food subsidies, food-for-work, and credit facilities for low-income borrowers. Beyond these measures, there is considerable debate on how far government intervention should go in providing what the private sector can. As Lord Bauer noted, if government sticks to the tasks just discussed and does them well, it won't have the time or the resources to do much else![2]

Most economists probably agree that government participation in the process of industrialization is usually necessary for it to be successful, but that intervention must be selective and well-designed. Obviously, it is advantageous to have able bureaucrats rather than ill-trained and politicized officials. Limited early expansion of industry may provide a necessary boost, giving technical experience to workers and managers. Tactical decisions are necessary. Light industries, such as textile and clothing production, require far less intervention by government and less capital investment than do heavy industries such as steel or automobiles, although heavy industries have done well in some countries, such as South Korea, Taiwan, and Brazil. Officials have to decide whether to base their decisions on a country's current markets, or on what they foresee as the condition of its markets some years into the future. Either decision involves a risk of error, the first being that the situation will change, and the second that it will not change as the officials predicted. Further decisions have to be made concerning whether to permit partial or complete foreign ownership, and on how liberal repatriation of profit is to be.

In spite of these risks, the idea that government assistance can give a jump-start to industrial development does appear to be reflected in the experience of the high-performing Asian economies. A head start toward industrialization may ultimately be one of the most important advantages in achieving economic progress. As Michael Porter has pointed out, the eventual development of industrial districts ("clusters" he calls them) results in the diffusion of ideas, attracts educational and technical institutions, and gives rise to pressures that keep industry competitive. The pressures include the motivation stemming from personal rivalries that frequently occur when firms are in close proximity. Such rivalries, according to Porter, are a central feature of successful industrialization.[3]

Government Intervention in Production

One of the great debates in development economics involves the role that government should play in the allocation of an economy's resources. The essential question is the extent to which an economy should be directed by a government's priorities rather than by the unplanned operation of a decentralized system of market prices.

Rather obviously, industrialization in *any* LDC will require some minimally adequate level of skills, education, and management ability. Even with supportive government policies in place, industrialization may still not be successful without a sufficient amount of these sorts of human capital. In their absence, investment in physical capital is likely to have a low payoff.[4]

Some economists go further, arguing that the appropriate model is Hong Kong: There, government intervenes hardly at all in actual production, which clearly cuts the risks of bad policy mistakes. But Hong Kong also has an exceptionally fine endowment of education, skills, entrepreneurship, and a good working infrastructure, most of which involve government effort. In effect, the Hong Kong model is not actually one of nonintervention, but of intervention by different means. LDCs interested in a similar policy of enhancing capabilities might find that this is actually harder to achieve than it is to intervene selectively to develop certain industries.

Advocates of a role for government suggest that an unimpeded market mechanism may not give optimal results for two reasons: First, the market may not work perfectly, and second, the market, when it works, may produce undesirable results.[5] Critics of this view will insist that all government interventions into production must be closely scrutinized. State-owned and state-operated enterprises may be inefficient, while increased taxation to support government activity, or measures that raise labor or other input costs, can undercut the profitability of private firms and cause them to fail. We trace the debate in this section.

Responses to Market Failures

1. Governments can help to disseminate information to dispel ignorance and add to the supply of information about markets. This can be especially important for investment decisions in which the lifetime of capital goods is long and the indivisibility of capital makes for "lumpy" investment and large economies of scale. Bold strategies pioneered by Japan's Ministry of Trade and Industry and emulated by the high-performing Asian economies, as we saw in Chapter 3, might pay dividends if governments can help to identify industries with a potential comparative advantage. The South Korean deliberation councils are a good example of how government can promote private–public cooperation. Other countries, mostly Asian, have adopted much the same approach—though clearly a competent bureaucracy is

required to make it work. One possible dynamic is that the information that private businesspeople receive from government can be of value to them, and so they may be willing to reveal some of their own plans in return.

2. Externalities can exist. Investors, employers, and landlords consider the private marginal product, not the social marginal product, of their activities. External economies do not lead to more of a given activity because the externality is reaped by others; external diseconomies are ignored because these costs are not felt by their perpetrator. Research and development activity and the training of skilled labor by a firm may benefit many other firms, not just the one undertaking the activity. In these cases, governments may assist, particularly with their policies on taxes, subsidies, foreign exchange, and credit. (Again, see the discussion of the high-performing Asian economies in Chapter 3 for a survey of how this might be done.)
3. Monopoly distortions can be widespread in an economy. Although estimates of the degree of monopoly power in the LDCs are rare, there are reasons to believe that such power may be more pervasive than in the developed countries. Imports may be constrained, antitrust laws are frequently nonexistent, the countervailing power of labor unions is often weak, small markets inhibit competition, and highly concentrated land ownership may mean some monopoly power in the agricultural sector as well as in industry. To the degree that the market does not allocate resources correctly, government action, such as lowering import barriers and establishing antitrust regulation, may be important.
4. Because of the economic structure of LDCs, a system of market prices may require large and destabilizing price changes to achieve useful results. Obstacles and bottlenecks of all kinds can exist. Resources may be immobile. Perhaps there is even a perverse ("backward-bending") response to price changes by labor, farmers, and small businesses. All these constraints may make supply so inelastic that large price changes are needed to call forth small adjustments, a position similar to the structural argument concerning inflation is discussed in Chapter 5. In such cases, governments may be able to assist in building institutions.[6] (Though it should be pointed out that a wealth of evidence from agriculture indicates that poor peasant farmers are quick to appreciate new opportunities for profit, as in the green revolution, or are quick to shift to lower-taxed crops, sell on the black market, or smuggle when taxation hits their staple. It is self-evident that migrants to the cities or overseas are responding in a dramatic way to economic incentives. This is certainly not to claim that all markets in LDCs work efficiently, but it is still a bit of a puzzle how the idea that market responses are generally weak or perverse in LDCs would gain such widespread credence.)[7]

The Decline of Planning

At one time, an opinion was current that even where markets work properly, they have undesirable results. Proponents of this view—epitomized by central planning in the former Communist countries, but reflected in the government planning undertaken in many non-Communist LDCs and developed countries as well—focus on the following:

1. A government might judge that there is a socially undesirable maldistribution of income that leads to the emphasis on production of items consumed by those with higher incomes at the expense of goods produced for those with lower incomes. In this view, markets might be working perfectly in all ways, but some people could still be living in deep poverty or even be starving.
2. Government might make a value judgment that it should weigh the interests of future generations more heavily than the market. Usually this meant government programs to boost capital investment to a higher level than the market would provide.

At the end of the colonial period, many LDCs acquired new governments with new leaders who were committed to fast future growth through capital investment and more equity in income distribution. They believed government planning could achieve both goals. These leaders went beyond the advocacy of government participation in the development process as a facilitator of private market activity. They argued that government should actually direct and undertake production of goods and services that *could* have been provided through private market forces.

What were the core characteristics of government plans?[8] (The use of past tense reflects the decline in enthusiasm for generalized planning, even though planning in one form or another still survives in numerous LDCs.) Government economic planning took three main forms: comprehensive, indicative, and formal. Comprehensive plans entailed substantial government intervention in the operation of the economy, with government directing most production and undertaking a considerable amount of that production itself. Indicative plans involved fully or largely planned government expenditure, with private spending influenced but not commanded by tax and subsidy policies. Formal plans were more a sketch for strategy than a blueprint actually to be implemented. Indicative and formal planning often emphasized sectoral models that focused on the relations between two or three industries. Such sectoral models were much easier to implement than was comprehensive planning, and are still in frequent use.[9]

Comprehensive Planning Comprehensive, or *dirigiste,* plans followed the Soviet command model, and covered a large part of the economy. Typically they employed direct government command to determine output, with inputs also specified in the plan under the system called "materials balancing." Karl Marx was not, by the way, the intellectual pioneer of comprehensive planning. He said little about it. That title falls more reasonably to Walter Rathenau, the mobilizer of Germany's World War I production effort. Rathenau made a number of the original arguments for planning, including market failure, many externalities and important scale economies (especially in the infrastructure), imperfect capital markets, and inadequate entrepreneurship.

Comprehensive planning was carried out for a large part of the economy, as was true of the USSR, Eastern Europe, and China; or it was applied mostly to heavy industry, as at one time or another in Bangladesh, Ethiopia, India, Sri Lanka,

Turkey, Algeria, Libya, and several others. The second Indian five-year plan of 1956 to 1961 was a typical partial effort. Government nationalized the economy's "commanding heights," adopted the licensing of enterprises, and established a wide variety of direct controls on private economic effort.

In LDCs, the major obstacles to carrying out comprehensive planning were lack of government support, weaknesses in information, inadequate staff, and poor coordination of industrial investment. Especially when the plan was highly mathematical but the planners were inadequate communicators, political support could be weak because the plan was not understood. Lack of government support also resulted when a plan required some economic restriction such as a tax, a tariff, or a control designed to lower consumption. Government paid lip service but then did not have the will to act. Often the separation of plan formulation from plan implementation contributed to this, because the people who prepared a plan had little or no authority to establish the policies (taxes, credit, money supply changes) needed to reach the targets.

Even given the will and the policies, aggregate planning faced severe difficulties. Weaknesses in underlying information of all kinds often meant that the plan was nothing but an elegant mathematical facade. As industrial output is easiest to measure, the lack of data in other areas biased the plan toward large industrial projects and against small projects and endeavors in agriculture. A plan covering several years was subject to interruption because of bottlenecks and poor "time-phasing." Delays in construction and equipping or inability to run a project at full capacity because of some shortfall in the planned supply of inputs were reasons for failure in meeting targets. Unanticipated problems of coordination in a plan led to costly bottlenecks. As an example, a plan that involved the simultaneous construction of a road, dam, hydroelectric power station, power grid, and electricity-using industry, if far out of sequence due to materials shortages, transport difficulties, or lack of skilled labor or management, could result in severe waste of resources. Even if the sequencing was adequate, completion under heavy pressure frequently resulted in shoddy construction and inefficient operation.

The main bottleneck in planning was usually the acute shortage of qualified personnel. Gerald Meier has noted that planning was sometimes put into effect with spectacular understaffing. Malawi did so at a time when the total number of economists plus accountants in the entire country was six, with no statisticians at all; the Ministry of Planning consisted of four officers, none of whom was an expert.* Inadequacies in training, incompetency, systems that shifted personnel between departments before a task was fully learned, jealousies among ministries, and the brain drain of the most qualified to developed countries or the World Bank, all reduced the effectiveness of planning performance. Rapid changes of government cut into continuity, and there were even cases (such as in Uganda) where nations utterly unable to maintain law and order nonetheless undertook to

---

*Meier, *Emerging from Poverty*, 51–52. Robert Christiansen, an expert on the Malawi economy, has told me that this plan was written by expatriates and generally ignored by the government.

plan.[10] Foreign advisors could be thrown into the breach, but the advisor who stayed a few weeks, made the initial decisions that included mistakes, and then left the local officials to take the responsibility when these mistakes became apparent, did little to improve the results. These difficulties appeared inherent in underdevelopment, hardly easier to solve than poverty itself.

Even the countries with excellent planning organizations and where good data were widely available (India, for example) found comprehensive planning difficult to carry through. By and large, their comprehensive plans were unable to surmount the shock that a changing economic environment might deliver. Unforeseen events of the 1970s and 1980s, such as the oil crises, the food shock, and the debt crisis, brought formidable and complex problems of reworking the planning structure. Events showed that governments with centralized decision making were no better able to anticipate these crises than governments with less comprehensive planning or none at all.

Only a minority of LDCs went through a period of comprehensive planning, though almost all other LDCs did actually adopt plans of their own. Over 300 separate national plans eventually emerged. But most of these were "formal" plans, attempts to present a national consensus or vision about economic policy rather than operating documents for managing an economy. Often such plans were designed to demonstrate rational development strategies to aid givers. Typically they emphasized forecasting, "strategic policies," and appraisal of individual projects rather than attempting to be comprehensive. Such plans often utilized a "capital–output ratio," which became the most familiar mathematical relationship in economic development. The appendix to this chapter discusses the use of capital–output ratios and the eventual loss of confidence in their utility.

Extensive national planning of any type faltered in the 1970s, with plan targets increasingly being missed.[11] In the 1980s, planning became moribund in most countries. The two main reasons for the misses were outside influences over which the planning country has no control and inside (domestic) problems with the plan. The outside influences were obvious. Very few plans were sufficiently resilient to survive the two oil shocks, the food shock, the interest rate shock, and the deepest recession since the 1930s, all occurring in the 1970s and 1980s. Wholesale scrapping of plans was a general result. Some LDCs brought their detailed planning to a complete halt; others quietly deemphasized the effort. Politicians and economists who supported planning came to see that plans can slip far behind events. Markets work better than plans when exogenous shocks hit and disrupt economies, because markets transmit the signals that a shock is in progress and provide the incentive for rapid reaction and adjustment, whereas planners usually have a much slower reaction time. Nowadays only Cuba and North Korea remain on the list of LDCs that undertake comprehensive planning.

What Survives? Sectoral Focusing and Project Appraisal

Planning still survives in modified form, even though the very word has become impolitic in many circles. Most LDCs have retrenched to a "lighter," less-detailed type of sectoral planning that applies more narrowly to the provision of basic human services and public goods, technology acquisition, and the like. More and more, governments have been retreating to this position, leaving production of the goods and services that the private sector can produce to private enterprise and market forces.[12]

A Sectoral Focus A focus on "key sectors" recognizes that in some economic activities, public initiative is essential, even in an economy that is reliant on private decision making through the price mechanism. The social infrastructure of basic human services—education, training, health, nutrition, and the control of population—is one area where private enterprise may have difficulties. The infrastructure of electricity, water, sewage, transport, and communication, irrigation, and agricultural support facilities, is another. Such investment is very "lumpy," and because of scale economies, the industry involved might otherwise be a private monopoly. A third area comprises efforts to aid in the acquisition of appropriate technologies and police the quality of exported products. This focus on basic human services, infrastructure development, and efforts in technology and quality have characterized the most successful contribution of governments in recent years.

A sectoral approach also implies that there are linkages among industries that private investors may find themselves unable to utilize, but which government activity could help to achieve. The main reasons why private investors might not take action on their own are lack of knowledge, unacceptable risk, and limited competition that restricts alternatives. Consider the potential problems of coordination between a small electricity-generating plant and a planned aluminum refinery. In a riskless world of perfect knowledge and competition, there would be no obstacle to coordination. The owners of the private generating plant would know that an aluminum refinery with a large demand for electrical power was planned and would move to expand accordingly in anticipation of higher profit. The aluminum promoters would go ahead with their plans, knowing that sufficient electricity will be forthcoming. Coordination takes place smoothly within the private market, and if either party reneges, potential competitors who see the profit opportunity will move to fill the gap.

Consider what may happen, however, in a world of imperfect knowledge, risk, high transactions costs, and limited competition. Again, the owners of the generating plant (call it *A*) are considering expansion, and the private backers of a proposed aluminum refinery (call it *B*) are considering construction. Yet *A* may take into account only the present level of electricity consumption, not knowing that *B* might be built. *B*, on the other hand, calculates its costs on the (expensive) price that *A* is presently charging for its current. Neither goes ahead with its plans. The problem introduced by imperfect knowledge is the lack of any motive for either *A* or *B* to increase its scale of operations in the first place, since neither knew of the other's plans.

Even if they did know, there is the risk that the plans would not actually be carried out. Neither party wants to move first because of this risk. If the power station expands but the aluminum refinery is not built, the extra electricity may have to be sold at marginal cost. If the refinery goes into operation, but the generating facility does not expand, then the required amount of current may be high in price. Neither company will move first, in a classic case of imperfect knowledge as to what will eventually happen, and risk aversion.

The lesson is that because of imperfect knowledge of the present and future, because of risk, and because there are no acceptable alternative sources of supply or demand, neither *A* nor *B* may expand, and this path toward economic growth is blocked. To counter the blockage, some arrangement for coordination and pooling of risk may be advantageous or even essential. There have been many attempts in the LDCs to overcome these problems of coordination. In practice, most attempts assume that government involvement will be necessary to overcome the imperfect knowledge, risk, and limited competition.

This sectoral focus on industrialization, based on the concept of coordinated investment, remains popular in the LDCs. A major advantage is its adaptability. It can be used to link small projects or large ones. It can apply to two firms or ten. It need not require direct government ownership and operation. Government may function as a broker, bringing private firms *A* and *B* together around the conference table. It might even be the catalyst for bringing about a merger of the firms. Alternatively, government might assume some of the risk of nonperformance. If *A* and *B* suffer from inferior entrepreneurship or a shortage of skills, a government advisory team may help. If imperfect capital markets mean limited access to capital, then government loan guarantees will perhaps suffice. At the far end of the spectrum, *A* and *B* might be government owned and operated so that the coordination is implemented directly—but the acceptability of production through state enterprises now has far less support than it once did, as we see later in the chapter. (All over the world, in the developed countries as well as the LDCs, the private market often achieves the same end when a large corporation "internalizes" these relationships. Major investments often involve a large amount of vertical coordination and information searching to overcome these problems.)

One warning, however: The idea that government can assist private enterprise in collecting and disseminating information assumes a reasonable degree of government competence and that the government's motives are above board. If one or the other of these assumptions does not hold, the outcome might be quite unsatisfactory.

Linkages A number of models envisage sectoral coordination by means of "vertical balancing" between industries or firms where a linkup would be most advantageous. Finding where such advantage might lie was an important part of the work of Albert O. Hirschman, who developed the concept of "linkage."[13] The term refers to the economic connection between a firm's operations and other sectors of the economy. The connection might be a product linkage, which in turn might be forward or backward. It is called forward when a firm's output is much used as an input by other firms and encourages investment by these subsequent users. In our previous example, the forward linkage was from electricity to aluminum production; other cases would be coal to steel, steel to light metalworking, and so on.

It is a backward linkage when a firm's output requires inputs from earlier stages of production and thus encourages investment in these earlier stages. To illustrate backward linkage, reverse the examples above (aluminum to electricity, steel to coal). It was once thought that there was little backward and forward linkage from agricultural and raw materials production, but that was before numerous LDCs began to produce fertilizers, simple farm machinery, milling and refining apparatus, and the like. Even Hirschman's reasonable assertion that the linkages may be to industries with technological requirements beyond the capacity of a typical LDC may not stop the effect from operating, since the linkages might attract multinational firms from abroad.

In addition to product linkages, which are direct, there are indirect consumption and fiscal linkages, larger or smaller depending on what is produced. When spent, the income generated by a new industry will raise demand for a wide spectrum of consumer goods producers. Even if the new spending goes for imports, a linkage is established to firms able to produce substitutes for those imports. Fiscal links emerge when government taxes the income generated by a new industry and channels the revenue into further productive investment. Such fiscal links may be especially important where a foreign-owned plantation or mining sector has little other impact on the domestic economy.

A sectoral focus on industrialization may thus come down to a measurement of the linkages (which are also sometimes called spread effects). Projects with the greatest total linkage are the ones that, once developed, will have the greatest overall effect in promoting further economic activity. Such projects will, it is hoped, become "growth centers" (*pôles de croissance*, as the original French phrase had it), their effects spreading more widely through the economy than would have been the case had there been no consideration of the linkages.

Linkages vertically between user and supplier have recently grown in the estimation of economists, who are impressed by the pioneering Japanese use of vertical coordination among firms. The Japanese have networks of vertical relationships called *keiretsu*, in which firms coordinate their research, product development, and input supply. The development is believed to have contributed to the successful product development and marketing, especially of automobiles and consumer electronics. The idea of mutually supporting, vertically related firms in close proximity to one another has been emulated by some of the high-performing Asian economies.[14]

Yet it must also be pointed out that in many LDCs, these linkage arguments have lost some force in recent years. They are still made and acted on, and they still hold the potential to be helpful. But experience has revealed difficulties in actually bringing about favorable coordination in the absence of market signals and market discipline. Moreover, government administrative weakness, political instability, and corruption have all been more damaging to successful coordination than proponents of this approach had anticipated. Significant government administrative competence appears to be essential in order to apply linkage arguments in specific and localized situations.[15]

Economies of Scale A sectoral focus and coordinated investment are related to the existence of scale economies. Coordination is necessary in the presence of imperfect knowledge and risk, so it is argued, because the high cost output of small-scale plants will present obstacles to firms utilizing that output as an input.

The argument involves the necessity of obtaining a minimum efficient scale large enough to avoid diseconomies of small scale either upstream (so keeping input prices reasonable) or downstream (so providing a sufficient market for a firm's output). A firm producing output for a small market at suboptimal scale means that other firms using that output as an input to their own production will find it expensive. Take our earlier example of a plant generating electricity on a small scale. The high costs of the electric power in a given area will presumably slow the development of any industry that is an important user of electricity. (For a case in point, China is saddled with many small-scale electricity-generating plants. These, not being very efficient, produce expensive power that would disadvantage electricity-using enterprises—except that the electricity is usually heavily subsidized, so transferring the problem to the government's budget.)[16]

In a riskless world of perfect knowledge, expansion in capacity would occur in response to new profit opportunities, bringing larger, more specialized machinery, further division of labor, and so lower average costs. In a competitive environment, the lower cost means a lower price. Potential users of electricity will be encouraged to expand their operations. The generating plant might then expand further, with users of the electricity finding that their costs are now even lower. This process goes forward as long as further expansion is profitable. If the combination of limited knowledge and risk halt the expansion, however, then scale may remain small with resulting long-term diseconomies.

The argument that small-scale production is high-cost production can be extended and generalized. If a large plant is the only kind that can achieve low long-run average costs (LRAC), as shown in Figure 12.1, then small LDCs with inadequate market size might have to pay a substantial penalty that is detrimental to development.

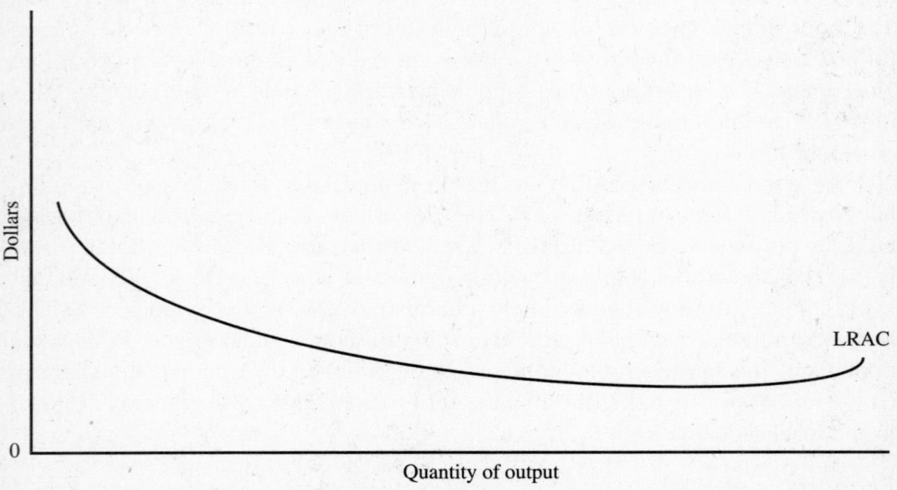

Figure 12.1 Economies of scale may be such that a large output is necessary for firms to minimize their costs.

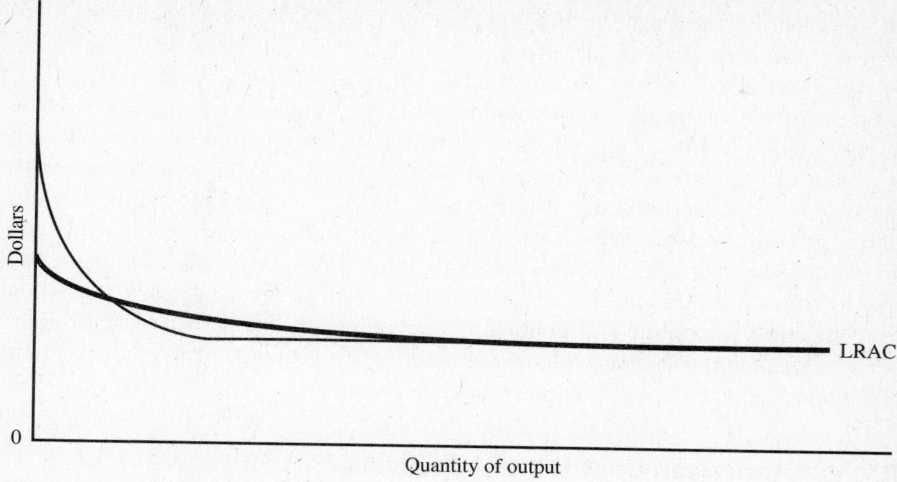

Figure 12.2 If a minimum efficient scale of production can be achieved at a relatively low level of output, then large-scale plants will be less advantageous.

Notice carefully, however, that a different view of costs would make necessary a substantial change in the predicted outcome. What if costs fall only a little with large-scale production, as along the broad curve of Figure 12.2? Or what if they fall rapidly but reach a minimum at a modest level of output, as along the narrow line of the same figure?

Unfortunately, the economic literature on this matter is neither abundant nor entirely conclusive, and the subject seems to be somewhat out of fashion. Early work based on U.S. data was done in the 1950s by Joe S. Bain; it suggested that scale economies were an overrated concept. According to Bain, most major countries had domestic markets large enough to support several plants of optimal scale in most industries. His figures led to the conclusion that numerous industries, both light and heavy, pay only a small penalty or no penalty at all when engaging in relatively small-scale production. Further research in the 1970s by F. M. Scherer and others working with him confirmed the broad thrust of Bain's pioneering efforts.[17] To the extent that Bain, Scherer, and the others are correct (and to that extent casting into doubt the traditional "received opinion" on the subject), the position of the LDCs is an easier one, with fewer pecuniary external diseconomies to suffer.

Work by other scholars over a broad range of countries typically reveals more mixed results, with scale economies important in some industries but not in others where they might logically be anticipated. Pan A. Yotopoulos and Jeffrey B. Nugent have surveyed seven studies containing a large number of estimates. These showed the greatest economies of scale in industrial gases (oxygen, chlorine, ethylene, methanol) and in some food processing (beer, fruit and vegetable canning, sugar refining). But economies were, perhaps surprisingly, far less important in some other areas (autos, computers, diesel engines, generators, machine tools, petroleum refining, rubber goods, shoes, and fish canning).[18] There seems no alternative to further careful studies of this type, but it is striking how few of them have actually been done in the LDCs.

Where does this leave the small LDC with a small domestic market and no prospect of ever achieving scale economies at home? The very question reveals the answer, which lies in exporting. A small country's foreign trade is its avenue of access to a large market—and always has been, as the developed-country examples of Belgium, the Netherlands, Luxembourg, Austria, Switzerland, all of Scandinavia, and New Zealand show conclusively. Small LDCs may even possess some economic advantages to offset the lack of a large domestic market. They are frequently freer from the divisive communal tensions of larger economies, and when they are, their economic and political organizations are likely to be less troublesome.[19] Such countries may well overcome the scale economy problem, especially if they find a niche in world markets for their exports.

Project Appraisal: Cost-Benefit Analysis and Shadow Prices

The sectoral focus on industrialization discussed above leads us to a next step: techniques for the appraisal and selection of projects. The major tool of appraisal is cost-benefit analysis (CBA), sometimes called the reverse, benefit-cost analysis (BCA).[20] Use of the technique is fairly recent in the LDCs; the very first published study employing CBA in a poor country was in 1972.[21]

Cost-benefit analysis is a method to identify projects that yield positive net social benefits, defined as benefits (willingness to pay) minus costs (compensation required). Conceptually, a measure of net social benefit can be obtained by using the demand curve shown in Figure 12.3. Say a new project reduces price from P to P_1. Total willingness to pay rises from $0DEQ$ to $0DE_1Q_1$, an increase of QEE_1Q_1. The actual payment, as opposed to the willingness to pay, is QAE_1Q_1. The net social benefit of the project is here equal to the shaded area AEE_1.

If all net benefits were realized immediately, the search would be at an end and the highest net benefit would identify the most desirable project. There is a complication, however. Some projects come to completion sooner, some later. One must employ discounting to find the net present value (NPV) of the net social benefit. The formula is the familiar one that sums the benefits at each time period Bt_1, Bt_2, Bt_3, etc., divided by $1 + r$, $(1 + r)^2$, $(1 + r)^3$, and so on, where r is the rate of interest. Often, when detailed information is lacking, a real rate of interest of 10% is used in these calculations. Planners who wish to make a choice among projects would select the ones with the highest NPVs. This is a result that most politicians are likely to find convincing, even those with little or no comprehension of the mechanics involved.

A further complication intrudes. What if an economy is distorted by such government controls as direct regulation of prices, an overvalued currency, laws requiring above-market wages in the modern sector, below-market interest rates, tariffs and quotas? This will mean that project costs do not reflect accurately the costs to society of resources used in a project. Under such conditions, a country appraising projects with the tool of net present value may choose to invest in activities that do not really fit the country's actual factor availabilities. Overly large

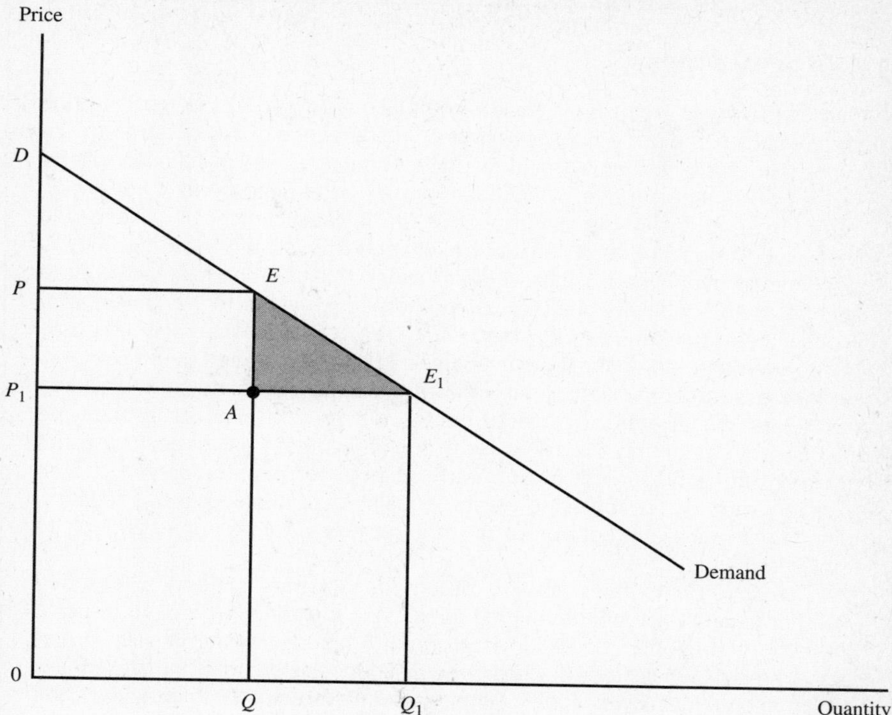

Figure 12.3 Calculating net social benefit as the difference in willingness to pay minus the actual payment, here equal to the shaded area AEE_1.

quantities of a scarce but price-controlled input may be used; too much capital and too little labor may be involved; export projects may look unprofitable because of the overvalued exchange rate; or use of cheap inputs from abroad may be retarded by tariffs and quotas. The list of potentially distorted decisions is as long as the list of distorted prices.

Problems with CBA Various difficulties affect the use of CBA. One is that the benefits of many sorts of projects are difficult to measure. A road is easier to analyze with CBA than is a health or education scheme or a prison, and so forth. For these, measurement problems may be so severe that simple cost minimization can actually be a better technique than CBA.[22] Peter Kilby of Wesleyan University has noted the illusion that can be involved in boiling down all the imponderables into a single ponderable "bottom line."[23]

A blunt warning is in order about the use of CBA. A planner can justify about any project by manipulating selected assumptions about shadow prices and linkages. Buried assumptions may be hard to trace, but even if implicitly, they may act to bias a decision. The power of government to pick and choose as it wishes is virtually

SHADOW PRICES

One possibility is an attempt to determine accurately what the market price for any output or input *would* have been in the absence of any distortion. This hypothetical price, called a "shadow price," could be used in calculating NPV instead of the actual price, which is affected by the distortions.[24] For goods traded internationally, the world price is an obvious choice, but this would have to be translated at a "shadow exchange rate" if the local currency is significantly overvalued. When there is a risk that the shadow price might change, then sensitivity analysis using alternative values for variables, with probabilities attached, can be used. If a project is assessed with shadow prices weighted for risk, then a positive NPV even under the most pessimistic assumptions would make that project a prime candidate for adoption. Even the effects of projects on the distribution of income could be included by weighting the NPVs, with higher weights assigned to income going to the poor. Project choice with weights for distribution may be an excellent method for achieving greater equality of income whenever political constraints make a direct approach (through taxes, for example) difficult to implement.

The arguments over how to determine accurate shadow prices and whether to employ welfare weights are of long standing.* It is hard to deny, however, that even crude shadow pricing, if employed systematically in project appraisal, would lead to less misallocation of investment than actually occurs in countries with a highly distorted price system. At the very least, the use of shadow prices tends to make previous misallocations more obvious.

It remains to warn the beginner in shadow pricing that there may be some mystery involved: The government that introduced the distortions in the first place, including its members, its allies, and its supporters who share the gains so generated, is often the same government toiling with shadow prices to correct for the distortions. Will there be a willingness to act on shadow prices if there is unwillingness to dismantle the controls and other distortions directly? Perhaps so, in cases where the government is rational but is politically unable to end the distortions. Perhaps not.[25]

*Among the countries that at one time or another have compiled full sets of shadow prices are India, Bangladesh, Sri Lanka, South Korea, Morocco, Kenya, and Jamaica; See Little, *Economic Development*, 397.

unlimited if its analysts are pliable—and there is plenty of circumstantial evidence that in some countries, from motives of personal gain, fear, or both, they *are* pliable. (Outside reappraisal on a sample basis would seem to be a good idea.)[26]

Even with all its problems, however, cost-benefit analysis ought to have a firm place in current development economics. As Andrew Kamarck has said, "even rough estimates are better than arbitrary, politically determined or purely intuitive decisions."[27] Requiring CBA project appraisal of every major project where it is feasible would be an excellent idea.[28]

There is a considerable way to go, however. Applications of CBA and shadow pricing are highly variable.[29] The apogee of the technique within the World Bank was in the early 1980s. Later, use of CBA with shadow pricing declined considerably, perhaps because of the scarcity of trained personnel who can do it properly, possibly because of the technical difficulties it poses for an older generation of economists, possibly because politicians dislike the way it can spoil their plans. Among LDC governments, Chile and India are major users, though even in India, which has long championed the technique, only about a third of the projects are appraised, and the only shadow price used is a shadow exchange rate. In a sample of 27 LDCs surveyed, only eight of them regularly used the techniques. Many countries do not apply CBA at all. The lack of use is unfortunate, given that CBA does involve measuring opportunity costs in a distorted economy and virtually forces economists (and presumably some politicians) to widen their view to include more than just the private outlays and revenues of projects. If the technique were more widely used, better knowledge would be available, thus reducing the chances that ill-conceived projects will be undertaken.

ELIMINATING DISTORTIONS: GOVERNMENT FAILURE IN THE LDCS

For two or three decades after World War II, development economics focused on market failures, which gave rise to extensive government interventions in economic activity. The 1980s and 1990s have seen more attention to government failures and renewed emphasis on the role of markets and the price system.[30] As we have seen in most of the chapters to this point, governments may serve to promote the self-interest of those in the government or those who can influence its behavior. "Rent-seeking behavior," that is, actions to obtain rewards from government in one form or another, has led to extensive intervention into markets and the price mechanism on the part of most LDCs.

Evidence has mounted that systematic distortions from free-market prices have systematic unfavorable effects on economic growth. The wide acceptance of the idea that government-induced distortions from market pricing could be damaging represented an important new departure in development economics. Only in the 1980s, however, was the point driven home statistically, in a World Bank analysis that showed significant correlation between the degree of distortion and low growth.[31] The analysis, reproduced here as Figure 12.4, examined the degree of interference in foreign exchange pricing, factor pricing, and product pricing, from which an index of distortion was compiled. High distortion was correlated with low economic growth (about two percentage points lower than average), and low distortion was correlated with high growth (about two percentage points higher than average). The regression equations employed suggest that about a third of

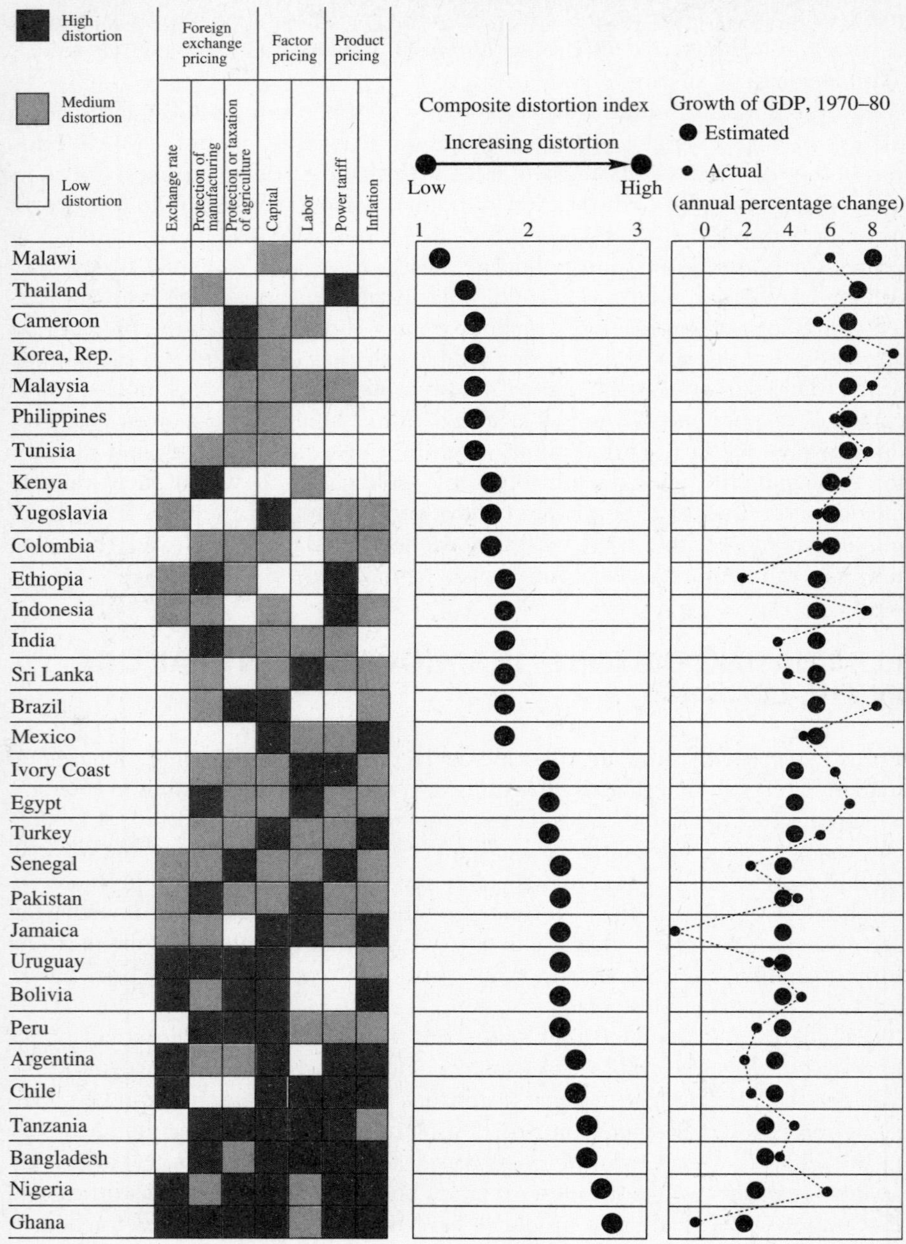

Figure 12.4 Price distortions and growth in the 1970s. *(WDR 1983, p. 62)*
In the figure countries are listed in order of increasing degree of distortion in prices. In the first section, the shading of the squares indicates the degree of distortion in the principal categories of prices. The middle section is a composite index of price distortion for each country. In the right-hand section, the small circles show the actual annual rate of growth of GDP; the large circles are estimates of GDP growth obtained by a regression relating growth to the distortion index.

the variation in growth is explained by the differences in distortion. This famous analysis has had its critics, who note that the degree of distortion leaves a considerable amount unexplained about how fast countries grow, and also that high distortion is not always due to government action. (Private monopolies can distort pricing too.) The critics note that the distortions may not be equally damaging, and that the order of their removal is not at all agreed on. Even so, opinion among development economists has swung strongly to the view that significant distortions can cause serious damage.[32]

Degrees of distortion as shown in Figure 12.4 are also strongly correlated with the ability to save and with the growth rate of exports, as shown in Table 12.1.

In development economics today, the tide is running strong in favor of greater use of the market mechanism and government efforts to strengthen and correct distortions in that mechanism, distortions rather often introduced by government itself. Building new institutions, such as a banking and credit system, a capital market, agricultural credit organizations, cooperatives, extension services, research and training facilities, and improving the transport, communications, and power systems have tended to take priority over a government role in production. These broad, market-based structural reforms, if successfully established, add up to an economic environment where individual enterprise and initiative are able to operate.

Case Studies of Industrial Reform in China and India

Two major examples of the recent market-based reforms are China and India. China's industrial economy for many years was planned on the Soviet model, with market forces playing only a limited role. India has exemplified much more reliance on the market, but government interference with these forces was standard practice. Both countries are now among the major reformers.

TABLE 12.1 PRICE DISTORTIONS, DOMESTIC SAVING, AND GROWTH OF EXPORTS, 1970s

Country Grouping	Distortion Index (average)	Domestic Saving (percent of income, average)	Growth Rate in Exports (percent per year, average)
Low distortion[a]	1.56	21.4	6.7
Moderate distortion[b]	1.95	17.8	3.9
High distortion[c]	2.44	13.8	0.7

Note: [a]The low distortion countries are the first ten listed in Figure 12.4, Malawi to Colombia inclusive.

[b]The moderate distortion countries are the nine countries Ethiopia to Turkey in Figure 12.4.

[c]The high distortion countries are the last 12 listed in Figure 12.4, Senegal to Ghana.

Source: *WDR 1983*, 60–61.

China China's move away from rigid central planning has attracted worldwide attention.[33] The original central planning dating from the early days of Chairman Mao was changed significantly when reforms that began in 1984 narrowed the scope of the plan. The number of items that were centrally planned was cut drastically. By 1993 fewer than 20 items were centrally planned compared to 700 or so in 1978; total output subject to planning has fallen to just over a quarter of the total. Industrial output from nonstate enterprises rose from 14% in 1979 near the start of the reforms to over half in the early 1990s. Central planning increasingly gave way to local government and provincial planning, with "local bargaining" of contracts carried out by firms and these smaller units of government. The contracts determined what share of profit would be retained by the firms, with the firms retaining any profits above what they have agreed to pay to government. The price mechanism has become much more important. By 1993, the scope of price controls was considerably reduced, and three-quarters of raw materials prices are now set by the market. The lure of higher earnings for firms had the predictable result on industrial output, which grew 12% per year in the five years centered in the mid-1980s. (The township enterprises in the countryside, discussed in the previous chapter, were a major part of this development.)

Though big industrial firms often remain in the state sector, the compensation of managers and workers is now closely tied to profitability, more directly than in most Western corporations. Large enterprises can keep their after-tax profits, financing their worker-management bonuses and their investment from this profit, and they can buy and sell input and output beyond what is planned. Investment has now become a local activity, with 95% of it outside the auspices of the central government. Wages in many companies now vary according to how much has been earned, and workers often have contracts.

A considerable amount of the investment in China is now foreign.[34] Chinese law now allows for three forms of foreign investment: (1) equity joint ventures, which are companies with foreign and Chinese partners. From 1979 to mid-1993, 87,810 of these have been approved, more than 70% in 1992 to 1993 alone. Much foreign participation in manufacturing is in this form, for example Beijing Jeep, Shanghai VW, and Daewoo refrigerators. (2) Contractual joint ventures are just that, a contract arrangement between a Chinese and foreign participant, with 22,304 approved from 1979 to mid-1993, nearly half during 1992–1993. An example is the coproduction agreement between McDonnell Douglas and Shanghai Aviation to make MD-82s airliners. (3) Wholly owned foreign enterprises have been permitted since 1988, with 23,818 approved so far to mid-1993. Of the total investment, nearly two-thirds has come to the southern provinces of Guangdong and Fujian, most of it to the special economic zones created to encourage such investment (and discussed further in Chapter 15). Hong Kong firms have invested the most, still about two-thirds of the total, with Taiwan second (since 1987 and mostly in Fujian directly across the Formosa Strait from Taiwan). The United States is the third-ranking investor, and Japan the fourth. Although the press gives much attention to the largest projects, most of the individual investments are relatively modest in size, and are in labor-intensive low-tech manufactured goods.

Up to now, the success of the Chinese reforms is not doubted; the move to decentralized decision making raised productivity and output considerably. Real growth averaged 10.3% per year during the period from 1980 to 1988, the highest in Asia. Recently it has exceeded even that, reaching 12% to 13% in 1992 and 1993, which ranks with Japan's best years. The growth has undoubtedly changed Chinese life. Food consumption has risen greatly. Most urban households now have a television set and a washing machine, and half have a refrigerator. In 1981, only six in a hundred households had washing machines, and fewer than one in a hundred had TVs and fridges. But macro stability has not been achieved. Inflation began to set in about 1988, and it has been a recurrent problem ever since, with a pronounced boom–bust cycle. For example, inflation fell from above 20% in 1988 to 2% in 1990, but growth slowed and business failures mounted, so credit was loosened once more in 1990. That unleashed the boom again, and the government has been trying to rein it in once more during 1993–1994, though still failing to bring it under control.

One reason for the inflation is that the regionalization of China has meant that regions go ahead with financial plans and the central government has little control over them. Another is that about two-thirds of the state enterprises make losses that remain heavily subsidized (with important exceptions such as refrigerators and television sets, the manufacture of which are profitable). The government appears to prefer the inflation to having to cope with the greater unemployment that would follow from closing more of these state enterprises. (It is thought that several million workers have already left the contracting state sector. China's unemployment is now mounting, with many reports of drifters moving around the country looking for work.) As a result, further liberalization of state enterprises has been suspended, with a new schedule announcing that it will not resume until 1996. Some price controls have been reintroduced, and the right to buy inputs at official prices remain an important component of a firm's success, thereby increasing corruption.

Among the economy's still-important weaknesses, services are very underdeveloped and the infrastructure of transport and communications is poor. Some provincial trade barriers are said to have sprung up, with imports from other provinces obstructed in order to stimulate local production. There is little in the way of a credit market, with the banks largely state-controlled, the central bank not very effective, government continuing to ration credit to some extent, and the investment decisions of some firms still requiring government approval. There is no code of private property rights nor a bankruptcy code, and the legal system is not an independent branch of government. The tax system is unusual, with taxes collected by the local governments and the provinces. Some of this revenue is then passed on to the central government, with considerable bargaining occuring as to how much.

For China, once the state sector problems are sorted out, it is perhaps likely that the economy will move toward a market system with considerable government intervention, along the lines of South Korea and Taiwan in the 1970s. If nothing else, Chinese manufacturing shows that partial and gradual reform can nonetheless be reasonably effective.

India India's very closed and controlled economy is undergoing rapid reform, the changes stimulated in part by the example of the high growth of the reformed Chinese economy.[35] The public sector extended far beyond the usual bounds, and private enterprise faced a maze of government controls that did not amount to comprehensive central planning, but was stifling nonetheless.

International trade was strictly policed, with many consumer-goods imports completely banned. To import many capital goods, firms had to show that a domestic product could not be supplied in a reasonable time period. When imports of parts and other intermediate goods *were* permitted, firms often had to institute a program for lowering the import content of their production. Technology imports could be prohibited if the government decided that the import requirements for the product produced were too high. Even after passing these hurdles, importers encountered high tariffs, in 1985 averaging 141% on consumer goods, 146% on intermediate goods, and 107% on capital goods. As a result, sales in the domestic market were more lucrative than in the world market, so the motive to export was reduced. The government responded with tax breaks for exporters and licenses to buy subsidized imports to use as inputs, adding to the bureaucracy and the red tape.

Licenses were required to set up new plants, or expand the capacity of old ones, or make a new product in an existing plant. The government approved only 40% to 50% of license applications in the early 1980s. The usual reason for refusal was that adequate capacity was already licensed in the industry. Yet some of the licenses were not actually used. Firms obtained them in part to preclude competition from other firms. It was especially hard to expand a given plant, so an economic structure of many smaller plants developed. Usually it also took several years to obtain antimonopoly clearance from the authorities, so, perversely, monopoly power stayed high. Most large enterprises that were making a loss found themselves in a dilemma. By law they were forbidden to close.

To offset some of these effects, the government made subsidies available, particularly to small businesses in sectors reserved for them. So many small and not very efficient firms emerged. Subsidies and rules exemptions were also provided for "backward areas," but these areas lack an adequate infrastructure, so the firms established there were often not very efficient. As Jagdish Bhagwati concluded,

> Admittedly, many learnt to bribe, evade, avoid, and generally live with the system. But it remained a thorn in one's side, a continuing reminder of an economic system out of control and a political system out of bounds.[36]

The system remained largely intact until 1992, when the government embarked upon a series of major reforms. A checklist of the reforms includes the following government actions:

1. It devalued the rupee and made it convertible.
2. It reduced import barriers, lowering the maximum rate of tariff from 400% to 65%.
3. It abolished most production licenses and eased antitrust restrictions on large firms. The public sector was reduced from 18 areas to eight. The removals from the public sector included aircraft, airlines, electric power and electrical equipment, iron and steel, and telecommunications equipment. The government has started to privatize state enterprises through the sale of shares. (See the next section for a discussion of how to privatize state enterprises.)
4. It gave partial tax exemption to profits from exports and made it easier for foreign firms to repatriate profits.

The Indian reforms have been gratifying for the IMF, which promoted many of the changes. Much remains to be done. Factories are difficult to close because of rules. Also, the politics of removing subsidies remain hard, and there are still many old-style central planners in the government. Growth is only a third of China's. Yet the progress is undeniable. India already possesses an effective court and contract code, a reasonably clear regulatory system, a stock market, and a good banking system. Added to these advantages, the reforms have caused a large surge of foreign investment, including stock purchases. One result is that U.S. investment in India during 1993 ($1.1 billion) was larger than the total investment India received from the United States between its independence in 1947 and 1992.

STATE-OWNED ENTERPRISES (SOEs)

A network of state-owned and state-run corporations (state-owned enterprises [SOEs], or parastatals) is characteristic of most of the LDCs whose economies are distorted by controls and other government intervention.[37] There are a number of arguments in support of SOEs, similar to those used to justify government planning. Capital may be lumpy and indivisible, the free market structure may be weak, and some given industry might otherwise have to be a private monopoly. Other common justifications advanced either explicitly or implicitly include ideology, generation of employment, regional development, national defense, and self-sufficiency.

The importance of these firms is attested to by the fact that at their peak they accounted for at least 10% of national product in the LDCs as a whole and a quarter or more of all capital formation. Sometimes the latter figure was (and sometimes still is) much higher, over 60%, for example, in Algeria, Burma/Myanmar, and Zambia. In Argentina, 118 state-controlled firms employed a quarter of the labor force. The government sector in Mexico consisted of about 550 companies; energy, petroleum, newspapers, airlines, railways, banks, and many other industries all were nationalized. Brazil had a huge state sector of just under 500 firms, with these SOEs carrying out 40% to 45% of Brazil's investment. This sector ran up

TABLE 12.2 INVESTMENT IN SOEs AS A PERCENTAGE OF TOTAL INVESTMENT, 1980–1985 AVERAGE

Turkey	68
Egypt	65
Côte d'Ivoire	61
Argentina	58
Colombia	40

Source: WDR 1987, 67.

about 65% of Brazil's total foreign debt during the debt crisis. The Indian government owned about two-thirds of the country's industrial assets. The importance of the SOEs in other countries' total investment can be seen in Table 12.2.

Flexibility of response is likely to be low among the managers of the state enterprises. They may be enmeshed in the net of price controls that stifle the signals of any shock, whether external or internal. Often they are not subject to the profit motive, with the government historically subsidizing them to cover their growing losses. For example, the combined net deficit of SOEs in the seven largest Latin American economies was 4% of GNP in 1980 to 1982, four times the figure in the mid-1970s. During the period from 1988 to 1990, the losses of state enterprises were over 3% of GDP in Bangladesh and Mexico, 4% in Turkey, 5% on average in sub-Saharan Africa, and 9% in Argentina.[38]

Not being held to accountability, they often do not respond rapidly to changing economic conditions. In any case, they know that the government will not allow them to fail because that would cause disruption in an important sector. This, too, limits their responsiveness. Finally, given the public "civil service" nature of their jobs, SOE managers are often risk averse rather than risk takers. No penalty attaches to very conservative management, no profit rewards innovation, better decision making, or cost cutting. If an innovation proves unsuccessful, however, the loss would be noticed, the manager would be blamed, and a promotion would be jeopardized—all good reasons for avoiding new ways of doing things. The question of how to select managers for SOEs has received far too little study. Clearly managers can rise by demonstrating no more than they have an ability to play the bureaucratic game, as often seems to occur in militaries everywhere. Beyond that, true managerial ability is very much needed for the SOEs of the developing countries.

Inflexibility is as a rule less important in industries where demand and supply conditions are relatively stable over long periods, as in the management of a sewer system, say, or public education. When demand or supply is volatile, however, the absence of a rapid response may cause considerable damage. Cases in point include energy-intensive industries, such as electric power when a country is hit by oil shocks; agriculture, which may be subject to severe supply fluctuations; or consumer goods such as shoes, where tastes change rapidly.

SOE performance has frequently been disappointing. Very often the firms are overstaffed. Overstaffing in the Indian public sector was estimated to be so great, perhaps 25% to 30%, that the suggestion was made that the marginal productivity of labor in that sector was negative. The SOEs can also be poorly managed, inert, and dependent on the government budget to make up their losses. Arguably, these firms are the exemplars of Harvey Leibenstein's "X-inefficiency." This is the concept, met with earlier, that given the quantity of resources used, output is less than otherwise could be obtained.[39]

In some fields, SOEs will presumably continue to be necessary. Numerous LDCs are likely to conclude that certain industries such as telecommunications, railways, electricity, and gas may possess such large economies of scale as to preclude competition, and ownership rather than regulation may be dictated because of imperfect capital markets. Where state enterprises are thought to be essential, in many cases there seems a need for rather thorough reform. Fortunately, there is no iron law that they *must* always be inefficient, and policy reformation can improve performance. Managers of state enterprises, given clear objectives with an incentive to succeed (a bonus system perhaps) and with their performance carefully monitored, may respond well.[40] (Losses have been virtually eliminated in the SOEs of Sri Lanka and Trinidad and Tobago by such methods.)[41] Long-term contracts between government and its enterprises are another possible path to reform. When SOEs are successful, usually (1) they are accountable for their losses; (2) the poor ones are closed, and the good ones are rewarded; (3) they are free from day-to-day interference by government—which may involve keeping down the price or high pay and overstaffing for workers—and are allowed to operate like a firm; and (4) they are allowed to face competition when that is practicable.

Privatizing the SOEs

Whatever the opportunities for making state enterprises more efficient, a movement has set in virtually worldwide to sell off these enterprises into private hands.[42] The privatization was motivated not just by the poor performance of the SOEs, but also by the necessity for cutting government spending and the chances for obtaining substantial revenue from the sales. The idea has spread even to LDCs considered "socialist." More than 2000 state enterprises have been privatized in the LDCs since 1980.[43] Table 12.3 shows the growth in sales.

The Western Hemisphere has been a leader.[44] In the years 1980 to 1991, 804 SOEs were privatized in Latin America and the Caribbean. Subsidies to Mexican SOEs decreased from 2.9% of GDP in 1982 to under 1.5% in 1991. The number of Mexican SOEs dropped from 1155 in 1982 to 234 in 1992 and will end up below

TABLE 12.3 LDC SALES OF SOEs, ASSET VALUE, 1988–1992 (BILLION U.S. DOLLARS)

1988	1989	1990	1991	1992
2.5	3.8	7.3	17.4	23.3

Source: Gerd Schwartz and Paulo Silva Lopes, "Privatization: Expectations, Trade-offs, and Results," *Finance and Development* 30, no. 2 (June 1993): 15.

200. The recent sale of Teléfonos de Mexico (Telmex), undertaken on Wall Street, was one of the world's major selloffs. Six of the ten biggest privatizations during the period 1988 to 1992 were in Mexico, as were 13 of the top 25. The Mexican government is withdrawing from all industrial production. Argentina has also been very active, privatizing Aerolineas Argentinas, Entel (the telephone company), major electrical companies, port facilities, the national gas, water, and sewage authorities, and the iron and steel industry. In addition to Argentina and Mexico, Chile and Venezuela have moved forward, and even Peru is going through major privatization under President Fujimori. In Asia, Bangladesh, Malaysia, and Singapore have made strides. There have also been many cases of privatization of management even when the underlying assets are not privatized, as in lease arrangements with rewards for managers dependent on better performance.

Privatization Concerns Early results of the privatizations are mixed. World Bank investigations of 12 cases of privatization show that the action led to higher productivity in 11 of the 12 cases.[45] But privatization works best when it is part of a macroeconomic reform program, and in many cases the results of privatization have fallen short of expectations because the reforms have not been sufficiently thoroughgoing.[46] Progress has been slow in sub-Saharan Africa. In many LDCs, the sales have largely been to foreign buyers because local capital markets cannot supply the necessary funds, giving the potential for future political problems. Unemployment may rise so there had better be some sort of safety net or further political and human problems will emerge. But providing for the laid-off workers can be expensive. Ghana, for example, decided it had to pay out a sum equal to two years of wages to workers dropped from the overstaffed Cocoa Board; Guyana laid off almost a quarter of the workers in its state enterprises, and in its civil service as well, but the costs in severance pay were so great that heavy borrowing was necessary to cover the bill.[47] Further, the sale process ought to be open and transparent, or firms may be taken over in ways involving corruption. Avoidance of secrecy will minimize public criticism. Early privatizations in Chile and Bangladesh involved government loans to buyers based on the collateral in the SOEs, the buyers then gleaning profits when they stripped off the firms' assets and sold them to others.[48]

Moreover, simply divesting the SOEs into private hands may involve significant problems because the result can be a private monopoly or a firm subject to lax regulation. Private exploitation can easily replace public corruption and inefficiency.[49] The process is often made more difficult because governments always prefer to sell the losers and retain the profitable ones, which limits the market. The bureaucracy will frequently oppose the sell-off. Returns may be less than anticipated because of the high opportunity cost in time and management, often made necessary because large state firms must be broken down into smaller competitive units before they are sold. Stock sales to the public may be difficult because capital markets may be very thin. Regional and ethnic differences may come into play. Rulers with a short time horizon may decide there are no gains from acting.[50]

Critics have noted that privatized SOEs have often been created to fill a vacuum that private enterprise did not enter in the first place. If the reaction against state firms is pushed to the point where none is welcome, will private enterprise move in? It must not be forgotten that the services delivered by a poorly managed SOE may bring more net advantages than no services at all.

WHERE WILL THE LABOR SUPPLY COME FROM?

Successful industrialization will require a large supply of labor. In most LDCs, the population is still mostly rural, 65% of it in 1992 in all LDCs, 79% in the least developed countries.[51] One of the great contributions that rural areas can make to economic development is to serve as the reservoir of labor to fuel industrialization.

The Lewis Model

Four decades ago, Princeton's W. Arthur Lewis had the major insight that low-productivity rural labor might be shifted in large quantities to manufacturing without a large sacrifice of agricultural output.[52] The labor's low productivity meant that at the margin it involved "disguised unemployment," a term coined during the Great Depression by Joan Robinson of Cambridge University and applied originally to the taking of jobs at a level of skill below what one was trained for during a time of depressed economic conditions. In the hands of Lewis and other theorists, disguised unemployment came to mean a surplus of labor in agriculture that might be mobilized for employment in a newly developing industrial sector.

The basic assumption of the model was that workers could be transferred to nonagricultural occupations with little or no loss of food output, because at the margin a worker's productivity was so low. Whenever a worker transferred from farm to factory, there would be less consumption of food on the farm equal to what the worker had been consuming before the move, but a negligible effect on output. With new income earned in a factory, the former farmer could afford to buy the now-surplus food. The model implied further that there is a perfectly elastic (unlimited) supply of labor available to the modern sector from the traditional sector.

The existence of some labor in agriculture with zero (or negative) productivity is important. If such a condition exists, it means that some workers can be shifted out of agriculture into industry without sacrificing agricultural output. It remains to be explained, however, how any labor at all would be employed if its marginal productivity is zero or less. The explanation lies in the practice, common in subsistence farming where food is raised for the household's own consumption, of sharing the total output among all family members. Everyone has a place at the family cooking pot. Under these circumstances the worker's income is the share of the family output, namely, the average (not the marginal) product of the family. It is certainly conceivable that the average product could be positive when the marginal product of the last worker is zero or below. (The baseball player who bats zero for four in today's game finds his season's batting average reduced, but not to zero. Mathematically, the logic is the same for marginal versus average product.)

Rural "traditional-sector" labor could be shifted to urban "modern-sector" manufacturing at a fixed wage with little or no loss of agricultural output until the growth of the modern sector depleted the labor supply in the traditional sector. At that point the productivity of rural labor would rise, in turn raising rural wages and eliminating the push out of agriculture. If labor scarcity eventually caused shortages of agricultural commodities, that would raise the relative price of those commodities vis-à-vis industrial goods and would also contribute to the rise of rural wages, thus ending the shift between sectors.

There was certainly logic to the claim of disguised unemployment in farming. Some authors pointed to historical experience for their evidence. Without disguised unemployment, how could a flood of peasant farmers into export production have occurred without some noticeable drop in food supplies? Yet for Burma's rice, Ghana's cocoa, Uganda's cotton, and Nigeria's palm oil and peanuts in the decades just before and after 1900, export production did increase rapidly without great changes in domestically produced food supplies and without imports of much staple food. How could rapid population growth occur in areas already overpopulated in relation to natural resource endowments and capital stock without contributing to disguised unemployment? How, finally, could the exodus from the farm to the city that has typified many LDCs in recent years take place without reducing farm output, unless there was significant disguised unemployment? Some empirical studies did indeed detect substantial disguised unemployment, including findings of 30% unutilized labor time in South Korea and 33% in West Bengal.[53]

Criticisms of the Lewis Model The logic of these arguments proved to be highly debatable, however. Authors attacked especially the confusion between marginal product at some given time as opposed to over the course of an entire year. Might not labor use in farming reflect seasonal unemployment together with high productivity during labor-intensive planting and harvest seasons? During the off-season for farming, farmers might indeed work with low intensity, carrying on temporary, low-productivity activities. During the planting, weeding, and harvesting of the crops, however, work might be intense, especially under tropical conditions of lush growth. Under such conditions, the yearly marginal product of labor could be positive; in fact, labor might even be short at the peak times of activity during the farmer's year. If it is added that farmers often carry on various other craft and transport activities during the year, and that the need for rest and recuperation is likely to be high in tropical farming, then the conclusion is suggested that output would not stay at the same level if workers were removed from agriculture.* This logic was supported by empirical evidence that disguised unemployment in underdeveloped countries was limited, even though considerable underutilization of labor did occur in the farming off-season.[54] (The possibilities

*The question of how the great expansion of cash crop exports from LDCs could have taken place without cutting food output still remains. One explanation is that the most intense periods of labor use in the production of these crops did not correspond exactly to the peak labor demands in food production.

for utilizing the underutilized labor in off-season rural manufacturing was addressed in Chapter 11.)

The Lewis Model Overtaken

The debate over the applicability of the Lewis model was still in progress when it was overtaken by two events, one highly favorable for the LDCs, the other less so. Especially during the 1970s, it became apparent that labor was indeed being transferred from agriculture to the cities and that farm output (with the major exception of some African countries) was not declining. The absence of a decline was due not to a zero marginal product of labor but to the technical changes that affected the farm sector of many countries. In an ironical twist, however, it became all too apparent that the movement of labor from rural areas to cities was *greater* than the Lewis model suggested it would be, with migrants from rural areas making up 60% or even 70% of urban population increase.[55]

Concerns grew that urban surplus labor would replace rural surplus labor. Theories were advanced that jobs for the migrants would be limited by a capital-intensive bias in manufacturing, the capital intensity made more so by policies such as overvalued foreign exchange rates that promote imports of capital but discourage exports that in labor-abundant countries would likely be labor-intensive. Another concern was that wages might be kept above market-clearing equilibrium in the cities by union pressure, by strict application of minimum wage laws, or by the payment of relatively high wages by government and foreign corporations. Michael Lipton's research did indicate that the urban–rural income difference was somewhat higher in the LDCs than it had been historically in today's developed countries. A differential of three to four times is usual in the LDCs, compared to under two for Germany, France, Italy, the Netherlands, Britain, and the United States, and between two and three for Sweden and Japan in the nineteenth century.[56]

So in many LDCs, the Lewis model of rural disguised unemployment was overtaken by the more "modern" idea that labor in agriculture would be freed by technical change, with the labor considering its alternatives and often choosing to migrate to urban areas without any government encouragement (or sometimes even outright *discouragement*). So rural areas could indeed be seen as a reservoir of labor that could be used for industrialization, though the mechanism was not exactly the one predicted by Lewis.

RURAL–URBAN MIGRATION

This section addresses the remarkable flows of labor from rural areas to the cities that have become a prominent feature of the LDCs. This migration from farms to cities has been numerically the largest in the world's history. From 1950 to 1975, on best estimate, some 330 million people made the journey.[57] Whereas only 22% of LDC inhabitants were urban in 1960, the figure was 35% in 1992, and the proportion is expected to reach one-half in the year 2000 or shortly thereafter. Brazil's urban population was 45% of the total in 1960, but 77% in 1992.[58] Mega-city size is now common: The world's top ten cities by size include seven in the LDCs, including Mexico City, 20.9 million; São Paulo (Brazil), 18.7 million; Seoul (South Korea), 16.8 million; Bombay (India), 12.1 million; Calcutta (India), 11.9 million, Rio de Janeiro (Brazil), 11.7 million; and Buenos Aires (Argentina), 11.7 million.[59]

The Todaro Model

Much research has focused on how individuals decide whether to migrate from a rural area to the city. A well-known earlier model formulated by Michael Todaro suggested that an economically rational rural laborer would migrate to a city if the present discounted value of an expected lifetime earnings stream in an urban location exceeded that stream for a rural location by more than the cost of moving.[60] This was a nice application of microeconomic theory to an important human issue and helped economists to understand a decision that for those involved may not be so easy to make. The Todaro model emphasized the risk that no job at all would be obtained in the city ("open unemployment"), or that employment would be not in a "modern sector" job but in the informal or "murky sector" of giving shoe shines, running errands, collecting thrown-away containers, producing handicrafts, selling individual cigarettes or aspirin tablets, and other low-productivity, low-wage, and irregular jobs. The Lewis model's term "disguised unemployment" was used to describe the situation, as were the alternative terms "underemployment" or "invisible unemployment." The proportion of the labor force in such low-productivity jobs, and with the training and capacity to earn more if better jobs were available, was thought to be high, perhaps 20% in Latin America, 40% in Africa, and much higher in many large cities.[61]

The potential migrant would also have to decide whether "murky-sector" employment would cut the eventual chances of getting a modern-sector job and what those chances were. These concerns would be larger the greater the flow of migrants, so reducing expected earnings and presumably halting the migration altogether when the expected income, weighted for the risk of unemployment, sinks to the level that could have been obtained in rural areas. The calculation would presumably take into account some advantages to city life that accrue even to those without a modern-sector job. Probably there would be much better access to public services, such as water and sewage systems, electricity, clinics, schools, and the mail, even if income earned in the murky sector is very low; and the "bright lights" surroundings will be there anyway. A last consideration is that some of the new migrants might personally prefer to go back to the country, but considering that they would lose face if they returned, they find themselves stuck with their mistake.

More Recent Views of Rural–Urban Migration

Recently the view of rural–urban migration has altered somewhat, with greater confidence that labor markets may in fact be working more smoothly in the process than was earlier believed. A number of developments have contributed to the new view, including the following.

1. First is skepticism that the urban–rural wage gap is as large or as meaningful as originally posited. Revisionist economists argued that some part of urban–rural wage differences compensate for the costs of training and higher urban living costs, seldom taken into account in the initial debate. Unions and minimum wage laws, often blamed for the gap, can be rather weak or perhaps laxly enforced. Nor were they becoming stronger; in most LDCs, minimum wages in real terms fell significantly during the 1980s. The evidence does not support the existence of rising wage gaps, even as rural–urban migration intensified.[62] A number of revisionists, Jeffrey Williamson outstanding among them, argue that the wage gap that does exist means that migration is simply pushing an economy to a microeconomic equilibrium in labor markets. He illustrates rural–urban migration with a conventional two-sector labor market model, shown in Figure 12.5.[63] Here D_{LA} is the demand for labor in agriculture, D_{LM}, is the demand for labor in manufacturing, and W° is the equilibrium wage. If there is a wage gap of *XY*, then labor must be misallocated by the quantity *LL′* Given a wage gap, asks Williamson, why is it said that there is too much migration?
2. Second is the changing view of unemployment, including some distrust of the figures of high open unemployment in cities. (Some cities have reported 15% to 20% open unemployment at one time or another.) The data are said by some economists to be inadequate and unreliable. A number of authorities claim that there is little evidence to indicate rising open unemployment in the cities.[64] It is clear that young educated workers do have high open unemployment, but to make this into a general case is misleading, according

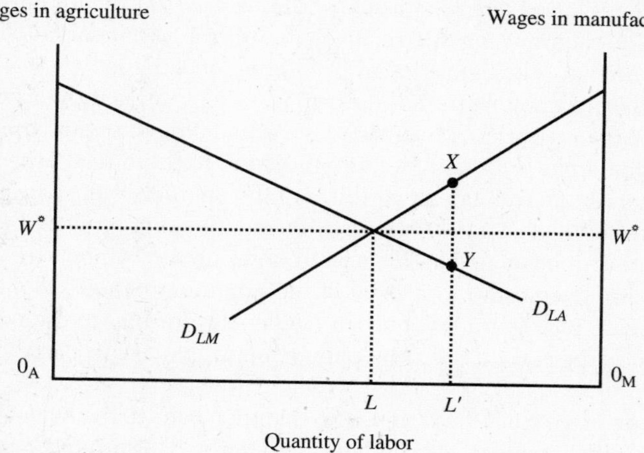

Figure 12.5 A simple model of a rural–urban wage gap. Given a higher wage in manufacturing than in agriculture, the gap being *XY*, a quantity of labor *LL′* will be influenced to move to the cities, pushing wages toward an equilibrium at W°.

to the critics, who argue that migrants do not face special unemployment or long unemployment problems.[65]

3. Next are assertions that the informal sector provides more employment at higher wages than had been believed. Migrants may voluntarily "queue up" for a modern sector job for a short time, and then rather soon take employment in the informal sector at a lower wage. Often that sector provides 40% of all urban jobs, up to 60% in parts of Africa and Latin America.[66] Some revisionist economists, again including Jeffrey Williamson, claim that this form of urban growth in LDCs is actually conventional by historical standards; the experiences of the developed countries at an earlier period are basically similar. Williamson argues that the informal sector is productive. Indeed, that sector does include many thousands of small machine shops and "factories" along with the menial services so often commented upon.
4. Lastly was a more careful identification of who does in fact migrate from rural areas to the cities.[67] The migrants are predominantly young people from their late teens to early thirties. Reflecting their awareness that many jobs in the city carry educational requirements that do not exist in the country, they are more highly motivated and consistently better educated than average. The closer they are to the city in the first place and the less productive the farming area in which they live, the more likely they are to pull up their roots. The migration may not be in one big move; the migrants may try life in a small town for a time before moving on. A survey in Mexico City revealed that only 4% of the migrants to that city had been searching for rural employment before their migration, and that 60% of the searchers found urban jobs within two weeks, at earnings in the range of 30% to 64% higher than their rural earnings had been.[68] Often the move takes place only after contacts have been established with relatives and friends already in the city.[69] The migrants include relatively few of the very poor landless, who often do not have the education to give them much hope for a decent job nor the financial support from their own resources or from their families to facilitate the migration. Meanwhile, the actual migrants with families back in the rural areas frequently send remittances to these relatives. The remittances, sent by an estimated two-thirds of the migrants, can amount to nearly a quarter of their income.[70] In case of need, the migrants can return to these farms. If recessions and associated high unemployment are bad enough, they can even cause a reversal of the migration. Since 1985, that has been the case in Nigeria, with urban residents returning to the countryside. (Ghana experienced the same phenomenon some years earlier.)

In short, flows take place from the farm to the city, then back to the farm, then perhaps another try, with financial help coming both ways. These intermingled flows, which imply that families utilize migration to diversify risks, have been underemphasized, according to the critics. More than is usually implied, unemployment in cities is focused on the educated (as noted above) and on people who have actually been in the city for some time.[71] In all of this, the basic argument is that labor markets are working better than originally posited. Williamson especially has been critical of the earlier approaches to rural–urban migration, which, he suggests, were either wrong or not proven in several major aspects. Among these are the views that (1) migration is a lottery system for the best-paid jobs, (2) migrants to cities have lower incomes than those originally there, (3) there is more unemployment among migrants, (4) wages are much lower in the informal sector, and (5) migrants earn less in cities when they first arrive than in the rural areas they left. This is criticism of the root-and-branch variety, and it leaves rather shaken the earlier conceptions of rural–urban migration.

Improving the Urban Sector

However this debate is concluded, some clear implications do emerge. The effects on the rural areas that the migrants leave behind may be striking. Shifts in labor use, involving less labor-intensive cropping patterns and more work for wages frequently occur, with these changes both a cause and a result of the migration. The increasing flow of labor to the cities obviously requires and will continue to require expensive extensions to social services and urban infrastructure. The expense will mean that in many LDCs, these facilities will often be inadequate, contributing to the perpetuation of slum conditions in urban areas, which involves not only poverty, but also pollution, crime, and social problems of all kinds. Presumably they will only grow worse as urbanization continues, with urban distress replacing rural distress, at least in terms of the numbers involved.

Programs to improve productivity in the informal employment will be valuable. Education and training, credit and extension services, all now familiar in rural development, have been widely ignored in the urban slums of the LDCs and could be much more widely utilized. Small-scale "slum production" by microenterprises and more support for these would be advantageous. Many legal barriers would have to be removed to regularize this sort of employment; until recently, formal lending for capital acquisition by tiny firms has not been available. Yet some calculations show that it takes 12 to 15 times more capital to create a job in the formal sector than it does in the informal sector. Progress in bringing assistance to microenterprises in the informal sector was slight until very recently, but figures such as these and the arguments made above have caused development economists to look again at this much-maligned sector. Finally, community participation in urban self-help projects may mobilize many in the development effort, just as they have in the rural sector as discussed in the previous chapter. The United Nations has recently showcased such projects in Cairo, Egypt, and Karachi, Pakistan.[72] In many other cities of the LDCs, new grassroots organizations are emerging in the slums, where they attempt to raise productivity in the informal sector of urban economies.

Politicians will be looking at these developments. The urban populations of the LDCs can be politically volatile, and poverty has moved into the cities along with the people. These people can act on disappointed aspirations, and can represent a threat to LDC governments. So efforts to raise productivity and incomes in this unstable setting are politically desirable as well as humane.

Whatever the dimensions of the threat, it is clear that one solution—using controls to restrict migration or to toss the migrants out of the cities and back to the farm (resorted to from time to time in China, Indonesia, the Philippines, and several African countries)—has worked poorly.[73] Better results have accompanied programs to make rural areas more attractive. But countries still continue to try to limit migration. Beijing city (population 11 million) announced in 1994 that new migrants moving permanently into the city would have to pay a fee of up to $11,600.[74]

CONCLUSION

Industrialization, particularly in processing and manufacturing that fits a country's factor proportions, has been the route to economic development followed by the most successful LDCs. Markets can fail to promote appropriate industrialization, which led to a long emphasis on comprehensive economic planning. But governments can fail, too, and evidence of the latter has led to renewed emphasis on market forces by both economists and politicians. Governments have a very important role to play when activities are better undertaken in the public sector, especially the provision of a legal framework, financial and banking services, and the provision of social overhead capital and other public goods. Where the private market can adequately provide goods and services, however, it is usually better to leave such activities to market forces.

APPENDIX

The Capital–Output Ratio

Whether economic planning involves a target actually aimed at, with government directing private decisions, or just a forecast, with government only influencing the private sector by means of taxes, subsidies, price controls, and similar means, planning during its heyday usually involved a measure called the capital–output ratio. Most popular of all the planning tools, the capital–output ratio was important in the work of the late Sir Roy Harrod of Oxford University and of Evsey Domar of MIT. The Harrod-Domar model is named for them.

In the hands of development economists the Harrod-Domar model relates the level of investment—that is, the growth in the capital stock—to the rate of growth in the national income. Development specialists working with the model believed that, for many countries, an investment of $100 would on average give rise to an increase in national income of between $25 and $33 per year. Or, stated another way, raising national income by 3% per year would be associated with yearly net investment of 9% to 12% of national income. These calculations embody the numerical relation between the amount of investment and the increase in output associated with that investment. Here the relation is between 3 and 4, because $^{9}/_{3} = 3$ and $^{12}/_{3} = 4$. Investment (change in capital) is in the numerator, output is in the denominator, hence the name capital–output ratio. When we speak of investment leading to growth in income, we are speaking of marginal or incremental changes. Investment is a change in the stock of capital, while growth in income constitutes a change also. So the measure is actually an *incremental* capital–output ratio, or ICOR. (Sometimes this is also called the marginal capital–output ratio.)

The appeal of models embodying such a ratio was seductive. The planning commissions in LDCs could see some signs of certainty in them. In many countries utilizing planning, a large share of investment was undertaken by government and was therefore directly controllable. A given capital–output ratio could simply be plugged arithmetically into a formula. If the planners wanted to achieve 4% growth in income and the capital–output ratio was 4, then the percent of this year's income that ought to be invested would be 16%, and this would also be the target for saving. Or, if it was thought that the maximum amount of investment that could possibly be squeezed out of the economy was 10%, then the rate of growth in income would be 2.5% per year.

Such simplicity attracted a very large following, and even today, capital–output ratios are often spoken of in the LDCs. But confidence in these ratios has long since dissipated. Growth and development are much too complex to allow for such simplistic analysis, and there is no guarantee that a ratio holding at this moment will continue to hold in the future. Many of the problems with models utilizing a capital–output ratio are technical in nature.* The most serious of the objections is, however, the easiest to understand. Concentrating on capital alone must lead to neglect of the noncapital elements in growth. These important elements may be, at worst, completely ignored, or they may be, at best, assumed to increase in just the right proportion as the capital stock increases.

To be sure, additions to capital increase output, and hence the capital–output ratio does have some justification. Think, however, of how much greater the increase in output would be if technological change accompanied the capital increase; if management improved; if the weather were better this year than last; if attitudes toward work altered; if health, nutrition, and education improved; if bribery and corruption in government and business were reduced; if onerous taxation and tariffs were lowered; or if the family system that previously discouraged saving and investment now encouraged it. All these changes are obscured by dependence on models that use a simple capital–output ratio. Any explanation of Japan's economy that uses such a ratio without discussing that country's pronounced emphasis on education and team achievement must be grossly inadequate. Any view of a green revolution that limits itself to capital as conventionally defined, without close attention to new seed, fertilizer, water, and extension services, is even more deficient.[75]

In spite of objections, logic is convincing that there will continue to be a use for capital–output ratios in which economists can still repose confidence. They do indicate an improving or worsening climate for new investment. Typically, the economies with the slowest growth are the ones with the highest ratios. In 1987 to 1992, the capital–output ratio was 3.5 for all LDCs, but it was 2.4 in the high-growth countries, 3.9 in the middle-growth countries, and 5.1 in the low-growth countries.[76] The effect of a high capital–output ratio can actually be more significant than a low level of investment.[77]

So the capital–output ratio, though much criticized as a planning device, continues to do useful service in measuring trends in the effectiveness of investment. Indeed, instead of

---

*Among the criticisms: (1) capital–output ratios are not fixed and will change over time—in particular, they will rise if capital waste or misinvestment increases, or if the economy shifts toward manufacturing (which uses more capital than agricultural or services); (2) the capital–output ratio implies that investment in a given year causes a rise in national income in that year, whereas in actuality investment has a gestation period, contributing to growth over a period of year; (3) capital–output ratios ignore the question of capacity utilization. It would be possible, obviously, to increase national income with no investment whatsoever if there were capital stock that could be more fully utilized. Even without any change in capacity utilization, there might be a more productive use of existing capital if better methods and techniques of production were applied.

the capital–output ratio, many observers now prefer to speak of the "efficiency of investment" or "investment productivity," which is the inverse of the capital–output ratio. Thus, a capital–output ratio of 4 would be the same as an efficiency of investment of 0.25.

For development success, it is very important that the capital–output ratio not rise, that is, the yield on investment not worsen. If it does, then an LDC's growth engine must be using more fuel while going slower. The very fact that investment has generally risen in many LDCs, while growth has slowed down, does unfortunately mean that capital–output ratios have risen and the efficiency of investment has fallen. One of the major questions in development economics today, involving all our lessons on what speeds growth and what impedes it, is why the capital–output ratio has fallen in some countries but risen in others. The trend on average has in fact been disturbing: Capital–output ratios in all LDCs averaged 4.5 in the mid-1970s, but that figure had risen to 6.2 in the mid-1980s.[78]

NOTES

1. See Sanjaya Lall, "Explaining Industrial Success in the Developing World," in V. N. Balasubramanyam and Sanjaya Lall, eds., *Current Issues in Development Economics* (New York, 1991), 118–155.
2. Partha Dasgupta, *An Inquiry into Well-Being and Destitution* (Oxford, 1993): 543–544. The United Nations has made much the same point in *HDR 1993*, 51–52.
3. See Michael E. Porter, *The Competitive Advantage of Nations* (New York, 1990).
4. Howard Pack, "Productivity and Industrial Development in Sub-Saharan Africa," *World Development* 21, no. 1 (January 1993): 1–16.
5. See Gerald M. Meier, *Emerging from Poverty* (New York, 1984), 49, 222–223; I. M. D. Little, *Economic Development: Theory, Policy, and International Relations* (New York, 1982), 125–136; and John Toye, *Dilemmas of Development*, 2nd ed. (Oxford, 1993), 135.
6. See H. W. Arndt, "The Origins of Structuralism," *World Development* 13, no. 2 (1985): 151–159.
7. Compare Little, *Economic Development*, 119.
8. See review articles by Francisco R. Sagasti, "National Development Planning in Turbulent Times: New Approaches and Criteria for Institutional Design," *World Development* 16, no. 4 (April 1988): 431–448; and Ramgopal Agarwala, *Planning in Developing Countries: Lessons of Experience*, World Bank Staff Working Paper No. 576 (1985). A practical survey of the subject is Warren C. Baum and Stokes M. Tolbert, *Investing in Development: Lessons of World Bank Experience* (New York, 1985). My background on this subject has been informed by W. Arthur Lewis, *Development Planning: The Essentials of Economic Policy* (New York, 1966); Michael P. Todaro, *Development Planning: Models and Methods* (Nairobi, 1971); and Albert Waterston, *Development Planning: Lessons of Experience* (Baltimore, 1974). A classic article is Tony Killick, "The Possibilities of Development Planning," *Oxford Economic Papers* 41, no. 4 (1976): 161–184. There is much of value in an earlier article by Andrew M. Watson and Joel B. Dirlan, "The Impact of Underdevelopment on Economic Planning," originally in the *Quarterly Journal of Economics* and reprinted by Theodore Morgan and George W. Betz, eds., *Economic Development: Readings in Theory and Practice* (Belmont, Calif., 1970), 416–423.
9. The classification of plans employed here is suggested in Agarwala, *Planning in Developing Countries.* The description in the next few paragraphs draws heavily on this publication.
10. P. T. Bauer, *Reality and Rhetoric* (Cambridge, Mass., 1984), 28.
11. See the lengthy discussion in Waterston, *Development Planning*.

12. This section has been informed by Howard Pack and Larry E. Westphal, "Industrial Strategy and Technological Change," *Journal of Development Economics* 22, no. 1 (June 1986): 114–115; Joseph E. Stiglitz, "Economic Organization, Information, and Development," in Hollis Chenery and T. N. Srinivasan, eds., *Handbook of Development Economics*, vol. 1 (Amsterdam, 1988), 93–160, especially 154–156; K. Basu, *The Less-Developed Economy: A Critique of Contemporary Theory* (Oxford, 1984); and Kevin M. Murphy, Andrei Shleifer, and Robert Vishny, *Industrialization and the Big Push*, NBER Working Paper No. 2708 (1988).
13. The concept was put forward in Hirschman's well-known book, *The Strategy of Economic Development* (New Haven, 1958). Some of Hirschman's later thinking on the subject may be found in his article, "A Generalized Linkage Approach to Development, with Special Reference to Staples," *Economic Development and Cultural Change* 25, supplement (1977): 67–98.
14. For the theory of vertical relationships, see P. A. Geroski, "Vertical Relations Between Firms and Industrial Policy," *Economic Journal* 102, no. 410 (January, 1992): 138–147; and for a discussion see Wilson B. Brown and Jan S. Hogendorn, *International Economics: Theory and Context* (Reading, Mass., 1993), chapter 8. For the idea of backward linkage expressed mathematically, see K. M. Murphy, A. Shleifer, and R. Vishny, "Industrialization and the Big Push," *Journal of Political Economy* 97 (October 1989): 1003–1026.
15. See Pranab Bardhan, "Economics of Development and the Development of Economics," *Journal of Economic Perspectives* 7, no. 2 (Spring 1993): 129–142.
16. Robert M. Wirtshafter and Ed Shih, "Decentralization of China's Electricity Sector: Is Small Beautiful?" *World Development* 18, no. 4 (April 1990): 505–512.
17. The pioneering work was Joe S. Bain, *Barriers to New Competition* (Cambridge, Mass., 1956). The later research of F. M. Scherer et al. is in *The Economics of Multi-Plant Operation: An International Comparisons Study* (Cambridge, Mass., 1975); it is surveyed together with the work of Leonard W. Weiss and C. F. Pratten in Scherer's *Industrial Market Structure and Economic Performance*, 2nd ed. (Chicago, 1980), 91–98.
18. The studies are summarized in Pan A. Yotopoulos and Jeffrey B. Nugent, *Economics of Development: Empirical Investigations* (New York, 1976), 152–153. Their methodologies vary substantially, and include cost functions, profit rates, value added, and engineering estimates. The results for petroleum refining were mixed. For an investigation of the issue, see Martin Williams and Prem S. Laumas, "Economies of Scale for Various Types of Manufacturing Production Technologies in an Underdeveloped Economy," *Economic Development and Cultural Change* 32, no. 2 (1984): 401–412.
19. Compare Hughes, *Policy Lessons of the Development Experience*, 14. For recent surveys of small-country advantages and disadvantages, see T. N. Srinivasan, "The Costs and Benefits of Being a Small, Remote, Island, Landlocked, or Ministate Economy," *World Bank Research Observer* 1, no. 2 (1986): 205–218; and Dwight H. Perkins and Moshe Syrquin, "Large Countries: The Influence of Size," in Hollis Chenery and T. N. Srinivasan, eds., *Handbook of Development Economics*, vol. 2 (Amsterdam, 1989), 1691–1753.
20. An authoritative review of the subject is Lyn Squire, "Project Evaluation in Theory and Practice," in Chenery and Srinivasan, eds., *Handbook of Development Economics*, vol. 2, 1093–1137. Standard works on the technique are I. M. D. Little and J. A. Mirrlees, *Manual of Industrial Project Analysis in Developing Countries*, vol. 2, *Social Cost-Benefit Analysis* (Paris, 1968); the same authors' *Project Appraisal and Planning for Developing Countries* (London, 1974); and their "Project Appraisal and Planning Twenty Years On," *Proceedings of the Annual World Bank Conference on Development Economics 1990* (Washington, D.C., 1991), 351–382; P. S. Dasgupta, S. A. Marglin, and A.

K. Sen, *Guidelines for Project Evaluation* (New York [UNIDO], 1972); A. Ray, *Cost-Benefit Analysis, Issues, and Methodologies* (Baltimore, 1984); E. J. Mishan, *Cost-Benefit Analysis: An Introduction* (New York, 1976); and Lyn Squire and Herman G. van der Tak, *Economic Analysis of Projects* (Baltimore, 1975). Application of the method in agriculture has its own specialized literature: See J. Price Gittinger, *Economic Analysis of Agricultural Projects* (Baltimore, 1982).

21. See Meier, *Leading Issues*, 4th ed., 642, citing I. M. D. Little and D. G. Tipping.
22. *WDR 1989*, 125.
23. Peter Kilby and David D'Zmura, *Searching for Benefits*, AID Special Study No. 28, U.S. Agency for International Development, 1985.
24. For evaluations of the general theory of shadow pricing, see Lyn Squire, "Project Evaluation in Theory and Practice," part 3; C. Blitzer, P. Dasgupta, and J. Stiglitz, "Project Appraisal and Foreign Exchange Constraints," *Economic Journal* 91, no. 361 (1981): 58–74; and Edward Tower and Gary Pursell, *On Shadow Pricing*, World Bank Staff Working Paper No. 792 (1986). A good critique is Sir Alec Cairncross, "The Limitations of Shadow Rates," in Sir Alec Cairncross and Mohinder Puri, eds., *Employment, Income Distribution, and Development Strategy: Problems of Developing Countries* (London, 1976).
25. See W. M. Corden, "Normative Theory of International Trade," in Ronald W. Jones and Peter B. Kenen, *Handbook of International Economics*, vol. 1 (Amsterdam, 1984), 105, and John Toye, *Dilemmas of Development* 2nd ed. (Oxford, 1993), 134.
26. I. M. D. Little and J. A. Mirrlees, "Project Appraisal and Planning Twenty Years On," *Proceedings of the Annual World Bank Conference on Development Economics 1990* (Washington, D.C., 1991), 358.
27. Kamarck, *Economics and the Real World*, 105.
28. *WDR 1989*, 125.
29. For this paragraph, see Little and Mirrlees, "Project Appraisal and Planning Twenty Years On," 358–364, 376; and Stern, "The Economics of Development: A Survey," 597–685.
30. Two works analyzing this transition are Charles Wolf, *Markets or Governments* (Cambridge, Mass., 1988); and David Osterfield, *Prosperity Versus Planning* (Oxford, 1992).
31. *WDR 1983*, 63. The methodology has, however, inspired controversy.
32. For these specific points, see John Toye, *Dilemmas of Development*, 2nd ed. (Oxford, 1993), 108–109, and Paul Mosley, "Structural Adjustment: A General Overview, 1980–9," in V. N. Balasubramanyam and Sanjaya Lall, *Current Issues in Development Economics*, eds. (New York, 1991), 227. For further critiques, see Keith Griffin, *Alternative Strategies for Economic Development* (London, 1989); David Evans, *Comparative Advantage and Growth: Trade and Development in Theory and Practice* (Hemel Hempstead, 1989); and David Evans and Parvin Alizadeh, "Trade, Industrialisation, and the Visible Hand," *Journal of Development Studies* 21, no. 1 (1984): 43–46.
33. I drew the material in this section from (alphabetically) Robert Ash and Y. Y. Kueh, eds., *The Chinese Economy in the 1990s* (Oxford, 1994); A. S. Bhalla, *Uneven Development in the Third World: A Study of China and India* (New York, 1992); William A. Byrd, ed., *Chinese Industrial Firms Under Reform* (Oxford, 1992); John Child, *Management in China During the Age of Reform* (Cambridge, Mass., 1994); Roger H. Gordon and Wei Li, "Chinese Enterprise Behavior Under the Reforms," *American Economic Review* 81, no. 2 (May, 1991): 202–206; Gary H. Jefferson, "Enterprise Reform in Chinese Industry," *Journal of Economic Perspectives* 8, no. 2 (Spring 1994): 47–70; D. Gale Johnson, "Economic Reforms in the People's Republic of China," *Economic Development and Cultural Change* 36, no. 3, supplement (April 1988): S225–S245; Kui-Wai Li, *Financial*

Repression and Economic Reform in China (Westport, Conn., 1994); Barry Naughton, *Growing Out of the Plan: Chinese Economic Reform, 1978–1993* (Cambridge, Mass., 1994); Dwight H. Perkins, "Completing China's Move to the Market," *Journal of Economic Perspectives* 8, no. 2 (Spring 1994): 23–46; Dwight H. Perkins, "Reforming China's Economic System," *Journal of Economic Literature* 26, no. 2 (June 1988): 601–645; Richard Pomfret, *Investing in China: Ten Years of the Open Door Policy* (Ames, Iowa, 1991); Thomas J. Rawski, "Progress Without Privatization: The Reform of China's State Industries," in Vedat Mellor, ed., *The Political Economy of Privatization and Public Enterprise in Post-Communist and Reforming Communist States* (Boulder, Colo., 1994); Thomas J. Rawski, "Chinese Industrial Reform: Accomplishments, Prospects, and Implications," *American Economic Review Papers and Proceedings* 84, no. 2 (May 1994): 271–275; Gang Yi, *Money, Banking, and Financial Markets in China* (Boulder, Colo., 1994); Shahid Yusuf, "China's Macroeconomic Performance and Management During Transition," *Journal of Economic Perspectives* 8, no. 2 (Spring 1994): 71–92; *International Economic Review*, July 1994; *The Economist*, June 1, 1991, October 5, 1991, November 28, 1992, March 5, 1994, September 17, 1994, October 22, 1994, and November 5, 1994; and *Christian Science Monitor*, December 1, 1992.

34. For the figures in this paragraph, see *International Economic Review* (July 1994).
35. See Jagdish Bhagwati, *India in Transition: Freeing the Economy* (Oxford, 1993); A. S. Bhalla, *Uneven Development in the Third World: A Study of China and India* (New York, 1992); J. S. Uppal, *Indian Economic Planning* (Delhi, 1984); *HDR 1993*, 59; *The Economist*, May 4, 1991, June 26, 1993, and April 9, 1994; and the *Wall Street Journal*, April 1, 1992, and June 6, 1994.
36. Jagdish Bhagwati, *India in Transition: Freeing the Economy*, 82.
37. For this section I utilized the work of Robert Bates, which is the subject of a series of papers edited by Howard Stein and Ernest J. Wilson III in *World Development* 21, no. 6 (June 1993): 1033–1081, with many citations of Bates's work; Sunita Kikeri, John Nellis, and Mary Shirley, "Privatization: Lessons from Market Economies," *World Bank Research Observer* 9, no. 2 (July 1994): 241–272; Tony Killick and Simon Commander, "State Divestiture as a Policy Instrument in Developing Countries," *World Development* 16, no. 12 (December 1988): 1465–1479; John Vickers, *Privatization* (Cambridge, 1988); Yair Aharoni, *Evolution and Management of State-Owned Enterprises* (Melrose, 1987); Hughes, *Policy Lessons of the Development Experience*, especially 20; Samuel Paul, "Privatization and the Public Sector," *Finance and Development* 22, no. 4 (1985): 42–45; *WDR 1987*, 67; *WDR 1983*, chapter 8; and many issues of *The Economist*.
38. *HDR 1993*, 48. Also see Kikeri, Nellis, and Shirley, "Privatization: Lessons from Market Economies," 241–272.
39. Leibenstein presents this concept and connects it to development studies in his *General X-Efficiency Theory and Economic Development* (New York, 1978).
40. See Heidi Vernon-Wortzel and Lawrence H. Wortzel, "Privatization: Not the Only Answer," *World Development* 17, no. 5 (May 1989): 633–641.
41. *HDR 1993*, 49.
42. For the privatizing of the SOEs, I have relied particularly on the following (in alphabetical order): Christopher Adam, William Cavendish, and Percy S. Mistry, *Adjusting Privatization: Case Studies from Developing Countries* (Portsmouth, N.H., 1992)—the title of this book refers to the adjustments that ought to be made to privatizing strategies in the LDCs, backed by case studies of seven countries; R. E. Christiansen, ed., "Privatization," a special issue of *World Development* 17, no. 5 (May 1989) and including especially R. E. Christiansen, "Editor's Introduction," 597–600, N. van de Walle, "Privatization in Developing Countries: A Review of the Issues," 601–616, Henry

Bienen and John Waterbury, "The Political Economy of Privatization in Developing Countries," 617–632, and Vernon-Wortzel and Wortzel, "Privatization Not the Only Answer," 633–642; Christopher Colclough and James Manor, eds., *States and Markets: Neo-Liberalism and the Development-Policy Debate* (Oxford, 1992), which is a book of essays pointing to the mistake of government doing what it should not have done (engaging in actual production, distorting the economy) and not doing what it should have done (improving the infrastructure); Dasgupta, *An Inquiry into Well-Being and Destitution*; and Sunita Kikeri, John Nellis, and Mary Shirley, "Privatization: Lessons from Market Economies," *World Bank Research Observer* 9, no. 2 (July 1994): 241–272.

43. See "Privatization: Eight Lessons of Experience," *World Bank Policy Research Bulletin* 3, no. 4 (August/October 1992).
44. For this paragraph, see *HDR 1993*, 48; *International Economic Review*, April 1992; Kikeri, Nellis, and Shirley, "Privatization: Lessons from Market Economies," 241–272; U.S. ITC, *Operation of the Trade Agreements Program 42nd Report* (Washington, D.C., 1991), 36; and *The Economist*, May 7, 1994, and August 21, 1993.
45. See "Privatization: Eight Lessons of Experience," *World Bank Policy Research Bulletin* 3, no. 4 (August/October 1992).
46. Gerd Schwartz and Paulo Silva Lopes, "Privatization: Expectations, Trade-offs, and Results," *Finance and Development* 30, no. 2 (June 1993): 17; *World Bank Policy Research Bulletin*, August–October, 1992: 2–4; Robert E. Christiansen, "Editor's Introduction," 597–599; van de Walle, "Privatization in Developing Countries: A Review of the Issues," 601–615.
47. Joan M. Nelson, "Organized Labor, Politics, and Labor Market Flexibility in Developing Countries," *World Bank Research Observer* 6, no. 1 (January 1991): 46.
48. "Privatization: Eight Lessons of Experience."
49. The need for antitrust regulation is emphasized by Dwight H. Perkins and Michael Roemer, eds., *Reforming Economic Systems in Developing Countries* (Cambridge, Mass., 1991).
50. Bienen and Waterbury, "The Political Economy of Privatization in Developing Countries," 617–632.
51. *HDR 1994*, 149.
52. See Lewis's famous article, "Economic Development with Unlimited Supplies of Labor," *Manchester School* 22 (1954): 139–191; as well as Gustav Ranis and J. C. H. Fei, *Development of the Labor Surplus Economy: Theory and Policy* (Homewood, Ill., 1964); and also A. Berry and R. H. Sabot, "Labour Market Performance in Developing Countries: A Survey," in Paul Streeten and Richard Jolly, eds., *Recent Issues in World Development* (Oxford, 1981), 149–192.
53. See Warren C. Robinson, "Types of Disguised Rural Unemployment and Some Policy Implications," *Oxford Economic Papers*, 21, no. 3 (1969): 373. See also Harvey Leibenstein, *General X-Efficiency Theory and Economic Development* (New York, 1978), chapter 4.
54. See Warren C. Robinson, "Types of Disguised Rural Unemployment," 373.
55. See *WDR 1979*, 55.
56. Michael Lipton, *Why Poor People Stay Poor: A Study of Urban Bias in World Development* (London, 1977), 435–437.
57. See Dennis J. Mahar, "Population Distribution Within LDCs," *Finance and Development* 21, no. 3 (1984): 15–17.
58. *HDR 1994*, 172–173.
59. The figures are for 1991. See *World Almanac 1994*.

60. The seminal early articles on decision making by migrants were Michael P. Todaro, "A Model of Labor Migration and Urban Unemployment in Less Developed Countries," *American Economic Review* 59, no, 1 (1969): 138–148; and John Harris and Michael Todaro, "Migration, Unemployment and Development: A Two-Sector Analysis," *American Economic Review* 60, no. 1 (1970): 126–142. A critique is William E. Cole and Richard D. Saunders, "Internal Migration and Urban Employment in the Third World," *American Economic Review* 75, no. 3 (1985): 481–494; and see Todaro's reply, "Internal Migration and Urban Employment: Comment," *American Economic Review* 76, no. 3 (1986): 566–569. A "Symposium on Advances in Migration Theory" was published as a special issue of the *Journal of Development Economics* 17, nos. 1–2 (January/February 1985); and there is a volume by Richard H. Sabot, *Migration and the Labor Market in Developing Countries* (Boulder, Colo., 1982). An application of sophisticated economic modeling to rural–urban migration in the LDCs is Allen C. Kelley and Jeffrey G. Williamson, *What Drives Third World City Growth? A Dynamic Equilibrium Approach* (Princeton, N.J., 1984). Peter Kilby of Wesleyan University provided me with some material for this section.
61. *WDR 1984*, 88.
62. See Subbiah Kannappan, "Urban Labor Markets and Development," *World Bank Research Observer* 3, no. 2 (July 1988): 189–206; Jeffrey G. Williamson, "Migration and Urbanization," in Hollis Chenery and T. N. Srinivasan, eds., *Handbook of Development Economics*, vol. 1 (Amsterdam, 1988), 425–465; and Friedrich Kahnert, "Re-examining Urban Poverty and Employment," *Finance and Development* 23, no. 1 (1986): 44–47.
63. Williamson, "Migration and Urbanization," 434.
64. Kahnert, "Re-examining Urban Poverty and Employment," 44–47; Mark R. Rosenzweig, "Labor Markets in Low-Income Countries," in Hollis Chenery and T. N. Srinivasan, eds., *Handbook of Development Economics*, vol. 1 (Amsterdam, 1988), 713–762.
65. Williamson, "Migration and Urbanization."
66. Williamson, "Migration and Urbanization;" Kahnert, "Re-examining Urban Poverty and Employment"; and information from the International Labor Office.
67. See Mahar, "Population Distribution Within LDCs," 16–17.
68. Peter Gregory, *The Myth of Market Failure: Employment and the Labor Market in Mexico* (Baltimore, 1986).
69. As documented for Delhi, India, by Biswajit Banerjee, *Rural to Urban Migration and the Urban Labor Market: A Case Study of Delhi* (Bombay, 1986).
70. Banerjee, *Rural to Urban Migration and the Urban Labor Market: A Case Study of Delhi*.
71. Williamson, "Migration and Urbanization."
72. *HDR 1993*, 86–87.
73. Compare *WDR 1984*, 98; and Mahar, "Population Distribution Within LDCs," 17.
74. *The Economist*, September 17, 1994.
75. See Andrew M. Kamarck, *Economics and the Real World* (Philadelphia, 1983), 74.
76. IMF, *World Economic Outlook 1993* (Washington, D.C., 1993): 47.
77. See *WDR 1985*, 52; *WDR 1986*, 26–27; and *WDR 1987*, 79.
78. IMF, *World Economic Outlook 1987*, p. 79.

Chapter 13

Trade and Economic Development

Does international trade lead to economic development?[1] The more or less standard opinion since the nineteenth century has been "yes." The famous British economist Alfred Marshall thought that trade was a major cause of progress, and his successor at Cambridge University, Dennis Robertson, called trade "the engine of growth."[2] (Even Robertson himself might by hindsight agree that expediter is a better term than engine, which gave rise to overly high expectations.)[3] Such opinions are based on the theory of comparative advantage, which argues that if countries produce what they can do best and leave to other nations what they can produce with less efficiency, then real output, income, and consumption will be higher than it could be in the absence of trade. The higher consumption means a bigger domestic market, increased specialization, greater economies of scale, and higher capacity utilization. The higher income lays the basis for expanded investment in domestic production. In turn, the wider markets and larger investment lead to even higher income, with further rounds of economic stimulation. Trade also includes imports of capital goods and technology, which speed the progress. Trade is indeed seen as an expediter of growth.

Such views have been challenged. In a reaction against the prevailing orthodoxy, many politicians and some economists have argued that international trade itself is to blame for underdevelopment. For a time, "dependency theory" and the "theory of unequal exchange," which arose largely in Latin America following World War II, became influential points of view. Among the leading voices of the trade counterrevolution were Samir Amin, Giovanni Arrighi, Arghiri Emmanuel,

André Gunder Frank, and Immanuel Wallerstein.[4] Trade is neither engine nor expediter of growth according to this school of thought. Rather, it locks LDCs into an inferior and worsening position in a world trade system dominated by, and for the benefit of, the rich. A revolutionary change in trading relations is required.

In this chapter we will explore the arguments that international trade leads to economic development, and the contrary case that trade is a poor prospect in the long run. The next chapter considers policies that lessen the beneficial impact from trade and recommends alternatives to those policies. Another chapter surveys the dangers of protectionist trade barriers and the difficulties facing primary product exporters. These three chapters reflect the decline in influence of the arguments that trade is responsible for poor economic growth in the LDCs.

TRADE AS A STIMULUS TO GROWTH

The idea that trade is a stimulus to growth is based on the theory of comparative advantage, which dates back to David Ricardo's famous Chapter 7, "On Foreign Trade," in his 1817 book, *The Principles of Political Economy and Taxation*. According to this theory, in the absence of barriers to trade, countries will specialize in the production of the goods they produce relatively cheaply (that is, goods in which they have a comparative advantage) and will import the goods in which other countries have a comparative advantage. Consumption and real income can thus be higher than in the absence of trade. The Ricardian model is surprisingly apt for modern development studies because Ricardo chose low-income Portugal and rich England to illustrate his case.[5]

The modern form of the theory uses production possibilities curves to illustrate Ricardo's point. (Readers familiar with the model may want to skip to the next section.) Figure 13.1 shows the simplest such model, with two countries, Poveria and Penuristan, producing only two commodities, food and clothing. At the top of Figure 13.1 we see that if all Poveria's factors of production were used for food farming, the result would be 80 units of food and no clothing, whereas if all factors were turned to clothing, 100 units of clothing and no food would be produced. Penuristan's output would be 120 units of food if it specializes on that commodity or 100 units of clothing if no food is produced, as shown at the bottom of the figure. Penuristan is clearly relatively more efficient at producing food than clothing; it is able to turn out more food than its trading partner, but the same amount of clothing. Reversing the logic, Poveria is relatively better at producing clothing, in which it is Penuristan's equal. But it is no match in food production.

In Poveria one unit of food costs $^{10}/_{8}$ of a unit of clothing; one unit of clothing costs $^{8}/_{10}$ of a unit of food. In. Penuristan, one unit of food costs $^{10}/_{12}$ of a unit of clothing; one unit of clothing costs $^{12}/_{10}$ of a unit of food. Under competitive conditions these will also be the price ratios in the two countries, as otherwise there would be an abnormal profit on one of the commodities and a loss on the other, leading resources to shift into the profitable item and away from the loss maker, so leading the ratio of prices toward the ratio of costs. Explicitly, the opportunity cost of clothing is lower in Poveria; the opportunity cost of food is lower in Penuristan.

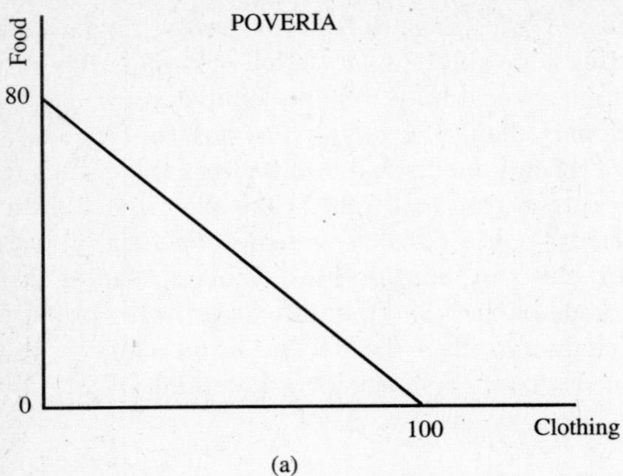

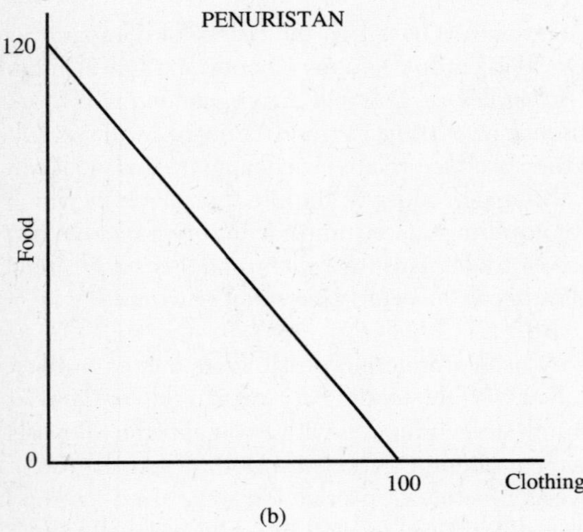

Figure 13.1 Production possibilities curves without international trade. In the absence of such trade, countries cannot consume combinations of output that lie outside their production possibilities curves.

Without international trade each country can consume only what it produces. There is no way either can reach a point of consumption outside its curve. This is only common sense, for how could a country's consumption ever exceed its production? Yet, in comparative advantage theory this is just what can occur if international trade is allowed to take place. Put the two curves on the same diagram, as in Figure 13.2. What if Poveria specializes on clothing (produced there with relatively greater efficiency) as at point *A* and sells some of it in Penuristan at the latter's prices? (Assume for the moment no transport costs or trade barriers.) Of the 100 clothing output, it could now export, say, 50 units and buy 60 units of food,

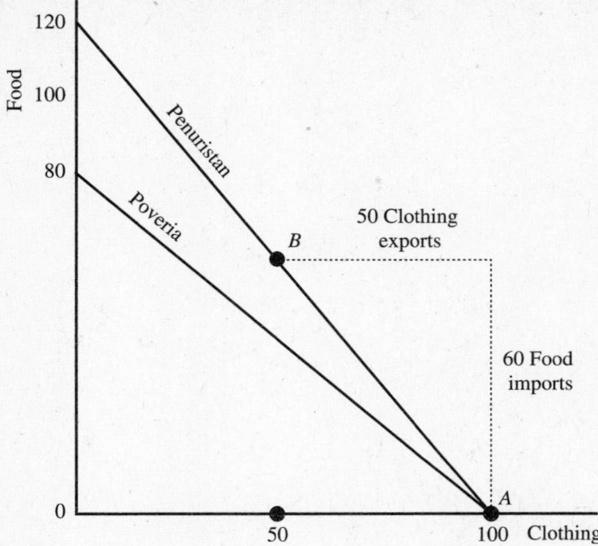

Figure 13.2 Poveria's gain from trade in the model of comparative advantage. By trading at Penuristan's prices, Poveria can end up consuming at a point such as *B*, located outside its production possibilities curve.

because if prices are in the ratio $^{12}/_{10}$ in Penuristan, then 50 clothing would buy 60 food. *Poveria thus consumes at point B outside its production possibilities curve.*

Penuristan, too, can gain from trade. As in Figure 13.3, Penuristan could specialize on food (at point *C*), which it produces more efficiently, and trade it at the Poverian price ratio of 8 food = 10 clothing. (To show this on the diagram, a dashed line is drawn from 120 food at a ratio of $^{8}/_{10}$. That is equal to $^{12}/_{15}$, so the line runs down to 150 clothing.) Penuristan can now export perhaps 48 units of food in return for 60 of clothing (because $^{48}/_{60}$ is in the same ratio as prices, $^{8}/_{10} = {}^{12}/_{15}$). *Penuristan can therefore also consume outside its production possibilities curve, at point D.*

The existence of exports and imports will mean, however, that prices will change. Food, now more abundant in Penuristan, will become cheaper there but more expensive in Poveria, where it becomes scarce. Clothing falls in price in Poveria, rises in Penuristan. Thus the actual price ratio after trade will fall somewhere in between the initial $^{8}/_{10}$ in Poveria and the initial $^{12}/_{10}$ in Penuristan. Whatever the resulting price, trade will allow both countries to consume outside their production possibilities curves at the same time. Such is the lesson of comparative advantage, which emphasizes the powerful point that gains from trade for one country are not losses for another. In the model of comparative advantage, trade is

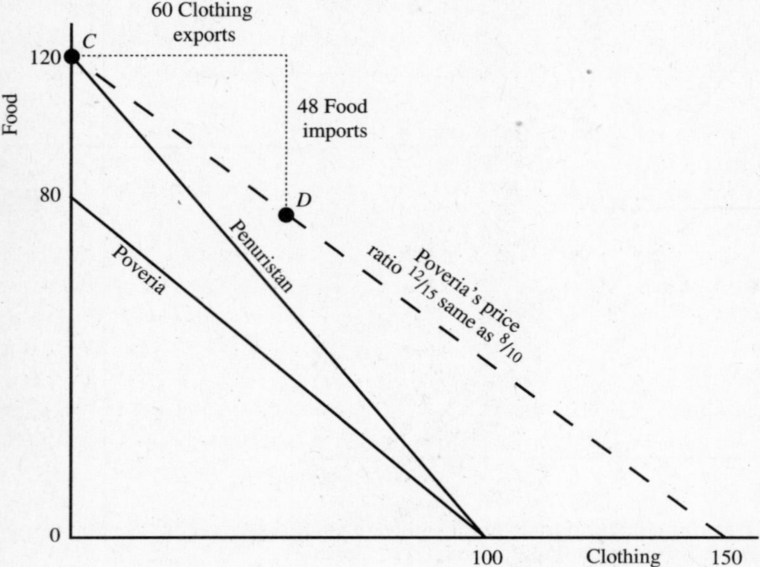

Figure 13.3 Penuristan's gain from trade in the model of comparative advantage. By trading at Poveria's prices, Penuristan can end up consuming at a point such as *D*, located outside its production possibilities curve.

a positive-sum game in which both participants gain.* Notice particularly that to establish gains from trade it does not matter whether the labor in one country is more or less productive than the labor in another country. The only matter at issue is whether a country gains or loses from producing a good itself instead of importing it.

*International trade textbooks use indifference curves to introduce demand, thus allowing a determination of exactly how much will be imported and exported by the two countries. They also show that diminishing returns, indicated by a production possibility curve bowed outward (concave to the origin), do not alter the essence of the model. Comparative advantage theory can easily be put in commonsense terms that have a remarkable validity. The town's best lawyer also is a careful, efficient, and fast-working mower of lawns. But the lawyer hires the neighbor kid to mow the lawn, even though the kid works more slowly at the job, for the obvious reason that the high earnings from an extra hour of legal work far outweigh the costs of paying the (less efficient) kid. Or take the dramatic example unearthed by Charles P. Kindleberger of MIT. Billy Rose was a noted impresario of stage and screen in the 1940s and made a fortune in his various promotions. Simultaneously and remarkably, he happened to be sensationally fast at typing and shorthand, having won numerous awards and actually holding a world championship in the skill at one time. He would obviously have encountered enormous difficulty in hiring a secretary who could perform nearly as well as he could. Still he hired secretaries, because even in this extreme case of being the world's best at the job, he could still earn much more in an hour spent manipulating his entertainment empire than he could in an hour of typing. Q.E.D.

What Establishes a Comparative Advantage? Why are comparative costs—and hence comparative advantages—what they are? The modern explanation was developed by the Swedish economists Eli Heckscher and Bertil Ohlin, who called attention to factor proportions as the most important element. Production possibilities curves have differing shapes because factor proportions differ: A resource (land, labor, capital) relatively scarce in one country is relatively abundant in another. Basically, the Heckscher-Ohlin idea is the simple one that nations export goods that intensively use their abundant factor and import those goods that embody the relatively large amounts of the scarce factor. A prediction of Heckscher-Ohlin theory is that labor-abundant LDCs will thus export goods produced with generous inputs of labor, or as in the case of many agricultural commodities, requiring inputs of such tropical conditions as hot weather and heavy rainfall. Developed countries will import these items and export those that are capital-intensive or contain sophisticated technology. The key point again is that both types of country will be gainers.

Evidence supports these conclusions of the Heckscher-Ohlin model. For example, the ratio of the labor content of manufactured imports to the labor content of manufactured exports is over 1 for all the major developed countries: France 1.32, Germany 1.31, Italy 1.15, Japan 1.38, Britain 1.19, and the United States 1.41.[6] The data indicate higher labor content in developed-country manufactured imports than in their exports, just what the theory suggests.

One conclusion of the Heckscher-Ohlin model is that when an LDC begins exporting, it will probably begin with primary products, then move to labor-intensive manufacturing. The labor-intensity will likely be higher the greater the density of the population. Japan's historical experience is an excellent case in point.[7] In that country, the share of silk (a primary product) in Japan's textile and clothing exports was 99% in 1880–82, 88% in 1900–02, 62% in 1924–26, and only 4% in 1953–55. Exports of (labor-intensive) textiles and clothing went from nothing in the middle of the nineteenth century to 25% of all Japan's exports in 1874–79 to 51% in 1890–99 to 56% in 1920–29. But a great fall then ensued, to 19% in 1960–69 and 4% in 1980–87, as a richer Japan could afford more capital and so became more capital-intensive in production. The labor-intensive finished textiles and standard clothing industries were the first to decline, while the capital-intensive synthetic fiber and fabric producers did not start to decline until much later.

The Heckscher-Ohlin model as amended by Wolfgang Stolper and Paul Samuelson further predicts that trade will increase the income of the most abundant factor because the exported item employs that factor intensively. The income of the scarce factor will, however, be reduced, as that factor predominates in the goods that are imported. There is an important conclusion from this "Stolper-Samuelson Theorem." Whenever these conditions hold, there should be a tendency for a labor-abundant LDC to find its income distribution shifting toward labor, probably leading to more income equality. Of course, there may be barriers. Monopoly, monopsony, government controls, and any other imperfection in the market mechanism can impede the expected result. But the tendency is strong enough so that numerous economists argue that unhindered trade is a workable way to increase the equality of income.

One problem with the Heckscher-Ohlin model is that it would seem to suggest that trade between the developed countries and the LDCs would be much larger in volume than trade among the developed countries themselves. Factor differences are much greater in the former case than in the latter. But trade among the developed countries predominates. Why? One reason is that explanations based on specialization, product differentiation, and increasing returns also explain the existence of international trade. Another is that barriers to trade are very high in many LDCs, while considerable protection also exists in the North against products exported from the South.[8]

THE VENT-FOR-SURPLUS

Ricardo (and Heckscher-Ohlin) showed that international trade allows already employed factors to be reallocated in a manner that enhances well-being. "Vent" models show how previously unemployed factors can be put to work. Trade may hold even more advantages than implied by Ricardo's model when an underdeveloped area formerly isolated by high transport costs is brought into contact with the world trading economy. The initial high transport costs, caused by poor or nonexistent roads, no railways, and the like, may mean that a country has unutilized supplies of productive factors, especially land and labor. Therefore, extensive underemployment of resources will be a characteristic. Improvements in international transport and communications will provide a market where none existed before, especially for agricultural commodities and minerals. Imported consumer goods become available and are the incentive for increased effort. Trade becomes a "vent-for-surplus," in the words first used by John Stuart Mill, building on a concept discussed originally by Adam Smith, and later made familiar by Hla Myint of the London School of Economics.[9] Examples suggested by Myint include the spurt in the export of rice in Burma/Myanmar, cocoa in Ghana, peanuts in Nigeria and Senegal, and cotton in Uganda.

The Myint model is portrayed diagrammatically in Figure 13.4. An LDC, with a food–clothing production possibilities curve shown here finds trade a way to move outside the curve, as in Ricardo's model. There is more to the movement, however, because the starting position at point *A* was one of heavy underemployment. The opportunity to export means that the underemployed factors can profitably be put to work. The gains from trade are proportionally greater even than in the Ricardo model. The vent does, however, cease to have its beneficial effect once the underutilized factors are absorbed into production. It is a once-for-all, noncumulative phenomenon. Furthermore, because there will be no effect at all in the absence of surplus resources, the model will certainly not apply to all countries.*

*Critics have contended that development by means of the vent leads inevitably to dependence on agricultural and mineral exports, both bad bets in the long run. They also argue that the imports of manufacturers made possible by the opening of trade can ruin local manufacturing and craft activities, stifling development along these lines. We will return to both points later.

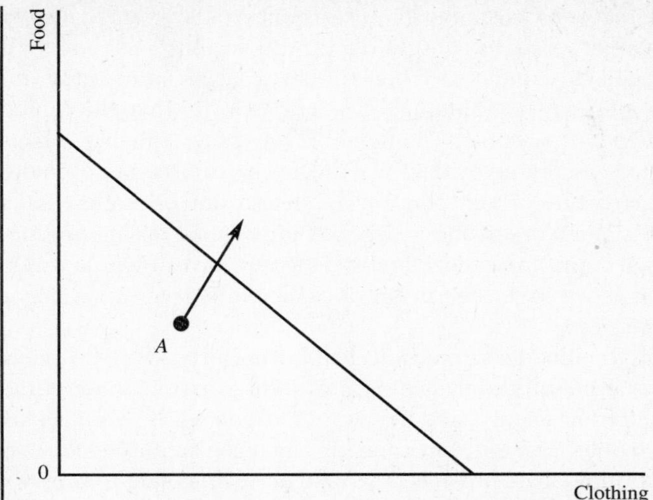

Figure 13.4 The Myint model implies movement to a point outside a given production possibility curve. The movement is partly due to the employment of underutilized factors of production, and partly to the ability to trade at a favorable price ratio as in Ricardian comparative advantage.

Dynamic Gains from Trade

Both the standard Ricardian model and the vent model share the problem that trade might leave comparative advantage unchanged over long periods of time. A country specializing in primary product exports produced by large quantities of unskilled labor, with little capital formation, minimal addition to knowledge and learning, and low levels of technical change, may find itself "locked in," for without enhanced skills, a greater capital stock, improved education, and technical change, new and potentially more profitable exports will not develop. Or, if it does develop, its scale will be too small. Proponents of trade see logic in this argument. That is why many economists believe that the main advantage of trade in development economics is not its static gains, as in the Ricardo and Myint models, but in the dynamic advantages of changing factor proportions and hence changing comparative advantage.

Dynamic benefits are not pictured with a fixed production possibilities curve. Such benefits lead to an outward shift in the curve itself, as in Figure 13.5. There is no guarantee that dynamic gains must accompany trade, and indeed, we shall see a number of cases where they were largely absent. Yet there are abundant examples where such gains were powerful, and a logical case can be made that, with proper economic management, they can be expected.

Outward shifts in production possibilities can come from imports of consumer goods, capital goods, and ideas.[10] New consumer goods have the potential to change tastes, expand wants, and so encourage the increased application of productive energy. At the very least, the mere existence of a popular import demonstrates that a market exists for the product, reducing the risks for local entrepreneurs who decide to compete. When the static gains from trade are invested, new capital goods may be accumulated at a price lower than the capital could have been produced for at home. The higher level of investment, perhaps financed from tax revenue generated by the fiscal linkage to exports, can promote both an improved infrastructure of transport, power, health, and education and a greater amount of capital per worker, and economies of scale, all raising productivity. These gains are, of course, maximized only if the new investment is wisely made. Where to invest, as we have seen in previous chapters, is always a major focus of development strategy.

The import of ideas as embodied in technical and managerial know-how may well be the most important of all the dynamic gains. John Stuart Mill noted the value of contact with different peoples and new ways of thinking. New skills may feed back into other activities; new entrepreneurship can make an impression and can be copied outside its immediate province; the road or rail line built to supply a foreign market with an exported good may be utilized for other economic purposes as well; simplification, standardization, specialization in subprocesses, and assembly-line methods are noted and copied.

Modern trade theory calls attention to the importance of "intra-industry trade," the idea that countries frequently end up exporting a product while importing basically the same product.[11] So Sweden exports Volvos and Saabs while importing BMWs and Volkswagens; and the United States exports design-

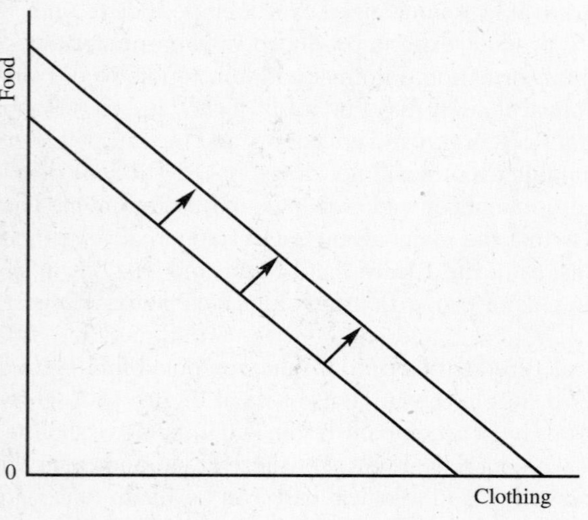

Figure 13.5 Dynamic gains bring an outward shift in the production possibilities curve.

er jeans and fashionable clothing but imports many standard items of apparel. The key to intra-industry trade is product differentiation. The richer consumers of the developed countries (and the LDCs as well) show persuasively that they prefer to buy more differentiated products rather than more standardized ones. Product differentiation is easier when production is more capital-intensive, and more difficult with the labor-intensive manufactured goods produced by most LDCs. Intra-industry trade is, indeed, closely correlated to the level of economic development. It averages 58.9% of all trade for industrial countries, 42.0% for the newly industrializing LDCs, and only 14.5% for the balance of the LDCs. Very low figures are common: Turkey 7.9%, Egypt 6.8%, Ghana 4.3%, Nigeria 0.2%.[12]

The "flexible factories" of modern industry are a widening avenue for intra-industrial trade. Their computer-assisted design and production, along with their robotics, are intended to allow faster and more flexible response to fickle consumer demand. Their ability to produce small batches without much sacrifice of scale economies means that they can give a comparative advantage based partly on their rapid response. But flexible factories have become important in only a few advanced LDCs because both are demanding in terms of capital, education, skills, and management. They will be out of reach of the low-income LDCs for years to come.[13]

In the establishment of comparative advantage based on dynamic change, production experience for both labor and management is thought to be particularly important. Experience, often called "learning-by-doing," may lower costs, so leading to a new comparative advantage that allows some former imports to be produced at home and also allows new exports beyond the initial range of primary product exports to develop. Learning-by-doing is now thought to be an especially important addition to the standard model of the gains from international trade. If the learning is specific to an industry, it may suggest a development strategy of deliberate early specialization in some selected line of activity. This would presumably be particularly attractive to countries where educational attainment is above average among the LDCs.

But it should be noted that the advantages from learning are easily eroded if a government permits protectionism, does not challenge monopoly power, and adopts other adverse economic policies.[14] For example, an automobile industry was established in India in the late 1940s, and even in the late 1970s, India was still producing more cars than Korea. But the Indian industry was stagnant, showing little sign that cumulative learning was much of an advantage to it. The drive to learn is obviously lessened in the presence of poor policies such as high trade barriers against foreign competition and monopoly power in the domestic market.

In short, dynamic trade models see international trade as contributing a sense of momentum, moving the curve of production possibilities outward. Michael Porter captures the difference between static and dynamic comparative advantage when he writes of the contrast between basic factors and advanced factors.[15] Countries move from a situation where basic factors such as natural resources and unskilled or semiskilled labor give comparative advantage, to a situation where human and physical capital investment, specialization, scale, and rapid response to market forces give the comparative advantage. In such cases, success can feed on itself, as new industries utilize processes introduced by old ones; as intermediate suppliers spring up (backward linkage again); and as industrial growth leads to lower transaction costs, a greater flow of information, and growing ties to the marketing networks of multinational firms.

Porter argues that the central task of governments' trade policy in the LDCs is encouraging movement from comparative advantage based on natural resources, cheap labor, locational factors, and other basic factors to creation of advanced factors. To accomplish this, a country must development human resources, a scientific and technological base, and an improved infrastructure. Fundamentally, he sees the economic benefits of intense domestic competition domestically among rival firms and in foreign markets as being a main source of benefits from the dynamic trade model. Governments can promote the process by not interfering with the development of competition. They might even stimulate it, perhaps along the lines of the competitive games run by countries such as South Korea concerning quality control, export credit, and the like. (The details of these games are described in Chapter 3 of this book).

The LDCs' Share of International Trade

The basic models of international trade suggest that trade brings higher incomes through static comparative advantage and through the dynamic change that alters comparative advantage and so increases incomes even further. The value of LDC trade has expanded greatly, by about four times from 1971 to 1991 in real terms.[16] Primary products were 90% of all LDC exports (excluding oil) in the mid-1950s, but this figure had fallen to 35% by the mid-1980s. Remarkably, during these years the LDCs' share of world manufactured exports was increasing from 5% in 1970 to 22% in 1993. But the success indicated by this advance is misleading because most of this rise was in Asia, where the increase was from a bit over 3% of the world total to a little over 17%. (In 1960, Hong Kong, Korea, Taiwan, and Singapore originated 5.6% of all LDC exports. In 1989 that figure was 32%.) The manufactured exports from the rest of the LDCs have only gone from about 2% of the world total to a little less than 5%.[17]

When *all* exports are included, the LDCs' share of total world trade has mostly been falling, rather than rising, as Table 13.1 shows. The developed countries, not the LDCs, have been doing better at expanding their trade.

TRADE AS A HINDRANCE TO GROWTH

The critical objections to international trade fall into three general categories. First, there is a school of thought that believes the doctrine of comparative advantage is itself fundamentally flawed and that trade is likely to result in "unequal exchange." This is the argument advanced by Arghiri Emmanuel.[18]

TABLE 13.1 SHARE OF WORLD EXPORTS, PERCENTAGE, 1950 AND 1990

	1950	1990
Industrial countries	63	74
(of which USA)	17	12
LDCs	37	26
Africa	5	2
Asia	11	14
Latin America and Caribbean	11	4

Source: Anne O. Krueger, *Economic Policies at Cross-Purposes* (Washington, D.C., 1993), 12.

Second, it is said that exports from the LDCs fail to stimulate development because of a low multiplier effect from that trade and because there is little "dynamic radiation" from trade. These are the so-called enclave or backwash arguments. The complaint is usually made with reference to primary products. Proponents of the backwash arguments often agree that trade along the lines of static comparative advantage may indeed be of benefit to all, but that some countries will benefit far more than others. An initial comparative advantage in high-technology manufacturing tends to be self-perpetuating, it is said, so locking LDCs into permanent and less-profitable production of agricultural goods and minerals with limited impact on the domestic economy.

Third, it is said that the prospect for exports from developing countries, especially primary products, are poor and that the prices of these exports have declined vis-à-vis the prices of goods exported by the industrial world. There is, further, little world capacity to absorb an increasing volume of exports from the LDCs. This is commonly known as the "terms of trade" argument.

All these North–South arguments concerning trade, when taken together, are called "dependency theory" by critics of trade, the name implying the locking of LDCs (the "periphery") into an inferior and worsening trading relationship with the industrial countries (the "center").[19] Various authors have used the word *dependency* in different ways. Many appear to mean merely that growth is much affected by actions in the metropole or capitalist world. This is, of course, true. In a strong version of this theory, however, the developed countries are blamed for creating underdevelopment. By destroying already existing industries, such as local textile manufacture and handicraft production, and by shifting farming from foods to cash crops for export, the gains from trade were, so it is claimed, nullified. Even when gains occur, arguably they are dissipated by wasteful consumption patterns introduced from the developed countries, by capital flight to foreign bank accounts for which urban elites are responsible, and by spending on "security" to maintain that elite in power. In a somewhat weaker version of the theory, the conditions surrounding foreign trade may not have created poverty, but they have prevented development in the LDCs from taking place.[20]

Either way, ending dependence is a synonym for throwing off poverty and grasping control over one's own destiny by lessening the degree of external relationships (including trade), by "delinking" the LDCs from the developed countries. The suggested strategy aims toward inward-looking self-reliance. Others consider ending dependence to mean pursuing an independent strategy in one's trade relations rather than lessening the degree of external relationships. In general, the dependency arguments have had less influence among economists than they have had in some other disciplines, such as sociology and political science. The debate has served, however, to identify more carefully the circumstances when trade may not be beneficial.

Arguments that trade is not an expediter of growth because of developed country trade barriers and flawed trade policies in the LDCs are less an attack on trade itself than on the particular strategies employed. These arguments are considered in Chapters 14 and 15.

On entering the thickets of this extensive debate, let us do so armed with our usual skepticism. Although trade is very important, it is easy to overrate that importance. The trade-to-income ratio for the world in 1988 (world exports divided by world income) was only 16%.[21] In large countries with a low trade-to-income ratio (Argentina 9%, Brazil 7%, India 8%), a fourfold improvement in export prices, with import prices unchanged, would raise national income only in the range of 28% to 36%. For India, it would require a rise in export prices of over 12 times to double national income. Obviously, for some important LDCs trade cannot possibly be the sole cause of poverty. Incomes are low in such countries basically because of their low productivity, not because of the conditions facing them in foreign trade. Productivity gains are the key to growth in the long run.[22]

The Unequal Exchange Argument

"The theory of comparative advantage is one of the few bits of statical logic that economists of all schools understand and agree with," writes Paul Samuelson of MIT.[23] A major exception is Arghiri Emmanuel, who argues that the poverty of the LDCs is caused by trade itself.[24] Much of Emmanuel's work considers the terms of trade, low multiplier effects, and the other points of a dynamic nature included in our second and third categories of objections to trade and examined in detail later in this chapter. An innovation in Emmanuel's argument is that even in a *static* situation, there can be an unequal exchange resulting in losses, not gains, for an LDC engaging in trade. Should this contention ever be borne out in practice, it would be revolutionary.

Emmanuel uses capital movements to make his case. International capital movements will, he argues, increase the supply of the scarce factor in capital-short countries (LDCs) and so lower profit rates there, while at the same time raising them in the capital-abundant countries (the rich). The lower profit component in LDC prices will mean the prices themselves fall, while in rich countries the higher profit component will boost prices. The capital flows will mean a poor country has to exchange more of its now-cheaper goods for less of the rich country's output. The LDC in this position is worse off than it would have been without trade. This case has attracted wide attention in the underdeveloped world and has been used to justify a strategy of self-sufficiency.

Paul Samuelson has mounted a powerful attack on the Emmanuel position. In his paper "The Illogic of Neo-Marxian Doctrine of Unequal Exchange," he states that the analysis assumes no change along the production possibilities curve after the opening of trade.[25] A move toward specialization alters Emmanuel's arithmetic greatly, says Samuelson. "It is a cruel hoax on the laborers in poor countries to pretend that there is some way of increasing their real incomes . . . by choking off trade. . . ." states Samuelson.[26] Indeed, the arithmetical counterexamples presented by Samuelson appear to cast grave doubt on the soundness of Emmanuel's position. We can reasonably conclude that in its static sense, the Ricardian theory of comparative advantage emerges still useful from this controversy, with Emmanuel's alleged flaw in comparative advantage theory unlikely to find acceptance among development economists generally. That leaves the dynamic objections—that trade in the long run brings declining benefits—still to be considered.

Enclave Arguments

A major criticism of trade as an expediter of growth, often associated with the Swedish economist Gunnar Myrdal, concerns the linkages and multiplier effects between the trading activity and the domestic economy. The ideal trading activity is easy enough to define. The optimum is a fast-growing export sector with a strong stimulus for investment, local employment, and local income. There would be considerable raising of skills of the employed labor and heavy purchases of local, rather than imported, raw materials by the export industry (backward linkage, in the language of Chapter 12). The labor force would use its new higher incomes to purchase domestically produced consumer goods instead of imports. At optimum, there will be also significant forward linkage from exports, as in the case of rice, where the brown husks left over after milling can be used for livestock feed.

To see the case at its best and worst, imagine the establishment of a canning factory. This exporter of canned fruits and vegetables provides fertilizer, seed, and technical advice to farmers and gives them long-term contracts. They and the labor employed in the cannery all receive higher incomes leading to a demand for more consumer goods and better food, so stimulating both local industry and local farming. These are the backward linkages. Farmers apply their new knowledge of techniques to other crops; the growing prosperity encourages banks to provide more credit to local farming and manufacturing; and cooperatives, brokers, and middlemen, all owing their existence initially to the cannery, have an impact on domestic pursuits as well. Trade expedites growth.

Now consider a more bleak alternative. The cannery fails to gain local supplies because farmers fear to switch from subsistence production. Raw materials must be imported. Labor is hired at subsistence wages, and the multiplier effect on income is therefore very low because there is little to be multiplied. Even those who do earn higher income use almost all of it to buy imported goods.

There are in fact stark examples of enclave economies where exports provided little domestic stimulus. Sri Lanka (then Ceylon) and its tea industry was a case in point. The capital equipment for the industry was purchased in Britain, the equipment and the tea were carried on British ships, and the managers were British, importing many of their consumer goods. The profits were largely repatriated to

London. Even the labor was imported from India, where it was cheaper. Sri Lanka was left with little in terms of new knowledge, multiplied incomes, and domestic industrialization. The same case has been made for the West Indies by the New World Group or Plantation Economy School. The perpetuation of absentee ownership and the foreign control of refining, marketing, shipping, and all associated finance arguably have political and psychological consequences far beyond their economic impact. All contribute to the inertia that characterizes an enclave economy.[27]

Some writers have concluded that the enclave problem is more serious in the production of primary product exports. Hans Singer of the United Nations emphasized the lesser degree of capital formation and the smaller "dynamic radiation" through the training of a skilled or semiskilled labor force. He believed industry was more suitable on both counts than agriculture and mining. That there is some validity to his argument is perhaps demonstrated by the examples of Germany in the nineteenth century and Japan in the twentieth.

Many economists, however, are far less certain of the conclusion. Dynamic radiation through training is much more likely to be important where agriculture is capital intensive and based on mechanical skill—and it is not obvious why this path is less desirable than the establishment of manufacturing industry. Nor is there reason to assume that an unskilled industrial labor force will give any external economies whatever in comparison with agriculture. Examples of countries developing through agriculture without sacrifice of external economies are not rare. They include the United States, Canada, Australia, New Zealand, and Denmark. The farmers of Iowa or the Australian Outback know considerably more about machinery, marketing, and production than do many city dwellers.

Moreover, it now is clear that manufacturing industry can lead to enclaves as easily as can primary production. The foreign firm that imports a capital-intensive technology may indeed pay relatively high wages and salaries but does not hire many workers. The lucky ones who do find employment may adopt a lifestyle that stimulates luxury imports rather than domestic production. Alternatively, domestic industry may be rather capital intensive, substituting for imports but at the same time relying heavily on imported inputs. Manufacturing in this sense provides not dynamic radiation, but just another enclave.

Most economists agree that "outpost investment" of the enclave sort is common in the LDCs. There is far less agreement, however, that international trade is the reason for the existence of enclaves. Enclaves and low multiplier effects can more realistically be blamed on other causes, impediments that are part of underdevelopment itself and not explained by reliance on trade or the nature of exports and imports. For example, a large subsistence sector in agriculture must result in a reduced domestic multiplier effect in rural areas when exports occur. A country such as Côte d'Ivoire with much cash marketing of food has a decidedly larger multiplier impact from its cocoa and coffee exports than does a country such as Uganda, whose cotton and coffee are grown together with food for the farmer's own family. As a general rule, the lower a country's income, the larger its subsistence sector, and therefore the smaller its domestic market and the less the opportunity to spend new income—whether from exports or any other internal activity unconnected with international trade—on locally produced goods. Similarly, the poorer a country is, the more it will be necessary to use imported capital, imported technology, and imported management with high repatriation of profits and salaries.

In addition to a large subsistence sector, another explanation of the existence of enclaves is the mass of unskilled labor available for employment at low wages. There may be overpopulation, underemployment, and a large sector of low-productivity farming. All this means low opportunity costs. With alternatives for employment poor or nonexistent, only a low wage is needed to attract labor into the export sector. The result is that exporting can become established and can begin to grow appreciably without as much stimulus to the economy as would be expected in a more developed country, where wages would rise significantly when the new demand for labor affects labor markets. For the same reason, any domestic activity in addition to exports (manufacturing for the local market, for instance) would radiate less stimulus to the rest of the economy.

Financial and political institutions may also contribute to enclaves. When a country's income is very low, banking and brokerage institutions often do not develop enough to provide further linkages from exports to the rest of the economy. Banks remain highly specialized, lending only for the traditional export crop or mineral. Foreign buyers and indigenous brokers also stay specialized, as when the local coffee buyer will not touch tobacco or cocoa. Frequently, the major reason for this conservatism is risk. With capital scarce and expensive and knowledge limited, neither bank nor broker feels the urge to leave the beaten track.

Another institutional element is the political process, which can work against linkages to and from farming. The tax system may, as we saw in Chapter 4, be biased against agriculture. The growing power of the urban workforce may result in price controls on food and subsidized food imports, both of which work to raise the urban real wage but also inhibit domestic agriculture. Again the enclave is seen to be associated with symptoms of underdevelopment in general, rather than with exporting in particular.

The conclusion must be that even a large initial stimulus from exporting, whether of primary products or manufactures, will not be passed on through a strong multiplier process if the domestic impediments are serious. These barriers will also be sizable for indigenous development based on production for the domestic market.

Some economists argue that the disadvantages of export enclaves have been overemphasized. No doubt, as Alec Cairncross suggests, there is little about an oil refinery that would bring transformation to the agriculture of an oil-producing state.[28] Yet what about the fiscal linkage of the tax mechanism? Even enclaves with no other conceivable connection to the domestic economy can be linked to it through the collection of taxes. Primary product enclaves were certainly important in the development of countries such as Japan (silk), the United States and Canada (grain), and Great Britain (first wool, then textiles, which once comprised over 70% of British exports). The enclaves producing such primary product staples are likely to find a strong linkage to the processing of those staples into semifinished and finished form. Any hindrance to the operation of this linkage will presumably be due more to politics in the developed world, especially high trade barriers against such processed items, than to any inherent weakness in trade itself. Even in the "worst case" of the Ceylonese tea discussed above, there were *some* linkages.[29] Railways and ports built or improved to handle the export item were useful for other economic activities. The higher tax revenues financed the first large investment in education and public health; this investment stemming from fiscal linkage became a hallmark of modern Sri Lanka. (Admittedly, in colonial days the tax revenues also paid for the army, the police, and the high salaries of the colonial administrators.) In sum, it would seem far more reasonable to attack the enclave effects of international trade with a combination of taxes and development programs than to attack the concept of international trade itself.

One element in the enclave debate is a rather bracing one.[30] Sometimes those who attack international trade as responsible for enclave development seem to assume that without such trade and its enclaves, the alternatives would be very bright. Would there, however, have been domestic investment to replace the foreign investment? Would local entrepreneurship be abundant? Above all, would the domestic market be sufficiently large to stimulate a wide range of new economic activity? There might be in all this a logical fallacy of contrasting what did occur (an export enclave) with some idyllic picture of what might have occurred at best. Unfortunately, the result without trade may be far less favorable: a stagnant idleness of the factors of production due to a very limited local market. For dozens of countries, export crops, mining, or production of some manufactures for export, even when their linkages are low and their future sales prospects not especially inviting, may be the only plausible way to start the development process. One thinks of the even worse poverty that would be found in Senegal without its peanuts; Uganda without coffee; Sudan without cotton; Bangladesh without jute; Zambia, Peru, and Bolivia without copper or tin; and, more obviously, Nigeria, Libya, and the Arab states without oil.

The Terms of Trade Argument

The terms of trade argument is a shorthand way of expressing a general pessimism on the prospects for exports from the LDCs, especially when these exports are primary products. Its chief advocates over a period of many years were Raul Prebisch of Argentina, former chairman of the UN Economic Commission for Latin America, and Hans Singer of the United Nations.

Several different elements are involved in the controversial assertion, all combining to mean that a typical LDC must export more and more to obtain the same quantity of imported goods as before. The argument is often expressed in the following manner. There is a secular (that is, long-run, lasting at least several decades) tendency for the terms of trade to turn against the exports, especially the primary product exports, of the LDCs. It is generally agreed that yearly or cyclical price changes, even when severe and disruptive, are not evidence of a long-run decline, can be due to very different causes, and are subject to other remedies considered in the next chapter.

"Terms of trade" is a measure economists use in attempting to express the relative prices of a country's exports and its imports. There are several ways to calculate the measure, but the most common version, called the commodity or net barter terms of trade, is an index of export prices divided by an index of import prices,

P_x/P_m. This calculation is itself turned into an index by setting it equal to 100 for some base year. If in later years export prices should rise faster than import prices (that is, P_x grows larger than P_m), then the index would be higher than 100, a so-called favorable movement in the terms of trade. Falling export prices relative to imports would result in an index number below 100, an unfavorable movement in the terms of trade. This most common version is published frequently for almost all countries.

One must be wary of the unqualified proposition that an improvement in the commodity terms of trade is necessarily good for a country or a fall in the index necessarily bad. In many cases this will be true, but a rising index is not always advantageous, and a falling index is sometimes favorable. Notice that the terms of trade alone say nothing about the resulting total revenues earned. For the LDCs as a whole or for large countries with some ability to influence market conditions, high and rising prices for exports might be reducing rather than increasing earnings, with the volume exported falling proportionately more than the price rise. This will, of course, depend on the elasticities involved. Conversely, lower export prices may stimulate sales and improve earnings. The "best" position is not simply some highest possible commodity terms of trade, but rather some optimum terms of trade that maximizes earnings.*

Significantly, a fall in export prices and hence an "unfavorable" movement in the terms of trade might be caused by an increase in productivity in the exporting industries. If the rise in productivity is greater than the fall in prices, then the enlarged quantity of exports may bring higher incomes from those exports in spite of the price decline. The productivity change causes the price decline, but it would not be correct to conclude that the country's economic situation is now worse. Economists for a number of years have attempted to calculate a version of the terms of trade that takes productivity changes into account. The major attempt is called the "single factoral terms of trade," a ratio between an index of income accruing to the factors of production engaged in producing for export and an index of import prices. The formula, for some base year and for the year to be measured, is an index of income to a fixed amount of factors used to produce a given quantity of exports divided by an index of import prices. Such a formulation would readily reveal the cases where export prices are falling, but where the falls are offset because factor incomes are stable or even rising, due to improvements in productivity.† Unfortunately, it is not easy to calculate the factoral terms of trade because of the difficulties in constructing an adequate index of productivity. Work is advancing, but progress is difficult because acceptable data are so rare. Even when the numbers are not available, however, the policymaker must be careful to make rough estimates, although these will admittedly be imperfect.

---

*International trade texts define an income terms of trade, P_xQ_x/P_m, that allows such trends to be measured. There is a similar situation on the side of imports. A decline in import prices (P_m) may reduce income in some foreign country, with a resulting fall in the volume and value of exports.

†There is also a double factoral terms of trade, an index of income to factors producing a given quantity of exports divided by an index of income to factors producing a given quantity of imports. This is of less concern to those interested in calculating a country's command over imports rather than its command over the quantity of foreign factors. It does figure, however, in the thinking of dependency theorists who believe that trade causes LDCs to fall behind rich countries.

Good examples of factoral considerations in practice are the United States and Canada, whose cheap grain captured many European markets in the late nineteenth and early twentieth centuries, and Japan, where there was a drastic decline in the commodity terms of trade between 1910 and 1920, again after 1930, and once again from 1960 to 1980.[31] The decline gave a vigorous push to exports, brought new markets, and accompanied rapid increases in per capita income. (Japan had the world's fifth-worst terms of trade performance between 1960 and 1980, the fall being from 150 to 77, with 1975 = 100. For that country, price competition was a key to economic success, not failure.)

It is therefore not enough to say that the commodity terms of trade are deteriorating for the LDCs, which are thus worse off. With this caveat in mind, we now turn to the reasons advanced by those who feel the commodity terms of trade are destined in the long run to decline against the LDCs.

THE TERMS OF TRADE ARGUMENTS AGAINST LDC EXPORTING

Each of the reasons purporting to explain why the terms of trade will turn against the LDCs has generated controversy of its own, and the points both pro and con are presented in this section.

The Main Cause for Declining Terms of Trade: Weak Demand for Primary Products

The main theoretical argument suggesting a decline in the terms of trade focuses on a supposed weakness in the long-run demand for primary products.[32] The argument is commonly associated with Raul Prebisch, Ragnar Nurkse, and Edward M. Bernstein. In this scenario a decline in the commodity terms of trade of the LDCs originates in their dependence on primary product exports, the demand for which rises more slowly than the demand for manufactures, turning prices against the former and in favor of the latter. Several different conditions are alleged to be the cause of this.

Engel's Law and the Demand for Food First, the demand for food rises more slowly than income rises. This well-known phenomenon is named Engel's Law after Ernst Engel,* a nineteenth-century Prussian statistician. Engel's Law is certainly correct for the developed countries. For example, the income elasticity of demand for food, which is the percentage increase in demand accompanying a 1% rise in

*Not Friedrich Engels, as is sometimes assumed. I used to tell my students that Engel was obscure, but then I discovered that he was a leader in the struggle against Bismarck's plan to militarize Germany. Eventually he was forced to resign his government post when, unfortunately, Bismarck won the battle.

income,* is in the range of only 0.2 to 0.3 in the United States, Canada, and Western Europe, and American per capita consumption of wheat was about the same in the 1980s as it was in 1900. The elasticities facing LDC food exporters are only a little more encouraging; their food exports are estimated to rise at about 0.6% for a 1% increase in developed-country incomes. The tropical specialties—sugar, tea, coffee, cocoa, pineapple, bananas—all have income elasticities less than 1.0, and most are lower even than the average 0.6 noted above, ranging from 0.3 to 0.5. In some cases, consumers are actually turning away from certain tropical products: coffee and tea to soft drinks, palm oil with its high cholesterol content to no-cholesterol corn oil. (Notice that the low elasticities do not apply to exports of *manufactured* goods from LDCs, which usually show income elasticities greater than 1.0.)

Export pessimists are surely correct in believing that markets for food in developed countries will grow slowly. The pessimism does not extend to these markets in the LDCs themselves, however. Population growth necessitates far larger quantities of food. In addition, Engel's Law has yet to take effect in the LDCs, and the income elasticity of demand for food is much higher, nearly 1.0 in India and Latin America and perhaps 0.8 for LDCs as a whole. Because of the growth in population and income, sales of food to LDCs will increase, and indeed has already done so. In just the 12 years between 1980 and 1992, cereal imports by the LDCs rose from 107 million tonnes to 170 million, a rise of nearly 60%.[33] As consumers in the LDCs become more affluent, their indirect consumption of grain will add further to demand in accordance with "Bennett's Law." Pioneer food economist M. K. Bennett observed in the 1930s how production tends to shift from calorie-efficient production of cereal grains and starches for human consumption toward the more costly and less efficient production of meat and poultry, which require more grain per calorie of human consumption.[34]

Food exporting might then be a leading sector for at least a few LDCs, those able to produce a large agricultural surplus after feeding their own population. Among the countries where food exporting could deliver a dynamic stimulus to economic development are Argentina, Brazil, Colombia, Indonesia, Thailand, Uruguay, and Vietnam. Numerous others may be able to join this group, particularly if the problems of scarce credit, limited capital, and inefficiency discussed in Chapter 12 can be overcome. The long-term prospects for food exporters are thus not nearly so bleak as is sometimes asserted.

Weak Demand for Natural Raw Materials A second condition assumed to lead to declining terms of trade for LDCs is a weak demand for primary product raw materials. For the world as a whole, food, fuel, and other primary commodity imports were 46% of all imports in 1965 but only 25% in 1992, a major decline.[35] Several reasons account for the weak demand. As income grows in developed countries, demand shifts to service industries with a low ratio of raw materials inputs to final output, as opposed to manufacturing where the reverse is true.

*Formally, the income elasticity of demand is percentage change in quantity demanded divided by percentage change in income.

Technological and engineering changes bring new substitutes: Natural nitrates were replaced by the synthetic product, cotton and silk have received heavy competition from artificial fabrics, and rubber has a man-made substitute.*

The substitution of synthetics for natural raw materials has had an especially pronounced effect on some metals, with plastics, ceramics, and silicon chips widely used as substitutes. Household goods from pens to coffeepots to computers show this. Autos and aircraft use large amounts of plastics and ceramics now. A car in the 1920s had a raw materials content of about 50% of its value; today's semiconductors in computers and appliances contain about 1% raw materials by value. Fiber optics, including the energy to produce them, have only a 12% raw materials content; the figure for copper cable, the predecessor to fiber optics, was 50%. A hundred pounds of fiber-optic cable can transmit as much as a ton of copper wire. Economies in the use of raw materials have also been put into place, including larger availability and better processing of scrap metal, electrolytic tin plating that conserves tin, and the like.

The result has been a dramatic decline in the use of several metals: 20% in the amount of copper used per unit of GNP, 30% for nickel, and 40% for tin, with plastics the usual substitute. Although plastics are derived from petroleum, they require less energy to produce than is used in the refining of most metals.[36] In any case, petroleum prices have been relatively stable in recent years, and their fall in real terms has given further advantage to petroleum-based plastics. The old rule of thumb that growth in manufacturing output will raise the consumption of metals is now questionable, with a serious loosening of ties between the rise of income in developed countries and the demand in these countries for raw materials inputs.

It certainly does appear then that LDCs face a declining demand for their primary product exports and therefore a shift in the terms of trade against them.†

Possible Counterarguments Despite the impressive nature of the arguments, there are serious reservations that do not support the case of the pessimists. Technical change does not always work against the demand for primary products; the reverse may be true. Increases in demand greater than GDP growth have already occurred or are projected for a number of materials including vanadium, uranium, tungsten, industrial diamonds, fluorspar, and phosphate rock among others, while demand for a wide range of minerals and raw materials is expected to keep pace with GDP growth.

Even demand falling behind GDP growth is no sign of an unfavorable turn in the terms of trade because price is also a matter of supply. Diminishing returns in the production of primary products, both mineral and agricultural, can mean rising

*Cotton declined from 41% of total fiber consumption in 1950 to only 29% in the 1970s. In the same period, natural rubber declined from 62% to 28% of total rubber consumption.

†Unexpected increases in supply can sometimes occur as well. The supply of both palm oil and cocoa have risen because of cloning and new hybrids. The supply of certain minerals exported from the old USSR, including bauxite, nickel, copper, and platinum, has risen as the former Communist countries have moved toward foreign trade.

prices and higher incomes whether or not demand is income inelastic. This was a traditional position in economics dating back to the work of Ricardo and Malthus on land scarcity. John Maynard Keynes warned of diminishing returns and supply constraints in a well-known *Economic Journal* article of 1923, and this view was resurrected with the Club of Rome's much publicized *Limits to Growth* report of 1972.[37] Developed countries are generally dependent on imports from the LDCs for their supplies of bauxite, chromium, copper, iron, manganese, nickel, and tin. Added to that, the mineral deposits being worked in the LDCs frequently are more richly concentrated than they are in the developed countries. This is true because of the serious transport problems common in LDCs, which makes it economically sensible to develop only the richer deposits. (Examples include the copper of Chile, Zambia, and Zaire; the iron ore of Liberia and Mauritania; the bauxite of Suriname and Guyana; the tin of Bolivia and Malaysia; and the phosphates of Morocco.) During the OPEC oil crisis the high concentration proved to be a major advantage to the LDCs because mining and processing less rich deposits is energy-intensive. Rising energy prices are thus likely to shift demand to the LDCs, where less energy must be expanded per ton of raw material recovered.

Finally, there are many alternative uses for resources in the rich industrial countries. With opportunity costs high, when mineral prices weaken we would expect these countries to shift out of minerals production long before an LDC does so. The United States or Canada would surely cut its copper output in the face of falling demand years before Chile or Zambia would make that decision. Developed-country metals producers are in fact shifting away from raw metal production and toward output of processed items that are higher in value. The more elastic supply would stand to benefit any LDC remaining in the field. The same arguments hold for LDCs that have better alternatives. Primary product exports fall as per capita income rises in all groups of LDCs, large and small, oriented toward manufacturing or agriculture, except for "small primary product exporting countries," some of which raise their primary product exports as their per capita income rises from about $300 to $800 or so. The fact that with growth some LDCs reduce their commodity exports must improve the situation, relatively, for those that continue to specialize in these exports.[38] So, as with food, the long-run prospects of mineral raw materials exporters perhaps do not warrant the extreme pessimism with which they are often viewed. Economies in their use and the substitution of synthetics may be considered not as the cause of a problem, but as a response that has the effect of supplementing a low elasticity of supply.

A final consideration is the possibility that LDC exports of food and raw materials might displace exports and production in developed countries. Developed nations are also large-scale producers of primary products, and their primary product exports are actually greater in quantity than are those of the LDCs. There is significant direct competition between the two groups of countries in numerous metals, fibers, sugar, fats and oils, and, indirectly, beverages and rubber. Competition tends to imply high price elasticities for individual commodities or countries. Alec Cairncross has pointed out that this high price elasticity, caused by the ready availability of competing primary products in developed countries, might well be responsible for what appears to be sluggish demand for these LDC exports.[39] If this is so, the practical significance would be that price stability, or a measure of price reduction in the LDCs (that is, a worsening of the commodity terms of trade), might actually be advantageous, leading to the eventual capture and retention of large markets at the expense of developed-country producers. More efficient methods in agriculture, more investment in mining, and lower taxes on exports would here be seen as playing on high price elasticities to offset the alleged income inelasticities of demand. If an exporter is small, then its situation is automatically better; the price elasticity of demand facing it will be high, and the market will be able to absorb large percentage increases in that country's output. Needless to say, if the developed countries maintain or increase their heavy protection of primary products facing competition from the LDCs, then the optimism of this paragraph would have to be much tempered. (Trade barriers against primary products are treated in Chapter 15.)

The observer attempting to be a fair-minded judge will perhaps conclude from this debate that general predictions of the overall price behavior of primary products are of far less significance to a given country than specific predictions for its individual exports. There will certainly be some primary product exports saddled with income inelasticity, subject to substitution through technical change, and unable to capture additional markets with calculated price cutting. Countries in this camp are well advised to look for alternative exports—perhaps other primary products, perhaps manufactures. Yet this prescription is not the same as sentencing all primary product exports to the certainty of declining terms of trade. Indeed, when John Cuddington looked at the performance of 26 primary products in recent years, he found the price behavior of 16 of these was essentially trendless while 5 more increased, compared to 5 that declined.[40]

The Productivity Argument

The second of the arguments pointing to a decline in the terms of trade is the productivity theory advanced by Hans Singer over three decades ago, but still very much a part of the current debate. Singer postulates that economic growth in the developed countries typically leads to higher income in the form of wages because labor supply is relatively inelastic. In Figure 13.6, economic growth increases the demand for labor and pushes up wages. Figure 13.7 shows the contrary position for a labor-abundant LDC, where growth pushes up labor demand, but along a highly elastic supply curve for labor. Adding to the problem, the growth in demand is faster in the rich countries because technical advances are concentrated there. Wage incomes in LDCs therefore do not rise or rise less than in the developed world. Goods prices then show a different secular tendency: rising due to increasing costs in the developed world with a less-elastic supply of labor; rising more slowly in the LDCs because of the high elasticity of labor supply.

The argument has received theoretical articulation in an article by Ronald Findlay of Columbia University.[41] Many economists see merit in the argument and agree that it does introduce a tendency for the terms of trade to decline against LDCs. Fortunately for those countries, however, this logic may not apply perma-

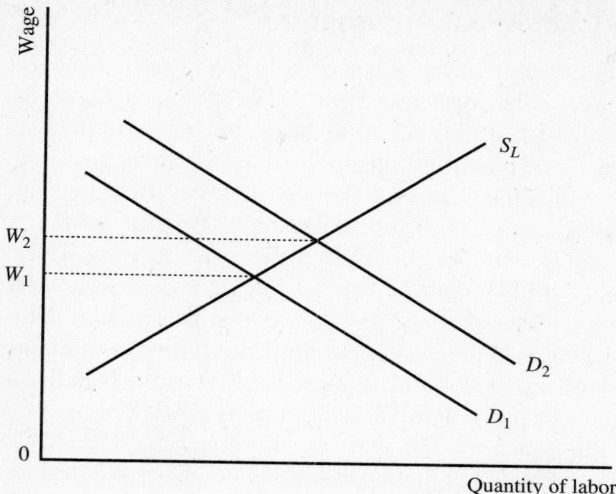

Figure 13.6 Growth in the demand for labor when labor supply is relatively inelastic will cause a significant rise in wages. This is the postulated case for the developed countries.

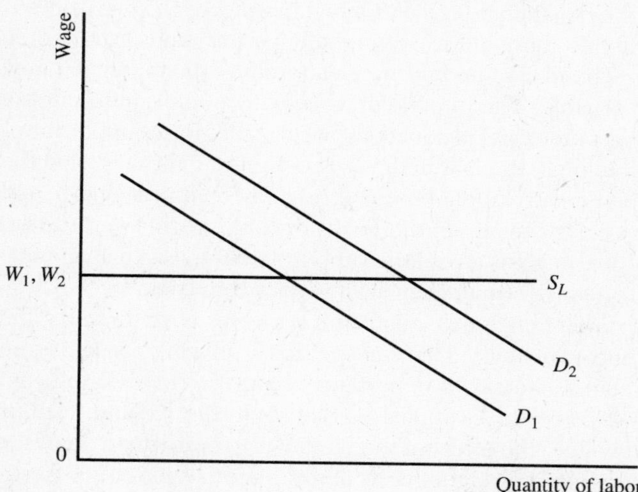

Figure 13.7 Growth in the demand for labor when labor supply is highly elastic will not cause a significant rise in wages. This is the postulated case for the LDCs.

nently. As development occurs, labor supplies may become less elastic, and the real wage will start to rise as it does in advanced countries. Here is another aspect to the need for limiting population growth.*

*The productivity theory has sometimes been used to justify concentration on industrial production rather than on primary products, but note that its implications affect both sorts of activity so long as labor supplies are relatively elastic.

The Monopoly and Ratchet Effect Argument

The third reason suggesting a decline in the commodity terms of trade concerns rigidities in the market structure of the developed world. The monopoly argument is most closely associated with Raul Prebisch and involves the "ratchet effect" of economic theory. In the developed countries, oligopolistic market structure characterizes industrial markets, with a resulting rent element in prices. In these same countries, but more rarely in the LDCs, strong trade unions bargain with large firms. Under these circumstances a ratchet effect may typify price patterns. Prices normally rise during a boom, with oligopolistic firms passing cost increases on to customers and unions, which perhaps pushes up wages beyond rises in productivity in a wage-push type of inflation. When a slump follows, both firms and unions work to avoid cuts in prices and wages. Prices rise more easily than they fall in the developed world; there are fewer barriers to the fall of prices elsewhere, and the terms of trade turn against the LDCs.

There is debate on this proposition. Charles P. Kindleberger has pointed out that trade union power alone is not enough to explain any such tendency. Firms must also have sufficient market power to pass cost increases through to consumers. Otherwise, competition in the product market results simply in reduced sales for any country with a cost-push inflation. Nor is it enough to say that there is strong market power within a national market. Only if the power to raise prices is international in scope will this argument work generally for the goods exported by the developed countries. The idea of an international product monopoly in many products does not seem tenable. The impression is actually one of quite intense global competition for most industrial products in world trade, for example, automobiles and trucks, shipbuilding, steel, aircraft, and computers. There is even the possibility that if developed-country monopoly leads to more technical change and hence lowers production costs over time, the terms of trade might even turn in favor of the LDCs. Statistical analysis gives little support to the thesis that an international ratchet results in a long-term decline against poor countries.[42]

Ronald Findlay has stated that as an explanation for terms of trade shifts, the monopoly argument is unconvincing.[43] There is perhaps a growing consensus on this point. The theory retains a kernel of importance, however, that is significant whenever there is market power in a national market sheltering behind tariff or nontariff barriers to trade. Here the effect of the ratchet is to exacerbate domestic inflation. If price rises are caused by higher costs of raw materials inputs, domestically the higher prices tend to remain even if the raw materials costs drop back later in the business cycle. Within a protected national market, then, the ratchet may have importance as a conveyer of inflation.

Lack of Flexibility

The fourth and last argument suggesting that the terms of trade will decline against LDC exports is the "inflexibility" theory advanced by Charles Kindleberger. A decline will occur because LDC economies are less capable of rapid shifts in production than are those of the developed world. Labor, land, capital, and entrepreneurial ability do

MONOPSONY BUYING IN THE DEVELOPED COUNTRIES

There is an additional argument that some markets for primary products are rigged on the side of the buyers. Such monopsony power may indeed exist in at least a few markets, thereby depressing the price paid to LDC producers.[44] There are said to be only about 12 independent copper smelters in the entire world who will buy from unintegrated mines. Perhaps only 20% of the Western world's aluminum production is marketed outside vertically integrated channels. Relatively few competitors are in the market to buy numerous other less well-known minerals. Gerald Helleiner has noted that some agricultural markets also have a limited number of buyers. Three firms, for example, are responsible for over two-thirds of the world's banana imports. The largest buyer involved in the purchase of cocoa beans has a share of the world market usually between 20% and 40%, and it publishes the most important market information on future demand and supply. The top three firms in the industry purchase 50% to 80% of the world cocoa crop. One firm buys 25% of the world's tea. Twelve buy 80% of the world's natural rubber.

There is, therefore, the possibility that where supply is inelastic, monopsony barriers can restrict the quantity purchased and thus reduce the price paid. The higher the elasticity of supply, the less exploitative a monopsony can be; supply will simply dry up as prices are pushed down. Producers have alternatives and will turn to them. Yet elasticity is sometimes low, with monopsony pricing possible if buying is concentrated. The case is questionable, however. In manufacturing, monopsony power seems limited because any exporting LDC can turn to alternative buyers in other countries as long as trade is open. The rapid growth of world commerce has presumably limited the problem by intensifying competition. In agricultural and mineral production, much capacity is now owned or supervised by government, and the output is sold by government marketing boards or is subject to an export tax or supply restriction. This would resemble a textbook bilateral monopoly model, with countervailing power used to offset the monopsony exploitation. The balance might even tilt far in the other direction, as with OPEC's oil. In one market, grain, in which the number of buyers is relatively small, studies have suggested that the large size of the firms is a reasonable reaction to market conditions and that the monopolistic consequences are slight.[45]

Monopsony power is also difficult to maintain, as exemplified by the decline of the United Fruit Company's banana empire in Central America, the ending of much market power in copper buying in Chile during the 1970s, and loss of position by the "Seven Sisters," which used to dominate world petroleum-buying. One need only add that countervailing action by LDC governments negotiating jointly or by developed countries applying their antitrust laws, or both, would seem called for whenever monopsony power is discovered among the firms of the rich countries. For then, more than would be likely at home, there is an indefensible exploitation of the poor by the rich.

It remains to point out that a further shift in the terms of trade against the LDCs because of monopsony power would presumably require the monopsony power to intensify.

not move as rapidly from one occupation to another because transportation is poor, communications and hence knowledge are limited, literacy is low, and skills in management and government are retarded. Even when decline for an export commodity is predictable, the shift away from that export toward other alternatives is sluggish. This low elasticity of supply for relative price decreases means a country can be locked for a lengthy period into a disadvantageous export, unable to pursue its changing comparative advantage.

Economists generally concede that the overall thrust of this argument is persuasive. Inflexibility is common enough in LDC exporting, with the familiar examples of countries staying with nitrates, jute, cotton, and natural rubber long after demand had dropped, and continuing with bananas, cocoa, and coffee after new and more competitive sources of supply had emerged elsewhere. Countries with exports suffering from declining terms of trade due to a fall in demand or greater and more competitive supply elsewhere will certainly want to consider shifting to alternatives. Where an inflexible economy hinders this, the situation is a difficult one.

The major weakness in the argument is the implication that primary product exporting is somehow to blame for the inflexibility. The reverse conclusion is more sensible: Inflexibility is the cause of unsuccessful exporting. Notice that this argument applies with equal force to any *manufactured* export from an LDC, and perhaps even more so because tastes change rapidly for many manufactured consumer goods. It applies also to producers of import substitutes, which, if inflexible, are more likely to be driven out of business by cheaper imports. Finally, it applies widely even to any domestic economic activity unrelated to international trade, where extra costs are incurred whenever response to changing internal demand and supply conditions is especially slow. It is not the nature of the commodity produced nor of international trade that is at fault here; it is underdevelopment itself. Even so, the Kindleberger position does make a sensible case that the terms of trade might turn against slow-reacting LDCs for long periods.

Summary

There is a plausible argument that long-run adverse shifts in the terms of trade might be experienced by LDCs. The risk is greatest for (1) exporters of foodstuffs and (2) exporters of primary product raw materials most subject to economies in use and replacement by synthetics. The potential for decline is more severe when (3) productivity gains result in price decreases in LDCs and (4) poor countries prove less flexible in moving away from exports with declining prospects.

TERMS OF TRADE: THE EVIDENCE

Debate on the actual behavior of the LDCs' terms of trade has occurred fitfully for over half a century.[46] Such studies are difficult to make because of changes in the quality of goods and alterations in transport costs. They are also uncertain in their interpretation because different beginning and ending dates for an annual series can radically alter the conclusion. (Thus studies that begin at the end of World War I and end during the Great Depression, or start during the Korean War worldwide commodity boom and end during the worldwide commodities slump of the 1980s, inexorably demonstrate a sharp decline in the LDCs' terms of trade, while series that begin in slumps and end in booms demonstrate the reverse conclusion.) Evidence that corrects for these problems appears to indicate some rather small deterioration in the terms of trade of the LDCs took place in the 60-odd years leading up to the start of World War II, then some improvement to the early 1960s, and then virtually no net change to the early 1970s. The terms of trade for the non-oil LDCs in 1971 and 1972 was an index number of 101, with 1963 equal to 100.[47]

Recent Trends in the Terms of Trade

From the early 1970s, the debate becomes complicated because of the oil shocks of 1973–1974 and 1979–1980. During those years the terms of trade of the oil-producing LDCs improved greatly, representing a transfer of welfare not just from rich countries to OPEC, but from many unlucky low-income countries to some lucky ones. The episode underscores how misleading it was ever to believe that there is some uniformity of economic behavior that applies generally to all LDC exports.

Table 13.2 shows the subsequent experience for the non-oil LDCs, which essentially shows terms of trade improvements during world economic recoveries and falls during recessions.* The table appears to bear out the contention by John Cuddington and Carlos Urzúa that for several decades now, the cycle of business activity in the developed countries has been the major factor in the LDCs' terms of trade, rather than any long-run deterioration.[48]

Still the debate goes on, with some scholars suggesting that a long-run decline in the terms of trade continues, while other scholars suggest that price behavior of primary products is essentially trendless. Working with similar data but different statistical and econometric techniques, E. R. Grilli and M. C. Yang see a significant downward trend while John Cuddington and C. M. Urzúa conclude that is no secular downward trend.[49]

TABLE 13.2 NON-OIL LDC TERMS OF TRADE (1963 = 100)

1972	1975	1978	1981	1982	1983	1984	1985	1986	1987	1988	1989	1990	1991
101	94	99	86	85	84	87	85	87	88	92	93	99	88

Source: Calculated by the author from the series in IMF, *International Financial Statistics Yearbook 1993* (Washington, D.C., 1993), 124–125.

*The table also illustrates a convention that sprang up in the 1970s, which was to make a separate terms of trade calculation for countries that export oil and those that do not. Given that the divergence between the two is sometimes large, this is reasonable. But it hardly needs to be said that one way to make movements in the terms of trade appear unfavorable is to exclude the items or countries that performed best during the period considered. The trained observer will keep that point well in mind.

CONCLUSIONS ON THE TERMS OF TRADE

Having completed this survey of the terms of trade and economic development, what conclusions can be drawn from the analysis? A large group of economists is inclined toward skepticism. The empirical evidence, such as it is, led Gottfried Haberler to conclude that the supply and demand for the exports of the LDCs are affected by such divergent conditions that movements in a broad, weighted index leaves us with little useful information. It led Alec Cairncross to say that averaging the experience of the LDCs is to "presume common elements that may have no real existence."[50] I. M. D. Little summarized the debate somewhat waspishly:

> Any reasonably objective observer would have been saying for many years now that the evidence cannot possibly be held to give grounds for maintaining that there is a trend in the terms of trade against developing countries. Theories have been invented to explain this non-existent trend: they are treated with respect even though they explain what does not exist.[51]

In Stephen Lewis's survey, the conclusion on the terms of trade is as broad as Little's:

> Despite the appeal of the Singer-Prebisch thesis, the evidence over the longer term has not been supportive of the basic idea of a consistent secular deterioration of . . . low-income countries as a group.[52]

Perhaps the major lesson conveyed by the statistics is that a general index conceals as much as it reveals. Some commodities are rising in price, while others fall; some LDCs prosper in their exporting, while others stagnate. Any overall average does not give sufficient information on which to base a country's decisions on whether to export and what to export. Only careful analysis of short- and long-run demand and supply for individual products can do that—and that is often much more difficult than compiling averages. The uncritical use of such averages certainly contributed to the bias against trade encountered for so long in so many LDCs, with costs discussed in more detail in the next chapter.

Yet the terms of trade issue refuses to go away. Logic does indicate that in the long term, some primary products and even manufactured exports may be bad bets, and some LDCs will need to worry about a secular decline in their terms of trade. Take Kenya's terms of trade between 1977 and 1987. With 1977 equal to 100, Kenya's 1987 figure was just 44. Over the same period, Colombia's terms of trade fell from 100 to 55, Sri Lanka's from 100 to 66, and Liberia's from 100 to 67.[53] These experiences, due to the poor performance of coffee ($2.29 per pound in 1977, $1.07 in 1987), tea ($1.22 per pound to $0.77 in those years), and natural rubber ($0.73 per pound in 1980, $0.44 in 1987), were bad indeed.[54] The fall in the price of exported goods may lead to increased sales and a greater command over imported goods, especially when the exports are manufactured goods—but in many cases it may not.[55]

Adverse terms of trade shifts can come at most inopportune times. For example, Uganda's coffee exports expressed in tons rose by about a quarter between

1986 and 1989 as production recovered from a time of serious political trouble in that country. But a shift in taste was taking place during those years away from Uganda's robusta to the arabica coffees grown elsewhere, while simultaneously coffee drinking was in general decline. The fall in the coffee price received by Uganda caused a decline in the revenue from its coffee exports of 30%, from $395 million to $273 million.[56]

When terms of trade declines are deep and long-lasting, programs to encourage a more flexible entrepreneurial response may have to be emphasized. These would include infrastructure development, education, freer markets, and the like. Diversification into other exports, including light industry, heavy industry, and services, may have to be pushed. Certainly the whole terms of trade issue becomes less important as the export of manufactured goods becomes more significant to the LDCs. The case that the terms of trade will decline in the long run against the LDC exporters of manufactured goods is far less persuasive than it is for primary product exporters. A move toward manufactures will actually help the countries that do remain specialized in primary products, the prices of which will benefit from the relative decline in supply. Unfortunately, one would expect the least-flexible and least-diversified economies to be also the poorest ones that would encounter the greatest difficulties in implementing remedies of any kind.

The message of this chapter is that trade has been an expediter of long-run growth in the LDCs and probably remains a good bet for the future. But governments had better stay constantly alert for signs of difficulty that will require policy action to correct. We should also note that there is no magic through which even successful trade will automatically solve the many problems considered in earlier chapters, such as inappropriate technologies, population pressure, agricultural backwardness, or market imperfections. There does seem to be some proclivity to blame the terms of trade and hence "international forces of capitalism" for a decline in export earnings even when the real problem is a decline in marketed supply due to economic policy or political disruption. Here, too, policymakers must simultaneously pursue other strategies if progress is to be made.

To this point we have considered international trade as a long-run strategy. The next two chapters will examine the numerous short-run problems that can impede trade's ability to expedite growth. Trade usually involves exchanges of currency, so ill-advised policies concerning foreign exchange rates can bring difficulties. Booms and slumps in the developed world, oil shocks, and food shocks cause LDC export prices and revenues to swing alarmingly. Protectionist barriers to trade can impede progress. Such developments are more painful to the LDCs, whose exports are heavily concentrated. The LDCs themselves may adopt trade policies that, however appealing politically, turn out to be economically ill-advised. All of these eventualities, even though they may be short run in nature, have the capability to reduce the effectiveness of international trade, as we shall see.

NOTES

1. Some parts of this introduction are taken from Wilson B. Brown and Jan S. Hogendorn, *International Economics: Theory and Context* (Reading, Mass., 1993). Several works considering the topic, listed alphabetically, are Bela Balassa, "Outward Orientation," Christopher Bliss, "Trade and Development," Henry Bruton, "Import Substitution," and Stephen R. Lewis, "Primary Exporting Countries," all in Hollis Chenery and T. N. Srinivasan, eds., *Handbook of Development Economics*, vol. 2 (Amsterdam, 1989), 1187–1240, 1541–1600, 1601–1644, and 1645–1689; Peter C. Y. Chow and Mitchell H. Kellman, *Trade—the Engine of Growth in East Asia* (Oxford, 1993); Sebastian Edwards, "Openness, Trade Liberalization, and Growth in Developing Countries," *Journal of Economic Literature* 31 (September 1993): 1358–1393; David Evans, *Comparative Advantage and Growth: Trade and Development in Theory and Practice* (Hemel Hempstead, 1989); David Greenaway, *Trade and Industrial Policy in Developing Countries: A Manual of Policy Analysis* (Ann Arbor, 1993); Keith Griffin, *Alternative Strategies for Economic Development* (London, 1989); Gerald K. Helleiner, *The New Global Economy and the Developing Countries: Essays in International Economics and Development*, (Aldershot, 1990); Gerald K. Helleiner, *Trade Policy, Industrialization, and Development: New Perspectives* (Oxford, 1991); and John Madeley, *Trade and the Poor: The Impact of International Trade on Developing Countries* (New York 1993).
2. See D. H. Robertson, *Essays in Monetary Theory* (London, 1940).
3. Irving B. Kravis has used the term *handmaiden* in his work. See Kravis, "Trade as a Handmaiden of Growth—Similarities Between the 19th and 20th Centuries," *Economic Journal* 80, no. 320 (1970): 850–872.
4. See the survey of the subject by Keith Griffin and John Gurley, "Radical Analyses of Imperialism, the Third World, and the Transition to Socialism: A Survey Article," *Journal of Economic Literature* 23, no. 3 (1985): 1089–1143. André Gunder Frank's *Latin America: Underdevelopment or Revolution* (New York, 1970) has been influential; see also his *Lumpenbourgeoisie and Lumpendevelopment* (New York, 1973). A vivid title in this genre is Walter Rodney, *How Europe Underdeveloped Africa* (London, 1972). Dependency theory is reviewed by Theotonio dos Santos, "The Structure of Dependence," *American Economic Review* 60, no. 2 (1970): 231–236; and by Gabriel Palma, "Dependency: A Formal Theory of Underdevelopment or a Methodology for the Analysis of Concrete Situations of Underdevelopment," in Paul Streeten and Richard Jolly, eds., *Recent Issues in World Development* (Oxford, 1981), 383–426. The term *unequal exchange* was popularized by Arghiri Emmanuel, *L'échange inégal* (Paris, 1969), translated into English as *Unequal Exchange* (New York, 1972). The concept also figures in the research of Samir Amin; see especially his *Neo-Colonialism in West Africa* (Harmondsworth, 1973). Also see Edmar L. Bacha, "An Interpretation of Unequal Exchange from Prebisch-Singer to Emmanuel," *Journal of Development Economics* 5, no. 4 (1978): 319–330; Giovanni Arrighi and John S. Saul, *Essays on the Political Economy of Africa* (New York, 1973); and Immanuel Wallerstein, *The Modern World System* (New York, 1974).
5. See Gerald M. Meier, *Emerging from Poverty* (New York, 1984), 129.
6. OECD data from *WDR 1987*, 143.
7. Young Il-Park and Kym Anderson, "The Rise and Demise of Textiles and Clothing in Economic Development: The Case of Japan," *Economic Development and Cultural Change* 39, no. 3 (April 1991): 531–548.

8. James R. Markusen and Randall M. Wiglee, "Explaining the Volume of North–South Trade," *Economic Journal* 100, no. 403 (December 1990): 1206–1215, which presents evidence that high protection explains low North–South trade. Note that this explanation is consistent with a Heckscher-Ohlin view of trade.
9. See Myint's well-known article, "The Classical Theory of International Trade and the Underdeveloped Countries," *Economic Journal* 68, no. 270 (1958): 317–337; and his *Export and Economic Development of Less-Developed Countries*, Fifth World Congress of the International Economic Association (Tokyo, 1977).
10. This and the next paragraph draw on W. M. Corden, *Trade Policy and Economic Welfare* (Oxford, 1974), 327–329; and on Gottfried Haberler's Cairo lecture reprinted in Gerald M. Meier, *Leading Issues in Economic Development*, 3rd ed. (Oxford, 1976), 702–707.
11. Discussion and analysis of intra-industry trade can be found in Brown and Hogendorn, *International Economics: Theory and Context*, chapter 3. Also see Jeffrey E. Bergstrand, "The Heckscher-Ohlin-Samuelson Model, the Linder Hypothesis and the Determinants of Bilateral Intra-Industry Trade," *Economic Journal* 100, no. 403 (December 1990): 1216–1229.
12. David Greenaway, "New Trade Theories and Developing Countries," in V. N. Balasubramanyam and Sanjaya Lall, *Current Issues in Development Economics*, eds. (New York, 1991), 165, citing O. Havrylyshyn and E. Civan, "Intra Industry Trade Among Developing Countries," *Journal of Development Economics* 18 (1985): 260. The data are from the year 1978.
13. Raphael Kaplinsky, "From Mass Production to Flexible Specialization: A Case Study of Microeconomic Change in a Semi-Industrialized Economy," *World Development* 22, no. 3 (March 1994): 337–353; David B. Yoffie, *Beyond Free Trade: Firms, Governments, and Global Competition* (Boston, 1993).
14. T. N. Srinivasan, "Comment on 'The Noncompetitive Theory of International Trade and Trade Policy,' by Helpman," *Proceedings of the World Bank Annual Conference on Development Economics 1989* (Washington, D.C., 1990): 217–221; Mrinal Datta-Chaudhuri, "Market Failure and Government Failure," *Journal of Economic Perspectives* 4, no. 3 (Summer 1990): 25–39.
15. See Michael E. Porter, *The Competitive Advantage of Nations* (New York, 1990).
16. Calculated from IMF, *International Financial Statistics Yearbook 1993*, 108–109, 120–121.
17. See *The Economist*, October 1, 1994; and Anne O. Krueger, *Economic Policies at Cross-Purposes* (Washington, D.C., 1991): 105.
18. Emmanuel, *Unequal Exchange*.
19. The survey by Griffin and Gurley, utilized in this section, has an extensive bibliography of the works of the major dependency theorists, including Paul Baran, Celso Furtado, E. Cardoso, O. Sunkel, P. O'Brien, and others, as well as the authors already mentioned in the text and in endnote 4. A recent look at dependency theory is Cristobal Kay, *Latin American Theories of Development and Underdevelopment* (London, 1989). A useful book by Anthony Brewer attempts, I believe successfully, to capture the essential features of these models in simplified form. See his *Marxist Theories of Imperialism: A Critical Survey* (London, 1980), especially parts III and IV. How to incorporate into their models the export success of the high-performing Asian economies and other NICs is a difficult problem for dependency theorists. The subject is examined by John Browett, "The Newly Industrializing Countries and Radical Theories of Development," *World Development* 13, no. 7 (1985): 789–803.

20. From Griffin and Gurley, "Radical Analyses of Imperialism," 1105–1116.
21. Calculated from IMF, *International Financial Statistics Yearbook 1993* and *WDR 1994*, 167.
22. Following the logic of David Greenaway and Chris Milner, "Trade Theory and the Less-Developed Countries," in Norman Gemmell, ed., *Surveys in Development Economics* (Oxford, 1987) and W. Arthur Lewis in *Growth and Fluctuations 1870–1913* (London, 1978), 244.
23. Paul A. Samuelson, "Illogic of Neo-Marxian Doctrine of Unequal Exchange," in David A. Belsley, Edward J. Kane, Paul A. Samuelson, and Robert M. Solow, eds., *Inflation, Trade, and Taxes* (Columbus, 1976), 96.
24. Emmanuel, *Unequal Exchange*.
25. Samuelson, "The Illogic of Neo-Marxian Doctrine of Unequal Exchange."
26. Samuelson, "The Illogic of Neo-Marxian Doctrine of Unequal Exchange," 107. Brewer's *Marxist Theories of Imperialism*, 226–230, advances and discusses other criticisms of Emmanuel's model.
27. For an example of the work of the New World Group, see Lloyd Best, "The Mechanism of Plantation Type Economies: Outline of a Model of Pure Plantation Economy," *Social and Economic Studies* 17 (1968): 283–326.
28. See A. K. Cairncross, *Factors in Economic Development* (London, 1962), excerpted in Meier, *Leading Issues*, 3rd ed., 712–717.
29. From Lloyd G. Reynolds, "Inter-Country Diffusion of Economic Growth, 1870–1914," in Mark Gersowitz et al., *The Theory and Experience of Economic Development* (London, 1982), 327, citing the work of J. E. Craig and D. Snodgrass.
30. Suggested by Hla Myint in Meier, *Leading Issues*, 4th ed., 504; and Gottfried Haberler's Cairo lecture, in Meier, *Leading Issues*, 3rd ed., 703.
31. For the earlier dates, see Benjamin Higgins, *Economic Development*, rev. ed. (New York, 1968), 624.
32. For the material in this section I used Alfred Maizels, *The Commodity Crisis of the 1980s and the Political Economy of International Commodity Prices* (Oxford, 1992); David Evans, "The Long-Term Determinants of North–South Terms of Trade and Some Recent Empirical Evidence," 657–671, in a special issue of *World Development* 15, no. 5 (May 1987), edited by Alfred Maizels, entitled "Primary Commodities in the World Economy: Problems and Policies"; Maizels's own remarks, "Commodities in Crisis: An Overview of the Main Issues," 537–549, in the same issue; John Madeley, *Trade and the Poor: The Impact of International Trade on Developing Countries* (New York, 1993); IMF, *World Economic Outlook 1987*; *South*, October, 1987; *The Economist*, April 18, 1987; Michael P. Todaro, *Economic Development in the Third World*, 2nd ed., 339, 352, 371, citing Alfred Maizels; and Meier, *Leading Issues*, 4th ed., 428, citing Bruce Johnston and John Mellor.
33. *WDR 1994*, 169.
34. See Thomas T. Poleman, "Quantifying the Nutrition Situation in Developing Countries," *Food Research Institute Studies* 18, no. 1 (1981): 29.
35. *WDR 1994*, 189; *WDR 1990*, 207.
36. *The Economist*, August 11, 1984, 61; *South*, no. 68 (June 1986): 103.
37. D. L. Meadows et al, *The Limits to Growth* (New York, 1972). That report, however, was criticized for failing to take into account future economies and substitutions in resource use due to scarcity-induced higher prices.
38. Moshe Syrquin, "Patterns of Structural Change," in Hollis Chenery and T. N. Srinivasan, eds., *Handbook of Development Economics*, vol. 1 (Amsterdam, 1988), 234.
39. Cairncross, *Factors in Economic Development*, reprinted in Meier, *Leading Issues*, 3rd ed., 712–717.

40. See John T. Cuddington, "Long-Run Trends in 26 Primary Commodity Prices," *Journal of Development Economics* 39, no. 2 (October 1992): 207–227.
41. Ronald Findlay, "The Terms of Trade and Equilibrium Growth in the World Economy," *American Economic Review* 70, no. 3 (1980): 291–299.
42. See A. P. Thirlwall and J. Bergevin, "Trends, Cycles and Asymmetries in the Terms of Trade of Primary Commodities from Developed and Less Developed Countries," *World Development* 13, no. 7 (1985): 805–817.
43. Findlay, "Terms of Trade and Equilibrium Growth."
44. The details here and in the next paragraph are from Gerald K. Helleiner, "World Market Imperfections in the Developing Countries," in William R. Cline, ed., *Policy Alternatives for a New International Economic Order* (New York, 1979); *International Economic Disorder: Essays in North–South Relations* (Toronto, 1981), chap. 2; "Freedom and Management in Primary Commodity Markets. U. S. Imports from Developing Countries," *World Development* 6, no. 1 (1978): 23–30; and other works by Helleiner on the subject.
45. Information provided to me by Wilson B. Brown of the University of Winnipeg.
46. See John Spraos, *Inequalising Trade: A Study of Traditional North-South Specialisation in the Context of Terms of Trade Concepts* (Oxford, 1983). This book grew out of an article by Spraos, "Have the Terms of Trade Declined?" *Economic Journal* 90, no. 357 (March 1980): 107–128. Spraos's work is much relied on here. Also see Dimitris Diakosavvas and Pasquale L. Scandizzo, "Trends in the Terms of Trade of Primary Commodities, 1900–1982: The Controversy and Its Origins," *Economic Development and Cultural Change* 39, no. 2 (January 1991): 231–264; section 2.2, "The Terms of Trade Issue," in Bela Balassa, "Outward Orientation," in Chenery and Srinivasan, *Handbook of Development Economics*, vol. 2, 1653–1659; Charles P. Kindleberger, *The Terms of Trade: A European Case Study* (New York, 1956), 239, 263–264; and Theodore Morgan, "The Long-Run Terms of Trade Between Agriculture and Manufacturing," *Economic Development and Cultural Change* 8, no. 1 (1959): 1–23.
47. Calculated by the author from the series in IMF, *International Financial Statistics Yearbook 1993* (Washington, D.C., 1993), 124–125.
48. John T. Cuddington and Carlos M. Urzúa, "Trends and Cycles in the Net Barter Terms of Trade: A New Approach," *Economic Journal* 99, no. 396 (June, 1989): 426–442.
49. For citations, see Cuddington, "Long-Run Trends in 26 Primary Commodity Prices," 207–227.
50. Gottfried Haberler, "Terms of Trade and Economic Development," in H. S. Ellis, ed., *Economic Development for Latin America* (New York, 1961), 275–297; and Cairncross, *Factors in Economic Development*, extracted in Meier, *Leading Issues*, 3rd ed., 714.
51. I. M. D. Little, "Economic Relations with the Third World—Old Myths and New Prospects," *Scottish Journal of Political Economy* 22, no. 3 (1975): 227.
52. Stephen R. Lewis, "Primary Exporting Countries," in Chenery and Srinivasan, *Handbook of Development Economics*, vol. 2, 1548.
53. All calculated by the author from the series in IMF, *International Financial Statistics Yearbook 1993*, 125.
54. The coffee price is "all coffee, New York." The tea price is "average auction, London." Rubber is "all origins, New York." They are taken from the commodity price table in IMF, *International Financial Statistics Yearbook 1993*, 164–167.
55. See Prabirjit Sarkar and Hans W. Singer, "Manufactured Exports of Developing Countries and Their Terms of Trade Since 1965," *World Development* 19, no. 4 (April 1991): 333–340; Matthias Lücke, "Developing Countries' Terms of Trade in Manufactures, 1967–87: A Note," *Journal of Development Economics* 29, no. 3 (April 1993): 588–595;

Paul Mosley and John Weeks, "Has Recovery Begun? 'Africa's Adjustment in the 1980s' Revisited," *World Development* 21, no. 10 (October 1993): 1583–1606; and Premachandra Athukorala, "Manufactured Exports from Developing Countries and Their Terms of Trade: A Reexamination of the Sarkar-Singer Results," *World Development* 21, no. 10 (October 1993): 1583–1606.

56. *HDR 1992*, 67.

Chapter 14

Trade Policy and Economic Development

In many developing countries, and for a long time, trade pessimism based on the arguments of the last chapter was both persistent and pervasive. To the degree that exports would have effects only of the enclave or backwash variety, with the terms of trade declining in the long run, the outlook was grim. The response by political leaders was widespread adoption of an "inward-looking" or "inward-oriented" strategy that was pessimistic concerning exports and designed to substitute domestic production for imports. Such policies involve high tariffs, strict quotas, licenses, and domestic content requirements on production, all designed to encourage the replacement of imports (especially of manufactured goods) by a country's own output. The fewer the imports, the less necessary it is to export to pay for them, and the less the thralldom to the rich countries. Many people, especially noneconomists, applauded the general idea of self-sufficiency, or "autarky" as it is sometimes called. But experience showed so many penalties had to be paid with such a policy that the good sense of that idea came to be much in doubt.

The purpose of this chapter is to survey the subject of inward-looking import substitution policy and contrast it to the opposite and presently much-recommended outward-looking strategy of removing policy biases and promoting exports. The following chapter will then consider the extent to which barriers to trade reduce the effects of export promotion.

INWARD-LOOKING (IMPORT SUBSTITUTION) POLICIES

Rational Policies for Import Substitution

Clearly some forms of import substitution are eminently sensible.[1] A very poor country with no local manufacturing will find that some lines of production are "naturally protected" by high transport costs. These goods are "market-oriented" and expensive to import; there is a clear advantage in producing them close to the market. Soft drinks and beer contain a great deal of water, and so the transport costs are high; bottling close to the market is obviously superior to paying for imported water. The water can easily be added by the bottler to the solid ingredients. Furniture can be imported assembled, but much space (between the table legs, for example) is wasted in transport. The volume to be shipped can be reduced if the furniture travels in unassembled form and is assembled at a local factory near the market. A similar assembly argument applies to cars and trucks. Perishable goods of all kinds, including many foods and tobacco, are also expensive to ship, and there will be a cost advantage in processing them close to the market. We would not be surprised to find imports of these types of goods rapidly giving way to domestic output, even if the domestic activity is merely the assembly of imported components, because of a comparative advantage based on transport.

Import substitution is also economically sensible when there is a comparative advantage based on production costs. Perhaps, as happened widely, a colonial government discouraged early attempts to industrialize. Some manufacturing industries, such as textiles, clothing, footwear, glassware, and the like may therefore not have developed, even though they would have been profitable. Imports of these labor-intensive light industrial products are obvious candidates for substitution, and their production can be the opening wedge for manufacturing. An equally good case for the replacement of imports holds when comparative advantage is changing, perhaps because the capital stock is rising; the human capital in the form of education, skills, health, and nutrition are improving; or learning-by-doing has enhanced performance. These cases may encompass the manufacture of office and telecommunications equipment, household appliances, machinery, transport equipment, chemicals, and so forth. For them, domestic production may become a reasonable proposition even though it was not earlier. Similarly, demand may expand to allow sufficient economies of scale for production to begin. Many imported products on the market for years become reasonable candidates for domestic production as income grows, perhaps giving vent to new middle-class tastes. With adequate demand, it may then pay to provide supportive retail personnel and equipment (the freezers for local ice cream, for example) without which local output will be limited. In all these cases, market forces would lead entrepreneurs to compete "naturally" with imports, without the need for a particular government policy to encourage its occurrence.

Any firm trying to start up may, however, encounter special problems. It might take months or even a few years to get the bugs out of production, for the workers and managers to learn their tasks, or for the purchase of inputs and marketing to go smoothly. Before this is accomplished, even firms that would eventually have a comparative advantage may find they cannot fight the flow of imports from abroad, and therefore succumb. Borrowing might tide a firm over this difficult infancy, but capital markets may be imperfect so that new entrepreneurs may find loans difficult to acquire from private sources. If government budgets are tight, then no assistance may be forthcoming from that source either. In any case, the new firm may have to bear the cost of training workers, who may then be bid away by competitors who incur no costs for training. There may also be strong externalities well worth having for the country as a whole but with little or no effect on the balance sheets of the originating firms, such as technical know-how that then becomes freely available. Lending will not cover these cases even if capital markets are efficient.

For these reasons, some limited protection on "infant industry" grounds early in a country's development may be warranted if there is already a domestic market for a product. Justifications for infant industry tariffs in LDCs are actually more persuasive than they are in developed countries, where capital markets are sophisticated and presumably well able to judge whether an industry has a chance to prosper. Protection of "good bets" for a period of, say, four to eight years, with infant industry tariffs kept in the range of 10% to 20%, would lead to a form of import substitution that, if not favored by economists who generally advocate improving capital markets or subsidies, would at least be tolerated.[2] Of course, a longer period may be needed to master a difficult new technology, but because of compounding, the consumer cost of the protection is then much more likely to outweigh the benefits.* The result would be a number of industries whose production would take the place of imports. If the choices were made correctly, these industries would eventually be able to compete without the trade barriers and perhaps even begin to export, as discussed later in the chapter.

The model is not just wishful thinking. The United States, Germany, France, and Japan all used it to advantage in their development experience. During World Wars I and II, the interruption of shipping to South America and unavailability of consumer and capital goods in that region acted widely as a regional form of infant industry protection, and the production of textiles, cement, food processing, and so forth boomed as entrepreneurs moved to fill the gap. The heavy industry of Brazil, Mexico, and South Korea, including steel and autos in all these countries, plus a broad range of manufacturing in these and other NICs, have benefited from a sensible application of the infant industry argument.† As Henry Bruton put it,

---

*Credit subsidies for infant industries might also be used. As with infant industry tariffs, the subsidies had better be kept relatively low and their duration relatively short, or their budgetary costs will rise markedly. Any such subsidies should be watched carefully, as it is easy to reintroduce a bias against agriculture by such methods.

†Brazil's case is the most recent, and in spite of horrendous macroeconomic difficulties in recent years the industrial growth of that country has been impressive. See the analysis by Simon Teitel and Francisco E. Thoumi, "From Import Substitution to Exports: The Manufacturing Exports Experience of Argentina and Brazil," *Economic Development and Cultural Change* 34, no. 3 (1986): 455–490.

> The message seems to be that evident profit opportunities plus non-distorting protection . . . produces the inducements for an economy to find ways to exploit its resources with ever-increasing effectiveness. . . .
>
> The idea that some form of protection is in order to enable a country to establish its place in the world economy, in order to establish an economy that is flexible and resilient, is a fundamental idea.[3]

Import substitution has, however, sometimes been implemented with such a battery of ill-designed policies that it is possible to lose sight of the fact that it sometimes makes eminently good sense.

Generalized Import Substitution Policy

In contrast to these rational applications of import substitution policy, a fair number of countries have generalized the strategy, using it across a wide range of imports even when there is no present comparative advantage in many of these and no likelihood that any changes in basic or advanced factors would lead toward one. This generalized inward-looking import substitution strategy was in its heyday from about the 1950s to the 1970s. While many governments have moved away from it, in some quarters the theory still has a major influence on the public and politicians. The idea seems to be based on a perception that if a substantial amount of some good is imported, then it should be produced locally. Often the justification centers on trade pessimism. Mixed with this is the presumption that important external economies and learning-by-doing will accompany local manufacturing of an industrial product. Frequently, the belief seems to be that the whole manufacturing sector is an infant, inefficient now, but lacking only a period of protection behind trade barriers in order to grow up. On occasion, the preference for domestic industry does not appear to be based on economics at all, but instead on considerations of morale and prestige. The production in some countries of steel or aircraft or cars at a considerable loss are cases in point.

A typical policy of generalized import substitution begins by protecting local producers of consumer goods. The umbrella of protection, by means of tariffs, quotas, licensing of foreign exchange, and other methods to be discussed, is usually not so much directed at capital goods and raw materials. Imports of these goods are thought to be more essential and are generally more difficult to produce or are completely unavailable domestically. Often, government decides in the first place which industries it wants to develop; these are the ones to receive the protection.

The High Costs of Generalized Import Substitution An overall, pervasive policy of import substitution is likely to be a high-cost strategy. More than anything else, the recognition of these costs has turned the great majority of economists against it and explains why the 1980s saw many LDCs abandoning their commitment to it.

Typically, the tariffs, quotas, and licensing of production will be costly for consumers because local prices are raised. (For an analysis, see the box entitled "Some Costs of Import Restriction" later in the chapter.) Trade barriers were the reason why Indonesian domestic steel prices in the 1980s were 45% above the world market price; plastics prices 20% more, and cement prices 100% more. The higher prices percolating through the economy, together with the distortions introduced by the policy controls, can be an inflationary mixture. It is endlessly fascinating to consider how often general protection means gains for a small group of well-to-do industrialists at the expense of the great mass of the population, who, because of the higher prices, lose some of their access to the imported "inducement goods" that are so effective in stimulating effort.

In some LDCs, the profits associated with import protection can run as high as 15% of GDP.[4] Not surprisingly, infant industry protection is hard to dismantle when the results pay the beneficiaries as well as this. The more quotas are used, the worse this problem will be. Quotas limit imports to a fixed quantity, whereas a tariff would cause import quantities to vary with supply-and-demand changes. As we saw in Chapter 2, these price-boosting effects of trade barriers lead to an artificially inflated importance of manufacturing in the GDP. Import substitution would look somewhat less appealing if GDP growth were not thereby overstated. I. M. D. Little suggests that growth rates for heavy import-substituting countries are exaggerated by up to about 0.5% per year because of the higher prices caused by the policy.[5]

Costs may be much higher yet, though difficult to quantify, because the system of controls will involve unexpected changes in the regulations, extensive red tape, and corruption. Costs are obvious if, as in Tanzania, applications for licenses to import had to be submitted three months in advance, or if, as in Indonesia, 25 to 100 pages of documentation were required for each piece of equipment imported.[6] With the quotas and licenses likely to be lucrative for the holder, the incentive for corruption increases. Import substitution can serve to enrich not only favored entrepreneurs but also government officials, as well as the smugglers and black marketeers who make their living by avoiding the controls. Not without reason is it sometimes said that a market price, rather than a controlled one, is a better policeman than the real thing.

Industries growing up under these hothouse conditions may be profitable enough for their owners, but they can be especially inefficient in a number of ways. Because the domestic market is relatively small in so many countries, there will be no economies of scale such as might have been attained in a larger market (that is, through exporting). Too many varieties of each good may be produced, and the industry's growth will be limited to the level and growth of local demand. Bangladesh, for example, has an industrial economy only 3% the size of Sweden's and 2% that of Canada's, and both of these two rich countries are generally thought to need international trade to obtain the benefits of scale economies. India, though its population is huge, has an industrial market estimated to be less than 25% that of Germany's.[7] With scale small, any gains from learning-by-doing will be reduced, as will any other dynamic advances in productivity that might be expected from high-volume output. Monopoly and oligopoly do tend to proliferate behind the barriers. These inexperienced firms, facing little competition, may turn out products substantially inferior to what could be imported. The problem will be noticed not only by consumers, but also by producers who use the protected goods as inputs and have no place to turn for better quality substitutes.

The character of the industries so established may not be satisfactory. The low barriers against imports of capital inputs mean the financial incentive to produce consumer goods of a less-essential type is higher even than it would otherwise have been. (The increased attraction involves the principle of "tariff escalation," which will be considered in Chapter 15.) The higher output of less-essential products is not in keeping with a goal of self-reliance, which is so often the initial motive for the policy.

The highest protection of all may apply to luxury goods, because tariffs against them will be thought fair; the incentives are then to produce these luxuries at home, for consumption by middle- or high-income consumers. The resulting industrial structure can therefore show signs of urban bias, even if unintended. (Discriminatory sales taxes can be used to offset the pull toward luxuries, but these taxes are difficult to collect in the lowest-income countries, as explained in Chapter 4.) Further, the industries established behind the protective barriers may largely be assembling activities, with little value added in production and few prospects for future expansion. From the easy beginnings, every further step may be more difficult because the imports substituted for must be ever more capital intensive and ever more subject to diseconomies due to small scale. Naturally, the products least difficult to produce and least sensitive to scale are undertaken first. At worst, the process ends with the economy more dependent on imports than before, with self-reliance actually diminished. Any disruption of imports that would formerly have affected only the flow of consumer goods now interrupts the supply of machinery, spare parts, and vital raw materials, causing production stoppages and layoffs.

A striking result is that the foreign exchange costs of the imported raw materials and capital may be higher than the foreign exchange costs of the imported product itself. Such has been the case with a number of products, including steel in Bangladesh and Egypt; tin cans in Kenya; autos in Thailand, Nigeria, and Turkey; and jet aircraft in Argentina, Egypt, and India.[8] (The technique for measuring these effects is addressed in the accompanying box.) In short, the confidence that import substitution increases independence is seriously exaggerated. This is ironic because the search for self-reliant independence was the justification for the policy in the first place.

An additional effect from the forced-draft expansion of industry is that scarce factors of production, including capital and talented entrepreneurs, will be attracted into the areas where trade barriers have raised profits. The relative cheapness of the imported capital, often exaggerated by interest rate subsidies, will lead to too much capital intensity and excess capacity. Because of the relative capital intensity, often the industries established do not provide as much employment of labor per unit of output as does exporting. The strong evidence for this assertion is presented in this chapter's section on export promotion. The artificial cheapness of capital is also very likely a major cause of the surprisingly low level of capacity utilization reported in the industries of many LDCs and the infrequency of shift work that would utilize capital more efficiently by applying to it larger quantities of abundant labor.

THE TECHNIQUE FOR MEASURING WHETHER FOREIGN EXCHANGE IS SAVED

The term *domestic resource cost* (DRC) is used to describe the ratio of the opportunity cost of all domestic resources used directly or indirectly to produce a good compared to the net foreign exchange saved from producing the good domestically rather than importing it. (Net because domestic production may require foreign exchange to pay for some inputs). A DRC coefficient for a project of less than 1 means that the local currency cost to gain foreign exchange by domestic manufacture is less than what the foreign exchange is worth in local currency. If the coefficient is greater than 1, then the cost in local currency to gain foreign exchange is greater than the local currency value of that foreign exchange. It is not unknown for projects actually to lose foreign exchange in their operation; that is, more foreign exchange is required to build and operate a project than would have been required to import the product. Formally,

$$DRC = \frac{\textit{value added at domestic prices in local currency}}{\textit{value added at world prices in foreign currency}}$$

The formula allows a prediction of whether an investment in an export industry or in an import substitution industry could earn or save foreign exchange that, when converted into local currency, would be a surplus over cost.[9]

The diversion of resources into the import substitution industries will inevitably penalize exports.[10] Exporting firms will also suffer because they use the expensive protected products as inputs, thus boosting their costs. More generally, domestic resources will be attracted into the production of import substitutes, raising the prices that exporters must pay for *all* inputs. To the extent that the exporters are selling in a competitive world market, they cannot pass on the higher costs to foreign consumers. Because the competition on world markets will prevent the price of exports from rising, the protection is like a tax on exporters. World Bank estimates of the size of this tax are 43% of the import duty in the Côte d'Ivoire and 95% in Colombia.[11] With exports penalized, there are likely to be chronic shortages of foreign exchange to purchase imports, requiring exchange controls and rationing. These controls themselves may be administered in such a way as to inflict even further damage, as explained in the next section on overvalued exchange rates. Of course, *potential* exporters will be hurt also. Products that could have been exported under neutral free-market conditions are poor bets because of the bias. Capital, including foreign investment by MNEs, has no incentive to flow toward export operations. As a case of "what might have been," this harm will be almost invisible to voters, politicians, or dictators. True, there will still be MNEs, but they will be there because of tariff jumping, taking advantage of the high profits available behind the trade barriers and competing with local firms for the quota licenses and the foreign exchange permits.

SOME COSTS OF IMPORT RESTRICTION

Import restriction attracts resources to a protected industry, raises prices for buyers of the product, shifts welfare from consumers to producers, and involves a deadweight loss.

Figure 14.1 shows the domestic supply and demand for a product that can be imported at the world price P_w. With free trade, domestic firms will produce a quantity Q_1; consumption will be Q_4; the gap Q_1Q_4 is filled by imports. A tariff P_wP_t will boost prices to P_1 and cut imports to Q_2Q_3. Alternatively, a quota limiting imports to Q_2Q_3 will have the same price-boosting effect; the price rises because of the supply limitation. In either case, domestic consumers cut back their consumption of the now higher-priced product from Q_4 to Q_3. A further result of either a tariff or a quota is new production by domestic firms Q_1Q_2, as these firms react to the higher price by raising their employment of resources.

Those with a knowledge of consumer and producer surpluses can also trace the shifts in welfare caused by a tariff or quota and identify a deadweight loss from protection. Consumer surplus is the area above the price paid and below

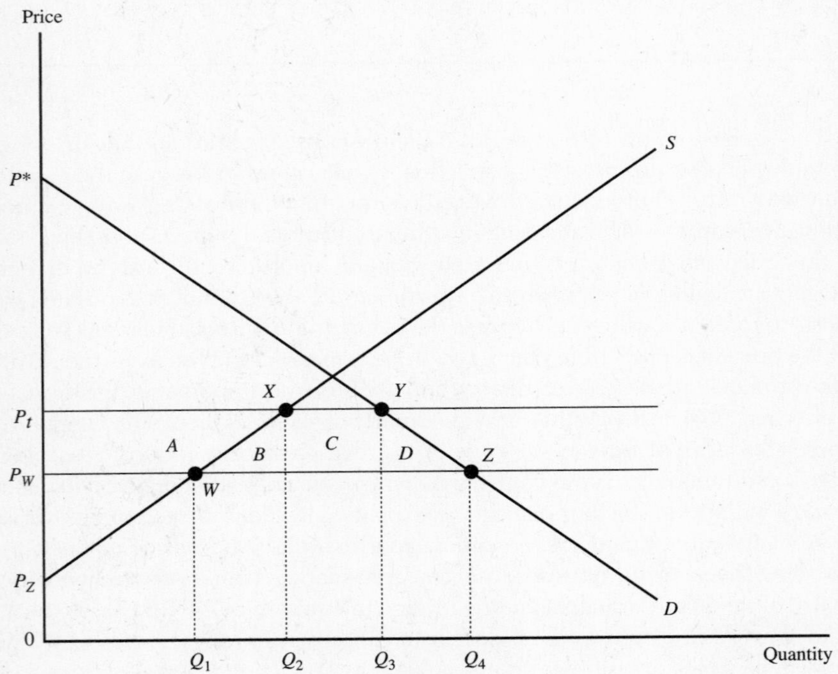

Figure 14.1 The effects of import restrictions include higher prices, lower quantities, and a deadweight loss (here equal to area $B + D$).

the demand curve. Before protection, it is P_wP^*Z, and after the tariff or quota is applied, it shrinks to P_tP^*Y, a reduction of areas $A + B + C + D$. Producer surplus is the area above the supply curve but below the price received. It rises from P_zP_wW to P_zP_tX, a rise of A. Under a tariff, government gets tariff revenue equal to the quantity of imports Q_2Q_3 times the tariff per unit P_wP_t, which amounts to area C. (Under a quota, usually given gratis to importers, C represents a transfer from consumers to those who receive the quota licenses.) Notice that the gains to producers and/or the government, $A + C$, are not as great as the loss to consumers, $A + B + C + D$. The remainder, $B + D$, is a deadweight loss in welfare, a penalty paid by society for choosing a protectionist policy.

Studies in developed countries show quite small deadweight losses from protection, usually 1% or less of national product. (Long-run losses are undoubtedly much higher; the large transfers from consumers to producers are not included in the estimates of deadweight loss.) Earlier studies of LDCs suggest much greater damage to those countries, sometimes as much as 9% to 10% of GNP or even more.[12] Work by Richard Harris emphasizes the dynamic gains from increased competition and from economies of scale. Harris suggests that realizing these through a dismantling of protection would yield a respectable rise in GNP in the range of 2.5% to 8.5%.[13] World Bank research suggests that removing just quotas from Turkey's structure of protection would have increased that country's GDP by 5.4%, while removing tariffs, quotas, and export taxation would have raised Philippine GNP by 5.2%.[14]

The country engaging in widespread import substitution is likely to discover that the panoply of price controls, foreign exchange rationing, and trade barriers required by the strategy makes its economy less flexible in the face of disturbances from inside or outside. A harvest failure requiring food imports or an OPEC oil shock that boosts fuel and fertilizer bills can wreak additional havoc. The extensive controls mean the economy is likely to respond less elastically. Low reserves of foreign exchange and little attractiveness to foreign bankers mean that imports may have to be restricted all at once, with consequent contraction of output of any industry using imported inputs.

The results of generalized import substitution seem so doleful that one wonders how such policies have survived. It is not very difficult to understand why. Every tariff, every quota, every import license or foreign exchange permit establishes a profitable vested interest in the maintenance of the system. While society as a whole is the loser, the favored individual firms—their owners, their managers, their workers—and the government officials who administer the system would all regret its passing and will fight hard for its retention.

That makes the reform of import substitution politically difficult, because withdrawal of the protectionist trade barriers would mean not only the collapse of many industries and perhaps a serious recession but also adamant opposition from the affected interests. At the same time there are potential benefits from setting up a new system that shakes up old ways of thinking and old political bases and alliances. A major debate surrounds the pace of reform: Should it be moderate, with incremental reductions of the barriers and increasing freedom from the controls, or should it be a sudden, once-for-all approach? Which policy will make the adjustment economically less painful and politically more acceptable? That subject is taken up later in the chapter.

OVERVALUED FOREIGN EXCHANGE RATES

Causes of Overvaluation

An overvalued foreign exchange rate is the usual companion of an import substitution policy. The overvaluation is often put in place by government to make imported capital goods cheaper for its industries. Producers with access to low-cost foreign exchange will find it easier to acquire imported capital and raw materials than would otherwise have been true. In effect, overvaluation acts as a subsidy to the firms selected. Such policies are most commonly used in Africa and Latin America and less so in Asia.

We use overvaluation to describe a price for a country's currency that is fixed above the price we guess would obtain in an unregulated market—for example, one U.S. dollar exchanging at a fixed rate of 100 Penuristan penuris when a free-market rate would have been 150 penuris for $1. The penuri is overvalued because it takes only 100 of them to buy a dollar, rather than the 150 that would have been needed if the rate had been market determined. To keep the exchange rate at a level different from what the market would dictate requires a system of foreign exchange controls enforced by administrative action.

Everyone will want dollars or other hard currencies at the favorable rate in order to import cheaply; the quantity of dollars demanded will exceed the supply of dollars when the penuri price of dollars is below equilibrium, as in Figure 14.2.

It will therefore be necessary to take one of three steps. (1) Monetary and fiscal policy can be made restrictive, contracting the economy and so lowering the demand for imports and the foreign exchange to buy it. This will be unpopular not only with citizens but also with economists, who will wonder why one would want to have an overvalued rate at the cost of chronic recession. (2) Borrowing abroad can be pursued to provide an extra supply of foreign exchange, thereby financing the deficit. Although obviously not a long-run solution, there has been some resort to this, especially by relatively prosperous borrowers such as Argentina, Chile, and Uruguay. By this route, overvalued exchange rates contributed to the debt crisis explored in Chapter 6. Given the reduction in private international bank lending, the tactic of borrowing to support an overvalued rate is now not practicable. (3) Finally, and much more generally, a country can establish trade controls to reduce the spending on imports and a system of rationing for foreign exchange, whereby the limited amount of hard currency available (*A* in Figure 14.2) is doled out to only a few of the many customers who will want much of it (*B*) at that price.

Overvaluation based on controls would not occur in a country with a freely floating exchange rate determined by movements in supply and demand. Yet only a minority of the LDCs allow their rates to float freely. In 1992, most of them had a fixed rate pegged to a major currency (23 to the U.S. dollar, 14 to the French franc, 5 to the SDR, 2 to the South African rand, 1 to the Indian rupee). Many others (24)

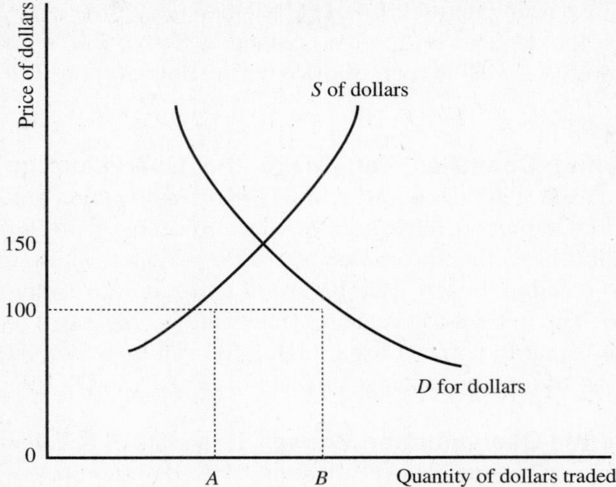

Figure 14.2 An overvalued exchange rate leads to an excess demand for foreign exchange, that is, a shortage.

pegged their rates to a market basket of foreign currencies.[15] Pegging is popular because freely floating foreign exchange rates may be highly variable where currencies are traded in only small quantities on thin markets. Extreme fluctuations in foreign exchange rates can generate uncertainty and reduce exports significantly.

The rest of the LDCs employed some sort of floating exchange rate, often managed by government controls and interventions, so that many of these currencies were overvalued too. In 1983, only three LDCs had freely floating rates: Lebanon, South Africa, and Uruguay. By 1993, the number had reached 26.* Some of these used foreign exchange auctions conducted by the central bank. There is, however, a growing trend toward floating with currencies bought and sold on an interbank market that includes not only private and central banks but also nonbank dealers. (The greater the competition in these exchange markets, the less the chances for market rigging by monopolistic buyers.) Most often, the floating had been adopted as part of required IMF stabilization programs, and the macroeconomic reforms adopted at the same time along with the removal of the overvaluation help to explain why economies usually perform better after a floating rate is adopted.[16]

Import Substitution Policies Can Cause Overvaluation Even without a government policy of deliberate overvaluation, import substitution measures such as tariffs and quotas can cause it anyway. These measures will ordinarily cut the

*Afghanistan, Bolivia, Brazil, Costa Rica, the Dominican Republic, El Salvador, Gambia, Ghana, Guatemala, Guyana, Haiti, Honduras, Jamaica, Lebanon, Mozambique, Nigeria, Paraguay, Peru, the Philippines, Sierra Leone, South Africa, Sudan, Uganda, Venezuela, Zaire, and Zambia. A small but growing number of LDCs, 23 in 1987, have forward foreign exchange markets, which helps to reduce fluctuations in the spot rate.

demand for foreign goods by pushing up their price. As compared with the situation without the protection, the demand for foreign exchange will thus fall, as in Figure 14.3, leading to a lower (overvalued) penuri price for the dollar of, say, 110 instead of 150.

The Penalty on Exporting Countries Can Make the Overvaluation Worse We have seen that exports are discouraged by an import substitution policy. Input prices are raised for exporters, who therefore have to charge more for their products. As a result, it is likely that the country earns fewer dollars, shifting the supply curve of dollars up and to the left, as in Figure 14.4. See how overvaluation becomes even greater. The free market exchange rate will become, say, 170 rather than 150. The result is that the official fixed rate of 100 will be under yet more strain, with the shortage of foreign exchange growing from Q_2Q_3 to Q_1Q_3.

Inflation Can Also Make the Overvaluation Worse If the rate of inflation is high, that, too, will contribute to growing overvaluation. With domestic prices rising, at the fixed exchange rate foreign goods will appear ever cheaper at home, and Penuristan's exports will look more expensive to foreigners. Penuristanis will thus want more foreign exchange to buy imports; foreigners will supply fewer dollars to buy that country's exports, with the result that both the supply and demand curves shift as in Figure 14.5, further widening the gap between the fixed official rate of 100 and the market equilibrium, which is now 200 rather than 150. At the official rate, the shortage of foreign exchange grows from to Q_2Q_3 to Q_1Q_4. The most common reason why exchange rates become overvalued is that rates of inflation are higher in LDCs than in developed countries.

An LDC's currency can also become more overvalued if it is pegged to a developed country's currency that is rising in value. Moneys tied to the dollar were pulled up as the dollar rose in value against other currencies in the mid-1980s. The LDCs that kept their pegged rates intact gradually found their dollar-linked currencies climbing against the pound, franc, mark, yen, and other currencies. Similarly, the rise in the French franc in the late 1980s and early '90s contributed to the heavy overvaluation of the CFA franc, which is tied to it and which is the currency of many of France's former colonies in West and Central Africa.

Further Effects of Overvaluation

A country that keeps its rate overvalued on a long-term basis is likely to find some further unfavorable consequences.[17] The damage to exports will lead to a demand for export subsidies from producers with enough political influence to get them. If enough firms are successful in obtaining them, the country's budget deficit will widen alarmingly. Because subsidies are expensive, they are usually applied selectively. The farm sector in LDCs seldom has the clout that manufacturing does, so agricultural exports may not receive them and will be especially hard hit. Nor are the subsidies likely to go to *potential* exporters, particularly the small ones, who might have found production for foreign markets profitable at a free market exchange rate. Finally, they may attract punitive measures (called countervailing duties) from developed countries that attempt to protect their own producers against these subsidies.

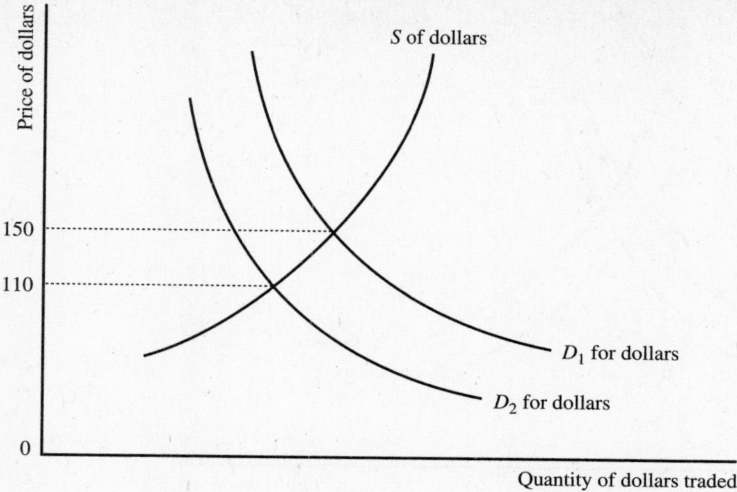

Figure 14.3 Trade barriers will reduce the demand for foreign currency, causing an overvaluation of the exchange rate.

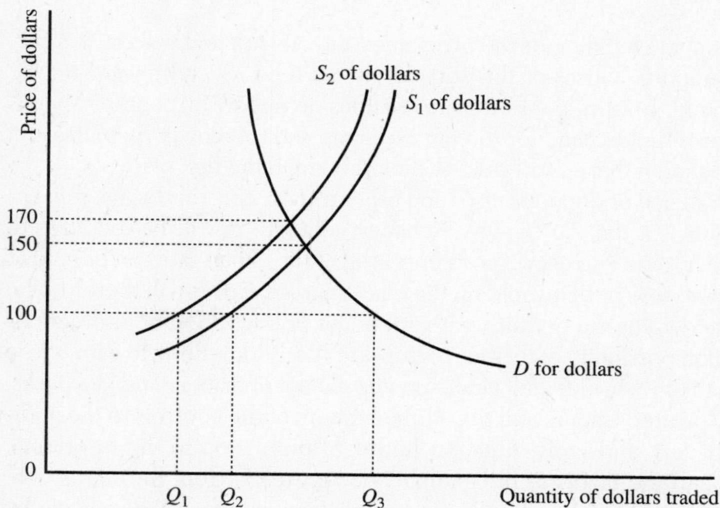

Figure 14.4 As exports decline, the supply of foreign currency is reduced, which contributes to an even greater overvaluation of the domestic currency.

The armor of protective devices will have to be extended and strengthened at the same time because any importable good produced at home but not yet protected will be penalized by the overvalued rate (imports will appear cheaper, remember). A perception on the part of the public that the protection will soon be extended, the

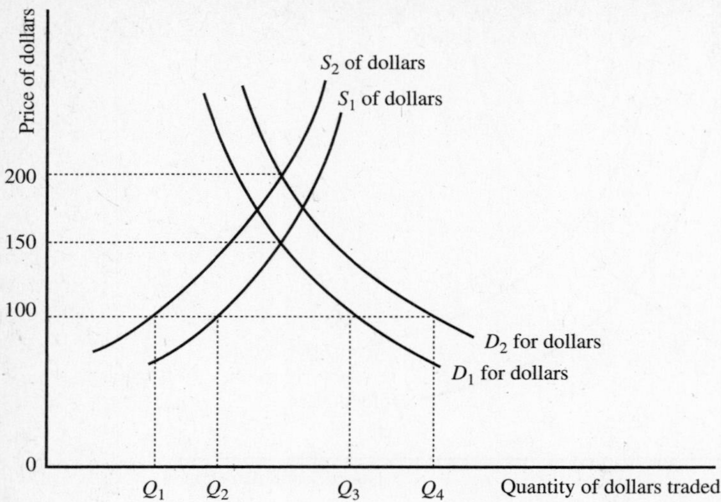

Figure 14.5 Inflation raises the demand for foreign currency and cuts its supply, thereby contributing to overvaluation.

exchange controls made tougher, or the overvalued rate abandoned will cause a further rush to buy imports. Crises of this sort do indeed tend to lead toward tighter restrictions all around. In turn, the further restrictions on imports, by cutting spending on them, reduces the demand for foreign exchange and thereby perpetuates and adds to the overvaluation that contributed to the problem in the first place.

Just as the existence of quota licenses and other import controls brings rents to the lucky recipients, so, too, do foreign exchange controls. It will be lucrative to acquire the scarce foreign currency; goods imported at the cheap rate can be sold at higher domestic prices or perhaps sold on the black market. Effort will therefore be thrown into the search for the permits, with attendant politicization of international trade and the high possibility of further corruption. With something to gain, there is also something to offer. Wider and wider spreads the net of bribery and kickbacks, from the circle of favored traders and the administrators of the controls to the auditors, police, politicians, and army officers who might put a stop to the favoritism. Both the bribers and the takers of bribes may benefit greatly from the status quo, along with the legions of black-market exchange dealers, who make their living by illegally avoiding the fixed rate. The police and armed forces may acquiesce for another reason as well; these politically vital arms of government can often count on getting the scarce permits when necessary for their own equipment, and so can buy imports cheaply. As the *The Economist* of London has noted only half jestingly, the president's cousins often want to run the department in charge of licensing the foreign exchange—fully understandable from their point of view.[18]

All contribute to the substantial corruption observed in many LDCs that run an overvalued exchange system. Honest behavior may not be the human way, but a free-market rate certainly cuts the potential profitability of corrupt practices in the foreign trade sector. The firms that can make the most efficient use of foreign exchange are then the ones willing and able to pay the bill for it, rather than the ones with the best lobbyists and the attention of the most important politicians.

The IMF notes that greatly overvalued exchange rates—sometimes by as much as 300% or more—have characterized exchange regimes in many LDCs. In recent years, among the countries with greatly overvalued rates have been Algeria, Egypt, Burma/Myanmar, Zambia, and the francophone African countries that use the CFA franc.[19] The impact of the overvaluation and the associated foreign exchange controls may be so strong that they can overpower any attempt to liberalize the foreign trade regime by removing trade barriers, such as tariffs and quotas. A fair number of LDCs have advertised that they are open to trade because their barriers are low, while at the same time overvaluation and exchange controls have thoroughly distorted their trade.[20] The distortions may actually become so serious that trade based on the purchase and sale of foreign exchange is superseded by *countertrade*, as explored in the box on page 485.

Evidence on the Effects of Overvaluation

Econometric studies of the effects of overvaluation typically compare the premium that has to be paid to buy foreign currency on the black market to the rate of economic growth.[21] They indicate that the adverse consequences of exchange rate overvaluation are serious.

Table 14.1 shows the data on the question covering the period 1971 to 1986. Take the first column: None of the countries with a low black-market premium (that is, with currencies that were not overvalued) had negative GDP growth, 13.6% of the countries with a low premium had GDP growth in the range of 0% to 2%, 27.3% of the countries had GDP growth of 2% to 4%, and so on. Each column adds to 100%.

Thus of 22 countries with low black-market premia on their exchange rates, 59.1% (13 countries) had economic growth of 4% or more, while only 18.5% (5) of

TABLE 14.1 BLACK-MARKET PREMIA AND GDP GROWTH IN 72 LDCs, 1971–1986, PERCENTAGE OF COUNTRIES IN EACH GROUP

Growth, Average Annual	Low Premium	Medium Premium	High Premium
Negative	0	0	3.7
0–2%	13.6	13.0	48.1
2%–4%	27.3	30.4	29.6
4%–6%	22.7	39.1	18.5
Over 6%	36.4	17.4	0

Source: IMF, *World Economic Outlook 1993* (Washington, D.C., 1993), 51. Low, medium, and high premia are defined as lying in the bottom third, middle third, and top third. There were 22 countries with low premia, 23 with medium premia, and 27 with high premia.

the 27 countries with high black-market premiums on their exchange rates had growth in this range.

Another study covering 24 LDCs examined the relationship between exchange rate misalignment (mostly overvaluation) and growth of both real GDP and exports. The study showed a significant negative correlation, with a 10% increase in misalignment associated with an average reduction in GDP growth of 0.8 percentage points and a reduction in export growth of 1.8 percentage points.[22]

Devaluation of the Exchange Rate

Official Devaluation as a Remedy for Overvaluation With all the demonstrated problems that predictably accompany an overvalued exchange rate, official devaluation of the rate would seem an obvious measure for adjustment.[23] There may even appear to be little choice, given the tendency for imports to increase and exports to stagnate, and with credit drying up as banks refuse any further bailouts. The IMF typically recommends devaluation as a remedy for overvalued currencies. A sufficient number of devaluations occurred between 1980 and 1988 that the average foreign exchange rates of approximately 80 LDCs studied by the World Bank, weighted by the trade of these countries and adjusted for inflation, fell by about 40%.[24]

This tool of exchange rate management is intensely unpopular, however, and will often be shunned by the government and the public alike. Why is this so, beyond the obvious point that those who have gained from the overvaluation will lose from the correction? A strong belief that national pride and national strength can be measured by the value of the currency is extremely common and seems almost visceral. The rate becomes symbolic: Bringing it down will appear to many to be proof of dependency and even of foreign neocolonialist machination; the country itself should decide, not the IMF or outsiders. Students riot over the issue; politicians wrapped in the flag declare they will never devalue.[25] Devaluing the exchange rate certainly does have its costs, as we shall see, but the intransigent opposition to it often seems to go far beyond any rational weighing of economic costs and benefits.

There is, incidentally, no reason to be surprised at this reaction. It is not a disease that affects the LDCs alone. Winston Churchill, when he was in charge of British finances in the 1920s, insisted on maintaining a strong pound as a monument to British greatness. It was ruinous policy that stifled exports and economic growth. In the 1980s, President Reagan argued for years that the high dollar was a symbol of U.S. economic vitality, even as the export sector rapidly sickened.

What positive results will a devaluation deliver? Although unpopular, it will undoubtedly have a shock effect that can be a valuable part of the political process, a sign of turning over a new leaf, so to speak. The main hope is that the devaluation will lower the country's price level relative to that of other countries. Much depends on what happens to these prices. Let us trace the possibilities.

If on world markets a country's exports are quoted in a foreign currency such as the dollar, then devaluation will not affect these prices. (Mexico's oil at $25 per

COUNTERTRADE

Eventually, if the official exchange regimen is on the way to breakdown and finance is failing, one expects to see the rise of *countertrade*.[26] This is the encompassing term for practices that avoid the use of foreign exchange. Included are counterpurchase and offsets (you buy from me, I will buy from you), switch-trading (chain bartering, so that *A* barters with *B*, *B* barters with *C*, and *C* barters with *A*, all as part of one transaction), and buy-backs (I build a plant in your country, and you pay me with some of the product that is produced).

Only about 15 countries had been involved in countertrade in the early 1970s, but the practice grew greatly in the 1980s and by 1990, nearly 90 countries were making use of the practice. At that time, some 20% of trade among the LDCs and 10% of trade between the developed countries and the LDCs was being carried out by these means.[27] Some nations—Brazil, India, Indonesia, Nigeria, China, and several nations in the Middle East, for example—have acquired a reputation for carrying on a significant proportion of their trade by these means. Agricultural commodities and oil figure most importantly. Vienna is the major venue for countertrade, with Singapore also an important center.

Countertrade is not cheap because often it involves the expensive services of lawyers, consultants, and bankers to work out the deals. Most big banks have had countertrade departments for several years now. These costs mean payments in countertrade transactions are usually higher, sometimes up to 30% or more, than in cash transactions. One reason for the higher payments is that countertrade often limits competition, because not every trading partner is willing to engage in it. Another is that it hides prices, so making it all too easy to fit in rake-offs, kickbacks, and other forms of corruption difficult to detect in a price-less environment. The risk of nondelivery because a deal falls through is high, and insurance against that is expensive. There are also many companies that refuse to do business this way, and some developed countries oppose the principle (though usually accepting it in practice). There have been cases of reduced trade concessions and foreign aid to LDCs pushing countertrade. All of this limits its benefits.[28]

Even so, countertrade may be a means by which LDCs can break into new markets. Products difficult to sell on one's own might find market access through the sales outlets of a multinational company in a countertrade relationship. Perhaps in time the products will be accepted and sold for cash through more normal channels. In any case, given the shortage of foreign exchange, the practice is unlikely to go away. It may even grow because an infrastructure supporting it has been built up, because computers have helped greatly in carrying it out, and because many firms have now learned how to use the various techniques.

barrel will still be $25 even if the peso's value is lowered).* This is common in the trade of the LDCs. But every dollar earned from exporting now means more local currency for the exporter: If the penuri, formerly at 100 to the dollar, is devalued to 150, then each dollar earned from sales abroad raises the revenues of exporters by 50 penuris. If local production costs do not change, profits rise accordingly.

Whether more *dollars* are earned from the exporting will depend crucially on the elasticity of supply of exports. If that is high, greater quantities will be exported and earnings in foreign exchange will rise. Indeed, only a zero elasticity of supply will prevent that from happening. Time helps: The longer the period considered, the more the enhanced profitability of exporting will attract resources into that activity, whereas in the short run there may be little impact. (The idea was once entrenched that low supply elasticities would make devaluations fruitless, but opinion has swung toward the belief that such elasticities are higher than once believed. That has put exchange rate adjustments in a more favorable light.)†

It also helps if adequate financing is available to expand capacity, if creating new capacity is easy; if a proper infrastructure of transport, communications, and public utilities is in place; and if resources are flexible and can respond smoothly to market incentives. The transition is even easier if the previously overvalued exchange rate has caused substantial excess capacity in the exporting industry and if the country has significant unemployment problems. Then the idle resources can simply be put back to work. Generally, experience shows that the rise in exports will be largest if the protection against imports is liberalized at the same time the currency is devalued. This suggests that unavailability of imported inputs had all along been constraining the growth of exports.

The export-raising consequences of devaluation are joined by a depressing effect on imports. It now takes more penuris to buy a dollar; consumers will therefore be less eager to purchase imported goods at their higher price in local currency and will turn to goods produced at home. Exporters, where possible, also switch away from imported inputs and purchase more local production. Both these results take effect at once and increase over time as new substitutes appear and knowledge about them grows. Analytically, any elasticity of demand for imports greater than zero will mean a reduction in dollar spending as prices rise and, therefore, will cause the demand for dollars to fail. The higher the elasticity, the greater the decline in imports and in the demand for dollars, and so the more successful the policy.

---

*If the oil had been priced in Mexican pesos, at 60 to the barrel, and the peso was devalued from 2.4 to 3.0 pesos per dollar, the dollar equivalent of one barrel sold at 60 pesos would fall immediately from $25 to $20. Foreign currency earnings would drop temporarily until the export quantities rise sufficiently to offset the fall. This so-called J-curve effect, named for the reversing pattern of foreign exchange earnings, is fortunately not a problem most LDCs have to worry about because their exports are so frequently priced in an important foreign currency, such as the dollar.

†A good case in point was the removal of the overvaluation of the CFA franc, used by numerous francophone African countries, in 1994. The devaluation from 50 CFA francs to 1 French franc to 100 to 1 was by far the largest devaluation of a convertible currency since World War II. But farmers turned to planting food crops on fallow land; farm incomes rose; and exports are increasing. For this devaluation, see the *International Economic Review*, August 1994.

The reduction in imports may be limited, however, if the country liberalizes its trade barriers at the same time. (A recent study by Sebastian Edwards concludes that in 20 of the 39 devaluations he investigated, the devaluation was accompanied by major removals of trade controls.)[29] The reduction in the barriers will work in some degree to offset the rise in prices. Also, spending on imports will not fall as much if more of them flow in as inputs to the newly expanding export industries and if the more efficient policies are causing a rise in real national income that fuels the inflow of goods from abroad. These are major reasons why studies often find the overall change in the trade balance is smaller than predicted.[30] Conceivably, the short-run results may even be in the wrong direction, though this will be reversed as exports pick up.

Unfavorable Consequences of Devaluation The path to an equilibrium exchange rate may not be an easy one, and several warnings are in order. If the country is a major producer of a commodity (Brazil of coffee or Côte d'Ivoire of cocoa), then it would have to worry about a decline in the world price as production of the export increases. This adverse turn in the terms of trade could be sharp if world demand is inelastic; if the country is heavily dependent on this export, it may find its foreign exchange earnings are falling. Meanwhile, imports are unlikely to be concentrated, so buying less of them will probably not depress the world price. The problem will be of no concern to an LDC that has little effect on world commodity prices, and various studies confirm that devaluation almost always raises the local currency returns to the production of exports, so that both the quantity exported and earnings rise.[31] But where a tendency toward an unfavorable shift in the terms of trade exists, it is a strong argument for long-run export diversification.

Perhaps the response of exports will be poor. A country specializing in tree crops that take a long time to bear or mineral products where new mines take years to develop, with its economy inflexible, its infrastructure inadequate, and financing for new projects scarce, may find the results of devaluation disappointing. In recent years some of the world's lowest supply elasticities have been reported for agricultural commodities in parts of sub-Saharan Africa. Under such conditions, it would be difficult to raise foreign exchange earnings. Where elasticities are so low, supply-side improvements in infrastructure, capital markets, provision of basic services, and so forth are obviously called for along with devaluation, but, unfortunately, these take a long time to bring about and can be expensive and unappealing to a country in crisis. Even at worst, however, the devaluation will make it potentially more profitable to export any suitable commodity, agricultural or industrial, and this incentive takes effect immediately. There is thus at least the hope of long-run improvement. (And some recent research indicates that African supply elasticities may be higher than once believed.)[32]

Another obstacle presents itself if numerous countries that are exporters or potential exporters of the same products all devalue at the same time. When one country devalues, it can compete more strongly against other producers. When many do so, the ability to make inroads into the markets of others is diluted. The more countries that attempt the strategy at the same time, the less well it will work.[33]

The devaluation must be real, meaning that it must not be offset by higher inflation, for then there would be no "expenditure switching" away from imports and toward exports and import substitutes—and so no change for the better. The intended impact is to lower domestic prices relative to other countries. (Remember that in dollar terms, export and import prices did not change, but all other local prices look lower, at least at the start, to holders of dollars.)[34] If the lower domestic prices quickly rise again because of inflation, the benefits of the devaluation are lost.

There is no immediate reason to expect general inflationary consequences. Imported goods do rise at once in local currency price, but if the demand for imports is elastic, there will be little feedback to the rest of the economy as consumption shifts to domestic substitutes when possible. If the demand for imports is on the contrary inelastic, perhaps because there are no substitutes, then the country's local currency spending on imports will rise. This will be deflationary for the economy as a whole, at least until the eventual expansion of export capacity increases revenues from exporting enough to offset it.[35] (Alternatively, there might not be much of a price rise for imports if such goods were largely being purchased before the devaluation at illegal black-market prices. The black market would already reflect the devalued price of foreign exchange. Prices may even fall because the risk element is reduced.)[36] The deflationary aspects of devaluation can cause unemployment whenever markets are not allowed to adjust. Thus, if workers' real wages are not allowed to fall because of union pressures, minimum wage laws, and the like, job losses may become serious.[37]

The domestic deflation that may result from a devaluation can be severe enough to make a piecemeal and gradual devaluation seem more sensible than an all-at-once one. That was once the orthodox advice, but then fears grew that a gradual movement would raise doubts about commitment and give more time to organize opposition. The World Bank and IMF now often advise immediate action.

Inflation May Follow the Initial Deflation Even if local prices do not rise at once, there are reasons to fear that in time they may do so, with the possibility of eventual inflationary consequences after all. The higher output of exports and domestic substitutes for imports may put pressures on factor markets, so that wages and other costs in these sectors start to rise, boosting the price of locally produced goods, even though the economy generally is suffering from deflation.* The resulting "stagflation" is likely to be a serious political problem for the government. That government may also be under intense pressure from unions because, as already noted, workers recognize that the prices of imports and import substitutes have risen and thus that the devaluation has cut their real wage. Perhaps the country has a comprehensive system of indexing incomes to reflect price rises. That, too, will transmit inflationary effects.

Sensible demand management can be of great help in these circumstances, but the government may respond instead with money creation to offset the original deflation and the decline in workers' real wages. If it does so, inflation can speed up to the point where exporting loses the advantages given it by the devaluation and imports again look attractive. In short, inflation causes the currency once again to be overvalued, and the "real exchange rate" has not changed. There are a

---

*For example, not long after the devaluation of francophone Africa's CFA franc from 1 French franc = 50 CFA francs to 1 Ffr = 100 CFA francs in 1994, the prices of locally produced goods rose in a range from 10% to 50%.

significant number of cases in which governments have responded in this fashion, canceling the real effects of the devaluation. Domestic monetary policy always has the capacity to ruin the reform; this threat has been particularly severe in Latin America. In response to this danger, Argentina decided in 1991 to tie its peso to the dollar and back all new issues of pesos with dollar holdings. That solution was drastic and expensive. It remains to be seen whether it will work in the long run.

At base, the argument that a strategy of devaluation will not work often boils down to an opinion that government will create money to avoid the adverse political effects of the real wage cuts. Entrepreneurs see this as fast or faster than anyone else.[38] If they believe that, following a devaluation, exporting will not be profitable for long because of continuing money-fueled inflation, then they are unlikely to raise the supply of exports in the first place. Although inflation often does not cancel the whole effect of the devaluation, experience shows that, unfortunately, much of the effect is indeed lost, and it is theoretically correct to say that inflation *could* entirely remove any real effect of the policy. Sebastian Edwards's examination of 39 cases of devaluation led him to conclude that in all the cases the benefit of a devaluation was partly eroded by continuing inflation after about four years. In 14 of the cases, the devaluation was fully offset by the inflation; here no "real" devaluation took place in the long run.[39] The conclusion is that devaluation must be accompanied by sound monetary and fiscal policy, and many countries with extensive indexing, politically minded labor unions, and oligopolistic industries are unable to mount such policies.

Sometimes when a country fears to devalue all at once, a "crawling" or "creeping" devaluation of the exchange rate is adopted. Perhaps it is introduced for some sectors before others by means of a temporary multiple exchange rate system.[40] It may also be possible temporarily to maintain or enlarge some of the transfer and subsidy programs that could alleviate the decline in labor incomes and counter the political backlash in that sector. The financing could come perhaps from further taxation of high incomes, tighter credit policies to replace cheap credit schemes, and lower defense spending. Of course, each of these steps immediately brings a new political problem of its own; in these circumstances foreign aid and IMF program assistance might help to prepare the path.*

It is frequently argued that a devaluation will make the country's distribution of income less equal. This could happen in the short run if exporters' revenues rise while the mass of urban wage earners suffer a fall in their real earnings. In the long run, however, the factors drawn into exporting will share in the gains, and this will be particularly true in rural areas, which often still contain the greater part of the population, as exports of agricultural cash crops grow. In any case, the rural areas will be less affected by the higher prices of imported goods.

Are There Alternatives to Devaluation? When a country's foreign exchange rate is badly overvalued, are there any alternatives to devaluation? Yes, several, but all with disadvantages of their own. We have already noted that policymakers could

*But then large amounts of aid result in bidding up the demand for local currency and so appreciating it.

A "WORST CASE"

All these unfavorable circumstances do not usually come to pass at the same time. They could, however, and it is instructive to examine a case of mismanaged devaluation to see what must be guarded against.[41] Chile moved away from an import substitution policy in the late 1970s but neglected to devalue the highly overvalued exchange rate. Other policies, such as 100% government bailouts of failing banks, spurred capital inflows by foreign lenders and caused further overvaluation of the exchange rate. The result was constricted exports, booming imports, and a balance of payments crisis. When devaluation eventually came, it caused a severe recession. In 1982, Chile's GDP fell 14%, far more than could have been expected from the effect of the world slowdown of production occurring (unhelpfully) at the same time. High unemployment was persistent. Meanwhile, Chile's system of almost complete indexation of wages picked up the rising cost of imports and transmitted an inflationary impulse in the midst of recession. Government created money to ease the recession and to make it possible to pay the higher wage bills caused by the indexing. All in all, the devaluation did not work well. The episode is an object lesson that there are no unbreakable promises of success in economic policy-making. Fortunately, the damage was not permanent. Chile's economy has recovered from this unfortunate episode, and is now considered a model of good macroeconomic management.

simply deflate the economy with monetary and fiscal policy to cure the excess of imports over exports. But deflating as a strategy is slow and painful, brings high unemployment, and does nothing to promote the exporting that has been suppressed by the overvaluation.

Another alternative is to use foreign exchange controls as a substitute for devaluation. These take effect at once, and because they do not work through the price mechanism, there is no resulting fall in national income as there is with devaluation. On first hearing, these are impressive advantages. But we have already examined these sorts of controls enough to anticipate the problems: The complex regulations are a fertile setting for corruption, as vested interests (import substitution industries, government officials in charge of the policies) rally to their support. The controls are usually stiffest against "nonessential" imports, thereby promoting local production of these very goods. Most importantly, controls do nothing to cure the underlying suppression of exports and therefore cannot cure the inefficient allocation of resources. That penalty is still paid. The discrimination against exporting could be offset by export subsidies, but these also usually discriminate, paid on some goods but not on others, such as traditional agricultural exports and the products of small firms lacking political influence. Further, if the subsidies offset high risks in some particular line of activity, then it is arguable that trade in that good should not have been taken up in the first place.

How Much Should a Country Devalue? Assuming that devaluation is selected as proper policy in spite of the difficulties, what should be the extent of the currency adjustment? This is not an easy question. There is no obvious benchmark. Freeing the exchange rate to float always has the disadvantage that trade in a given LDC's currency may be thin, contributing to high volatility. One would not want Sierra Leone's leone, Burma/Myanmar's kyat, Honduras's lempira, or a hundred others to fall sharply because a new electric generator has been purchased or to rise in a rush because customers abroad have just paid for a shipload of export produce. The arbitrageurs who normally iron out these fluctuations may avoid these currencies because of the unpredictability of government policy and because information about the day-to-day trade in them is not as good as it is for a developed country. This potential for high volatility explains the reluctance of most LDCs to adopt floating rates.

Elasticity studies that would allow for analysis and prediction are scarce or perhaps have not been done at all. Black markets can give clues, but expectations of future devaluation in these markets may mean the rate there is actually more devalued than a free-market rate would be. Further, trading in a black market is usually limited by the fear of discovery, making rates highly volatile to shifts in even thinner supply and demand than that noted above. Finally, the investigator has to balance the foreign exchange overvaluation against the existing structure of trade barriers, preferential tax and credit schemes, export subsidies, and other government intervention in the market. These have to be taken into account if any are reformed at the time of the devaluation.[42]

The IMF and World Bank have sometimes suggested aggressive currency devaluations greater than actually needed to bring exports and imports into balance. This is the "fast track" idea to bring rapid encouragement to exports and discouragement of imports. Aggressive devaluation may go too far. First, any resulting inflation is likely to break out faster, with more rapid removal of the devaluation's effects. Second, the results can be seriously detrimental if a country cannot switch output to domestic production because of supply inelasticities or if export revenues do not rise because foreign demand is inelastic. At worst, aggressive devaluation may even reduce domestic investment because of the higher prices for imported capital goods and the reduction in real domestic incomes. That would in time mean a serious loss of output. Recent research indicates that these factors have caused aggressive devaluation to be of less benefit to African primary product exporters than it has been to other LDCs. Where the economic environment is not propitious, aggressive devaluation may be ill advised.[43]

OUTWARD-LOOKING (EXPORT PROMOTION) STRATEGY

The detrimental consequences of inward-looking policies, those that involve generalized import substitution buttressed by trade barriers and overvalued exchange rates, are all too clear. This package of policies is likely to retard growth in the LDCs, when, as everyone will agree, the goal is to do just the opposite.

It might be thought that the cure would be an outward-looking policy of export promotion, and indeed that term is widely used.[44] But export promotion does not mean exactly what it says. The term is misleading in that a literal interpretation would indicate an indiscriminate push for all exports and no attention at all to the replacement of imports. Such a policy would have distortions of its own in a direction opposite to those of import substitution. We shall avoid this misunderstanding by defining export promotion as the removal of the bias toward import substitution and the achievement of neutrality toward trade.* Therefore an economically rational replacement of imports, based on comparative advantage, would still be recommended along with exports of goods, also based on comparative advantage.

Figure 14.6 demonstrates the argument. *AA* is a production possibility curve, with exportable goods (*X*) on the horizontal axis and importables (*M*) on the vertical. The ratio *PP* shows a distorted price relationship, with trade barriers, subsidies, and discriminatory credit policies all combining to make imports and import substitutes relatively dear and exports relatively cheap. (See how *PP*, if extended to each axis, would show a smaller amount of expensive *M* goods exchanging for a larger quantity of cheaper *X* goods.) Entrepreneurs respond with higher quantities of *M* and lower amounts of *X*. Were the distortions removed so that the stimulus for *M* goods is eliminated and *X* goods are on an equal footing with them (price line *P'P'*), the production of exportables would rise and that of importables would fall. If distortions were introduced to favor exports—for example, export subsidies and cheap credit—then the price line would swing to *P"P"*. The case examined in detail here is the middle one (*P'P'*), where there is no attempt to maintain a bias of any sort in foreign trade.

The accompanying box analyzes the same case in terms of exchange rates.

Advantages of a Growing Export Sector

Several outstanding advantages should be expected from an outward-looking strategy that removes the bias toward import substitution and against exports. Undistorted prices will better reflect the actual scarcities of the factors of production. Studies generally show that export-promoting countries have fewer distortions in their price systems than do countries with an import substitution strategy.[45]

An immediate and important consequence is job creation. Export promotion will generally create more employment. Labor is usually abundant in LDCs, and comparative advantage should lie in goods that contain a large relative input of the abundant factor of production. A. H. M. M. Rahman noted two decades ago that 80% of the manufactured goods exported by LDCs were more labor intensive than the factor proportions in world exports as a whole. Studies in a number of countries confirm the heavy use of labor in exporting, for example, in Chile 28% more employment per dollar of value added in exports than in import-competing production; double or more in Brazil, Indonesia, and Thailand; and nearly that in Uruguay. In South

*Lal and Rajapatirana make the point that a neutral trade regime is one where incentives for import substitution are the same as those for export promotion. That can be achieved either by offsetting government interventions or by means of a liberal regime where no such interventions occur. Both are neutral. See Deepak Lal and Sarath Rajapatirana, "Foreign Trade Regimes and Economic Growth in Developing Countries," especially 213.

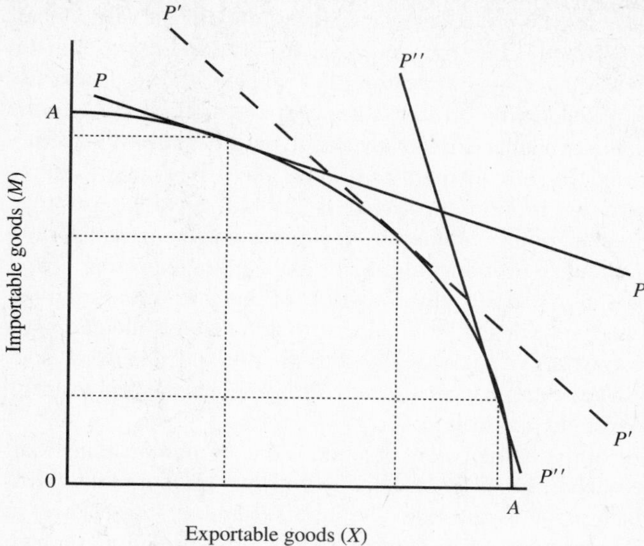

Figure 14.6 Trade distortions. The price line $P'P'$ shows a set of undistorted prices. PP shows distorted prices with importables more expensive and exportables cheaper. $P''P''$ shows distorted prices with exportables more expensive and importables cheaper.

DISTORTIONS DESCRIBED BY MEANS OF THE "EFFECTIVE EXCHANGE RATE"

Removing the bias can also be described as establishing an "effective exchange rate" that is the same for both imports and exports.[46] If the official fixed foreign exchange rate is 100 penuris = $1, then an importer must pay 100 penuris in local currency to buy a dollar's worth of imports from abroad. With the structure of tariffs and quotas, however, that dollar's worth of imports sells domestically for perhaps 200 penuris, or the equivalent of $2. In practice, the importer was able to buy $2 for 100 penuris, for an effective exchange rate of 50 penuris = $1. Meanwhile, an exporter would receive 100 penuris for each dollar earned, giving an effective exchange rate of 100:$1. This is an import bias. An opposite export bias would occur if subsidies or cheap credit were given for each unit exported. If the official foreign exchange rate is 100 penuris = $1, an exporter would earn 100 penuris for each dollar's worth of goods exported plus the subsidy from the government of, say, another 100 penuris. That makes 200 in all per dollar, so that the effective exchange rate when exports are subsidized is 200:$1. In the meantime, importers must pay 100 penuris to buy $1 for importing; their effective rate is 100:$1. This is an export bias. If there had been no trade barriers, cheap credit, or subsidies, then both importers and exporters would have faced the same effective exchange rate, perhaps 100:$1. There would be no foreign trade bias; policy is neutral.

Korea, production of manufactures for export was 33% more labor intensive than production of manufactures for the domestic market, and 50% more so than in industries that specifically competed against imports.[47] This demonstrated capacity to create employment for unskilled labor in LDCs is a major attraction of an export promotion policy. (If the labor available is relatively skilled and the country's overall trade strategy is well designed, the employment creation is likely to be greater yet.)

The effect of outward orientation on saving is also likely to be positive because, first, the higher real incomes obtained from exporting will encourage saving, and second, because the entrepreneurs and firms engaged in exporting probably save more than the average. (Admittedly, the effect of outward orientation on saving has been little studied empirically.)[48] The larger market that trade can provide may also facilitate economies of scale and lead to greater specialization, and although by and large these advantages have not received proper empirical testing, these consequences are certainly plausible.

A further consequence of the employment creation is the strong possibility that the distribution of income will become more equal. The growing number of new jobs for thousands and eventually millions of originally unskilled laborers has played a major role in bringing relatively high equality of incomes to South Korea, Taiwan, and other export promoters. The effect is certainly not true of all exports. Oil revenues have often not contributed much to income equality, and mining also has limitations in this regard. But for agricultural commodities, especially when produced by small holders, and for a wide range of manufactures, the statement seems justified.

The environment in exporting is usually quite different from that found behind trade barriers. Improved economies of scale are a possibility because the boundaries of the market are worldwide rather than the nation's own borders. There is a constant incentive to compete more effectively by reducing any internal inefficiencies, whether in choosing how to combine the factors of production, what goods to produce, or how to squeeze the most output out of a given stock of resources (so achieving X-efficiency). With no built-in bias toward cheap imported capital, as occurs with import substitution, there is no reason to expect overexpansion of capacity; all other things being equal, the likelihood is that capacity utilization in industry will rise. The receipts will be paid in foreign exchange, thus loosening that constraint on development and allowing further imports of capital and intermediate goods.

In short, the resource cost of earning a unit of foreign exchange through exporting is quite likely to be less than the resource cost of saving a unit of foreign exchange by means of import substitution, as explained earlier in the chapter.[49]

Dynamic Gains from Outward Orientation As is usual in foreign trade, the static gains may be overshadowed by the less easily measured dynamic gains. As time passes, exporters obtain new insights into technology, design, quality control, organization, and management, especially from buyers in developed countries willing to pass on the latest information. Large exporting firms spread this knowledge to smaller firms by contracting for inputs. Government agencies can assist in locating suitable subcontractors and helping with quality control. Exports of entirely new products may spring up at once if the developed countries lead in subcontracting to the LDCs. In these circumstances foreign MNEs may provide the specifications, the technology, the capital, and joint management. Inflows of direct investment from developed countries are in fact increasingly associated with exporting.

With the incentives now favoring export expansion, the limited number of old traditional export commodities expands also. This gives more flexibility if supply shocks occur or if problems develop in overseas markets. Banks become more interested in lending because the rising revenues from exporting make debt servicing easier. In some ways the opportunity may be greatest for the low-income countries. These have the lowest wages, so their labor-intensive exports will be strongly competitive in world markets. The ease with which technology can be transferred or copied gives broad opportunities for rapid productivity increases in manufacturing, and developed-country trade barriers apply more lightly to the lowest-income LDCs. But the obstacles of imperfect and limited capital markets, little original experience with manufacturing, inadequate human capital, an underdeveloped infrastructure of services such as banking, transport, communications, and insurance, and all the other concomitants of severe poverty are obvious limitations for the least developed countries.[50] The strong correlation between exporting and economic growth discussed in the next section is, unfortunately, weakest for the countries with the lowest incomes.

Another dynamic advantage is that the efficiency with which an economy operates tends to improve with outward orientation. This can be seen in the comparative data on incremental capital–output ratios, which appear to fall (that is, the efficiency of investment rises) with outward orientation. The data to this effect are presented in Table 14.2.

More broadly, total factor productivity—the output obtained from a given quantity of inputs—is likely to rise. When Hollis Chenery pursued this subject in a study of 20 LDCs, he found that the annual increase in total factor productivity exceeded 3% in the strongly outward-oriented economies but was less than 1% annually and sometimes negative in the strongly inward-oriented economies.[51]

There is another, largely unsung outcome, that for some countries may well be the most important of all. A market structure of undistorted pricing, with trade barriers and subsidies reduced and with overvaluation of the exchange rate eliminated, leaves far fewer opportunities for rent-seeking behavior. Less is to be gained from influence-peddling, bribery, and concealment, so the incidence and costs of lobbying and corruption may drop dramatically.

TABLE 14.2 INCREMENTAL CAPITAL–OUTPUT RATIOS IN THE LDCs

	1963–73	1973–85
Strongly outward-oriented	2.50	4.50
Moderately outward-oriented	2.50	5.00
Moderately inward-oriented	3.33	6.25
Strongly inward-oriented	5.26	9.09

Source: World Bank data cited in *The Economist,* September 23, 1989, 26.

Economic modeling on the subject largely conforms to the logic that outward orientation will increase the efficiency of an economy and improve its economic growth. Various macroeconomic models predict that elimination of trade barriers and the introduction of a neutral trade bias would raise GNP 5.4% for Turkey, 5.2% for the Philippines, and in a range from 5% to 15% for a group of six other countries for which specific studies exist.[52] These predicted gains were far above the 1% to 2% forecast by static analysis, which does not take productivity growth into account. The dynamic gains from trade due to productivity growth thus lie in the range of 3 to 14 percentage points above the static gains. Even broad macroeconomic models may miss the further gains from higher capacity utilization and the elimination of rent-seeking behavior, and they do not capture the longer-run results on productivity.[53]

The potential for dynamic gains is impressive, but there is little doubt that a strategy emphasizing growth in foreign trade also increases risks of various types. A country that specializes in a limited range of exported manufactures or primary products might find itself facing unexpected trade barriers erected by the developed countries, with the risk of protectionist action greatest for the most successful exporters. If sharp swings in prices occur, especially of agricultural commodities and minerals, then export revenues may not be very stable. By their nature, small countries will be the most vulnerable of all; because of their size, they will usually be specialized in just a few exports. (All of these subjects are returned to in Chapter 15.)

These adverse dynamic effects are not necessarily immutable, however. Developed countries might be persuaded that their own interests militate against protection. Sensible economic policies in individual countries may make it possible to reduce the impact of the fluctuations in export revenue, and even international action in pursuit of revenue stabilization might be taken. Policies to encourage resource flexibility and development itself, both often having the same effect, can reduce the trauma of a declining market for a major export.

Even so, there is no gainsaying that certain sorts of risks do increase in international trade. Then again, there are obvious risks in being poor, too—the risks of hunger, illness, and blighted human potential. If trade based on comparative advantage offers a good possibility of escaping poverty, then even if success is not guaranteed, the idea will command attention. Indeed, the empirical evidence on growth by means of trade does command attention, as we see below.

Empirical Studies of Outward Versus Inward Orientation

Evidence of a high correlation between the rate of growth of exports and the rate of growth of GDP is frequently cited. A wide range of studies utilizing both cross-country and time-series data conclude that the relationship between export performance and growth performance is significant.[54] Anne Krueger, for example, finds that "an increase in the rate of growth of export earnings of one percentage point annually was associated with an increase in the rate of growth of GDP of about 0.1 percentage point."[55] Studies using statistical methods quite different from the original work on the subject typically continue to support the conclusion that outward-oriented policies are correlated with superior growth in GDP.[56]

Correlation does not prove anything about what is cause and what is effect. The usual hypothesis is that the export growth causes the output growth, but the causation could be the other way, from GDP growth to exports. Consider that a country's output may be rising because of human and physical capital accumulation, learning-by-doing, or new technology inflows to some industries, which thereupon produce more than can be absorbed in domestic consumption. Such industries would export, and here it would be reasonable to say that the growth caused the exports. An alternative hypothesis would be that exporting and GDP expansion are both correlated to some other causal determinant. Further, one could hypothesize that economic growth will raise the local demand for exported goods and so eventually reduce those exports. Jung and Marshall, using statistical tests for causality in their 1985 study, found numerous cases where each of these different explanations appeared to be significant.[57]

The important conclusion from this debate is the degree to which policies to reduce distortions and increase exports do appear to stimulate growth, whatever the immediate cause of the larger exports. Whether the superior performance of export-promoting policies is due primarily to the less distortionary economic structure or to the dynamic gains from foreign trade is not entirely clear. Export promotion policies appeared to help especially in making adjustments to the oil and food shocks of the 1970s.[58] During this period of disturbances, the correlation between an outward-looking policy stance and output growth was particularly marked for countries that were pursuing export promotion when they were first struck by the shocks. Earlier data covering the 1960s and 1970s are shown in Table 14.3.

Subsequent studies published by the World Bank have extended the analysis to 1992 for a sample of 41 economies. According to the Bank, the data suggest that outward orientation is more successful than inward-looking strategy in terms of economic growth, industrialization, and agricultural development.[59] The key evidence is presented in Table 14.4, where the first row and the last cover the countries classified as strongly outward-oriented and strongly inward-oriented.

An expanded sample covering 95 LDCs also points to the growth enhancement from outward orientation.[60]

As posited earlier, most authorities suggest that the major connection between trade orientation and growth in output appears to involve a combination of static gains—getting more out of one's resources—and dynamic gains, such as increased competition, increased investment, economies of scale, transmission of technology, and use of best-practice techniques.

Criticisms of The Data Many authorities have, however, called attention to a number of worrisome points concerning this analysis. The highly outward-oriented countries in the study were a small sample that included only South Korea, Hong Kong, and Singapore. Of these, South Korea (and also Taiwan and Japan before it, neither included in the study) was well known for utilizing an infant-industry strategy of strengthening export industries as part of its outward-oriented policy. Thus outward orientation does not necessarily mean immediate trade liberalization, and the reductions in these countries' trade barriers have been gradual.[61]

TABLE 14.3 EXPORT GROWTH AND GNP GROWTH, 1960–1973 AND 1973–1981

Real Annual Growth (percent)	Period	Exports	GNP		Period	Exports	GNP
World	1960–73	8.1	5.0	World	1973–81	3.8	2.5
		Countries with "Balanced" (Neutral) Trade Incentives					
Brazil	1968–73	13.6	11.2	Chile	1975–80	12.0	7.5
Hong Kong	1962–73	13.6	10.1	Hong Kong	1973–81	8.5	9.1
Côte d'Ivoire	1960–73	11.2	7.6	Côte d'Ivoire	1973–81	4.5	5.7
Korea	1960–73	14.0	8.9	Korea	1973–81	15.7	8.8
Malaysia	1965–73	8.8	7.1	Malaysia	1973–81	4.2	7.3
Singapore	1965–73	12.6	12.7	Singapore	1973–81	12.1	8.0
Group average		12.3	9.6	Group average		9.5	7.6
		Countries with "Inward-looking" Trade Policies					
Argentina	1960–73	4.0	4.1	Argentina	1974–81	5.3	0.4
Chile	1960–68	3.7	4.4	Ghana	1973–81	—	–2.4
Ghana	1961–73	1.5	2.7	India	1973–78	7.7	5.1
India	1960–73	3.0	3.5	Pakistan	1974–81	6.4	5.4
Pakistan	1960–73	2.9	6.2	Sudan	1974–81	2.6	3.8
Turkey	1960–73	7.3	5.9	Turkey	1973–80	0.3	4.0
Group average		3.9	4.5	Group average		3.7	3.7

Source: Anne O. Krueger and Constantine Michalopoulos, "Developing-Country Trade Policies and the International Economic System," in Ernest Preeg, ed., *Hard Bargaining Ahead: U.S. Trade Policy and Developing Countries* (New Brunswick, N.J., 1985). Also see Shailendra J. Anjaria, Naheed Kirmani, and Arne B. Petersen, *Trade Policy Issues and Developments,* IMF Occasional Paper No. 38 (1985), table 66.

TABLE 14.4 TRADE ORIENTATION AND ANNUAL REAL GDP GROWTH PER CAPITA (PERCENT), 1963–1973 TO 1986–1992

	1963–73	1974–85	1986–92
Strongly outward-oriented	**6.8**	**8.0**	**7.5**
Moderately outward-oriented	4.8	4.3	4.8
Moderately inward-oriented	3.8	4.4	2.4
Strongly inward-oriented	**1.6**	**2.3**	**2.5**

Source: WDR 1987, 84, for the figures for 1963–1973, which are calculated by the author from the Bank's graphical presentation and are therefore approximate. For 1974–1985 and 1986–1992, see IMF, *World Economic Outlook 1993* (Washington, D.C., 1993): 76.

Critics further contend that it is not especially easy to determine what policy actually was at various times. South Korea, for example, is considered strongly outward-oriented in all periods though admittedly its policies were quite different in the periods. Outliers exist as well. Several LDCs have above-average shares of trade and have grown slowly (Jamaica, Uruguay), while other LDCs trade at relatively low levels but have grown rather rapidly (Colombia, Brazil).[62]

Moreover, critics note that the moderately inward-oriented countries performed slightly better in GDP growth during 1974 to 1985 than did the moderately outward-oriented, and the strongly inward-oriented slightly better than the moderately inward-oriented in 1986–1992. David Evans posits that there is little to indicate that a shift from moderately inward-oriented to moderately outward-oriented, or from moderately outward-oriented to strongly outward-oriented, would do much to improve economic performance.[63] Howard Pack states that there is "no clear confirmation that outward-oriented countries are more efficient" and debates the issue at length.[64] Hans Singer and Gerald Helleiner attack the World Bank's analysis (which underlies Table 14.4 above) by making the point that the lower-income LDCs face more difficulties generally, and that export promotion has worked less well in all time periods the poorer a country is.[65] Singer notes that world demand for countries' exports is usually more important than the effects of trade policy in the success of an outward-oriented policy and that the correlation between outward orientation and growth is strong only when market conditions are favorable.[66] Using similar arguments, Nicholas Stern judges the World Bank's analysis sternly, though he does agree that the performance of the strongly inward-oriented economies is especially weak.[67] The critics appear more or less to agree that to become a successful exporter in any reasonable space of time, a country must have already developed some minimal industrial base and possess some minimal degree of technical skills. Even the many economists who generally have confidence in an outward-oriented policy would in large measure accept these caveats.

Warily, then, understanding that empirical studies have been few and somewhat controversial, let us take the view that outward orientation holds advantages over strong inward-looking strategies of import substitution at the macro level by increasing economic growth and at the level of the firm by raising efficiency. The next step is to move to a discussion of what form outward orientation should take.

Adopting an Outward-Oriented Policy For countries discouraged by the results of a generalized import substitution strategy, an important question is how to move toward outward orientation with the greatest efficiency and least cost. Without doubt, one of the major topics of modern development economics is how to manage this transition. The startup is likely to be difficult because of the wide range of politically important groups benefiting from the previous policy of high trade barriers, overvalued exchange rates, and so forth. Ironically, the move is probably easier to make in crisis conditions. A huge balance of payments deficit, hyperinflation, and a drought in foreign lending will concentrate minds wonderfully. Under these circumstances, even the beneficiaries of import substitution policy will see the need for wholesale reform.

The initial step will most likely be to ensure that the economy is macroeconomically stable. Trade and exchange rate measures will achieve little until the huge money creation and budget deficits that are the cause of hyperinflation are eliminated.[68] This is the time to be rid of price controls, industrial licensing, wasteful subsidies, and the rigging of labor markets. The next question is whether simultaneously to reduce trade barriers, or whether this step should wait until the macroeconomy is stabilized.[69] The argument for delay emphasizes that simultaneous action may make allies of the part of the community that wants to retain trade barriers and those that oppose the stabilization program. Moreover, macro stabilization may cause unemployment at the very time that removing trade barriers may also be costing jobs in protected industries. So simultaneous adjustment may be unacceptably costly. Arguments *for* simultaneous action emphasize that a macro crisis may make it politically possible to undertake thoroughgoing reform, and if the moment is lost, it may not come again.

Whatever the timing, a major reduction in trade barriers will be an important component because healthy exporting will require the purchase of imported inputs. These must be available, and the price paid must be at world levels, not higher, if the potential exporter is to compete on even terms. The reduction of protection will encourage entrepreneurs and resources to enter exporting rather than huddling behind the trade barriers. (If capital markets including interest rates are freed before this step is taken, then new resources might unfortunately be attracted into the still-protected industries.) The new export ventures are most likely to be light manufactured goods of a labor-intensive nature, with low capital–output ratios.

With the reduction in protection can come the dismantling of the bias against agriculture, which will give a boost to traditional agricultural exports. Export taxation of agricultural commodities should be eased whenever the foreign price elasticity of demand is high, but it can be judiciously maintained for items with very low elasticities of demand and supply. The import substitution that continues will generally be limited to labor-intensive, nondurable consumer goods. Many of the less-viable industries established under the previous trade regime will not survive as the heat is turned down in the hothouse. Their labor, capital, and management are freed for more efficient uses.

When trade barriers begin to be dismantled, economists usually recommend that import quotas be the first to go. They are thought to be an especially damaging form of protectionism because they promote monopoly power and lead to rent-seeking behavior.[70] The quotas and licenses can be streamlined and relaxed and be replaced by tariffs; this will ensure that imports cannot be completely cut off and should also increase trade straightaway. Then the tariffs can be lowered and rationalized by reducing the dispersion between high and low ones.

In this process a choice among several specific actions may be made. Among the steps that could be taken are (1) raising the size of existing quotas until they are no longer binding; (2) eliminating quotas on a product-by-product basis; (3) converting quotas to tariffs and then reducing the tariffs (the conversion will raise government revenue for a time, while at the same time causing less damage to the economy); (4) auctioning the quotas rather than giving them to importers, as do Australia and New Zealand and as Brazil did between 1953 and 1957 (that would make them more like tariffs and generate government revenue); (5) converting quotas to tariff quotas, with a lower tariff applying to a certain quantity of imports and a higher tariff applying to additional imports.

Because governments of the low-income LDCs are often overly dependent on tariff revenues, trade liberalization and tax reform may have to be undertaken at the same time. Adopting a value-added tax simultaneously with the reduction in tariffs is a good idea.[71] But it is likely that tax reform will take time, so structural adjustment assistance from the IMF and World Bank may be necessary at this point. Finally, a devaluation of the exchange rate may be in order, the inflationary consequences of which will likely be dampened if liberalization of foreign trade is taking place at the same time.

Among the many countries that have recently engaged in important trade liberalization are Argentina, Bolivia, Brazil, Chile, Côte d'Ivoire, Gambia, Ghana, India, Jamaica, Kenya, Mexico, Morocco, Nigeria, Pakistan, Peru, Senegal, Sri Lanka, Turkey, and Venezuela. Indeed, the IMF usually requires a liberalizing of trade before countries can obtain loans from it. The earlier advice was that the liberalizing process had better be cautious and gradual to avoid short-run dislocations. Fears have intensified, however, that this would reveal lack of commitment to reform on the part of the government and give more time to organize opposition. A recent study by the World Bank that examines 36 trade-reform programs in 19 countries concluded that governments need strong and immediate rather than gradual reform of trade policy to avoid this outcome.[72] In general, trade liberalization in a "big bang" has been most common in Latin America, with a slower approach used in much of Asia and least progress, either suddenly or gradually, in Africa.

Unfortunately, an immediate trade reform is likely to mean that existing firms may be damaged by free trade before new ones spring up to export. Thus there may be a critical point in the transition where unemployment may rise and governments may be tempted to inflate to provide unemployment benefits. In fact, the unemployment from trade liberalization may not be very serious if economic performance is already so bad anyway that unemployment does not increase or increase much. The World Bank study of 36 trade reforms cited in the last paragraph does not indicate great cause for worry on this score, but as already noted, Chile was a major exception in the late 1970s. In the five-and-a-half years that took that country to virtually free trade, there were major job losses in manufacturing, perhaps 11% to 12% of the labor force. Although much of this labor eventually found reemployment, the transition costs were exceptionally high.[73]

Encouraging Exports The final step is to encourage exporting. The infant-industry tariffs discussed earlier in the chapter are a common method for establishing a new industry that may eventually be able to export without government assistance, as in the case of Japanese and South Korean cars, electronic goods from much of Asia, aircraft from Brazil, and the like. Credit subsidies for potential exporters may be better yet, as they do not raise so many international objections from trading partners. As in the HPAEs, initial successes can be rewarded by more credit.

A variety of other promotional tactics can be employed as well.[74] Exporters may receive tax relief, including holidays on income tax and rebates of sales tax. Government may make available land and buildings at zero or subsidized rent, fund market research, or provide insurance. Government can guarantee credit lines to the overseas customers for the exports, though currently fewer than half of the LDCs have an adequate structure for export credit finance and export information. Often the central bank is the only agency that can help, and it is not specialized.[75] (The high-performing economies of East Asia all have excellent export-credit schemes. The United Nations has been investigating whether an interregional trade-financing facility could be established and be commercially viable. Such a facility might increase LDC South-South trade by an additional 6% per year, according to United Nations Commission on Trade and Development (UNCTAD.)[76]

Government help might also be useful whenever an LDC's manufacturing is penalized by quality problems and lack of trustworthy brand names.[77] Left to their own devices, manufacturers may choose a short-run low-quality approach that does not engender consumer confidence and penalizes other potential sellers. A reputation for "lemons" may attach to all firms in the country. A vicious circle develops. Your firm has no reason to emphasize quality if your output is going to be considered low in quality in any case, but since you produce low-quality output, the bias against you is justified. Originally the Japanese government, and later the governments of South Korea and other high-performing Asian economies, used selection of export firms and inspection and certification of their products to overcome the bias, and in this they appear to have been eminently successful. The alternative is for firms to borrow an already-existing reputation by allying themselves with multinational firms.

Encouragement of exporting can also be accomplished by exempting raw materials, semifinished inputs, and spare parts from tariffs and allowing the issue of special import licenses to outflank whatever trade barriers survive. Perhaps free trade zones can be established, as explored in the accompanying box. Of course, any use of subsidies or subsidy-like devices to promote exports creates the danger that vested interests will fight to retain the subsidies and special treatment, so these tactics will have to be carefully monitored or even eschewed if the government is unable to control their use. Some of these tactics have been widely used in the high-performing Asian economies, as discussed in Chapter 3.

By this or other means, encouraging industrial flexibility is extremely important. Among consumers, tastes change rapidly, and trade barriers can arise unexpectedly in a key market. Sure knowledge of what exports will be successful five years from now, or even next year, is unobtainable. Helping to instill flexibility is therefore an important aim of government policy, far more so than bureaucratic "picking of winners," which is largely mythical—understandably so, because why should a bureaucrat do better at this than entrepreneurs who stand to profit from a correct choice and risk their capital on mistakes? A government can probably accomplish more by not permanently propping up losers than it can by attempting to pick winners; this is an essential element in encouraging flexibility.

A government seriously inclined toward export promotion might attempt to emulate the high-performing Asian economies' technique of consultation and liaison between business, public officials, and academics, with frequent and regular discussions of appropriate trade policies. The consultation and liaison might advantageously extend to government contacts with MNEs abroad. The surge of investment in the fabrication, subassembly, and processing of imported components in the LDCs, mostly destined for eventual reexport, often involves government negotiations over foreign trade zones and a package of inducements such as low tax and full repatriation of profits. This remarkable development has been spurred by low labor costs and the willingness of rich countries to apply their tariffs only to the value added abroad rather than the complete product.

FOREIGN TRADE ZONES

If a country is politically unable to reduce trade barriers throughout its territory, it may be able to do so in "foreign trade zones" (FTZs), sometimes also called export processing zones.[78] In these zones, which are spreading rapidly, no tariffs and quotas are applied. In many LDCs, an array of tax breaks and incentives to attract foreign investment is joined to the free trade aspect, leading to the use of one more name, "investment promotion zones." Recently there were about 400 in 80 countries, with some 10% of global trade routed through zones of this sort. Manufacture can be undertaken within the zone and the output exported under free trade conditions; any restrictions the country has apply only when the goods cross the boundary of the FTZ.

Foreign trade zones, always carefully policed and often behind real walls, have played a growing part in export promotion strategy during recent years. The whole of Hong Kong and most of the island-nations of Singapore and Mauritius are FTZs. Sri Lanka has a major program, with the FTZ near Colombo originating most of the country's textile production. FTZs are important in the Dominican Republic and elsewhere in the Caribbean, in Costa Rica, and in Guatemala. The large zone at Colon, Panama, at the Atlantic end of the canal, is well-known. In Asia, by the early 1980s there were about 35 export-processing zones.

The Chinese "special economic zones" have been a remarkable innovation. They export electronics, machinery, and textiles and clothing, while the rest of China does basic machinery and primary products.[79] In 1980, China established four special economic zones; Zhuhai, Shenzhen (these two near Hong Kong), Shantou in Guangdong, and Xiamen in Fujian opposite Taiwan. In 1984, 14 coastal cities were allowed most of the privileges of the SEZs. In 1988, a fifth SEZ was added—the large island of Hainan. In 1990, part of the city of Shanghai was given more liberal status, allowing foreign firms to engage freely in banking, accounting, real estate, and retail sales; trade freely in foreign exchange; build and operate ports; establish insurance companies; and engage in free foreign trade. Many of these rules were extended to the other SEZs in 1992. Also in 1992, 23 inland cities and 13 more along borders were subject to liberalized rules as well. An important development was the 1992 easing of restrictions against foreign firms selling their products within China.[80]

Most foreign investment is in these zones. Hong Kong firms have invested the most, encompassing about two-thirds of the total. The Shenzen region, on China's border with Hong Kong, is the most prosperous Chinese zone. It has registered growth in industrial output, trade, and foreign investment of about 40% per year. The Xiamen zone could soon surpass Shenzen, however, because of its proximity to Taiwan.

In spite of the success of these zones in China and elsewhere, they generally represent limited enclave-style development. For example, it has been charged that the Chinese zones have led to prosperity for those who live there but have produced shortages elsewhere, and that little more will be accomplished until a general nationwide trade reform is undertaken.[81] Clearly, the more well-off a country becomes, the less it will want or need zones of this type. Liberalizing only within a zone can deflect attention from illiberality outside the zone and leave the situation worse than before.[82] They do give employment, a view of modern-sector work, and on-the-job training, but it is easy to exaggerate their significance.

Trade of this kind, with the developed country as exporter of component and importer of final product, depends on transport costs being low enough for a given item to stand both the outward and the inward shipment. It includes some unlikely examples. The cores of 95% of U.S. baseballs are exported from the United States to Haiti, where their covers are sewn on, and then they are flown back. Similarly, semifinished clothes, gloves, and leather luggage are sewn in Southeast Asia, Mexico, and the West Indies and then reexported. Over 20 American companies have located their data processing in the Caribbean, about half in Barbados, and with other important centers in the Dominican Republic and Jamaica. Data tapes are flown from the United States for keypunching. Data processing is also done in Southeast Asia, India, and China; sometimes the data are transmitted via satellite. (This new industry, which was pioneered by American Airlines, is supported mostly by airlines, hotels, credit card companies, and car rental agencies. The workers are mostly women, who sit behind keyboards with video-display terminals.) Auto components are worked on in Taiwan, South Korea, Mexico, Thailand, and India. The semiconductors, valves, and tuners, used for a variety of electronic equipment, are manufactured in Hong Kong, Singapore, Taiwan, Mexico, and elsewhere.[83] Along with electronics items, the most important segment of this trade is apparel.

Export Subsidies

Perhaps more controversial than any other measure for export promotion is government subsidization of the exports.[84] Such subsidies have the plain effect of increasing exports over what they would otherwise have been, as seen in Figure 14.7. Assume that the world price is *W* and that because Penuristan is a small country, any quantity of the item can be exported without affecting that price. Penuristan would thus export *AB* widgets. By paying a subsidy equal to *WS* per unit exported, government will cause exports to rise to *CD*. Local consumption of the product falls because the price rises; producers would always want to sell at prices including the subsidy rather than accept less for domestic sales. Trade barriers against imports will have to be employed to keep a backflow from entering the country to profit from the above-market price.

If the export subsidies are provided to all exports, then there is a uniform degree of bias and the subsidies are equivalent to a partial devaluation of the currency. If they are doled out selectively, however, they have distortionary impacts similar to a nonuniform structure of tariffs. That, in turn, could easily cause a country to specialize in the "wrong" exports, that is, those produced less efficiently than some unsubsidized ones.

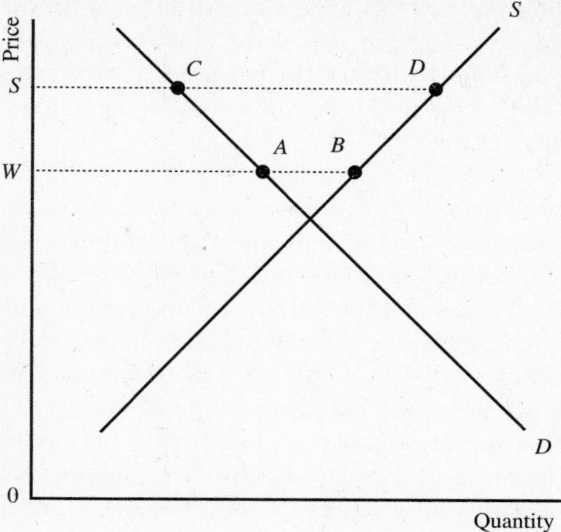

Figure 14.7 Government subsidization of exports increases the amount exported, as shown from *AB* to *CD*.

The General Agreement on Tariffs and Trade (GATT) in Geneva, the forum for carrying on negotiations in international trade, has rules on export subsidies. Under the subsidies code dating from the Tokyo Round of 1979 and earlier GATT rules, the rich industrial countries cannot legally subsidize exports of manufactured goods and minerals. Agricultural commodities cannot be subsidized either if that results in the substantial displacement of the exports of other countries. Under the subsidies code, however, LDCs are permitted to use export subsidies for manufactured goods as long as they do not cause serious prejudice to the trade and production of another signatory. No presumption is to be made that LDC export subsidies will have an adverse effect. The LDC is expected, however, to reduce or eliminate the subsidies as its national product grows, although no graduation procedure is prescribed. This clause has led to controversy, with the United States insisting on rigorous adherence to it.*

The main uses for export subsidies are to encourage infant industries and to offset past policies that have harmed exporting, such as import protection and overvalued foreign exchange rates. Most economists would probably argue that they are unobjectionable or desirable for LDCs as long as they are phased out when an industry either fails to grow up or becomes competitive. They are less acceptable for the prosperous NICs because capital markets are more able to loan to industries that are developing a comparative advantage, thus tiding them over

*Domestic subsidies to firms, not just on exports but to help cover costs of operation generally, are also legal. The code provides for consultations if harm is caused to industry in another country. These operating subsidies used to be less controversial, though recently some developed countries, including the United States, have directed substantially more countervailing duty actions against them.

the period of infancy. It would seem reasonable to allow importing countries to impose countervailing duties against the subsidies only if the subsidized exports have passed some relatively large threshold level and if there is proof of substantial harm so caused. Whether the behavior of the developed countries has been tolerant in this regard is examined in the next chapter.

Disadvantages of Export Promotion All the measures discussed in the past few pages can clearly be pursued too far, turning export promotion based on a reasonable expectation of comparative advantage into costly export bias. A bias toward exports, with firms lacking comparative advantage and permanently kept alive by subsidies, is no more defensible than generalized import substitution policy, and no better economics either. Overdoing it is perhaps not as likely, however, because the costs are generally in the government budget and are therefore highly visible. Another reason why overzealous export promotion is relatively rare is that the initial bias toward import substitution in many LDCs was very strong. Wide-ranging measures for export promotion could be taken and still do no more than correct the underlying imbalance. Furthermore, a major part of export promotion strategy is intended to work through market prices rather than controls. Even if subsidies are granted, the freeing of the price mechanism reduces the damage.

Sometimes governments may use criteria other than comparative advantage in selecting the export industries they want to promote. Malaysia's much-criticized industrialization program seems to fit this description. The tires, furniture, palm oil products, and other goods chosen for emphasis were apparently selected because the raw materials were produced domestically and not because the export promised to be profitable.

The type of industry established may have limited effects on the economy as a whole. The processing of materials in a foreign trade zone may fit well the description of enclave exporting discussed in Chapter 13. On top of their enclave character, an MNE's assembly operations may be quite footloose, quick to move on at any perceived slight. The LDC may have little bargaining strength, there being no control either over the imported input or the output decided on by the MNE and then exported. What does one do with an Apex stereo tuner besides install it in an Apex product?[85] This conundrum may give MNEs engaged in the assembly activities more than usual influence in domestic politics. It may also mean that further progress in exporting will be in the hands of foreign firms. Clearly, the decision to welcome this sort of investment carries costs as well as benefits.

Finally, an outward-looking strategy of export promotion can have a wide array of undesirable side effects, making it incumbent on government to lessen the damage. For example, perhaps the tendency is to concentrate land-holding in the hands of an elite because some plantation crop has a comparative advantage. Perhaps richer farmers are advantaged by credit market imperfections and by the aid made available for capital-intensive machinery. In such cases and many other cases as well, political influence may block reversal of these policies. The government that abdicates its social responsibilities in these areas cannot very well argue that the advantages of outward orientation are being maximized.

Summary

Whatever the costs, we have seen that the benefits of a policy mix that promotes exports are large. Productivity increase is the key to growth in the long run, and trade can help greatly in reallocating a country's factors of production to more efficient uses. There is wide agreement that productivity growth is faster when a country's economic policies are outward-looking.[86]

What remains to be seen is whether the environment will be as receptive to outward-looking strategies in the future as it has been over the past two decades. The major fears are twofold: that world growth will be slow, thus providing inadequate demand for new exports by the LDCs, and that the developed countries will turn to trade restrictions to protect their industries from competitive pressures. These two topics are currently among the most important in our discipline, and they are considered in the next chapter.

NOTES

1. Useful studies on which I have drawn are (alphabetically) Bela Balassa, "Outward Orientation," Henry Bruton, "Import Substitution," and Sebastian Edwards and Sweder van Wijnbergen, "Disequilibrium and Structural Adjustment," all in Hollis Chenery and T. N. Srinivasan, eds., *Handbook of Development Economics*, vol. 2 (Amsterdam, 1989), 1481–1533, 1601–1644, and 1645–1689; Graham R. Bird, *International Financial Policy and Economic Development* (Basingstoke, 1987); Rudiger Dornbusch, "The Case for Trade Liberalization in Developing Countries," *Journal of Economic Perspectives* 6, no. 1 (Winter 1992): 69–85; Sebastian Edwards, *Economic Adjustment and Exchange Rates in Developing Countries* (Chicago, 1986); Sebastian Edwards, *Exchange Rate Misalignment in Developing Countries* World Bank Occasional Paper, N.S., no. 2 (1988); Anne O. Krueger, "Comparative Advantage and Development Policy Twenty Years Later," in M. Syrquin, L. Taylor, and L. Westphal, eds., *Economic Structure and Performance: Essays in Honor of Hollis B. Chenery* (New York, 1984); Deepak Lal and Sarath Rajapatirana, "Foreign Trade Regimes and Economic Growth in Developing Countries," *World Bank Research Observer* 2, no. 2 (July 1987): 189–217; Gerald M. Meier, *Leading Issues in Development Economics*, 5th ed. (New York, 1989), part VIII; Hubert Schmitz, "Industrialization Strategies in Less Developed Countries: Some Lessons of Historical Experience," *Journal of Development Studies* 21, no. 1 (1984): 1–21; and his *Technology and Employment Practices in Developing Countries* (London, 1985); and *WDR 1987*, which focuses on international trade. A classic article that I used is Henry J. Bruton, "The Import-Substitution Strategy of Economic Development: A Survey," *Pakistan Development Review* 10, no. 2 (1970): 123–146.
2. See David Evans and Parvin Alizadeh, "Trade, Industrialization, and the Visible Hand," *Journal of Development Studies* 21, no. 1 (1984): 23, for a discussion. In his "Alternative Perspectives on Trade and Development," in Chenery and Srinivasan, eds., *Handbook of Development Economics*, vol. 2, 1292, Evans notes that these guidelines are conservative when judged by the experience of South Korea and Taiwan, where the infant industry protection was applied for a longer period.
3. Henry Bruton, "Import Substitution," in Chenery and Srinivasan, *Handbook of Development Economics*, vol. 2, 1612, 1641.
4. *WDR 1983*, 52.

5. I. M. D. Little, *Economic Development: Theory, Policy, and International Relations* (New York, 1982), 280.
6. *WDR 1983*, 55.
7. See Anne O. Krueger, "Import Substitution Versus Export Promotion," *Finance and Development* 22, no. 2 (1985): 22.
8. In part from *WDR 1983*, 58.
9. Meier, *Leading Issues*, 5th ed., 399.
10. For the penalties paid by exporters, see *WDR 1987*; Anne O. Krueger, *Trade and Employment in Developing Countries*, vol. 3, *Synthesis and Conclusions* (Chicago, 1983); and her *Foreign Trade Regimes and Economic Development: Liberalization Attempts and Consequences* (Cambridge, Mass., 1978). See also Jagdish N. Bhagwati, *Foreign Trade Regimes and Economic Development: Anatomy and Consequences of Exchange Control Regimes* (Cambridge, Mass., 1978).
11. *WDR 1987*, 80.
12. See, for example, Bela Balassa et al., *The Structure of Protection in Developing Countries* (Baltimore, 1971).
13. See Richard Harris, "Applied General Equilibrium Analysis of Small Open Economies and Imperfect Competition," *American Economic Review* 74, no. 5 (1984), 1016–1032.
14. *WDR 1987*, 90.
15. *IMF Survey*, October 26, 1992. Details are in IMF, *Annual Report on Exchange Arrangements and Exchange Restrictions* (Washington, D.C.). For discussions, see Ricardo J. Caballero and Vittorio Corbo, "The Effect of Real Exchange Rate Uncertainty on Exports: Empirical Evidence," *World Bank Economic Review* 3, no. 2 (May 1989): 263–278; and Peter J. Quirk and Hernán Cortés-Douglas, "The Experience with Floating Rates," *Finance and Development* 30, no. 2 (June 1993): 28–31.
16. Quirk and Cortés-Douglas, "The Experience with Floating Rates," 28–31. Also see Rudiger Dornbusch, ed., *Policymaking in the Open Economy: Concepts and Case Studies in Economic Performance* (Oxford, 1993).
17. A short summary of the adverse effects can be found in Guy Pfeffermann, "Overvalued Exchange Rates and Development," *Finance and Development* 11, no. 1 (1985): 17–19.
18. January 19, 1985, 72.
19. IMF, *World Economic Outlook 1994* (Washington, D.C., 1994), 62.
20. A point that emerges from John Whalley, ed., *Developing Countries and the Global Trading System*, 2 vol. (London, 1989).
21. For a survey of such markets see C. Jones and M. Roemer, eds., "Parallel Markets in Developing Countries," *World Development* 17, no. 12 (December, 1989).
22. The period covered was 1960 to 1983. See Domingo F. Cavallo, Joaquin Cottani, and M. Shahbaz Khan, "Real Exchange Rate Behavior and Economic Performance in LDCs," background paper for the 1986 *World Development Report*, summarized on 31–32 of that report; Sebastian Edwards, *Real Exchange Rates, Devaluation, and Adjustment* (Cambridge, Mass., 1989); and *The Economist*, April 15, 1989.
23. The analysis in this section relies on Graham Bird, "Should Developing Countries Use Currency Depreciation as a Tool of Balance of Payments Adjustment? A Review of the Theory and Evidence, and a Guide for the Policy Maker," *Journal of Development Studies* 19, no. 4 (1983): 461–484; W. Max Corden, "Exchange Rate Policies for Developing Countries," *Economic Journal* 103, no. 416 (January 1993): 198–207; the works of Edwards, Edwards and van Wijnbergen, and Bird cited in this chapter's note 1; Sebastian Edwards, "Openness, Trade Liberalization, and Growth in Developing Countries," *Journal of Economic Literature* 31, no. 3 (September 1993): 1358–1393; and Thorvaldur Gylfason and Marian Radetzki, "Does Devaluation Make Sense in the Least Developed Countries?" *Economic Development and Cultural Change* 40, no. 1 (October 1991): 1–25.

24. *The Economist*, November 24, 1990.
25. For a survey of the difficulties, see David B. H. Denoon, *Devaluation Under Pressure, India, Indonesia, and Ghana* (Cambridge, Mass., 1986).
26. I utilized Grant T. Hammond, *Countertrade, Offsets and Barter in International Political Economy* (London, 1990); Jack L. Hervey, "Countertrade—counterproductive?" Federal Reserve Bank of Chicago *Economic Perspectives* (January/February 1989): 17–24; "Countertrade Reconsidered," *Finance and Development* 24, no. 2 (June 1987): 46–49; the Group of 30, *Countertrade in the World Economy* (New York, 1986); Bart S. Fisher and Kathleen M. Harte, *Barter in the World Economy* (New York, 1985); Frieder Roessler, "Countertrade and the GATT Legal System," *Journal of World Trade Law* 19, no. 6 (1985): 604–614; Gary Banks, "The Economics and Politics of Countertrade," *The World Economy* 6, no. 2 (1983): 159–182; *International Economic Review*, October 1994; and various issues of *The Economist*.
27. *International Economic Review*, August, 1992.
28. See Thomas B. McVey, "Why Countries Find Countertrade a Double-Edged Sword," in Group of 30, *Countertrade in the World Economy*.
29. Edwards, "Openness, Trade Liberalization, and Growth in Developing Countries," *Journal of Economic Literature*, 1358–1393. Also see Edwards, *Exchange Rate Misalignment in Developing Countries*, World Bank Occasional Paper, N.S., no. 2 (1988).
30. See, for example, the lack of a consistent pattern in the 22 episodes of devaluation studied by Anne Krueger in her *Foreign Trade Regimes and Economic Development*.
31. See Graham Bird, "Should Developing Countries Use Currency Depreciation?" 465, quoting studies by Cooper, Connolly, Taylor, and Krueger. Norman S. Fieleke, "Price Behavior During Balance of Payments Adjustment," *New England Economic Review* (November/December 1984), 42, comes to the same conclusion. There is strikingly little empirical evidence that devaluation causes the terms of trade to deteriorate.
32. Edwards, "Openness, Trade Liberalization, and Growth in Developing Countries," 1358–1393. Edwards cites Bela Balassa for supply elasticities in 16 countries. Also see Edwards, *Exchange Rate Misalignment in Developing Countries*.
33. See Morris Goldstein, "Global Effects of Fund-Supported Programs," IMF Occasional Paper No. 42 (1985).
34. How prices change following a devaluation is nicely surveyed by Fieleke, "Price Behavior."
35. Sebastian Edwards and Sweder van Wijnbergen suggest that, in the short run, a 10% devaluation will on average lead to a fall of about 1% in GNP. See their "Disequilibrium and Structural Adjustment," in Chenery and Srinivasan, eds., *Handbook of Development Economics*, vol. 2, 1529. Richard Cooper's evidence that devaluation is initially deflationary has been influential. See Cooper, "Currency Devaluation in Developing Countries," in Gustav Ranis, ed., *Government and Economic Development* (New Haven, 1971), 504.
36. See Michael Nowak, "Quantitative Controls and Unofficial Markets in Foreign Exchange: A Theoretical Framework," *IMF Staff Papers* 31, no. 2 (1984): 404–431.
37. The effect of devaluation on output can be more complex than described in the text. Several variations are discussed by Edwards and van Wijnbergen, "Disequilibrium and Structural Adjustment," in Chenery and Srinivasan, eds., *Handbook of Development Economics*, Vol. 2, 1481–1533; Liaquat Ahamed, "Stabilization Policies in Developing Countries," *World Bank Research Observer* 1, no. 1 (1986): 97–98; and Thorvaldur Gylfason and Marian Radetzki, "Does Devaluation Make Sense in the Least Developed Countries?" *Economic Development and Cultural Change* 40, no. 1 (October 1991): 1–25. These works cite numerous sources. This is an area of theoretical debate.
38. Compare Little, *Economic Development*, 82.

39. Edwards, "Openness, Trade Liberalization, and Growth in Developing Countries," 1358–1393. For discussion of the cases, which occurred between 1962 and 1982, see Edwards, *Real Exchange Rates, Devaluation, and Adjustment* (Cambridge, Mass., 1989). Other similar evidence is surveyed by Edwards and van Wijnbergen, "Disequilibrium and Structural Adjustment," 1525–1528.
40. Choosing the speed for a crawl or creep can be a delicate and complex task. See the discussion in Ahamed, "Stabilization Policies," 84–85.
41. Five interesting articles contributed to this paragraph: Arnold C. Harberger, "Observations on the Chilean Economy, 1973–1983," *Economic Development and Cultural Change* 33, no. 3 (1985): 451–462; Sebastian Edwards, "Stabilization with Liberalization: An Evaluation of Ten Years of Chile's Experiment with Free-Market Policies, 1973–1983," *Economic Development and Cultural Change* 33, no. 2 (1985): 223–254; Edwards's "Monetarism in Chile, 1973–1983: Some Economic Puzzles," *Economic Development and Cultural Change* 34, no. 3 (1986): 535–559; Ricardo Ffrench-Davis, "The Monetarist Experiment in Chile: A Critical Survey," *World Development* 11, no. 11 (1983): 905–926; and *The Economist*, August 10, 1985, 60–62. Also see Rodrigo Briones, "The Chilean Malaise," *Challenge* 27, no. 1 (1984): 57–60.
42. The subject is surveyed by G. G. Johnson, "The Formulation of Exchange Rate Policies in Adjustment Programs," IMF Occasional Paper No. 36 (1985). Bela Balassa has led in investigating ways to measure the effects of preferential tax and credit arrangements. See Balassa et al, *Development Strategies in Semi-Industrial Countries* (Baltimore, 1982). I also utilized Michael Nowak, "Black Markets in Foreign Exchange," *Finance and Development* 22, no. 1 (1985): 20–23; and Jones and Roemer, eds., "Parallel Markets in Developing Countries."
43. See Riccardo Faini and Jaime de Melo, "Adjustment, Investment and the Real Exchange Rate in Developing Countries," *Economic Policy* (October 1990); and *The Economist*, November 24, 1990.
44. In addition to the specific references in the following sections on outward orientation, I utilized Henry Bruton, "Import Substitution," and Bela Balassa, "Outward Orientation," both in Chenery and Srinivasan, *Handbook of Development Economics*, vol. 2, 1601–1644 and 1645–1689; Deepak Lal and Sarath Rajapatirana, "Foreign Trade Regimes and Economic Growth in Developing Countries," *World Bank Research Observer* 2, no. 2 (July 1987): 189–217; *WDR 1983*, 54–56; *WDR 1984*, 13, 103; *WDR 1985*, 70; much of *WDR 1987*, which focuses on the issue; Meier, *Leading Issues*, 5th ed., part VIIIB; Anne O. Krueger, "Import Substitution Versus Export Promotion," 20–23; and Anne O. Krueger "Trade Strategies and Employment in Developing Countries," *Finance and Development* 21, no. 2 (1984): 23–26.
45. The advantages of a growing export sector, including the many nonquantifiable ones, are traced understandably by Jagdish N. Bhagwati, "Export-Promoting Trade Strategy: Issues and Evidence," *World Bank Research Observer* 3, no. 1 (January 1988): 27–57. Anne O. Krueger's research on this topic is conveniently summarized in her "Trade Strategies and Employment in Developing Countries," especially 25.
46. See Gerald M. Meier, *Leading Issues*, 5th ed., 408–410; and Meier, *Emerging from Poverty* (New York, 1984), 178–179, for a discussion.
47. The evidence is from Anne O. Krueger et al, eds., *Trade and Employment in Developing Countries*, vol. 1, *Individual Studies* (Chicago, 1981), and vol. 3, *Synthesis and Conclusion* (Chicago, 1983); *WDR 1984*, 103; A. H. M. M. Rahman, *Exports of Manufactures from Developing Countries* (Rotterdam, 1973); Larry E. Westphal, "The Republic of Korea's Experience with Export-Led Industrial Development," *World Development* 6, no. 3 (1978): 347–382; and Meier, *Leading Issues*, 4th ed., 533.

48. *WDR 1987*, 91.
49. Following the statement in Meier, *Emerging from Poverty*, 176.
50. The volume by Hollis B. Chenery, Sherman Robinson, and Moshe Syrquin, *Industrialization and Growth: A Comparative Study* (Washington, D.C., 1986), was an important advance in reaching this conclusion.
51. Hollis B. Chenery, "Growth and Transformation," in Chenery, Robinson, and Syrquin, eds., *Industrialization and Growth: A Comparative Study*, table 2.2.
52. See Oli Havrylyshyn, "Trade Policies and Productivity Gains in Developing Countries: A Survey of the Literature," *World Bank Research Observer* 5, no. 1 (January 1990): 18–20.
53. Havrylyshyn, "Trade Policies and Productivity Gains in Developing Countries: A Survey of the Literature," 18–20. Also Dornbusch, *Policymaking in the Open Economy: Concepts and Case Studies in Economic Performance*.
54. Good places to start are the balanced and thoughtful essay by Havrylyshyn, "Trade Policies and Productivity Gains in Developing Countries, 1–24; Bela Balassa, "Outward Orientation," in Chenery and Srinivasan, *Handbook of Development Economics*, vol. 2, 1645–1689; and Moshe Syrquin and Hollis Chenery, "Three Decades of Industrialization," *World Bank Economic Review* 3, no. 2 (May 1989): 145–181. Also see Hollis B. Chenery, "Growth and Transformation," in Hollis B. Chenery, Sherman Robinson, and Moshe Syrquin, *Industrialization and Growth: A Comparative Study* (Washington, D.C., 1986); and two essays by Chenery and Syrquin in the same volume: "Typical Patterns of Transformation," and "The Semi-Industrial Countries." Among the studies are those of R. Emery, 50 countries, 1967; A. Maizels, 9 countries, 1968; C. Voivodas, 22 countries, 1973; M. Michaely, 41 countries, 1977; B. Balassa, 10 countries, 1978; R. Williamson, 22 countries, 1978; O. Fajana, 20 countries, 1979; W. Tyler, 55 countries, 1981; C. Schenzler, 30 countries, 1982; G. Feder, 31 countries, 1983; *WDR 1987*, 41 countries; and D. Dollar, 95 countries, 1992. Also see the citations in *WDR 1987*; David Dollar, "Outward-oriented Developing Economies Really Do Grow More Rapidly: Evidence from 95 LDCs, 1976–1985," *Economic Development and Cultural Change* 40, no. 3 (April 1992): 523–544; Rudiger Dornbusch, "The Case for Trade Liberalization in Developing Countries," *Journal of Economic Perspectives* 6, no. 1 (Winter 1992): 69–85; Edwards, "Openness, Trade Liberalization, and Growth in Developing Countries," 1358–1393; Bernard Heitger, "Import Protection and Export Performance: Their Impact on Economic Growth," *Weltwirtschaftliches Archiv* 123, no. 2 (1987): 249–261; Woo S. Jung and Peyton J. Marshall, "Exports, Growth and Causality in Developing Countries," *Journal of Development Economics* 18, no. 1 (1985): 1–12; and the rather less confident conclusion of Dominick Salvatore and Thomas Hatcher, "Inward Oriented and Outward Oriented Trade Strategies," *Journal of Development Studies* 27, no. 3 (April 1991): 7–23, that the claim that outward orientation causes growth "is partially supported by the econometric results."
55. See her study *Foreign Trade Regimes and Economic Development* for the statistical detail. The sample size involved was ten countries. The quotation is from her article, "The Effects of Trade Strategies on Growth," *Finance and Development* 20, no. 2 (1983): 7.
56. See, for example, Heitger, "Import Protection and Export Performance: Their Impact on Economic Growth," 249–261. Edwards, "Openness, Trade Liberalization, and Growth in Developing Countries," 1389–1390, surveys recent theoretical work by Paul Romer, Danny Quah, James Rauch, Gene Grossman, and Elhanan Helpman as well as by Edwards himself that attempts to explain more thoroughly why export orientation promotes GDP growth. These studies have become increasingly influential among international economists.

57. Jung and Marshall, "Exports, Growth and Causality," 9. Sebastian Edwards addresses the direction of causality in his "Openness, Trade Liberalization, and Growth in Developing Countries," especially 1381–1382 and 1388.
58. Bela Balassa, "Exports, Policy Choices, and Economic Growth in Developing Countries After the 1973 Oil Shock," *Journal of Development Economics* 18, no. 1 (1985): 23–35. Balassa's figures suggest that the improved performance was true even for the lowest-income LDCs, where the correlation between export growth and GNP growth had heretofore been weaker. See also Balassa's "Policy Responses to Exogenous Shocks in Developing Countries," *American Economic Review* 76, no. 2 (1986): 75–78; and his book *Change and Challenge in the World Economy* (London, 1985).
59. The original study of the 41 countries dates from 1987, and the evidence is surveyed at length in *WDR 1987*. Updates have taken the analysis to 1992.
60. Dollar, "Outward-oriented Developing Economies Really Do Grow More Rapidly: Evidence from 95 LDCs, 1976–1985," 523–544.
61. Neng Liang,"Beyond Import Substitution and Export Promotion: A New Typology of Trade Strategies," *Journal of Development Studies* 28, no. 3 (April 1992): 447–472.
62. See Desmond F. McCarthey, Lance Taylor, and Cyrus Talati, "Trade Patterns in Developing Countries, 1964–1982," *Journal of Development Economics* 27 (1987): 5–39. Criticisms of how the 41 countries are classified are discussed by Edwards, "Openness, Trade Liberalization, and Growth in Developing Countries," 1386–1387.
63. David Evans, "Alternative Perspectives on Trade and Development," in Hollis Chenery and T. N. Srinivasan, eds., *Handbook of Development Economics*, vol. 2 (Amsterdam, 1989), 1293.
64. Howard Pack, "Industrialization and Trade," in Hollis Chenery and T. N. Srinivasan, eds., *Handbook of Development Economics*, vol. 1 (Amsterdam, 1988), 333–380, especially 346–358.
65. H. W. Singer, "The *World Development Report 1987* on the Blessings of 'Outward Orientation': A Necessary Correction," *Journal of Development Studies* 24, no. 2 (January 1988): 232–236; G. K. Helleiner, "Trade Strategy in Medium-Term Adjustment," *World Development* 18, no. 6 (June 1990): 879–897.
66. Hans W. Singer and Patricia Gray, "Trade Policy and Growth of Developing Countries: Some New Data," *World Development* 16, no. 3 (March 1988): 395–403.
67. Nicholas Stern, "The Economics of Development: A Survey," *Economic Journal* 99, no. 397 (September 1989): 633.
68. As advocated by *WDR 1987*, 109. See Dornbusch, *Policymaking in the Open Economy: Concepts and Case Studies in Economic Performance*.
69. Rod Falvey and Cha Dong Kim, "Timing and Sequencing Issues in Trade Liberalisation," *Economic Journal* 102, no. 413 (July 1992): 908–924.
70. Falvey and Kim, "Timing and Sequencing Issues in Trade Liberalisation," 908–924; and Rudiger Dornbusch, "The Case for Trade Liberalization in Developing Countries," *Journal of Economic Perspectives* 6, no. 1 (Winter 1992): 69–85.
71. Pradeep Mitra, "The Coordinated Reform of Tariffs and Indirect Taxes," *World Bank Research Observer* 7, no. 2 (July 1992): 195–218.
72. Demetris Papageorgiou, Michael Michaely, and Armeane Choksi, eds., *Liberalizing Foreign Trade* (Oxford, 1991), especially vol. 7, *Lessons of Experience in the Developing World*, Chapter 6, 80. For a critique of this work, see David Greenaway, "Liberalising Foreign Trade Through Rose-Tinted Glasses," *Economic Journal* 103, no. 416 (January 1993): 208–222.
73. *WDR 1987*, 107–108.
74. See Falvey and Kim, "Timing and Sequencing Issues in Trade Liberalisation," 908–924.

75. *International Economic Review*, May 1992.
76. USITC, *The Year in Trade 1991*, 60.
77. Chong Ju Choi, "Marketing Barriers Facing Developing Country Manufactured Exports: A Comment," *Journal of Development Studies* 29, no. 1 (October 1992): 166–171.
78. For surveys and analyses of the zones, see Peter G. Warr, "Export Processing Zones: The Economics of Enclave Manufacturing," *World Bank Research Observer* 4, no. 1 (January 1989): 65–88; Walter H. Diamond and Dorothy B. Diamond, *Tax-Free Trade Zones of the World* (New York, 1977); and D. L. U. Jayawardena, "Free Trade Zones," *Journal of World Trade Law* 17, no. 5 (1983): 427–444.
79. See Michael W. Bell and Kalpana Kochhar, "China: An Evolving Market Economy—A Review of Reform Experience," IMF Working Paper 92/89 (November 1992); World Bank, *China: Between Plan and Market*, World Bank Country Study (Washington, D.C., 1990); and Nicholas R. Lardy, *Foreign Trade and Economic Reform in China. 1978–1990* (Cambridge, 1990).
80. See the *International Economic Review*, July 1994; and *The Economist*, October 5, 1991. China's experience has not been altogether favorable. When China authorized firms to buy abroad, deals by officials especially on Hainan Island resulted in serious loss of foreign exchange reserves.
81. *The Economist*, December 10, 1988.
82. Warr, "Export Processing Zones," 85.
83. A recent volume on overseas assembly activities is Joseph Grunwald and Kenneth Flamm, *The Global Factory: Foreign Assembly in International Trade* (Washington, D.C., 1985).
84. See Belayneh Seyoum, "Export Subsidies under the MTN: An Analysis with Particular Emphasis on Developing Countries," *Journal of World Trade Law* 18, no. 6 (1984): 512–541.
85. Repeating a question asked by Meier, *Leading Issues*, 4th ed., 396, and also reflecting the work of G. K. Helleiner quoted there.
86. David Greenaway and Chris Milner, "Trade Theory and the Less-Developed Countries," in Norman Gemmell, ed., *Surveys in Development Economics* (Oxford, 1987).

Chapter **15**

The Future for the International Trade of the LDCs

Whether exports can continue to act as a powerful expediter of economic growth in the LDCs depends largely on three main considerations. First, will incomes in the developed countries rise enough to increase their demand for imports and thus provide a growing market for the LDCs? Second, will the successful conclusion of the Uruguay Round of trade negotiations in 1994 usher in a new period of declining trade barriers, or will that promise ultimately fail? Third, will the LDCs lower their high trade barriers against one another? Failure on any of these three counts, but especially the first two, would significantly reduce the likelihood of export-led development.

DEVELOPED-COUNTRY GROWTH IS IMPORTANT FOR LDC EXPORTS

The 1970s and 1980s brought unmistakable signs of a slowdown in developed-country growth. The slowdown has serious implications for developing countries, first, because about two-thirds of LDC exports still go largely to those countries (63% in 1987, about the same as the 65% of 1973) and, second, because industrial-country GDP and LDC export revenue are closely connected.[1]

This close connection between developed-country growth and LDC export revenue works through two routes. The first involves the price changes discussed in Chapter 13, which are pronounced for primary products. A study by Data Resources, Inc., suggests that when developed-country growth averages less than 2.6% annually, commodity prices will fall.[2] An alternative calculation by the IMF indicates that a 1% fall in industrial production causes a decline in commodity prices of about 2%. Metals and agricultural raw materials are the exports most sensitive to reductions in developed-country growth. Prices do not change nearly so much with manufactured exports, but the quantity of these exports usually falls, on average about 2.7% for a 1% fall in developed-country GDP. On both counts, the falling terms of trade mostly of primary products and the falling volume mostly of manufactures means a decline in the export revenues earned by the LDCs. The elasticity is about 2; that is, a 1% fall in developed-country GDP causes a fall in LDC export revenues of about 2%. This, in turn, is associated with a 0.2% to 0.3% decline in the real GDP of the exporting LDCs, with the figure as high as 0.7% for some countries. (Exports from LDCs to developed countries account for 12% of the LDCs' GDP.)[3]

Economic growth did fall in the developed world, about 25% between the 1965 to 1980 average and the 1980 to 1991 average, though the reasons for the slowdown in developed-country growth are complex and not entirely clear.[4] One cause is the shift toward the service sector, which has meant a tendency toward lower GDP growth because the productivity of services is difficult to augment. Stagflation stemming from the several oil shocks played a role. So did labor market rigidities, especially in Europe, with unemployment high in part because wage cuts were politically unacceptable. The great U.S. federal budget deficit together with tight monetary policy led to higher interest rates and crowding out, especially of exports due to the resulting strong dollar. Whatever the reasons, the end result was a long-term slowdown in growth. All students of economic development should be aware that the development prospects of the LDCs depend in large measure on the use of sensible macroeconomic policies in the developed-countries themselves. Slow growth there can easily delay progress in the LDCs.

The "Reverse Linkage"

The link between income and exports does not run just from the developed countries to the LDCs. Developed-country exports to the LDCs are growing more important, and in a "reverse linkage" these exports depend on the buyers' income. Trade fosters an interdependence of nations. In 1993, developed-country exports to LDCs were about 4% of developed-country GDP (4.1% in Japan and 3.1% in the United States). The exports involved were about 42% of total U.S. exports, 48% of Japan's, and 20% of Western Europe's. From 1990 to 1993, U.S. exports to LDCs grew six times faster than did growth in U.S. exports to developed countries. In effect, the LDCs were helping to pull the developed countries out of the recession taking place at that time, and faster growth in the LDCs feeds back into faster growth in the developed countries as well.[5]

The LDCs stimulate the developed countries not just by buying their exports. Growth in LDC markets also brings valuable competition for the developed countries, helping to strengthen the competitive abilities of its companies. It brings lower prices to developed-country consumers. And it has the potential to provide greater scale economies all around.[6]

DEVELOPED-COUNTRY TRADE BARRIERS AND LDC GROWTH

A major obstacle to LDC export growth would be the maintenance of developed-country barriers to trade, or even a rise in such barriers.[7] The long-awaited signing in 1994 of a new international agreement called the Uruguay Round. The agreement which was negotiated under the General Agreement on Tariffs and Trade, or GATT, makes it likely that most trade barriers will be going down. The new World Trade Organization that began operations in 1995, will be of great help to the LDCs—and to the developed countries as well—in policing the new agreement. But history demonstrates that trade disputes and trade wars may spring up unexpectedly, spoiling many plans. To a large degree, economic development through trade depends on whether the developed countries will allow the paths of trade to continue to open up.

In this section, we will adopt the following plan. First, we will sketch the reasons why rising trade barriers will continue to be a danger in the developed countries no matter how many international agreements are signed on the matter. Then we shall examine the major existing barriers to the LDCs' exports to the developed countries, and consider the effect of the Uruguay Round on these barriers.

Why Trade Barriers Will Remain a Danger

Trade barriers in the developed countries will continue to be a danger as long as commercial interests and the public believe that low wages in the LDCs will undercut developed-country firms—that is to say, indefinitely. The typical argument, exemplified in the writings and speeches of many politicians and, in particular, Ross Perot in the United States runs as follows: Low wages in the LDCs mean that costs of production in these countries are low. The low costs make it possible for LDC competitors to undercut the prices that developed-country firms have to charge. Import penetration by the products of the LDCs will continue to increase, thereby costing many jobs in the developed countries.*

The claim of low wages in the LDCs is certainly correct. Table 15.1 shows average 1993 hourly labor cost in manufacturing:

---

*Some commentators argue that LDCs will cost the developed countries even more jobs because the latter in the long term will run a balance of trade deficit with the LDCs, importing more from them than they export to them, and also that LDCs will suck capital for investment out of the developed countries. It is, however, impossible for both these eventualities to occur at the same time. A trade deficit must mean a capital inflow, as we discussed in Chapter 4. Much more likely is a developed-country trade *surplus*, and a capital inflow to the LDCs.

TABLE 15.1 AVERAGE HOURLY LABOR COST IN MANUFACTURING, 1993

Germany (West)	$24.87
Japan	$16.91
United States	$16.40
Britain	$12.37
Taiwan	$5.46
Singapore	$5.12
South Korea	$4.93
Hong Kong	$4.21
Mexico	$2.41
Thailand	$0.71
Philippines	$0.68
China	$0.54

Source: Wall Street Journal, September 30, 1994.

The claim of greater import penetration by the LDCs is also correct. For example, U.S. imports of manufactured goods from LDCs rose from 5% of the value of all manufacturing output in 1978 to 11% in 1990. The rise has also been substantial, though slower, in Japan and Europe.

In any general sense, the argument that low wages abroad must undercut the domestic economy are, of course, false. The question is not the wage, but the amount produced per dollar spent, that is, the productivity of the labor. High productivity explains why the United States, Germany, and Japan are the world's largest exporters, while cheap-labor countries are not. Were cheap labor the only key, then China (and India, Indonesia, and Bangladesh, all of which have wages at or under $0.50 per hour) would be the world's export leaders.

The higher productivity of labor in the developed countries, and indeed in the Asian countries occupying the middle of Table 15.1, allows these countries to compete successfully. For example, Taiwan's T-shirts incur labor costs only 50% more than the labor costs in Thailand, even though Taiwan's average wage in the production of that item are four times higher than Thailand's.[8] The increasing labor productivity in these countries causes their wages to rise—8% per year over the last 20 years in South Korea compared to less than 2% per year in the developed countries. And it would not help the LDCs to compete if they try artificially to hold down wages. That would cause them to generate a surplus of exports over imports, which in turn would appreciate the currency, with the same effect as higher wages.[9]

Nor does high import penetration signify that employment must be declining in the affected country. An LDC that exports large amounts is an LDC earning the foreign exchange that allows it to buy imports from the developed countries. New rich-country jobs open up in exporting as old ones disappear in industries affected by imports.[10] They also open up elsewhere in an economy, because trade in accord with comparative advantage promotes efficiency and hence higher incomes. Many of these new jobs are likely to be in the service sector. The higher import penetration might actually be signaling even greater developed-country competitiveness than before.[11]

Unfortunately, however, there may be a problem in matching the workers who have lost their jobs because of imports and the new jobs that open up because of exporting and a more prosperous economy. The problem is acute when the jobs lost require few skills and little educational attainment. The developed countries have no comparative advantage in producing goods that require mostly inputs of unskilled labor and simple technology. If the unskilled workers of the developed countries have been inadequately educated, with associated poor reading and math ability, it will be difficult to shift these workers into other activities. The countries that have neglected their education and training will face long-term difficulties reemploying workers "locked in" to their jobs by their limited abilities.

Empirical evidence is mounting that the unskilled workers of the developed countries will be under pressure. One study concludes that imports from LDCs have caused about a 6% fall in the demand for unskilled labor in U.S. manufacturing.[12] That effect of competition from the LDCs has been strong enough, according to Paul Krugman of Stanford University, so that overall U.S. wages have been reduced, though he estimates the reduction to have been less than 1%.[13] But the major implication of trade with the LDCs is that it tends to raise the demand for skilled labor because of exports and reduce the demand for unskilled labor because of imports. Research suggests that about 15% to 25% of the 11 percentage point rise in the gap in earnings between U.S. high school and college graduates during the period 1980 to 1985 was due to the increased U.S. trade deficit.[14]

So LDC exports of manufactured goods *do* cause job losses among an already disadvantaged group of people in the developed countries. It is possible to argue that any such effect is swamped by the effect of overall changes in labor productivity. Only about 2% of the fall in manufacturing employment in six developed countries (the United States, France, Germany, Italy, Japan, and Great Britain) is estimated to be from trade, and the rest to rising labor productivity.*

The workers whose wages are under pressure, or who fear for their jobs, the managers and stockholders in the industries concerned, the townspeople in an affected community, not to mention those with a xenophobic attitude in the first place, will be in the van of those demanding that trade barriers be maintained or increased. Sometimes the appeal for such barriers can extend to a moral plane, as with child labor discussed in the accompanying box.

Trade Barriers in the Developed Countries

By the 1980s, over four-fifths of all manufactured imports and nearly two-thirds of all agricultural imports entered the developed countries freely, which was a helpfully high figure.[15] Unfortunately, however, the remaining industrial-country protection is believed to cost the LDCs about 3% of their GDP according to the World

---

*Adrian Wood, "How Much Does Trade with the South Affect Workers in the North?" *World Bank Research Observer* 6, no. 1 (January 1991): 19–36. True, foreign trade may prompt developed-country businesses to raise their productivity in a defensive reaction, so the real effect of imports from the LDCs is presumably larger than indicated here. But the effect is still small, unlikely to be responsible for causing more than 0.5% of the labor force per year to change jobs compared to about 20% of the labor force that changes jobs every year from all causes, as Wood points out.

CHILD LABOR

An outcry against the exploitation of child labor has become part of the debate on developed-country trade with the LDCs. The International Labor Office states that 58 million children work for wages in the LDCs. Fair-minded people agree on the undesirability and even horror of children working in "dark satanic mills." Yet they are also uncomfortable about erecting trade barriers in the developed countries to exclude goods made by child labor because using protection would probably make things worse for the children. They would have to work in industries that produce for the domestic market, and they would presumably earn less. Or they would beg, or engage in prostitution, or starve. There is a danger that special interests seeking trade barriers will

> seek to use human rights as just another way to raise old-fashioned barriers against poor countries' exports, caring little for human rights, caring nothing for the plight of the third world's poor, caring nothing for the freedoms of industrial-country consumers. The argument is ugly—but it will run and run.[16]

Would it not be better to leave the question of child labor to the UN's International Labor Office, rather than to ban imports of goods made by child labor, so making the children worse off? Perhaps.

Bank. For some LDCs, the costs range up to 9% of their GDP.[17] A reduction in developed-country protection would clearly increase the chances for export-led development in the LDCs.

Tariff Issues

Developed-country tariffs have come down considerably since World War II. But there are remaining "peaks" or "spikes"—some high tariff rates among many lower ones—on numerous goods, usually labor-intensive ones, of great interest to the LDCs. In this group are footwear, textiles and clothing, color television sets, and agricultural products.

Effective Protection LDCs face a problem of "effective protection," often called "tariff escalation." The nominal or apparent tariff rate—5% on widgets, for example—may differ substantially from the effective or actual rate.[18] Let us explain why this is so with a tale of the tariff on pearls. The nominal rate on strung pearls imported into the United States used to be about 50%, thus amounting to $50 on a necklace that could be purchased abroad in Greece for $100. There was no tariff at all on raw pearls. Boring the pearls and stringing them added only about $1 to their value. No sane Greek exporter would ever be willing or able to pay a $50 tariff on the strung pearls because that would be a tax of $50 on just $1 of value added for the stringing.[19] The tariff on the strung pearls was "effectively" 5000%, enormously higher than the 50% nominal rate. The processing of a raw material or semifinished commodity would not occur in the exporting country under these conditions. All processing

THE GENERALIZED SYSTEM OF PREFERENCES

For a long time, the LDCs have been granted certain tariff preferences by the developed countries. An outcome of much publicized negotiations in the 1970s, the Generalized System of Preferences (GSP) was a primary aim of LDC policymakers. It is also constantly held up as a major concession by the rich nations. The European Community (EC or Common Market) first offered GSP in 1971. The United States began its GSP with a ten-year plan inaugurated on January 1, 1976, the nineteenth industrial country to do so. This law was renewed in 1985, for eight-and-a-half more years. When it expired on July 4, 1993, another renewal was difficult because Congress did not want to give up any further tariff revenue. A renewal of only 15 months until early 1995 was all that could be negotiated.[20] Eventually over 4000 products imported from the LDCs were covered by the variants on the GSP established by almost all of the industrial countries. By increasing the return on exports from LDCs, the GSP increased trade—though the effect has been relatively small, probably not more than about 2%. Even so, the GSP has probably contributed to faster economic growth.[21]

In spite of the growth in trade that did occur, there is no escaping the fact that GSP has been a disappointment. Developed countries unilaterally reserved the right to remove the preferences, both by commodity and by country. From the start, the EC excluded all primary products (a serious blow) and base metals to the ingot stage, plus a long list of manufactures and semi-manufactures that made up over three-fifths of the dutiable imports from LDCs to the EC. The United States always excluded textiles, clothing, shoes, some electronic goods, some steels, watches, and glassware, the first four of these especially important to many LDCs. Goods could also be removed from the preferential list; the United States did so a number of times. In the United States, automatic exclusion was built in under the "competitive need" formula, applied when 50% of the total imports of a product came from one country or when imports of a product reached a certain dollar figure ($97 million annually in 1991, the figure adjusted every year). If the president determines that a GSP country is more competitive than other beneficiaries, then this competitive need limit is reduced even more to just $37.5 million or 25% of total imports. About half of the trade that would otherwise have been eligible does not get U.S. GSP treatment because of these limits.

Moreover, the president can "graduate" a country, declaring it ineligible for GSP treatment because of its successful development. Taiwan, South Korea, Hong Kong, and Singapore, four of the five countries that had garnered the greatest benefits from GSP, were eliminated from the U.S. program in 1989, drastically reducing its importance. This was a discretionary decision—the law does not require graduation until per capita income reaches $8500 in 1985 dollars indexed to the rate of U.S. economic growth. Bahrain, Bermuda, Nauru, and Brunei have been graduated this way. (Arguably, graduation is eminently reasonable policy. A country deserves more normal treatment and full incorporation into the regular system when it becomes rich.) In 1993, imports entering duty free were $19.5 billion, which was 16% of all imports from eligible countries and 3.4% of all U.S. imports. The top four—Mexico, Malaysia, Thailand, and Brazil—accounted for over half of the GSP imports in that year.[22] The EC has also slashed preferences for a similar group of countries. Politics involving Communist insurgencies or oil embargoes often led to the removal of countries from the eligible list.

Further clauses in the U.S. law allow the president to cancel the preferences if a beneficiary fails to provide reasonable access to its markets and require recipients to assure "internationally recognized worker rights," including trade unions and "acceptable" conditions of work. GSP can also be denied for noncooperation with drug policies. Among the countries that have lost their U.S. GSP treatment for these reasons are Burma/Myanmar, the Central African Republic, Chile, Mauritania, Nicaragua, Paraguay, Romania, and Sudan. The AFL-CIO files numerous petitions to remove GSP preferences, with pending cases against the Dominican Republic and Malaysia in 1994.[23]

The uncertainty as to what countries and what goods will be covered and for how long, has very likely cut investment in the Third World that would otherwise have occurred to take advantage of GSP. Notice that none of this maze of exceptions and limitations would have been possible had tariffs simply been reduced across the board. In that case, the ancient rule of "most favored nation" would have applied, meaning that no country can be specially discriminated against and all must receive the same benefits as the most favored trading partner. There seems little doubt that further tariff cuts, as in the Uruguay Round, make more economic sense than does the GSP. Such cuts are permanent, whereas all GSP programs include time limits.

Probably the vast attention given to GSP in the past two decades was misplaced. It made the developed countries feel better, and it convinced the LDCs they had won a battle for a concession even while putting them at risk of being pushed politically by threats of removing the benefits. The broad decline in tariffs negotiated over the years within GATT has brought much greater gains to LDCs than GSP ever did, and the Uruguay Round tariff cuts will continue these gains. The tariff cutting clearly serves to reduce the importance of GSP. If a recommendation may be made, it would be to phase out the preferences and their associated restrictions and discrimination, include the LDCs as full partners in world trade, and replace the GSP with further general tariff cuts.

would take place in the importing country. The conclusion is that whenever the rate of duty is higher on finished commodities than it is on raw materials or semifinished goods, the exporting country will be less likely to undertake the processing, even if otherwise that country would have a strong comparative advantage in doing so.

A formula to calculate the degree of effective protection is

$$\textit{Effective rate of protection} = \frac{(y - b) - (x - a)}{x - a}$$

where x is the international price of the finished commodity, y is the domestic price of the finished commodity, a is the international price of the imported component, and b is the domestic price, including the tariff, of the imported component.

TABLE 15.2 TARIFF ESCALATION IN THE 1980s: AVERAGE DEVELOPED-COUNTRY TARIFFS, PERCENT

Coffee	6.8	Processed coffee	9.4
Cocoa	2.6	Chocolate	11.8
Rubber	2.3	Rubber articles	6.7
Hides and skins	0.0	Leather goods	8.2
Semimanufactured wood	1.8	Furniture	6.6

Source: WDR 1987, 138.

For ease of calculation, say the tariff on strung pearls is only $1; the stringing of $100 worth of pearls also costs $1, and there is no duty on raw pearls. In this case the nominal tariff is 1%, but the effective tariff through escalation is

$$\frac{(102 - 100) - (101 - 100)}{101 - 100} = \frac{1}{1} = 100\%$$

How easy it would be to dismiss a 1% tariff; but 100% is a different story. The examples in Table 15.2 show some of the many examples where average tariff rates are higher for processed items than for raw materials, meaning high effective protection for the processing.

In 1987, the overall average tariff rate for the industrial countries was 0.3% on raw materials, 4% on semifinished manufactures, and 6.5% on finished manufactures.[24] There are egregious examples.[25] The EC duty on fresh mangoes is 7%, on canned mangoes it is 30%, and on mango juice it is 40%. Peanuts enter the EC free of duty, but peanut butter pays a 17% tariff. Japan allows cocoa beans entry without tariff, but charges 27.4% on chocolate. The United States has no duty on hides and skins, but puts a 14.4% charge on leather goods. Thus even though average nominal tariffs are now quite low, tariff escalation still exists, and the LDCs have a legitimate complaint. The chances for these countries to process commodities when there is a comparative advantage in doing so are reduced. (There is no reason to believe that any conspiratorial malevolence against the LDCs has caused this, incidentally. It is obvious that developed-country manufacturers would lobby for low tariffs on inputs and high tariffs on output.)

More local processing of primary products could generate substantial earnings for the LDCs. An UNCTAD study using data from the 1970s puts the potential increase for ten important commodities at one-and-a-half times the value of the unprocessed commodities themselves, not far below the value of all foreign aid.[26] More recently, the World Bank stated that removal of tariffs from processing by the developed countries would increase such activity by about 80% in the case of coffee, by 76% for wool, and by 52% for cocoa.[27]

Developed-Country Tariffs and the Uruguay Round A major decline in tariffs was agreed on in the Uruguay Round, and benefits will accrue to the LDCs that export manufactured goods. Industrial countries will cut their tariffs on manufactured goods by about 40% in five equal annual steps starting in 1995. Tariffs will be completely eliminated in ten product sectors, raising the overall percentage of duty-free trade from 20% to 43%. The weighted average tariff on manufactures will go from slightly over 6% to just under 4%. Tariff escalation will continue to be a problem however, interfering with the processing of raw materials in the LDCs.

Nontariff Barriers (NTBs) in Manufactures

Nontariff barriers in the developed countries have hit LDCs' exports of manufactured goods hard. NTBs are quota-type arrangements, either in the form of a normal quota imposed by the importing country or voluntary export restraints (VERs). VERs are analytically quite similar to quotas, except that the import licenses awarded under a quota become export licenses usually allocated to foreign producers by the foreign government that agreed to the VER. Of the 284 known VERs at the start of 1991, 121 were aimed at LDCs.[28] In the late 1980s, they covered about a quarter of the products exported by the LDCs, slightly more than the impact on developed-country exports.[29]

Economic theory indicates clearly that quotas and VERs, inflexible and bringing no tariff revenue to the country where imports are limited, are more damaging than tariffs. Quotas are more profitable for producers receiving the protection whenever demand rises or supply falls, and they have the ability to convert potential monopoly power into actual monopoly power. Because the licenses to import are usually given away, what would have been tariff revenue usually accrues to importing firms lucky enough to obtain a share of the quota. In a VER, the country whose exporters are restraining themselves can sell their products at a higher price within the protected market. They collect what would have been the tariff revenue. Either way, quotas and VERs carry greater welfare losses for consumers than do tariffs.

Several of the most stringent NTBs are directed explicitly at manufactured goods such as textiles, clothing, leather goods, shoes, some electronic goods, wood products, paper, glass products, electrical equipment, and transport equipment, in many lines of which the LDCs appear to have a comparative advantage. Steel, produced efficiently by some more advanced LDCs, also faces high trade barriers. It is clear enough that the main reason this is so is because the LDCs have less bargaining capacity and ability to defend themselves in trade battles than do important developed countries.

The Multi-Fiber Arrangement in Textiles and Clothing The harm to the LDCs is undoubtedly greatest in the area of textiles and clothing; the most interesting and important trade restrictions concern these products.[30] The products make up 10% of world trade, about a quarter of the total manufactured exports of non-oil LDCs and nearly a third of their exports to developed countries. In numerous LDCs, textiles and clothing together are the largest nonagricultural export and provider of employment.

The LDCs have a healthy comparative advantage in the many lines of production where low labor costs are crucial and rapid delivery is not important, But it is also clear that these are areas of very long-lasting protection against them, with high barriers against textile and clothing imports and with an extremely well-organized political lobby devoted to keeping them in place. Because of this protection specifically directed against the LDCs, their share in the exports of these products has grown much more slowly than the share of the developed world.

A Multi-Fiber Arrangement (MFA) was first cobbled together in 1974, the name indicating that it applies to fiber made from, cotton, wool, and synthetics. Textiles and clothing had been protected for many years before the arrangement was negotiated. Several renewals have taken place. Under the terms of the agreement came hundreds of bilateral, and sometimes unilateral, VERs and quotas that limit the growth of exports. For example, textile and clothing imports from Hong Kong, South Korea, and Taiwan are limited under the MFA to increases of just 1% per year. These limits on trade in textiles and clothing apply only to the LDCs but not to the developed countries (except Japan). With that single exception, the MFA does not control the exports of the developed countries.

The MFA has now grown to a labyrinthine complexity of 69 clauses, some 20,000 annexes, and about 3000 bilateral quotas on different countries and products within the arrangement. Taking U.S. agreements as an example, the MFA covered imports from 48 countries in 1991, including Guam, which is U.S. territory![31] Each agreement covers a wide range of individual items, with some countries subject to over 100 categories of restraint. Underutilized product quotas cannot be transferred to other products or other countries, so the MFA is more restrictive than it otherwise appears. The MFA's mass of impenetrable detail means that even when imports would otherwise be permitted, great uncertainty faces exporters. As an example of what can happen, in 1987 a U.S. government computer error caused the publication of information that the quota on Chinese-made cotton coats was still open. When the error was discovered, the quota was immediately closed, and importers who acted on the incorrect information suffered serious loss when they had to renege on their contracts. The enormous complexity creates uncertainties that undoubtedly have their worst effect on small suppliers with limited expertise and potential exporters who are discouraged.

An IMF study indicates that complete liberalization of the MFA would allow developing countries to raise their textile exports by 82% and their clothing exports by 93%. The cost of the MFA to the LDCs is estimated at about $50 billion per year, or about the same as the total flow of foreign assistance.[32] The most efficient producers, the very ones that have signified their belief in trade, not aid, are the most penalized.

The Uruguay Round and NTBs The Uruguay Round represents a major advance for the LDCs in the area of NTBs.[33] All VERs will be eliminated at the start of 1999, with the exception of one grandfathered VER for each member that will be allowed to extend for one more year. The MFA is subject to special rules. It will be phased out in four stages over ten years, a shorter period than the 15 years originally favored by the United States. Current permitted growth rates of products that stay controlled by quotas during the ten-year period will be raised in three stages, first by 16%, then 25%, and then 27%. Importing countries will determine the order in which products are liberalized. Tariffs on textiles and clothing will remain high, with more than 25% of the imports of these products subject to duties of over 15%.[34]

Unfair Trade Practices

As other trade barriers have declined, a group of protective measures that allow tariffs to be imposed against "unfair trade practices" has assumed new significance. These practices include dumping and subsidies. Charges of dumping and subsidization have become an effective way to harass potential LDC exporters and a major route to protection for industries in developed countries.

Dumping Laws The first of the unfair trade practices is dumping, originally defined as selling abroad at a price below that in the home market.[35] The United States extended the definition in 1974 to encompass sales below cost of production; other countries are also adopting this extended definition. Under the U.S. antidumping statutes, when dumping is proven, the Department of Commerce applies an antidumping duty as an offset. The president has no discretion to interfere.

Numerous but obscure regulations and rulings have been adopted that make it ever easier to prove that dumping is occurring.* Producers in the developed countries have also come to see that they can harass foreign competitors by bringing dumping charges even if in the end the government determines that dumping is not occurring. Protectionist interests fully exploit the provisions in the U.S. law that accused firms receive no reimbursement for a successful defense against the charges, and nondumping firms from any given country get hit with antidumping investigations right along with the guilty parties. Indeed, over a third of all antidumping investigations find that no dumping has occurred.[36]

Not surprisingly, as the possibilities for protection through this route were understood, a large increase in the number of antidumping cases occurred. At the start of 1994, of the 57 countries affected by U.S. antidumping duties, 32 were LDCs.[37] The EC, Australia, and Canada use this tool with special frequency against the LDCs, though Japan's dumping law is rarely used against anybody.

Most economists would find it reasonable to retaliate against dumping when that tactic is used to run domestic firms out of business and then boost prices to claim the monopoly rewards. This practice is rare, however, because there would have to be international, not just national, monopoly power and because the high prices would stimulate domestic competition once again. There is no doubt that even when not predatory, the idea of charging a lower price abroad than at home does seem to violate the producers' sense of fair play. But why is nonpredatory dumping thought to be so bad if a foreign firm charges more at home because it has some monopoly power there? Is it sensible to claim that others, too, should pay monopoly prices for the product? And why is it argued that sales below average cost are "unfair" when

*Among the U.S. rules are the following: Transport costs, distribution costs, and tariffs are not counted in the U.S. price; any sales of the import above the U.S. price are ignored; even tiny differences in price can trigger a dumping charge; foreign firms can subtract distribution costs only up to the amount of such costs in the United States, even if they are higher abroad; and changes in the exchange rate must immediately be reflected in the U.S. price no matter what that would do to sales of the imported good. For a more detailed treatment, see Brown and Hogendorn, *International Economics: Theory and Context*, chapter 7.

domestic firms very often do exactly that, on a massive scale, during a recession?* Add the thought that dumping, however nasty the word, does benefit consumers by bringing lower prices, and a conclusion emerges: The concept of the antidumping laws in the United States and other developed countries is fundamentally unsound.

The Uruguay Round and Dumping Law The Uruguay Round will not cause much change in the dumping laws. Now the margin of dumping must be more than 2% of the export product price for antidumping duties to be imposed, and the total amount of imports from the dumping country must be at least 3% of total imports of the product into the country bringing the charge. There is also now a five-year sunset clause, so that antidumping duties must be reexamined rather than being kept in place forever. These measures represent progress. But, disquietingly, VERs—which otherwise are slated to disappear—will still be allowed in settlement of dumping cases.[38]

Countervailing Duties Against Subsidies Countervailing duties against subsidies are another remedy for an unfair trade practice.[39] Recently, U.S. firms have been bringing many cases under laws dating back to 1897. These laws require a countervailing duty to be imposed when proof is forthcoming that a foreign government is subsidizing exports to the United States or, under the amendment of 1922, is granting domestic subsidies to a selected industry or group of industries. As with antidumping duties, the president has no discretion to interfere. Most other major countries have similar laws, but countervailing duties are most used by the United States. Even tiny subsidies (as low as 0.75% in a case involving Thailand) could trigger an investigation and prosecution, and the law does not take into account whether the United States is also subsidizing the same good.†

Over the years, the definition of a subsidy expanded, amoeba-like. Cases were brought against regional development subsidies for poor areas of a country (even though the cost of production might be very high in these areas because of a lack

---

*A new departure has been to use the dumping laws against countries such as China where average cost is impossible to establish directly because market pricing is not used. In recent cases, the Chinese cost of production was established by proxy, estimated by what it would have been if the product had been produced in some other country. For Chinese paintbrushes, 27% dumping was found by using a Sri Lankan firm as the proxy. In steel wire nails, South Korea was the surrogate. Malaysia and the Republic of Guinea were used for Chinese wax candles; Pakistan for steel; Paraguay for menthol; and a weighted figure for Japan, Canada, Switzerland, Germany, the Netherlands, and France for porcelain-on-steel cooking ware. Because labor costs in all these other countries are higher than China's, sometimes very much so, the results seem irrelevant and the method badly flawed.

†For example, Argentine wool growers have been hit by a U.S. countervailing duty after a finding of a 6% subsidy, even though Argentina was levying a 17% export tax and even though U.S. wool growers get direct government payments that boost the return to wool growing by about 50%. A countervailing duty was imposed against imports of rice from Thailand after various subsidies were found, including some price support, mortgage assistance, discounts to rice millers, and government assistance to cooperatives. But at the same time Thailand was collecting a large export tax that was over five times as high as the subsidy, and the United States was paying large export subsidies to its own rice farmers. The U.S. program was transferring over $1 million per year to the average American grower, while the Thai program was transferring about $100 to the average Thai farmer per year before payment of the export tax. James Bovard, "The Myth of Fair Trade," 9–10.

of infrastructure), against low prices for government-owned resources such as timber, against subsidized inputs even though the offending product itself was not subsidized, and against subsidies that had effect only on sales to other countries, not the country bringing the charge (the justification being that export sales would be lost). About the only subsidies that the courts generally found could not be prosecuted were "generally available" ones applying to all industries, such as government-funded health care for workers. The justification for not attacking such subsidies was that they would tend to make all exports cheaper to foreign buyers, meaning that the demand for the exporting country's currency will rise, so appreciating the value of that currency and offsetting the subsidy.

Many subsidy cases involve the LDCs—22 of the 34 countries affected by U.S. countervailing duties at the start of 1994 were in that category.[40] The countervailing duties affect a wide range of commodities, including bricks, cement, tile, steel, chemicals, clothing, and lime. Australia, Canada, and the EC also have countervailing duty laws, but these are used less frequently than is U.S. law. The Japanese law is almost never enforced.

Most economists would probably agree that there is an element of unfairness when exports caused by long-term subsidies harm domestic firms. They would note, however, that there is a world of difference between a subsidy designed to allow the controlled running down of a declining industry or to compensate for some government regulation such as above-market minimum wage laws, and a subsidy designed to increase market share at the expense of other producers. All are treated alike under the law, however.

The Uruguay Round and Countervailing Duties The Uruguay Round trade negotiations clarified some of these issues, and the LDCs emerged in a better position than was the case with the dumping laws.[41] The agreement divides subsidies into prohibited, actionable, and nonactionable. Export subsidies contingent on export performance and subsidies contingent on using locally produced goods are prohibited, though low-income LDCs with per capita incomes under $1000 can continue to use these for eight years after 1995. General export subsidies are prohibited as well, with the exception that the low-income LDCs can continue to use them. As the agreement notes, "subsidies are recognized as a legitimate tool of economic development." Subsidies paid on output or inputs are defined as actionable if they distort trade or production; a subsidy exceeding 5% of the cost of the product, or covering the loss of making the product will establish a presumption of distortion. Nonactionable subsidies are defined as aid for research and development expenses up to 75% of industrial research costs and 50% of "precompetitive development activity" up to the first noncommercial prototype; aid to disadvantaged regions if this aid is generally available in these regions; and aid to lessen environmental consequences up to 20% of the costs of doing so. A sunset clause is imposed on countervailing duties after five years of use. (Subsidies and export subsidies for agricultural products are treated quite differently, as is discussed below.)

In general, the developing countries have agreed to phase out subsidies when they are no longer needed for development or for competitive purposes, although there is no stated procedure for doing so.[42]

Other Unfair Trade Practices In the United States, prosecutions of several other examples of unfair trade practices have recently been emphasized. Under Section 337 of the U.S. trade act, goods can be excluded if they violate patents, infringe copyrights and trademarks, or involve false labeling. Of the 51 outstanding Section 337 exclusions at the start of 1994, 39 were against LDCs, with Taiwan and Hong Kong most heavily represented. The United States has also become aggressive in responding to what it perceives as foreign government actions limiting access to markets or involving unfair competition under provisions concerning violation of trade agreements (Section 301 and Super 301). Among the LDCs recently investigated under Section 301 are Argentina, Brazil, China, India, South Korea, and Thailand.

Admittedly, the infringement cases have represented a real and growing problem, and the Section 301 cases have been limited in number and directed toward especially serious examples of foreign trade policies that seem to go beyond normal infant-industry protection. They do, however, represent yet another route by which developed-country trade barriers could intensify.

Uruguay Round Advances Under the Uruguay Round, several new regulations were adopted. Patent protection will be generally extended for 20 years, which was a victory for the developed countries, traded by the LDCs against their gains elsewhere in the agreement.[43] In another gain for the developed countries, computer software will be protected as literary works under the Berne Convention on copyrights.

Agricultural Protection

Just as manufactured goods must contend with protectionist barriers, so must agricultural and mineral commodities, though usually only when developed countries also produce the item in question.[44] Of course, LDCs will never be able to compete in some temperate zone crops for reasons of climate, and many LDC commodity exports face little or no competition from developed-country producers, and therefore encounter no trade barriers at all. In between the commodities that LDCs do not produce and those on which there is no protection is an area of competition in which LDCs with a comparative advantage could gain from trade in the absence of barriers. Major protection against imports from the LDCs occurs against sugar, peanuts and peanut oil, beef, cotton, tobacco, and fresh fruits and vegetables.

Developed-country trade barriers are erected because they are needed to maintain the structure of agricultural price supports. Governments that buy a portion of the crop to keep prices high for farmers know that without protection, there would be a huge influx of foreign imports. They generally have used quotas for this purpose, permissible because of a GATT rule exemption covering agricultural quotas dating from 1955 and instigated by the United States. The pattern of this protection differs significantly among the developed countries.

U.S. Trade Barriers in Agriculture The United States has significant barriers against trade in agricultural commodities. U.S. cotton quotas virtually exclude imports of upland cotton, which are limited to 28,000 bales, or about 0.002% of the market. (The higher cost of the protected cotton is one reason why the textile industry has sought the barriers against LDC exports discussed in the previous chapter.) Peanuts receive virtually ironclad protection, with the import quota on them, unchanged since 1953, amounting to 775 metric tonnes which is 0.00055% of the market. The butter and cheese quotas are also extremely restrictive, with possible producers face a quota equivalent to 0.06% of U.S. butter production and cheese quotas of 0.3% to 14% of U.S. production, depending on the type of cheese. Beef is subject to quotas figured on a base adjusted for cyclical domestic production. Although restrictions have not usually been applied in recent years, strict quotas come into force when imports exceed a certain trigger level, causing some countries "voluntarily" to limit their exports.

The U.S. sugar quotas have the worst effect on the LDCs because sugarcane can be grown efficiently in at least 100 countries, some of them very poor and with no other good export opportunities.[45] Sugar refining may be the start of industrialization; long-run prospects are promising because of the high income elasticity of demand in LDCs. U.S. quotas, which date in their modern form from 1982, keep U.S. prices at about 22¢ per pound, often double or triple the world price.[*] The U.S. sugar program is estimated to have reduced world sugar prices by 21% to 33%. The disastrous result for exporters of sugar to the United States was that their earnings, about $2 billion in 1981, were only $390 million in 1987. Half or more of the workers in the sugar industry lost their jobs in some Caribbean countries (the Dominican Republic, St. Kitts-Nevis). U.S. consumers pay approximately $3.2 billion more, or about $100 extra for a family of four, for their sugar, equivalent to a 92% tax. It is estimated that the 12,600 U.S. growers glean over $260,000 per grower from this system, with the biggest producers collecting the biggest benefits (an average of $1.6 million per producer in Florida). Six large companies own all the Florida mills. No wonder sugar producers are the third largest contributors of funds in American politics, behind only lawyers and doctors.

Not only does protection keep some commodities out, lowering the revenues that can be earned by the LDCs, but subsidies are paid on the export of some items, so lowering LDC sales further yet. High cotton, rice, and beef export subsidies are cases in point.

Japanese Agricultural Protection Japan's agriculture is heavily protected, with the costs of the protection amounting to more than half the value of total farm output, about 2% of GDP. Wheat is 11 times more expensive than world prices, some cuts of steak sell in Japan for ten times the price in U.S. supermarkets, and strict limits on sugar imports raise the domestic selling price in a range usually two to three times over the world price. Rice is the most famous case, with farmers receiving eight to

[*]A GATT panel ruled the sugar quotas illegal in 1989. The United States changed the rules somewhat, adopting a tariff-quota scheme that took effect in 1990. Imported sugar beyond a quota of 1.725 million metric tons is now charged a tariff of 16¢ per pound. Imports did not increase much; the change was mostly "window dressing" to stay within the GATT rules.

nine times the world price, though consumers pay less (about six times) because of expensive rice subsidies. The very high prices for these products, due to price support programs, in turn necessitate barriers against imports that would otherwise flood in. (Rice imports, for example, have been completely forbidden for many years.)

EC Agricultural Protection The most costly protection is in the EC, under the Common Agricultural Policy (CAP).[46] The EC's principal tool is the simple purchase of surpluses at a floor price; until very recently there have been few provisions for controls on acreage and production. The main protected products of interest to the LDCs are wheat, dairy products, beef, wine, and sugar, especially the latter. All are about 30% to 60% higher in price within the EC than their price in world trade. Over half the value added in farming comes from the CAP. To maintain the supports, imports must of course be restricted. This is accomplished by quotas and by the so-called variable levy, a tariff that rises when world prices fall and vice versa.

Thus protected, the EC pursues its purchases to maintain price, with farm surpluses the inevitable result. Some of the "mountains" of surplus commodities were at record highs in the early 1990s, as shown in Table 15.3. About a quarter of the EC's farmland produces nothing but this surplus.

The EC has subsidized the export of its surpluses to world markets, where the commodities are sold in competition with domestic production and the exports of other countries.[47] The general result is that the EC's share of all world food exports, less than 3% in 1970, and still only 8.3% in 1976, was 18.3% by 1981. The EC is now the world's largest agricultural exporter, having passed the United States in 1986. A net importer of dairy products, sugar, and beef as late as 1974, it is now the world's largest exporter of dairy products, poultry, eggs, and veal, vies with Argentina for the number-two position as a beef exporter, and is number three in wheat. Instead of being a net importer of sugar, as it was in the early 1970s, the EC is now the free world's largest exporter of that commodity, produced from sugar beets. The subsidies have serious repercussions as prices are forced down for local farmers in importing countries and as other exporters lose their markets. For the LDCs, the whole episode amounts to being kicked when you are down. Not only are markets lost because of the protection, but the subsidized EC exports capture other markets outside the Community. The United States retaliated with some subsidies of its own, to which the EC often counter-retaliated. World prices were forced lower yet, and LDC exporters were harmed even more than before.

The clear result of the widespread protection of developed-country agriculture is harm for the LDCs in their export markets, and harm to their domestic production as well, because commodity prices are pushed lower by the developed-country export subsidies. Thus the wide web of price support and income maintenance for developed-country farmers not only involves extreme expense for the consumers there but also unforgivably holds back the prospects for the world's poor farmers. (Admittedly, LDC consumers get the advantage of lower prices.)

The Uruguay Round and Agriculture The difficulties in reaching agreement on agricultural trade were the major cause of the long delay in completing the

TABLE 15.3 SIZE OF EC SURPLUS COMMODITY "MOUNTAINS" AND WINE "LAKE"

Cereal grains	18.0 million metric tons (record high)
Beef	0.7 million metric tons (record high)
Butter	0.3 million metric tons
Milk powder	0.3 million metric tons
Wine	80.0 million liters

Source: EC Commission. The figures are for January 1991. In recent years a combination of some CAP reforms, a U.S. drought, but mostly redoubled efforts to subsidize the export of the mountains brought large falls in some of the figures. Butter, for example, had been as high as 1.2 million metric tons in 1987, while wine was 740 million liters in 1988.

Uruguay Round. They came close to wrecking the negotiations entirely. In the end, a substantial advance was made that should be beneficial to LDC exporters.[48]

The *market access agreement* requires all countries to convert their agricultural trade barriers to tariffs. The developed countries will be required to reduce their tariffs by 36% on average over six years, 1995 to 2000, with a minimum 15% reduction for each product. A minimum of 3% of the domestic market in 1995 and 5% in 2000 must consist of imports. The rules for LDCs are less stringent. They must transform their barriers into tariffs, then reduce by 24% over ten years, 1995 to 2004. Their guaranteed minimum access is 3% of the domestic market in 1995 and 5% in 2004. The lowest-income countries will not be required to make any reduction at all, though their barriers will have to be turned into tariffs.

Special import access rules were negotiated in specific cases for "developing-country dietary staples." A minimum access of 1% of domestic access must be allowed initially, rising by 0.25% per year to 2% in 1998 and 4% in 2004. The rule applies, for example, to South Korea's rice market. Japan was also allowed to have the special rule for rice, rising from 4% in 1995 to 8% in 2000. After that, the market would be open but a high declining tariff would apply.

A *domestic support agreement* will require developed countries to reduce their domestic agricultural subsidies by 20% over six years 1995 to 2000 from a 1986 to 1988 base period. For LDCs, the reduction is 13.3% over ten years, 1995 to 2004. The lowest-income countries will not be required to reduce their subsidies, though they must cap their level of support.

An *export subsidies agreement* requires a reduction of 36% in the value of export subsidies and 21% in the volume of goods benefiting from such subsidies by 2000 compared to a base of 1986 to 1990. The reductions have to apply to each product group; they are not just an average. For LDCs, the percentages are 23% and 14% for ten years, 1995 to 2004. The lowest-income countries are exempt from these rules.

The liberalization of agricultural trade will greatly help the exporters of Latin America and Asia. Argentina presently loses more from overseas agricultural protection ($2.4 billion) than it does from debt service as one of the hardest-hit participants in the debt crisis. Thailand should benefit from a large rise in rice exports to Japan. Africa, however, is likely to lose because food prices there have been pushed quite low by the subsidized exports of the developed countries. These prices will rise somewhat.[49]

The LDCs Made Concessions in the Uruguay Round

In the Uruguay Round, the LDCs made significant concessions to the developed countries. At least they called them concessions, though the steps would have been beneficial to the LDCs even if they had been undertaken unilaterally.

Tariffs and NTBs The LDCs themselves maintain many barriers to trade.[50] In 1987, the average tariff in the LDCs was 32%, much higher than the average in the developed countries. The highest regional protection was in South Asia, at 77%. Maximum tariffs in the range of 100% to 150% are not uncommon. LDCs also apply NTBs to over a quarter of their imports (28% in 1987). Quota coverage is often even greater than this, over 50% of all imports in India, Pakistan, Latin America, and Africa.[51] Tariff escalation, discussed earlier in the chapter, is pronounced in many LDCs just as it is in developed countries; imported inputs to manufacturing are often allowed in duty-free, so causing the escalation.*

As a result of the Uruguay Round, LDCs will drop their tariffs significantly, many by more than the developed countries, as shown in Table 15.4.

The decrease in the LDCs' own trade barriers is more than a quid pro quo for reduced developed-country barriers. It will also help to expand South–South trade in manufactures, processed food, beverages, and semifinished materials. With growing prosperity in the LDCs, markets there will enlarge, benefiting not just themselves but also the developed countries that will find new markets for their exports.

Services and the LDCs LDCs are becoming ever more avid in protecting against imports of services as these have become easier to buy abroad.[52] For example, foreign insurance, banking, transport, communications, computer hardware and software, and professional services such as auditing and accounting are sometimes excluded from the LDCs even when the developed countries have an obvious and large comparative advantage in them. But services are necessary to development. Without them, manufacturing cannot be supported, and specialization cannot be as great.

Allowing the importation of such services as insurance, banking, transport, communications, and professional work obviously brings pause to many politicians in the LDCs who consider services to be quite "intrusive" from a cultural and political point of view. Services may therefore be kept off limits to foreigners even though free trade would appear to give cheaper access to them.

There are numerous examples. Brazil jealously guards its information and technology sector. Major international disputes have erupted around its protec-

*Another problem is that the collection of tariffs by customs officials in the LDCs is often corrupt. Recently nearly 30 countries were using private customs agents for preshipment inspection of their imports in the exporting country (say, on the docks in London or New York) to counter border fraud and stop capital flight. The practice also has the effect of cutting customs delays, in Indonesia from 40 days to three. The cost of the private services is about 1% of the value of the goods they check. For an article on the subject, see William van Raab, "Pre-Shipment Inspections: Improved Administration of an International Trade Regime," *Journal of World Trade* 25, no. 5 (October 1991): 87–97.

TABLE 15.4 LDCs TARIFFS, PERCENT

	Before Uruguay Round	After Uruguay Round
Argentina	38	31
Brazil	41	27
Chile	35	25
Colombia	44	35
India	71	32
South Korea	18	8
Malaysia	10	9
Sri Lanka	29	28
Thailand	36	28
Venezuela	50	31

Source: IMF Survey, November 14, 1994.

tionist measures against telephone switching, computers, and software from the United States and elsewhere. In insurance, some LDCs (India for one) do not allow any underwriting of any kind. All exports from and imports to Mexico, among others, must have insurance from domestic underwriters. Only South Korean companies are allowed to write life and fire insurance policies in that nation. About two dozen countries allow foreigners to write coverage only if the type of insurance the foreigner is providing is not available locally. Though a company that can insure cargo could be located anywhere, commonplace local insurance requirements are said at least to double the transport and insurance costs on about half of all imports into the LDCs. Many governments require that exports be insured domestically; some require that *both* imports and exports must be insured that way (for example, Bangladesh, Burundi, Cameroun, Cuba, the Dominican Republic, Malta, Mexico, Rwanda, Senegal, Tanzania). It is a nice problem as to what happens when these countries trade with one another. Reinsurance must be 25% local in Kenya and Turkey, 80% in the Philippines, 100% in Brazil.[53]

In banking, laws that discriminate against foreign banks are commonplace. In Taiwan, for example, foreign banks are prohibited outside Taipei and Kaohsiung and are excluded from the credit card business. Professional services (accounting, legal, and so forth) involve considerable discrimination. Accountants practicing their skills in Brazil must possess a Brazilian degree. In Argentina, Mexico, Peru, and Venezuela local accountants must supervise foreign auditors. No foreign lawyers are permitted to practice in some countries.

Television, advertising, and film may also be heavily protected. Argentina, among others, restricts broadcast of commercials of foreign origin on the television or radio. South Korea prohibits foreign investment in advertising. In Brazil, prints of color feature films must be processed in that country if shown there. Taiwan limits imports of foreign films to six copies each.

In shipping, 15 of the 18 countries that run cargo reservation schemes to help their national carriers are LDCs. More widely, "liner codes" fix market share (40% of cargoes for the exporter, 40% for the importer, and 20% left for free trade), and rates as well. Transport costs from the LDCs can therefore be higher than justified by costs, thereby boosting the prices of imported goods and reducing the price paid for exports.[54] The problem is worse in the least developed countries, especially in Africa and the Caribbean, than it is elsewhere because the lower level of cargo volume attracts less competition from nonscheduled shipping. Efforts to dismantle the monopoly power and encourage competition would seem eminently justified, but the UN Liner Code negotiated in 1974 and in effect from 1983 permits and even encourages continuation of restrictive practices in ocean shipping. Of the 71 countries that had signed by 1988, many were LDCs. It seems a clear case of special interest economics and national prestige (boosted, so it is said, by ships flying one's own flag) winning out over economic efficiency. Similarly, landing rights and airport facilities for the national airline often have priority over those for foreign carriers. Their flights may be legally limited, their ticket counters cramped and ill-lit, and their passengers subjected to more rigorous entry and exit controls.

The General Agreement on Trade in Services Yet there has been growing awareness that an underdeveloped service sector can hinder development. A General Agreement on Trade in Services (GATS) to cover all service trade has been pursued for some years, kept technically separate from the trade talks but held simultaneously in Geneva. The talks have been spurred on by the United States, which is the largest service exporter.* They have proved contentious, with strong opposition especially from Brazil and India.† Eventually the opponents did seem to appreciate that concessions in this area could be exchanged for freer trade in manufactured goods and agricultural commodities. One would have thought that it might also have been persuasive to such countries that poor services such as insurance, banking, telephones, and transportation can clearly damage the prospects for exporting manufactured goods or indeed anything at all. At the same time, it is fair to say that developed-country governments have not generally been very sympathetic toward measures for maintaining cultural independence. A greater degree of tolerance, for example, in attitudes toward television and radio regulation, would increase the chances for a compromise settlement.

There are still many loose ends in the GATS negotiations, with little progress to report in some areas, such as ocean shipping. In these talks, unity among the LDCs splintered. This was perhaps not surprising, as the NICs, the agricultural exporters, and the lowest-income countries all had quite different aims.[55] Negotiations are continuing.

---

*The United States held 11% of the world total of service exports, or $56 billion, in 1987. France was close in second place at $53 billion. Japan was well back at $28 billion.

†Some LDCs, however, have become important exporters of services. South Korea, Singapore, Hong Kong, and Mexico are all in the world's top 20. They do not side with most of the other LDCs.

Further Gains from the Uruguay Round

The Uruguay Round Final Act was signed at Marrakech, Morocco, in April 1994. Ratifications by the national governments involved followed. Only U.S. approval was ever in doubt, but the treaty was ratified by healthy majorities late in the year.

The LDCs stand to gain in particular from the improvement in how disputes are settled under international trade rules. A new World Trade Organization (WTO) succeeded the GATT in 1995. Dispute settlement will be far more automatic than it was. Under the GATT, countries that didn't like a ruling by a GATT settlement panel could simply refuse to accept it, and there the matter would end. Under the WTO, however, panel reports will be speeded up and automatically adopted unless there is a consensus not to or there is an appeal to a new appellate body. The penalty if a country refuses to accept a finding will be suspension of some of the trade concessions already made to it by the offended country.[56] The advantage to LDCs will be that their relative powerlessness in negotiations with large industrial countries will be somewhat offset by the WTO's existence, which will reduce the scope for unilateral action by the large industrial economies.*

Several studies concur that the increase in global real income from the Uruguay Round's full implementation in 2005 will be about 1% of the world's 1992 GDP, assuming implementation in 1995 and completion in 2005.[57] Four separate projections suggest figures for world gains of $212 billion, $213 billion, $230 billion, and $274 billion. Predicted gains for Europe (where the damage from agricultural protection is large) would range from $61 billion to $98 billion; for Japan, the gain would be $27 to $42 billion; for the United States $28 to $67 billion. Merchandise trade is predicted to grow by more than 12% ($745 billion in 1992 dollars) over what would have been the case with present growth rates. All of these developed-country gains will stimulate imports and hence exports from the LDCs.[58] Only one study shows the gains for the LDCs by region, totaling $78 billion in 1992 dollars. This is a net figure. Disaggregating by continents, most of Asia and Latin America are expected to register modest gains, with high-income Asia likely to obtain large gains while Africa will incur a slight loss.[59] The major reason for Africa's loss will be the decline in the subsidization of food exports.

These predicted gains from the Uruguay Round are the outcome of just the tariff and quota reductions. They are an underestimate because some other favorable impacts have been difficult to quantify. They include the elimination of VERs, the more structured treatment of subsidies, the GATS liberalization of trade in services, the freeing of international investment, and improvements in dispute settlement.[60]

*Some U.S. opponents of the treaty claimed that voting in the WTO will be one country, one vote. That is quite true. But that was also the voting method in GATT, where no votes have been undertaken since the late 1950s. Consensus has been the universal method of decision making in GATT, and that will continue as the normal method under the WTO.

The LDCs emerged from the negotiations with concerns of their own. They believe they got no credit during the negotiations for their efforts to reduce foreign exchange controls. Admittedly, overvalued exchange rates can overpower other types of trade barriers, and there is a strong case that exchange rate policies should have been joined with tariff and nontariff policies during the negotiations. Moreover, for years the IMF has required reductions in trade barriers as part of conditionality agreements, and many LDC governments believe they did not get sufficient credit for this either. The LDCs also complain that during the negotiations they did not adequately build coalitions of mutual interest among themselves, link trade and other issues, or bargain as a bloc.

Yet much of the opposition to the agreement in the Third World seems based on nothing more than misinformation. For example, rioters in India charged that the WTO's new rules will cause a cut in farmers' subsidies (not true because India's subsidies are below the threshold), that subsidized ration shops for food will have to be closed (no such rule exists), and that India will become less self-sufficient (true, but remember the gains from trade based on comparative advantage).[61]

CUSTOMS UNIONS TO ENCOURAGE TRADE

Under the rules of international trade, countries can join "customs unions" or "free trade areas" that reduce and eventually eliminate tariffs among the members while maintaining barriers against outsiders. Technically, customs unions and free trade areas are different. In a customs union, the members adopt a "common external tariff" against outsiders. In a free trade area, the members maintain different national barriers. Below, we use the term customs union to describe both sorts of arrangement.

In certain circumstances, customs unions are capable of generating a great increase in trade among their members (called "trade creation" in the literature). Further unilateral reductions in the barriers against the whole world could achieve even more trade creation, but this may not be politically feasible. Some of these unions are among the LDCs themselves, while others are alliances that involve developed countries as well as LDCs.

South–South Customs Unions

It should be understood that in the abstract there is no reason to encourage South–South trade for its own sake. Comparative advantage will work to identify who will be the largest trading partners. In general, one would expect North–South trade to be of greater importance for years to come because factor proportions differ more than in South–South trade; the North offers the larger markets, and LDC protection is higher.[62] However, there is little question that some goods developed for an LDC market will have an appeal for similar market segments in like countries elsewhere and will become profitable exports. Additionally, many LDCs with high trade barriers may find it much easier to grant trade preferences to other LDCs than to lower barriers to the developed countries.

If a customs union with other LDCs is the only politically acceptable way to reduce protection in a country, then the opportunity may well be worth taking because of the scale and learning effects. If groups of LDCs lower barriers against one another, the result can be larger markets, greater economies of scale, more learning by doing, and more diversification of exports. Especially important is that any backwash effect from specializing in primary products might be avoided by diversifying into manufactures for consumption within the union. The great fear is that such mutual lowering of barriers might be trade diverting, with countries buying from LDCs at higher prices what they used to buy from developed countries at lower prices.

A union joining together a number of countries that previously had high tariffs will be most successful when the following six conditions are met.[63]

1. If the elasticity of demand in the member countries is high, a cut in the barriers against fellow members of the customs union will lower prices and cause a large increase in consumption. Much additional trade is generated. The higher the duties in the first place, the more positive the result.
2. If the elasticity of supply in the member countries is high, production within the union will rise rapidly to take the place of the former imports from nonmembers when a demand increase occurs because of the fall in tariffs.
3. If the low-cost producers of any given good also belong to the customs union, there will be only a small sacrifice in shifting trade from nonmembers to members. It follows that the larger the customs union the better, for there is more chance that there will be low-cost producers among the membership, thus lessening the diversion of trade away from cheaper producers on the outside.
4. If the member countries are large, with only a small percentage of their consumption imported, then diversion of trade to a higher-cost source within the union will make little difference.
5. If in negotiating the union the external tariff against outsiders is more or less an average of the previous rates existing in the member countries, then the dispersion of tariffs is likely to be reduced. This is an advantage. When very high and very low tariffs exist together, incentives become skewed toward and away from the various industries concerned. A smaller variation in tariffs means comparative advantage has a greater chance to work.
6. If the union is large enough that its external tariff can affect the world market for an imported item, it may be able to manipulate the tariff to alter the terms of trade in its favor. (It may be able to do the same thing with exports if export taxes are standardized.)

These six conditions are worrisome for the success of LDC customs unions. Consider them one by one. LDC imports often contain a high proportion of essential inputs (capital goods, oil), and demand may be quite inelastic. A low-income economy is an inflexible one; LDCs have more government controls over economic activity, an inadequate infrastructure, low levels of literacy and education, and so forth; supply may be inelastic as a result. Customs unions among LDCs often have a rather limited membership, do not contain low-cost producers of manufactured goods, and consist of relatively small countries. The conclusion is that policymakers must be especially alert to possible trade diversion when preference arrangements are made. Even with all these disadvantages, a union still might be worthwhile if the dynamic effects—economies of scale in intraunion sales, higher investment, improved marketing, a greater spur to productive efficiency, better management, and technical change—are large enough to more than offset the trade diversion. But there is no guarantee that this will be so, and the record of such South–South unions so far has not been particularly encouraging.

A new wave of enthusiasm for South–South unions is sweeping the criticisms away, however, particularly in Latin America and Asia where major countries such as Brazil, Argentina, Malaysia, Thailand, and Indonesia have joined one or another of the unions. An accounting of such unions is contained in Table 15.5

In almost every case progress in these LDC customs unions has come easily at first as the intraunion duties are lowered initially on goods of which there is no local production in any member country. When production already exists in one country but not the others, progress is not so simple. The country with the lead typically wants to eliminate protection rapidly; the others obstruct in the hope that they can catch up; the advance slows. The unions tend to be weakest when the level of industrialization is low, for then new industries do not spring up easily and are high in cost. There is too much chance for trade diversion and monopoly creation. Often enough, the unions have quite high external barriers against outsiders, which increase the chances of trade diversion. As Anne Krueger has written,

> While there is undoubtedly scope for gainful intradeveloping country trade, it seems clear that the type of trade in manufactures that has been encouraged under regional trading arrangements has generally been more the outcome of the import-substitution type of incentives than of the incentives that accompany a genuinely export-oriented trade strategy.[64]

General Trade Preferences Among the LDCs

If they could be arranged, general trade preferences among all LDCs would be more useful than regional preferences. Because the wider the customs union, the less the chances of trade diversion, a super union among the LDCs makes good sense. Negotiations began in 1986 for a global system of trade preferences (GSTP) that would cover both manufactured goods and primary products and involve reductions in both tariffs and nontariff barriers. In 1988, 48 LDCs agreed to establish a GSTP with bilateral deals, most-favored nation treatment for the signatories, safeguard provisions, balance of payments exclusions, and a dispute settlement mechanism. Refik Erzan, Samuel Laird, and Alexander Yeats suggest that duty-free South–South trade might increase 17% above existing levels if a 100% preference is given and NTBs are relaxed, or 8.5% with a 50% margin, or 1% or so with a preference of just 10%.[65] The idea certainly seems better than the present one of regional preference arrangements with high barriers against the outside. A concern about GSTP is that in the short run more of its benefits would probably accrue to the better-off LDCs, especially those in Asia, than to the poorest, especially those in Africa.

Customs Unions with a Rich Patron

A last alternative is for one or more LDCs to join a customs union with one or a group of rich countries. Some of these arrangements are one-way, with the

TABLE 15.5 REGIONAL TRADE ARRANGEMENTS AMONG LESS-DEVELOPED COUNTRIES

KEY TO THE TABLE		
Short Name (Full Name), Year Founded Member Comments	Intraunion trade as % of total (where available) 1960	 1990
AFRICA		
East African Community, 1967 Kenya, Tanzania, Uganda Defunct. At its inception perhaps the most widely discussed of all the efforts to form an economic arrangement outside of Europe. But intractable disputes arose, the community disintegrated, and borders were closed.		
CEEAC (Communauté Economique des Etats de l'Afrique Centrale), 1981 Burundi, Cameroun, Central African Republic, Chad, Congo, Equatorial Guinea, Gabon, Rwanda, São Tomé and Principe, Zaire Name means Economic Community of Central African States. Little success.		
CEAO (Communauté Economique de l'Afrique de l'Ouest), 1974 Benin, Burkina Faso, Côte d'Ivoire, Mali, Mauritania, Niger, Senegal Name means West African Economic Community. Reasonably good performance. A cut in nontariff barriers and an expansion of intraunion trade to 10% have taken place.		
CEPGL (Communauté Economique Pays des Grands Lacs) Burundi, Rwanda, Zaire Name means Economic Community of the Great Lakes States. Has not yet been able to lower barriers.	1.0%*	0.2%†
ECOWAS (Economic Community of West African States), 1976 Benin, Burkina Faso, Cape Verde, Côte d'Ivoire, Gambia, Ghana, Guinea, Guinea-Bissau, Liberia, Mali, Mauritania, Niger, Nigeria, Senegal, Sierra Leone, Togo Was scheduled to abolish all tariffs in 1989, but "progress negligible," and "virtual paralysis in the mutual reduction of trade barriers."[a] Very strict rules of origin are a hindrance. Problems have arisen because the former French colonies in ECOWAS (see the CEAO above) use the strictly managed CFA franc while other members (Ghana, Nigeria, Siena Leone) have had much looser money management and rapid inflation.Also, the CEAO has trade rules not always compatible with those of ECOWAS. The influence of Nigeria grates on the smaller members.	1.2%	5.5%
MRU (Mano River Union), 1973 Guinea, Liberia, Sierra Leone The Mano River touches all three of these West African countries. Rendered ineffective by 1990s civil war in Liberia and armed insurgency in Sierra Leone.	0.2%*	0.3%

TABLE 15.5 REGIONAL TRADE ARRANGEMENTS AMONG LESS-DEVELOPED COUNTRIES *(Continued)*

KEY TO THE TABLE		
Short Name (Full Name), Year Founded Member Comments	Intraunion trade as % of total (where available) 1960	1990
PTA (Preferential Trading Arrangement), 1984 Burundi, Comoros, Djibouti, Ethiopia, Kenya, Lesotho, Malawi, Mauritius, Mozambique, Rwanda, Somalia, Swaziland, Tanzania, Uganda, Zambia, Zimbabwe Full name is Preferential Trading Arrangement for Eastern and Southern African States. Aiming to eliminate tariffs and reduce NTBs by 2000. "Some progress in reducing tariffs."	8.4%	8.5%
SADCC (Southern African Development Coordination Council), 1980 Angola, Botswana, Lesotho, Malawi, Mozambique, Swaziland, Tanzania, Zaire, Zimbabwe More concerned with growth projects than with reductions in trade barriers. Squabbles over its domestic content rules.	2.4%	3.9%
UDEAC (Union Douanière et Economique de l'Afrique Centrale), 1966 Cameroun, Central African Republic, Chad, Congo, Equatorial Guinea, Gabon Name means Central African Customs and Economic Union.One of the oldest of the world's attempts, small, still not properly organized. "Almost complete nonimplementation."	5.0%*	4.6%
Lagos Plan of Action, 1980 All African countries A move to construct a framework to facilitate an eventual African common market. No progress to report.		
ASIA		
ASEAN (Association of Southeast Asian Nations), 1967 Brunei, Indonesia, Malaysia, the Philippines, Singapore, Thailand Move to an Asian Free Trade Area (AFTA) within ASEAN agreed on only in 1993, to take 15 years. NTBs—of which there are many—are not addressed. Now only some 20% of intraregional trade is at preferential rates. Indonesia has high tariffs while Singapore's are virtually zero. Strict rules of origin to qualify for preferences (50% of a given product's value added must be local) limit the benefits yet further. ASEAN's attempts to establish joint ventures are proceeding very slowly, partly due to the opposition of Singapore, which does not approve of protection. Indonesia and the Philippines, the poorest members, are the least inclined to move rapidly. Brunei joined in 1984; 1991 announcement that Burma (Myanmar), Cambodia, Laos, and Vietnam would eventually be allowed to join.	20.7%*	16.6%

TABLE 15.5 REGIONAL TRADE ARRANGEMENTS AMONG LESS-DEVELOPED COUNTRIES *(Continued)*

KEY TO THE TABLE		
Short Name (Full Name), Year Founded Member Comments	Intraunion trade as % of total (where available) 1960	 1990
LATIN AMERICA AND THE CARIBBEAN		
CARICOM (Caribbean Community), 1973 Antigua and Barbuda, Bahamas, Barbados, Belize, Dominica, Grenada, Guyana, Jamaica, Montserrat, St. Kitts-Nevis, St. Lucia, St. Vincent and the Grenadines, Trinidad and Tobago An earlier West Indian Federation fell apart due to internal dissension. Many deadlines missed; FTA in effect 1991; common external tariff not yet adopted.	4.5%	6.3%‡
CACM (Central American Common Market), 1960 Costa Rica, El Salvador, Guatemala, Honduras, Nicaragua Included allocation of industries. Rousing start, with about 95% of items traded having duty-free status by 1969 and intraunion trade reaching 26% of all trade. Trade diversion is believed to have outweighed trade creation, however, with considerable oligopolistic behavior instead of specialization and scale economies.[66] William R. Cline believes that in spite of the trade diversion, other static and dynamic gains were sufficient to bring a net benefit—perhaps 3% of GDP for the CACM as a whole;[67] 1969 "Soccer War" between El Salvador and Honduras caused temporary breakup. Honduras withdrew in 1970, stopped trade with El Salvador, and reestablished duties with the rest. Costa Rica was expelled in 1972.[68] Revived from 1986, aiming first for a 20% ceiling on its (quite high) tariffs and then at free trade at the start of 1996. El Salvador and Guatemala already have bilateral free trade. Panama is now part of the talks.	7.0%	14.8%
LAFTA (Latin American Free Trade Area), 1961 Argentina, Brazil, Bolivia, Chile, Colombia, Ecuador, Mexico, Paraguay, Peru, Uruguay, and Venezuela Expired 1980. Tried but failed to eliminate tariffs in 10 years and to allocate industries among member countries. Some studies indicate significant trade diversion.[69]		
LAIA (Latin American Integration Association), 1980 Same as LAFTA Less-ambitious successor to LAFTA. Internal duties not yet eliminated. No common external tariff yet, though Argentina, Brazil, and Mexico have removed tariffs on many imports from other members. Relatively succesful.	7.9%	10.6%

TABLE 15.5 REGIONAL TRADE ARRANGEMENTS AMONG LESS-DEVELOPED COUNTRIES *(Continued)*

KEY TO THE TABLE

Short Name (Full Name), Year Founded Member Comments	Intraunion trade as % of total (where available) 1960	1990
Andean Group, 1969 Bolivia, Ecuador, Colombia, Peru, Venezuela Formed partly to escape from Brazil's influence. "Many postponements." Chile withdrew in 1976, and Peru temporarily in 1992. FTA in 1992 but only for Bolivia, Colombia, and Ecuador.Others supposed to join in 1993. A customs union with a common external tariff was planned for 1994, but Venezuela has erected new barriers; 75% of interregional trade is now duty-free. Large static gains have been claimed, although some authorities state that these gains are exaggerated.[70]	0.7%	4.6%
Mercosur, 1991 Argentina, Brazil, Paraguay, Uruguay Mercosul in Portuguese. Common market planned from January 1, 1995, with a low common external tariff to average 5% and ranging from 0 to 20%, free movement of services,capital, and labor. About 15% of all trade will be excluded, including capital goods, advanced electronics, and petrochemicals. Common external tariffs in these areas will be delayed to the period 2001–2006, and the common external tariff will be high when it *is* adopted. Hindered by extreme differences in rates of inflation (Brazil high, Argentina low) and in economic policy as well. Brazil and Argentina continue to exclude hundreds of items on which tariffs still exist. IntraMercosur trade nearly doubled between 1991 and 1993.		
Miscellaneous A Chile–Mexico free trade agreement went into effect in 1991 to be complete in 1996, and a Chile–Venezuela agreement in 1993 (to eliminate almost all tariffs by 1997). Chile–Bolivia free trade dates from 1993 for a wide but not complete range of goods, and Chile–Brazil and Chile–Columbia talks are going on.[71] Colombia–Venezuela–Mexico free trade was agreed on for the future in 1994. This "G3" is also discussing a trade zone with Caricom countries. A Caricom–Colombia free trade agreement has been agreed on, to take effect in 1995 with the duty reductions phased in over five years. A Caricom–Venezuela trade accord dates from 1992. In the agreements with Caricom, the Latin American partner granted immediate trade preferences, while the Caricom preferences will come from that group's advanced countries only. In 1991 the CACM negotiated bilateral free trade accords with Mexico and Venezuela to be in place by 1996. Bolivia–Mexico and Brazil–Mexico free trade agreements are being negotiated. Brazil is pushing for a South American Free Trade Area (SAFTA) by the year 2005. All the countries mentioned may join with the United States in a free trade agreement.		

TABLE 15.5 REGIONAL TRADE ARRANGEMENTS AMONG LESS-DEVELOPED COUNTRIES *(Continued)*

KEY TO THE TABLE		
Short Name (Full Name), Year Founded Member Comments	Intraunion trade as % of total (where available) 1960	 1990
MIDDLE EAST		
GCC (Gulf Cooperation Council), 1981 Bahrain, Kuwait, Oman, Qatar, Saudi Arabia, United Arab Emirates Tariffs abolished 1983, with common external tariff to have been introduced in 1993. Little accomplished because trade among the members is small.	3.0%*	4.4%
Miscellaneous Plans for an Arab Common Market and a Mahgreb (North African) Customs Union exist, but little progress has been made.		

Source: This table is reproduced with updating and amendment from Brown and Hogendorn, *International Economics: Theory and Context,* chapter 9. See de la Torre and Kelly, *Regional Trade Arrangements,* 20, 26–27, 30, 32; Fieleke, "One Trading World, or Many: The Issue of Regional Trading Blocs," *New England Economic Review* (May/June 1992): 4–5; David Greenaway and Chris Milner, "South–South Trade: Theory, Evidence, and Policy," *World Bank Research Observer* 5, no. 1 (January 1990): 47–68; and World Bank, *WDR 1991,* 107. Some information is from "Market-Integration and Market-Sharing Schemes," in B. P. Menon, *Bridges Across the South* (New York, 1980), 106–111; and Constantine V. Vaitsos, "Crisis in Regional Economic Cooperation (Integration) among Developing Countries: A Survey," in Paul Streeten and Richard Jolly, eds., *Recent Issues in World Development* (Oxford, 1981). The comments in quotes are from de la Torre and Kelly, pp. 26–27, except [a] which is from Fieleke, p. 9. The 1960 data are for the membership before the formation of the arrangement. *1970 figure. †1983 figure. ‡1987 figure.

developed-country members extending more preferences than the LDC members do. There is a certain colonial pattern to such action, as it usually ties the trade of the LDC partner tightly to the metropolitan economy of the "patron." Counting the aid, technical help, and defense umbrella that may accompany the deal, it may still be worth doing from the LDC's point of view.

The oldest of these preferences are those advanced by the EC to the former colonies of its members, the African–Caribbean–Pacific (ACP) states. Lower tariffs and guaranteed access outside quota barriers and VERs are commonly granted to this group.* The EC also has preferential trade agreements with Israel (dating from 1975), Algeria, Egypt, Jordan, Lebanon, Morocco, Tunisia, and Yugoslavia (all in 1978); and associate agreements with Turkey (1963), Malta (1970), and Cyprus

*Arguably, the preferences to the ACP countries have had limited benefits. The margins are slim, trade diversion has predominated, monopsonistic European buyers have captured some of the preferences, sometimes the "diversification of exports" that are reported have occurred only because entrepreneurs want to move goods to the duty-free list, and the poorest ACP states have not been flexible enough to take much advantage of the arrangement. See *WDR 1986,* 144.

(1972). The United States is involved in four such unions, one with the Caribbean countries, one with Israel, one with Mexico (NAFTA, which also includes Canada), and one with several Andean countries under the Andean Trade Preference Act.

The Caribbean Basin Economic Recovery Act A Caribbean Basin Economic Recovery Act (CBERA) took effect January 1, 1984. The name Caribbean Basin Initiative (CBI) is also used. All Caribbean territories are included except Cuba and Suriname, which have not qualified for political reasons, and Anguilla, the Cayman Islands, and the Turks and Caicos Islands, which have had tax disagreements with the United States. The CBERA was originally scheduled to expire in 1995, but it has now been extended indefinitely.[72] The rules are more liberal than they are in the U.S. GSP scheme. There are fewer listed exceptions to duty-free treatment, less strict rules of origin, no "competitive need" restrictions, and no plans to "graduate" countries when they hit a certain income level. But the Multi-Fiber Arrangement on textiles and clothing remains in force, as do the prohibitive restrictions on U.S. imports of peanuts, cotton, and sugar, with the sugar exclusion especially damaging. The result of the exclusions is that the impact of the CBERA has been strictly limited, in 1992 affecting only about 16% of the region's total trade with the United States.* Many CBERA countries are seeking membership in NAFTA, as we will see below.

The U.S.–Israel Free Trade Agreement The second of the U.S. preference agreements took effect on September 1, 1985, when the United States and Israel promised to eliminate virtually all tariff and nontariff barriers against one another over a ten-year period.[73] The union appears to pose some threat of trade diversion for Israel, with more expensive U.S. exports substituting to some extent for what Israel could buy at cheaper world market prices. From the Israeli point of view, however, that problem is no doubt completely overshadowed by the further evidence of a strong political and economic alliance with the United States. Any costs of diversion are well offset.

The North American Free Trade Agreement NAFTA, the North American Free Trade Agreement among the United States, Canada, and Mexico, was signed at the end of 1993.[74] Against bitter resistance, it passed by the close vote of 234 to 200 in the U.S. House of Representatives. Opponents of the agreement, including most U.S. trade unions and certain politicians, such as Ross Perot, insisted against the weight of the economic evidence that Mexico's cheap labor would lure very large numbers of American firms to Mexico, involving the loss of jobs for many American workers. Supporters pointed to the jobs that would be created by the growth of American exports to Mexico. Supplementary agreements on labor and the environment had to be added before the U.S. Congress would approve the treaty. Under NAFTA, tariffs will go to zero over a period of 15 years, though about

---

*Outside the CBERA rules, trade between these countries and the United States has been boosted by special U.S. tariff rules. HTS headings 9802.00.60 and5525 9802.00.80 allow producers to deduct from dutiable value the value of U.S.-produced components assembled abroad and returned in a final product.

50% of them were abolished immediately. Many restrictions on trade are being dropped, including the Mexican limits on foreign delivery of services and many U.S. barriers to the import of fresh fruits and vegetables. Many CBERA countries want to be included in NAFTA.

The United States has been negotiating agreements with virtually all the Latin American and Caribbean countries to work toward free trade. A "Free Trade Area of the Americas" (FTAA) was being pushed by the Clinton administration and some Republicans as well. But there was little support in the quarters that had opposed NAFTA, and Mexico itself seemed to lack enthusiasm for the move.

The Andean Trade Preference Act An Andean Trade Preference Act (ATPA) was passed by the U.S. Congress in 1991 and went into effect in 1992/1993.[75] It establishes a duty-free arrangement resembling the CBERA for Bolivia, Colombia, Ecuador, and Peru. The exclusions of textiles, clothing, sugar, and the like, and the rules of origin, are similar to those of the CBERA. ATPA is designed to compensate for the impact of the "War on Drugs" on coca exports. The act will expire in ten years, unlike the other three U.S. agreements, which are permanent.

Rich–Poor Customs Unions: A Conclusion

All of these unions involving rich and poor countries involve a tendency for patrons and clients to be cemented into trading blocs that discriminate against one another, and with the client states becoming wedded to their privileges. Intransigent opposition to the similar imperial preferences of the British and French colonial days was a hallmark of U.S. foreign policy for half a century.[76] There is some irony in the United States joining in that game.* No single customs union may have the capacity to do much harm. But these unions could possibly be subterfuges to keep barriers intact against outsiders, and it seems clear that some of their supporters intend exactly that. Together, by making trade discrimination commonplace, they might cause the new World Trade Organization to be shouldered aside. A Japanese bloc in the Far East, a U.S. bloc in Latin America and the Caribbean, a European bloc in Africa and the Middle East, could grow into "trade fortresses" that reduce world welfare. The more such agreements proliferate, the greater the likelihood that countries may end up importing from higher-cost suppliers that face no trade barriers, while lower-cost suppliers outside the walls lose their access. Large regional blocs might be "halfway houses to global free trade or the battlements from which future trade wars will be fought."[77] No one can be sure, and vigilance will be needed.

*The British Commonwealth Preference scheme was established in 1932. That marked the British decision to limit foreign trade with its colonies. Before that time, trade with the British colonies had been reasonably free.

THE FUTURE FOR PRIMARY PRODUCT EXPORTS

One aspect of the international trade of the LDCs is that so many countries are still highly specialized on primary product exports. More than 70 LDCs still rely on primary commodities for over half their exports. Often, the countries most dependent on primary product exports also have the lowest income; primary products make up 61% of the exports of the least-developed LDCs but only 48% of the exports of the upper-middle-income LDCs.[78]

The degree of specialization can sometimes reach extraordinary levels: In recent years, some 30 LDCs obtained over 80% of their export revenues from no more than three primary products, and there were about 30 more where the figure lay between 60% and 80%. Oil makes up over 90% of the exports of Iran, Nigeria, Venezuela, and the Arab oil states. Coffee exceeds 70% for El Salvador, 90% for Uganda, and 97% for Burundi. Copper is over 80% of Zambia's total. The figure is 50% to 60% for Bangladeshi jute and Jamaican bauxite and alumina; 40% to 50% for Sudanese cotton; and 30% to 40% for Zaire's copper and Bolivia's tin. Compare this with America's largest, corn, which generates less than 5% of U.S. export revenue.

Price and Income Volatility in Primary Products

The dependence on primary product exports is awkward for the LDCs because there is a notorious tendency for the prices of these products to be unstable in the short run. When prices fluctuate violently, so in some degree may the income earned from exporting. This problem has generated interesting and controversial ideas on how to dampen the fluctuations.

There are economic reasons to expect and evidence to indicate that price fluctuations for primary products are on average considerably greater than they are for manufactured goods. The pattern of surge and collapse will, it is said, have a serious detrimental effect on the progress of countries exporting these commodities. The price changes may cause the incomes of producers to rise and fall. Income changes, if they occur, will cause a spreading multiplier effect, with the sales of those who supply inputs for commodity producers and those who produce goods consumed by them directly affected. The country's tax revenues will swing sympathetically, especially if export taxes are important. The supply and demand for credit is likely to gyrate also and, therefore, so will interest rates, generating further instability in investment.[79]

The difficulties are greatest when a country is highly specialized in exporting, for then there is little spreading of the risk. Some time-series analysis does indeed support a conclusion that commodity concentration is an important cause of the instability of export proceeds.[80] A country should be cautious, however: It is easy to assume that diversifying exports would therefore always be advantageous. Not so. The exports a country diversifies into may not be as profitable as the original ones, and that country may end up with less price variability but with the average price received lower, and therefore a lower average level of income as well. Here, the diversification would have been an expensive failure.

Evidence of High Variability in Prices Primary product prices generally fluctuate strongly with the business cycle, with the swings both frequent and intense. The average fluctuation expressed as movement around a trend line during three- to five-year periods is commonly 20 to 40% or even more.[81] For example, the world economic recovery in the year 1994 increased the demand for primary products, causing a boomlet during which metals prices climbed about a quarter, food by about half, and all items by about 40%, though the increase was from low levels caused by the preceding recession.[82]

How is it possible that these price fluctuations are so large? The answer lies in the elasticities of the demand and supply curves and in the considerable shifts that these curves typically undergo. First let us consider the elasticities. Elementary analysis indicates that large price shifts will occur if demand and supply are highly inelastic, as in Figure 15.1. Any small shift either in supply or demand causes a large change in price. (Figure 15.1(a) shows a small rise in supply and a large fall in price; Figure 15.1(b) shows a minor increase in demand and a major rise in price.)

Most agricultural commodities do have very low short-run supply elasticities, often near zero, because it is so difficult to obtain any increase in output between one harvest and the next. The means for increasing yields in the middle of the growing season are very limited. Tree crops (cocoa, coffee, tea, rubber, palm oil) have even greater price inelasticities of supply, as they take several years to bear following a first planting. Mineral production can often be increased only by large-scale investment in mining or drilling, a slow and expensive process. The supply elasticities shown in Table 15.6 are long-run; the short-run supply elasticities are much lower yet.

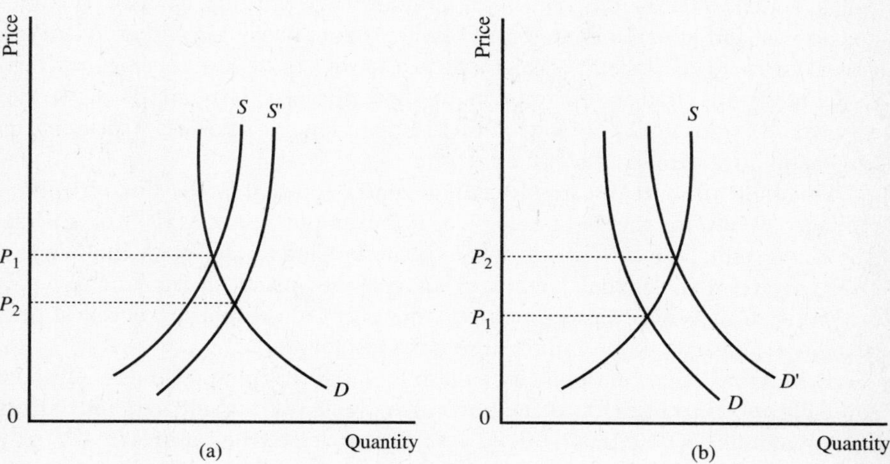

Figure 15.1 When demand and supply are inelastic, shifts in either of the curves lead to large price fluctuations.

TABLE 15.6 LONG-RUN SUPPLY AND DEMAND ELASTICITIES, VARIOUS PRIMARY PRODUCTS

	Price elasticity of supply	Price elasticity of demand
Coffee	0.5	–0.6
Cocoa	0.8	–0.4
Tea	0.6	–0.2
Sugar	0.8	–0.3
Cotton	0.4	–0.4
Rubber	0.2	–0.8
Jute	0.8	approx. 0.0
Sisal	0.3	approx. 0.0
Copper	0.2	–0.2
Tin	0.2	–5.0

Source: From Jere R. Behrman, "International Commodity Agreements: An Evaluation of the UNCTAD Integrated Commodity Programme," in William R. Cline, ed., *Policy Alternatives for a New International Economic Order* (New York, 1979), 118–121.[83]

Moreover, there is no well-organized international market for numerous minor crops produced in the LDCs. Examples include cloves, cashews, sesame, shea, sisal, ginger, pyrethrum, mangoes, avocados, green beans, asparagus, and cut flowers. Markets may be thin and hence volatile.[84]

A low price elasticity of developed-country demand for tropical agricultural commodities is also well documented. Most of the foods and beverages absorb little of the consumer's total food bill, but are also important in most people's lives. By their nature, their use does not expand or contract greatly as prices rise or fall. (Sugar, coffee, cocoa, and tea fit this description.) For the industrial raw materials, such as sisal and jute, the limited uses of the product make demand even less sensitive to price. The demand elasticities are also thus quite low, as shown in Table 15.6. The figures cited are long run; in the short run, as with the supply elasticities, they would be lower. These low elasticities go a long way toward explaining the long-standing instability of commodity prices.

Variability of short-run supply is the second important factor. For agricultural products, weather is the great unknown. For example, episodes of frost in Brazil have often ruined the coffee crop; given the underlying inelasticities, the swings in price have been substantial. Adding to the volatility, producers may behave as in the "cobweb theorem," raising and lowering output in response to cyclical price changes in a fashion that reinforces the price instabilities.

Finally, variations in demand can also be large for some products. Although generally not true of the foods and beverages, demand instability certainly affects many minerals because that demand is so closely tied to the business cycle in the developed countries, As income swings in these countries, so demand swings in the LDC producers. Income elasticities of demand as high as 5.0 have been noted (for tin); for many metals and minerals used as inputs, a given percentage rise or fall in output of the final product results in a rise or fall in purchases of the input of approximately the same percent. A "minerals accelerator" has even been reported, with falling demand for a final product resulting in a proportionally greater fall in mineral demand as producers draw down their raw material inventories, and vice versa.[85]

How Harmful Is the Price Variability? Given the obvious ill effects that would seem to stem from highly variable export prices, it may come as rather a surprise to find that the degree of harm is debatable. Alasdair MacBean's initial study produced little statistical evidence that instability of export earnings is detrimental to economic growth. Economists were perhaps a bit skeptical at first, but these results have now been replicated a number of times by other scholars.[86] Apparently, the fluctuations in export revenue sometimes even lead to higher levels of saving to avoid risks, which, in turn, leads to a higher level of investment. Anne Krueger writes,

> It seems reasonable to conclude that if there are negative feedbacks from instability to growth, they are sufficiently small in magnitude relative to other factors contributing to growth that it is difficult to find robust empirical tests that detect them.[87]

It would appear that price instability for primary products is less damaging than common sense would lead one to expect. Perhaps, as Jere Behrman suggests, the major damage may be adverse political consequences for the leaders of the LDCs.[88] This is ironic because the volatility of prices is the usual reason given to justify schemes to stabilize primary product prices by means of the international commodity agreements discussed below. Yet where economic damage does occur, it is likely to be worse for poor countries whose exports are highly concentrated. Once again, sub-Saharan Africa appears to be the major loser.[89]

PRICE AND REVENUE STABILIZATION

The idea that primary product prices and/or revenues can be manipulated is of long standing. One plan is to adopt a mechanism that would stabilize prices. More radically, one could attempt to raise prices. Another idea is to stabilize export revenues by means of loans or grants. We treat the economics of such plans in this section.

Stabilizing or Raising Prices by Means of International Agreements

International agreements to stabilize the swings in commodity prices or to increase those prices, or both, have a long intellectual history, and there have been more practical examples than is generally realized.[90] There was an agreement to restrict sugar output and raise prices as early as 1902, and at the Bretton Woods Conference of 1944, John Maynard Keynes suggested an international commodity system. Soon thereafter, the American economist Benjamin Graham advocated that price stabilization for commodities be funded by the new IMF. Although nothing came of these proposals at the time, they eventually did germinate.

There have always been two distinct alternative arrangements for commodities. One could try to restrict output by means of export quotas or export taxes and so raise prices, or one could maintain an international stockpile ("buffer stock") of a given commodity to achieve price stabilization, adding to it when prices are low and selling from it when they are high. The two aims are of course very different in their appeal. Producers typically prefer higher prices to stabilization; consumers typically support either stabilization or a free market. Much about the politics of commodity agreements becomes clearer when this is understood.

Raising Prices by Means of Quotas on Output Quota arrangements to restrict output have had a much longer history than have buffer stocks. Long ago it was realized that few countries had much chance of influencing world prices through individual action because a single country generally provided too small a proportion of total supply to affect the world market to any great extent. Only rarely (Chile with nitrates before World War I, Brazil with coffee before World War II, Pakistan with jute and Ghana with cocoa briefly after that war, and Saudi Arabia with oil in the 1970s) has a single country been able to exercise substantial commodity power. The importance of elasticity conditions in determining when it is profitable for a single country to restrict supply was considered at length when we discussed export taxation in Chapter 4.

What an individual country lacked in monopoly power might be rectified if it joined a cartel of producers. The first attempts on an international level were crude quota arrangements wherein producers agreed to limit output, with the limits usually adjustable according to the state of the market. Generally, any fall in prices would be resisted by tightened quotas; less frequently, higher prices would result in liberalized quotas. In a fully formed quota arrangement, shares are assigned, usually based on past performance, and the building up of new production capacity in the member countries is prohibited. Within each member a mechanism is put into place for allocating a share of the country's quota to existing producers. In addition to the original sugar agreement of 1902, other early examples include tin (1921), tea (1933), rubber (1934), and coffee (1962). The International Coffee Organization, set up to administer the 1962 agreement, urged its members to limit production by uprooting trees. Brazil, which exported about 40% of the world's coffee at the time, tore up a sufficient number to cut its crop by a quarter. In 1993, a series of failures to negotiate a new coffee agreement led to a confederation of coffee producing countries that agreed to hold coffee off the export market when prices are low and release it when prices are high. The new confederation still provides for quotas on exporters, automatically tightened when the coffee price hits a floor (recently 75¢ per pound), increased when the price hits certain levels (75¢ and 80¢), and a release of stocks when price reach a ceiling of 85¢.

Economists have traditionally looked askance at quota schemes, not because they cannot work in the interests of the LDCs, but because the circumstances in which they do work are so limited. The price elasticity of demand for the product must be low, meaning consumers cannot easily shift to substitutes if prices are forced up by the quotas. Otherwise, falling sales volume may offset the gain in price. Income elasticity of demand should be high, so that economic growth will cause growth in the demand for the product. There ought to be only a small number of members in the cartel, and they ought to believe that joint action is in their best interests. This will make policing easier and limit the incentives to cheat. Supply should continue to be inelastic even after several years. So the entry of new members should be difficult because of technological problems, absence of a necessary resource such as a mineral deposit, or lack of the right kind of agricultural land. If there are substitute products, the members would prefer the long-run supply elasticities of these substitutes to be low so their production cannot easily expand. Profit maximizing should perhaps not be pushed too far, with prices kept low enough to discourage the entry of competitors who would find high prices attractive. (Technically, this is a "limit price.") It helps if the commodity is storable at low cost (metals, oil, rubber, coffee) and does not always have to be put on the market as soon as it is produced (bananas, fresh meat). Finally, it will be an advantage if the members of the cartel have similar cost structures and market shares, for then there will be less debate on where to set prices and how to allocate production.

A quota scheme that initially succeeds in raising prices and hence earnings will predictably encourage additional production both in members and in nonmembers of the cartel and a search for substitutes by consumers. Jere Behrman's study of 51 attempts to raise prices found many did not sufficiently satisfy the conditions noted above. The median length of time before the attempt was abandoned was two-and-a-half years.[91] Behrman concluded that the major cause of failure where quotas were employed has been competition among the members, each knowing that if it could increase its market share at the high cartel price, it could greatly increase revenues.

A second important cause of failure has been the development of production in nonmembers. Typically, a cartel attempts to control this by attracting the nonmembers into membership. Doing so necessitates granting them handsome quotas, however, and so dilutes the advantages to the original members. Another possibility is to include consuming countries in the cartel, obtaining their help in policing the agreement. Consumers might be enticed by more generous prices than the cartel would otherwise offer. Yet this has proved to be difficult. Consumers and producers are uncomfortable bedfellows: The cartel members may spend most of their time debating the degree of supply restriction and the price to be defended.

Substitute products also pose a serious problem for price-raising cartels. Most important primary products do face potential competition if their prices are raised, as shown in Table 15.7. For some products (rubber, jute) the price of the competing substitutes now governs the market. For others (such as tin, sugar, copper) it is important. Only a few commodities (including coffee and tea) have no direct competitors, and even here the possibility that consumers would switch to other beverages limits the possibilities for price enhancement. Cola drinks, for example, have already made major inroads into the coffee market among the under 30 age group in the United States.

Finally, it should be noted that even if the cartel works perfectly to raise long-run prices and incomes, the results might not be fully desirable from the standpoint of the LDCs. Low-income countries consume these products, too; have-nots lose at the expense of the haves, and the have-nots might be poorer. Nor is there any guarantee that a cartel will do much for the mass of the population even in a

TABLE 15.7 COMPETITION FACING IMPORTANT PRIMARY PRODUCTS

Primary Product	Competition
Rubber	Synthetic rubber, plastics
Cotton	Other natural and synthetic fibers
Tin	New technology permitting thinner tin plating; plastic can lining; paper, aluminum, and plastic containers
Jute	Polypropylene and polyethylene
Sugar	High-fructose corn sweeteners
Copper	Aluminum, glass fiber, plastics
Bauxite	Plastics, aluminum recycling
Cocoa	Artificial chocolate flavoring, vegetable oil extenders

Source: Dennis T. Avery, "International Commodity Agreements," Department of State Special Report No. 83 (June, 1981).

country clearly receiving benefits. It has not escaped notice that producer interests—plantations, landowners, merchant firms, transport companies, banks—are usually first in line to lobby for cartels of this sort and fierce in their defense.

OPEC AND ITS QUOTAS

Supply restriction for one product, oil, proved to be a remarkably special case. The Organization of Petroleum Exporting Countries (OPEC) succeeded for some time in limiting supplies and raising prices.

OPEC, with Venezuela leading in its formation, was at first weak and cautious. But the Arab–Israeli Yom Kippur War of October 1973 brought cohesion to OPEC as it never had before and served to divide the consuming nations as well. A temporary oil embargo was succeeded by a new sense of determination by OPEC to control production and force prices up. OPEC was able to raise prices to $12 to $13 per barrel by 1975, where they stayed for some time.

The second incident was the great Khomeini oil shock of 1979 to 1980. This time Iran's and Iraq's oil deliveries were sharply cut back as war broke out between these countries. The other OPEC members deliberately did not make up the difference. The result was that oil eventually reached $34 per barrel. (The two names Yom Kippur and Khomeini are, incidentally, convincing testimony that there would have been an oil crisis even if there never had been an OPEC.)

In its heyday, OPEC rigged the market by establishing export quotas set in quantity terms. Many of the requisites for a successful quota scheme were present. Both supply and demand elasticity appeared to be low; it would not be easy to develop new sources of supply or substitutes in consumption. There was plenty of political cohesion at first, and the oil could just be left in the ground. One producer, Saudi Arabia, had and still has such vast reserves that its own actions could influence the world price substantially. It could act as OPEC's policeman.[92]

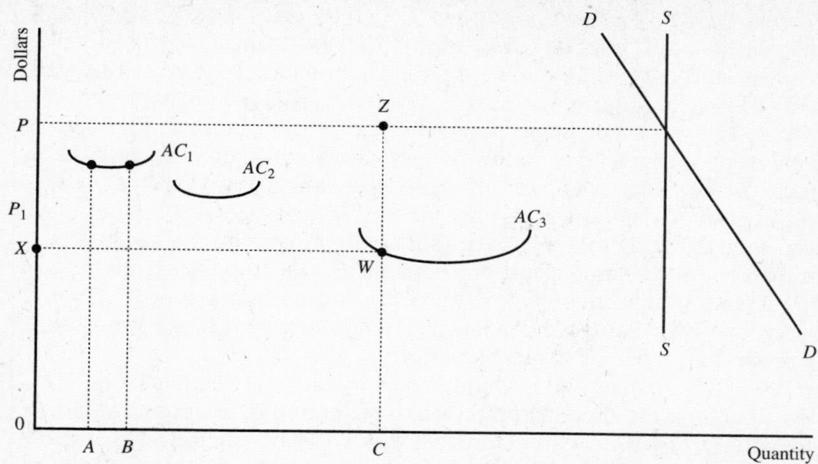

Figure 15.2 The oil cartel was able to maintain an "umbrella" price by limiting the supply on the market.

Analytically, the cartel maintained an "umbrella" price by manipulating supply, as in Figure 15.2. Given the world demand curve *DD*, the cartel needed only to limit total supply to the level *SS* to accomplish its aim of a high price at *P*. The limitation was achieved by agreeing on an overall production figure and allocating shares of that to each individual member. The policy was effective because at the time OPEC first struck in 1973, it controlled 92% of world crude oil exports.

Saudi Arabia (Country 3 in Figure 15.2) had much lower costs than some other members, say Ecuador (Country 1) and Indonesia (Country 2), as shown by the average cost curves AC_1, AC_2, and AC_3. By expanding production, Saudi Arabia could easily have driven prices below P_1 and thereby have eliminated Ecuador and Indonesia from the world market. It did not do so, usually pumping only about half of what it was capable of, because by tolerating the other countries at the high umbrella price, it vastly increased its own profits. (If Arabia's output is *C*, its total profit is *WXPZ*.)

The members with high costs either had to agree to stay within their allocated share or somehow be policed. There was always a motive for them to cheat to increase revenues by pushing up their production from some allocated figure such as *A* to a higher figure *B*. Perhaps they could be accommodated with a Saudi Arabian cut, or perhaps the threat that Saudi Arabia would increase production would suffice to restrain them. There was additional tension between countries with limited, rapidly depleting reserves and those with large reserves. The former would, of course, prefer pumping now at the high cartel price; the latter would prefer a limit price strategy to restrain new exploration and guard against technological change.

The economic impact of the two oil crises on the LDCs was profound. Countries that exported oil milked their cash cow; countries without oil paid dearly to fuel their cars, trucks, pumps, and machinery, and to make or buy the petroleum-based fertilizer that was so important in agriculture. OPEC's strategy also slowed economic growth in the rich countries and thereby diminished their demand for LDC exports. Even for the oil exporters, some citizens of which grew fabulously rich, there were disappointments. These were caused largely by the waste of going too quickly, of costly ill-planned projects, and of inefficiencies generated by broad new subsidies for consumption. This illustrates the paradox that a large endowment of natural resources *may* be a disadvantage for development, a sort of "resource curse." The resources may enable a country to carry on with misguided micro and macroeconomic policies, and they are likely to give rise to rent-seeking ("sharing the spoils") by groups that may be tolerated longer and become more entrenched.[93] It is stunning to realize that the greatest development successes of recent history—first Japan and later South Korea, Taiwan, Hong Kong, and Singapore—had few or no natural resources to aid their effort.

To the OPEC countries, a large stock of national resources hardly seemed a curse at the time, and the wealth generated by oil was extraordinary. Eventually, however, market forces brought a response. Because of the special nature of oil, this response was very slow, but by 1986 it had gathered momentum. Conservation in the developed countries proved to be possible, as power stations shifted to coal and natural gas. Drivers traded in their eight-cylinder gas guzzlers for four-cylinder compact cars, and government mileage standards helped to propel the move. Homeowners turned down the thermostat and used natural gas and wood. The energy to GDP ratio (tons of oil per $1000 of GDP) fell in almost all major countries, by an average of 20% between 1973 and 1985. In some years this economizing saved more oil than the entire amount of OPEC's output. Even in the LDCs, where conservation was more difficult, oil as a percent of energy consumption fell from 53.5% in 1973 to 45% in 1983. In Figure 15.2, the demand curve moved to the left.

Meanwhile, non-OPEC production soared. Alaska and the North Sea came on-line; Britain alone produced more oil than any OPEC members except Saudi Arabia and Iran. As this occurred, developed-country exports of oil as a percent of the total went from only 3.7% in 1973 to 12.5% in 1983. Even more impressive was the rise of non-OPEC production in LDCs that did not join—Mexico especially, but also Egypt, Oman, Angola, Malaysia, China, and others—from 4% of total exports in 1973 to 18.7% in 1983. In the process, Mexico became the world's third largest free-world producer, after the United States and Saudi Arabia. In some LDCs, small deposits previously not worth bothering about were brought into production, "topping up" domestic use in countries where major finds are not expected: Cameroun, Ghana, the Côte d'Ivoire, Sudan, Guatemala, the Philippines, and India are cases in point. Elsewhere, efforts were made where possible to develop hydroelectric sites, coal mines, and even nuclear power (in Argentina, Brazil, India, Pakistan, and South Korea). Brazil moved quickly into ethanol production, and eventually about half of Brazil's cars were running on this product of sugarcane.* In Figure 15.2, the supply curve moved to the right.

OPEC began to crack, with constant reports of discounting (cheating) by some of the members and pumping quotas exceeded by perhaps 20%. OPEC could have kept the price high by cutting production, of course, but it was unable to do so. The price plummeted from $28 per barrel in late 1985 to only $9 per barrel in mid-1986. OPEC hastily wove together some new supply limitations in 1986/1987, but nothing like what had triggered the two earlier crises. Except for some reduced supply and panic buying that temporarily accompanied Iraq's invasion of Kuwait in 1990, oil prices have been relatively moderate ever since. Saudi Arabia, especially, seemed to have learned the lesson that it had sufficient power to discipline the rest of OPEC, and that if it did not, then high prices would drive consumers to conserve and to shift to substitute fuels. The economic principles that had stymied all the other primary product cartels this century had at last caught up with OPEC.†

---

*When oil prices fell in 1986, Brazil's ethanol program turned sour. It came to cost twice as much as gasoline to produce, and sugar had to be subsidized to get enough of it. See *Wall Street Journal,* September 28, 1989.

† If OPEC were to attempt another large output reduction, the developed countries would find consumption would not be so easy to cut this time around because the obvious economies have already been made. But it would also find much more cooperation among those countries, with an International Energy Association pledged to maintain stocks sufficient to replace 90 days' worth of imports, to equalize the drawing down of stocks in case of need, and to share oil in an emergency. The U.S. strategic petroleum reserve of 500 million barrels stored underground, with room for 750 million barrels if desired, is another stabilizing factor.

Stabilizing Price by Means of Buffer Stocks In addition to quota limits on production, the other major method for intervening in world markets for primary products is a buffer stock system that influences prices by buying and selling commodities.[94] Buffer stocks are a poor way to *raise* prices, because, obviously, the stock must continuously and expensively accumulate the commodity in order to keep prices above the market-clearing level. Buffer stocks have, however, been favored for *stabilizing* prices and have thus been a major element in the proposals for a "New International Economic Order" favored for years by the United Nations Commission on Trade and Development (UNCTAD). UNCTAD includes all UN members and usually holds a general meeting every four years, the most recent at Cartagena, Colombia, in 1992. The next meeting, the ninth, is scheduled for 1996.[95]

A suitably managed system of buffer stocks could conceivably dampen the severe short-run price fluctuations that afflict most primary product exporters. The elementary theory of buffer stock operation is simple enough and is analyzed in Figure 15.3. A tin buffer stock is illustrated, tin providing the outstanding historical example of a buffer stock in action. It starts operation with a stockpile of the metal and a war chest of cash; these are its working tools. The market supply and demand for the metal are S and D, respectively. The buffer stock manager must determine a floor and ceiling price at which action will be taken; in the diagram these are P_C and P_f. No actions are taken as long as supply and demand equilibrate at prices within the floor–ceiling range. The manager ignores any price changes in this range.

Should either demand or supply (or both) change by enough to give a market price above the ceiling or below the floor, the buffer stock manager reacts. If, for example, there is an increase in demand for tin to D', to keep the price from rising to the high level P_1 sufficient krypton is released onto the market from the buffer stock so that the price does not rise above P_c. The amount needed is exactly AB. Or, if a decline in demand to D'' would otherwise push prices down to a low P_1, the buffer stock manager uses some of the cash reserve to buy just enough tin (XY) to keep the price at P_f. Supply changes can be analyzed in the same way, with tin sold from the stock to keep prices from rising or purchased to keep them from falling.

Several buffer stocks were established. An International Tin Agreement was first implemented in 1956. It was the oldest and for a long time the most successful of the buffer stocks, though as we shall see its winning reputation did not last. The buffer stock was intended to be some 40,000 metric tons; when it was at this size, production quotas were to be imposed. From 1980, the International Natural Rubber Agreement had a buffer stock that reached 360,000 tons of rubber in 1987. From 1981, the International Cocoa Agreement had a buffer stock intended to reach 250,000 metric tons, financed by a 2¢ per pound fee on exports. Finally, the International Sugar Agreement had a buffer stock for a time. Countries interested in the buffer stock idea established a "Common Fund" to provide financing. Funds were contributed by both exporters and importers. The Common Fund began operations in 1989. The IMF assisted with a Buffer Stock Financing Facility that provided loans for this purpose (up to 45% of the member's IMF quota). The facility was used for financing the commodity agreements in tin, rubber, and sugar. The United States generally opposed the formation of new buffer stocks, however. Conservatives disliked the intervention in free markets, while liberals wondered why the aid to set them up was better used for this purpose than to assist the poorest LDCs—which are generally not the countries participating in buffer stock arrangements.[96]

Doubts Concerning Stabilization by Buffer Stocks Many economists have always been skeptical about the efficacy of buffer stocks as a device for stabilization. One concern has been that the stocks, instead of having a stabilizing influence, might actually destabilize commodity markets. The buffer stock must be sufficiently large and adjust with sufficient rapidity to long-term trends in prices, so that it exhausts neither its cash nor its supply of commodity. The buffer stock that runs out of either, because it is too small or because the manager did not pick up an underlying price trend soon enough, could conceivably face a change in price much greater (because of panic and speculative overshooting) than would have occurred with no intervention whatsoever. Certainly, any price change when the stock is "broken" is likely to be very large and very sudden.

In practice, speculators tended to bet that the stock would run out of money or commodity. They would sometimes buy at the stock's ceiling price, to profit later when the price is pushed through the roof following the stock's collapse.[97]

Unfortunately, the pessimism was fully confirmed by a disastrous episode involving the collapse of the tin buffer stock in late 1985. The Tin Agreement had a long-standing reputation for success in spite of some incidents when the price fell through the floor or broke through the ceiling for a short time. Most of the time, it worked rather smoothly. The 1985 collapse was caused by defense of a price range that was too high. Quotas kept production down in the members, but that led to substitutions by consumers and new and highly rewarded production in nonmem-

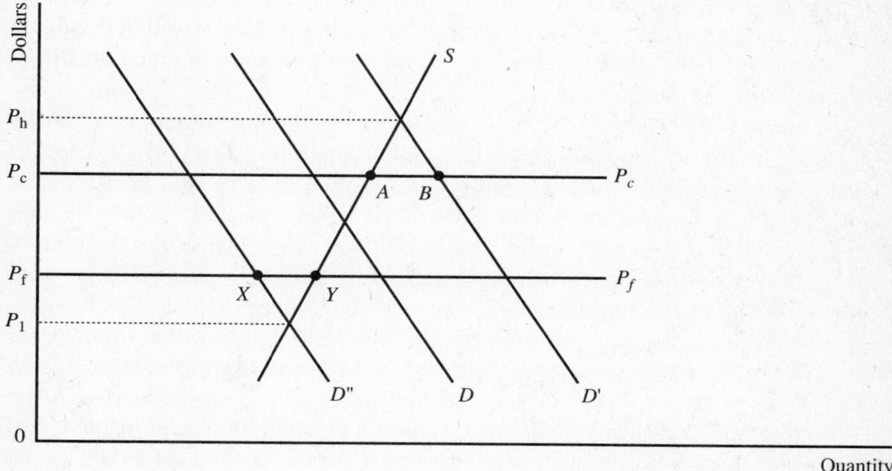

Figure 15.3 The buffer stock manager buys with the stock's cash when the price falls to the floor P_f and sells from the stockpile when the price rises to the ceiling P_c, so keeping price within a given range.

bers, especially Brazil and China. By 1985 about 40% of the world's tin was being produced by nonmembers, nearly half of that by Brazil. Twenty years before, nonmembers had been responsible for only 20% of world output.

The buffer stock manager struggled from his headquarters near the London Metals Exchange to buy sufficient tin to keep the price at the floor level. Eventually, the stock reached 50,000 to 60,000 metric tons, with another 68,000 metric tons contracted for.[98] On a shocking day in October 1985, the manager announced to the Metals Exchange that he could not fulfill the contracts already made and that the member countries would not come up with the $90 million or so needed to avoid default. The price of tin plunged almost 10% in a few minutes and 17% in the first week. Amidst consternation the London Metals Exchange closed, and so did tin trading around the world.

After the failure of the tin buffer stock, the price of tin went from £8000 per metric ton to £3400 in 1986. The Tin Agreement expired, unlamented, in mid-1989, a decision already having been taken in 1986 not to go ahead with a new tin pact. Because the Tin Agreement had been set up by governments, a major question was whether these governments would back the unpaid debts run up by the buffer stock manager. After a long delay they did so in a 1990 out-of-court settlement that included nearly 40% of the claims. The London metals exchange suspended tin trading permanently, and trading has moved mostly to Kuala Lumpur, Malaysia. A new Association of Tin Producing Countries agreed on production quotas, and Brazil and China, which are not members, promised not to take advantage of the quota system by raising their own output. With the export quotas in use, tin prices recovered to some extent.[99]

The whole episode seems to have handed opponents of price-stabilizing buffer stocks the best evidence they could want that such stocks are actually destabilizing. The mismanagement had repercussions far beyond the world of tin; many authorities believe that the tin fiasco may have been the coup de grâce for price-stabilizing buffer stocks.[100]

The cocoa buffer stock came to an end as well, though its demise was hardly as dramatic as the tin case. An initial attempt to operate a stock in 1981 led to exhaustion of funds the next year. Another try from 1987 involved an $0.87 per pound "must buy" intervention point and a $1.27 "must sell" point. (Actually, the values were in SDRs so they could vary in dollar terms.) There was mandatory adjustment if prices were not within the intervention limits by 115 SDRs per ton, and the buffer stock manager had bought or sold 75,000 tons in the last six months. The buffer stock manager made purchases through 1987, but he quickly spent over half his $250 million in cash in a failed effort to keep prices above the intervention point. Quotas were hard to agree on, and the buffer stock was ineffective in the face of oversupply and shrinking demand. The stock ran out of money in 1988, and the manager's power to fix price ended abruptly. Prices reached a 14-year low in 1990. When a new five-year cocoa agreement was negotiated in 1993, it was decided to liquidate the buffer stock of 230,000 metric tons in monthly sales over four-and-a-half years. The new agreement will not regulate prices or use quotas.

The rubber agreements of 1980 and 1988 had a buffer stock, but the buffer stock manager could not borrow as the tin manager could. Floor and ceiling prices were adjusted by at least 5% whenever the market price was above the ceiling or below the floor. The stock, supposed to contain 400,000 metric tons, had run out of rubber in 1989, in another defeat for stabilization. Even so, with the collapse of the tin and cocoa buffer stocks, the rubber agreement is now the last with a continuing aim to stabilize price.

Other agreements exist for sugar, jute, wheat, and tropical timber, but none of these attempts to manipulate price by quotas or buffer stocks. Mostly they are confined to research and development, market promotion, and conservation.

It remains to ask why official buffer stocks are thought necessary when private trading by commodity speculators buying when prices are low and selling when they are high works toward the same end of stabilizing prices.[101] Futures markets could be a substitute for price stabilization through buffer stocks. A major reason why so many economists have opposed the buffer stock idea is that they believe efforts to encourage futures markets would ultimately have a higher payoff than stabilizing through stocks. Futures markets are currently available only for the larger producers of the more important products. Most economists would no doubt agree that their development should be encouraged whenever possible.

Stabilizing Export Revenue

Even if the prices of exported commodities are stabilized by buffer stocks, the revenues earned from these exports could still fluctuate with changes in supply. A bumper crop at a fixed price would return a much higher income; a drought would reduce revenues. It would be fair to ask why, if revenues remain unstable, would one bother with smoothing price at all? Why not focus on revenue stability alone and simplify matters? The answer appears to be a tactical one. Stabilization of primary product export revenues might be of great value to the LDCs, but it is of little direct value to the buyer of the commodity. Buffer stocks working on price will, on the other hand, promise some benefits to consumers if the fluctuations are dampened. Consuming nations would, of course, have to come up with large amounts of the funding in either case. This is a major reason why both price and revenue stabilization are often advocated at the same time.

There are presently two rather small schemes for stabilizing revenue: the Compensatory and Contingency Financing Facility of the IMF and the Stabex scheme of the European Community that applies to its associated ACP states.

The Compensatory and Contingency Financing Facility An IMF Compensatory and Contingency Financing Facility (CCFF) dates from 1988, and is a descendant of a program begun in 1963. In part, it is a revenue-smoothing device that allows lending to countries where a shortfall in export earnings has occurred.[102] Along with compensation for temporary shortfalls in export earnings, the CCFF also provides for loans on contingencies such as shocks to import prices and interest rates.

Export revenue shortfalls are measured in a sophisticated manner: A five-year trend in revenue is established statistically, based on the evidence from the previous two years and projections as to what is most likely in the two following years. For this year, if revenue is below the trend, the member country can borrow a maximum of 80% of quota to cover the deficiency. Repayment is required after three to five years. Loans for the purpose have been relatively small, usually amounting to about a billion dollars at a given time. Full conditionality applies, meaning that the IMF may require some policy reforms as in its regular leading.

Critics of this policy change are quite correct in pointing out that the revenue shortfall may have been caused by a policy action in some developed country, but that no remedial steps are required of them by the IMF. Critics also point out that the loans have to be repaid in a rather short period of time even if earnings continue to fall. It should also be noted that linking the borrowing to quota size is not entirely sensible in that some countries with large IMF quotas export few primary products, while others are very dependent on these exports but have small quotas. UNCTAD has suggested that the CCFF be divorced from IMF quotas and that repayments be delayed until the contingency ends, but there is little likelihood of this in an era of budget stringencies.

Stabex The other revenue-stabilizing scheme currently in use is the EC's Stabex, which dates originally from 1975.[103] The scheme usually covers only exports to the EC and not to the rest of the world. It is less sophisticated than the IMF's CCFF in that the shortfall in export performance is based only on the average of earnings in the past four years, with no account taken of the future trend. (The main result is that Stabex always lags behind any inflation or deflation of prices, whereas the CCFF keeps up by making projections of price behavior.)

Stabex is the most distinctive feature, and often the most controversial one, of the Lomé Conventions between the EC and its associated ACP states. There are currently 70 of these states.* (Lomé is the capital of Togo, where the four different treaties have been signed.) Under the Lomé IV agreement of December 1989, which is to last for ten years, some 50 products of the 68 member countries are covered up to the financial limits of the scheme, which is now set at about $2 billion. Stabex will pay on a given export even if export earnings are rising on other commodities; this is unlike the IMF's CCFF. There are dependency thresholds and fluctuation thresholds, so that the more a country depends on an export and the more earnings from it fluctuate, the more likely that Stabex payments will be received. When and if export revenues again increase, repayment is eventually required from all but the poorest countries, to which the money goes as grants. Also unlike the IMF's CCFF, the loans are interest free and there is no limit on receipts. Receipts under the scheme have been important for some countries. For example, at times in the 1980s they amounted to as much as 10% or more of all export revenue in Senegal, Sudan, and Mauritania.† (It should be noted that the Lomé Conventions channel much more aid to the LDC members than does Stabex. The treaties also include development cooperation, rural development, food security programs, and infrastructure promotion.)

Though Stabex is a wide-ranging and liberal idea, it has faced mammoth problems. The funding is not adequate to meet anywhere near all the legitimate claims, so Stabex has run out of money several times when world recessions have affected primary products. In some years only about half or less of the claimed amounts have actually been paid. In 1994, the EC proposed that its Stabex aid be made conditional on democratic political reforms and economic liberalization.

The Stabex scheme probably leads to more production of the commodities that are covered and less production of uncovered ones. Certainly non-ACP states with no recourse to Stabex are put at a disadvantage. Finally, potential benefits in agriculture are much diminished because the EC is so restrictive on imports of commodities, especially sugar, that compete with community production.

The Future for Revenue Stabilization Aid through the IMF's CCFF or the EC's Stabex to stabilize export revenue along some moving trend line would appear to lessen the difficulties facing primary product exporters. Yet the enthusiasm has definitely been muted. The developed countries fear that stabilization will

*A few non-ACP developing countries were made eligible for Stabex aid in 1986. Historically, Britain was unable to engineer entry into the ACP of India, Pakistan, Burma, and Sri Lanka; the Netherlands could not get Indonesia in; and Spain did not manage the entry of Latin America.

†There is also a small program (currently slightly over half a billion dollars) for minerals called Sysmin, or sometimes Minex, dating from 1980. A country is eligible for Sysmin funds if 15% of its export earnings come from a covered mineral (copper, cobalt, phosphate, manganese, bauxite, tin, or iron ore). By special dispensation on a case-by-case basis, the payments will be made on any mineral (except oil, natural gas, and precious metals and stones) that makes up at least 20% of export revenue. (The figures are 10% and 12%, respectively, for least developed, landlocked, and island countries.) The payments are used to improve production and infrastructure and to reduce capacity.

THE BANANA CASE AS A RESULT OF EC POLICIES

The ongoing banana case shows how the preferences for the ACP states can have broader effects. Bananas produced in the ACP countries are relatively high in cost compared to those produced in Latin America, which generally has the comparative advantage. Germany had no client states in the LDCs and was content to import bananas duty-free from any source. But the EC's single market arrangement of 1992 brought this to an end, for otherwise low-cost Latin American bananas could be imported to Germany and reexported from there to members such as Britain and France which had preferences for their former colonies. So the EC adopted a tariff-quota, with Latin American fruit limited to exports of 2 million metric tons with a tariff of 20%; additional fruit would pay 170%. The EC would not accept a GATT panel finding against the scheme, and the ensuing dispute surrounding this prohibitive duty almost caused a delay in the signing of the Uruguay Round. Then the EC offered improved terms of Latin America, which were accepted by four countries—Colombia, Costa Rica, Nicaragua, and Venezuela—but not by others. A new agreement giving preferential treatment to these four countries was scheduled to come into effect on January 1, 1995. Germany is challenging the EC decision in the European Court of Justice. The United States is also attacking the arrangement because of its detrimental effect on Chiquita, a firm that exports many Latin American bananas to Europe.[104] The ramifications of the EC's patronage to its client states are not always benign.

become a compulsory transfer mechanism for aid funds, and so they oppose further enhancements. Some LDCs, the ones that export few primary products or products unlikely to be covered, are also opposed. It is probably fair to say that most economists would favor extensions in this area over enhanced price stabilization, and even more over measures to boost commodity prices. In the present political climate, however, developed-country governments have taken a dim view of all such policies.

Conclusion

The future for international trade as an expediter of the LDCs' economic growth is clouded by the ties between exports and the business cycle in the developed countries, by the existence of barriers to trade in the developed countries and the LDCs alike, by the dangers of trade-diverting customs unions, and by the failure of price stabilization for primary products. Yet international trade has uniformly shown itself to be a positive element in the growth of the best-performing countries of the Third World. That being so, it is heartening that the world's developed countries at last found the courage to enact the Uruguay Round of trade reforms and establish the new World Trade Organization. That will lower many of the barriers that have in the past reduced the ability of international trade to expedite growth. Assuming that the new trade rules hold and that liberalization continues, trade is likely to become an even greater stimulus to economic development than before.

NOTES

1. For the figures, see *WDR 1987*, 146.
2. The DRI study is cited in Allen Wallis, "Commodity Markets and Commodity Agreements," *U.S. Department of State Current Policy No. 791* (1986).
3. *WDR 1991*, 123; *The Economist*, October 1, 1994; and David Goldsborough and Iqbal M. Zaidi, "Transmission of Economic Influences from Industrial to Developing Countries," Staff Studies for the World Economic Outlook (Washington, D.C., 1986). Also see Margaret Kelly, Naheed Kirmani, Miranda Xafa, Clemens Boonekamp, and Peter Winglee, "Issues and Developments in International Trade Policy," IMF Occasional Paper No. 63 (1988), 129; and IMF, *World Economic Outlook, 1986* (Washington, D.C., 1986), 11.
4. *HDR 1994*, 206.
5. *The Economist*, October 1, 1994.
6. *The Economist*, October 1, 1994.
7. Good recent sources are David Evans, ed., *Developing Countries and the International Economy: Issues in Trade, Adjustment and Debt* (London, 1991); Dominick Salvatore, ed., *Protectionism and World Welfare* (Cambridge, 1993); John Whalley, ed., *Developing Countries and the Global Trading System*, vol. 1, *Thematic Studies*, and vol. 2, *Country Studies* (London, 1989); and David B. Yoffie, *Beyond Free Trade: Firms, Governments, and Global Competition* (Boston, 1993).
8. *The Economist*, November 16, 1991.
9. *The Economist*, October 1, 1994.
10. Adrian Wood, "How Much Does Trade with the South Affect Workers in the North?" *World Bank Research Observer* 6, no. 1 (January 1991): 19–36.
11. See Douglas Cleveland, "It's Time to Retire the Import Penetration Ratio," *Challenge* 28, no. 4 (1985): 50–53.
12. Jeffrey Sachs and Howard Shatz, "Trade and Jobs in U.S. Manufacturing," *Brookings Papers on Economic Activity* (1994). See Adrian Wood, *North–South Trade, Unemployment, and Inequality* (Oxford, 1994), for a study making the case that imports from the LDCs have been a major factor in the poor situation for unskilled workers in developed countries.
13. *The Economist*, October 1, 1994.
14. Adrian Wood, "How Much Does Trade with the South Affect Workers in the North?" 26; George Borjas, Richard Freeman, and Lawrence Katz, *On the Labor Market Effects of Immigration and Trade*, NBER Working Paper No. 3761.
15. The figure is for 1983. See W. Max Corden, *Protection and Liberalization: A Review of Analytical Issues*, IMF Occasional Paper No. 54 (1987). Also see J. Michael Finger and Sam Laird, "Protection in Developed and Developing Countries—An Overview," *Journal of World Trade Law* 21, no. 6 (December 1987): 9–23.
16. *The Economist*, April 9, 1994. Also see Steve Charnowitz, "Fair Labor Standards and International Trade," *Journal of World Trade Law* 20, no. 1 (1986): 61–78.
17. See *WDR 1988*, 16; *HDR 1992*, 63; and, for comments on the effects of developed-country protection on economic growth, see Bernard Heitger, "Import Protection and

Export Performance: Their Impact on Economic Growth," *Weltwirtschaftliches Archiv* 123, no. 2 (1987): 257.

18. The history and analysis are covered thoroughly by W. M. Corden, *The Theory of Protection* (Oxford, 1971), 35–40, 245–249.
19. The tale is from Don D. Humphrey, *The United States and the Common Market* (New York, 1964), 61. In actuality, the pearls were bored and temporarily threaded abroad because these steps did not transform them into "strung pearls" under U.S. law. They were put on a permanent string and provided with a clasp in the United States.
20. *International Economic Review*, August, 1993.
21. For estimates of trade expansion under the GSP see John Whalley, "Non-Discriminatory Discrimination: Special and Differential Treatment Under the GATT for Developing Countries," *Economic Journal* 100, no. 403 (December 1990): 1324, citing G. Karsenty and S. Laird, and C. R. MacPhee; *WDR 1990*, 124; *The Economist*, January 9, 1988; and R. E. Baldwin and T. E. Murray, "MFN Tariff Reductions and Developing Country Trade Benefits under the GSP," *Economic Journal* 87, no. 345 (1977); 30–46. Also see T. E. Murray, *Trade Preferences for Developing Countries* (London, 1977); and Robert E. Baldwin, "Trade Policies in Developed Countries," in Ronald W. Jones and Peter B. Kenen, eds., *Handbook of International Economics*, vol. 1 (Amsterdam, 1984), 598–600. Some of the figures in this section are from the annual issues of the U.S. International Trade Commission (ITC), *The Year in Trade* (Washington, D.C.).
22. All from USITC, *The Year in Trade 1993* (Washington, D.C., 1994), 130–131.
23. *The Economist*, January 29, 1994, and April 30, 1994.
24. See Kelly et al, "Issues and Developments in International Trade Policy" (1988), 118, and C. Fred Bergsten and William R. Cline, "Trade Policy in the 1980s: An Overview," in Cline, *Trade Policy in the 1980s*, 72. There is an analytical study by Stephen S. Golub and J. M. Finger, "The Processing of Primary Commodities: Effects of Developed-Country Tariff Escalation and Developing-Country Export Taxation," *Journal of Political Economy* 87, no. 3 (1979): 559–577. With the development of large econometric models in the rich countries, it has become possible to trace more carefully the effects of any change in nominal tariffs, so the subject has gone somewhat out of fashion. But it remains an important issue for the LDCs. See Peter Kenen, *The International Economy* (Englewood Cliffs, N.J., 1985), 184.
25. For some of these, see Emmanuel Opoku Awuku, "How Do the Results of the Uruguay Round Affect the North–South Trade?" *Journal of World Trade* 28, no. 2 (April 1994): 75, citing E. Mayo.
26. Quoted in Brandt Commission, *North–South: A Programme for Survival* (London, 1980), 141–142.
27. *WDR 1990*, 125.
28. Margaret Kelly and Anne Kenny McGuirk, *Issues and Developments in International Trade Policy* (Washington, D.C., 1992), 117.
29. Kelly et al, *Issues and Developments in International Trade Policy* (1988), 27.
30. See Sri Ram Khanna, *International Trade in Textiles: MFA Quotas and a Developing Exporting Country* (New Delhi, 1991); Kelly et al, *International Trade Policy* (1988), 72–75, 160, 162; Xiaobing Tang, "Textiles and the Uruguay Round of Multilateral Trade Negotiations," *Journal of World Trade* 23, no. 3 (June 1989): 51–68; Robert Z. Lawrence and Charles L. Schultze, *An American Trade Strategy: Options for the 1990s* (Washington, D.C., 1990), 44; Madhaul Majmudar, "The Multi-Fibre Arrangement (MFA IV) 1986–1991: A Move Towards a Liberalized System?" *Journal of World Trade* 22, no. 2 (April 1988): 109–125; Martin Wolf, "Managed Trade in Practice:

Implications of the Textile Arrangement," in Cline, Trade Policy in the 1980s, 455–482; and all recent issues of the USITC, *The Year in Trade*. I also consulted numerous articles in *The Economist*. Much of the material in this section also appears in Wilson, B. Brown and Jan S. Hogendorn, *International Economics: Theory and Context* (Reading, Mass., 1993).

31. USITC, *The Year in Trade 1992* (Washington, D.C., 1993), 102.
32. *HDR 1994*, 66. Also see Refik Erzan, Samuel Laird, and Alexander Yeats, "On the Potential for Expanding South–South Trade Through the Extension of Mutual Preferences Among Developing Countries," *World Development* 16, no. 12 (December 1988): 1441–1454.
33. USITC, *The Year in Trade 1993*, 50.
34. Richard Harmsen, "The Uruguay Round: A Boon for the World Economy," *Finance and Development* 32, no. 1 (March 1995): 24–26.
35. Dumping is analyzed by Brown and Hogendorn, *International Economics: Theory and Context*, chapter 7. Also see John H. Jackson and Edwin A. Vermulst, eds., *Antidumping Law and Practice* (Ann Arbor, 1989); and Richard Boltuck and Robert E. Litan, eds., *Down in the Dumps*, (Washington, D.C., 1991).
36. Kelly et al, "Issues and Developments in International Trade Policy" (1988), 26.
37. USITC, *The Year in Trade 1993*, 13, 175–180.
38. *The Economist*, December 24, 1994.
39. See Brown and Hogendorn, *International Economics: Theory and Context*, chapter 7; Gary Clyde Hufbauer and Joanna Shelton Erb, *Subsidies in International Trade*, (Washington, D.C., 1984), especially chapter 3; Kelly et al., *Issues and Developments in International Trade Policy*, (1988), 130; Jagdish Bhagwati, *Protectionism* (Cambridge, Mass., 1988), 52, 116; James Bovard, "The Myth of Fair Trade," *Policy Analysis* 164 (November 1, 1991): 9–11; N. David Palmeter, "Injury Determination in Antidumping and Countervailing Duty Cases—A Commentary on U.S. Practice," *Journal of World Trade Law* 21, no. 2 (1987): 123–161; and the coverage in USITC, *The Year in Trade* and the *International Economic Review*.
40. USITC, *The Year in Trade 1993*, 183–185.
41. USITC, *The Year in Trade 1993*, 17–18.
42. Bela Balassa, "Subsidies and Countervailing Measures: Economic Considerations," *Journal of World Trade* 23, no. 2 (April 1989): 74–79.
43. Emmanuel Opoku Awuku, "How Do the Results of the Uruguay Round Affect the North–South Trade?" *Journal of World Trade* 28, no. 2 (April 1994): 75–93.
44. Most of the material on agricultural protection in the sections that follow is taken from Brown and Hogendorn, *International Economics: Theory and Context*, chapter 4. For a specialized work on the subject, see Fred H. Sanderson, ed., *Agricultural Protection in the Industrialized World* (Washington, D.C., 1990).
45. For details see Brent Borrell and Ronald C. Duncan, "A Survey of the Costs of World Sugar Policies," *World Bank Research Observer* 7, no. 2 (July 1992): 171–194; U.S. Department of Commerce, "United States Sugar Policy: An Analysis" (1988); *WDR 1990*, 122; Kelly et al., "International Trade Policy" (1988), 62; U.S. Department of Agriculture, annual reports, "Sugar and Sweetener"; all recent reports of USITC, *The Year in Trade*; and *The Economist*, December 12, 1992.
46. See Sanderson, *Agricultural Protection in the Industrialized World*; Enzo Grilli, *The European Community and the Developing Countries* (Cambridge, 1992); Ulrich Koester and Malcolm D. Bale, "The Common Agricultural Policy: A Review of Its Operation and Effects on Developing Countries," *World Bank Research Observer* 5, no. 1 (January 1990): 95–121; Julius Rosenblatt, *The Common Agricultural Policy of the European Community: Principles and Consequences*, IMF Occasional Paper No.

62 (November 1988); and Brian E. Hill, *Common Agricultural Policy: Past, Present, and Future* (London, 1984).

47. *WDR 1986*, 129–131. This edition of the *WDR* concentrates, in part, on protection in agriculture.
48. USITC, *The Year in Trade 1993*, 7–8. For a specific study, see A. J. Rayner, K. A. Ingersent, and R. C. Hine, "Agriculture in the Uruguay Round: An Assessment," *Economic Journal* 103, no. 421 (November 1993): 1513–1527.
49. Margaret Kelly and Anne Kenny McGuirk, *Issues and Developments in International Trade Policy* (Washington, D.C., 1992): 59.
50. This section relies heavily on Margaret Kelly and Anne Kenny McGuirk, *Issues and Developments in International Trade Policy* (Washington, D.C., 1992), 43; Kelly et al, "Issues and Developments in International Trade Policy"; and *WDR 1991*, especially p. 98. There is a lengthy catalog of protective measures in LDCs in the various issues of a publication of the Office of the United States Trade Representative, *Annual Report on National Trade Estimates* (Washington, D.C.).
51. *WDR 1991*, 98; Kelly et al, "Issues and Developments in International Trade Policy," 22; and see W. M. Corden, *The Theory of Protection*, 199.
52. See A. F. Ewing, "Why Freer Trade in Services Is in the Interest of Developing Countries," *Journal of World Trade Law* 19, no, 2 (1985): 147–169.
53. Brian Hindley, "Economic Development and Services," in V. N. Balasubramanyam and Sanjaya Lall, *Current Issues in Development Economics*, eds. (New York, 1991), 206–208.
54. See, for example, Alexander Yeats, "Do African Countries Pay More for Imports," *Finance and Development* 27, no. 2 (June 1990): 38–40.
55. Emmanuel Opoku Awuku, "How Do the Results of the Uruguay Round Affect the North–South Trade?" *Journal of World Trade* 28, no. 2 (April 1994): 92.
56. USITC, *The Year in Trade 1993*, 34–36.
57. For the figures in this paragraph, see IMF, *World Economic Outlook 1994*, 84–87. The studies, one by GATT, one by the OECD, and two by independent investigators, are cited and discussed in that publication.
58. See Marcelo de Paiva Abreu, "Developing Countries and the Uruguay Round of Trade Negotiations," *Proceedings of the World Bank Annual Conference on Development Economics 1989* (Washington, D.C., 1990), 27, for an estimate of the gains.
59. T. Nguyen, C. Perroni, and R. Wingle, "An Evaluation of the Draft Final Act of the Uruguay Round," *Economic Journal* 103, no. 421 (November 1993): 1540–1549.
60. IMF, *World Economic Outlook 1994*, 84–85.
61. *The Economist*, April 2, 1994.
62. Oli Havrylyshyn explores the factor differences and advances criticisms of South–South trade in "The Direction of Developing Country Trade: Empirical Evidence of Differences Between South–South and South–North Trade," *Journal of Development Economics* 19, no. 3 (1986): 255–281.
63. See Brown and Hogendorn, *International Economics: Theory and Context*, chapter 9, for a more extended discussion.
64. Anne O. Krueger, "Trade Strategies and Employment in Developing Countries," *Finance and Development* 21, no. 2 (1984): 25.
65. Refik Erzan, Samuel Laird, and Alexander Yeats, "On the Potential for Expanding South–South Trade Through the Extension of Mutual Preferences Among Developing Countries," *World Development* 16, no. 12 (December 1988): 1441–1454. Even greater effects are predicted by Hans Linnemann and Harmen Verbruggen, "GSTP Tariff Reduction and Its Effects on South–South Trade in Manufactures," *World Development* 19, no. 5 (May 1991): 539–551.

66. L.N. Willmore, "Trade Creation, Trade Diversion and Effective Protection in the Central American Common Market," *Journal of Development Studies*, 12 (1976): 396–414.
67. William R. Cline, "Benefits and Costs of Economic Integration in Central America," in W. Cline and C. Delagado, eds., *Economic Integration in Central America: A Study*, (Washington, D.C.), 1978.
68. *International Economic Review*, April 1991.
69. de la Torre and Kelly, *Regional Trade Arrangements*, 37, citing R. George, Rolf J. Langhammer, and Dean Spinanger.
70. de la Torre and Kelly, *Regional Trade Arrangements*, 37, citing K. Khazeh and D. Clark.
71. *International Economic Review*, December 1993, January 1994, and September 1994.
72. There is an annual accounting of the CBERA in USITC, *The Year in Trade*.
73. See Sidney Weintraub, "A U. S.–Israel Free-Trade Area," *Challenge* 28, no. 3 (1985): 47–50; and the annual reports on this agreement in USITC, *The Year in Trade*.
74. See Mario F. Bognanno, ed., *The North American Free Trade Agreement: Labor, Industry, and Government Perspectives* (Westport, Conn., 1993); and Peter M. Garber, *The Mexico–U.S. Free Trade Agreement* (Cambridge, 1993).
75. *International Economic Review*, October 1994.
76. Richard Pomfret, "The Quiet Shift in U.S. Trade Policy," *Challenge* 27, no. 5 (1984): 61–64.
77. Christian E. Petersen, "Trade Conflict and Resolution Methodologies," *American Economic Review* 82, no. 2 (May 1992): 65.
78. *WDR 1994*, 190–191.
79. W. M. Corden, *Trade Policy and Economic Welfare* (Oxford, 1974), 314.
80. James Love, "Commodity Concentration and Export Earnings Instability: A Shift from Cross-Section to Time Series Analysis," *Journal of Development Economics* 24, no. 2 (December 1986): 239–248.
81. See *WDR 1982*, 12.
82. *The Economist*, July 23, 1994.
83. I used Behrman's "median of available estimates" where given. As he explains, for a number of reasons these elasticities are probably biased upward to some degree, adding to the strength of the case. The supply figure for tin is Behrman's own, as are the demand estimates for cotton, jute, sisal, and tin. In many cases Behrman's own estimates are lower than the "median of available estimates." The higher long-run supply elasticities are also presented by Behrman. Alternative figures are in *WDR 1986*, 68.
84. H. Laurens van der Laan, "Boosting Agricultural Exports? A 'Marketing Channel' Perspective on an African Dilemma," *African Affairs* 92, no. 367 (April 1993): 182.
85. See Paul D. Reynolds, *Commodity Agreements and the Common Fund* (New York, 1978), 22.
86. See A. I. MacBean, *Export Instability and Economic Development* (Cambridge, 1966). Further studies by Peter Kenen and C. S. Voivodas did not alter the basic conclusion. A nice treatment of the issue is D. Lim, "Export Instability and Economic Growth: A Return to Fundamentals," *Oxford Bulletin of Economics and Statistics* 38, no. 4 (1976): 311–322. The debate is summarized by Stephen R. Lewis, Jr., "Primary Exporting Countries," in Hollis Chenery and T. N. Srinivasan, eds., *Handbook of Development Economics*, vol. 2 (Amsterdam, 1989), 1541–1600, especially 1551–1552.
87. Anne O. Krueger, "Trade Policies in Developing Countries," in Ronald W. Jones and Peter B. Kenen, eds., *Handbook of International Economics*, vol. 1 (Amsterdam, 1984), 5.
88. Jere R. Behrman, "Commodity Price Instability and Economic Goal Attainment in Developing Countries," *World Development* 15, no. 5 (May 1987): 570.

89. See Lewis, "Primary Exporting Countries," in Chenery and Srinivasan, *Handbook of Development Economics*, vol. 2, 1551–1552, citing Lewis's own "Africa's Trade and the World Economy," in R. J. Berg and J. S. Whitaker, eds., *Strategies for African Development* (Berkeley, 1986); and G. K. Helleiner, "Outward Orientation, Import Instability and African Economic Growth: An Empirical Investigation," in S. Lall and F. Stewart, eds., *Theory and Reality in Economic Development* (London, 1986).
90. The subject is surveyed by Fiona Gordon-Ashworth, *International Commodity Control: A Contemporary History and Appraisal* (London, 1984); by Reynolds, *Commodity Agreements and the Common Fund*; and by Christopher P. Brown, *The Political and Social Economy of Commodity Control* (London, 1980).
91. Jere R. Behrman, "Stabilizing Prices Through International Buffer Stock Commodity Agreements," *National Development* (May 1980): 49–54.
92. A very readable account is Daniel Yergin, *The Prize* (New York, 1991).
93. See Richard M. Auty, "Industrial Policy Reform in Six Large Newly-Industrializing Countries: The Resource Curse Thesis," *World Development* 22, no. 1 (January 1994): 11–26; and Gustav Ranis and Syed Akhtar Mahmood, *The Political Economy of Development Policy Change* (Oxford, 1992).
94. For this section I have utilized Jere R. Behrman, "The Analytics of International Commodity Agreements," in Carl K. Eicher and John M. Spatz, eds., *Agricultural Development in the Third World* (Baltimore, 1984); Behrman, "International Commodity Agreements," in Cline, *Policy Alternatives for a New International Economic Order*; and Christopher P. Brown, *Political and Social Economy of Commodity Control*.
95. Grant P. Taplin, "Revitalizing UNCTAD," *Finance and Development* 29, no. 2 (June 1992): 36–37.
96. Analysis can be found in Alasdair MacBean and Duc Tin Nguyen, "International Commodity Agreements: Shadow and Substance," and Christopher L. Gilbert, "International Commodity Agreements: Design and Performance," both in *World Development* 15, no. 5 (May 1987): 575–590, 591–616.
97. Another problem is that stabilizing price may not necessarily stabilize revenue. For this analysis, which is technical, see Jere R. Behrman, *Development, the International Economic Order, and Commodity Agreements* (Reading, Mass., 1978). Also see Ezriel Brook, Enzo Grilli, and Jean Waelbroeck, "Commodity Price Stabilization and the Developing Countries," *Banca Nazionale del Lavoro Quarterly Review*, no. 124 (March 1978): 79–99. Debate on this issue is considered by Walter C. Labys, "Commodity Price Stabilization Models: A Review and Appraisal," *Journal of Policy Modeling* 2, no. 1 (1980): 121–136. This article also considers welfare implications of stabilization and directs the reader to the earlier studies of B. F. Massell, F. V. Waugh, and Walter Oi.
98. Figures differ. I have generally followed "Tin Crisis in London Roils Metals Exchange," *Wall Street Journal*, November 13, 1985. Other details in this section are from *South*, no. 66 (April 1986): 15; and see John Toye, *Dilemmas of Development*, 2nd ed. (Oxford, 1993): 189.
99. Ronald W. Anderson and Christopher L. Gilbert, "Commodity Agreements and Commodity Markets: Lessons from Tin," *Economic Journal* 98 (March 1988): 1–15; *South*, March 1990.
100. Gilbert, "International Commodity Agreements: Design and Performance," 591–616.
101. The question is asked in *WDR 1986*, chapter 7.
102. For details see Roger Pownall and Brian Stuart, "The IMF's Compensatory and Contingency Financing Facility," *Finance and Development* 25, no. 4 (December 1988): 9–11; Nihad Kaibni, "Evolution of the Compensatory Financing Facility," *Finance and Development* 23, no. 2 (1986): 24–27; and *WDR 1986*, 138–139, 141. For critical

reviews, see Sidney Dell, "The Fifth Credit Tranche," *World Development* 13, no. 2 (1985): 245–249; and J. M. Finger and Dean A. Derosa, "The Compensatory Finance Facility and Export Instability," *Journal of World Trade Law* 14, no. 1 (1980): 14–22.

103. Details and analysis may be found in Shada Islam, "Europe Toughens Terms for ACP Countries," *Africa Recovery* 7, nos. 3–4 (December 1993–March 1994): 21; Adrian P. Hewitt, "Stabex and Commodity Export Compensation Schemes: Prospects for Globalization," *World Development* 15, no. 5 (May 1987): 617–631; Adrian Hewitt, "Stabex: An Evaluation of the Economic Impact over the First Five Years," *World Development* 11, no. 12 (1983): 1005–1027; Hamisi S. Kibola, "Stabex and Lomé III," *Journal of World Trade Law* 18, no. 1 (1984): 32–5 1; Gerrit Faber, "The Economics of Stabex," *Journal of World Trade Law* 18, no. 1 (1984): 52–62; Michael Blackwell, "Lomé III: The Search for Greater Effectiveness," *Finance and Development* 22, no. 3 (1985): 31–34; *WDR 1986*, 139–144; and various issues of *IMF Survey* and *The Economist*.

104. *International Economic Review*, June 1994 and December 1994; *The Economist*, March 20, 1993.

Chapter 16

The Environment and the LDCs

John Maynard Keynes said that in the long run, we are all dead. One hopes he was not a clairvoyant speaking of environmental problems. When Keynes died in 1946 and the pioneers of development economics were beginning to erect the structure of this discipline, the environmental considerations of economic progress were patently of little concern to those pioneers. It was understood by them that regard for the environment tends to lag behind appreciation for a higher income and the advantages of an escape from poverty. This was, after all, exactly what had happened in all the developed countries. England's "dark satanic mills," in the evocative phrasing of William Blake, had their counterparts in all the economies that industrialized during the nineteenth century. The smoke and grit, the coal-fed fogs and polluted water, and the dangerous working conditions in industry were understood to be a penalty paid for eventual economic improvement and a better life as incomes grew. The English Midlands, Pittsburgh, the Ruhr, and dozens of other industrial areas were indeed wastelands, but wastelands with rising incomes where, albeit gradually, poverty was retreating.

If interviewed today, the pioneers of development economics would surely express no surprise that for many years there was only slight concern in the LDCs for environmental pollution, nor that until very recently pollution control policies were rare in the LDCs. With condolences, but also with equanimity, they would show understanding for cases such as present-day China with its grim levels of pollution. China is the world's leading producer of coal, and that coal is very high in sulfur content. Yet the dirty urban environment has been of little concern to the average Chinese, who realizes that the new industries pay much higher wages than could be earned pulling rickshaws or working all day knee-deep in rice paddies. Much richer Taiwan is almost as dirty, its air so polluted that it is officially classified as harmful to public health for a total of two months out of every year. Here, too, people appear to believe that the foul odor is the "smell of money."

The pioneers of development economics would explain that, to most people in most LDCs, square meals are preferred to clean air. Mrs. Gandhi's statement that the worst pollution is poverty would undoubtedly receive enthusiastic support from the masses in the LDCs. The past decisions by these countries to opt for higher income at the cost of some local degradation in the environment is by this logic entirely understandable. As a general rule, the decisions to allow or control local pollution could properly be left to the internal political processes of the countries concerned. In this view, the rarity of LDCs with environmental protection agencies (the number hardly exceeding ten in the early 1970s) would be temporary and in the long run relatively harmless. Eventually the problem would prove to be self-correcting as a country grew out of its poverty. It could then afford to make a turn toward cleaning up. In fact, with two decades of reasonable growth in the LDCs, the number of such agencies *did* increase, to well over 100 in the 1980s. With economic growth, so it appears, comes more sensitivity to environmental harm and more ability to do something about it.

LOCAL CONCERNS

The first concerns for environmental matters to spoil the prevailing calm were basically local ones, pertaining to individual countries.[1] It was becoming clear that population increases could harm the prospects for development by increasing the scarcity of land and water while at the same time degrading their quality. As more people are driven to marginal hillside land, the clearing and farming of the hillsides can erode land and silt up waterways, irrigation channels, and hydroelectric facilities. In Africa, there is concern that soil erosion could severely reduce agricultural production.[2] There is also heavy soil erosion in China, Latin (especially Central) America, and in parts of South Asia. The environmental deterioration makes the poor population, living close to the land, even poorer. (Fortunately, soil conservation and prevention of erosion can be quite low in cost. Mulching, contour cultivation, and grass contour hedges slow runoff, prevent erosion, and at the same time increase water retention and hence fertility. Tree planting of fast-growing tree varieties to anchor the soil can help. Eucalyptus is a favorite for this, though it adds few nutrients to the soil.)[3]

A major reason why population growth has become a major cause of environmental decline is the cutting down of forests for farms and firewood. Much forest cover has already been lost in many LDCs, with the problems acute in many countries and perhaps greatest in Haiti, Nepal, and in the African countries that border the Sahara. In Africa, some 90% of the population uses fuelwood for cooking, with consumption equal to about 1.5 tons of oil per family per year. Cutting outpaces the increment to tree growth by 75% in northern Nigeria, by 70% in Sudan, by 150% in Ethiopia, and by 30% in all countries of the African Sahel.[4] In the Philippines, about 60% of the land was forested in the 1950s, compared to about 10% now.[5] Worldwide, it is estimated that today ten trees are being cut down for every one planted, and the claim is made that 23 countries have essentially run out of wood for fuel. The wood burning for cooking and heating raises the local amount of particulate matter in the atmosphere substantially.[6] Overgrazing by cattle has similar roots in population growth and has destructive consequences.[7] "Desertification" can be one of the results. This transformation of grazing land to desert is caused by the rapid erosion and greater exposure to sun and wind of overgrazed land. It is estimated that six million hectares, equal to the size of Ireland, are being lost to desert every year, beyond a practicality of reclamation. Three-and-a-half times more than that is rendered unprofitable for farming or grazing. Water goes short as too many farmers attempt to irrigate and too many wells are sunk; overfishing spoils fish stocks in rivers and lakes.

As LDCs struggle to produce more output for their ever-growing populations; they run up against an even wider range of environmental hazards: Major use of pesticides can adversely affect people. DDT, now banned in the developed countries, is still produced today by many LDCs, including India and Brazil. The last U.S. DDT-making plant was dismantled in 1983, but the plant was sold to Indonesia and reassembled there. Even various agencies of the United Nations still sponsor applications of DDT.[8] One recent estimate is that pesticide poisoning kills from 3,000 to 20,000 people per year in the LDCs, while 800,000 to 1.1 million others suffer adverse effects to their health. In some countries, significant amounts of groundwater are badly polluted by pesticides.[9] In Guatemala and Nicaragua, very high levels of DDT in humans have been recorded.[10] Moreover, the pesticides may make more resistant the very pests marked for elimination. Irrigation can lead to flooding, salinization, and waterborne disease; chemical fertilizers may bring chemical runoff into water supplies; increasing industrialization can pollute the air and contaminate ground water with effluent.[11] All can degrade human health and hence productivity.

These consequences were far more serious than the pioneers of development economics had anticipated. Yet it remained true that the effects were felt only in the countries where the environmentally damaging activities were taking place. The concerns were still local ones, and national policies could be adopted (or not adopted) in response. Indeed, that is how in earlier chapters we treated the environmental side to population growth, agricultural growth, or industrial growth—as costs to be dealt with by the country concerned, and essentially its own business. In any case, development itself was partly the cause of the harm, and in spite of the pollution, income and output were growing. Hopes that a better environment would flow from development itself could be considered bright.

Certainly considerable evidence emerged that development *could* be combined with a cleaner environment. Figure 16.1 shows for the developed countries how economic growth (actually about 80% in the time period shown) was linked with no greater or even *less* pollution in various forms.[12] This decrease in pollution was achieved with expenditures of about 0.8% to 1.5% of GDP, with about half the

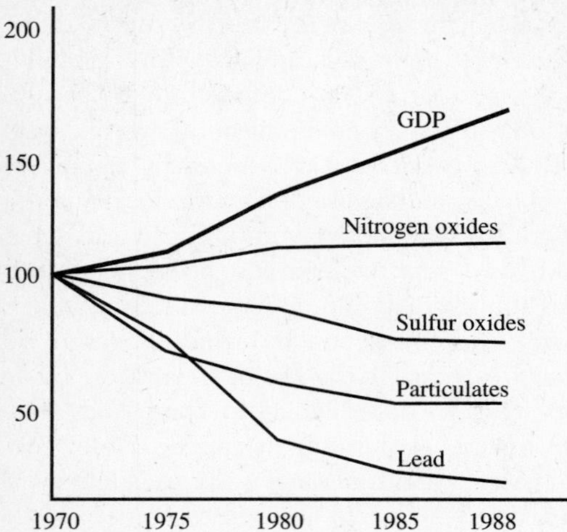

Figure 16.1 Considerable economic growth (here about 80%) has been accompanied by a substantial decline in a number of pollutants in the developed countries.

cost incurred by private firms and about half by governments. As noted, the growth in GDP during the period was about 80%.

Several reasons combine to make richer countries cleaner countries. Economic growth makes cleaning up desirable as well as more affordable, and it helps to cut increases in population. All are powerful weapons for a cleaner environment.[13]

GLOBAL CONCERNS

Then it came to be realized that, distressingly, environmental harm can have a global impact. The global aspect raises obvious questions about economic growth. If the greater production of the LDCs increases environmental damage to other countries, either just across the border or around the world, then the net positive effects of growth will be reduced, others will be damaged, and political roadblocks to growth are sure to arise, particularly in the area of international trade. The global problems of most concern to development economics are the proven and non-controversial destruction of the ozone layer, and the less certain and more debatable prospect of global warming from the so-called greenhouse effect. We examine them in detail.*

*Acid rain could in the future be another environmental issue for the LDCs, but at present it appears a less-pressing problem than ozone depletion and global warming. Acid rain carries sulfur emissions a relatively short maximum distance of some 200 to 600 miles, and so is often a national rather than an international problem. Corrective technology, though expensive, is available.

Destruction of Ozone

Thomas Midgley, Jr., was the discoverer of chlorofluorocarbons (CFCs) in 1930.[14] Undeniably, it was a major event. CFCs are neither toxic nor flammable, and they are effective and inexpensive coolants for use in refrigerators. Three-quarters of all food in the developed countries was said to be chilled with them at some point. Air-conditioning, including that in businesses, homes, and autos, used them in huge quantities, especially the large machinery in shopping malls, arenas, and high-rise buildings. CFCs also served as aerosol propellants for hair spray, polish, deodorants, and many other products, and they found further use as rigid insulation, packing, and the like, as with Dow Chemical's Styrofoam. They were even employed in dry cleaning and computer maintenance as a cleaning solvent. Table 16.1 shows the purposes to which CFCs were put worldwide in the mid-1980s.

Unfortunately, experience showed that escaping CFCs float upward through the atmosphere, reaching the stratosphere in six to eight years. There they survive for up to 100 years. Each chlorine atom, the chloro in chlorofluorocarbon, is capable of destroying tens of thousands of ozone molecules. Chlorine in the upper atmosphere grew from 0.6 parts per billion in the early 1960s to 2.7 parts per billion in the late 1980s.[15]

In 1985, British scientists broke the news that the ozone level in the atmosphere was shrinking and that a vast hole in the ozone layer had been opening over Antarctica since 1979. The news came as a complete surprise.[16] Subsequent studies revealed that in the years 1960 to 1986, ozone had decreased 1.7% to 3% in a Northern Hemisphere band encompassing the United States and Europe. Winter loss was greater, 2.3% to 6.2%. Unfortunately, because of the long delay before the escaping chlorofluorocarbons destroy atmospheric ozone, the destruction being seen then was due only to the releases that had occurred up to the late 1970s. The ozone layer screens out hazardous ultraviolet and infrared radiation in sunlight. The predicted results of ozone depletion include more skin cancers, eye cataracts, crop losses, and damage to marine life.[17] CFCs also contribute to the greenhouse effect and global warming, which is discussed below, so they are doubly damaging.

As attention focused on the reasons for ozone depletion, other chemicals became suspect as well. These included methyl bromine (one of the most common industrial chemicals, used for fumigation), halons (used in fire fighting), carbon

TABLE 16.1 GLOBAL PERCENTAGE SHARE OF CFC USE, 1985

Aerosols	25
Rigid foam insulation	19
Solvents	19
Air-conditioning	12
Refrigeration	8
Flexible foam	7
Other	10

Source: Cynthia Pollock Shea, "Protecting the Ozone Layer," in Lester R. Brown et al., *State of the World 1989* (New York, 1989), 86.

TABLE 16.2 GLOBAL CFC USE BY REGION, 1986, PERCENT

United States	29
Other industrial countries	41
USSR, other Eastern European countries	14
China, India	2
Other LDCs	14

Source: Cynthia Pollock Shea, "Protecting the Ozone Layer," in Lester R. Brown et al., *State of the World 1989*, 87.

tetrachloride, and methyl chloroform. All are employed in quantities much smaller than CFCs, but their uses have been growing rapidly. The bromine escaping into the atmosphere is an even greater destroyer of ozone than is chlorine.

The LDCs and Ozone The level of CFC use is correlated closely to a country's level of income, as Table 16.2 illustrates. The rich industrial countries utilized far more of this substance than did the LDCs, with per capita CFC consumption highest in the United States and Europe, and Japan close behind. It caused considerable apprehension that in most LDCs, including Brazil, China, India, and Indonesia, the ownership of refrigerators and air conditioners was small, with tremendous potential to grow. Just one in ten Chinese households, for example, had a refrigerator. The likelihood of enormous expansion in the use of CFCs by the LDCs meant a bleak outlook for the ozone layer unless control measures could be implemented.[18]

The Montréal Convention on Ozone The world's reaction was encouraging. Rather expeditiously, without too much friction, a Montréal Convention of 1987, amended later in London in 1990, set schedules to phase out 15 CFCs, three halons, carbon tetrachloride, and methyl chloroform. In 1991, however, assessments that ozone depletion was more severe than predicted resulting in a speedup of the phaseouts. Halon production ended in 1994. Production of CFCs, carbon tetrachloride, and methyl chloroform is to cease in 1996. Already the Montréal Convention has worked to reduce the annual increase in CFC concentration, which was steady at 4% per year in the 1980s, to 2% now. A Copenhagen Amendment of 1994 scheduled a phaseout of CFC's replacement, hydrochlorofluorocarbons (HCFCs), which are now being used in refrigerators and air conditioners. HCFC output is to be ended by 2030. Another decision at Copenhagen has caused most uses of methyl bromide to be frozen at current levels. The Montréal Convention now has 132 signatories, representing 4.7 billion people and including China and India which were initially holdouts. They were induced to sign partly by threats of trade restrictions; under the convention, trade between signatories and nonsignatories in the substances themselves, or in products made with or containing them, was banned. Another reason for their accession was that the LDCs were permitted a later phaseout date than was agreed on by the developed countries.[19] There is now considerable hope that the ozone depletion emergency has found an acceptable solution.

Global Warming

Global warming is the term used for the possible rise in world temperatures resulting from a greenhouse effect of various gases in the atmosphere.[20] The main natural greenhouse gases are water vapor (the largest source), CO_2, methane, nitrous oxide, and ozone. Among the purely man-made ones are CFCs. Recent additions of CO_2 come mostly from burning fossil fuels (including auto exhaust), with deforestation and other land clearing contributing one-fifth to one-half as much. The burning of forests to clear land is a direct contributor of CO_2, and cutting trees and vegetation also has the indirect effect of preventing them from removing CO_2 from the atmosphere. Half the world's rain forests in Latin America, Africa, and Asia have already been destroyed.* Methane comes from decaying wood, termite eating, fermenting decay in rice paddies and wetlands, livestock flatulence, landfills, coal mining, burning of biomass, and natural gas production and transmission. (Except for the last of these, methane emissions are difficult to combat.) Human sources of nitrous oxide include biomass burning, fertilizer use, automobile exhaust, and coal-fired power plants. The greenhouse gases are not equally harmful per unit. A single unit of methane can have 30 times the effect of a unit of CO_2 in terms of its greenhouse effect. A unit of CFCs can have an impact as much as 15,000 times more.[21]

The man-made sources of greenhouse gases are shown in Figure 16.2.

The atmospheric emission of carbon dioxide is currently increasing at about one-half of 1% per year. The CO_2 emissions act in effect like an extra blanket that retains heat. From the preindustrial era until 1990, the atmospheric concentration of CO_2 increased by 26%, of methane by 115%. Estimates for 1990 to 2025 are for further increases of 23% and 51% respectively.[22]

The damage from the warming effect could be severe, in some locales even catastrophic. Higher average world temperatures could disrupt agriculture. Trees might die out in large parts of their former range, and animal and plant species unsuited to the new climate could become extinct. Grain and corn belts may shift position by hundreds of miles, with a probable decline in productivity because little advantage will accrue from a warming of Siberia and northern Canada, the soils of which are inadequate. (Even so, the northernmost tier of countries stand to gain something from a warmer climate, which adds to the difficulty of negotiating a solution with the LDCs.) Rainfall cycles could be disrupted; the margins between forests and rangeland could shift substantially. Warming could also spread malaria and other tropical diseases into new areas, with further negative effects.

---

*Economics explains most of the deforestation. Population growth raises the demand for land and firewood as already noted. Much Latin American land clearing has taken place for ranching to supply beef (hamburger) for consumption in the United States, while considerable Asian deforestation has occurred because Japan uses 12 billion disposable chopsticks per year. Tropical forests are rarely managed. Government royalties are often very low, and logging rights are never auctioned. Global warming is not the only possible outcome. The rain forest comprises a rich genetic bank, loss of which would be an ecological disaster because wild strains have to be reintroduced continuously into hybrids by plant breeders.

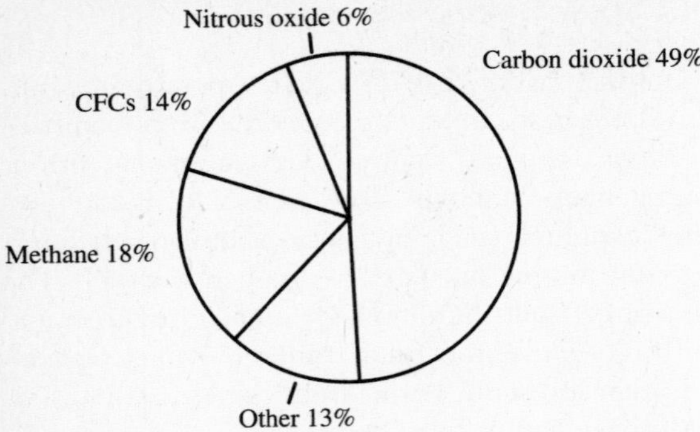

Figure 16.2 Man-made contributions to the greenhouse effect, 1980s.[23]

The warming could also cause melting of the polar ice caps, which would result in further warming as the polar regions fail to reflect as much sunlight as before. The melting ice would cause the sea level to rise, by perhaps by one to two meters according to the most alarming predictions. Even a one-meter rise would cost Bangladesh an estimated 14% of its land area and 13% of its GDP. A height of two meters is a Maldive or Tuvalu mountain, and these island countries would disappear if the sea were to rise this much. The prospect of sinking beneath the sea like a modern Atlantis is understandably a daunting one for these countries. The barriers and dikes that would be built to protect islands such as Manhattan or low-lying cities such as New Orleans would be far too expensive for these and other small and poor LDCs.

The consequences for the LDCs from all this could obviously be doleful. Pronounced global warming might be so damaging that the LDCs would have to cut back on their economic growth. Their economies are the less-flexible ones, closer to the margin, so adjustments would be more painful for them than for the developed countries. The costs could be greatest for tropical LDCs that are not mainly responsible for the global warming.

A Doubtful Outcome? But considerable uncertainty surrounds global warming. First, any warming will be long delayed because it will take many years to alter ocean temperatures. So the full effects of greenhouse gases emitted now will not be fully felt for many years. Second, the quantity of emissions will in large part determine how much warming occurs, so the predicted warming differs greatly depending on assumptions concerning economic growth and technical change. The estimates of warming from 1900 to the year 2100 vary widely, ranging from about 2°C to about 10°C. Third, there is considerable disagreement over how great the costs would be if nothing were done. The estimates run from nothing to about 16% of world output. Fourth, the costs of treating the problem also involve considerable uncertainty. Stabilizing the world emissions of carbon dioxide at 1990 levels would carry an annual cost of less than 1% to about 9% of total world output, depending on the estimate.[24]

Many experts are skeptical. They note that there has been warming of about 0.6°C in the century after 1880, but that most of the greenhouse gas emissions occurred after 1940, whereas most of the temperature rise occurred before that date. Meteorological records show little temperature change in the 1980s, whereas most models of global climate change predicted at least some temperature increase during this period. Some recent models of sea-level changes predict increases far less than the 15 to 25 feet suggested in the early 1980s. A few models even predict a decrease. The skeptics emphasize the modest and uncertain nature of the damage from global warming, and argue that decisions should be delayed until the climate change actually starts to take place. According to them, encouragement of economic growth will yield the resources that growing economies can eventually mobilize to support sea defenses, drought resistance in plants, and other gradual adaptations to the warming. *The Economist* magazine is included among the skeptics. It recently argued that

> Water pollution kills more people than global warming is likely to do; soil erosion leaves more people hungry;. . . deforestation has locally (and perhaps internationally) dramatic effects on climate. The world has only so much wealth to devote to solving environmental problems. Any one of these deserves greater priority than global warming.[25]

The Economist suggests that if evidence does in time emerge that warming is substantial, then large reductions in emissions can be made at that time as needed.

LDC Growth and Global Warming Thus there is a debate between those who believe that action against global warming should be stern and immediate, and those who advocate caution. The LDCs have a very large stake in the outcome. Obviously the situation could become much worse as the LDCs clear more land, as the proportion of heavy industry in their economies grows, and as they begin to acquire many more polluting products, such as automobiles. Imagine what it would be like if everyone had a car. There are 800 million bicycles in the world today, compared with just 400 million cars; China in particular has 540 bicycles for every car.[26] If growth were to bring a chicken to every pot and a car to every garage, as in the old political slogan, then pollution problems would worsen considerably. Economic development pushes in this direction anyway, but rapid population growth makes the environmental prospects worse yet.[27] Table 16.3 gives some indication of the dangers involved.

Close examination of Table 16.3 shows the cause for concern. The column on the far right indicates that the major LDCs emit very little carbon per person of population. Nigeria, for example, has nearly half the population of the United States but emits less than one-fiftieth as much carbon per person. Even if that country were to raise its carbon emissions per person just to the level of the carbon-stingy Japanese, the rise would still be over 20 times. That is not all. Their income being low, the LDCs cannot afford the pollution control equipment that has become common in the rich countries. Their emissions of carbon per unit of GNP are often higher—in China's case by seven times—than the figure for the United States, which itself exceeds the figure for most other developed countries.*

*It should be noted that big falls have occurred in carbon per dollar of GNP in developed countries—by a third in the United States—since 1960.

TABLE 16.3 WORLD CARBON EMISSIONS, 1987

	Carbon (million tons)	Carbon per Dollar of GNP (grams)	Carbon per Capita (tons)
World average	5599	327	1.08
United States	1224	276	5.03
Canada	110	247	4.24
USSR	1035	436	3.68
Germany (West)	182	223	2.98
Britain	156	224	2.73
Japan	251	156	2.12
Mexico	80	609	0.96
China	594	2024	0.56
Brazil	53	170	0.38
India	151	655	0.19
Nigeria	9	359	0.09

Source: Christopher Flavin, "Slowing Global Warming," in Lester R. Brown et al., *State of the World 1990* (New York, 1990), 17–38.

Economic growth in the LDCs will certainly mean that a substantial increase in carbon emissions will occur unless steps are taken. At current rates of increase, carbon emissions by the LDCs will increase from 1990's 1.8 billion tons to 5.5 billion tons in 2025.[28] Consider some of the details lying behind this projection. Energy use in the LDCs grew by three times from 1970 to 1990 and is now 27% of the world total. By 2010, LDC energy consumption is expected to reach 40% of the world total, and growth between 2000 and 2010 will be as much as Western Europe consumes today. By 2030, LDC consumption of energy could be more than twice as great as it is in the developed countries, even though in per capita terms it would probably still be only about a third of the consumption in the developed countries. More electrical-generating capacity is expected to be built between now and 2020 than was constructed in the last century.[29] Even now, energy consumption in China has risen 22 times since 1952. Since 1978, the number of electric fans in China has risen by 20 times, the number of washing machines in use has risen from virtually none to 97 million, and rising oil consumption has turned China into an oil importer for the first time since oil discoveries in the early 1970s. If China's electricity use rises just to the South Korean level over the next 20 years, the resulting 500% increase would be larger than total electricity use in the United States today, but still leave China consuming only about a third of the electricity used by Americans.[30]

Unfortunately, a large part of this energy is generated by burning coal, which is an exceptionally dirty practice. By 2000, China is expected to be producing a third of the world's coal, which emits over 75% more CO_2 than does natural gas. One result is that in winter, the smog in China's northern cities can be six to 20 times worse than the most severe smog encountered in the developed countries. But even if China raises its energy consumption by an apparently huge 85% and

India (which starts behind) by 145%, both would still be consuming less than *one-fifth* of the energy consumed by the average American.[31]

Cutting back on carbon emissions will be very painful for the LDCs, increasing their costs and limiting their ability to enjoy the fruits of development at the level that the developed countries do. Costs of stabilizing emissions of greenhouse gases are likely to be higher for LDCs than for developed countries—perhaps twice the world average—for three reasons: (1) Manufacturing does not permit easy economizing on energy, and the LDCs are moving rapidly toward more manufacturing to propel their development. (2) Scarcity of funds for investment will make pollution control measures difficult to take. (3) The LDCs' heavy reliance on cheap coal discussed above means that they may have to move toward more expensive sources of energy. (Of course, the coal is cheap only when the negative externalities are ignored. Analysis indicates that if the environmental damage from burning coal were factored into its price, that price would have to rise by over four times.)[32] It is estimated that the losses from limiting CO_2 emissions to double their 1990 level by the year 2030 might be (though it is bold to predict) as much as 5% to 10% of GDP for some countries, such as China.[33] The expense would also be particularly heavy for India. Both would point out that virtually all of the developed countries depended on coal for *their* development.[34]

The leaders of the LDCs will therefore certainly insist that the evidence of global warming be persuasive and that the analysis of damage to the world be convincing before action is taken. Remember that some estimates indicate that controlling global warming would be much more costly in lost output than the damage from the warming, while other estimates show the damage to be much greater than the control costs. A mistake would be potentially very injurious for the LDCs. The most sensible course will therefore be to obtain the best available information on the consequences and their costs; to weigh the probabilities of the various possible outcomes as likely, possible, or highly implausible; and then to take the course that appears to be the most reasonable. Halting population growth is a key to all this.

Some Official Polices Have Been Harmful

Fortunately, a certain amount of the global warming problem can be traced not to economic development, but to misguided government policies. "Fortunately" because mistaken policies can be fixed much more easily than a slowdown in development can be engineered.

The policy areas of greatest import are subsidies for energy, water, pesticides, and ranching, lack of titles for farmers' land, credit difficulties, public ownership of enterprises, inefficient charges for public utilities, and inadequate evaluation of the environmental consequences of government projects.[35] In the case of the subsidies, the case is strong that many of them reduce economic efficiency at the same time that they increase environmental damage. Reforming this situation would therefore "kill two birds with one stone," raising economic efficiency and yielding an improved environment at the same time.

Let us review some recent cases involving these causes. Consider first subsidies for energy, which are common in the LDCs. Where subsidies are used, charges for electric power are only a little more than half of the charges in developed countries, a little over 4¢ per kilowatt hour compared to 8¢. Subsidizing electricity leads to an excessive quantity demanded, 20% or so higher than it would be under unsubsidized conditions, and keeps revenues low, thus discouraging investment in environmentally cleaner methods of production and leading to poor service as well.[36] China's electricity is particularly cheap (half the price charged in India) and as a result, many big, dirty, coal-fired plants are being built. The cheap power delays attempts to provide buildings with insulation and storm windows, contributing to the fact that Chinese buildings use three times as much energy for heating as do U.S. buildings. Proper market pricing would help.[37] In general, it is believed that for most LDCs, eliminating energy subsidies would decrease carbon emissions in the range of 10% to 20%.[38]

The cutting of the Brazilian rain forests is an outstanding example of a regrettable impact of public policy on the environment. Brazil has about a third of the world's rain forest. Deforestation there is very rapid, faster even than had been previously believed.[39] The reasons are partly those of Brazilian official policy, which for many years has led to increasing forest destruction.[40] Among these actions are the following: (1) Macroeconomic mistakes have led to high inflation, so holders of wealth buy land as a hedge against the rising prices. (2) Brazil has very low land taxes on acreage that is farmed, so settlers denude the forest on their holdings as soon as they can in order to lower their tax bill. (3) Tax credits exist for projects like ranching; these have been as high as 75% of operating costs. (4) There are rural credit subsidies, again with ranches eligible. The implicit subsidies for ranching amounted to over $1 billion from 1975 to 1986, said to be the biggest subsidy in all of history for environmental destruction. (5) Brazil's equivalent to homestead laws are strongly protective of what might be called "squatters' rights." (6) There has been little environmental policing by the government.

In a free market, these forests might have been more valuable for their fruit, rubber, and carefully harvested timber than they are as farmland, especially because much Brazilian frontier land is of poor quality. But the explicit and implicit subsidies tip the balance and lead to continued land clearing. (The World Bank has been making the case generally that greater returns can be obtained from not cutting the trees in the rain forest. Obviously many entrepreneurs do not agree, and in any case, as seen above, policy often works to offset the market's signals.)[41]

The underlying cause of the increasing pressure to move toward the frontier is that Brazil's population growth is high, and its land ownership badly skewed toward the rich. That country has chosen to promote the movement of people rather than to address the politically difficult issue of land reform. It is true that Brazil is undergoing a major change in public opinion on the subject, with 300 conservation groups having sprung up to protect the environment in that country. Yet damaging government policies still exist, and eliminating them would be a major environmental gain.

About the time the effects of these Brazilian policies were being realized and understood in environmental circles, it became apparent that some World Bank lending was another factor contributing to the increasing movement of settlers to rain forest areas.* The Bank helped finance a huge agricultural land settlement project, Polonoroeste, in Brazil's northwest. That project involved the heavy cutting of forest along with the dispossession of thousands of Indians. World Bank money was also used to construct Brazil's major highway, BR 364, into the rain forest areas. These funds were cut off in 1985 over the question of inadequate protection for the forests and the Indians. (Eventually Brazil did comply with the Bank's demands, and the money was restored.) Highway BR 364 has caused a tidal wave of settlers into the jungles of Rondônia, costing that state 15% of its forest cover in less than five years. Other roads into the rain forest elsewhere in the north and northwest have brought the same problems.[42]

It should be noted that policies of the LDCs and the international agencies are not the only ones that cause harm to the environment in low-income countries. Protection against LDC exports, such as textiles and clothing, indirectly produces the same unfortunate outcome. The protection keeps a potentially large quantity of LDC exports out of the developed countries. Without these policies, many people would have found jobs in the exporting industries and so would not have moved to the frontier, would not have burned rain forest to carve out a plot for subsistence farming, and would not have plowed a steep hillside because they were hungry. Here the employment in exporting would help the environment; trade protection, however, keeps the employment from occurring, and the developed countries bear most of the responsibility.

WHAT CAN BE DONE ABOUT THE ENVIRONMENT?

What to do about the environmental problems associated with growth is a major dilemma of modern development economics. Much can be done within the LDCs themselves. Removal of the subsidies that lead to the overuse of energy, irrigation water, and pesticides, and to the over-cutting of forests, are clearly called for. Much pollution in the LDCs is actually due to unsound agricultural practices and not to industrial development. Therefore substantial improvement to the environment could potentially accompany higher agricultural productivity if, say, subsistence farmers were able to earn enough income to begin the practice of terracing or planting binding grasses to stop hillside erosion. If adequate capital markets existed, farmers could borrow to support their conservation measures. The clarification of ownership rights to land, forests, and fisheries would help to stop the exploitation of common property. Much overgrazing would come to a rapid end if land

*Other World Bank projects beyond Brazil have attracted the adverse attention of environmentalists. We have already discussed (in Chapter 7) the displacement of people by dams, which have also caused heavy waterlogging and salinization. The Bank has become sensitive to these charges, and policy changes have been implemented. An Office of Environmental and Scientific Affairs (OESA) now screens all proposed Bank and IFC investment projects, numbering about 300 per year, for their environmental impact. The Bank will not finance those projects that bring adverse ecological consequences, affect public health, cause harm to another country, or violate a treaty.

reform put the ownership of common grazing lands into private hands. Private ownership could also help in areas where nationalized forests are being overcut. For example, when Nepal nationalized its forests in 1957, the government found it was incapable of protecting them. Management had been better when the forests were in private hands.[43]

To help in propelling this process, there are now respectable environmental movements in a number of LDCs, including Argentina, Brazil, Ecuador, India, Indonesia, Kenya, Malaysia, and Mexico among others.* These can help to educate and involve local people so they can see where their self-interest actually lies. The key is to produce more with less pollution, not to give up too much of the environment or sacrifice too much economic growth. Fortunately, diminishing returns works in favor of cleaning up the environment in the LDCs, because easy environmental victories are possible when a cleanup effort first begins. Perhaps 80% of the LDCs' pollution can be cleaned up with only modest increases in cleanup costs.[44] World Bank lending for environmental purposes will help, as will the increased sensitivity among developed-country aid-giving agencies.

Specific Steps

A number of specific steps can be recommended.[45]

1. Stabilizing the population sooner rather than later is exceptionally important. Lowering population growth will remove a major source of increasing pressure on the environment.
2. Giant reforestation projects supported by levies on the activities that dirty the environment and foreign aid could reverse the decline of the rain forest and reduce global warming. It is estimated that 130 million hectares of planting in LDCs would cut carbon release by 8% to 11%.[46] Any new factories that burn fossil fuel might be required to plant large numbers of trees in partial recompense. Billions of new trees growing to maturity would raise the supply of fuelwood and help to stop erosion as well. A Tropical Forests Action Plan sponsored jointly by the World Bank, FAO, UN Development Program, and World Resources Institute has existed since 1987. It aims to achieve a balance between harvesting and planting by the year 2000.
3. Focused and subsidized research on energy could lead to lower use of fossil fuels and more reliance on benign sources of energy. There is a bright future for photovoltaic and solar-thermal power production in the tropical LDCs. Improved turbines running on natural gas can increase fuel efficiency. Great improvement can be made in appliance efficiency: Compact 18-watt fluorescent bulbs give the same illumination as 75-watt incandescent bulbs; recycling the heat from electricity generation could save as much as 30% of the energy expended on this activity. A shift to more fuel-efficient transport will cut back on exhaust release; mass transit, mandato-

*But little in the way of Green parties, which now exist in 16 European countries and several U.S. states.

ry mileage standards requiring cars to obtain 50 mpg, and taxes as discussed below could cut carbon emission in half. Cars that run on hydrogen produce almost no CO_2. Even nuclear power may qualify as relatively benign if global warming does prove to be damaging.

4. Suitable taxes, on gasoline in a simple alternative, or on the amount of carbon used in fuels in a more complex variant, would more accurately reflect the true costs of fossil fuel use, would aid in economizing on consumption, and would provide incentives for recycling, hence lessening environmental harm.* A $1 per million BTU tax on coal and $0.60 per million BTU tax on oil would raise some $53 billion annually just in the United States.[47] Taxes on the emission of the other greenhouse gases could also be implemented. The taxes should be agreed on globally, perhaps with an international fund to ease the transition for the LDCs.[48] In all these cases, the developed countries are certainly in a position to lead by example if they choose to. At the 1992 Earth Summit held at Rio de Janeiro, some European countries advocated a carbon tax, and a few, including the Netherlands, Denmark, Norway, Finland, and Sweden already have one. *Any* plan should aim to reduce emissions the most in countries where it costs the least to do so, but that points especially to the coal burning in China and India. A carbon tax would be especially disadvantageous for China and India, the LDCs with most of the coal. They would have to be persuaded, presumably by technical and financial aid. Additionally, the rich oil exporting countries would be the biggest losers of all, and will object. They may have to be bought off, even given their affluence. If the burden is *not* shared, the countries standing to lose the most will have an incentive to stay out of any international agreement, or if they sign, to cheat on the agreement.

Financial Help for the LDCs

The LDCs will need financial help to cope with pollution problems if they are to achieve a cleaner environment before economic growth would bring that about. In fairness, the major share of the blame for global pollution up to the present time should not be placed on the LDCs. The developed world with its immensely greater production and fuel use is clearly the major immediate source of the greenhouse gases, emitting over four-fifths of these by volume, and will remain so for many years to come. The rich countries benefited economically by doing so before the problem was recognized, and it would be proper to demand that the rich move first and help the LDCs as well.

---

*Taxes are preferable to regulations for achieving this purpose. Regulations can go wrong. Mexico City and Athens limit trips by license plate. For example, certain numbers are permitted into a city only on certain days of the week. But that limits accessibility even for those who put a high value on the trips, whereas taxing gasoline or carbon emissions would avoid that problem. In Mexico City, people bought old polluting clunkers for a second car so they could still drive on all days, making the pollution problem worse. See *WDR 1992*, 75; and Gunnar S. Eskeland, "Attacking Air Pollution in Mexico City," *Finance and Development* 29, no. 4 (December 1992): 28–30.

Loans and Grants The main responsibility to develop the necessary technologies and equipment for control must lie with the rich countries and not the poor. Once these are evolved, they can be made available to the LDCs, who would thus not have to bear the burden of financing their development. The UN Environmental Program created a new fund (some $200 million) in 1990 to assist LDCs willing to control their pollution. Some World Bank loans are now made directly for environmental improvement, and nearly two-fifths of total World Bank loans now have some environmental elements in them. U.S. foreign aid has developed in the same way, with USAID required to identify and modify projects that it considers to be environmentally unsound.

A new Global Environmental Facility (GEF) has been set up by the World Bank to channel developed countries' money into projects that bring environmental gains. The GEF, first established as a pilot program in 1991, was made permanent in 1994. It deals with climate change, destruction of biological diversity, pollution of international waters, and ozone depletion. Land degradation is also covered if it has effects in the four main areas. Decision making involves a double majority—a 60% majority of the membership (now over 80 countries) with each country having one vote, and approval by donor countries contributing at least 60% of the funding. Thus in effect both the LDCs and the developed countries have a veto. Over $2 billion has been pledged by donors; $750 million had been committed to more than a hundred projects by early 1994. Technical assistance and advice will be a part of the activity. The GEF has grown very rapidly, which shows how high up on the agenda environmental matters have moved.[49]

Emissions Trading? If a decision were taken to move soon against global warming, many economists would recommend that an international system of "emissions trading" might be the most appropriate way to do it. International quotas on greenhouse gases could be established, with the quotas bought and sold as needed. The problem is how to distribute the quotas. If the quotas were distributed by population, they would go mostly to the poor countries, and it would be very expensive for the rich to buy the transferable permits they would need. (The World Bank estimates that it would cost the rich countries $70 billion to buy the permits for one year's total emissions.) If, on the other hand, the quotas were distributed by income level, then the rich would receive most of them, which would be very unfair. In any case, there are as yet no examples at all of international emissions trading.

Debt for the Environment One excellent idea to provide assistance to the LDCs that are coping with global environmental deterioration is to link this effort to reductions in their debts. It is noteworthy that over two-thirds of global deforestation occurs in the same 14 developing countries that ran up about half of the international debt during the debt crisis.

The first trade of debt for ecology was with Brazil in 1987.[50] By 1992, there had been 16 such arrangements, including swaps with Costa Rica, Ecuador, Madagascar, and the Philippines. Here is a typical effort that occurred in 1992. Nature Conservancy, a U.S. group, bought $2.192 million in face value of Brazil's debt at a discounted price of 35% to 37.5% of the debt's face value. Nature Conservancy donated the debt instruments to a Brazilian foundation, which then traded the instruments for government local currency bonds paying 6%. The funds were used to conserve and manage the Grande Sertão Verdeas Park, 200,000 acres of savanna land in central Brazil, a park that had previously existed only on paper.[51] Most of the conservation swaps have been between private organizations and LDCs, but some developed-country governments are now participating, including those of the Netherlands and Sweden.

The economics of debt-for-nature swaps is often very favorable. For example, it costs about $4 in prevention of forest destruction in Brazil to keep one ton of CO_2 from entering the atmosphere. The cost of preventing a ton of CO_2 from being emitted by U.S. factories and autos is much greater, about $10, while the cost of Brazilian reforestation that would reduce CO_2 release by one ton is about $30.[52]

The idea is promising. One could envisage banks donating their LDC debt to environmental groups in return for tax credits. Then the groups could sell the debt to LDC governments at a discount, turning over the local currency to the LDCs to finance an environmental fund, to be used for protecting the ecology and for population control. The creation of local currency could be monitored by the IMF and World Bank to ensure that it is not inflationary. A special tax on fossil fuels in the developed countries could raise revenue that could add to the environmental fund. The concept of reducing debt while doing battle with pollution might be just the catalyst that could mobilize political support in both the developed countries and the LDCs, convincing rich-country taxpayers and donors that their sacrifice is worthwhile, while persuading LDCs that environmental protection really pays.[53] In theory, such swaps could be used not only for environmental protection but for population control.

INTERNATIONAL TRADE AND THE ENVIRONMENT

The connection between international trade and the environment may not be benign for the LDCs. Three sorts of considerations arise. First, an LDC's exports may result in long-term harm to its own environment. Second, the developed countries might attempt to dispose of their toxic materials in pliant LDCs willing to take them for payment. Third and most important, the developed countries might choose to use trade barriers to enforce environmental regulation on the LDCs.

Damaging Exports from the LDCs

Exporting can bring ecological harm. Exported commodities and minerals are cases in point. We have already discussed the possible effects on the environment of agricultural practices, such as clearing land for farming or ranching, use of fertilizers and pesticides, erosion, and silting. Mining can bring obvious problems, such as contaminated soils, slag heaps, open pits, and the like. The energy used to produce a country's manufactured exports may be obtained mostly from dirty coal.

Governments must therefore be alert to the negative externalities, which private enterprise might be willing to ignore.

Sometimes the harm is more subtle. An outstanding case of damaging exporting involves the trade in frogs' legs from Bangladesh. In the 1970s, Bangladesh began to export this gourmet food product, and by the 1980s, more than 50 million frogs were being exported per year. The frog population was thought to have fallen to only 400 million. Eventually came the realization that fewer than 50 frogs can keep an acre of paddy fields insect-free, protecting crops and suppressing malaria. As a result of the decline in the frog population, pesticide imports rose. Finally, frog exports were banned in 1989. The episode was a good example of a negative externality that had to be recognized and corrected by government.[54]

The Disposal of Toxic Substances

The disposal of toxic substances is cause for ecological concern. Serious cases have arisen where the entrepreneurs of one country, faced with national laws against the dumping of toxic wastes, exported the wastes to countries where such laws were weaker or did not exist. A recent Basel Convention on waste export requires exporters to inform the governments of recipient countries of a shipment and obtain permission for it. The treaty, dating from 1989, came into effect in 1992.[55]

This will help when private interests are the guilty parties, but it will do little when government officials in an LDC are willing to inflict costs on citizens while pocketing the payments. The poor West African nation of Guinea-Bissau was paid $40 per metric ton to take dangerous U.S. and European materials, a ridiculously low figure if the potential damage to local residents had been considered. But the transaction gerenated revenues that totaled more than half the governments's budget until the perverse nature of the bargain was recognized. At one point, Guinea-Bissau was offered $500 million, three times the country's annual GNP, to accept just one load of (very) hazardous waste. (The offer was turned down.)[56] The nearby Republic of Bénin accepted just $4 a ton to dispose of some toxic shipments, a bargain on a private basis for those that made the decision without bearing the costs, but incomprehensible when the externalities are factored in. The political leaders of these countries apparently made no plans at all to protect their citizens from the dangerous materials. News of the dumping of toxic material from abroad has also emanated from Morocco, Senegal, Guinea, Nigeria, Equatorial Guinea, the Congo Republic, and Djibouti.

Polluting Developed-Country Firms May Flee to the LDCs

Is there not a danger that as environmental regulations become more strict in the developed countries, polluting firms will transfer their operations to LDCs with laxer controls? In theory, yes. The reduced level of environmental regulation and lower standards of enforcement in LDCs could make these countries a favored destination for firms that pollute. In practice, however, there is little hard data to support a "pollution-haven hypothesis."[57] Up to now, the costs of controlling pollution in the developed countries have not been large enough to make much of a difference. These abatement costs have been only 0.5% of output on average for U.S. industries (1988 figure), and 3% for the dirtiest industries, which has not been enough to offset other costs such as those for labor, capital, technology, and natural resources.

In any case, multinational firms are not the biggest polluters. They often find it cheaper to use standard equipment as used already in developed countries, and this equipment often embodies controls on the emission of pollution. Small companies, which have more difficulties moving abroad, have that dubious distinction. Moreover, the uncertainty and possible impermanence of the welcome for polluting firms discourages their movement. Countries generally show an increasing tendency to back away from accepting developed-country polluters, exemplified by the growing antipathy of the public and governments of Spain and Ireland toward accepting the EC's polluters, and the similar case of Mexico and U.S. polluters.[58]

No very significant shift of polluting industries to low-income countries has yet been perceived. Some anecdotal evidence does exist, pointing to movements by U.S. furniture makers to Mexico to avoid California's air quality laws, and other shifts by asbestos, dye, and pesticide producers. Mining companies have been active in expanding their multinational operations in LDCs, especially Latin America, where environmental opposition is weaker and much of the old hostility to foreign mining companies has died away.[59] (Mexico has even abolished mining royalties.)* But all these movements still seem quite limited at present. No doubt, however, a potential does exist that polluting industries will move to more hospitable countries in order to escape environmental regulation.

TRADE BARRIERS AND ENVIRONMENTAL CONCERNS

To what extent might environmental concerns lead to trade barriers against the exports of the LDCs? The question attracted little importance until recently. Just as the use of prison labor has always been considered an unfair way to produce exports and has traditionally been subject to trade barriers, so some environmental practices might fairly be considered beyond the pale, to be combated with trade sanctions. The question is, "what practices?"

International Conventions and Treaties

International treaties that exclude some imports for environmental reasons date back to the beginning of this century.[60] In 1906, long before the General Agreement on Tariffs and Trade, an import ban on white phosphorus matches was agreed on. (The white phosphorus caused a loathsome occupational disease.) Regulations against sealing and the hunting of sea otters date from 1911.

---

*It should be said that the mines usually pay much higher wages than are available elsewhere in the LDC for similar levels of skill and effort, and recently their environmental awareness has been much better than it was formerly.

Examples of international action include the "Convention on Trade in Endangered Species" (CITES) of 1975. CITES banned the trade in ivory, rhinoceros horn, rare turtle shells, and other animal products as well where extinction is an issue, and instituted a permit system for trade in endangered species. A 1986 treaty stopped commercial whaling. The Montréal Convention of 1987 on CFCs and the Basel Convention of 1989 on movements of hazardous waste have already been discussed.

Admittedly, international agreements may not always work as planned. For example, barriers against log exports from the LDCs, intended to protect the environment, could cause more environmental damage if the forests are cut to clear land. Halting exports of ivory might lead local farmers to kill off the elephant population entirely. Still, well-designed international treaties embodying environmental objectives established by world consensus address necessary ends and arguably justify the use of trade barriers to police them. But a major problem arises if there is no consensus and no international treaty. In that case, one country's use of trade barriers to change another country's environmental practices is likely to engender considerable controversy—especially if the practices do not have a direct effect on the country erecting the barrier.[61]

Imposition of Trade Barriers by One Country Against Another

Barriers to exclude products for environmental reasons when the barriers are not called for by international treaty are a difficult matter.[62] Under GATT's Article XX, countries may pass "measures necessary to protect" public morals, human, animal, or plant life, maintain health, or conserve natural resources, so long as they are not a "disguised restriction on international trade" and the regulations apply to domestic producers as well as foreign ones. This language was retained in the Uruguay Round negotiations. Tens of thousands of environmental regulations have been adopted all around the world in recent years, of which GATT has found only a handful illegal under its rules. In effect, a country can pass any environmental law to restrict imports that also applies to its own goods.

But there are grey areas and quandaries hidden in Article XX.[63] The article does not explicitly mention protection of the atmosphere, the ozone, the oceans, and other global questions. A country may find it is challenged at GATT if it attempts to exclude goods from another country in order to address environmental damage outside its borders. Also, GATT cases have interpreted the words "measures necessary to protect" to mean the measure least harmful to trade that could still accomplish the mission. So in GATT cases arguments often erupt as to whether some substitute measure would be better for the task at hand. Finally, Article XX focuses on products, not on how the products are produced in their country of origin. A country concerned about the environment is free to control production processes within its borders, but not to use trade barriers to control production processes in a country from which it imports. Environmentalists have been disturbed to find that if a product is made by methods that add to global pollution, GATT rules do not allow barriers against the import of the product.

Many "Greens" appear to favor trade restrictions as a way to force other countries to enter into environmental agreements and to police these. For example, they would argue that a ban on wood imported from countries that do not use sustainable logging practices would force them to do so, and halt the forest destruction that is a cause of global warming. This might seem reasonable.

But there is also plenty of scope for abuse if one country could legally employ trade barriers for any and all environmental reasons. Such legality could play into the hands of protectionists in the industries that would benefit from barriers against trade and could end up costing the public more than the benefits they deliver. Where would the limits be, for example, if one country were allowed to erect barriers against production processes in another?[64] Does this mean that barriers could be erected against any import produced with electricity from a country where the electricity generation is dirty? Could "precautionary" barriers be put in the way of goods that *might* cause harm? Could trade with the Central African Republic be embargoed if that country failed adequately to preserve okapis and gorillas? Obviously, the doors of world trade could swing closed against many LDCs if protectionists and environmentalists allied on these issues.

A Reasonable Compromise A reasonable compromise would be to allow trade barriers—unless the violator is willing to pay compensation—when one country's production processes cause significant harm to the global environment or cause damaging cross-boundary pollution (particulates, acid rain) that significantly affects a neighbor. But where global or cross-boundary pollution is charged, the standard of proof should be high. The threat to an ecosystem or species ought to be significant. In this view, the greater the harm, the more the justification for trade sanctions, just as is true of political disputes that lead to trade sanctions. It would also be appropriate to insist that good faith diplomatic efforts always be made before trade sanctions are employed.[65]

It is more difficult to justify trade barriers where the harm is purely local within another country, or where some amenity is being neglected, as when North Americans love bluebirds but their winter habitat in the Republic of Paraná is being cut over. In such cases, a country reaping the externality (enjoyment of the bluebirds) should logically be expected to share in the costs of preserving their winter habitat.[66]

Examples of Protectionism in the Guise of Environmentalism Unfortunately, numerous examples of trade protectionism under the guise of saving the environment have already come to light. Most of the cases discussed below involve trade barriers among the developed countries, but they all indicate how environmental issues might be used to exclude imports from the LDCs. Here are some of the outstanding ones.[67]

Denmark required beer and soft drink bottlers to use specially shaped bottles, arguing that this facilitated cleaning and reuse. The European Court of Justice ruled in 1988 that this was protectionism in disguise, designed to benefit Denmark's own bottlers. Ontario put a 10¢ environmental tax on aluminum beer cans (most imports from the United States are in cans), but exempted the bottles favored by Ontario's own breweries. A dispute with the United States is ongoing. Similarly Germany put a deposit on plastic bottles (often imported) but not the glass bottles preferred by Germany's own bottlers. Shopkeepers often did not want to go to the trouble of dealing with the imported plastics. (Under pressure this law was modified.) Germany has a new law that requires all sellers to take back the packaging their goods came in. Also, carmakers must recycle their cars when they are junked. Because of the logistics involved, recycling would be much harder on foreign producers than it would be on EC producers. Foreigners would either have to shift their carmaking to Germany or ship their junk back home.

Another example involves the Corporate Average Fuel Economy (CAFE) standards in the United States. These standards are fleetwide, imposing a tax on fleets (that is, all cars of all models produced by a company) that average less than 27.5 miles per gallon. U.S. manufacturers can meet the standards because they produce small cars as well as big ones, but European producers, such as Volvo, BMW, and Mercedes, typically cannot because they have no small cars in their fleets. A higher gasoline tax would have avoided this problem, which clearly contains elements of trade protectionism.[68]

In other dubious cases, the United States banned tuna imports from Canada in order to conserve the species, but somehow neglected to limit its own tuna catch. Not to be outdone, Canada limited exports of herring and salmon, again for conservation, but failed to put limits on its own fishing industry's catch for domestic use. In both cases GATT found that the restrictions were not meant for conservation, but were protectionist. France's February 1994 special health inspection of imported fish took so long that it caused the fish to rot. It had nothing to do with health but was a means for appeasing angry French fishermen who were complaining about the competition.[69] Thailand seemed to be guarding public health when it recently banned cigarette imports. A GATT panel called by the United States ruled against the Thais, however. Imports can certainly be banned for health reasons, but Thailand did nothing to stop the sale of domestically produced cigarettes. The profits of local manufacturers were being protected, not the health of consumers.*

Clearly, a way must be found to make informed decisions on the reasonability of environmental measures, and to expose and defeat those environmental measures that are protectionism in disguise. As Arthur Dunkel, GATT's former director-general, has stated, the world must guard "against the risk of the environment being kidnapped by trade protectionist interests."[70]

The Tuna–Dolphin Case A fine example of the conflict between environmental goals and international trade is the U.S. law of July 1991 that banned the impor-

*For more cases of abuse of health, safety, and technical standards, see Brown and Hogendorn, *International Economics: Theory and Context*, chapter 5. My personal favorite is the ban Japan once imposed on imports of Dunlop tennis balls, the justification being that the high pressure in the cans posed a risk to public health.

tation of fish from countries that allow "large-scale driftnet fishing." Driftnet fishing for tuna has the side effect of killing dolphins. The driftnet fishing law also banned tuna imports from third countries that have bought tuna from the country that did the fishing. Mexico, whose fishermen use driftnets, objected and took a case (Tuna/Dolphin I) to GATT. A GATT panel found in Mexico's favor, stating that "in principle it is not possible under GATT's rules to make access to one's own market dependent on the domestic environmental policies of the exporting country."[71]

Though it did not make the argument quite this way, Mexico's case was that it should not have to give up an efficient fishing method that provides its low-income people with cheap protein and provides it with some export earnings, too, but does *not* threaten a species' existence. (The dolphin is not an endangered species.) Mexicans asked why their country should automatically have to adopt the dolphin fetish that Americans share? GATT saw the matter Mexico's way in a sweeping ruling stating that laws cannot be applied to production practices in other countries.

Environmentalists were outraged, though they perhaps did not see that the law was in fact flawed. The Tuna/Dolphin I case was never actually concluded because both parties decided to withdraw it from the GATT process and they entered into a bilateral accord on the matter. (Mexico still uses drift nets but is limiting its catch.)[72] At that point, the European Community took up the case, returning it to GATT as Tuna/Dolphin II (1994). The EC, representing the Netherlands Antilles, which imports tuna from Mexico and also exports tuna, continued the case on the ground that the number of dolphin kills permitted to Mexico was determined retroactively and variably after the U.S. kills. It charged that this was unfair, as indeed it seemed to be.[73]

Labeling as an Alternative Ironically, the tuna case was conclusively settled by the market before GATT ever got to Tuna/Dolphin II. "Dolphin-safe" labeling made it very difficult to sell "unsafe" tuna in the United States. In Tuna/Dolphin I, GATT explicitly approved ecolabeling, that is, clear warnings on labels, and called such programs a better way to handle the problem than trade restrictions. This appears to be very good advice. Consumers can vote in a sense, and they may even be willing to pay a premium.[74] The United States has done little with labeling, preferring to use trade barriers, but Germany's Blue Angel scheme, Canada's environmental choice programs, and the similar efforts by the Nordic Council in Scandinavia, are examples of what can be done.[75]

Could There Be a Comparative Advantage in Production That Pollutes?

Could a comparative advantage arise in LDCs that allow methods of production that pollute? If so, then would not "clean" producers of similar products in the developed countries be disadvantaged? Alternatively, would not the environmental standards of the developed countries be eroded by a rush to the lowest common denominator?

Many environmentalists do indeed believe that LDCs with lax environmental standards will obtain a comparative advantage in dirty output that acts to undermine rigorous environmental regulation elsewhere.[76] They call for trade restrictions in the form of "ecodumping duties" as the solution to the problem.*

Such a position misses the point that differences between countries are at the heart of comparative advantage. Countries may choose different levels of environmental regulation for several reasons: climate, prevailing winds, existing pollution, economic needs, risk preferences, and population density.[77] Ecodumping duties would negate comparative advantage, and would be subject to capture by protectionists. Countries that are poorer should probably be free to choose a lower level of environmental protection if the effect is felt by them alone. Doing so would enable them to choose more economic growth for a time.

The LDCs themselves strongly oppose environmental policing in the form of trade restrictions, with Brazil and India leading the opposition. This opposition is

REDUCING TRADE BARRIERS MAY *IMPROVE* THE ENVIRONMENT

Some environmentalists support trade barriers to improve the environment, but there are reasons to believe that *lower* trade barriers may actually accomplish more in this regard. Freer international trade means that LDCs will be able to raise their exports of textiles, clothing, steel, and other manufactured goods now subject to restraint. Production of these goods is likely to cause less environmental harm than do pesticides and clear-cutting in agriculture. Opening trade would also be expected to raise national incomes, and as pointed out at the beginning of the chapter, richer countries both desire and can afford a cleaner environment. Some pollutant emissions, for example suspended particles, decrease as income rises at all levels of income. Others, including major ones such as sulfur dioxide and smoke, rise with income when income is low but then turn down at an income level of about $5000 per capita.[78] (Carbon dioxide and carbon monoxide emissions, among others, clearly *rise* as income grows, however, and must await a change in attitudes to bring them down.) Moreover, a major environmental improvement would likely follow freer trade in agriculture. The heavily protected farmers of Europe and Japan use extraordinary amounts of fertilizer in their agricultural production. Not nearly so much is needed to produce agricultural commodities in the countries that have the comparative advantage.

*There is a marked split among the major environmental organizations in their view toward the costs and benefits of free trade. For example, groups favoring the North American Free Trade Area included the National Wildlife Foundation, the Environmental Defense Fund, the Natural Resources Defense Council, the Audubon Society, the World Wildlife Fund, and Conservation International. Groups opposed included the Sierra Club, the Friends of the Earth, and many grassroots local organizations. See Esty, *Greening the GATT*, 28.

probably a political mistake, perhaps based on inadequate appreciation of how strong environmental forces are in the developed countries, or perhaps on bargaining brinkmanship. Whatever the reasons, the LDCs believe that they are being asked to bear costs that, so far, are due mostly to the growth of the developed countries, and that reflect the developed countries' environmental priorities. They believe that the main cause of world environmental problems is the failure of developed countries to make producers and consumers pay the costs of their pollution, which stems from a resource-intensive and consumption-oriented lifestyle.[79]

THE ENVIRONMENT AND TRADE: A NEW BODY IS NEEDED

Disputes between the developed countries and the LDCs on trade and the environment are likely to be common. Already sanctions have been used by the developed countries, and countersanctions by the LDCs are making an appearance. (When Austria banned tropical timber imports in 1992, various Asian nations threatened an embargo of trade with Austria, causing that country to back down six months later.)[80] Unless some compromise can be engineered, these disputes will surely only grow more bitter, with Pandora's box pried open bit by bit. One could even imagine rapidly growing hostility, perhaps with the developed countries insisting that resource use be frozen (thereby keeping LDCs in poverty), while the LDCs insist that resources be devoted to grain production for people rather than for animals to produce the meat eaten in the developed countries.[81]

Internationally negotiated agreements among trading partners, rich and poor, to raise their level of environmental protection need to be pursued in a more formal setting than is now possible. A new body for negotiation and agreement is needed. Establishment of such a body would ensure that trade barriers could be used for the necessary policing of vital environmental actions. It would also ensure that barriers are not protectionism in disguise or unwarranted unilateral action not justified by the seriousness of an issue.[82] Up to now, GATT and the succeeding World Trade Organization have sometimes had to operate outside their field of technical competence in making decisions regarding trade and the environment. A new environmental body to judge such issues would be an improvement.[83]

If a new Global Environmental Organization (GEO) were to be established alongside the WTO, it could coordinate international agreements against global environmental harm. Its dual task would be to police the use of trade restraints to enforce these agreements and see that trade flows are kept open and uncorrupted by protectionists posing as environmentalists. A GEO could review all trade measures to protect the environment, and decide whether they are appropriate for the amount of harm they are attempting to prevent or whether they are protectionism in disguise. Such an organization would solve the problem that no present world body has a mandate to protect the environment.[84] Many in the LDCs would grumble, as might some environmentalists for the opposite reason. But low-income countries would benefit just as the rich ones would from the scientific guidance that a GEO could bring to an area where emotion, not fact, has been playing an important role.

SUSTAINABLE DEVELOPMENT

The term *sustainable development* gained wide attention from the 1987 Brundtland Commission Report, named for Norway's prime minister, Mrs. Brundtland.[85] Surely economists, politicians in the developed countries and the LDCs alike, and the common people of these countries can agree that in some sense development ought to be sustainable. The meaning of the term is, however, debatable. Some ecologists and biologists use it to express the idea of not depleting resources or cutting trees.[86] Economists generally do not agree and would advise that the costs of sustainable growth would then be very great. They believe that long before any given resource runs out, its price would rise and a switch made away from that resource to substitutes. In any case, with population growth raising population by three to four times in 50 or so years, it is hard to imagine development occurring without some significant encroachment on the world's stock of resources.

The idea of sustainable development is more convincing if it is interpreted to mean that a given rate of growth may be unsustainable if the environment degrades catastrophically, or if greater income inequality leads to revolution, or if population growth runs out of control, or if agricultural land is being fragmented and thus lessening productivity.[87] A useful definition might be that *un*sustainable development is development where damage to the environment penalizes economic growth.[88] The Brundtland report used a looser definition, defining sustainable development to mean "meeting the needs of the present generation without compromising the needs of future generations."[89] Yet care must be taken not to define it as having the next generation be just as poor as the present one—for who could approve of sustainable poverty?

Sustainable development could also be interpreted to mean macroeconomic policies, and perhaps international cooperation, designed to stabilize the rate of growth and avoid stop-go performance, too fast in periods of prosperity and too slow during slumps. It would also be sensible to include in the term progress in income distribution and basic human needs provision so that economic policies receive broad support from the population.[90] Finally, if sustainable growth means only that due consideration should be given to environmental problems, then as a broad goal it is fully acceptable.

All this amounts to saying that those who use the term should be careful to give it adequate definition. However it is defined, it has become a "buzz phrase." The World Bank has decided to hold annual conferences starting 1994 on the sustainability of development and has created a vice-president of environmentally sustainable development.[91] The attention accurately reflects the growing concern that economic growth may harm the environment.

NOTES

1. For a general examination of environmental problems, see A. V. Kneese and J. L. Sweeney, eds., *Handbook of Natural Resource and Energy Economics* (Amsterdam, 1988). For the impact of the environment on the LDCs, I relied on Edward Dommen,

Fair Principles for Sustainable Development: Essays on Environmental Policy and Developing Countries (Aldershot, 1993); and Tom Tietenberg, *Environmental and Natural Resource Economics*, 3rd ed. (New York, 1992), chapter 22.

2. For this statement see Lester R. Brown and John E. Young, "Feeding the World in the Nineties," in Lester R. Brown et al., *State of the World 1990* (New York, 1990), 60.
3. *WDR 1992*, 138–139.
4. Dennis Anderson, "Declining Tree Stocks in African Countries," *World Development* 14, no. 7 (July 1986): 854.
5. *The Economist*, June 25, 1994; *WDR 1992*, 75.
6. *WDR 1992*, 53; *South*, September 1987.
7. James Lee and Robert Goodland, "Economic Development and the Environment," *Finance and Development* 23, no. 4 (December 1986): 36–39.
8. *Christian Science Monitor*, July 21, 1987.
9. *The Economist*, September 2, 1989.
10. *WDR 1992*, 140.
11. *WDR 1988*, 118.
12. *WDR 1992*, 40. The figures are an average for the OECD countries.
13. *WDR 1992*, 43, 51.
14. See Cynthia Pollock Shea, "Protecting the Ozone Layer," in Lester R. Brown et al., *State of the World 1989* (New York, 1989), 85; *WDR 1992*, 63; *Christian Science Monitor*, June 1, 1994; and *The Economist*, September 2, 1989.
15. Shea, "Protecting the Ozone Layer," 87.
16. Shea, "Protecting the Ozone Layer," 77.
17. *WDR 1992*, 63; Lester R. Brown, Christopher Flavin, and Sandra Postel, "A World at Risk," in Lester R. Brown et al., *State of the World 1989* (New York, 1989), 4.
18. Shea, "Protecting the Ozone Layer," 86, 93.
19. *Christian Science Monitor*, June 1, 1994; Daniel C. Esty, *Greening the GATT: Trade, Environment, and the Future* (Washington, D.C., 1994), 232; *WDR 1992*, 157.
20. In particular I used the "Symposium on Global Climate Change," especially the articles by Richard Schmalensee and William D. Nordhaus, in the *Journal of Economic Perspectives* 7, no. 4 (Fall 1993): 3–86; and William Cline, *The Economics of Global Warming* (Washington, D.C., 1992).
21. Anthony A. Churchill and Robert J. Saunders, "Global Warming and the Developing World," *Finance and Development* 28, no. 2 (June 1991): 30.
22. *WDR 1992*, 61.
23. World Resources Institute Information, reprinted in *The Economist*, March 11, 1989.
24. Fxor a study of the costs in the long run, see William R. Cline, *The Economics of Global Warming* (New York, 1992). For the 9% figure, see Dale W. Jorgenson, "Comment on 'Climate and Development,' by Nordhaus," *Proceedings of the World Bank Annual Conference on Development Economics 1993* (Washington, D.C., 1994): 378.
25. *The Economist*, May 30, 1992, S24.
26. Michael Renner, "Rethinking Transportation," in Lester R. Brown et al., *State of the World 1989* (New York, 1989), 112.
27. Christopher Flavin, "Slowing Global Warming," in Lester R. Brown et al., *State of the World 1990* (New York, 1990), 20.
28. Nicholas Lenssen, "Providing Energy in Developing Countries," in Lester R. Brown, ed., *State of the World 1993* (New York, 1993), 106.
29. *The Economist*, June 18, 1994; *WDR 1992*, 114–115.
30. *The Economist*, October 1, 1994.
31. *The Economist*, June 18, 1994.

32. Esty, *Greening the GATT*, 16, citing work of Robert Cullen.
33. Stated in *The Economist*, September 15, 1990.
34. *WDR 1992*, 160; *The Economist*, March 6, 1993.
35. Lawrence H. Summers and Vinod Thomas, "Recent Lessons of Development," *World Bank Research Observer* 8, no. 2 (July 1993): 252.
36. *WDR 1992*, 117.
37. Nicholas Lenssen, "Providing Energy in Developing Countries," in Lester R. Brown, ed., *State of the World 1993* (New York, 1993): 109.
38. Bjorn Larsen and Anwar Shah, "Combatting the 'Greenhouse Effect'," *Finance and Development* 29, no. 4 (December 1992): 20–23.
39. Brown, Flavin, and Postel, "A World at Risk," 4.
40. From Hans Binswanger, "Fiscal and Legal Incentives with Environmental Effects on the Brazilian Amazon," World Bank Discussion Paper No. 69 (1989); and *The Economist*, March 18, 1989.
41. Lester R. Brown et al., *State of the World 1989* (New York, 1989), 21.
42. *Wall Street Journal*, July 3, 1987.
43. *The Economist*, May 3, 1987.
44. The environment was the main topic of *WDR 1992*. For the points in this paragraph, see pp. 2, 10–12, 35, 128. For a discussion of policies, also see Gunnar S. Eskeland and Emmanuel Jimenez, "Policy Instruments for Pollution Control in Developing Countries," *World Bank Research Observer* 7, no. 2 (July 1992): 145–169. The earlier Brundtland Report, named for Norway's prime minister, made much the same points.
45. These suggestions were mostly culled from various annual issues of Lester R. Brown et al., *State of the World*.
46. Lester R. Brown, Christopher Flavin, and Sandra Postel, "Outlining a Global Action Plan," in Lester R. Brown et al., *State of the World 1989* (New York, 1989), 176–178, 180.
47. T. H. Tietenberg, "The Poverty Connection to Environmental Policy," *Challenge* 33, no. 5 (September/October 1990): 30, citing William Ruckleshaus.
48. Tietenberg, "The Poverty Connection to Environmental Policy," 30–31.
49. Mohamed El-Ashry, "The New Global Environmental Facility," *Finance and Development* 31, no. 2 (June 1994): 48; Esty, *Greening the GATT*, 87.
50. *WDR 1992*, 169.
51. *Christian Science Monitor*, May 12, 1992.
52. *The Economist*, December 7, 1991.
53. See David Bigman, "A Plan to End LDC Debt and Save the Environment Too," *Challenge* 33, no. 4 (July/August 1990): 33–37.
54. *Guardian Weekly*, June 26, 1994.
55. Hilary F. French, "Reconciling Trade and the Environment," in Lester R. Brown, ed., *State of the World 1993* (New York, 1993): 165.
56. *Christian Science Monitor*, March 24, 1989.
57. See Maureen L. Cropper and Wallace E. Oates, "Environmental Economics: A Survey," in *Journal of Economic Literature* 30 (June 1992): 675–740; Hilary F. French, "Reconciling Trade and the Environment," in Lester R. Brown et al., *State of the World 1993* (New York, 1993); H. Jeffrey Leonard, *Pollution and the Struggle for the World Product* (Cambridge, 1988); and *WDR 1992*, 67.
58. Hilary F. French, "Reconciling Trade and the Environment," in Lester R. Brown, ed., *State of the World 1993* (New York, 1993): 167.
59. Marj Charlier, "U.S. Mining Firms, Unwelcome at Home, Flock to Latin America," *Wall Street Journal*, June 18, 1993.

60. Much of the material in this section is from Wilson B. Brown and Jan S. Hogendorn, *International Economics: Theory and Context* (Reading, Mass., 1993), chapter 5. That work draws on Steve Charnovitz, "Exploring the Environmental Exceptions in GATT Article XX," *Journal of World Trade* 25, no. 5 (October 1991): 37–55, and Kym Anderson and Richard Blockhurst, eds., *The Greening of World Trade Issues* (Ann Arbor, 1992). A more recent important source is Daniel C. Esty, *Greening the GATT: Trade, Environment, and the Future* ((Washington, D.C., 1994).
61. Esty, *Greening the GATT*, 166–167.
62. For this paragraph, see Esty, *Greening the GATT*, 47–52, 102–103.
63. Esty, *Greening the GATT*, 49–51, 134.
64. See *The Economist*, May 30, 1992.
65. Esty, *Greening the GATT*, 124–125, 131.
66. Esty, *Greening the GATT*, 126.
67. See Brown and Hogendorn, *International Economics: Theory and Context*, chapter 5.
68. Esty, *Greening the GATT*, 45, 269.
69. Esty, *Greening the GATT*, 45.
70. *Wall Street Journal*, February 12, 1992.
71. *Wall Street Journal*, February 12, 1992.
72. See Esty, *Greening the GATT*, 29–32, 188, 190; and *International Economic Review*, November, 1994.
73. Esty, *Greening the GATT*, 30, 107–108.
74. Esty, *Greening the GATT*, 134, 171.
75. Esty, *Greening the GATT*, 252.
76. Esty, *Greening the GATT*, 2–3.
77. Esty, *Greening the GATT*, 106.
78. Gene Grossman and Alan Krueger, *Environmental Impacts of a North American Free Trade Area*, NBER Working Paper No. 3914 (1992).
79. Esty, *Greening the GATT*, 181–183.
80. Esty, *Greening the GATT*, 189.
81. *International Economic Review*, November 1994.
82. Esty, *Greening the GATT*, 5–6, 159–161, 163–164.
83. Esty, *Greening the GATT*, 31–32.
84. Esty, *Greening the GATT*, 54–58, 79, 128, 230–231.
85. See Edward Dommen, *Fair Principles for Sustainable Development: Essays on Environmental Policy and Developing Countries* (Aldershot, 1993); and Michael Redclift, *Sustainable Development: Exploring the Contradictions* (London, 1987).
86. Clem Tisdell, "Sustainable Development: Differing Perspectives of Ecologists and Economists, and Relevance," *World Development* 16, no. 3, (March 1988): 373–384.
87. *HDR 1994*, 13.
88. H. W. Arndt, "Sustainable Development and the Discount Rate," *Economic Development and Cultural Change* 41, no. 3 (April 1993): 651–661.
89. *WDR 1992*, 8.
90. *IMF Survey*, July 24, 1989.
91. *The Economist*, December 25, 1993, September 16, 1989.

Chapter **17**

Lessons Learned

Now we reach a short epilogue, where we shall attempt to evaluate what economists know about how to develop in the long run. Perhaps the best way to put into perspective the lessons learned in this book is to make the attempt to "teach" them to someone else. Of course, mastering one book in development economics doth not a development advisor make: that will require additional years of further training, reading, and often most important of all, field experience. Yet imagining that we have been asked to serve as consultants to the government of Poveria, to make and explain policy recommendations, can be a useful final exercise. Suppose this morning we find ourselves flying into Poveria's international airport, scheduled this afternoon to discuss development issues in a North–South round table with economists and politicians. Which of the principles of development economics we have studied here would we want to emphasize as most generally useful? Permitting ourselves the freedom to make uninhibited policy recommendations to rich and poor countries alike, what would that advice be?

Development Is Complex

We begin with what may be the hardest of all lessons for us and for our well-trained colleagues to learn: One must be always open-minded yet skeptical and questioning, always willing to learn from other schools of economics and from other disciplines, and always willing to adjust theory to the reality of empirical evidence. In this field of economics, certainty can come uncomfortably close to intellectual arrogance. The principles we believe to be generally valid all too often will have many exceptions, unavoidable because of the great variety of social, political, and economic conditions in the world of the LDCs. History has had a way of treating poorly some of the most widely supported policy recommendations of the past, the "slaying of beautiful hypotheses by ugly facts" in the words of Thomas Huxley.

Then let us admit that our economic modeling does not always capture well the complexity of the barriers to development in the LDCs. We have examined a long list of such barriers, including inadequate knowledge; poor organization; social and religious constraints on women, ethnic minorities, and entrepreneurship; government policies that distort economic incentives; rule by an economic elite or by the military; corruption; and so forth.

Whenever this is so, then internal constraints may block any number of otherwise promising paths toward development, and rather than being an inevitable, scientific movement, progress is likely to involve a process of "searching, probing, trials and errors, willingness to abandon trials that are errors."[1] We know that more resources are needed for development, but long before the full potential of what is available can be used, a country may encounter internal barriers that are difficult to breach and perhaps were not even anticipated until development caused them to be encountered. Economic growth may appear as in Figure 17.1, with a country's actual growth rate always lying below its potential growth rate.[2] An understanding that development is more like negotiating a maze than it is like walking a straight line, always likely to yield less than it could, is humbling no doubt, but it will lessen the sense of surprise when a strategy goes wrong or performs disappointingly and will encourage a flexible approach by economists.

Policy Recommendations for the LDCs

The heart of the development effort is to raise productivity, for this is the key to income growth. What can the LDCs do for themselves? Promoting domestic saving and investment, and increasing the efficiency of that investment, are crucial elements in productivity increase, but more difficult the lower a country's income. Government assistance to establish financial institutions can help, and so can the use of market rates of interest, for that will encourage savers and avoid overly great capital intensity. Government budget surpluses financed from tax revenue and made available through lending agencies to private entrepreneurs could play a much more important role than they currently do. But the tax mechanism employed to collect the revenues for these purposes must be carefully managed; it is too easy to discourage saving, penalize agriculture, distort foreign trade, and generate wholesale tax avoidance with an ill-designed tax system. Probably the most promising tax for LDCs is the value added tax, with its broad base, its self-policing aspect, and its nonapplication to savings or the interest on savings. To promote both equity and ease of collection, VAT might be charged at a higher rate on luxuries and supplemented with a moderate income tax, might exempt foodstuffs, and might not be collected from petty traders in local markets. The earlier a VAT replaces specific taxes on agriculture and imported goods, the better.

We shall insist, with Nicholas Stern, that there is now "enough experience of economic development to know that growth in aggregate income cannot, by itself, be guaranteed to eliminate deprivation."[3] It is important to improve the quality of Poveria's population directly. Economic growth could (and with luck perhaps

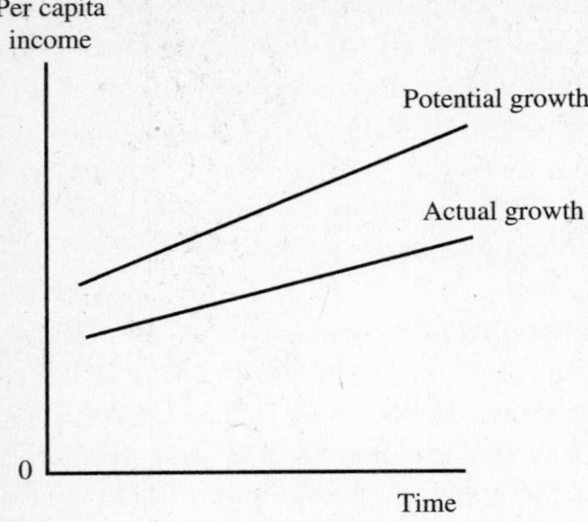

Figure 17.1 Constraints in the LDCs may lower actual growth below potential growth.

would) eventually bring this about without government effort, but even if it happens, the process is likely to take many years, with the longest delays for those in the lowest income groups. The provision of basic human services in education, health, and nutrition can raise productivity now and thereby boost incomes. Primary health care, research on crops consumed by the poor, programs to provide income to the poor including "food for work," and food subsidies based on need are all sensible ideas. By reducing infant mortality and providing some rudimentary welfare measures, such policies can counteract two important reasons for choosing to bear large numbers of children, in turn reducing the burden of dependency and making it easier to increase the stock of capital per person. A well-designed family planning program will work toward the same end, but to the degree that it goes beyond reasonable peer pressure and financial incentives to involve direct compulsion, it will probably run into difficulties. By improving conditions in villages and on farms through rural development efforts, including provision of basic human services, higher incomes through research and extension services, rural credit, and also mobilizing the off-season labor surplus for infrastructure improvement and employment in rural factories, policy can reduce the motive for further migration to the cities and improve the lot of the largest part of the population.

Concentrating on the quality of the population also augments the ethical dimension to the economics of development. It reflects a belief that economic growth must be accompanied by humane treatment for the poorest and that growth is not real progress if in spite of it many people, especially children, are still going hungry every day.[4] At the same time, policies to rectify extreme unevenness in land ownership, including a well-designed land tax, can be a major tool for bringing more equality to the distribution of income.

"Appropriateness" should be a watchword. Appropriate technology means in particular more attention to a country's factor proportions when selecting the type of capital to employ. Appropriate education programs mean more emphasis at the primary level on basic literacy and numeracy, agricultural technique, and health; more emphasis at the secondary level on technical training of the type useful in the development effort and linked to job openings; and less emphasis on expensive university education, especially where the government's spending is focused on the already well-to-do. Emphasis on women's education is important in its own right not only because it is fair and because of the neglect of the past, but also because of its positive indirect effects on nutrition and health and the reinforcement that it brings to efforts to reduce population growth.

Next we turn to the official development policies already in place in Poveria. We have a little list of policies that, if we find them in use, will cause us immediate unease.[5] To be sure, as polite advisors and skeptics of revealed wisdom, even when it is our own, we must give our hosts every opportunity to explain the origins and justifications for these policies, and perhaps we will find their reasoning is convincing. But we are well aware that the policies are on our little list because, at many other times and places, they have been counterproductive. A little pressure along with the advice may pay dividends.

1. *Urban bias*. Is there favoritism toward the cities and a prejudice against the interests of the countryside? Do we find urban wages higher than justified by labor productivity, expensive general food subsidies in the cities, low procurement prices in agriculture, high taxation of farmers by means of marketing boards and export levies? Are village schools and rural health care far below urban standards? Do rural residents live without electricity, without adequate transport, and without an effective communications system? Do private bank loans and government assistance find their way overwhelmingly to manufacturing enterprise in the cities, and not to agriculture or rural improvement? Then truly we have identified urban bias and rural neglect. In general the greater this bias, the worse the result for a country's past economic growth and its future economic prospects. Even if a country has begun to correct for this bias with subsidies for agricultural inputs and credit, we must examine whether these subsidies go predominantly to bigger farmers, whether they encourage misallocations such as a lower demand for agricultural labor, and whether the inputs are distributed inefficiently by government marketing organizations.
2. *Inflationary bias*. Does the government habitually boost its spending and support real wage growth in excess of productivity gains by running large fiscal deficits financed by rapid increases in the money supply? Then we shall have to warn our Poverian hosts that, however much they justify the government spending and money creation as providing capital for development or improving the lot of the poor and the working class, the policy will be inflationary. If the politicians are not realistic in determining what the country can afford, the resulting inflation will absorb private saving, will repel foreign investment, will risk a breakout of hyperinflation that will ravage the growth figures, and will be difficult to stop. We shall also have to remind them that to bring the inflationary bias under control, they will have to maintain credible reform policies even though the political risk will be

high. Stop-go flipflops and halfhearted attempts at reform are sure to undermine the government's credibility and in the end are likely to fail.

3. *Distortions of foreign trade*. Is the foreign exchange rate sharply overvalued, and are high trade barriers utilized against a wide range of imports? Is effective protection far more stringent than implied by the nominal rates, and does a high dispersion of tariff rates and quota amounts skew incentives sharply? Are quotas and controls emphasized more than tariffs? Behind the trade barriers do we find inefficient "hothouse" industries that could not survive on their own? Does the combination of an overvalued exchange rate and artificially low real interest rates on government-approved loans mean capital intensity is far higher than we would expect given the relative abundance and cheapness of labor, with labor saving encouraged rather than labor use? Here we have found an import substitution policy that has probably been carried too far. We will strongly consider advising Poveria to eliminate the biases.

By and large, in all these cases we will support the use of market pricing intelligently used. The replacement of controls and interventions with market pricing will be a long step forward in erasing the common favoritism toward urban areas, capital-intensive manufacturing, and the production of goods in which the country has no comparative advantage. Facing the market's realities, buyers and sellers in those markets can make more rational economic decisions based more firmly on the information conveyed by those prices; foreign trade can be based on comparative advantage; and entrepreneurs are encouraged to deal with people outside their circle of friends, relatives, and political allies. When government undertakes activities, these will preferably be to improve the capabilities of the private sector and to do what that sector cannot do, or does poorly, rather than government operation of activities that could be performed privately, guided by the signals of the market. All too often, when government ownership and operation expands beyond these sensible limits, the activity ends up inefficiently done, at high cost, in politicized surroundings. Where state-operated enterprises remain in government hands, they should behave like private companies, governed by the same rules. Much remains to be accomplished in structuring these operations so that managers are rewarded on the basis of their performance. They should not be permitted to exclude private firms from the market by price-cutting made possible by government subsidies. Yet if it is decided to sell the state-operated enterprises when possible, consider that little or nothing may be gained if they end up as unregulated monopolies in the hands of the rich or expatriate interests. Care is needed.

Worrying about state-operated enterprises is decidedly not the same as saying that government activity should be minimized, as some conservatives would have it. There are many areas where well-designed government participation in the development process is essential, and this is likely to be the more true the lower a country's income is. An important area is the infrastructure of law and order (including fuller definition and protection of property rights), finance and banking, the power grid, large irrigation systems, transport, and communications. These activities will require government control or operation because, if left to the private sector, they might be provided in inadequate amounts or would otherwise be private monopolies. Most of these also possess demonstrable and strong external economies. Public goods such as education, health, family planning, agricultural research, and extension services will also often be most successfully organized by government. It is especially important to repair and maintain the infrastructure: impassable roads and railways, water systems and telephones that do not work, power outages, and garbage that goes uncollected all represent areas of failure that governments must be involved in addressing. From the standpoint of efficient production, government participation in these sectors, with the remainder of the economy following the path indicated by market forces, appears to us vastly preferable to the more comprehensive forms of economic planning.*

A grave problem with planning is its demands on institutional capacity, which is likely to be limited because of the scarcity of trained administrators. Indeed, some reforms that are called for in any case will serve to reduce the need for scarce talent, thereby increasing the payoff. Fitting this description are the removal of quotas on imports, liberalizing the marketing of agricultural commodities, and freeing regulated markets.

Broad and damaging inequalities of income may remain, however, and if they do, government will have to implement programs to raise the productivity and employability of the poor. In examining *any* government plan of action, we will cast a critical eye at the degree to which policy neglects to improve the capacity of the poor to improve their lives. Some of these poor people will have been harmed by the very reforms we have been recommending. Both in urban and rural areas there are people whose poverty will be increased, temporarily at any rate, because we have allowed agricultural prices to rise. Workers in industries protected by trade barriers will suffer when trade is liberalized, some state enterprises will downsize their labor force as privatization occurs, and some civil servants will be dismissed as we reduce the government's efforts to control the economy. Cushioning the negative effects of reform on losers is not only the humane thing to do, but it may reduce the outcry from these losers when the reforms are made.

Policy Recommendations for the Developed Countries

There is no doubt that our recommendations to take important and worthwhile steps involve costs to the LDCs that exceed their available revenues. That is why aid from the developed countries can be crucial, the more so for the lowest income countries. As advisors, we find ourselves favoring restoration of the funds for IDA so valuable to the least-developed LDCs, and more multilateral aid for the poorest part of the population of the lowest-income countries, rather than bilateral aid to

*As Nicholas Stern notes, those who suggest that government should do less have in mind questions of cost and efficiency in what the government does do, but often they say little about what the market does not do. Those who suggest that the government should do more are thinking of what the government does not do, but they are obligated to show how government can raise revenues without excessive damage to the economy. See Stern, "The Economics of Development: A Survey," *Economic Journal* 99, no. 397 (September 1989): 674.

the better-off part of the population in LDCs, which need it less. But we also agree that aid can be and often has been misused within an environment of damaging economic policies. Projects undertaken primarily because aid is available to support them are unlikely to be the most successful ones. Structural adjustments in return for the assistance and adequate, preferably international, supervision of its use would seem to be reasonable requirements.

The aid could be increasingly valuable if a greater amount of it focused on developing more appropriate technologies that utilize labor without sacrificing output and on assisting small farms and small businesses where credit has been especially scarce. Support for funding population programs is essential, including especially the neglected field of research into new contraceptive techniques. So is aid to assist the LDCs in reducing the harm to the environment from economic growth.

Obviously, budgetary problems in the developed countries will limit the amount of foreign aid for years to come, and conservative politicians will continue to attack it. If we are in a bold mood, we could recommend a new revenue source that could raise enough money to finance aid for these humanitarian purposes, but with few adverse side effects. That source is international purchases and sales of foreign exchange. As James Tobin has suggested, a worldwide 0.05% sales tax on currency transactions could yield about $150 billion per year. The tax would be so low as a percent of the transactions that it would be unlikely to cause serious disruptions in the financial markets. Even if it did cut down such transactions to some small extent, there is presently over *100 times* more turnover in foreign exchange than there is investment in plant and equipment, so it is unlikely that any harm would be appreciable—whereas the benefits to development and the environment might be substantial.[6]

Perhaps above all is the potential for progress in the promotion of trade flows and the potential for damage if trade barriers are erected against the LDCs. Nothing would be so discouraging for these countries as to find their growth prospects choked off by selfish developed-country protection, nothing more encouraging than stable prospects for following their comparative advantage in trade. In the long term, this vital topic transcends the question of aid, which could double or triple in amount and still accomplish little if trade is stifled. The completion of the Uruguay Round promises a bright future, but storms could arise overnight if the developed countries come to believe that development in the LDCs threatens their jobs, or if regional free trade areas turn protectionist.

Policy Recommendations Involving Mutual Gains

During our discussions in Poveria we will emphasize that progress will be easier whenever contending parties such as the LDCs and the developed countries can see, or be convinced, that mutual gains will result from some possible policy change. Although this was a major thrust of the Brandt Commission report of 1980, the large scope for exploiting such mutual gains is still too little appreciated. All chances should be seized, for positive-sum games will always be easier to play than zero or negative-sum ones.

This recommendation should not be misunderstood. Mutual gain ordinarily does not result in unanimous support, because gain to all countries is not the same as gain to all individuals. It is very difficult to find any policy changes that will leave every person better off without any further action by government. Such movements, which harm no one, are easy to bring about (there being no rational opposition to them), but this being so, the changes will probably already have been carried out. Another easy case involves policies that bring mutual gain in the sense that the total benefits are sufficiently large so that gainers can pay full compensation to losers, leaving society as a whole better off if the policies are adopted. Such "Pareto-optimal" movements will not be resisted on economic grounds either.[7]

Many cases are harder ones, however. For LDCs, there are two major reasons why losers might not actually be compensated for their losses. First, the tax and transfer mechanisms may not be up to the task, and second, the gainers may think the losers undeserving and therefore will not support the compensation. (This second reason frequently applies in developed countries also.) Those who lose will therefore resist, and if they are politically powerful, their resistance may be decisive in preventing the implementation of a policy change that could have been advantageous to all if compensation were paid.

Whether to undertake any given policy change when compensation is not paid then becomes a more difficult question involving some concept of justice and fairness on which there will never be unanimous agreement. There will be some economists who would state bluntly that no welfare judgment can be made if a policy change makes group A better off and group B worse off.

Such "welfare pessimism" does not appear to be very current among development economists, however. Most appear to take two approaches to the subject when compensation of losers is not possible, and in our round table discussions we will do so, too.[8] One is a presumption that adopting sensible policies with the promise of enhanced growth will, in time, be likely to make everyone better off, even those who lose initially. This seems especially apt for an LDC such as Poveria, where even the people who gain from faulty policies are relatively poor and are likely to gain more from long-run economic progress than from policy favoritism. The second approach is to take a normative position based on a communal value judgment. Thus, if a proposal would increase aggregate income greatly and harm a small number of rich slightly, then society might well be comfortable with the decision even if the rich were not compensated for their loss. But if a policy would bring widespread uncompensated harm to a large middle class while bringing only a slight net gain to society, then as a value judgment society might be equally comfortable rejecting that policy. In between these easy decisions, the effect of higher income for society as a whole will have to be weighed in a normative judgment against the uncompensated losses to those with higher incomes, and the good chance that through growth losers, too, will eventually gain. There is also the further chance that compensation will eventually be paid after all. Such decisions will no doubt often be difficult, but in many LDCs they will be made easier whenever past policies boosted the incomes of the already wealthy while depressing the incomes of the already poor.

This whole question is extremely important because there is a general perception that gains for the LDCs will be losses for the developed countries, and vice versa. Perhaps more than any other reason, this perception explains why international development conferences have so frequently achieved so little or have even had negative results. What could be constructive negotiations deteriorate all too often into a "vicious circle of suspicion, skepticism, indifference, hostility, and stalemate," with "counterproductive procedures and one-sided agendas."[9] It is self-evident that the LDCs have the most to gain from successful cooperation, because any given improvement in income to a poor person or country will have more significance than the same gain to a rich one. This being so, it would seem crucial that the South take the initiative wherever possible for altering the pattern of negotiations, pressing for the adoption of positive-sum policies whenever they are identified.

Consider some of the policies involving mutual gains that we have recognized in the course of the book.

1. *Promoting growth*. Policies to promote economic growth in the LDCs bring obvious benefits. But if the rich countries would themselves adopt policies more oriented toward their own growth (lower budget deficits and interest rates in the United States, deregulation of price-boosting government policies in Europe, encouragement of consumption in Japan, for example), then not only would their own citizens benefit, but the high growth would fuel the export engine of the LDCs. That in turn would generate income there, cause increased exports from the developed countries, and add further to *their* growth in a "virtuous circle."
2. *Restructuring agriculture*. If developed countries would restructure their farm support schemes and reduce their agricultural protection, then consumers there would gain just as LDCs benefit from being able to export far greater quantities of commodities in which they have a comparative advantage. A similar, though smaller, effect would flow from liberalization of agricultural protection in the LDCs. Recall the World Bank estimate that the overall gains to both groups of countries from dismantling trade barriers in agriculture would in value terms be more than double the amount presently paid out in foreign aid. It should also be noted that there is a surprising amount of complementarity between agricultural production in the LDCs and the developed countries, with growth in one leading to growth in the other. The successful completion of the Uruguay Round of trade negotiations means that progress is in the offing, though vigilance will be needed to ensure that the promised reductions in price supports and protection will actually be taken.
3. *Reducing trade barriers against industrial products*. In the developed countries, oligopolies and trade unions will seek protection to maintain their market power. In the LDCs, similar motives plus general import substitution strategies are the cause of the high tariffs and quotas. If both groups of countries were to resist these policies, reducing their protection of industrial products, then each would increase the exports of products in which it has a comparative advantage. An open, multilateral trading system brought huge benefits to the developed countries in the decades since World War II, and trade has been instrumental in the progress of the most successful LDCs as well. These advantages must not be lost. Again, the

promised steps of the Uruguay Round and its new World Trade Organization holds much promise, but supporters of open trade will have to be alert to an uprising of protectionist interests. For political reasons, perhaps the LDCs will find it easier to promote trade in the context of South–South and North–South customs unions. If these are not too trade-diverting, they will be better than the status quo, but continuing overall reduction of barriers among all countries would be better yet.

4. *Stimulating capital and technology flows*. Given the importance for development of both capital investment and appropriate technology, keeping open the channels for their flow and stimulating their movement stands to be advantageous both to the LDCs that put them profitably to use and the rich countries that make them available at a profit. Recently there has been a substantial increase in private capital flows to the LDCs. But a huge potential for further mutually beneficial expansion in capital flows exists if the pension funds of the developed world enlarge their purchase of equity shares in LDC markets. The pension funds could earn the higher average returns often paid in these markets, and the LDCs would receive a welcome infusion of new financing. The host LDCs can assist by policing their own macroeconomic policies. Misguided policies can spook bond- and shareholders, leading to panic capital flight. Keeping open the flow of technology also involves mutual gains for the developed countries in the form of profits, and for the LDCs because the productivity of their capital and labor is raised. "Appropriate technology" is an area for research that could yield substantial returns if more international assistance were provided.
5. *Averting deterioration of the global environment*. Self-evidently, both rich countries and low-income ones stand to gain from sensible programs to avert environmental harm. As it will surely be necessary for the developed countries to pay most of the bills for an international effort along these lines, the prospect opens of an opportunity not only to protect the environment but also to reduce the burden of LDC debt at the same time. It may actually be a small blessing that the environment and reduction of LDC debt issues can be linked together, for that increases the odds that the dangers from both can be reduced at the same time. One conclusion is all too obvious: failure to cope with long-term environmental issues could be quite injurious to the LDCs' prospects for development.

All this advice is not meant as a recommendation for "maximum openness" in an economy, with complete noninterference with free trade and no limits on the operation of the marketplace. In LDCs there are certainly important roles for government policy. These include promotion of infant industries through identifying changes in comparative advantage and overcoming barriers that block the realization of the new advantage. Preferably the policies will encourage quality enhancement and technology improvement, perhaps with start-up subsidies and even with tariffs if budget constraints are intense. The high-performing Asian economies present impressive examples of how encouragement of competitive industries and dynamic achievement of new comparative advantage can be accomplished.

For the LDCs, "economic self-reliance" and "reducing dependency" are understandable and laudable goals of government action if they mean policies to encourage diversification into areas of increasing comparative advantage, or prudent promotion of alternative exports to reduce risk in a single-product economy, or judicious controls on firms with market power, or development of production at home when that promises to be more efficient than importing the product.

But if "economic self-reliance" means following policies of blind import substitution, attempting to delink from the world economy, unpoliced appropriation of the intellectual property rights of foreign firms, and taking action that repels foreign investment, then we believe the evidence shows a country becomes less self-reliant, and more dependent, because its economy is weakened. All in all, we advocate a large degree of freedom for trade flows and for investment as the best strategy. Exactly what "large degree" means in practice for any specific country is certainly debatable and cannot be answered by averages or by referring to the experience of rich countries. The answer will vary in different countries at different stages of development and requires careful, specialized research. Finally, we would warn that complete freedom for private enterprise may not always be optimal. The behavior of firms with monopoly or monopsony power needs to be carefully monitored and controlled, or the public will suffer.

Further Afield

Because we are economics advisors, we shall avoid political topics during our official sessions, but that will not keep us from making a few salient points as we enjoy a social evening with our hosts (though perhaps at some risk of reducing the conviviality!). Too commonly, we shall say, democratic ideals are thought to be irrelevant to economic progress. But the military government of the generals, the junta, the dictatorship, with their censorship and rule of bullet not ballot, are likely to mean that the political process is very narrow. Where the political process is narrow, special interests allied to the oligarchs will glean their reward—appointments to positions of responsibility not based on talent, access to loans at low rates of interest, permits to acquire scarce foreign exchange, licenses to bring in scarce imported goods.

Where the political process is not open, where the press is not free, graft and corruption are likely to flourish; little light penetrates to these dark corners. We might hint at our conviction that authoritarian practices may spring up partly because governments find they must become more coercive if they are to continue policies that have such clear losers—the rural sector victimized by high taxes on agriculture, the many would-be businesspeople and farmers unable to borrow because the cheap loan policy makes credit scarce, the exporters ruined by the overvalued foreign exchange rate—and if the winners are to retain their gains. Indeed, authoritarian measures may be needed to overturn these policies, because long habituation to their perquisites may make vested interests violent in their defense. Economic growth together with encouragement of democratic institutions may be the best way out of this dilemma, because growth will reward even those who lose the benefits of discriminatory policies. As economists, we are not specialists in these often complicated issues of domestic politics. But we can certainly acknowledge their broad importance, and point out that political and civil disturbances and violence are only short of war itself as destroyers of economic growth.

Pessimism or Optimism?

We have encountered many reasons that could justify a pessimistic view of the development prospects of the LDCs. The population explosion, slow growth in the developed countries, the continuing debt overhang, the shortage of capital for investment and the decline of aid, the growing fears of trade with the LDCs, the politicization of economic policy, global environmental concerns, and the poor performance of Africa are among the many challenges still to be faced in bringing about successful economic development.

Yet there are many reasons for hope. Economic growth, though not uniform, has been more rapid in the LDCs than anticipated by the first generation of development economists, and some of the best performances have been in countries such as South Korea and Taiwan where prospects were at one time thought to be extremely poor. The effects of international trade have been sufficiently favorable that, if its critics are not confounded, they must be greatly surprised. Progress has been made in controlling population, especially in Asia and Latin America. Sensible rural development and appropriate technology seem in the ascendant; the more questionable forms of planning are in full retreat. Private investment is now treated with much more appreciation for the benefits it brings and with more confidence that its costs can be limited and controlled. In the new climate, the flow of investment has increased dramatically to some countries. There appears to be less acrimony in North–South relations than was true only a short while ago.

Evidence mounts that scarcity of natural resources in any particular LDC, or even the total absence of such resources, is not fatal for development prospects or even much of a disadvantage, just as was true for now-developed countries such as Denmark, the Netherlands, Switzerland, and more recently and impressively, Japan. Although it is satisfying to have natural resources, these can be imported and processed; the greatest economic successes among the NICs are rather resource-poor (South Korea and Taiwan) or have none at all (Hong Kong and Singapore). A capable and energetic population can overcome this problem, and one suspects that the lack of natural resources may even unleash work effort in a sort of "we try harder" among nations.

A Parting Word

Perhaps the proper frame of mind in which to conclude is to suggest that the many daunting problems of economic development we have encountered in this book can be viewed either as an unalterable destiny requiring a supine and fatalistic acceptance or as a challenge to be faced with untiring effort and commitment. Much of that challenge lies in overcoming the passivity and inertia of the idea that "nothing can be done." The instructive tale of two salesmen sent to a poor country by a shoe company will make the point.[10] The first reported back, NO PROSPECTS HERE. NO ONE WEARS SHOES. The second sent a far different report: IMMENSE PROSPECTS HERE. MILLIONS WITHOUT SHOES. The LDCs need the spirit of the second salesman.

A final word to the voters and public officials of the developed countries: There is little choice but to help the LDCs to develop. The challenges to peace and order in the twenty-first century will very probably come from the planet's low-income countries, not its rich ones. Even if the moral imperative and obvious justice of helping the poor to better themselves fails to impress, the stark fact that continuing widespread poverty is dangerous certainly *ought* to do so. Recognizing that the developed countries must do a better job of promoting growth in the LDCs is, after all, no more than recognizing their own self-interest.[11]

NOTES

1. Henry J. Bruton, "The Search for a Development Economics," *World Development* 13, no. 10/11 (1985): 1116.
2. Meier, *Leading Issues*, 5th ed., 66.
3. Nicholas Stern, "The Determinants of Growth," *Economic Journal* 101, no. 404 (January 1991): 132.
4. Echoing Dudley Seers, "The Meaning of Development," in David Lehmann, ed., *Development Theory: Four Critical Studies* (London, 1979), 21.
5. In making the list, I was stimulated by Arnold C. Harberger, ed., *Economic Policy and Economic Growth* (San Francisco, 1984), 9–16; Meier, *Leading Issues*, 5th ed., 526–530; *WDR 1991*, 152; and the suggestions in Robert Klitgaard's very readable *Tropical Gangsters* (New York, 1990). (This last consists of the personal reminiscences of a development economist working in Equatorial Guinea, and is the best of this genre.)
6. *HDR 1994*, 68; Daniel C. Esty, *Greening the GATT: Trade, Environment, and the Future* (Washington, D.C., 1994), 239.
7. An understandable review of Pareto improvements is Edmund S. Phelps, *Political Economy* (New York, 1985), chapter 9.
8. See W. M. Corden, "Normative Theory of International Trade," in Ronald W. Jones and Peter B. Kenen, eds., *Handbook of International Economics*, vol. 1 (Amsterdam, 1984), 66–69, whose analysis I followed here.
9. Thomas G. Weiss, "Alternatives for Multilateral Development Diplomacy: Some Suggestions," *World Development* 13, no. 12 (1985): 1187–1209.
10. David Morawetz, "On the Origins of Theories," *World Development* 13, no. 12 (1985): 1308.
11. This paragraph concludes my principles of economics textbook, Jan S. Hogendorn, *Modern Economics* (Englewood Cliffs, N.J., 1995). I cannot improve on it.

Name Index

Subject Index